Equal Protection
Cases and Materials

FIRST EDITION

EQUAL PROTECTION
CASES AND MATERIALS

FIRST EDITION

by

ROBERT C. FARRELL
Professor of Law
Quinnipiac University School of Law

ALISON E. CONROY
Member of the Bar
State of Connecticut

VANDEPLAS PUBLISHING, LLC
UNITED STATES OF AMERICA

Equal Protection: Cases and Materials
First Edition 2013

Farrell, Robert C. & Conroy, Alison E.

Published by:

Vandeplas Publishing, LLC – March 2013

801 International Parkway, 5th Floor
Lake Mary, FL. 32746
USA

www.vandeplaspublishing.com

Copyright © 2013 by Robert C. Farrell & Alison E. Conroy
All rights reserved.
No part of this book may be reproduced, stored in a retrieval system, or transmitted by any means, electronic, mechanical, photocopying, recording, or otherwise, without written permission from the author.

ISBN 978-1-60042-189-1

For Mary-Jean, Aileen, Maureen, and Deirdre
--R.C.F.

For Cameron, Avery, and Davis
--A.E.C.

Omnibus Paribus

TABLE OF CONTENTS

Preface xv

INTRODUCTION 1

CHAPTER 1. RATIONAL BASIS REVIEW 5
A. How the Notion of Equality Leads to the Rational Basis Standard 5

B. Deferential Rational Basis Review 7
Massachusetts Bd. of Retirement v. Murgia 7

C. How Do We Determine the Purpose of a Law? 11
U.S. Railroad Retirement Board v. Fritz 12

D. What Is the Required Correlation Between Classification and Purpose? 19
State of Minnesota v. Clover Leaf Creamery Co. 19

E. Deference So Great as to Amount to No Review at All 23
Federal Communications Commission v. Beach Communications, Inc. 23
Heller v Doe 26

F. More Demanding Rational Basis Review 29
U. S. Dept. of Agriculture v. Moreno 30
City of Cleburne, Tex. v. Cleburne Living Center 35
Romer v. Evans 38

G. The Class of One Claim 45
Village of Willowbrook v. Olech 45
Engquist v. Oregon Dept. of Agriculture 47

H. Other Theoretical Models of Equal Protection 52
1. The Anti-Subordination Model 53
2. The Substantive Equality Model 54

Chapter 2. Race Classifications ... 55
A. Racial Classifications Before the Adoption of the Fourteenth Amendment ... 55
    1. Slavery in the Original Text of the Constitution ... 55
    2. Slavery and Racial Classifications Before the Civil War ... 56
    3. The Adoption of the Post-Civil War Amendments ... 57

B. The Original Understanding of the Equal Protection Clause ... 57
    Strauder v. West Virginia ... *58*
    Yick Wo v. Hopkins ... *61*
    Plessy v. Ferguson ... *63*

C. The Strict Scrutiny Standard ... 66
    United States v. Carolene Products Co. ... *67*
    Korematsu v. United States ... *69*
    McLaughlin v. Florida ... *72*

D. Racial Segregation in Schools ... 78
    Brown v. Board of Education ... *78*
    Cooper v. Aaron ... *81*
    Green v. County School Board of New Kent County, Va. ... *84*
    Swann v. Charlotte-Mecklenburg Board of Education ... *86*
    Keyes v. School District No. 1, Denver, Colo. ... *91*
    Milliken v. Bradley ... *94*
    Parents Involved in Community Schools v. Seattle School Dist. No. 1 ... *97*

E. The Requirement of Racially Discriminatory Purpose ... 98
    Washington v. Davis ... *99*
    Village of Arlington Heights v. Metropolitan Housing Development Corp. ... *102*
    Personnel Administrators of Massachusetts v. Feeney ... *105*
    McClesky v. Kemp ... *106*

F. Affirmative Action ... 111
    Regents of University of California v Bakke ... *112*
    City of Richmond v. J.A. Croson Co. ... *122*
    Adarand Constructors Inc. v. Pena ... *128*
    Grutter v. Bollinger ... *132*
    Gratz v Bollinger ... *141*
    Parents Involved in Community Schools v. Seattle School Dist. No. 1 ... *142*

G. What is a Racial Classification? What is a National Origin Classification? ... 153

Chapter 3. Gender Classifications ... 155
A. Traditional Thinking ... 155

B. The Road to Intermediate Scrutiny: 1971-1976 ... 158
    1. The Supreme Court Precedents ... 158
    Reed v. Reed ... *158*
    Frontiero v. Richardson ... *160*
    Craig v. Boren ... *164*

	2. What Factors Make a Classification Suspect?	169
C.	**Prohibited Gender Classifications**	**175**
	1. In the Calculation of Social Security Benefits	175
	2. In the Award of Alimony	175
	3. In the Required Parental Consent for Adoption	176
	4. In the Right to Control the Disposition of Real Property	176
	5. All-Female University Programs	176
	Mississippi University for Women v. Hogan	*176*
	6. Excluding Women from the Jury	179
	J.E.B. v. Alabama	*179*
	7. All-Male University Programs	184
	United States v. Virginia	*184*
D.	**Permitted Gender Classifications**	**197**
	1. Based on Genuine Biological Differences Between the Sexes	197
	Michael M. v. Superior Court of Sonoma County	*197*
	Nguyen v. I.N.S.	*201*
	2. To Remedy the Effects of Past Discrimination Against Women	208
	Kahn v. Shevin	*208*
	Califano v. Webster	*209*
	3. Justified by a Broader and Unchallenged Gender-Based Difference	211
	Scheslinger v. Ballard	*211*
	Rostker v. Goldberg	*213*
	4. Classifications That Are Treated As If They Are Not Gender Classifications	217
	Geduldig v. Aiello	*217*
	Personnel Administrator of Massachusetts v. Feeney	*219*
E.	**Current Issues of Gender Equality**	**223**
	1. Gender Classifications in Government-Run Sports Programs	223
	2. Gender-Segregated Public School Classrooms	225
	3. Military Combat Exclusion	226
	4. Gender Segregation in Prisons	227

CHAPTER 4. CLASSIFICATIONS DISADVANTAGING NONMARITAL CHILDREN

....229

A.	**The Common Law Rules That Disadvantaged Nonmarital Children**	**229**
B.	**The Court's Uncertain Movement Toward Intermediate Scrutiny of Classifications Disadvantaging Nonmarital Children**	**230**
	1. The Court Invalidates Certain Classifications Using Rational Basis Review	230
	Levy v. Louisiana	*230*
	Glona v. American Guarantee & Liability Insurance Co.	*231*
	Weber v. Aetna Casualty & Surity Co.	*232*
	Gomez v. Perez	*236*
	2. The Court Upholds Certain Classifications Using Something Like Rational Basis Review	237
	Labine v. Vincent	*238*
	Mathews v. Lucas	*241*

Lalli v. Lalli 248
3. The Court Adopts Intermediate Scrutiny for Classifications That Disadvantage Nonmarital Children. 252
Mills v. Habluetzel 253
Pickett v. Brown 256
Clark v. Jeter 260
4. Should Nonmarital Children Be Considered a Quasi-Suspect Class? 262
5. Does the Availability of Reliable DNA Evidence Eliminate the Final Remaining Justification for Treating Nonmarital Children Differently? 264
6. Is the Battle Over–Are Nonmarital Children Now the Equals of Marital Children? 265

CHAPTER 5. CLASSIFICATIONS THAT DISADVANTAGE ALIENS 267
A. **The Legal Tradition of Treating Aliens Differently From Citizens** 267

B. **Strict Scrutiny of Alienage Classifications by State Governments** 268
    1. Should Aliens Be Considered a Suspect Class? 268
    Graham v. Richardson 268
    2. The Political Function Exception to Strict Scrutiny of Alienage Classifications 274
    Sugarman v. Dougall 274
    Foley v. Connelie 278
    Ambach v. Norwick 279
    Cabell v Chavez-Salido 280
    Bernal v. Fainter 281

C. **The Federal Government's Power to Classify Aliens** 285
    Mathews v. Diaz 285

D. **Recent Issues on the Classification of Aliens** 289
    1. The Hybrid State/Federal Classification of Aliens 289
    2. The Treatment of Undocumented and Nonimmigrant Aliens 290
        a. Undocumented Aliens 290
        b. Nonimmigrant Aliens 290

CHAPTER 6. CLASSIFICATIONS BASED ON SEXUAL ORIENTATION 293
A. **The Longstanding Tradition of Treating Gay Men and Women as Less Worthy** 293
    1. Public School Teaching 294
    2. Immigration 295
    3. Parenting 295
    4. Service in the Military 296
    Dronenburg v. Zech 296
    5. Criminalization of Sexual Activity 299
    Bowers v. Hardwick 302

B.	**Closer Review of Sexual Orientation Classifications in the Supreme Court**	302
	Romer v. Evans	302
	Lawrence v. Texas	304
C.	**What is the Proper Standard of Review of Classifications that Disadvantage Gay Men and Women?**	313
	1. Traditional Deferential Rational Basis Review	314
	2. More Demanding Rational Basis Review	315
	3. Heightened Scrutiny of Sexual Orientation Classifications Because Gay Men and Women are a Quasi-Suspect Class	317
	Kerrigan v. Commissioner of Public Health	318
	Windsor v United States	328
	4. Heightened Scrutiny of Sexual Orientation Classifications Because They Infringe on the Fundamental Right of Privacy	334
	Witt v. Department of Air Force	334
D.	**Current Issues on Sexual Orientation Classifications**	341
	1. The Exclusion of Gay Men and Women from the Military	341
	Log Cabin Republicans v. United States	342
	2. State Rules Limiting Marriage to a Man and a Woman	346
	Citizens for Equal Protection v. Bruning	347
	Perry v. Brown	350
	3. The Federal Defense of Marriage Act	359
	In re Kandu	360
	Massachusetts v. U.S. Dept. of Health and Human Services	364
	Windsor v United States	371

CHAPTER 7. NONSUSPECT CLASSIFICATIONS 377

A.	**Poverty Is Not a Suspect Classification**	377
	1. The Court Initially Suggests that Poverty Is as Suspect as Race	377
	2. The Court Concludes that Wealth is *Not* A Suspect Classification	378
	San Antonio Independent School District v. Rodriguez	379
	3. Government's Failure to Fund the Poor Does Not Implicate a Suspect Class	383
B.	**Mental Disability Is Not a Suspect Classification**	385
	City of Cleburne v. Cleburne Living Center	386
C.	**Age Is Not a Suspect Classification**	390
	Massachusetts Board of Retirement v. Murgia	390

CHAPTER 8. IMPLIED FUNDAMENTAL RIGHTS & THE EQUAL PROTECTION CLAUSE 395

A.	**The Relationship Between Implied Fundamental Rights under the Due Process Clause and Implied Fundamental Rights Under the Equal Protection Clause**	395
B.	**Procreation and Marriage**	396
	Skinner v. Oklahoma	396
	Zablocki v. Redhail	400

C.	**Voting** **404**
	1. Access to the Voting Booth and the Right to Have One's Ballot Counted Equally 404
	Reynold v. Sims *404*
	Harper v. Virginia Board of Elections *408*
	Kraemer v. Union Free School District *411*
	2. Restrictions on Candidates 415
	Williams v. Rhodes *415*
	Anderson v. Celebrezze *418*
	3. When the Strict Scrutiny Standard Applies 422
	Clements v. Fashing *422*
	Burdick v. Takushi *426*
	Crawford v. Marion County Election Board *429*
	4. The Case That Must Not Be Named 436
	Bush v. Gore *436*
D.	**Access to the Judicial Process** **445**
	Griffin v. Illinois *445*
	Douglas v. California *448*
	Boddie v. Connecticut *451*
	Mayer v. Chicago *455*
	M.L.B. v. S.L.J. *457*
E.	**The Right to Travel** **466**
	1. The Court Applies Strict Scrutiny to Infringements on the Right to Travel 466
	Shapiro v. Thompson *466*
	Dunn v. Blumstein *471*
	2. The Court Applies Less Demanding Scrutiny to Infringements on the Right to Travel 475
	Sosna v. Iowa *475*
	Vlandis v. Kline *476*
	3. The Court Reconceptualizes the Implied Fundamental Right to Travel 478
	Saenz v. Roe *478*
F.	**Interests That Are Not Fundamental** **483**
	1. Food and Shelter 483
	Dandridge v. Williams *483*
	Lindsey v. Normet *486*
	2. Education 488
	a. Not a Fundamental Right 488
	San Antonio School District v. Rodriquez *488*
	b. But Not Just Another Benefit 494
	Plyler v. Doe *494*

CHAPTER 9. CONGRESSIONAL POWER TO ENFORCE THE EQUAL PROTECTION CLAUSE 501

A. **Congressional Power Under the Commerce Clause and Under Section 5 of the Fourteenth Amendment** **501**

B. **The Principle of Congruence and Proportionality** **502**
    City of Boerne v. Flores *502*
    Kimel v. Florida Board of Regents *507*
    Board of Trustees of University of Alabama v. Garrett *513*
    Nevada Department of Human Resources v. Hibbs *516*
    Tennessee v. Lane *520*
    Coleman v. Court of Appeals of Maryland *525*

PREFACE

Subject Matter

This casebook deals with the substantive law of equal protection, both under the Fourteenth Amendment as applied against state governments, and under the implied equal protection component of the Fifth Amendment as applied against the federal government. The book focuses on decisions of the United States Supreme Court, except in the chapter on sexual orientation, where most of the recent developments have been in state supreme courts and the lower federal courts. The casebook limits its coverage to the constitutional doctrine of equal protection; it does not cover civil rights or anti-discrimination statutes, nor does it include materials on procedural issues such as the existence of causes of action or of jurisdiction.

The book includes the following topics: rational basis review, racial classifications, the different tiers of review, gender classifications, classifications affecting nonmarital children, classifications of aliens, classifications on the basis of sexual orientation, implied fundamental rights under the Equal Protection Clause, and Congressional power to enforce the Equal Protection Clause.

Organization

There are two obvious ways to organize an equal protection casebook—historically or conceptually. The historic model has the advantage of focusing on the way in which the origins of the Equal Protection Clause give meaning to its terms. This historic method gives appropriate weigh to the centrality of slavery and racism to the meaning of the Equal Protection Clause and provides the opportunity to view all other forms of prohibited classifications in comparison to racial classifications.

The downside to an historical model, particularly in a book meant to be used as a teaching vehicle in a classroom, is that it forces one to deal with doctrinal structures before the foundation for those doctrines has been laid. Thus, for example, the Supreme Court uses strict scrutiny to review racial classifications--a requirement that the classification be narrowly tailored to achieve a compelling purpose. This strict scrutiny standard makes far more sense if one learns it after learning why classifications are relevant to the doctrine of equality and the ordinary standard that a classification must be rationally related to a permissible interest. A book organized around the conceptual idea of equality is able to address these and other foundational issues first and that it is the organizational model that this book adopts.

Editing of Cases

The cases in this book are, of necessity, heavily edited. Constitutional law cases in the Supreme Court often run in excess of 100 pages. In order, therefore, to produce a book that is of manageable size and that focuses on the most important equal protection issues we have edited the cases in accordance with the following guidelines:

(1) Omit all material in the case on issues other than equal protection. This means, for example, that if, in addition to its equal protection component, a case includes a discussion on the First Amendment or a statutory cause of action, those materials are omitted.

(2) Omit the factual and procedural histories of the case. In their place we have written our own very brief summaries of the facts and placed those summaries in brackets at the beginning of the case.

(3) Omit from within the cases the Court's citations to other cases and to statutes, except where those citations have a substantive relevance to the outcome of the case.

(4) Omit concurring and dissenting opinions, except where these opinions make important points that are not made elsewhere in these materials.

(5) Do not use ellipses. We have not followed the Bluebook rule that requires that omissions be indicated with ellipses, that is, with three periods separated by commas. In a book with as many cases as this and with as many omitted passages as this, we would have filled the book up with ellipses if we had followed the Bluebook rule. What this means, then, is that omission of words or of entire passages is not noted. There is a danger that selective editing without notation can mislead the reader about the sense of a passage, but the authors have taken great care to assure that the cases, even when heavily edited, are true to the spirit of the full version of the case.

Previous Publications

Some of the commentary on the cases in this book is based on material that originally appeared in the following articles previously published by one of the authors:

The Two Versions of Rational Basis Review and Same-Sex Relationships, 86 Washington L. Rev. 281 (2011);

The Equal Protection Class-of-One Claim: Olech, Engquist, and the Supreme Court's Misadventure, 61 South Carolina L. Rev. 1 (2009);

An Excess of Methods: Identifying Fundamental Rights in the Supreme Court, 26 St. Louis University Public Law Review 203 (2007);

Classes, Persons, Equal Protection, and Village of Willowbrook v. Olech, 78 Washington L. Rev. 367 (2003);

Successful Rational Basis Claims in the Supreme Court from the 1971 Term through Romer v. Evans, 32 Indiana L. Rev. 357 (1999);

Classifications That Disadvantage Newcomers and the Problem of Equality, 28 University of Richmond L. Rev. 547 (1994);

Legislative Purpose and Equal Protection's Rationality Review, 37 Villanova L. Rev. 1 (1992).

Acknowledgments

The authors thank the students at Quinnipiac University School of Law who took the Equal Protection course over the past twenty years and who endured many different versions of the materials that became this casebook. In particular, the authors thank Arunan Arulampalam, Malika Sheth, and John Wylam, who helped with this version of the materials.

INTRODUCTION

America's Declaration of Independence begins by identifying certain truths as self-evident. The first of these is that "all men are created equal." The prominence of this assertion suggests that equality was to be a foundational principal of the newly independent country. When, however, the United States Constitution was adopted eleven years later, that document contained no equality provision whatever. Worse than that, the original version of the Constitution contained sections that mandated inequality—those sections that recognized and thereby endorsed slavery in the United States. The first of these sections counted slaves as three fifths of a person for purposes of determining the number of Congressmen for each state. The second took from Congress the power to prohibit the importation of slaves into the United States until 1808. The third provided that a slave who escaped and arrived in a free state had to be returned to his owner in his former slave state.

On the issue of slavery, no workable compromise could be reached between the northern and southern states and the matter was not resolved until the two sides fought a Civil War. Abraham Lincoln described that war as a conflict to determine whether a nation "conceived in liberty and dedicated to the proposition that all men are created equal" could long endure. That nation did endure and the Union was preserved. At the end of that war, three amendments were added to the American Constitution. The Thirteenth Amendment abolished slavery and the Fifteenth Amendment prohibited racial discrimination in voting. The Fourteenth Amendment contained a citizenship clause, a privileges or immunities clause, a due process clause, and, most importantly for our purposes, an equal protection clause—"nor [shall any state] deny to any person within its jurisdiction the equal protection of the laws."

For the first time in United States history, state governments were held to a standard of equality. The promise of the Declaration of Independence—that all men are created equal—was now a constitutional command. The full scope of that command, however, was yet to be defined with precision. Given the historical context in which it was adopted, it was clear the Equal Protection Clause did address the issue of slavery and discrimination against former slaves. Since slavery in America had been a system operated entirely on racial grounds, it was clear that the Equal Protection Clause prohibited racial discrimination by states against black Americans. But did it do more than that?

In the early years after the adoption of the Equal Protection Clause, the Supreme Court expressed the view that the clause was limited to addressing issues of race discrimination. In

Strauder v. State of West Virginia, 100 U.S. 303 (1879), the Court found a violation of equal protection in a state law that excluded black citizens from jury service, since "[t]he existence of laws in the States where the newly emancipated negroes resided, which discriminated with gross injustice and hardship against them as a class, was the evil to be remedied." But the Court suggested that the amendment might not address issues other than race:

> We doubt very much whether any action of a State, not directed by way of discrimination against the negroes, as a class, will ever be held to come within the purview of this provision . . . [The state] may confine the selection [of jurors] to males, to freeholders, to citizens, to persons within certain ages, or to persons having educational qualifications. We do not believe the Fourteenth Amendment was ever intended to prohibit this. Looking at its history, it is clear it had no such purpose. Its aim was against discrimination because of race or color.

Despite this strong statement on limitation of the Equal Protection Clause to racial classifications, the Court did not follow its own directive. The language of the clause was written as a generalized command to treat persons equally rather than as a specific prohibition of racial classifications. In a series of cases shortly before and after 1900, the Court confirmed this broader view of equal protection. These cases indicated that the Equal Protection Clause was to be treated as a general limit on state action that singles out certain groups for different treatment from the general public without adequate justification. See Chapter 1, *infra*. The Equal Protection Clause, then, is not limited to addressing racial classifications but establishes a more general principal of equality.

In the 1940s, the Court took an additional major step toward developing equal protection doctrine. In 1942, in *Skinner v. Oklahoma*, 316 U.S. 535 (1942), the Court invalidated a state statute that required the sterilization of certain three-time felons. In explaining its decision, the Court noted that the statute affected procreation, a fundamental right, and that the Court would therefore strictly scrutinize the classification involved in the statute. *Skinner* became the foundation for the Court's subsequent precedents on the application of strict scrutiny to classifications that affect a fundamental right. Two years later, in *Korematsu v. United States*, 323 U.S. 214 (1944), the Court considered the military regulation that required the internment of Japanese-Americans during World War II. Although the Court upheld the regulation, it announced that legal restrictions on the rights of a racial group are "immediately suspect" and will be subjected to "the most rigid scrutiny." *Korematsu* thus became the foundation for the Court's subsequent precedents on strict scrutiny of suspect classifications.

During the 1960s and 1970s, the Court further developed its jurisprudence of heightened scrutiny of suspect classifications and implied fundamental rights. The Court determined that alienage classifications, like racial classifications, are suspect and thus deserving of strict scrutiny. In addition, the Court found that classifications based on gender and illegitimacy are quasi-suspect, and therefore deserving of a newly created intermediate level of review. In the course of doing so, the Court created its three tiers of equal protection review—(1) rational basis for most classifications, requiring that a classification be rationally related to a permissible interest, (2) strict scrutiny for suspect classifications and of government actions that invade fundamental rights, requiring that a classification be narrowly tailored to achieve a compelling interest, and (3) intermediate scrutiny of gender and illegitimacy classifications, requiring that a classification be substantially related to an important governmental interest.

The Supreme Court has described the history of the Equal Protection Clause in the following terms: "A prime part of the history of our Constitution . . . is the story of the extension of constitutional rights and protections to people once ignored or excluded." *United States v.*

Virginia, 518 U.S. 515 (1996). Since 1976, however, the Supreme Court has effectively been out of the business of creating additional suspect classifications. In the lower federal courts and in state courts, however, there has been a recent and steady stream of cases holding that classifications based on sexual orientation are at least quasi-suspect, and should therefore be subject to at least intermediate scrutiny.

The State Action Requirement

All equal protection decisions are limited by the state action requirement: by its terms the Equal Protection Clause only requires that the *state* shall not deny to any person the equal protection of the law. By its own terms, then, the Clause does not apply to, and therefore does not limit, conduct by private parties. In the absence of federal or state anti-discrimination legislation, private persons are free to discriminate all they want, on the basis of any trait, and there is no legal recourse for the adversely affected party.

The Equal Protection Clause of the Fourteenth Amendment has no application to the federal government and there is no explicit equal protection clause that binds and limits the federal government. The federal government is, however, subject to the same equal protection limitations as are the states. The Fifth Amendment to the Constitution clearly does apply to the federal government and the Supreme Court has held that its Due Process Clause includes an implied equal protection component. In *Bolling v. Sharpe*, 347 U.S. 497 (1954), a companion case to *Brown v. Board of Education,*, the court noted that "'equal protection of the laws' is a more explicit safeguard of prohibited unfairness than 'due process of law,'" but that "[i]n view of [the] decision that the Constitution prohibits the states from maintaining racially segregated public schools, it would be unthinkable that the same Constitution would impose a lesser duty on the Federal Government." The Court confirmed this understanding in *Adarand Constructors, Inc. v. Pena*, 515 U.S. 200 (1995), where it stated that the state and federal obligations under the Fourteenth and Fifth Amendment were congruent: "Equal protection analysis in the Fifth Amendment area is the same as that under the Fourteenth Amendment.

CHAPTER 1

RATIONAL BASIS REVIEW

A. How the Notion of Equality Leads to the Rational Basis Standard

The command of equality is essentially comparative. It requires a comparison of one entity with another entity. Thus, it makes sense to say that "A equals B," but it would be nonsense to assert that "A equals." When it is asserted that "A equals B," that assertion is usually followed by a claim that A and B are entitled by their equality to a certain treatment. What kind of treatment does A's and B's equality entitle them to? As an initial matter, it makes sense to argue that if A and B are equal, they are entitled to the *same* treatment. Thus, a teacher would be treating each student in his class equally if he gave each of them the same set of course materials. This idea that equal treatment of two entities involves the *same* treatment of those entities has been a powerful claim in constitutional law cases. Thus, for example, early cases challenging racially segregated schools typically involved the claim that black students should be treated *the same as* white students, and early cases challenging gender classifications involved the claim that women should be treated *the same as* men.

This notion, however, that equal treatment of persons requires the *same* treatment of those persons turns out to be a hollow and ineffective claim in many situations. Thus, for example, while it is fine for the teacher to give all his students the same course materials, it would probably not be acceptable for the teacher to give all the students in the course the same grade. And it would be foolish for a doctor to treat all his patients by prescribing aspirin to each one of them. In these two cases, treating everyone the same does not turn out to be very satisfactory. It turns out, then, that while equal treatment means *the same* treatment in many cases, that notion of equal treatment is inadequate to explain the requirement of equality in more complicated situations. Since Aristotle, the idea of equality has been understood to involve the comparative command, not simply that everyone be treated the same, but rather that those similarly situated be treated similarly.

In equal protection cases, the question of who is similarly situated to whom is usually asked not about individual persons, but about groups of people. Although it is possible to make an equal protection argument involving only two persons or two entities (such as a claim that a parent ought to give each of her ten-year old twins the same bedtime), in fact, most equal protection cases involve a comparison of two different classes. To classify is to identify a trait that makes a person a member of a class (all those over age fifty, for example) and then to ascribe a certain treatment (such as forced retirement) for those who, having the trait, are members of that class. The typical equality challenge to this kind of classification compares one class of persons (those who have the trait) with a second class of persons (those without the trait) and argues that, because the two classes are similarly situated, the members of both classes should be treated similarly. The question then becomes—who is similar to whom and therefore entitled to similar treatment?

This question of similarity is unanswerable in the abstract. On the one hand, all human beings are similar to all other human beings in having, for example, a human genome, and are therefore arguably entitled to similar treatment. At the same time, all human beings are unique— each person with his or her own genes and life experience—and thus different from everyone else and entitled to different treatment. The difficulty in solving this conundrum is substantial. Peter Westen has called it an impossible task—one that makes the idea of equality an empty thing. *See* Peter Westen, *The Empty Idea of Equality*, 95 Harv. L. Rev. 537 (1982).

Courts applying the Equal Protection Clause have addressed the problem of identifying who is similar to whom by referring to an external criterion—the purpose for which the classification was made. Thus, for example, all persons over the age of fifty share a trait that makes them members of a class. Are they similarly situated to individuals in a class made up of people younger than fifty? It depends on whether this age classification is relevant to its purpose. If the purpose of the classification is to identify individuals who still have sufficient vigor to perform a physically demanding job like police work, then the two classes might be considered differently situated, as fitness declines with age. If, however, the purpose of the classification is to determine who is eligible to vote, then the two classes appear to be similarly situated, because physical vigor bears little relation to voting ability. It is on this understanding—that there must be some correlation between classification and purpose—that the U.S. Supreme Court has developed equal protection's rational basis standard. In order to determine whether or not two classes are similarly situated, then, we ask if the two classes are related in the same way to the purpose of the law. If they are, then the notion of equality requires that the two classes be treated the same; if not, then the classes can be treated differently. This required correlation between classification and purpose is the underlying genesis of the rational basis standard that the Supreme Court has adopted under the Equal Protection Clause—that a classification must be rationally related to a legitimate governmental interest or purpose.

The classic treatment of the process of classification and its place in the making of equal protection arguments is Joseph Tussman & Jacobus tenBroek, *The Equal Protection of the Laws*, 37 Calif. L. Rev. 341 (1949). For a more recent exploration of the history and meaning of the "similarly situated" standard, *see* Giovanna Shay, *Similarly Situated*, 18 Geo. Mason L. Rev. 581 (2011).

In order to apply this standard, a court must (1) identify the classification, (2) identify the purpose, and (3) determine whether or not the classification is adequately correlated with that purpose. The Supreme Court has, however, applied this standard in two different ways, the first, an extremely deferential standard that sometimes gives the appearance of being no review at all, and the second, a more demanding form of rationality. The next two sections examine the idea of equality under both versions of rational basis review.

B. DEFERENTIAL RATIONAL BASIS REVIEW

Massachusetts Bd. of Retirement v Murgia
427 U.S. 307 (1976)

[Under Massachusetts law, Robert Murgia, a State Police Officer, was required to retire at age 50. Murgia filed an action claiming his mandatory retirement was a violation of the Equal Protection Clause.]

PER CURIAM.

This case presents the question whether the provision of Mass.Gen.Laws Ann . . . that a uniformed state police officer "shall be retired . . . upon his attaining age fifty," denies appellee police officer equal protection of the laws in violation of the Fourteenth Amendment.

The primary function of the Uniformed Branch of the Massachusetts State Police is to protect persons and property and maintain law and order. Specifically, uniformed officers participate in controlling prison and civil disorders, respond to emergencies and natural disasters, patrol highways in marked cruisers, investigate crime, apprehend criminal suspects, and provide backup support for local law enforcement personnel. As the District Court observed, "service in this branch is, or can be, arduous." "(H)igh versatility is required, with few, if any, backwaters available for the partially superannuated." Thus, "even (appellee's) experts concede that there is a general relationship between advancing age and decreasing physical ability to respond to the demands of the job."

These considerations prompt the requirement that uniformed state officers pass a comprehensive physical examination biennially until age 40. After that, until mandatory retirement at age 50, uniformed officers must pass annually a more rigorous examination, including an electrocardiogram and tests for gastro-intestinal bleeding. Appellee Murgia had passed such an examination four months before he was retired, and there is no dispute that, when he retired, his excellent physical and mental health still rendered him capable of performing the duties of a uniformed officer.

The record includes the testimony of three physicians: that of the State Police Surgeon, who testified to the physiological and psychological demands involved in the performance of uniformed police functions; that of an associate professor of medicine, who testified generally to the relationship between aging and the ability to perform under stress; and that of a surgeon, who also testified to aging and the ability safely to perform police functions. The testimony clearly established that the risk of physical failure, particularly in the cardiovascular system, increases with age, and that the number of individuals in a given age group incapable of performing stress functions increases with the age of the group. The testimony also recognized that particular individuals over 50 could be capable of safely performing the functions of uniformed officers. The associate professor of medicine, who was a witness for the appellee, further testified that evaluating the risk of cardiovascular failure in a given individual would require a number of detailed studies.

In assessing appellee's equal protection claim, the District Court found it unnecessary to apply a strict-scrutiny test, see Shapiro v. Thompson, 394 U.S. 618 (1969), for it determined that the age classification established by the Massachusetts statutory scheme could not in any event withstand a test of rationality, see *Dandridge v. Williams*, 397 U.S. 471 (1970). Since there had been no showing that reaching age 50 forecasts even "imminent change" in an officer's physical condition, the District Court held that compulsory retirement at age 50 was irrational under a scheme that assessed the capabilities of officers individually by means of comprehensive annual physical examinations. We agree that rationality is the proper standard by which to test whether compulsory retirement at age 50 violates equal protection. We disagree, however, with the District Court's determination that the age 50 classification is not rationally related to furthering a legitimate state interest.

III

We turn then to examine this state classification under the rational-basis standard. This inquiry employs a relatively relaxed standard reflecting the Court's awareness that the drawing of lines that create distinctions is peculiarly a legislative task and an unavoidable one. Perfection in making the necessary classifications is neither possible nor necessary. *Dandridge v. Williams*, *supra*, 397 U.S., at 485. Such action by a legislature is presumed to be valid.

In this case, the Massachusetts statute clearly meets the requirements of the Equal Protection Clause, for the State's classification rationally furthers the purpose identified by the State: Through mandatory retirement at age 50, the legislature seeks to protect the public by assuring physical preparedness of its uniformed police. Since physical ability generally declines with age, mandatory retirement at 50 serves to remove from police service those whose fitness for uniformed work presumptively has diminished with age. This clearly is rationally related to the State's objective. There is no indication [the statute] has the effect of excluding from service so few officers who are in fact unqualified as to render age 50 a criterion wholly unrelated to the objective of the statute.

That the State chooses not to determine fitness more precisely through individualized testing after age 50 is not to say that the objective of assuring physical fitness is not rationally furthered by a maximum-age limitation. It is only to say that with regard to the interest of all concerned, the State perhaps has not chosen the best means to accomplish this purpose. But where rationality is the test, a State "does not violate the Equal Protection Clause merely because the classifications made by its laws are imperfect." *Dandridge v. Williams*, 397 U.S., at 485.

We do not make light of the substantial economic and psychological effects premature and compulsory retirement can have on an individual; nor do we denigrate the ability of elderly citizens to continue to contribute to society. The problems of retirement have been well documented and are beyond serious dispute. But "(w)e do not decide today that the (Massachusetts statute) is wise, that it best fulfills the relevant social and economic objectives that (Massachusetts) might ideally espouse, or that a more just and humane system could not be revised." We decide only that the system enacted by the Massachusetts Legislature does not deny appellee equal protection of the laws.

The judgment is reversed.

NOTES

1. The Court's opinion in *Murgia* is a good example of traditional rational basis review. The first element of the analysis--identifying the classification--is usually the simplest. Most commonly, the classification in a statute or regulation is explicit. In *Murgia*, the statute required all state police officers to retire at age fifty. This is an explicit age classification. A statute that

prohibits the sale of milk in plastic containers would be a classification of milk container makers. A regulation that forbids the hiring of anyone using narcotics would be a classification of narcotics users. In equal protection cases, it is rare that the parties dispute the nature of the classification. On occasion, however, the nature of the classification is hidden. Thus, for example, a state provision that freezes property tax assessments at the time of purchase could be viewed as a disguised classification distinguishing between newcomers and established residents; and a statute that caps the benefits that the state will provide to families in its welfare program could be viewed as a wealth classification. Notwithstanding these last two examples, however, the identification of the classification is, in general, the most straightforward and least controversial element of a rational-basis argument.

2. In *Murgia*, the Massachusetts legislature had created a class by identifying a trait—age 50—and then assigning a certain treatment to members of the class—mandatory retirement. Was it rational to treat police officers over age fifty differently from police officers under age fifty? It would be rational if the two groups were differently situated in relation to the purpose of the law. The court determined that the purpose of the law was to assure physical preparedness of the uniformed police. Are those over and under fifty differently situated to this purpose? The Court determined that the answer was yes, since fitness tends to decline with age. Thus, it was rational for the Massachusetts legislature to assume that more of those in the class of over-fifties would be unfit than would those in the class of under-fifties.

Borrowing from Joseph Tussman and Jacobus tenBroek, *The Equal Protection of the Laws*, 37. Cal. L.Rev. 341 (1949), we can illustrate this correlation graphically:

CLASSIFICATION

Those *with* the trait that makes one a member of the class

Those *without* the trait that makes one a member of the class

PURPOSE

Those *tainted by the mischief* at which the law aims

Police Officers Over Age 50

Police Officers Under Age 50

Physically Unfit Police Officers

The two circles on the left indicate, first, the group that has the trait that makes one a member of the class (over-fifties) and, second, the group that does not have the trait that makes one a member of the class (under-fifties). The circle on the right correlates with the purpose of the law, that is, if the purpose of the law is to eliminate unfit police officers, then those tainted by the mischief at which the law aims will be unfit police officers. To determine the rationality of the law, we must compare how the two groups on the left relate to the group on the right. If the group that has the trait (over-fifty police officers) is more likely to be within the group tainted by the mischief (unfit police officers) than is the group without the trait (under-fifty police officers), then the classification is rational.

This, in effect, is what the Court found in *Murgia* when it said that physical ability declines with age. Although the Court did not list any percentages, this conclusion must mean that, absent the mandatory retirement rule, a greater percentage of those over fifty would be unfit than would be the percentage of those under fifty. So even if only 20% of police officers over fifty would be unfit, it would still be rational to have a mandatory retirement age at fifty if, for example, only 5% of police officers under fifty would be unfit. As for Robert Murgia himself, the rule worked very unfairly since, as the Court conceded, he was very fit. Murgia's individual fitness did not matter, however, so long as the rule created a reasonable classification. Since the generalization embodied in the rule about fifty-year-olds was true, it did not matter that the generalization was not true as to a particular member of the over-fifty class.

3. The previous discussion illustrates what are sometimes spoken of as the problems of overinclusion and underinclusion. The mandatory retirement rule in *Murgia* was overinclusive in that the legislature painted with too broad a brush—not all those over fifty were unfit, that is, not all of those with that trait were tainted by the mischief. Robert Murgia himself was in that category—over fifty yet very fit. The rule is also presumably underinclusive—some of those that do *not* have the trait *are* tainted by the mischief—that is, there are likely to be some under fifty who are not fit. But, under the deferential purpose of rational basis review, overinclusion and underinclusion do not create a constitutional problem. Once it has been determined that there is a rational relation between the classification and the purpose of the law, there is no requirement that the generalizations embodied in the law be true in every case.

It might seem that the Massachusetts legislature could have attacked the problem of unfit police officers more directly. Instead of presuming that fifty-somethings are unfit and forcing them to retire, why not simply have a rule that unfit police officers have to retire, without regard to age? Such a rule would have the benefit of directness but it would have the effect of replacing a simple, easily-applied rule (all those over fifty must retire) with a much more complicated, difficult-to-administer rule, since each police officer would have to undergo regular physical exams. Moreover, as the court noted, not even those individual exams would turn up every case of unfitness. Thus, it makes sense for the legislature to adopt a broad, prophylactic rule that is clear and readily applied.

4. *NY City Transit Authority v Beazer*, 440 U.S. 568 (1979), is another good example of rational basis review at work. In that case, the New York City Transit Authority, in order to ensure safety and efficiency in the workplace, had a policy against hiring employees who were drug users. The Authority considered those using methadone, a synthetic drug prescribed by physicians as part of a heroin detoxification program, to be within its definition of drug user. The plaintiffs, who were part of a methadone maintenance program, claimed that the policy violated the Equal Protection Clause in that at least certain identifiable subgroups within the methadone program were as employable as the general population. The argument was that those who had completed a certain portion of the program were similarly situated with the general public in relation to the purpose of the law—safety and efficiency. Those with the trait (methadone users) were similarly situated to

those without the trait (the general public) in relation to the purpose of the law (ensuring workplace safety and efficiency). The Court conceded that many in the methadone program were employable but determined that "there are relevant differences between persons using methadone regularly and persons who use no narcotics of any kind." According to the Court, "the 'no drugs' policy now enforced by TA is supported by the legitimate inference that as long as a treatment program (or other drug use) continues, a degree of uncertainty persists," and thus that "an employment policy that postpones eligibility until the treatment program has been completed, rather than accepting an intermediate point on an uncertain line, is rational." In the course of upholding the Transit Authority rule, the Court quoted Justice Holmes on both the necessity, and the arbitrariness, of legislative line-drawing, and the corresponding need for judicial restraint:

> When a legal distinction is determined, as no one doubts that it may be, between night and day, childhood and maturity, or any other extremes, a point has to be fixed or a line has to be drawn, or gradually picked out by successive decisions, to mark where the change takes place. Looked at by itself without regard to the necessity behind it the line or point seems arbitrary. It might as well or nearly as well be a little more to one side or the other. But when it is seen that a line or point there must be, and that there is no mathematical or logical way of fixing it precisely, the decision of the legislature must be accepted unless we can say that it is very wide of any reasonable mark. *Louisville Gas & Electric Co. v. Coleman*, 277 U.S. 32, 41 (Holmes, J., dissenting).

C. How Do We Determine the Purpose of a Law?

A rule that insists that a classification be rationally related to the purpose of a law assumes that there is such a thing as the purpose of a law and that that purpose can be identified. The claim underlying this assumption is not without criticism. As a starting point, there is not even agreement on meaning of the expression, "the purpose of the law." At one extreme, it is urged that the very idea of a law's having a purpose is incoherent, because (1) a legislature does not have a mind that could form a purpose,[1] (2) a multi-member body cannot have a single intent,[2] (3) the alleged purpose of a law varies significantly depending on the generality with which the purpose is expressed,[3] and (4) laws frequently serve more than one purpose.[4] To the extent this critique of the idea of legislative purpose is accurate, then the rational-basis standard, which requires a certain relationship between legislative classification and the law's purpose, is itself incoherent.

The courts have adopted a more objective, pragmatic understanding of the concept of "the purpose of a law." In this understanding, the purpose of a law does not depend on a legislature's having a mind or on complete unanimity of the legislators who voted for the law. The purpose of a

---

[1] Robert W. Bennett, *"Mere" Rationality in Constitutional Law: Judicial Review and Democratic Theory*, 67 CALIF. L. REV. 1049, 1071 (1979) ("The concept of 'purpose,' even more than that of rationality, presumes individual intelligence."); Gerald C. MacCallum, Jr., *Legislative Intent*, 75 YALE L.J. 754, 764 (1966) ("Legislation is a group activity and it is impossible to conceive a group mind or [group] cerebration." (quoting ALBERT KOCOUREK, AN INTRODUCTION TO THE SCIENCE OF LAW 201 (1930))).

[2] . *See, e.g.*, Note, *Legislative Purpose, Rationality, and Equal Protection*, 82 YALE L.J. 123, 142 (1972) ("How is a court to determine which consequences a majority of the legislators had in mind when each legislator might have had several motivations and no majority had the same set of motivations?").

[3] *See* Robert C. Farrell, *Legislative Purpose and Equal Protection's Rationality Review*, 37 VILL. L. REV. 1, 15–17 (1992).

[4] *Id.* at 17–20.

law is the end at which a law is directed.[5] This end may be stated negatively as "the elimination of a public 'mischief,'" or affirmatively as "the achievement of some positive public good."[6] This understanding of legislative purpose, while not requiring a legislative mind or legislative unanimity, does assume that there is some distinction between the classification created by a law and the purpose on account of which the law was enacted. We cannot derive the purpose of a law solely from its operative effect. Thus, for example, we might ask, "What is the purpose of a law that requires state police officers to retire at age fifty?" It would not be useful to say the purpose of that law is to assure that state police officers retire at age fifty. By collapsing the difference between classification and purpose and thus "presuming purpose from result," the analysis is "reduce[d] . . . to tautology."[7] Rational basis review assumes that a law has a purpose independent of its effect. Thus, it is likely that the purpose of a law that requires police officers to retire at age fifty is to promote public safety by assuring that officers are physically fit. The rational basis question would then be whether or not the classification (police officers over fifty) is adequately correlated with the purpose of the law (eliminating unfit police officers).

Once it is conceded that a law has a purpose, the next question is how a court should go about identifying that purpose. Courts applying the traditional, deferential version of rational basis review do not attempt to discern the actual purpose of a statute. Rather, a large part of the deference that courts show in rational basis cases is related to the court's willingness to hypothesize the purpose of a law or to rely on the suggestions of government attorneys defending the law. *U.S. Railroad Retirement Board v. Fritz*, the case that follows, shows the Court's willingness to hypothesize a legislative purpose that will save a law from an equal protection challenge, even in the face of strong evidence to the contrary.

U.S. Railroad Retirement Board v. Fritz
449 U.S. 166 (1980)

[The Railroad Retirement Act of 1974 was passed to address fiscal problems in the Railroad Retirement system and to correct a potential retirement benefit windfall: Railroad Employees who qualified for both a railroad pension (after 10 years of service) and social security benefits (for at least 10 years of work performed outside the Railroad industry) would receive a dual benefit that was larger than the benefit earned by employees who worked for a comparable amount of time in only one of the two retirement systems. The Act modified the system to eliminate the disparity in benefit calculation.

Congress included a grandfather provision that preserved windfall benefits for certain employees who had already earned vested retirements in both systems but were not yet retired and therefore were not receiving the dual benefit. From this group of vested employees, the statute allowed continued receipt of the dual benefit only for three subgroups: (1) those who had performed some railroad service in 1974, or (2) those who had a "current connection" with the railroad industry of 12/31/1974, (defined as employment in the railroad industry in 12 of the preceding 30 calendar months) and (3) those who had completed 25 years of railroad service as of 12/31/1974.

In a class action lawsuit, individuals who would no longer qualify for the dual benefit asserted that the amended statute impermissibly distinguished between classes of annuity recipients and, as such, was unconstitutional under the Due Process Clause of the Fifth Amendment.]

---

[5] *Id.* at 3.

[6] Joseph Tussman and Jacobus tenBroek, *The Equal Protection of the Laws*, 37. Cal. L.Rev. 341, 346 (1949).

[7] *See* U.S.R.R. Ret. Bd. v. Fritz, 449 U.S. 166, 187 (1980) (Brennan, J., dissenting).

CHAPTER 1: RATIONAL BASIS REVIEW

Justice REHNQUIST delivered the opinion of the Court.

The initial issue presented by this case is the appropriate standard of judicial review to be applied when social and economic legislation enacted by Congress is challenged as being violative of the Fifth Amendment to the United States Constitution. There is no claim here that Congress has taken property in violation of the Fifth Amendment, since railroad benefits, like social security benefits, are not contractual and may be altered or even eliminated at any time. And because the distinctions drawn in § 231b(h) do not burden fundamental constitutional rights or create "suspect" classifications, such as race or national origin, we may put cases involving judicial review of such claims to one side. *San Antonio Independent School District v. Rodriguez*, 411 U.S. 1 (1973); *Vance v. Bradley*, 440 U.S. 93 (1979).

Despite the narrowness of the issue, this Court in earlier cases has not been altogether consistent in its pronouncements in this area. In *Lindsley v. Natural Carbonic Gas Co.*, 220 U.S. 61, 78-79 (1911), the Court said that "[w]hen the classification in such a law is called in question, if any state of facts reasonably can be conceived that would sustain it, the existence of that state of facts at the time that the law was enacted must be assumed." On the other hand, only nine years later in *F.S. Royster Guano Co. v. Virginia*, 253 U.S. 412, 415 (1920), the Court said that for a classification to be valid under the Equal Protection Clause of the Fourteenth Amendment it "must rest upon some ground of difference having a fair and substantial relation to the object of the legislation. . . ."

In more recent years, however, the Court in cases involving social and economic benefits has consistently refused to invalidate on equal protection grounds legislation which it simply deemed unwise or unartfully drawn.

Thus in *Dandridge v. Williams*, 397 U.S. 471 (1970), the Court rejected a claim that Maryland welfare legislation violated the Equal Protection Clause of the Fourteenth Amendment. It said:

> In the area of economics and social welfare, a State does not violate the Equal Protection Clause merely because the classifications made by its laws are imperfect. If the classification has some 'reasonable basis,' it does not offend the Constitution simply because the classification 'is not made with mathematical nicety or because in practice it results in some inequality.' *Lindsley v. Natural Carbonic Gas Co.*, 220 U.S. 61, 78. 'The problems of government are practical ones and may justify, if they do not require, rough accommodations-illogical, it may be, and unscientific.' *Metropolis Theatre Co. v. City of Chicago*, 228 U.S. 61, 68-70 . . .
>
> [The rational-basis standard] is true to the principle that the Fourteenth Amendment gives the federal courts no power to impose upon the States their views of what constitutes wise economic or social policy.

Applying those principles to this case, the plain language of § 231b(h) marks the beginning and end of our inquiry. There Congress determined that some of those who in the past received full windfall benefits would not continue to do so. Because Congress could have eliminated windfall benefits for all classes of employees, it is not constitutionally impermissible for Congress to have drawn lines between groups of employees for the purpose of phasing out those benefits. *New Orleans v. Dukes, supra,* at 305.

The only remaining question is whether Congress achieved its purpose in a patently arbitrary or irrational way. The classification here is not arbitrary, says appellant, because it is an attempt to protect the relative equities of employees and to provide benefits to career railroad employees. Congress fully protected, for example, the expectations of those employees who had already retired and those unretired employees who had 25 years of railroad employment. Conversely, Congress denied all windfall benefits to those employees who lacked 10 years of railroad employment. Congress additionally provided windfall benefits, in lesser amount, to those employees with 10 years' railroad employment who had qualified for social security benefits at the time they had left railroad employment, regardless of a current connection with the industry in 1974 or on their retirement date.

Thus, the only eligible former railroad employees denied full windfall benefits are those, like appellee, who had no statutory entitlement to dual benefits at the time they left the railroad industry, but thereafter became eligible for dual benefits when they subsequently qualified for social security benefits. Congress could properly conclude that persons who had actually acquired statutory entitlement to windfall benefits while still employed in the railroad industry had a greater equitable claim to those benefits than the members of appellee's class who were no longer in railroad employment when they became eligible for dual benefits. Furthermore, the "current connection" test is not a patently arbitrary means for determining which employees are "career railroaders," particularly since the test has been used by Congress elsewhere as an eligibility requirement for retirement benefits. Congress could assume that those who had a current connection with the railroad industry when the Act was passed in 1974, or who returned to the industry before their retirement, were more likely than those who had left the industry prior to 1974 and who never returned, to be among the class of persons who pursue careers in the railroad industry, the class for whom the Railroad Retirement Act was designed.

Where, as here, there are plausible reasons for Congress' action, our inquiry is at an end. It is, of course, "constitutionally irrelevant whether this reasoning in fact underlay the legislative decision," *Flemming v. Nestor*, 363 U.S., at 612, because this Court has never insisted that a legislative body articulate its reasons for enacting a statute. This is particularly true where the legislature must necessarily engage in a process of line-drawing. The "task of classifying persons for ... benefits ... inevitably requires that some persons who have an almost equally strong claim to favored treatment be placed on different sides of the line," *Mathews v. Diaz*, 426 U.S. 67, 83-84 (1976), and the fact the line might have been drawn differently at some points is a matter for legislative, rather than judicial, consideration.

Finally, we disagree with the District Court's conclusion that Congress was unaware of what it accomplished or that it was misled by the groups that appeared before it. If this test were applied literally to every member of any legislature that ever voted on a law, there would be very few laws which would survive it. The language of the statute is clear, and we have historically assumed that Congress intended what it enacted. To be sure, appellee lost a political battle in which he had a strong interest, but this is neither the first nor the last time that such a result will occur in the legislative forum. What we have said is enough to dispose of the claims that Congress not only failed to accept appellee's argument as to restructuring *in toto*, but that such failure denied him equal protection of the laws guaranteed by the Fifth Amendment.

For the foregoing reasons, the judgment of the District Court is *Reversed*.

Justice STEVENS, concurring in the judgment.

Justice BRENNAN correctly points out that if the analysis of legislative purpose requires only a reading of the statutory language in a disputed provision, and if any "conceivable basis" for a discriminatory classification will repel a constitutional attack on the statute, judicial review will constitute a mere tautological recognition of the fact that Congress did what it intended to do. Justice BRENNAN is also correct in reminding us that even though the statute is an example of "social and economic legislation," the challenge here is mounted by individuals whose legitimate expectations of receiving a fixed retirement income are being frustrated by, in effect, a breach of a solemn commitment by their Government. When Congress deprives a small class of persons of vested rights that are protected--and, indeed, even enhanced-- for others who are in a similar though not identical position, I believe the Constitution requires something more than merely a "conceivable" or a "plausible" explanation for the unequal treatment.

I do not, however, share Justice BRENNAN's conclusion that every statutory classification must further an objective that can be confidently identified as the "actual purpose" of the legislature. Actual purpose is sometimes unknown. Moreover, undue emphasis on actual motivation may result in identically worded statutes being held valid in one State and invalid in a neighboring State. I therefore believe that we must discover a correlation between the classification and either the actual purpose of the statute or a legitimate purpose that we may reasonably presume to have motivated an impartial legislature. If the adverse impact on the disfavored class is an apparent aim of the legislature, its impartiality would be suspect. If, however, the adverse impact may reasonably be viewed as an acceptable cost of achieving a larger goal, an impartial lawmaker could rationally decide that that cost should be incurred.

In this case we need not look beyond the actual purpose of the legislature. As is often true, this legislation is the product of multiple and somewhat inconsistent purposes that led to certain compromises. One purpose was to eliminate in the future the benefit that is described by the Court as a "windfall benefit" and by Justice BRENNAN as an "earned dual benefit." That aim was incident to the broader objective of protecting the solvency of the entire railroad retirement program. Two purposes that conflicted somewhat with this broad objective were the purposes of preserving those benefits that had already vested and of increasing the level of payments to beneficiaries whose rights were not otherwise to be changed. As Justice BRENNAN emphasizes, Congress originally intended to protect *all* vested benefits, but it ultimately sacrificed some benefits in the interest of achieving other objectives.

Given these conflicting purposes, I believe the decisive questions are (1) whether Congress can rationally reduce the vested benefits of some employees to improve the solvency of the entire program while simultaneously increasing the benefits of others; and (2) whether, in deciding which vested benefits to reduce, Congress may favor annuitants whose railroad service was more recent than that of disfavored annuitants who had an equal or greater quantum of employment.

My answer to both questions is in the affirmative. The congressional purpose to eliminate dual benefits is unquestionably legitimate; that legitimacy is not undermined by the adjustment in the level of remaining benefits in response to inflation in the economy. As for the second question, some hardship--in the form of frustrated long-term expectations--must inevitably result from any reduction in vested benefits. Arguably, therefore, Congress had a duty--and surely it had the right to decide--to eliminate no more vested benefits than necessary to achieve its fiscal purpose. Having made that decision, any distinction it chose within the class of vested beneficiaries would involve a difference of degree rather than a difference in entitlement. I am satisfied that a distinction based upon currency of railroad employment represents an impartial method of identifying that sort of difference. Because retirement plans frequently provide greater benefits for recent retirees than for those who retired years ago-and thus give a greater reward for recent service than for past service of equal duration-the basis for the statutory discrimination is supported by relevant precedent. It follows, in my judgment, that the timing of the employees' railroad service is a "reasonable basis" for the classification as that term is used in *Lindsley v. Natural Carbonic Gas Co.,* 220 U.S. 61 and *Dandridge v. Williams,* 397 U.S. 471, as well as a "ground of difference having a fair and substantial relation to the object of the legislation," as those words are used in *F.S. Royster Guano Co. v. Virginia,* 253 U.S. 412.

Accordingly, I concur in the judgment.

Justice BRENNAN, with whom Justice MARSHALL joins, dissenting.

The purposes of the Railroad Retirement Act of 1974 are clear, because Congress has commendably stated them in the House and Senate Reports accompanying the Act. A section of the Reports is entitled "Principal Purpose of the Bill." It notes generally that "[t]he bill provides for a complete restructuring of the Railroad Retirement Act of 1937, and will place it on a sound financial basis," and then states:

> Persons who already have vested rights under both the Railroad Retirement and the Social Security systems will in the future be permitted to receive benefits computed under both systems just as is true under existing law. H.R.Rep.No.93-1345, pp. 1, 2 (1974); S.Rep.No.93-1163, pp. 1, 2 (1974); U.S.Code Cong. & Admin.News 1974, p. 5702.

Moreover, Congress explained that this purpose was based on considerations of fairness and the legitimate expectations of the retirees:

> [A]ny plan to eliminate these dual benefits should include protection of the equities of existing beneficiaries and employees with claims upon such benefits. Dual beneficiaries cannot fairly be criticized, since they have merely secured the benefits to which they are entitled under existing law. That is why their equities should be preserved. H.R.Rep.No. 93-1345, at 11; S.Rep.No. 93-1163, at 11; U.S.Code Cong. & Admin.News 1974 at 5710.

Thus, a "principal purpose" of the Railroad Retirement Act of 1974, as explicitly stated by Congress, was to preserve the vested earned benefits of retirees who had already qualified for them. The classification at issue here, which deprives some retirees of vested dual benefits that they had earned prior to 1974, directly conflicts with Congress' stated purpose. As such, the classification is not only rationally unrelated to the congressional purpose; it is inimical to it.

III

The Court today avoids the conclusion that § 231b(h) must be invalidated by deviating in three ways from traditional rational-basis analysis. First, the Court adopts a tautological approach to statutory purpose, thereby avoiding the necessity for evaluating the relationship between the challenged classification and the legislative purpose. Second, it disregards the actual stated purpose of Congress in favor of a justification which was never suggested by any Representative or Senator, and which in fact conflicts with the stated congressional purpose. Third, it upholds the classification without any analysis of its rational relationship to the identified purpose.

A

The Court states that "the plain language of [45 U.S.C.] § 231b(h) marks the beginning and end of our inquiry." This statement is strange indeed, for the "plain language" of the statute can tell us only what the classification is; it can tell us nothing about the purpose of the classification, let alone the relationship between the classification and that purpose. Since § 231b(h) deprives the members of appellee class of their vested earned dual benefits, the Court apparently assumes that

Congress must have *intended* that result. But by presuming purpose from result, the Court reduces analysis to tautology. It may always be said that Congress intended to do what it in fact did. If that were the extent of our analysis, we would find every statute, no matter how arbitrary or irrational, perfectly tailored to achieve its purpose. But equal protection scrutiny under the rational-basis test requires the courts first to deduce the independent objectives of the statute, usually from statements of purpose and other evidence in the statute and legislative history, and second to analyze whether the challenged classification rationally furthers achievement of those objectives. The Court's tautological approach will not suffice.

B

The Court analyzes the rationality of § 231b(h) in terms of a justification suggested by Government attorneys, but never adopted by Congress. The Court states that it is "constitutionally irrelevant whether this reasoning in fact underlay the legislative decision." In fact, however, equal protection analysis has evolved substantially on this question since *Flemming* was decided. Over the past 10 years, this Court has frequently recognized that the actual purposes of Congress, rather than the *post hoc* justifications offered by Government attorneys, must be the primary basis for analysis under the rational-basis test. In *Weinberger v. Wiesenfeld*, 420 U.S. 636, 648, n. 16 (1975), we said:

> This Court need not in equal protection cases accept at face value assertions of legislative purposes, when an examination of the legislative scheme and its history demonstrates that the asserted purpose could not have been a goal of the legislation.

Thus, in *San Antonio Independent School District v. Rodriguez*, 411 U.S. 1, 17 (1973), this Court stated that a challenged classification will pass muster under "rational basis" scrutiny only if it "rationally furthers some legitimate, *articulated* state purpose" (emphasis added), and in *Massachusetts Board of Retirement v. Murgia*, 427 U.S., at 314, we stated that such a classification will be sustained only if it "rationally furthers the purpose *identified by the State*." (Emphasis added.) Moreover, in *Johnson v. Robison*, 415 U.S., at 381-382, we upheld a classification on the finding that "[t]hese quantitative and qualitative distinctions, *expressly recognized by Congress*, form a rational basis for Congress' classification. . . ." (Emphasis added.) See also *Califano v. Goldfarb*, 430 U.S. 199, 212-213 (1977).

From these cases and others it is clear that this Court will no longer sustain a challenged classification under the rational-basis test merely because Government attorneys can suggest a "conceivable basis" upon which it might be thought rational. The standard we have applied is properly deferential to the Legislative Branch: where Congress has articulated a legitimate governmental objective, and the challenged classification rationally furthers that objective, we must sustain the provision. In other cases, however, the courts must probe more deeply. Where Congress has expressly stated the purpose of a piece of legislation, but where the challenged classification is either irrelevant to or counter to that purpose, we must view any *post hoc* justifications proffered by Government attorneys with skepticism. A challenged classification may be sustained only if it is rationally related to achievement of an *actual* legitimate governmental purpose.

The Court argues that Congress chose to discriminate against appellee for reasons of equity, stating that "Congress could properly conclude that persons who had actually acquired statutory entitlement to windfall benefits while still employed in the railroad industry had a greater equitable claim to those benefits than the members of appellee's class who were no longer in railroad employment when they became eligible for dual benefits." This statement turns Congress' assessment of the equities on its head. As I have shown, Congress expressed the view that it would be inequitable to deprive any retirees of any portion of the benefits they had been promised and that they had earned under prior law. The Court is unable to cite even one statement in the legislative history by a Representative or Senator that makes the equitable judgment it imputes to Congress. In the entire legislative history of the Act, the only persons to state that the equities justified eliminating appellee's earned dual benefits were representatives of railroad management and labor, whose self-serving interest in bringing about this result destroys any basis for attaching weight to their statements.

Therefore, I do not think that this classification was rationally related to an *actual* governmental purpose. I respectfully dissent.

NOTES

1. There is clear disagreement among members of the Court over what the purpose of the amendment to the Railroad Retirement law was and how the Court was supposed to ascertain that purpose. The majority suggested two different methods to use in identifying purpose, but the two methods contradict each other. On the one hand, the majority initially insisted that the plain language of the statute marks the beginning and end of its inquiry. But as the dissenters pointed out, the "plain language" of a statute can only identify the statutory classification; it cannot identify the law's purpose. The majority opinion at this point seemed to suggest that, because the statute in fact accomplishes a particular result, then the legislature must have intended that result. Thus, in *Fritz*, if the law deprives retirement benefits to certain vested employees, then Congress must have intended to deny benefits to that subgroup, and therefore the purpose of the law must be to deny benefits to that subgroup. If this is an accurate method of identifying purpose, then there would always be a perfect correlation between classification and purpose. As the dissenters make clear, this is nonsense. The purpose of a law cannot be derived from its operative effect. To do so would be to reduce rational basis review to a tautology in that you could say of every law that its purpose is to accomplish exactly what it in fact accomplishes.

As the previous paragraph indicates, there must be some distance between the classification created by the express language of a statute and that statute's purpose. Even conceding the necessity of this distance, however, the majority and dissenters differed on the proper method for determining purpose. On its face, the statutory distinctions that rewarded some vested workers but denied benefits to other vested workers made no obvious sense. The majority was able to make sense of those distinctions by hypothesizing a statutory purpose—preserving the benefits of "career railroaders." The majority latched onto this purpose although there was no evidence that Congress had ever considered it and even though the first time that purpose was advanced was during the litigation in question, when it was brought forth as a "post-hoc rationalization proffered by government attorneys." This technique of hypothesizing legislative purpose, even without any evidence to support that assertion, is a cornerstone of deferential rational basis review.

The dissenters pointed out that there was, in fact, clear evidence of the actual purpose of the law and that evidence was contained in the official House and Senate Reports that accompanied the Act. According to these Reports, the purpose of the amended law was to protect those whose benefits had already vested. In relation to this purpose, the statutory distinctions among those with vested benefits made no sense in that all of those whose benefits had vested were similarly situated in relation to that purpose, and thus all should be treated the same. This emphasis by dissenters on looking for the actual purpose of a law has no place in the traditional, deferential version of rationality review, but, as the latter part of this chapter will make clear, focus on the actual purpose of a law is an essential element of heightened rational basis review.

D. WHAT IS THE REQUIRED CORRELATION BETWEEN CLASSIFICATION AND PURPOSE?

Once a court has identified the classification made by a statute and the statute's purpose, it must then determine if the classification is adequately correlated with the purpose. The classification and the purpose are supposed to be "rationally related." As the next case shows, under traditional deference, that standard requires very little connection between the two.

State of Minnesota v. Clover Leaf Creamery Co.
449 U.S. 456 (1981)

[A Minnesota statute banned the retail sale of milk in plastic containers that were not returnable or refillable but did not forbid the sale of milk in paperboard containers. The stated purpose of the statute was to address waste management and environmental concerns surrounding the production and use of plastics. During the legislative process, opponents of the statute had challenged the purported environmental benefits and claimed that the ban merely reflected a bias in favor of the Minnesota pulpwood industry. Parties involved in the sale of milk in nonreturnable plastic containers filed an action in state court alleging that the statute violated the Equal Protection Clause.]

Justice BRENNAN delivered the opinion of the Court:

The parties agree that the standard of review applicable to this case under the Equal Protection Clause is the familiar "rational basis" test. See *Vance v. Bradley*, 440 U.S. 93, 97, (1979); *New Orleans v. Dukes*, 427 U.S. 297, 303 (1976). Moreover, they agree that the purposes of the Act cited by the legislature--promoting resource conservation, easing solid waste disposal problems, and conserving energy--are legitimate state purposes. Thus, the controversy in this case centers on the narrow issue whether the legislative classification between plastic and nonplastic nonreturnable milk containers is rationally related to achievement of the statutory purposes.

A

Respondents apparently have not challenged the *theoretical* connection between a ban on plastic nonreturnables and the purposes articulated by the legislature; instead, they have argued that there is no *empirical* connection between the two. They produced impressive supporting evidence at trial to prove that the probable consequences of the ban on plastic nonreturnable milk containers will be to deplete natural resources, exacerbate solid waste disposal problems, and waste energy, because consumers unable to purchase milk in plastic containers will turn to paperboard milk cartons, allegedly a more environmentally harmful product.

But States are not required to convince the courts of the correctness of their legislative judgments. Rather, "those challenging the legislative judgment must convince the court that the legislative facts on which the classification is apparently based could not reasonably be conceived to be true by the governmental decisionmaker." *Vance v. Bradley*, 440 U.S., at 111. Although parties challenging legislation under the Equal Protection Clause may introduce evidence supporting their claim that it is irrational, *United States v. Carolene Products Co.*, 304 U.S. 144, 153-154 they cannot prevail so long as "it is evident from all the considerations presented to [the legislature], and those of which we may take judicial notice, that the question is at least debatable." *Id.*, at 154. Where there was evidence before the legislature reasonably supporting the classification, litigants may not procure invalidation of the legislation merely by tendering evidence in court that the legislature was mistaken.

B

The State identifies four reasons why the classification between plastic and nonplastic nonreturnables is rationally related to the articulated statutory purposes. If any one of the four substantiates the State's claim, we must reverse the Minnesota Supreme Court and sustain the Act.

First, the State argues that elimination of the popular plastic milk jug will encourage the use of environmentally superior containers. There is no serious doubt that the plastic containers consume energy resources and require solid waste disposal, nor that refillable bottles and plastic pouches are environmentally superior. Citing evidence that the plastic jug is the most popular, and the gallon paperboard carton the most cumbersome and least well regarded package in the industry, the State argues that the ban on plastic nonreturnables will buy time during which environmentally preferable alternatives may be further developed and promoted.

As Senator Spear argued during the Senate debate:

> [T]his bill is designed to prevent the beginning of another system of non-returnables that is going to be very, very difficult [to stop] once it begins. It is true that our alternative now is not a returnable system in terms of milk bottles. Hopefully we are eventually going to be able to move to that kind of a system, but we are never going to move to a returnable system so long as we allow another non-returnable system with all the investment and all of the vested interest that is going to involve to begin.

The Minnesota Supreme Court dismissed this asserted state interest as "speculative and illusory." 289 N.W.2d, at 86. The court expressed doubt that the Minnesota Legislature or Pollution Control Agency would take any further steps to promote environmentally sound milk packaging, and stated that there is no evidence that paperboard cartons will cease to be used in Minnesota.

We find the State's approach fully supportable under our precedents. This Court has made clear that a legislature need not "strike at all evils at the same time or in the same way," *Semler v. Oregon State Board of Dental Examiners*, 294 U.S. 608, 610 (1935), and that a legislature "may implement [its] program step by step, ... adopting regulations that only partially ameliorate a perceived evil and deferring complete elimination of the evil to future regulations." *New Orleans v. Dukes*, 427 U.S., at 303. The Equal Protection Clause does not deny the State of Minnesota the authority to ban one type of milk container conceded to cause environmental problems, merely because another type, already established in the market, is permitted to continue in use. Whether *in fact* the Act will promote more environmentally desirable milk packaging is not the question: the Equal Protection Clause is satisfied by our conclusion that the Minnesota Legislature *could rationally have decided* that its ban on plastic nonreturnable milk jugs might foster greater use of environmentally desirable alternatives.

Second, the State argues that its ban on plastic nonreturnable milk containers will reduce the economic dislocation foreseen from the movement toward greater use of environmentally superior containers. The State notes that plastic nonreturnables have only recently been introduced on a wide scale in Minnesota, and that, at the time the legislature was considering the Act, many Minnesota dairies were preparing to invest large amounts of capital in plastic container production. As Representative Munger, chief sponsor of the bill in the House of Representatives, explained:

> Minnesota's dairy market is on the verge of making a major change over from essentially a paperboard container system to a system of primarily single use, throwaway plastic bottles. The major dairies in our state have ordered the blow-mold equipment to manufacture in plant the non-returnable plastic milk bottle. Members of the House, I feel now is an ideal time for this legislation when only one dairy in our state is firmly established in manufacturing and marketing the throwaway plastic milk bottle.

Moreover, the State explains, to ban both the plastic and the paperboard nonreturnable milk container at once would cause an enormous disruption in the milk industry because few dairies are now able to package their products in refillable bottles or plastic pouches. Thus, by banning the plastic container while continuing to permit the paperboard container, the State was able to prevent the industry from becoming reliant on the new container, while avoiding severe economic dislocation.

The Minnesota Supreme Court did not directly address this justification, but we find it supported by our precedents as well. In *New Orleans v. Dukes* we upheld a city regulation banning pushcart food vendors, but exempting from the ban two vendors who had operated in the city for over eight years. Noting that the "city could reasonably decide that newer businesses were less likely to have built up substantial reliance interests in continued operation," we held that the city "could rationally choose initially to eliminate vendors of more recent vintage." This case is not significantly different. The state legislature concluded that nonreturnable, nonrefillable milk containers pose environmental hazards, and decided to ban the most recent entry into the field. The fact that the legislature in effect "grandfathered" paperboard containers, at least temporarily, does not make the Act's ban on plastic nonreturnables arbitrary or irrational.

Third, the State argues that the Act will help to conserve energy. It points out that plastic milk jugs are made from plastic resin, an oil and natural gas derivative, whereas paperboard milk cartons are primarily composed of pulpwood, which is a renewable resource. This point was stressed by the Act's proponents in the legislature. Senator Luther commented: "We have been through an energy crisis in Minnesota. We know what it is like to go without and what we are looking at here is a total blatant waste of petroleum and natural gas. . . ." Representative Munger said in a similar vein:

> A sweep to the plastic throwaway bottle in the gallon size container alone would use enough additional natural gas and petroleum to heat 3,100 homes each year in Minnesota when compared to a refillable system and 1,400 compared to the present paperboard system. Plastic containers are made from a non-renewable resource while the paperboard is made from Minnesota's forest products.

The Minnesota Supreme Court held, in effect, that the legislature misunderstood the facts. The court admitted that the results of a reliable study support the legislature's conclusion that less energy is consumed in the production of paperboard containers than in the production of plastic nonreturnables, but, after crediting the contrary testimony of respondents' expert witness and altering certain factual assumptions, the court concluded that "production of plastic nonrefillables requires less energy than production of paper containers."

The Minnesota Supreme Court may be correct that the Act is not a sensible means of conserving energy. But we reiterate that "it is up to legislatures, not courts, to decide on the wisdom and utility of legislation." *Ferguson v. Skrupa*, 372 U.S. 726, 729 (1963). Since in view of the evidence before the legislature, the question clearly is "at least debatable," *United States v.*

Carolene Products Co., 304 U.S., at 154, the Minnesota Supreme Court erred in substituting its judgment for that of the legislature.

Fourth, the State argues that the Act will ease the State's solid waste disposal problem. Most solid consumer wastes in Minnesota are disposed of in landfills. A reputable study before the Minnesota Legislature indicated that plastic milk jugs occupy a greater volume in landfills than other nonreturnable milk containers. This was one of the legislature's major concerns. For example, in introducing the bill to the House of Representatives, Representative Munger asked rhetorically, "Why do we need this legislation?" Part of his answer to the query was that "the plastic non-refillable containers will increase the problems of solid waste in our state." Transcript of the Debate of the Minnesota House of Representatives on H.F. 45, p. 1 (Mar. 10, 1977).

The Minnesota Supreme Court found that plastic milk jugs in fact take up less space in landfills and present fewer solid waste disposal problems than do paperboard containers. But its ruling on this point must be rejected for the same reason we rejected its ruling concerning energy conservation: it is not the function of the courts to substitute their evaluation of legislative facts for that of the legislature.

We therefore conclude that the ban on plastic nonreturnable milk containers bears a rational relation to the State's objectives, and must be sustained under the Equal Protection Clause.

The judgment of the Minnesota Supreme Court is *Reversed.*

NOTES

1. Which milk container is more environmentally harmful—the plastic or the paperboard? The statute enacted by the Minnesota legislature assumed that plastic containers are more harmful and therefore prohibited their use. But was the legislature's assumption correct? There was substantial evidence before the legislature that *paperboard* containers were more harmful than plastic. Even if one assumed that plastic containers were only similarly harmful rather than more harmful, rational basis review would seem to require the legislature to treat the two containers the same.

That analysis, however, overlooks the deferential nature of rational basis review in evaluating the required correlation between classification and purpose. As the *Minnesota Creamery* Court made clear, there does not have to be an actual correlation between classification and purpose. Equal protection simply requires that "the Minnesota Legislature *could rationally have decided* that its ban on plastic nonreturnable milk jugs might foster greater use of environmentally desirable alternatives," *even if the legislature was mistaken.*

This standard is extraordinarily forgiving of governmental error. If we look back at the statute involved in the Murgia case, for example, what if it turned out in fact that those over fifty were *not* less fit to do police work than those under fifty? Would that invalidate the statute? According to the Court in *Clover Leaf Creamery*, it would not, so long as it could be argued that the Massachusetts legislature could rationally have decided that over-fifties were less fit, even if the legislature was mistaken. Note also the almost impossible burden placed on those challenging a classification under traditional deferential rational basis review—"those challenging the legislative judgment must convince the court that the legislative facts on which the classification is apparently based could not reasonably be conceived to be true by the governmental decisionmaker." The two cases in the next section are good examples of a review that is so deferential as to amount to no review at all.

E. DEFERENCE SO GREAT AS TO AMOUNT TO NO REVIEW AT ALL

Federal Communications Commission v. Beach Communications, Inc.
508 U.S. 307 (1993)

[In providing for the regulation of cable television facilities, Congress drew a distinction between facilities that serve separately owned and managed buildings and those that serve one or more buildings under common ownership or management. Cable facilities in the latter category were exempted from regulation as long as they provided services without using public rights-of-way.]

JUSTICE THOMAS delivered the opinion of the Court.

Whether embodied in the Fourteenth Amendment or inferred from the Fifth, equal protection is not a license for courts to judge the wisdom, fairness, or logic of legislative choices. In areas of social and economic policy, a statutory classification that neither proceeds along suspect lines nor infringes fundamental constitutional rights must be upheld against equal protection challenge if there is any reasonably conceivable state of facts that could provide a rational basis for the classification. See *Sullivan v. Stroop*, 496 U.S. 478, 485 (1990); *Bowen v. Gilliard*, 483 U.S. 587, 600–603 (1987); *United States Railroad Retirement Bd. v. Fritz*, 449 U.S. 166, 174–179 (1980); *Dandridge v. Williams*, 397 U.S. 471, 484–485 (1970). Where there are "plausible reasons" for Congress' action, "our inquiry is at an end." *United States Railroad Retirement Bd. v. Fritz, supra*, 449 U.S., at 179. This standard of review is a paradigm of judicial restraint. "The Constitution presumes that, absent some reason to infer antipathy, even improvident decisions will eventually be rectified by the democratic process and that judicial intervention is generally unwarranted no matter how unwisely we may think a political branch has acted." *Vance v. Bradley*, 440 U.S. 93, 97 (1979).

On rational-basis review, a classification in a statute such as the Cable Act comes to us bearing a strong presumption of validity, and those attacking the rationality of the legislative classification have the burden "to negative every conceivable basis which might support it," *Lehnhausen v. Lake Shore Auto Parts Co.*, 410 U.S. 356, 364 (1973). Moreover, because we never require a legislature to articulate its reasons for enacting a statute, it is entirely irrelevant for constitutional purposes whether the conceived reason for the challenged distinction actually motivated the legislature. *United States Railroad Retirement Bd. v. Fritz, supra*, 449 U.S., at 179. Thus, the absence of "'legislative facts'" explaining the distinction "[o]n the record," 294 U.S.App.D.C., at 389, has no significance in rational-basis analysis. See *Nordlinger v. Hahn*, 505 U.S. 1, 15 (1992) (equal protection "does not demand for purposes of rational-basis review that a legislature or governing decisionmaker actually articulate at any time the purpose or rationale supporting its classification"). In other words, a legislative choice is not subject to courtroom fact-finding and may be based on rational speculation unsupported by evidence or empirical data. See *Vance v. Bradley, supra*, 440 U.S., at 111. See also *Minnesota v. Clover Leaf Creamery Co.*, 449 U.S. 456, 464 (1981). "'Only by faithful adherence to this guiding principle of judicial review of legislation is it possible to preserve to the legislative branch its rightful independence and its ability to function.'" *Lehnhausen, supra*, 410 U.S., at 365.

These restraints on judicial review have added force "where the legislature must necessarily engage in a process of line-drawing." *United States Railroad Retirement Bd. v. Fritz*, 449 U.S., at 179. Defining the class of persons subject to a regulatory requirement—much like classifying governmental beneficiaries—"inevitably requires that some persons who have an almost equally strong claim to favored treatment be placed on different sides of the line, and the fact [that] the line might have been drawn differently at some points is a matter for legislative, rather than judicial, consideration." The distinction at issue here represents such a line: By excluding from the definition of "cable system" those facilities that serve commonly owned or managed buildings without using public rights-of-way, § 602(7)(B) delineates the bounds of the regulatory field. Such scope-of-coverage provisions are unavoidable components of most economic or social legislation. In establishing the franchise requirement, Congress had to draw the line somewhere; it had to choose which facilities to franchise. This necessity renders the precise coordinates of the resulting legislative judgment virtually unreviewable, since the legislature must be allowed leeway to approach a perceived problem incrementally.

Applying these principles, we conclude that the common-ownership distinction is constitutional. There are at least two possible bases for the distinction; either one suffices. First, Congress borrowed § 602(7)(B) from pre-Cable Act regulations, and although the existence of a prior administrative scheme is certainly not necessary to the rationality of the statute, it is plausible that Congress also adopted the FCC's earlier rationale. Under that rationale, common ownership was thought to be indicative of those systems for which the costs of regulation would outweigh the benefits to consumers. Because the number of subscribers was a similar indicator, the Commission also exempted cable facilities that served fewer than 50 subscribers. See 47 CFR § 76.5(a) (1984).

This regulatory-efficiency model provides a conceivable basis for the common-ownership exemption. A legislator might rationally assume that systems serving only commonly owned or managed buildings without crossing public rights-of-way would typically be limited in size or would share some other attribute affecting their impact on the welfare of cable viewers such that regulators could "safely ignor[e]" these systems.

Respondents argue that Congress did not intend common ownership to be a surrogate for small size, since Congress simultaneously rejected the FCC's 50–subscriber exemption by omitting it from the Cable Act. Whether the posited reason for the challenged distinction actually motivated Congress is "constitutionally irrelevant," *United States Railroad Retirement Bd. v. Fritz, supra,* 449 U.S., at 179, and, in any event, the FCC's explanation indicates that both common ownership and number of subscribers were considered indicia of "very small" cable systems. Respondents also contend that an SMATV operator could increase his subscription base and still qualify for the exemption simply by installing a separate satellite dish on each building served. The additional cost of multiple dishes and associated transmission equipment, however, would impose an independent constraint on system size.

Furthermore, small size is only one plausible ownership-related factor contributing to consumer welfare. Subscriber influence is another. Where an SMATV system serves a complex of buildings under common ownership or management, individual subscribers could conceivably have greater bargaining power vis-à-vis the cable operator (even if the number of dwelling units were large), since all the subscribers could negotiate with one voice through the common owner or manager. Such an owner might have substantial leverage, because he could withhold permission to operate the SMATV system on his property. He would also have an incentive to guard the interests of his tenants. Thus, there could be less need to establish regulatory safeguards for subscribers in commonly owned complexes. Respondents acknowledge such possibilities and we certainly cannot say that these assumptions would be irrational.

There is a second conceivable basis for the statutory distinction. Suppose competing SMATV operators wish to sell video programming to subscribers in a group of contiguous buildings, such as a single city block, which can be interconnected by wire without crossing a public right-of-way. If all the buildings belong to one owner or are commonly managed, that owner or manager could freely negotiate a deal for all subscribers on a competitive basis. But if the buildings are separately owned and managed, the first SMATV operator who gains a foothold by signing a contract and installing a satellite dish and associated transmission equipment on one of the buildings would enjoy a powerful cost advantage in competing for the remaining subscribers: He could connect additional buildings for the cost of a few feet of cable, whereas any competitor would have to recover the cost of his own satellite headend facility. Thus, the first operator could charge rates well above his cost and still undercut the competition. This potential for effective monopoly power might theoretically justify regulating the latter class of SMATV systems and not the former.

III

The Court of Appeals quite evidently believed that the crossing or use of a public right-of-way is the only conceivable basis upon which Congress could rationally require local franchising of SMATV systems. As we have indicated, however, there are plausible rationales unrelated to the use of public rights-of-way for regulating cable facilities serving separately owned and managed buildings. The assumptions underlying these rationales may be erroneous, but the very fact that they are "arguable" is sufficient, on rational-basis review, to "immuniz[e]" the congressional choice from constitutional challenge. *Vance v. Bradley*, 440 U.S., at 112.

The judgment of the Court of Appeals is reversed, and the case is remanded for further proceedings consistent with this opinion. *So ordered.*

NOTES

1. The result in *Beach Communications* is not at all surprising in that the Court is particularly deferential to the legislature when the legislature is regulating business affairs. The language of the Court's opinion, however, is surprising in its breadth, for it states a standard of review that is so deferential, so unconnected with evidence of the real world, that it is hard to imagine any statute that could not satisfy the Court's requirements. The Court insists (1) that those attacking the rationality of the legislative classification have the burden "to negative every conceivable basis which might support it," (2) that the legislature need not articulate its reasons for enacting a statute, (3) that it is entirely irrelevant whether the conceived reason for the challenged distinction actually motivated the legislature, (4) that the absence of "legislative facts" explaining the distinction on the record has no significance in rational-basis analysis, (5) that a legislature or governing decisionmaker need not actually articulate at any time the purpose or rationale supporting its classification, and (6) that a legislative choice is not subject to courtroom fact-finding but rather may be based on rational speculation unsupported by evidence or empirical data. The effect of this kind of deference is that "the resulting legislative judgment [is] virtually unreviewable."

2. For a trenchant and scathing commentary on the deferential version of rational basis review at its extreme, *see* Clark Neily, *No Such Thing: Litigating Under the Rational Basis Test*, 1 NYU J. Law & Liberty 898 (2005):

> The original legal definition of insanity is the inability to tell right from wrong. So it is the first irony of the "rational" basis test that it is, according to that definition, insane. The word "basis" is likewise a misnomer, since the rational basis test is concerned not with the *actual* basis for challenged legislation, but with speculative and hypothetical purposes instead. Finally, the word "test" is inappropriate, at least insofar as it suggests some meaningful analytical framework to guide judicial decision-making, because the rational basis test is nothing more than a Magic Eight Ball that randomly generates

different answers to key constitutional questions depending on who happens to be shaking it and with what level of vigor. Mendacious as the rational basis test is in name, however, that is nothing compared to the intellectual dishonesty it engenders in actual litigation.

3. *Beach Communications* thus creates a very strong presumption of nonreviewability in the standard rational basis case, arising in the commercial context. The next case arises in a context where previous Court precedents seem to have suggested a more demanding review but the Court cites *Beach Communications* and applies an equally deferential standard.

Heller v Doe
509 U.S. 312 (1993)

[By statute in the Commonwealth of Kentucky, commitment proceedings differ based on whether an individual being evaluated for civil involuntary commitment is alleged to be mentally retarded or mentally ill. At a commitment hearing based on mental retardation, the burden of proof for involuntary commitment is clear and convincing evidence. In addition at such a hearing, third parties who are guardians or immediate family members are permitted to participate, and this participation includes the right to present evidence and to appeal the hearing decision. On the other hand, at a commitment hearing based on mental illness, the burden of proof is beyond a reasonable doubt, and there is no third party right to participate in the proceedings.

The respondents were mentally retarded persons who had been involuntarily committed to Kentucky institutions. They argued that the distinction made between the mentally retarded and the mentally ill was irrational and violated the Equal Protection Clause of the Fourteenth Amendment.]

Justice KENNEDY delivered the opinion of the Court.

We many times have said, and but weeks ago repeated, that rational-basis review in equal protection analysis "is not a license for courts to judge the wisdom, fairness, or logic of legislative choices." *FCC v. Beach Communications, Inc.,* 508 U.S. 307, 313 (1993). Nor does it authorize "the judiciary [to] sit as a superlegislature to judge the wisdom or desirability of legislative policy determinations made in areas that neither affect fundamental rights nor proceed along suspect lines." *New Orleans v. Dukes,* 427 U.S. 297, 303, (1976) *(per curiam).* For these reasons, a classification neither involving fundamental rights nor proceeding along suspect lines is accorded a strong presumption of validity. Such a classification cannot run afoul of the Equal Protection Clause if there is a rational relationship between the disparity of treatment and some legitimate governmental purpose. See, *e.g., Nordlinger v. Hahn,* 505 U.S. 1, 11 (1992). Instead, a classification "must be upheld against equal protection challenge if there is any reasonably conceivable state of facts that could provide a rational basis for the classification." *Beach Communications, supra,* 508 U.S., at 313.

A State, moreover, has no obligation to produce evidence to sustain the rationality of a statutory classification. "[A] legislative choice is not subject to courtroom factfinding and may be based on rational speculation unsupported by evidence or empirical data." *Beach Communications, supra,* 508 U.S., at 315. A statute is presumed constitutional and "[t]he burden is on the one attacking the legislative arrangement to negative every conceivable basis which might support it," *Lehnhausen v. Lake Shore Auto Parts Co.,* 410 U.S. 356, 364 (1973), whether or not the basis has a foundation in the record. Finally, courts are compelled under rational-basis review to accept a legislature's generalizations even when there is an imperfect fit between means and ends. A classification does not fail rational-basis review because it "'is not made with mathematical nicety or because in practice it results in some inequality.'" *Dandridge v. Williams, supra,* 397 U.S., at 485. "The problems of government are practical ones and may justify, if they do not require, rough accommodations—illogical, it may be, and unscientific." *Metropolis Theatre Co. v. Chicago,* 228 U.S. 61, 69–70 (1913). We have applied rational-basis review in previous cases involving the mentally retarded and the mentally ill. See *Cleburne v. Cleburne Living Center, Inc.,* 473 U.S. 432 (1985); *Schweiker v. Wilson, supra.* In neither case did we purport to apply a different standard of rational-basis review from that just described.

True, even the standard of rationality as we so often have defined it must find some footing in the realities of the subject addressed by the legislation. That requirement is satisfied here. Kentucky has proffered more than adequate justifications for the differences in treatment between the mentally retarded and the mentally ill.

A

Kentucky argues that a lower standard of proof in commitments for mental retardation follows from the fact that mental retardation is easier to diagnose than is mental illness. That general proposition should cause little surprise, for mental retardation is a developmental disability that becomes apparent before adulthood. By the time the person reaches 18 years of age the documentation and other evidence of the condition have been accumulated for years. Mental illness, on the other hand, may be sudden and may not occur, or at least manifest itself, until adulthood. Furthermore, as we recognized in an earlier case, diagnosis of mental illness is difficult. Kentucky's basic premise that mental retardation is easier to diagnose than is mental illness has a sufficient basis in fact.

This difference between the two conditions justifies Kentucky's decision to assign a lower standard of proof in commitment proceedings involving the mentally retarded. In assigning the burden of proof, Kentucky was determining the "risk of error" faced by the subject of the proceedings. If diagnosis is more difficult in cases of mental illness than in instances of mental retardation, a higher burden of proof for the former tends to equalize the risks of an erroneous determination that the subject of a commitment proceeding has the condition in question. From the diagnostic standpoint alone, Kentucky's differential burdens of proof (as well as the other statutory distinction at issue) are rational.

There is, moreover, a "reasonably conceivable state of facts," *Beach Communications,* 508 U.S., at 313, from which Kentucky could conclude that the second prerequisite to commitment— that "[t]he person presents a danger or a threat of danger to self, family, or others,"—is established more easily, as a general rule, in the case of the mentally retarded. Previous instances of violent behavior are an important indicator of future violent tendencies. Mental retardation is a permanent, relatively static condition, so a determination of dangerousness may be made with some accuracy based on previous behavior. We deal here with adults only, so almost by definition in the case of the retarded there is an 18-year record upon which to rely.

This is not so with the mentally ill. Manifestations of mental illness may be sudden, and past behavior may not be an adequate predictor of future actions. Prediction of future behavior is complicated as well by the difficulties inherent in diagnosis of mental illness. For these reasons, it would have been plausible for Kentucky to conclude that the dangerousness determination was more accurate as to the mentally retarded than the mentally ill.

A statutory classification fails rational-basis review only when it "'rests on grounds wholly irrelevant to the achievement of the State's objective.'" *Holt Civic Club v. Tuscaloosa,* 439 U.S.

60, 71 (1978). Because ease of diagnosis is relevant to two of the four inquiries, it is not "wholly irrelevant" to the achievement of Kentucky's objective, and thus the statutory difference in the applicable burden of proof survives rational-basis review. In any event, it is plausible for Kentucky to have found that, for purposes of determining the acceptable risk of error, diagnosis and dangerousness are the most critical factors in the commitment decision, so the appropriate burden of proof should be tied to them.

There is a further, more far-reaching rationale justifying the different burdens of proof: The prevailing methods of treatment for the mentally retarded, as a general rule, are much less invasive than are those given the mentally ill. The mentally ill are subjected to medical and psychiatric treatment which may involve intrusive inquiries into the patient's innermost thoughts, see and use of psychotropic drugs,. By contrast, the mentally retarded in general are not subjected to these medical treatments. Rather, "'because mental retardation is ... a learning disability and training impairment rather than an illness,'" *Youngberg v. Romeo,* 457 U.S. 307, 309, n. 1 (1982,

It is true that the loss of liberty following commitment for mental illness and mental retardation may be similar in many respects; but the different treatment to which a committed individual is subjected provides a rational basis for Kentucky to decide that a greater burden of proof is needed before a person may be committed for mental illness. The procedures required before the government acts often depend on the nature and extent of the burden or deprivation to be imposed. See *Addington v. Texas,* 441 U.S., at 423–424. For example, because confinement in prison is punitive and hence more onerous than confinement in a mental hospital, the Due Process Clause subjects the former to proof beyond a reasonable doubt, *In re Winship,* 397 U.S. 358 (1970), whereas it requires in the latter case only clear and convincing evidence, *Addington v. Texas, supra.* It may also be true that some persons committed for mental retardation are subjected to more intrusive treatments while confined. Nonetheless, it would have been plausible for the Kentucky Legislature to believe that most mentally retarded individuals who are committed receive treatment that is different from, and less invasive than, that to which the mentally ill are subjected. "States are not required to convince the courts of the correctness of their legislative judgments." *Minnesota v. Clover Leaf Creamery Co.,* 449 U.S. 456, 464 (1981). Thus, since "'the question is at least debatable,'" *Western & Southern Life Ins. Co. v. State Bd. of Equalization of Cal.,* 451 U.S. 648, 674 (1981), quoting *United States v. Carolene Products Co.,* 304 U.S. 144, 154 (1938), rational-basis review permits a legislature to use just this sort of generalization.

These distinctions may explain, too, the differences in treatment between the mentally retarded and the mentally ill that have long existed in Anglo–American law. At English common law there was a "marked distinction" in the treatment accorded "idiots" (the mentally retarded) and "lunatics" (the mentally ill). 1 F. Pollock & F. Maitland, The History of English Law 481 (2d ed. 1909) (hereinafter Pollack and Maitland). As Blackstone explained, a retarded person became a ward of the King, who had a duty to preserve the individual's estate and provide him with "necessaries," but the King could profit from the wardship. In contrast, the King was required to "provide for the custody and sustentation of [the mentally ill], and preserve their lands and the profits of them," but the King was prohibited from profiting thereby.

Ancient lineage of a legal concept does not give it immunity from attack for lacking a rational basis. That the law has long treated the classes as distinct, however, suggests that there is a commonsense distinction between the mentally retarded and the mentally ill. The differentiation continues to the present day. A large majority of States have separate involuntary commitment laws for the two groups and many States as well have separate agencies for addressing their needs.

Kentucky's burden of proof scheme, then, can be explained by differences in the ease of diagnosis and the accuracy of the prediction of future dangerousness and by the nature of the treatment received after commitment. Each of these rationales, standing on its own, would suffice to establish a rational basis for the distinction in question.

B

[The Court also determined that there was a rational basis also for Kentucky's rule that allows close relatives and guardians to participate as parties in proceedings to commit the mentally retarded but not the mentally ill.]

NOTES

1. While the Court makes some attempts in *Heller* to explain how it in fact makes sense to treat civil commitment for mental retardation differently from civil commitment for mental illness, ultimately, as the Court makes clear, none of that really matters. "[A] legislative choice is not subject to courtroom factfinding and may be based on rational speculation unsupported by evidence or empirical data." What this appears to mean is that it doesn't matter if there are in fact relevant differences between the mentally ill and the mentally retarded. All that matters is that the legislature might rationally have speculated that there might be relevant differences. The Court assumes that "rational speculation" is possible even in the absence of evidence or empirical data that might support differences in treatment. One might ask how any speculation could be termed "rational" if it is not based on any evidence, but the Court's suggestion that this is a standard method of rational basis review suggests how completely deferential the standard usually is.

2. The very deferential version of rational basis review that has been examined in this section is the method the Court uses in almost all rational basis cases. Between 1971 and 1996, the Supreme Court decided 110 cases in which it used some form of rational basis review. Of these 110 cases plaintiffs prevailed in only ten.[8] Thus, it is generally true to say that rational basis review is usually tantamount to no review at all. The next section, however, examines that small number of rational basis cases in which plaintiff claims were successful.

F. MORE DEMANDING RATIONAL BASIS REVIEW

As the previous section noted, the rational basis standard is extraordinarily deferential. This deference arises, substantively, because of the respect that courts have for the workings of other branches of government and, procedurally, through the techniques the Court uses in applying the deferential rational basis standard. As to technique, the deferential version of rational basis review does not insist on any evidence of purpose nor that there be any correlation in fact between classification and purpose. This section examines cases where the Court does not follow these techniques of deference but rather looks for evidence of the actual purpose of a law and also looks to see if the legislative classification is in fact correlated with the purpose identified. Further, this section includes instances in which the Court, applying this heightened version of rational basis review, is willing to rule out certain legislative purposes as impermissible. The next case is the first modern case in which the Court applied this kind of heightened rational basis scrutiny.

---

[8] *See*, Robert C. Farrell, *Successful Rational Basis Claims in the Supreme Court from the 1971 Term Through Romer v. Evans*, 32 Ind.L.Rev. 357, 370 (1999).

U. S. Dept. of Agriculture v. Moreno
413 U.S. 528 (1973)

[The federal food stamp program determines eligibility on the basis of the household unit rather than on an individual basis. Before 1971, a household was defined as "a group of related or non-related individuals . . . living as one economic unit sharing common cooking facilities and for whom food is customarily purchased in common." A 1971 amendment to the Food Stamp Act redefined "household" to include only groups of related individuals. Households who were denied food stamps under the amended definition brought this suit. One household included a mother and her hearing impaired daughter who shared an apartment with another indigent individual so they could live closer to the daughter's school for the deaf. Another consisted of a single woman, suffering from diabetes, who combined her resources with another woman and her three children. The petitioners argued that the "related" classification is irrational and, as such, a violation of the Due Process clause of the Fifth Amendment.]

Mr. Justice BRENNAN delivered the opinion of the Court.

Under traditional equal protection analysis, a legislative classification must be sustained, if the classification itself is rationally related to a legitimate governmental interest. See Jefferson v. Hackney, 406 U.S. 535, 546 (1972). The purposes of the Food Stamp Act were expressly set forth in the congressional 'declaration of policy':

> It is hereby declared to be the policy of Congress . . . to safeguard the health and well-being of the Nation's population and raise levels of nutrition among low-income households. The Congress hereby finds that the limited food purchasing power of low-income households contributes to hunger and malnutrition among members of such households. The Congress further finds that increased utilization of food in establishing and maintaining adequate national levels of nutrition will promote the distribution in a beneficial manner of our agricultural abundances and will strengthen our agricultural economy, as well as result in more orderly marketing and distribution of food. To alleviate such hunger and malnutrition, a food stamp program is herein authorized which will permit low-in-come households to purchase a nutritionally adequate diet through normal channels of trade. 7 U.S.C. § 2011.

The challenged statutory classification (households of related persons versus households containing one or more unrelated persons) is clearly irrelevant to the stated purposes of the Act. As the District Court recognized, '(t)he relationships among persons constituting one economic unit and sharing cooking facilities have nothing to do with their abilities to stimulate the agricultural economy by purchasing farm surpluses, or with their personal nutritional requirements.'

Thus, if it is to be sustained, the challenged classification must rationally further some legitimate governmental interest other than those specifically stated in the congressional 'declaration of policy.' Regrettably, there is little legislative history to illuminate the purposes of the 1971 amendment of § 3(e). The legislative history that does exist, however, indicates that that amendment was intended to prevent so-called 'hippies' and 'hippie communes' from participating in the food stamp program. See H.R.Conf.Rep.No.91-1793, p. 8. The challenged classification clearly cannot be sustained by reference to this congressional purpose. For if the constitutional conception of 'equal protection of the laws' means anything, it must at the very least mean that a bare congressional desire to harm a politically unpopular group cannot constitute a legitimate governmental interest. As a result, '(a) purpose to discriminate against hippies cannot, in and of itself and without reference to (some independent) considerations in the public interest, justify the

1971 amendment.' 345 F. Supp. at 314 n. 11.

Although apparently conceding this point, the Government maintains that the challenged classification should nevertheless be upheld as rationally related to the clearly legitimate governmental interest in minimizing fraud in the administration of the food stamp program. In essence, the Government contends that, in adopting the 1971 amendment, Congress might rationally have thought (1) that households with one or more unrelated members are more likely than 'fully related' households to contain individuals who abuse the program by fraudulently failing to report sources of income or by voluntarily remaining poor; and (2) that such households are 'relatively unstable,' thereby increasing the difficulty of detecting such abuses. But even if we were to accept as rational the Government's wholly unsubstantiated assumptions concerning the differences between 'related' and 'unrelated' households we still could not agree with the Government's conclusion that the denial of essential federal food assistance to all otherwise eligible households containing unrelated members constitutes a rational effort to deal with these concerns.

At the outset, it is important to note that the Food Stamp Act itself contains provisions, wholly independent of § 3(e), aimed specifically at the problems of fraud and of the voluntarily poor. For example, with certain exceptions, § 5(c) of the Act, 7 U.S.C. § 2014(c), renders ineligible for assistance any household containing 'an able-bodied adult person between the ages of eighteen and sixty-five' who fails to register for, and accept, offered employment. Similarly, § 14(b) and (c), 7 U.S.C. § 2023(b) and (c), specifically impose strict criminal penalties upon any individual who obtains or uses food stamps fraudulently. The existence of these provisions necessarily casts considerable doubt upon the proposition that the 1971 amendment could rationally have been intended to prevent those very same abuses.

Moreover, in practical effect, the challenged classification simply does not operate so as rationally to further the prevention of fraud. As previously noted, § 3(e) defines an eligible 'household' as 'a group of related individuals . . . (1) living as one economic unit (2) sharing common cooking facilities (and 3) for whom food is customarily purchased in common.' Thus, two unrelated persons living together and meeting all three of these conditions would constitute a single household ineligible for assistance. If financially feasible, however, these same two individuals can legally avoid the 'unrelated person' exclusion simply by altering their living arrangements so as to eliminate any one of the three conditions. By so doing, they effectively create two separate 'households' both of which are eligible for assistance. Indeed, as the California Director of Social Welfare has explained:

> The 'related household' limitations will eliminate many households from eligibility in the Food Stamp Program. It is my understanding that the Congressional intent of the new regulations are specifically aimed at the 'hippies' and 'hippie communes.' Most people in this category can and will alter their living arrangements in order to remain eligible for food stamps. However, the AFDC mothers who try to raise their standard of living by sharing housing will be affected. They will not be able to utilize the altered living patterns in order to continue to be eligible without giving up their advantage of shared housing costs.

Thus, in practical operation, the 1971 amendment excludes from participation in the food stamp program, not those persons who are 'likely to abuse the program,' but, rather, only those persons who are so desperately in need of aid that they cannot even afford to alter their living arrangements so as to retain their eligibility. Traditional equal protection analysis does not require that every classification be drawn with precise "mathematical nicety." *Dandridge v. Williams*, 397 U.S., at 485. But the classification here in issue is not only 'imprecise,' it is wholly without any rational basis. The judgment of the District Court holding the 'unrelated person' provision invalid under the Due Process Clause of the Fifth Amendment is therefore affirmed.

NOTES

1. It is clear that if the Court in *Moreno* had applied the traditional, deferential version of rational basis review, the food stamp amendment would have survived scrutiny. The government argued that households made up of unrelated members were more likely to defraud the program than would households made up of related members. This suggests a plausible, if not even likely, reason for excluding unrelated households from the program—the prevention of fraud—and a plausible connection between unrelated households and that purpose. And as the Court had made clear in its earlier rational basis decisions, there was no need for the government to introduce any evidence either of the legislative purpose or of the connection between the classification and that purpose.

The *Moreno* Court, however, adopted an entirely different tack. Characterizing these assertions as *"unsubstantiated assumptions* concerning the differences between 'related' and 'unrelated' households," the Court determined that the "unrelated individual" rule was not a rational effort to deal with concerns about fraud. Rather, the Court explained that the *"practical effect"* of the challenged classification "simply does not operate so as rationally to further the prevention of fraud," and that *"in practical operation,* the . . . amendment excludes from participation in the food stamp program, not those persons who are 'likely to abuse the program,' but rather only those who . . . cannot even afford to alter their living arrangements so as to retain their eligibility." (emphases added). The Court's rejection of "unsubstantiated assumptions," and its careful review of the "practical effect" and the "practical operation" of the program are quite clearly inconsistent with the view the Court would advance in *Beach Communications* that the purpose of the law and the correlation between classification and purpose could be identified by "rational speculation," even without evidence or empirical support.

2. The *Moreno* Court took one additional significant step that was inconsistent with traditional deference. Having determined that deterring fraud was not the actual purpose of the amendment, the Court looked to see what that actual purpose was. Although there was very little legislative history that would have identified the purpose of the amendment, the Court decided that the actual purpose was "to prevent [so-called] 'hippies' and 'hippie communes' from participating in the food stamp program." That purpose, the Court explained in words that would be much cited, was not permissible:

> For if the constitutional conception of "equal protection of the laws" means anything, it must at the very least mean that a bare congressional desire to harm a politically unpopular group cannot constitute a legitimate governmental interest. As a result, "[a] purpose to discriminate against hippies cannot, in and of itself and without reference to [some independent] considerations in the public interest, justify the . . . amendment.

This statement by the Court here constitutes the bedrock of heightened rationality. It shows that, not only will the Court look to find the actual purpose of a law, but it will rule out certain purposes as impermissible.

3. What purposes are impermissible? The *Moreno* Court ruled out the "desire to harm" a particular group as impermissible. This kind of legislative purpose can be called "naked antagonism." The idea of naked antagonism accepts the fact that virtually any law will have the effect of benefitting some persons and disadvantaging others, but the disadvantaging of a

particular group must be an unintended side effect of the law, not the very purpose of a law. Thus, as Justice Stevens pointed out in his concurring opinion in *Fritz*, "adverse impact may reasonably be viewed as an acceptable cost of achieving a larger goal, [and] an impartial lawmaker could rationally decide that that cost should be incurred," but where "the adverse impact on the disfavored class is an apparent aim of the legislature, its impartiality would be suspect," and such a purpose would not be permissible. Thus, for example, it is acceptable for the Massachusetts legislature to adopt a mandatory retirement policy as a means to promote public safety, even though that policy disadvantaged all those over fifty. If, however, the very purpose of the law was to disadvantage older people for its own sake, that would have been an impermissible purpose.

Although the U.S. Supreme Court has not formalized a test for determining what constitutes an impermissible purpose, it has found that the following are all impermissible purposes:

(a) naked antagonism toward a particular group, *Korematsu v. United States*, 323 U.S. 214, 216 (1944) ("Pressing public necessity may sometimes justify the existence of such restrictions; racial antagonism never can.");

(b) a mere desire to harm a particular group, *U.S. Dep't of Agric. v. Moreno*, 413 U.S. 528, 534 (1973) ("For if the constitutional conception of 'equal protection of the laws' means anything, it must at the very least mean that a bare congressional desire to harm a politically unpopular group cannot constitute a legitimate governmental interest.");

(c) prejudice against a particular group, *City of Cleburne v. Cleburne Living Ctr.*, 473 U.S. 432, 450 (1985) ("The short of it is that requiring the permit in this case appears to us to rest on an irrational prejudice against the mentally retarded;");

(d) the public endorsement of private bias, ("Private biases may be outside the reach of the law, but the law cannot, directly or indirectly, give them effect.");

(e) disadvantaging a particular group based on animus or animosity toward the group, *Romer v. Evans, 517 U.S. 620, 632, 634 (1996)* ("[T]he amendment seems inexplicable by anything but animus toward the class it affects; it lacks a rational relationship to legitimate state interests. . . . [L]aws of the kind now before us raise the inevitable inference that the disadvantage imposed is born of animosity toward the class of persons affected."); and

(f) giving effect to stereotypical views about the roles of a particular class, *Miss. Univ. for Women v. Hogan*, 458 U.S. 718, 725 (1982) ("Care must be taken in ascertaining whether the statutory objective itself reflects archaic and stereotypic notions. Thus, if the statutory objective is to exclude or 'protect' members of one gender because they are presumed to suffer from an inherent handicap or to be innately inferior, the objective itself is illegitimate.").

4. As Tussman and tenBroek explain, the rule that a classification must be rationally related to a permissible purpose makes no sense unless we limit the universe of acceptable purposes:

[T]he requirement that laws be equal rests upon a theory of legislation quite distinct from that of pressure groups--a theory which puts forward some conception of a "general good" as the "legitimate public purpose" at which legislation must aim, and according to which the triumph of private or group pressure marks the corruption of the legislative process." *Tussman and tenBroek*, 37 Cal. L. Rev. at 349-50.

Cass Sunstein, in *Naked Preferences and the Constitution*, 84 Columbia L. Rev. 1689 (1984), has developed the public value model of Constitutional law and has found support for it in the historical background and structure of the Constitution. Sunstein distinguishes "naked preferences"--unprincipled distributions of resources and opportunities that reflect the view that it is intrinsically desirable to treat one person better than another--from "public values," defined negatively as "any justification for government action that goes beyond the exercise of raw political power." Professor Sunstein's argument is that a number of clauses in the Constitution, including the Equal Protection Clause, can best be explained as prohibiting naked preferences, thereby insisting that laws must promote public purposes.

More recently, in *Unconstitutional Animus,* 81 Fordham L. Rev. 887 (2012), Susannah W. Pollvogt focuses on the concept of "animus" as constituting the most coherent explanation of what is *not* a permissible purpose under the Equal Protection Clause. She says, "In short, animus, including hostility toward a particular social group, is never a valid basis for legislation or other state action. . . . So while the Court has discerned the presence of unconstitutional animus on only a few occasions, when animus is found, it functions as a doctrinal silver bullet."

5. The principal competitor of the public value model of government is a theory variously called the interest group model, pressure group theory, or public choice theory. This model purports to describe the legislative process as it is, not as it ought to be, and leaves no room for altruism, or the public interest, in the legislative process it describes. Tussman and tenBroek identified the "pressure group" theory of government, which holds that "a law is properly the resultant of pressures exerted by competing interests." *Tussman & tenBroek*, at 350. Politics is considered to be a struggle between interest groups. Each group pursues its own advantage and hopes to gain benefits at the expense of less powerful, or less well-organized, interest groups. In such a model, success is defined as getting your way at the expense of others. Thus, the purpose of government, from the perspective of the interest group theory, is the aggregation of individual preferences and not the identification of public values. This means that the successful passage of a law by a majority of the legislature is itself a sufficient justification for the law, requiring no independent public welfare basis.

The contemporary version of the interest group model applies economic principles of the market to the legislative process. This model is called the public choice theory. Under the public choice theory, legislators and interest groups are presumed to act in their own self-interest. Legislators want to get re-elected; interest groups want to advance their interests. Therefore, legislators and interest groups make deals that allow both to achieve their goals, even though this results in "rent-seeking" at the expense of the general public. With regard to the permissibility of legislative purposes, it should be obvious that the interest group theory of government turns the public value model on its head. The unprincipled distribution of resources to A instead of B for A's own sake, rather than being a prohibited naked preference, turns out to be the very essence of the democratic process.

It is quite clear, however, that if we take rationality review as our starting point, the Constitution insists on the public value model of government and is inconsistent with the interest group theory. Rationality review, after all, insists that legislative judgments be directed towards a public good, while under the interest group model, the passage of a law by a majority is itself sufficient justification for that law. The Supreme Court, by continuing to announce the rule that a classification must be correlated with a permissible purpose, at least implicitly accepts the public value model of legislation.

6. In identifying the purpose of the law as a desire to harm a particular group, the *Moreno* Court did not hypothesize what the purpose might be but rather looked for evidence of the actual

purpose of the law. In that case, the Court cited a House Conference Report and a statement of Senator Holland recording in the Congressional Record as evidence that the real purpose of the law was to prevent hippies from participating in the program. In general, when a Court, applying heightened rational basis review looks for the actual purpose of a law, it will look at (1) the statutory language itself, which sometimes, as in *Minnesota Creamery, supra*, specifically identifies the purpose of a law, or (2) the legislative history, as the dissenters did in *Fritz* and the majority did in *Moreno*. At other times, as in the next two cases, the Court surmises the actual purpose of a law by process of elimination, that is, when it has found all the proffered purposes to be implausible, the Court will determine that that the only remaining purpose is that of impermissible discrimination against a particular group.

City of Cleburne, Tex. v. Cleburne Living Center
473 U.S. 432 (1985)

[Cleburne Living Center, Inc. (CLC) rented a four-bedroom home with the intent of creating a supervised group home for 13 mentally retarded men and women. The city initially classified the project as a "hospital for the feeble-minded," a designation that required a special use permit under city zoning ordinances, and then denied the permit. CLC argued that the home was a residence and that the permit would have been granted but for the mental condition of the proposed occupants. They filed suit on behalf of themselves and their potential residents, alleging the ordinance violated the Equal Protection Clause.]

Justice WHITE delivered the opinion of the Court.

The Equal Protection Clause of the Fourteenth Amendment commands that no State shall "deny to any person within its jurisdiction the equal protection of the laws," which is essentially a direction that all persons similarly situated should be treated alike. *Plyler v. Doe*, 457 U.S. 202, 216 (1982). The general rule is that legislation is presumed to be valid and will be sustained if the classification drawn by the statute is rationally related to a legitimate state interest. *Schweiker v. Wilson*, 450 U.S. 221, 230 (1981). When social or economic legislation is at issue, the Equal Protection Clause allows the States wide latitude, *United States Railroad Retirement Board v. Fritz, supra*, 449 U.S., at 174, and the Constitution presumes that even improvident decisions will eventually be rectified by the democratic processes.

[The Court then determined that the mentally retarded were not a quasi-suspect class and that a classification based on mental retardation would therefore not be entitled to heightened scrutiny.]

Our refusal to recognize the retarded as a quasi-suspect class does not leave them entirely unprotected from invidious discrimination. To withstand equal protection review, legislation that distinguishes between the mentally retarded and others must be rationally related to a legitimate governmental purpose. This standard, we believe, affords government the latitude necessary both to pursue policies designed to assist the retarded in realizing their full potential, and to freely and efficiently engage in activities that burden the retarded in what is essentially an incidental manner. The State may not rely on a classification whose relationship to an asserted goal is so attenuated as to render the distinction arbitrary or irrational. See *Zobel v. Williams*, 457 U.S. 55, 61-63 (1982); *United States Dept. of Agriculture v. Moreno*, 413 U.S. 528, 535 (1973). Furthermore, some objectives--such as "a bare ... desire to harm a politically unpopular group," *id.*, at 534--are not legitimate state interests. Beyond that, the mentally retarded, like others, have and retain their substantive constitutional rights in addition to the right to be treated equally by the law.

IV

We turn to the issue of the validity of the zoning ordinance insofar as it requires a special use permit for homes for the mentally retarded. We inquire first whether requiring a special use permit for the Featherston home in the circumstances here deprives respondents of the equal protection of the laws. If it does, there will be no occasion to decide whether the special use permit provision is facially invalid where the mentally retarded are involved, or to put it another way, whether the city may never insist on a special use permit for a home for the mentally retarded in an R-3 zone. This is the preferred course of adjudication since it enables courts to avoid making unnecessarily broad constitutional judgments.

The constitutional issue is clearly posed. The city does not require a special use permit in an R-3 zone for apartment houses, multiple dwellings, boarding and lodging houses, fraternity or sorority houses, dormitories, apartment hotels, hospitals, sanitariums, nursing homes for convalescents or the aged (other than for the insane or feebleminded or alcoholics or drug addicts), private clubs or fraternal orders, and other specified uses. It does, however, insist on a special permit for the Featherston home, and it does so, as the District Court found, because it would be a facility for the mentally retarded. May the city require the permit for this facility when other care and multiple-dwelling facilities are freely permitted?

It is true, as already pointed out, that the mentally retarded as a group are indeed different from others not sharing their misfortune, and in this respect they may be different from those who would occupy other facilities that would be permitted in an R-3 zone without a special permit. But this difference is largely irrelevant unless the Featherston home and those who would occupy it would threaten legitimate interests of the city in a way that other permitted uses such as boarding houses and hospitals would not. Because in our view the record does not reveal any rational basis for believing that the Featherston home would pose any special threat to the city's legitimate interests, we affirm the judgment below insofar as it holds the ordinance invalid as applied in this case.

The District Court found that the City Council's insistence on the permit rested on several factors. First, the Council was concerned with the negative attitude of the majority of property owners located within 200 feet of the Featherston facility, as well as with the fears of elderly residents of the neighborhood. But mere negative attitudes, or fear, unsubstantiated by factors which are properly cognizable in a zoning proceeding, are not permissible bases for treating a home for the mentally retarded differently from apartment houses, multiple dwellings, and the like. It is plain that the electorate as a whole, whether by referendum or otherwise, could not order city action violative of the Equal Protection Clause, *Lucas v. Forty-Fourth General Assembly of Colorado*, 377 U.S. 713, 736-37 (1964), and the City may not avoid the strictures of that Clause by deferring to the wishes or objections of some fraction of the body politic. "Private biases may be outside the reach of the law, but the law cannot, directly or indirectly, give them effect." *Palmore v. Sidoti*, 466 U.S. 429, 433 (1984).

Second, the Council had two objections to the location of the facility. It was concerned that the facility was across the street from a junior high school, and it feared that the students might harass the occupants of the Featherston home. But the school itself is attended by about 30 mentally retarded students, and denying a permit based on such vague, undifferentiated fears is again permitting some portion of the community to validate what would otherwise be an equal protection violation. The other objection to the home's location was that it was located on "a five hundred year flood plain." This concern with the possibility of a flood, however, can hardly be based on a distinction between the Featherston home and, for example, nursing homes, homes for convalescents or the aged, or sanitariums or hospitals, any of which could be located on the

Featherston site without obtaining a special use permit. The same may be said of another concern of the Council--doubts about the legal responsibility for actions which the mentally retarded might take. If there is no concern about legal responsibility with respect to other uses that would be permitted in the area, such as boarding and fraternity houses, it is difficult to believe that the groups of mildly or moderately mentally retarded individuals who would live at 201 Featherston would present any different or special hazard.

Fourth, the Council was concerned with the size of the home and the number of people that would occupy it. The District Court found, and the Court of Appeals repeated, that "[i]f the potential residents of the Featherston Street home were not mentally retarded, but the home was the same in all other respects, its use would be permitted under the city's zoning ordinance." Given this finding, there would be no restrictions on the number of people who could occupy this home as a boarding house, nursing home, family dwelling, fraternity house, or dormitory. The question is whether it is rational to treat the mentally retarded differently. It is true that they suffer disability not shared by others; but why this difference warrants a density regulation that others need not observe is not at all apparent. At least this record does not clarify how, in this connection, the characteristics of the intended occupants of the Featherston home rationally justify denying to those occupants what would be permitted to groups occupying the same site for different purposes. Those who would live in the Featherston home are the type of individuals who, with supporting staff, satisfy federal and state standards for group housing in the community; and there is no dispute that the home would meet the federal square-footage-per-resident requirement for facilities of this type. In the words of the Court of Appeals, "[t]he City never justifies its apparent view that other people can live under such 'crowded' conditions when mentally retarded persons cannot."

In the courts below the city also urged that the ordinance is aimed at avoiding concentration of population and at lessening congestion of the streets. These concerns obviously fail to explain why apartment houses, fraternity and sorority houses, hospitals and the like, may freely locate in the area without a permit. So, too, the expressed worry about fire hazards, the serenity of the neighborhood, and the avoidance of danger to other residents fail rationally to justify singling out a home such as 201 Featherston for the special use permit, yet imposing no such restrictions on the many other uses freely permitted in the neighborhood.

The short of it is that requiring the permit in this case appears to us to rest on an irrational prejudice against the mentally retarded, including those who would occupy the Featherston facility and who would live under the closely supervised and highly regulated conditions expressly provided for by state and federal law.

The judgment of the Court of Appeals is affirmed insofar as it invalidates the zoning ordinance as applied to the Featherston home. The judgment is otherwise vacated, and the case is remanded. *It is so ordered.*

NOTES

1. Throughout its opinion, the *Cleburne* Court repeatedly referred to group disadvantaged by the permit denial as the "mentally retarded." The term "retarded" has been widely considered acceptable for a long time. In recent years, however, both federal and state governments, as well as private mental health organizations, have begun to use different terminology, based on the understanding that the term "retarded" can be demeaning. This matter is discussed *infra*, at Chapter 7.B.

2. The *Cleburne* court made no attempt to hypothesize a permissible purpose for the disadvantage imposed on the mentally retarded, nor did it imagine a conceivable connection between the classification and such a hypothesized purpose. Instead, the Court insisted on an actual correlation between the classification and the alleged purposes, and then it searched the record for evidence of such a correlation. The Court twice referred to the absence of any evidence in "the record" that would explain why, in relation to the legitimate concern with the size of a home and the number of occupants, the city treated this one group home (made up of the mentally disabled) differently from other group homes (such as those used as boarding houses, nursing homes, family dwellings, fraternity houses, or dormitories). The Court was demanding evidence in the record that the city was in fact "right" that the mentally disabled were different in relation to the purpose. Nowhere in the opinion does the Court ask whether there is any conceivable set of facts under which it might be appropriate to treat the mentally disabled differently from those who occupied other group homes.

The *Cleburne* Court also rejected a number of hypothetical permissible purposes as implausible, because the mentally disabled were no different from any of the other, non-regulated groups in relation to those purposes. The Court then assessed the city's actual purpose in denying the permit: "The short of it is that requiring the permit in this case appears to us to rest on an irrational prejudice against the mentally retarded." This, as the Court made clear, was not a permissible purpose, for some "objectives-- such as 'a bare . . . desire to harm a politically unpopular group,'--are not legitimate state interests." That is, "mere negative attitudes, or fear, unsubstantiated by factors which are properly cognizable in a zoning proceeding, are not permissible bases for treating a home for the mentally retarded differently from apartment houses, multiple dwellings, and the like," and "[p]rivate biases may be outside the reach of the law, but the law cannot, directly or indirectly, give them effect."

Romer v. Evans
517 U.S. 620 (1996)

[Various municipalities in Colorado adopted ordinances barring discrimination based on sexual orientation. In 1992, the voters of Colorado adopted "Amendment 2" of the Constitution of the State of Colorado, which stated:

> No Protected Status Based on Homosexual, Lesbian or Bisexual Orientation. Neither the State of Colorado, through any of its branches or departments, nor any of its agencies, political subdivisions, municipalities or school districts, shall enact, adopt or enforce any statute, regulation, ordinance or policy whereby homosexual, lesbian or bisexual orientation, conduct, practices or relationships shall constitute or otherwise be the basis of or entitle any person or class of persons to have or claim any minority status, quota preferences, protected status or claim of discrimination. This Section of the Constitution shall be in all respects self-executing. *Colo. Const., Art. II, § 30b.*

Plaintiffs were gay men and women who alleged that the amendment violated the Equal Protection Clause.]

Justice KENNEDY delivered the opinion of the Court.

One century ago, the first Justice Harlan admonished this Court that the Constitution "neither knows nor tolerates classes among citizens." *Plessy v. Ferguson,* 163 U.S. 537, 559 (1896) (dissenting opinion). Unheeded then, those words now are understood to state a commitment to the law's neutrality where the rights of persons are at stake. The Equal Protection Clause enforces this principle and today requires us to hold invalid a provision of Colorado's Constitution.

II

The State's principal argument in defense of Amendment 2 is that it puts gays and lesbians in the same position as all other persons. So, the State says, the measure does no more than deny homosexuals special rights. This reading of the amendment's language is implausible.

We rely not upon our own interpretation of the amendment but upon the authoritative construction of Colorado's Supreme Court. The state court, deeming it unnecessary to determine the full extent of the amendment's reach, found it invalid even on a modest reading of its implications. The critical discussion of the amendment, set out in *Evans I,* is as follows: "The immediate objective of Amendment 2 is, at a minimum, to repeal existing statutes, regulations, ordinances, and policies of state and local entities that barred discrimination based on sexual orientation. *See* Aspen, Colo., Mun.Code § 13-98 (1977) (prohibiting discrimination in employment, housing and public accommodations on the basis of sexual orientation); Boulder, Colo., Rev.Code §§ 12-1-2 to -4 (1987) (same); Denver, Colo., Rev. Mun.Code art. IV, §§ 28-91 to -116 (1991) (same); Executive Order No. D0035 (December 10, 1990) (prohibiting employment discrimination for 'all state employees, classified and exempt' on the basis of sexual orientation); Colorado Insurance Code, § 10-3-1104, 4A C.R.S. (1992 Supp.) (forbidding health insurance providers from determining insurability and premiums based on an applicant's, a beneficiary's, or an insured's sexual orientation); and various provisions prohibiting discrimination based on sexual orientation at state colleges. "The 'ultimate effect' of Amendment 2 is to prohibit any governmental entity from adopting similar, or more protective statutes, regulations, ordinances, or policies in the future unless the state constitution is first amended to permit such measures." 854 P.2d, at 1284-1285, and n. 26.

Sweeping and comprehensive is the change in legal status effected by this law. So much is evident from the ordinances the Colorado Supreme Court declared would be void by operation of Amendment 2. Homosexuals, by state decree, are put in a solitary class with respect to transactions and relations in both the private and governmental spheres. The amendment withdraws from homosexuals, but no others, specific legal protection from the injuries caused by discrimination, and it forbids reinstatement of these laws and policies.

The change Amendment 2 works in the legal status of gays and lesbians in the private sphere is far reaching, both on its own terms and when considered in light of the structure and operation of modern anti-discrimination laws. That structure is well illustrated by contemporary statutes and ordinances prohibiting discrimination by providers of public accommodations. "At common law, innkeepers, smiths, and others who 'made profession of a public employment,' were prohibited from refusing, without good reason, to serve a customer." *Hurley v. Irish-American Gay, Lesbian and Bisexual Group of Boston, Inc.,* 515 U.S. 557, 571 (1995). The duty was a general one and did not specify protection for particular groups. The common-law rules, however, proved insufficient in many instances, and it was settled early that the Fourteenth Amendment did not give Congress a general power to prohibit discrimination in public accommodations, *Civil Rights Cases,* 109 U.S. 3 (1883). In consequence, most States have chosen to counter discrimination by enacting detailed statutory schemes.

Colorado's state and municipal laws typify this emerging tradition of statutory protection and follow a consistent pattern. The laws first enumerate the persons or entities subject to a duty not to discriminate. The list goes well beyond the entities covered by the common law. The Boulder ordinance, for example, has a comprehensive definition of entities deemed places of "public accommodation." They include "any place of business engaged in any sales to the general public and any place that offers services, facilities, privileges, or advantages to the general public or that receives financial support through solicitation of the general public or through governmental subsidy of any kind." Boulder Rev.Code § 12-1-1(j) (1987). The Denver ordinance is of similar breadth, applying, for example, to hotels, restaurants, hospitals, dental clinics, theaters, banks, common carriers, travel and insurance agencies, and "shops and stores dealing with goods or services of any kind," Denver Rev. Municipal Code, Art. IV, § 28-92 (1991).

These statutes and ordinances also depart from the common law by enumerating the groups or persons within their ambit of protection. Enumeration is the essential device used to make the duty not to discriminate concrete and to provide guidance for those who must comply. In following this approach, Colorado's state and local governments have not limited antidiscrimination laws to groups that have so far been given the protection of heightened equal protection scrutiny under our cases. Rather, they set forth an extensive catalog of traits which cannot be the basis for discrimination, including age, military status, marital status, pregnancy, parenthood, custody of a minor child, political affiliation, physical or mental disability of an individual or of his or her associates---and, in recent times, sexual orientation.

Amendment 2 bars homosexuals from securing protection against the injuries that these public-accommodations laws address. That in itself is a severe consequence, but there is more. Amendment 2, in addition, nullifies specific legal protections for this targeted class in all transactions in housing, sale of real estate, insurance, health and welfare services, private education, and employment.

Not confined to the private sphere, Amendment 2 also operates to repeal and forbid all laws or policies providing specific protection for gays or lesbians from discrimination by every level of Colorado government. The State Supreme Court cited two examples of protections in the governmental sphere that are now rescinded and may not be reintroduced. The first is Colorado Executive Order D0035 (1990), which forbids employment discrimination against "'all state employees, classified and exempt' on the basis of sexual orientation." 854 P.2d, at 1284. Also repealed, and now forbidden, are "various provisions prohibiting discrimination based on sexual orientation at state colleges." *Id.,* at 1284, 1285. The repeal of these measures and the prohibition against their future reenactment demonstrate that Amendment 2 has the same force and effect in Colorado's governmental sector as it does elsewhere and that it applies to policies as well as ordinary legislation.

Amendment 2's reach may not be limited to specific laws passed for the benefit of gays and lesbians. It is a fair, if not necessary, inference from the broad language of the amendment that it deprives gays and lesbians even of the protection of general laws and policies that prohibit arbitrary discrimination in governmental and private settings. At some point in the systematic administration of these laws, an official must determine whether homosexuality is an arbitrary and, thus, forbidden basis for decision. Yet a decision to that effect would itself amount to a policy prohibiting discrimination on the basis of homosexuality, and so would appear to be no more valid under Amendment 2 than the specific prohibitions against discrimination the state court held invalid.

[E]ven if, as we doubt, homosexuals could find some safe harbor in laws of general application, we cannot accept the view that Amendment 2's prohibition on specific legal protections does no more than deprive homosexuals of special rights. To the contrary, the amendment imposes a special disability upon those persons alone. Homosexuals are forbidden the safeguards that others enjoy or may seek without constraint. They can obtain specific protection against discrimination only by enlisting the citizenry of Colorado to amend the State Constitution or perhaps, on the State's view, by trying to pass helpful laws of general applicability. This is so no matter how local or discrete the harm, no matter how public and widespread the injury. We find nothing special in the protections Amendment 2 withholds. These are protections taken for granted by most people either because they already have them or do not need them; these are protections against exclusion from an almost limitless number of transactions and endeavors that constitute ordinary civic life in a free society.

III

The Fourteenth Amendment's promise that no person shall be denied the equal protection of the laws must coexist with the practical necessity that most legislation classifies for one purpose or another, with resulting disadvantage to various groups or persons. *Personnel Administrator of Mass. v. Feeney,* 442 U.S. 256, 271-272 (1979); *F.S. Royster Guano Co. v. Virginia,* 253 U.S. 412, 415 (1920). We have attempted to reconcile the principle with the reality by stating that, if a law neither burdens a fundamental right nor targets a suspect class, we will uphold the legislative classification so long as it bears a rational relation to some legitimate end. See, *e.g., Heller v. Doe,* 509 U.S. 312, 319-320 (1993).

Amendment 2 fails, indeed defies, even this conventional inquiry. First, the amendment has the peculiar property of imposing a broad and undifferentiated disability on a single named group, an exceptional and, as we shall explain, invalid form of legislation. Second, its sheer breadth is so discontinuous with the reasons offered for it that the amendment seems inexplicable by anything but animus toward the class it affects; it lacks a rational relationship to legitimate state interests.

Taking the first point, even in the ordinary equal protection case calling for the most deferential of standards, we insist on knowing the relation between the classification adopted and the object to be attained. The search for the link between classification and objective gives substance to the Equal Protection Clause; it provides guidance and discipline for the legislature, which is entitled to know what sorts of laws it can pass; and it marks the limits of our own authority. In the ordinary case, a law will be sustained if it can be said to advance a legitimate government interest, even if the law seems unwise or works to the disadvantage of a particular group, or if the rationale for it seems tenuous. By requiring that the classification bear a rational relationship to an independent and legitimate legislative end, we ensure that classifications are not drawn for the purpose of disadvantaging the group burdened by the law. See *Railroad Retirement Bd. v. Fritz,* 449 U.S. 166, 181 (1980) (STEVENS, J., concurring) ("If the adverse impact on the disfavored class is an apparent aim of the legislature, its impartiality would be suspect").

Amendment 2 confounds this normal process of judicial review. It is at once too narrow and too broad. It identifies persons by a single trait and then denies them protection across the board. The resulting disqualification of a class of persons from the right to seek specific protection from the law is unprecedented in our jurisprudence. The absence of precedent for Amendment 2 is itself instructive; "[d]iscriminations of an unusual character especially suggest careful consideration to determine whether they are obnoxious to the constitutional provision." *Louisville Gas & Elec. Co. v. Coleman,* 277 U.S. 32, 37-38 (1928).

It is not within our constitutional tradition to enact laws of this sort. Central both to the idea of the rule of law and to our own Constitution's guarantee of equal protection is the principle that government and each of its parts remain open on impartial terms to all who seek its assistance. "'Equal protection of the laws is not achieved through indiscriminate imposition of inequalities.'" *Sweatt v. Painter,* 339 U.S. 629, 635 (1950) (quoting *Shelley v. Kraemer,* 334 U.S. 1, 22 (1948)). Respect for this principle explains why laws singling out a certain class of citizens for disfavored legal status or general hardships are rare. A law declaring that in general it shall be more difficult for one group of citizens than for all others to seek aid from the government is itself a denial of equal protection of the laws in the most literal sense. "The guaranty of 'equal protection of the laws is a pledge of the protection of equal laws.'" *Skinner v. Oklahoma ex rel. Williamson,* 316 U.S. 535, 541 (1942) (quoting *Yick Wo v. Hopkins,* 118 U.S. 356, 369 (1886)).

[L]aws of the kind now before us raise the inevitable inference that the disadvantage imposed is born of animosity toward the class of persons affected. "[I]f the constitutional conception of 'equal protection of the laws' means anything, it must at the very least mean that a bare ... desire to harm a politically unpopular group cannot constitute a *legitimate* governmental interest." *Department of Agriculture v. Moreno,* 413 U.S. 528, 534 (1973). Even laws enacted for broad and ambitious purposes often can be explained by reference to legitimate public policies which justify the incidental disadvantages they impose on certain persons. Amendment 2, however, in making a general announcement that gays and lesbians shall not have any particular protections from the law, inflicts on them immediate, continuing, and real injuries that outrun and belie any legitimate justifications that may be claimed for it. We conclude that, in addition to the far-reaching deficiencies of Amendment 2 that we have noted, the principles it offends, in another sense, are conventional and venerable; a law must bear a rational relationship to a legitimate governmental purpose, *Kadrmas v. Dickinson Public Schools,* 487 U.S. 450, 462 (1988), and Amendment 2 does not.

The primary rationale the State offers for Amendment 2 is respect for other citizens' freedom of association, and in particular the liberties of landlords or employers who have personal or religious objections to homosexuality. Colorado also cites its interest in conserving resources to fight discrimination against other groups. The breadth of the amendment is so far removed from these particular justifications that we find it impossible to credit them. We cannot say that Amendment 2 is directed to any identifiable legitimate purpose or discrete objective. It is a status-based enactment divorced from any factual context from which we could discern a relationship to legitimate state interests; it is a classification of persons undertaken for its own sake, something the Equal Protection Clause does not permit. "[C]lass legislation ... [is] obnoxious to the prohibitions of the Fourteenth Amendment. . . ." *Civil Rights Cases,* 109 U.S., at 24.

We must conclude that Amendment 2 classifies homosexuals not to further a proper legislative end but to make them unequal to everyone else. This Colorado cannot do. A State cannot so deem a class of persons a stranger to its laws. Amendment 2 violates the Equal Protection Clause, and the judgment of the Supreme Court of Colorado is affirmed. *It is so ordered.*

NOTES

1. *Romer* is the last of the trio of paradigmatic heightened rationality cases. The State asserted that the amendment served three state interests--"that it put gays and lesbians in the same position as all other persons"; that it respected freedom of association, particularly "the liberties of landlords or employers who have personal or religious objections to homosexuality . . ."; and that it conserved resources "to fight discrimination against other groups." The Court was unwilling to accept the State's assertions that these were the purposes of the amendment, calling them "implausible" and "impossible to credit." Nor did the Court make any attempt to hypothesize a permissible purpose. Instead, focusing on the "sheer breadth" of the amendment (in terms of the substantial number of statutes, ordinances, and state regulations and practices it affected) along with the fact that the amendment directed its adverse consequences at a very specific group, the Court found that the amendment was "inexplicable by anything but animus toward the class it affects." In addition, the amendment raised "the inevitable inference that the disadvantage imposed is born of animosity toward the class of persons affected," and it classified gay persons

"not to further a proper legislative end but to make them unequal to everyone else" and "stranger[s] to its laws." The Court explained equal protection's basic limit on governmental purpose--"that classifications are not drawn for the purpose of disadvantaging the group burdened by the law." Instead, laws must be justified "by reference to legitimate public policies which justify the incidental disadvantages they impose on certain persons."

2. Other examples of heightened rational basis review include *Zobel v. Williams*, 457 U.S. 55 (1982) and *Eisenstadt v. Baird*, 405 U.S. 438 (1972). In *Zobel,* the Court used rational-basis review to invalidate an Alaska statute that would have provided for the distribution of income from the state's oil fund on the basis of years of residency in Alaska. The Court first found that the years-of-residency classification was not in fact adequately correlated with the permissible purposes of the statute. The Court never asked whether a reasonable legislator might have believed that there was an adequate correlation between classification and purpose. Further, the Court found that one of the state's asserted purposes--rewarding citizens for past contributions--was not a legitimate state purpose. The Court concluded that "[t]he only apparent justification for the retrospective aspect of the program, 'favoring established residents over new residents,' is constitutionally unacceptable."

Eisenstadt v. Baird is another example. There, the Court invalidated a statute that prohibited the sale of contraceptives to unmarried persons. The Court looked carefully for evidence of the actual purpose of the law and found that the purposes identified by the courts below were implausible. The Court then considered whether the statute's purpose could be identified as equivalent to its effect--preventing the use of contraceptives. Assuming that prohibiting the use of contraceptives was both a permissible purpose and the actual purpose of the statute, the Court determined that the statutory classification that prohibited only unmarried persons from using contraceptives was not adequately correlated with that purpose. The Court explained that married and unmarried persons were similarly situated in relation to that purpose. For the Court, this problem of under-inclusion was decisive because the guaranty of equal protection means "that the principles of law which officials would impose upon a minority must be imposed generally."

3. The heightened, more demanding version of rationality review that can be seen in *Moreno, Cleburne,* and *Romer* is not typical of rational basis review. The very deferential version examined in the first part of this chapter is the standard method that the Court uses in the vast majority of its cases. Between 1971 and 1996, of the 110 cases the Supreme Court decided using some form of rational basis review, plaintiffs prevailed in only ten. *See*, Robert C. Farrell, *Successful Rational Basis Claims in the Supreme Court from the 1971 Term Through Romer v. Evans*, 32 Ind. L. Rev. 357, 370 (1999).

4. Since the Court is ordinarily quite deferential in rationality cases, what is it that explains the different level of review in the heightened rationality cases? Several explanations will be examined but none is particularly satisfactory.

(a) The first of these explanations examines the nature of the disadvantaged class: the groups disadvantaged in the heightened rationality cases—*e.g.,* the poor, the mentally retarded, gay men and women—share many of the characteristic of groups to which the Court has formally given heightened scrutiny—blacks, women, nonmarital children, and aliens. Although this is a plausible claim initially, it does not hold up.

First, we have to deal with the language of the Court itself, language that apparently rejects the notion that the nature of the class affected is a significant factor in these cases. In *Cleburne,* for example, the Court explicitly rejected the notion that the mentally retarded were a quasi-suspect class and thus entitled to heightened scrutiny. In several other cases, the

Court insisted that it did not need to decide the issue of heightened scrutiny, because the classification did not even survive rational basis review. And in *Romer,* the Court completely ignored the question of heightened scrutiny. The first problem is thus that the Court opinions give no indication that the nature of the class affected is relevant to the decision in the case.

But perhaps we should pay more attention to what the Court does, and less attention to what it says it is doing. By this standard, are not the groups involved in the heightened rationality cases similar to the existing suspect and quasi-suspect classifications? Even if one were to answer this question affirmatively, it still would not explain why the Court used heightened rationality in these cases but not others. Specifically, why were the mentally retarded treated as a quasi-suspect class in *Cleburne* but not in *Heller*? Why was animus against gays an impermissible purpose in *Romer* but only part of a valid attempt to promote morality in *Bowers v. Hardwick*, 478 U.S. 186 (1986). And why were the poor a special concern in *Moreno* but not worthy of any special consideration in *San Antonio Ind. School Dist. v. Rodriguez,* 411 U.S. 1 (1973)? Certainly, the Court has never attempted to answer these questions and it is doubtful that any reasoned set of distinctions would explain the different results.

(b) The second attempt to explain these ten cases is by reference to the nature of the benefit that was involved, that is, the more significant the interest at stake, the more likely the Court would apply some kind of heightened scrutiny. Thus, the interests involved in the preceding cases were food, housing, and access to the political process. Once again, in search of a pattern that could explain heightened scrutiny, one could identify some similarities between the government benefits denied in these cases and fundamental rights that the Court has explicitly recognized and to which it has formally adopted stricter scrutiny. This would help explain why the Court used heightened rationality to review cases that limited access to the political process since it is closely related to the existing fundamental right to vote. Further, at least an argument could be made, notwithstanding the Court's protestations to the contrary, that there ought to be fundamental claim to some minimum level of food and housing.

Once again, though, the attempt to identify a consistent principle by reference to the nature of the benefit at issue fails. For example, why would food stamps have been considered quasi-fundamental in *Moreno* but not so in *Knebel v. Hein,* 429 U.S. 288 (1977); *Lyng v. Castillo,* 477 U.S. 635 (1986); or *Lyng v. International Union,* 485 U.S. 360 (1988)? Why was housing quasi-fundamental in *Cleburne* but not so in *Lindsey v. Normet,* 405 U.S. 56 (1972). And finally, why would some equal access to the political process be fundamental in *Romer,* but not so in *Salyer Land Co. v. Tulare Lake Basin Water Storage District,* 410 U.S. 719 (1973). Ultimately, the attempt to identify a consistent principle by reference to the nature of the benefit affected is unsuccessful.

(c) A more realistic explanation of how the Court determines which method of rationality to be used is simply the result of shifting majorities on the Court, with the Justices holding conflicting viewpoints in particular factual situations. Obviously, the more demanding version of rationality review is more likely to be an example of judicial activism while the deferential version is, by definition, deferential to the other branches of government. But the concept of judicial activism is very hard to pin down, and Justices identified as liberal or conservative appear to be equally likely to be activists, only in different situations.

This search for an underlying principle that would explain when the Court will use heightened rationality appears to be futile. Rather, it appears that the Court, without explanation, decides in a particular case to use heightened rationality and thus the claim succeeds. The Court continues to write opinions as if they matter, but, in a rational basis case, it is difficult to predict what standard the Court will use.

G. THE CLASS OF ONE CLAIM

As the previous materials have made clear, in most contexts, the basic role of the Equal Protection Clause is to act as a limit on government classifications. Under this view of equal protection as a limitation on government classification, it is sufficient that a classification be rationally related to a permissible purpose, without regard to the classification's effect on individual persons. Once it is determined, for example, that an age classification is reasonably correlated with fitness for police work, it does not matter what adverse effect the classification will have on an individual member of the class. Since, the classification makes use of a generalization about age that is reasonably accurate, it does not matter that the generalization is not true as to a particular member of that class. Thus, the ordinary equal protection doctrine appears to provide no protection to individuals from being harmed by classifications that embody generalizations that are not true as to the individual. In this context, it is very hard to make sense of the claim that equal protection is a personal, individual right.

That being said, in two cases decided in recent years, the Supreme Court has recognized a "class of one" claim where the plaintiff was an individual who did not identify herself as a member of a class and yet was found to have stated a claim under the Equal Protection Clause. The first of these cases follows.

Village of Willowbrook v. Olech
528 U.S. 562 (2000)

[The Olechs were landowners in the village of Willowbrook. In their complaint, the Olechs alleged as follows. They had asked the Village to connect their home to the municipal water supply. Although other neighboring property owners were required to grant the Village merely a 15-foot easement for that access, the Village demanded that the Olechs grant a 33-foot easement. This, the Olechs alleged, was in retaliation for their filing an unrelated suit against the Village several years earlier. Although access to the water supply was ultimately provided in exchange for a 15-foot easement, the Olechs filed suit against the Village, claiming that the village's original demand was arbitrary, irrational, and in violation of their 14th Amendment right to Equal Protection.]

PER CURIAM.

We granted certiorari to determine whether the Equal Protection Clause gives rise to a cause of action on behalf of a "class of one" where the plaintiff did not allege membership in a class or group.

Our cases have recognized successful equal protection claims brought by a "class of one," where the plaintiff alleges that she has been intentionally treated differently from others similarly situated and that there is no rational basis for the difference in treatment. See *Sioux City Bridge Co. v. Dakota County,* 260 U.S. 441 (1923); *Allegheny Pittsburgh Coal Co. v. Commission of Webster Cty.,* 488 U.S. 336 (1989). In so doing, we have explained that "'[t]he purpose of the equal protection clause of the Fourteenth Amendment is to secure every person within the State's jurisdiction against intentional and arbitrary discrimination, whether occasioned by express terms of a statute or by its improper execution through duly constituted agents.'" *Sioux City Bridge Co., supra,* at 445 (quoting *Sunday Lake Iron Co. v. Township of Wakefield,* 247 U.S. 350, 352 (1918)).

That reasoning is applicable to this case. Olech's complaint can fairly be construed as alleging that the Village intentionally demanded a 33-foot easement as a condition of connecting her property to the municipal water supply where the Village required only a 15-foot easement from other similarly situated property owners. See *Conley v. Gibson,* 355 U.S. 41, 45-46 (1957). The complaint also alleged that the Village's demand was "irrational and wholly arbitrary" and that the Village ultimately connected her property after receiving a clearly adequate 15-foot easement. These allegations, quite apart from the Village's subjective motivation, are sufficient to state a claim for relief under traditional equal protection analysis. We therefore affirm the judgment of the Court of Appeals, but do not reach the alternative theory of "subjective ill will" relied on by that court. *It is so ordered.*

Justice BREYER, concurring in the result.

The Solicitor General and the village of Willowbrook have expressed concern lest we interpret the Equal Protection Clause in this case in a way that would transform many ordinary violations of city or state law into violations of the Constitution. It might be thought that a rule that looks only to an intentional difference in treatment and a lack of a rational basis for that different treatment would work such a transformation. Zoning decisions, for example, will often, perhaps almost always, treat one landowner differently from another, and one might claim that, when a city's zoning authority takes an action that fails to conform to a city zoning regulation, it lacks a "rational basis" for its action (at least if the regulation in question is reasonably clear).

This case, however, does not directly raise the question whether the simple and common instance of a faulty zoning decision would violate the Equal Protection Clause. That is because the Court of Appeals found that in this case respondent had alleged an extra factor as well--a factor that the Court of Appeals called "vindictive action," "illegitimate animus," or "ill will." 160 F.3d 386, 388 (C.A.7 1998). And, in that respect, the court said this case resembled *Esmail v. Macrane,* 53 F.3d 176 (C.A.7 1995), because the *Esmail* plaintiff had alleged that the municipality's differential treatment "was the result not of prosecutorial discretion honestly (even if ineptly-even if arbitrarily) exercised but of an illegitimate desire to 'get' him." 160 F.3d, at 388.

In my view, the presence of that added factor in this case is sufficient to minimize any concern about transforming run-of-the-mill zoning cases into cases of constitutional right. For this reason, along with the others mentioned by the Court, I concur in the result.

NOTES

1. It was certainly unexpected that a garden-variety land-use dispute between a village and one of its residents would reach the Supreme Court, but it happened. The Supreme Court opinion in the case also had to be surprising as well, particularly in its brevity and in the casualness with which the Court treated the problem before it. The entire per curiam opinion consisted of five paragraphs. The first three paragraphs summarized the facts and procedural history below, and then concluded with the Court's identification of the issue as "whether the Equal Protection Clause gives rise to a cause of action on behalf of a 'class of one' where the plaintiff did not allege membership in a class or group." The Court's entire substantive response to this question consisted of exactly two short paragraphs.

In the first of these paragraphs, the Court stated that "[o]ur cases have recognized successful equal protection claims brought by a 'class of one,' where the plaintiff alleges that she has been intentionally treated differently from others similarly situated and there is no rational basis for the difference in treatment." It was certainly open to debate whether the Court's previous cases in fact "recognized" a class of one claim, in as much as this kind of claim appeared to be inconsistent with the Court's ordinary focus in equal protection cases on the reasonableness of government classification. Thus, the case appeared to be breaking new ground. In addition, the Supreme Court reframed the issue from the way it had been addressed below by Judge Posner in the Seventh Circuit. Judge Posner had given weight to the allegation that the Village had vindictively singled out Mrs. Olech in retaliation for a previous lawsuit. Judge Posner's theory required a plaintiff to produce evidence of the defendant officials' subjective motivation, but not necessarily evidence of similarly situated persons being treated differently. The Supreme Court's explanation, on the other hand, required a plaintiff to produce evidence that similarly situated persons were treated differently, but not any evidence of the defendant's subjective motivation for the conduct being challenged. The Supreme Court explicitly distanced itself from the "subjective ill will" theory that had been relied on by Judge Posner below.

In the aftermath of the Supreme Court's decision in *Olech* there was the concern at "the prospect of turning every squabble over municipal services, of which there must be tens or even hundreds of thousands every year, into a federal constitutional case." *Olech v. Village of Willowbrook*, 160 F.3d 386, 388 (7th Cir. 1998). Lower federal courts attempted to find limiting principles on what could have been a major expansion of equal protection doctrine. In 2008, the Court returned to the class of one claim and, in the next case, announced its own limiting principle.

Engquist v. Oregon Dept. of Agriculture
553 U.S. 591 (2008)

[Anup Engquist worked for the Oregon Department of Agriculture and was laid off after her position was eliminated. Engquist brought a class of one claim in federal district court and won a jury verdict of $175,000 in compensatory damages and $250,000 in punitive damages. The jury found that the employees in her department "'intentionally treat[ed] [Engquist] differently than others similarly situated with respect to the denial of her promotion, termination of her employment, or denial of bumping rights, without any rational basis and solely for arbitrary, vindictive or malicious reasons.'" The United States Court of Appeals for the Ninth Circuit reversed, holding that the class of one theory was "inapplicable to decisions made by public employers with regard to their employees." Because there was a dispute among the circuits on the issue, the Supreme Court granted certiorari and affirmed the Ninth Circuit's decision, carving out a government employment exception to the *Olech* class of one claim.]

Justice ROBERTS delivered the opinion of the Court.

The question in this case is whether a public employee can state a claim under the Equal Protection Clause by alleging that she was arbitrarily treated differently from other similarly situated employees, with no assertion that the different treatment was based on the employee's membership in any particular class. We hold that such a "class-of-one" theory of equal protection has no place in the public employment context.

II

Engquist argues that the Equal Protection Clause forbids public employers from irrationally treating one employee differently from others similarly situated, regardless of whether the different treatment is based on the employee's membership in a particular class. She reasons that in *Olech, supra,* we recognized in the regulatory context a similar class-of-one theory of equal protection; that the Equal Protection Clause protects individuals, not classes; that the Clause proscribes "discrimination arising not only from a legislative act but also from the conduct of an administrative official," and that the Constitution applies to the State not only when it acts as regulator, but also when it acts as employer. Thus, Engquist concludes that class-of-one claims can be brought against public employers just as against any other state actors, and that differential treatment of government employees—even when not based on membership in a class or group— violates the Equal Protection Clause unless supported by a rational basis.

We do not quarrel with the premises of Engquist's argument. It is well settled that the Equal Protection Clause "protect[s] persons, not groups," *Adarand Constructors, Inc. v. Peña,* 515 U.S. 200, 227 (1995) and that the Clause's protections apply to administrative as well as legislative acts, see, *e.g., Raymond v. Chicago Union Traction Co.,* 207 U.S. 20, 35–36 (1907). It is equally well settled that States do not escape the strictures of the Equal Protection Clause in their role as employers. See, *e.g., New York City Transit Authority v. Beazer,* 440 U.S. 568 (1979); *Harrah Independent School Dist. v. Martin,* 440 U.S. 194 (1979) (*per curiam*); *Massachusetts Bd. of Retirement v. Murgia,* 427 U.S. 307 (1976) (*per curiam*). We do not, however, agree that Engquist's conclusion follows from these premises. Our traditional view of the core concern of the Equal Protection Clause as a shield against arbitrary classifications, combined with unique considerations applicable when the government acts as employer as opposed to sovereign, lead us to conclude that the class-of-one theory of equal protection does not apply in the public employment context.

A

We have long held the view that there is a crucial difference, with respect to constitutional analysis, between the government exercising "the power to regulate or license, as lawmaker," and the government acting "as proprietor, to manage [its] internal operation." *Cafeteria & Restaurant Workers v. McElroy,* 367 U.S. 886, 896 (1961). This distinction has been particularly clear in our review of state action in the context of public employment. Thus, "the government as employer indeed has far broader powers than does the government as sovereign." *Waters v. Churchill,* 511 U.S. 661, 671 (1994) (plurality opinion).

In light of these basic principles, we have often recognized that government has significantly greater leeway in its dealings with citizen employees than it does when it brings its sovereign power to bear on citizens at large. Our precedent in the public employee context therefore establishes two main principles: First, although government employees do not lose their constitutional rights when they accept their positions, those rights must be balanced against the realities of the employment context. Second, in striking the appropriate balance, we consider whether the asserted employee right implicates the basic concerns of the relevant constitutional provision, or whether the claimed right can more readily give way to the requirements of the government as employer. With these principles in mind, we come to the question whether a class-of-one theory of equal protection is cognizable in the public employment context.

B

Our equal protection jurisprudence has typically been concerned with governmental classifications that "affect some groups of citizens differently than others." *McGowan v. Maryland,* 366 U.S. 420, 425 (1961). See, *e.g., Ross v. Moffitt,* 417 U.S. 600, 609 (1974) ("'Equal Protection' ... emphasizes disparity in treatment by a State between classes of individuals whose situations are arguably indistinguishable"); *San Antonio Independent School Dist. v. Rodriguez,* 411 U.S. 1, 60 (1973) (Stewart, J., concurring) ("[T]he basic concern of the Equal Protection Clause is with state legislation whose purpose or effect is to create discrete and objectively identifiable classes"). Plaintiffs in such cases generally allege that they have been arbitrarily classified as members of an "identifiable group." *Personnel Administrator of Mass. v. Feeney,* 442 U.S. 256, 279 (1979).

Engquist correctly argues, however, that we recognized in *Olech* that an equal protection claim can in some circumstances be sustained even if the plaintiff has not alleged class-based discrimination, but instead claims that she has been irrationally singled out as a so-called "class of one." [The Court here summarized its *Olech* holding.]

Recognition of the class-of-one theory of equal protection on the facts in *Olech* was not so much a departure from the principle that the Equal Protection Clause is concerned with arbitrary government classification, as it was an application of that principle. That case involved the government's regulation of property. Similarly, the cases upon which the Court in *Olech* relied concerned property assessment and taxation schemes. We expect such legislative or regulatory classifications to apply "without respect to persons," to borrow a phrase from the judicial oath. As we explained long ago, the Fourteenth Amendment "requires that all persons subjected to ... legislation shall be treated alike, under like circumstances and conditions, both in the privileges conferred and in the liabilities imposed." *Hayes v. Missouri,* 120 U.S. 68, (1887). When those who appear similarly situated are nevertheless treated differently, the Equal Protection Clause requires at least a rational reason for the difference, to assure that all persons subject to legislation or regulation are indeed being "treated alike, under like circumstances and conditions." Thus, when it appears that an individual is being singled out by the government, the specter of arbitrary classification is fairly raised, and the Equal Protection Clause requires a "rational basis for the difference in treatment." *Olech,* 528 U.S., at 564.

What seems to have been significant in *Olech* and the cases on which it relied was the existence of a clear standard against which departures, even for a single plaintiff, could be readily assessed. There was no indication in *Olech* that the zoning board was exercising discretionary authority based on subjective, individualized determinations—at least not with regard to easement length, however typical such determinations may be as a general zoning matter. Rather, the complaint alleged that the board consistently required only a 15–foot easement, but subjected Olech to a 33–foot easement. This differential treatment raised a concern of arbitrary classification, and we therefore required that the State provide a rational basis for it.

In *Allegheny Pittsburgh,* cited by the *Olech* Court, the applicable standard was market value, but the county departed from that standard in basing some assessments on quite dated purchase prices. Again, there was no suggestion that the "dramatic differences in valuation" for similar property parcels were based on subjective considerations of the sort on which appraisers often rely. *Sioux City Bridge,* also cited in *Olech,* was the same sort of case, recognizing an equal protection claim when one taxpayer's property was assessed at 100 percent of its value, while all other property was assessed at 55 percent, without regard to articulated differences in the properties.

There are some forms of state action, however, which by their nature involve discretionary decisionmaking based on a vast array of subjective, individualized assessments. In such cases the rule that people should be "treated alike, under like circumstances and conditions" is not violated when one person is treated differently from others, because treating like individuals differently is an accepted consequence of the discretion granted. In such situations, allowing a challenge based on the arbitrary singling out of a particular person would undermine the very discretion that such state officials are entrusted to exercise.

Suppose, for example, that a traffic officer is stationed on a busy highway where people often drive above the speed limit, and there is no basis upon which to distinguish them. If the officer gives only one of those people a ticket, it may be good English to say that the officer has created a class of people that did not get speeding tickets, and a "class of one" that did. But assuming that it is in the nature of the particular government activity that not all speeders can be stopped and ticketed, complaining that one has been singled out for no reason does not invoke the fear of improper government classification. Such a complaint, rather, challenges the legitimacy of the underlying action itself—the decision to ticket speeders under such circumstances. Of course, an allegation that speeding tickets are given out on the basis of race or sex would state an equal protection claim, because such discriminatory classifications implicate basic equal protection concerns. But allowing an equal protection claim on the ground that a ticket was given to one person and not others, even if for no discernible or articulable reason, would be incompatible with the discretion inherent in the challenged action. It is no proper challenge to what in its nature is a subjective, individualized decision that it was subjective and individualized.

This principle applies most clearly in the employment context, for employment decisions are quite often subjective and individualized, resting on a wide array of factors that are difficult to articulate and quantify. As Engquist herself points out, "[u]nlike the zoning official, the public employer often must take into account the individual personalities and interpersonal relationships of employees in the workplace. The close relationship between the employer and employee, and the varied needs and interests involved in the employment context, mean that considerations such as concerns over personality conflicts that would be unreasonable as grounds for 'arm's-length' government decisions (*e.g.,* zoning, licensing) may well justify different treatment of a public employee." Unlike the context of arm's-length regulation, such as in *Olech,* treating seemingly similarly situated individuals differently in the employment context is par for the course.

Thus, the class-of-one theory of equal protection—which presupposes that like individuals should be treated alike, and that to treat them differently is to classify them in a way that must survive at least rationality review—is simply a poor fit in the public employment context. To treat employees differently is not to classify them in a way that raises equal protection concerns. Rather, it is simply to exercise the broad discretion that typically characterizes the employer-employee relationship. A challenge that one has been treated individually in this context, instead of like everyone else, is a challenge to the underlying nature of the government action.

Of course, that is not to say that the Equal Protection Clause, like other constitutional provisions, does not apply to public employers. Indeed, our cases make clear that the Equal Protection Clause is implicated when the government makes class-based decisions in the employment context, treating distinct groups of individuals categorically differently. See, *e.g., Beazer,* 440 U.S., at 593 (upholding city's exclusion of methadone users from employment under rational-basis review); *Martin,* 440 U.S., at 199–201 (classification between teachers who had complied with a continuing-education requirement and those who had not is rational and does not violate the Equal Protection Clause); *Murgia,* 427 U.S., at 314–317 (upholding a mandatory retirement age—a classification based on age—under rational-basis review). The dissent's broad statement that we "excep[t] state employees from the Fourteenth Amendment's protection against unequal and irrational treatment at the hands of the State," *post,* at 2158 (opinion of STEVENS, J.), is thus plainly not correct. But we have never found the Equal Protection Clause implicated in the specific circumstance where, as here, government employers are alleged to have made an individualized, subjective personnel decision in a seemingly arbitrary or irrational manner.

State employers cannot, of course, take personnel actions that would independently violate the Constitution. But recognition of a class-of-one theory of equal protection in the public employment context—that is, a claim that the State treated an employee differently from others for a bad reason, or for no reason at all—is simply contrary to the concept of at-will employment. The Constitution does not require repudiating that familiar doctrine.

In concluding that the class-of-one theory of equal protection has no application in the public employment context—and that is all we decide—we are guided, as in the past, by the "commonsense realization that government offices could not function if every employment decision became a constitutional matter." If, as Engquist suggests, plaintiffs need not claim discrimination on the basis of membership in some class or group, but rather may argue only that they were treated by their employers worse than other employees similarly situated, any personnel action in which a wronged employee can conjure up a claim of differential treatment will suddenly become the basis for a federal constitutional claim. Indeed, an allegation of arbitrary differential treatment could be made in nearly every instance of an assertedly wrongful employment action—not only hiring and firing decisions, but any personnel action, such as promotion, salary, or work assignments—on the theory that other employees were not treated wrongfully. On Engquist's view, every one of these employment decisions by a government employer would become the basis for an equal protection complaint.

Engquist assures us that accepting her view would not pose too much of a practical problem. Specifically, Engquist argues that a plaintiff in a class-of-one employment case would have to prove that the government's differential treatment was intentional, that the plaintiff was treated differently from other similarly situated persons, and that the unequal treatment was not rationally related to a legitimate government purpose. And because a "governmental employment decision is ... rational whenever the discrimination relates to a legitimate government interest," it is in practice "difficult for plaintiffs to show that the government has failed to meet this standard." *Id.,* at 41. Justice STEVENS makes a similar argument, stating "that all but a handful [of class-of-one complaints] are dismissed well in advance of trial."

We agree that, even if we accepted Engquist's claim, it would be difficult for a plaintiff to show that an employment decision is arbitrary. But this submission is beside the point. The practical problem with allowing class-of-one claims to go forward in this context is not that it will be too easy for plaintiffs to prevail, but that governments will be forced to defend a multitude of such claims in the first place, and courts will be obliged to sort through them in a search for the proverbial needle in a haystack. The Equal Protection Clause does not require "[t]his displacement of managerial discretion by judicial supervision." *Garcetti v. Ceballos,* 547 U.S. 410, 423 (2006).

In short, ratifying a class-of-one theory of equal protection in the context of public employment would impermissibly "constitutionalize the employee grievance." *Connick,* 461 U.S., at 154. "The federal court is not the appropriate forum in which to review the multitude of personnel decisions that are made daily by public agencies." *Bishop, supra,* at 349. Public employees typically have a variety of protections from just the sort of personnel actions about which Engquist complains, but the Equal Protection Clause is not one of them.

The judgment of the Court of Appeals is affirmed. *It is so ordered.*

NOTES

1. The *Engquist* Court insisted that it was deciding only one thing: that the class-of-one theory of equal protection has no application in the public employment context. The language of the *Engquist* opinion, however, suggests it will have a much broader effect. In explaining why the

Olech class-of-one claim does not apply in the context of government employment, the Court adopted a principle much broader than the factual context of government employment—the Court explained that class of one claims are ill-fitted, and therefore do not apply, to government acts that involve the exercise of discretion. The Court explained:

> There are some forms of state action, however, which by their nature involve discretionary decisionmaking based on a vast array of subjective, individualized assessments. In such cases the rule that people should be "treated alike, under like circumstances and conditions" is not violated when one person is treated differently from others, because treating like individuals differently is an accepted consequence of the discretion granted. In such situations, allowing a challenge based on the arbitrary singling out of a particular person would undermine the very discretion that such state officials are entrusted to exercise.

The Court then explained that the exercise of discretion is readily applicable in the employment context, "for employment decisions are quite often subjective and individualized, resting on a wide array of factors that are difficult to articulate and quantify."

After *Engquist*, a number of federal courts have read the case as applying not simply to cases involving government employment but also to all discretionary decisionmaking by government. Thus, federal courts have determined that *Engquist*'s exception for discretionary government action in employment was equally applicable to the criminal justice system, government regulation, land use regulation, education, and government contracting. *See* Robert C. Farrell, *The Equal Protection Class of One Claim: Olech, Enquist, and the Supreme Court's Misadventure*, 61 South Carolina L. Rev. 107 (2009).

William D. Araiza has written critically about the *Engquist* case. He notes that in the post-*Olech* world, the lower federal courts had developed a number of methods to cabin the class-of-one claim, by "impos[ing] appropriate pleading requirements, sift[ing] carefully through the facts, and thus cull[ing] meritless claims at early stages of litigation while allowing the potentially meritless claims to progress." The *Engquist* opinion, by contrast, adopted a "blunt, categorical rule' for class-of-one claims in the governmental workplace and rejected the "more nuanced way [used by lower courts] that more accurately strikes the balance" between the countervailing interests. *See* William D. Araiza, *Constitutional Rules and Institutional Roles: The Fate of the Equal Protection Class of One and What It Means for Congressional Power to Enforce Constitutional Rights*, 62 SMU L. Rev. 27 (2009).

H. OTHER THEORETICAL MODELS OF EQUAL PROTECTION

The model of equal protection set forth in this chapter is a model that focuses on classifications and their relationship to statutory purpose. This could be called a "reasonable classification" model, or more commonly, an "anti-classification" model. This "anti-classification" model most closely tracks the reasoning of the Supreme Court equal protection opinions, but it is not the only model that might be used to explain the requirements of equal protection. Scholars have suggested several alternate models that would explicate the command of equality and this section examines these.

1. *THE ANTI-SUBORDINATION MODEL*

Under the anti-classification, the concern is with unreasonable classifications, that is, classifications that are not adequately correlated with their purpose. The anti-subordination model, on the other hand, focuses on government acts that aggravate or perpetuate the subordinate position of a specially disadvantaged group. *See* Owen M. Fiss, *Groups and the Equal Protection Clause*, 5 Philosophy and Public Affairs 107, 157 (1976). The two models will often produce similar results but, in certain important contexts, they diverge. The anti-subordination model is most frequently called on to do work in the areas of race and gender discrimination, but it is mentioned here because it is typically contrasted with the reasonable classification model set forth in this chapter.

A couple of well-known examples will illustrate the models. If, in *Brown v. Board of Education*, 347 U.S. 483 (1954), the wrong was that children were classified by race and then assigned to racially segregated schools, then the constitutional problem is racial classification. If, on the other hand, the wrong in *Brown* was that black children were treated as inferior to white children, then the constitutional problem is anti-subordination. Similarly, if the problem in *United States v. Virginia*, 518 U.S. 515 (1996) was that VMI was classifying students by gender in a way that was not relevant to its mission, the problem is one of gender classification. If, on the other hand, the problem at VMI was that the exclusion of women tended to create or perpetuate the legal, social, and economic inferiority of women, then the problem is one of anti-subordination.

As the examples in the preceding paragraph indicate, the anti-classification and anti-subordination models will frequently produce the same results: racial segregation in public schools and the exclusion of women from VMI will violate the Equal Protection Clause under either model. There are, however, two contexts in which the models will likely produce different results: affirmative action and actions with disproportionate impact on a particular disadvantaged group. Consider the case of a state institution that makes race-conscious admissions decisions to benefit those who have historically been excluded. Under the first model, that is a racial classification which is constitutionally just as troublesome as a state action that is designed to disadvantage a racial minority and will be very difficult to justify. *See* Chapter 2, *infra*. Under the second model, however, since that action attempts to undo rather than perpetuate the subordination of a disadvantaged class, it will not raise constitutional concerns. Further, under the anti-classification model, a facially neutral law that has a disproportionately disadvantageous effect on blacks is not considered a racial classification, and therefore, will not be given any special scrutiny. Under the anti-subordination model, however, since the effects of the law exacerbate the disadvantages of a subordinate class, it will be constitutionally suspect.

Some scholars are of the view that the anti-subordination model expresses the spirit of the Equal Protection Clause better than does the anti-classification model. *See*, Ruth Colker, *Anti-Subordination Above All: Sex, Race, and Equal Protection,*, 61 N.Y.U. L. Rev. 1003, 1011 (1986) (arguing that "the anti-subordination principle better explains both much of the law and the aversions we feel to race and sex discrimination."); Jack M Balkin and Reva B. Siegal, *The American Civil Rights Tradition: Anticlassification or Antisubordination?*, 58 U. Miami L. Rev. 9, 32-33 (2003) (arguing that the anti-subordination principle is "the expression of the American revolutionary tradition in our own time, the living source of our commitment to the Declaration and its promises of equality, the warm lifeblood of the American spirit.").

In affirmative action cases, the Supreme Court has tended to favor the anti-classification model over the anti-subordination model. The Court treats all racial classifications, whether invidious or remedial as equally suspect, and all subject to the same level of strict scrutiny. These cases are examined in Chapter 2.

2. THE SUBSTANTIVE EQUALITY MODEL

The feminist critique of the reasonable classification model of equality is that, with its emphasis on treating similarly those similarly situated, it produces a superficial equality in which women must be like men in order to be equal. This means that men are the standard by which equality is measured. Even conceding this point, it is still true that the formal equality model works for women in some contexts. As Lucinda Finley has pointed out, this formal view of equality "has been particularly useful for gaining access to traditionally male prerogatives within the public sphere." Lucinda Finley, *Transcending Equality Theory: A Way Out of the Maternity and the Workplace Debate*, 86 Columbia L. Rev.1118, 1142 (1986). The argument that women should be treated like men helped women eliminate gender discrimination in probate court appointments, payment of alimony, and admission to VMI. *See infra* Chapter 3. So the formal equality argument does work for women in some contexts.

Where the formal equality model tends to fail is in those situations where the law deals with the effects of pregnancy. Finley explains:

> This conception of the ideal world that underlies equality jurisprudence is precisely why it is limited and problematic in the pregnancy context, and in other gender contexts where women have qualities or perspectives that can enhance the male sphere and should not be dispensed with. Pregnancy is essential to the human race, and it is an area in which women cannot and should not act like men. It is "female behavior" that is not going to gradually wither away. Where gender distinctions arise from biological facts, or where they have culturally existed, women are not similarly situated to men. Existing institutional structures therefore have distinct implications for women and men. Given this reality, equality doctrine is not going to advance women very far. The doctrine inherently assumes that the goal is assimilation to an existing standard without questioning the desirability of that standard and thus it limits the debate to what policies will best achieve the assimilation. *Id.*

The Court's adoption of an intermediate standard of review of gender classifications makes it more likely that courts will be able to recognize those situations in which men and women are not similarly situated and in which, therefore, even under the traditional anti-classification model, they ought not to be treated similarly.

CHAPTER 2

RACE CLASSIFICATIONS

A. RACIAL CLASSIFICATIONS BEFORE THE ADOPTION OF THE FOURTEENTH AMENDMENT

1. SLAVERY IN THE ORIGINAL TEXT OF THE CONSTITUTION

The original text of the United States Constitution contained no equality provision that would have mandated that the state or federal government treat persons equally. In fact, there were provisions in the original version of the Constitution that mandated inequality—the sections that gave effect to, and thereby endorsed, slavery, even without using the term "slavery." These sections were:

- Article I, Section 2, Clause 3—"Representatives and direct Taxes shall be apportioned among the several States which may be included within this Union, according to their respective Numbers, which shall be determined by adding to the whole Number of free Persons, including those bound to Service for a Term of Years, and excluding Indians not taxed, three fifths of all other Persons." This provision counted slaves as three fifths of a person for purposes of determining the number of Congressmen for each state.

- Article I, Section 9, Clause 1—"The Migration or Importation of such Persons as any of the States now existing shall think proper to admit, shall not be prohibited by the Congress prior to the Year one thousand eight hundred and eight, but a Tax or duty may be imposed on such Importation, not exceeding ten dollars for each Person." This provision meant that Congress could not outlaw the slave trade until 1808, thus guaranteeing that the importation of slaves into the United States would continue for twenty-one years after the adoption of the Constitution.

- Article IV, Section 2, Clause 3—"No Person held to Service or Labour in one State, under the Laws thereof, escaping into another, shall, in Consequence of any Law or Regulation therein, be discharged from such Service or Labour, but shall be delivered up on Claim of the Party to whom such Service or Labour may be due." This provision guaranteed that a slave who escaped and arrived in a free state could still be returned to his owner in his former slave state. Congress gave effect to this constitutional provision in the 1793 Fugitive Slave Act.

2. SLAVERY AND RACIAL CLASSIFICATIONS BEFORE THE CIVIL WAR

Prigg v. Com. of Pennsylvania, 41 U.S. 539 (1842), is an example of the fugitive slave provision of the Constitution at work. In that case, Edward Prigg went to Pennsylvania to recover a slave who had escaped from Maryland. Prigg did so, but his act violated a Pennsylvania statute that barred the transporting of persons by force and violence to be returned to a life of servitude, and he was convicted of kidnapping. Prigg appealed his conviction to the United States Supreme Court where it was overturned on the ground that the Pennsylvania law was unconstitutional in that it was inconsistent with the fugitive slave provision of the Constitution as well as inconsistent with Fugitive Slave statute. The Court explained the importance of the fugitive slave provision of the Constitution:

> Historically, it is well known, that the object of this clause was to secure to the citizens of the slave-holding states the complete right and title of ownership in their slaves, as property, in every state in the Union into which they might escape from the state where they were held in servitude. The full recognition of this right and title was indispensable to the security of this species of property in all the slave-holding states; and, indeed, was so vital to the preservation of their domestic interests and institutions, that it cannot be doubted, that it constituted a fundamental article, without the adoption of which the Union could not have been formed. Its true design was, to guard against the doctrines and principles prevalent in the non-slave-holding states, by preventing them from intermeddling with, or obstructing, or abolishing the rights of the owners of slaves.

The infamous *Dred Scott* decision, *Dred Scott v. Sandford*, 60 U.S. 393 (1856), was another case involving a slave who had moved to a free state. In that case, Dred Scott had been taken as a slave into the free state of Illinois. Scott sued his owner, claiming that he was free. The Supreme Court ruled that Scott, a slave, was not a citizen of the United States and therefore the Court did not have jurisdiction based on diversity of citizenship. In addition, the Court declared that the Missouri Compromise, which had ruled out extending slavery to United States territories, was unconstitutional since it interfered with an owner's property rights in his slaves.

Even apart from slavery, racial discrimination in the years before the Civil War was widespread. A telling example of this racism is the case of *People v. Hall*, 4 Cal. 399 (1854), in which the California Supreme Court approved of a state statute under which "No Black, or Mulatto person, or Indian, shall be allowed to give evidence in favor of, or against a white man." In that case, a white male defendant had been convicted of murder upon the testimony of Chinese witnesses. The Court had no problem with the act itself; the problem was determining whether or not a Chinese person was black or Indian. The court decided the case in the alternative. On the one hand, a Chinese person could not testify because he was "Indian," the reasoning being that American Indians likely came over the Behring's Straits from Asia, and therefore, the term "Indian" included "Asiatics." In the alternative, a Chinese person was "Black" because the term "Black" must be taken in its generic sense and thus exclude all races other than the Caucasian. The court noted the problems that would result from any other conclusion:

> We have carefully considered all the consequences resulting from a different rule of construction, and are satisfied that even in a doubtful case we would be impelled to this decision on grounds of public policy. The same rule which would admit them [the Chinese witnesses] to testify, would admit them to all the equal rights of citizenship, and we might soon see them at the polls, in the jury box, upon the bench, and in our

legislative halls. This is not a speculation that exists in the excited and over-heated imagination of the patriot and statesman, but it is an actual and present danger.

The anomalous spectacle of a distinct people, living in our community, recognizing no laws of this State except through necessity, bringing with them their prejudices and national feuds, in which they indulge in open violation of law; whose mendacity is proverbial; a race of people whom nature has marked as inferior, and who are incapable of progress or intellectual development beyond a certain point, as their history has shown; differing in language, opinions, color, and physical conformation; between whom and ourselves nature has placed an impassable difference, is now presented, and for them is claimed, not only the right to swear away the life of a citizen, but the further privilege of participating with us in administering the affairs of our Government.

3. *THE ADOPTION OF THE POST-CIVIL WAR AMENDMENTS*

The problem of slavery, America's original sin, was not resolved until the Civil War was fought. At its conclusion, the nation adopted three amendments that would finally address the problem:

- The Thirteenth Amendment, which abolished slavery—"Neither slavery nor involuntary servitude, except as a punishment for crime whereof the party shall have been duly convicted, shall exist within the United States, or any place subject to their jurisdiction.

- The Fourteenth Amendment—"All persons born or naturalized in the United States, and subject to the jurisdiction thereof, are citizens of the United States and of the State wherein they reside. No State shall make or enforce any law which shall abridge the privileges or immunities of citizens of the United States; nor shall any State deprive any person of life, liberty, or property, without due process of law; nor deny to any person within its jurisdiction the equal protection of the laws."

- The Fifteenth Amendment—"The right of citizens of the United States to vote shall not be denied or abridged by the United States or by any State on account of race, color, or previous condition of servitude."

For the first time in United States history, state governments were held to a standard of equality. The promise of the Declaration of Independence—that all men are created equal—was now a constitutional mandate as well. It was, however, not at all clear what the command of equality demanded. The Court began to address that question shortly after the adoption of the Fourteenth Amendment and still struggles to answer it today.

B. THE ORIGINAL UNDERSTANDING OF THE EQUAL PROTECTION CLAUSE

It is often assumed that the Equal Protection Clause was given little effect by the Supreme Court during the nineteenth century. This viewpoint is probably colored by the prominence of a late nineteenth century case, *Plessy v. Ferguson*, 163 U.S. 537 (1896), in which the Court endorsed the doctrine of "separate but equal" and thereby seemed to read most of the substance out of the Equal Protection Clause. Before *Plessy*, however, the Court had given substantive effect to the Equal Protection Clause in cases prohibiting certain governmental racial classifications. This section examines two prominent cases of that type and considers how the result in the *Plessy* case might have been justified by the lawyers of that day.

Strauder v. State of West Virginia
100 U.S. 303 (1879)

[A West Virginia statute provided that only white males could serve as jurors. Strauder, "a colored man," was convicted of murder in a West Virginia Court. On appeal, he asserted that the impaneling of an all-white jury violated the Equal Protection Clause.]

MR. JUSTICE STRONG delivered the opinion of the court.

[The court is asked to consider] whether, by the Constitution and laws of the United States, every citizen of the United States has a right to a trial of an indictment against him by a jury selected and impanelled without discrimination against his race or color, because of race or color.

[The question] is not whether a colored man, when an indictment has been preferred against him, has a right to a grand or a petit jury composed in whole or in part of persons of his own race or color, but it is whether, in the composition or selection of jurors by whom he is to be indicted or tried, all persons of his race or color may be excluded by law, solely because of their race or color, so that by no possibility can any colored man sit upon the jury.

The question . . . demand[s] a construction of the recent amendments of the Constitution. If the defendant has a right to have a jury selected for the trial of his case without discrimination against all persons of his race or color, because of their race or color, the right, if not created, is protected by those amendments, and the legislation of Congress under them. The Fourteenth Amendment ordains that 'all persons born or naturalized in the United States and subject to the jurisdiction thereof are citizens of the United States and of the State wherein they reside. No State shall make or enforce any laws which shall abridge the privileges or immunities of citizens of the United States, nor shall any State deprive any person of life, liberty, or property, without due process of law, nor deny to any person within its jurisdiction the equal protection of the laws.'

This is one of a series of constitutional provisions having a common purpose; namely, securing to a race recently emancipated, a race that through many generations had been held in slavery, all the civil rights that the superior race enjoy. The true spirit and meaning of the amendments, as we said in the *Slaughter-House Cases* (16 Wall. 36), cannot be understood without keeping in view the history of the times when they were adopted, and the general objects they plainly sought to accomplish. At the time when they were incorporated into the Constitution, it required little knowledge of human nature to anticipate that those who had long been regarded as an inferior and subject race would, when suddenly raised to the rank of citizenship, be looked upon with jealousy and positive dislike, and that State laws might be enacted or enforced to perpetuate the distinctions that had before existed. Discriminations against them had been habitual. It was well known that in some States laws making such discriminations then existed, and others might well be expected. The colored race, as a race, was abject and ignorant, and in that condition was unfitted to command the respect of those who had superior intelligence. Their training had left them mere children, and as such they needed the protection which a wise government extends to those who are unable to protect themselves. They especially needed protection against unfriendly action in the States where they were resident. It was in view of these considerations the Fourteenth Amendment was framed and adopted. It was designed to assure to the colored race the enjoyment of all the civil rights that under the law are enjoyed by white persons, and to give to that race the protection of the general government, in that enjoyment, whenever it should be denied by the States. It not only gave citizenship and the privileges of citizenship to persons of color, but it denied to any State the power to withhold from them the equal protection of the laws, and authorized Congress to enforce its provisions by appropriate legislation. To quote the language used by us in the *Slaughter-House Cases*, 'No one can fail to be impressed with the one pervading purpose found in all the amendments, lying at the foundation of each, and without which none of them would have been suggested,--we mean the freedom of the slave race, the security and firm establishment of that freedom, and the protection of the newly made freeman and citizen from the oppressions of those who had formerly exercised unlimited dominion over them.' So again: 'The existence of laws in the States where the newly emancipated negroes resided, which discriminated with gross injustice and hardship against them as a class, was the evil to be remedied, and by it [the Fourteenth Amendment] such laws were forbidden. If, however, the States did not conform their laws to its requirements, then, by the fifth section of the article of amendment, Congress was authorized to enforce it by suitable legislation.' And it was added, 'We doubt very much whether any action of a State, not directed by way of discrimination against the negroes, as a class, will ever be held to come within the purview of this provision.'

[The amendment] ordains that no State shall deprive any person of life, liberty, or property, without due process of law, or deny to any person within its jurisdiction the equal protection of the laws. What is this but declaring that the law in the States shall be the same for the black as for the white; that all persons, whether colored or white, shall stand equal before the laws of the States, and, in regard to the colored race, for whose protection the amendment was primarily designed, that no discrimination shall be made against them by law because of their color? The words of the amendment, it is true, are prohibitory, but they contain a necessary implication of a positive immunity, or right, most valuable to the colored race--the right to exemption from unfriendly legislation against them distinctively as colored--exemption from legal discriminations, implying inferiority in civil society, lessening the security of their enjoyment of the rights which others enjoy, and discriminations which are steps towards reducing them to the condition of a subject race.

That the West Virginia statute respecting juries--the statute that controlled the selection of the grand and petit jury in the case of the plaintiff in error--is such a discrimination ought not to be doubted. The very fact that colored people are singled out and expressly denied by a statute all right to participate in the administration of the law, as jurors, because of their color, though they are citizens, and may be in other respects fully qualified, is practically a brand upon them, affixed by the law, an assertion of their inferiority, and a stimulant to that race prejudice which is an impediment to securing to individuals of the race that equal justice which the law aims to secure to all others.

We do not say that within the limits from which it is not excluded by the amendment a State may not prescribe the qualifications of its jurors, and in so doing make discriminations. It may confine the selection to males, to freeholders, to citizens, to persons within certain ages, or to persons having educational qualifications. We do not believe the Fourteenth Amendment was ever intended to prohibit this. Looking at its history, it is clear it had no such purpose. Its aim was against discrimination because of race or color.

The Fourteenth Amendment makes no attempt to enumerate the rights it designed to protect. It speaks in general terms, and those are as comprehensive as possible. Its language is prohibitory; but every prohibition implies the existence of rights and immunities, prominent among which is an immunity from inequality of legal protection, either for life, liberty, or property. Any State action that denies this immunity to a colored man is in conflict with the Constitution.

The judgment of the Supreme Court of West Virginia will be reversed, and the case remitted with instructions to reverse the judgment of the Circuit Court of Ohio County; and it is *So ordered.*

NOTES

1. The Court's opinion in *Strauder* is important for two propositions. The first is that, even in 1879, long before the civil rights revolution of the 1960s and 1970s, the Court was construing the Equal Protection Clause to prohibit explicit racial classifications that disadvantaged former slaves, at least in the context of jury service. The Court explained that this result followed from the historical purpose underlying the adoption of the Fourteenth Amendment—"the freedom of the slave race, the security and firm establishment of that freedom, and the protection of the newly made freeman and citizen from the oppressions of those who had formerly exercised unlimited dominion over them."

Once it stated in strong terms that the purpose of the Fourteenth Amendment was the protection of the former slaves, however, the Court suggested that this was the Amendment's only purpose:

> [The state] may confine the selection to males, to freeholders, to citizens, to persons within certain ages, or to persons having educational qualifications. We do not believe the Fourteenth Amendment was ever intended to prohibit this. Looking at its history, it is clear it had no such purpose. Its aim was against discrimination because of race or color.

Of course, the Court's 1879 prediction that the Equal Protection Clause would only address racial discrimination against former slaves turned out to be incorrect. Although the Equal Protection Clause had been adopted to address a specific problem, the Clause itself was written much more broadly than the original problem. Instead of drafting a somewhat limited prohibition such as "No state may discriminate on the basis of race," the Equal Protection Clause was drafted in much more general terms—no state "may deny any person the equal protection of the law. It soon became clear that *Strauder's* very limited reading of the Equal Protection Clause would not be adopted in subsequent opinions of the Court and it is not the Court's understanding today.

A NOTE ON TERMINOLOGY

In 1909, when the NAACP was founded, it was still acceptable to refer to black Americans as "colored." In 1954, when the Supreme Court decided *Brown v. Board of Education*, it was not considered improper for the Court to make repeated references to "the Negro race." Both of those terms have long since come to be considered unacceptable.

Today both the United States Census Bureau and the Associated Press Stylebook adopt the view that the terms "African American" and "black" are both acceptable, although the AP includes a hyphen between "African" and "American" while the Census Bureau does not.

A Gallup poll of black Americans taken in 2007 indicated that, for 61% of those polled, it did not matter whether they were called black or African-American, 24% preferred to be called African-American, and 13% preferred to be called black.

Yick Wo v. Hopkins
118 U.S. 356 (1886)

[In 1880, the city of San Francisco passed an ordinance requiring a permit for the operation of a laundry in a wooden building. The permit was to be granted at the discretion of the board of supervisors. Of the 320 laundries in the city at that time, 240 had Chinese owners and all but 10 were operated in wooden buildings. After the ordinance was in place, *all* applications by Chinese laundry operators were denied, while only one non-Chinese owner was denied a permit.]

MATTHEWS, J.

In the case of the petitioner, brought here by writ of error to the supreme court of California, our jurisdiction is limited to the question whether the plaintiff in error has been denied a right in violation of the constitution, laws, or treaties of the United States.

The ordinance drawn in question in the present case ... does not prescribe a rule and conditions, for the regulation of the use of property for laundry purposes, to which all similarly situated may conform. It allows, without restriction, the use for such purposes of buildings of brick or stone; but, as to wooden buildings, constituting nearly all those in previous use, it divides the owners or occupiers into two classes, not having respect to their personal character and qualifications for the business, nor the situation and nature and adaptation of the buildings themselves, but merely by an arbitrary line, on one side of which are those who are permitted to pursue their industry by the mere will and consent of the supervisors, and on the other those from whom that consent is withheld, at their mere will and pleasure. And both classes are alike only in this: that they are tenants at will, under the supervisors, of their means of living. The ordinance, therefore, ... differs from the not unusual case where discretion is lodged by law in public officers or bodies to grant or withhold licenses to keep taverns, or places for the sale of spirituous liquors, and the like, when one of the conditions is that the applicant shall be a fit person for the exercise of the privilege, because in such cases the fact of fitness is submitted to the judgment of the officer, and calls for the exercise of a discretion of a judicial nature.

The rights of the petitioners, as affected by the proceedings of which they complain, are not less because they are aliens and subjects of the emperor of China. The fourteenth amendment to the constitution is not confined to the protection of citizens. It says: 'Nor shall any state deprive any person of life, liberty, or property without due process of law; nor deny to any person within its jurisdiction the equal protection of the laws.' These provisions are universal in their application, to all persons within the territorial jurisdiction, without regard to any differences of race, of color, or of nationality; and the equal protection of the laws is a pledge of the protection of equal laws. The questions we have to consider and decide in these cases, therefore, are to be treated as involving the rights of every citizen of the United States equally with those of the strangers and aliens who now invoke the jurisdiction of the court.

It is contended on the part of the petitioners that the ordinances for violations of which they are severally sentenced to imprisonment are void on their face, as being within the prohibitions of the fourteenth amendment, and, in the alternative, if not so, that they are void by reason of their administration, operating unequally, so as to punish in the present petitioners what is permitted to others as lawful, without any distinction of circumstances,--an unjust and illegal discrimination, it is claimed, which, though not made expressly by the ordinances, is made possible by them.

When we consider the nature and the theory of our institutions of government, the principles upon which they are supposed to rest, and review the history of their development, we are constrained to conclude that they do not mean to leave room for the play and action of purely personal and arbitrary power. Sovereignty itself is, of course, not subject to law, for it is the author and source of law; but in our system, while sovereign powers are delegated to the agencies of government, sovereignty itself remains with the people, by whom and for whom all government exists and acts. And the law is the definition and limitation of power. It is, indeed, quite true that there must always be lodged somewhere, and in some person or body, the authority of final decision; and in many cases of mere administration, the responsibility is purely political, no appeal lying except to the ultimate tribunal of the public judgment, exercised either in the pressure of opinion, or by means of the suffrage. But the fundamental rights to life, liberty, and the pursuit of happiness, considered as individual possessions, are secured by those maxims of constitutional law which are the monuments showing the victorious progress of the race in securing to men the blessings of civilization under the reign of just and equal laws, so that, in the famous language of the Massachusetts bill of rights, the government of the commonwealth 'may be a government of laws and not of men.' For the very idea that one man may be compelled to hold his life, or the means of living, or any material right essential to the enjoyment of life, at the mere will of another, seems to be intolerable in any country where freedom prevails, as being the essence of slavery itself.

In the present cases, we are not obliged to reason from the probable to the actual, and pass upon the validity of the ordinances complained of, as tried merely by the opportunities which their terms afford, of unequal and unjust discrimination in their administration; for the cases present the ordinances in actual operation, and the facts shown establish an administration directed so exclusively against a particular class of persons as to warrant and require the conclusion that, whatever may have been the intent of the ordinances as adopted, they are applied by the public authorities charged with their administration, and thus representing the state itself, with a mind so unequal and oppressive as to amount to a practical denial by the state of that equal protection of the laws which is secured to the petitioners, as to all other persons, by the broad and benign provisions of the fourteenth amendment to the constitution of the United States. Though the law itself be fair on its face, and impartial in appearance, yet, if it is applied and administered by public authority with an evil eye and an unequal hand, so as practically to make unjust and illegal discriminations between persons in similar circumstances, material to their rights, the denial of equal justice is still within the prohibition of the constitution.

The present cases, as shown by the facts disclosed in the record, are within this class. It appears that both petitioners have complied with every requisite deemed by the law, or by the public officers charged with its administration, necessary for the protection of neighboring property from fire, or as a precaution against injury to the public health. No reason whatever, except the will of the supervisors, is assigned why they should not be permitted to carry on, in the accustomed manner, their harmless and useful occupation, on which they depend for a livelihood; and while this consent of the supervisors is withheld from them, and from 200 others who have also petitioned, all of whom happen to be Chinese subjects, 80 others, not Chinese subjects, are permitted to carry on the same business under similar conditions. The fact of this discrimination is admitted. No reason for it is shown, and the conclusion cannot be resisted that no reason for it exists except hostility to the race and nationality to which the petitioners belong, and which, in the eye of the law, is not justified. The discrimination is therefore illegal, and the public administration that enforces it is a denial of the equal protection of the laws, and a violation of the fourteenth amendment of the constitution. The imprisonment of the petitioners is therefore illegal, and they must be discharged. To this end the judgment of the supreme court of California in the *Case of Yick Wo*, and that of the circuit court of the United States for the district of California in the *Case of Wo Lee*, are severally reversed, and the cases remanded, each to the proper court, with directions to discharge the petitioners from custody and imprisonment.

NOTES

1. As a starting point, the Court's *Yick Wo* opinion, which came only seven years after *Strauder's* language limiting the Equal Protection Clause to discrimination against those who had been enslaved, made clear that the scope of protection was somewhat broader. The *Yick Wo* court held that the provisions of the Equal Protection Clause "are universal in their application, to all persons within the territorial jurisdiction, without regard to any differences of race, of color, or of nationality." The group subject to discrimination in *Yick Wo* was not made up of former slaves, but rather of Chinese immigrants, yet they too received the protection of the Equal Protection Clause. Thus, the Court's *Yick Wo* opinion was the first to suggest that the Court will treat discrimination based on national origin as the constitutional equivalent of discrimination based on race.

2. The *Yick Wo* case is still widely cited for another reason. The challenged ordinance did not contain an explicit racial classification, that is, it did not say, "No Chinese person may operate a laundry. Rather, it was a racially neutral ordinance--restricting laundries in wooden buildings--administered in a racially discriminatory manner. The Court explained that the administration of the ordinance was "directed so exclusively against a particular class of persons as to warrant and require the conclusion that, whatever may have been the intent of the ordinances as adopted, they are applied . . . with a mind so unequal and oppressive as to amount to a practical denial by the state of that equal protection of the laws." This issue of racially neutral rules that have a racially discriminatory effect is taken up in Part E of this chapter.

Plessy v. Ferguson
163 U.S. 537 (1896)

This case turns upon the constitutionality of an act of the general assembly of the state of Louisiana, passed in 1890, providing for separate railway carriages for the white and colored races.

The first section of the statute enacts 'that all railway companies carrying passengers in their coaches in this state, shall provide equal but separate accommodations for the white, and colored races, by providing two or more passenger coaches for each passenger train, or by dividing the passenger coaches by a partition so as to secure separate accommodations: provided, that this section shall not be construed to apply to street railroads. No person or persons shall be permitted to occupy seats in coaches, other than the ones assigned to them, on account of the race they belong to.'

The information filed in the criminal district court charged, in substance, that Plessy, being a passenger between two stations within the state of Louisiana, was assigned by officers of the company to the coach used for the race to which he belonged, but he insisted upon going into a coach used by the race to which he did not belong. Neither in the information nor plea was his particular race or color averred.

The petition for the writ of prohibition averred that petitioner was seven-eighths Caucasian and one-eighth African blood; that the mixture of colored blood was not discernible in him; and that he was entitled to every right, privilege, and immunity secured to citizens of the United States of the white race; and that, upon such theory, he took possession of a vacant seat in a coach where passengers of the white race were accommodated, and was ordered by the conductor to vacate said coach, and take a seat in another, assigned to persons of the colored race, and, having refused to comply with such demand, he was forcibly ejected, with the aid of a police officer, and imprisoned in the parish jail to answer a charge of having violated the above act.

The constitutionality of this act is attacked upon the ground that it conflicts both with the thirteenth amendment of the constitution, abolishing slavery, and the fourteenth amendment, which prohibits certain restrictive legislation on the part of the states.

[The Court determined that the act did not violate the Thirteenth Amendment, since it did not constitute involuntary servitude.]

By the fourteenth amendment, all persons born or naturalized in the United States, and subject to the jurisdiction thereof, are made citizens of the United States and of the state wherein they reside; and the states are forbidden from making or enforcing any law which shall abridge the privileges or immunities of citizens of the United States, or shall deprive any person of life, liberty, or property without due process of law, or deny to any person within their jurisdiction the equal protection of the laws.

The object of the amendment was undoubtedly to enforce the absolute equality of the two races before the law, but, in the nature of things, it could not have been intended to abolish distinctions based upon color, or to enforce social, as distinguished from political, equality, or a commingling of the two races upon terms unsatisfactory to either. Laws permitting, and even requiring, their separation, in places where they are liable to be brought into contact, do not necessarily imply the inferiority of either race to the other, and have been generally, if not universally, recognized as within the competency of the state legislatures in the exercise of their police power. The most common instance of this is connected with the establishment of separate schools for white and colored children, which have been held to be a valid exercise of the legislative power even by courts of states where the political rights of the colored race have been longest and most earnestly enforced.

In this connection, it is also suggested by the learned counsel for the plaintiff in error that the same argument that will justify the state legislature in requiring railways to provide separate accommodations for the two races will also authorize them to require separate cars to be provided for people whose hair is of a certain color, or who are aliens, or who belong to certain nationalities, or to enact laws requiring colored people to walk upon one side of the street, and white people upon the other, or requiring white men's houses to be painted white, and colored

CHAPTER 2: RACE CLASSIFICATIONS 65

men's black, or their vehicles or business signs to be of different colors, upon the theory that one side of the street is as good as the other, or that a house or vehicle of one color is as good as one of another color. The reply to all this is that every exercise of the police power must be reasonable, and extend only to such laws as are enacted in good faith for the promotion of the public good, and not for the annoyance or oppression of a particular class.

So far, then, as a conflict with the fourteenth amendment is concerned, the case reduces itself to the question whether the statute of Louisiana is a reasonable regulation, and with respect to this there must necessarily be a large discretion on the part of the legislature. In determining the question of reasonableness, it is at liberty to act with reference to the established usages, customs, and traditions of the people, and with a view to the promotion of their comfort, and the preservation of the public peace and good order. Gauged by this standard, we cannot say that a law which authorizes or even requires the separation of the two races in public conveyances is unreasonable, or more obnoxious to the fourteenth amendment than the acts of congress requiring separate schools for colored children in the District of Columbia, the constitutionality of which does not seem to have been questioned, or the corresponding acts of state legislatures.

We consider the underlying fallacy of the plaintiff's argument to consist in the assumption that the enforced separation of the two races stamps the colored race with a badge of inferiority. If this be so, it is not by reason of anything found in the act, but solely because the colored race chooses to put that construction upon it. The argument necessarily assumes that if, as has been more than once the case, and is not unlikely to be so again, the colored race should become the dominant power in the state legislature, and should enact a law in precisely similar terms, it would thereby relegate the white race to an inferior position. We imagine that the white race, at least, would not acquiesce in this assumption. The argument also assumes that social prejudices may be overcome by legislation, and that equal rights cannot be secured to the negro except by an enforced commingling of the two races. We cannot accept this proposition. If the two races are to meet upon terms of social equality, it must be the result of natural affinities, a mutual appreciation of each other's merits, and a voluntary consent of individuals. Legislation is powerless to eradicate racial instincts, or to abolish distinctions based upon physical differences, and the attempt to do so can only result in accentuating the difficulties of the present situation. If the civil and political rights of both races be equal, one cannot be inferior to the other civilly or politically. If one race be inferior to the other socially, the constitution of the United States cannot put them upon the same plane.

The judgment of the court below is therefore *affirmed.*

NOTES

1. It is far easier to identify the flaws in *Plessy v. Ferguson* than to find anything that would justify it. The *Plessy* Court seemed to forget what it had said about the purpose of the post-Civil War amendments in *Strauder,* seventeen years earlier:

> The true spirit and meaning of the amendments . . . cannot be understood without keeping in view the history of the times when they were adopted, and the general objects they plainly sought to accomplish. At the time when they were incorporated into the Constitution, it required little knowledge of human nature to anticipate that those who had long been regarded as an inferior and subject race would, when suddenly raised to the

rank of citizenship, be looked upon with jealousy and positive dislike, and that State laws might be enacted or enforced to perpetuate the distinctions that had before existed.

This seems to be exactly what was going on in *Plessy*—an attempt to use state law to perpetuate the discriminatory distinctions that had existed before.

The Court, declaring that the Equal Protection Clause did not reach a statute that required racially segregated railway cars, relied on a distinction between civil and political rights, on the one hand, and social relationships, on the other. According to the *Plessy* Court, the Equal Protection Clause required equality only in the areas of civil and political rights. These rights presumably included the right to vote, to run for political office, to serve on a jury, and to testify as a witness at a trial. The right to travel on a particular train car, however, was not considered a civil or political right and therefore not protected by the Equal Protection Clause. The fact that blacks or whites chose not to socialize with one another, on railway cars or anywhere else, did not create any constitutional issue.

Even by the precedents available to it in 1896, the *Plessy* decision is highly questionable. When the Court in *Yick Wo* found a constitutional violation only ten years earlier, it certainly did not limit the scope of the Equal Protection Clause to encompass only civil and political rights. Operating a laundry in a wooden building is hardly a civil right and it is hardly distinguishable from riding a railroad. With regard to the *Plessy* Court's claim that the Equal Protection Clause could not demand equality in social relations, the Court confused private conduct with the coercive power of a state law. Certainly, there would have been no constitutional issue if blacks and whites decided on their own to sit in separate railway cars. But this separation was *required* by state law, and seemed to directly conflict with the Court's language in *Yick Wo*, that "the equal protection of the laws is a pledge of the protection of equal laws."

2. The legacy of *Plessy* was toxic. The Court's approval of separate but equal railway cars was taken as a general endorsement of the principal of separate but equal. For almost sixty years, until *Brown v. Board of Education* overturned it, *Plessy* was used to justify racial segregation in public schools, parks, swimming pools, public restrooms, and courtroom seating.

C. THE STRICT SCRUTINY STANDARD

It is now firmly established that governmental racial classifications will be subjected to strict scrutiny. In the modern day version of that test, a racial classification must be either "necessary to promote a compelling governmental interest," or "are narrowly tailored to achieving a compelling governmental interest." This demanding standard is readily distinguishable from the rational basis standard, usually applied in a very deferential way, which requires only that a classification be rationally related to a permissible interest.

The exact nature of the strict scrutiny standard has not always been clear and has developed over time. A complicating factor is that the strict scrutiny standard in constitutional law is not limited to the review of suspect classifications under the Equal Protection Clause. It also extends to infringements on implied fundamental rights under the Equal Protection and Due Process Clauses and to First Amendment issues affecting free speech, freedom of association, and the free exercise doctrine. See Richard H. Fallon, *Strict Judicial Scrutiny*, 54 U.C.L.A. Law Rev. 1267

(2007).

In early cases that invalidated race classifications such as *Strauder* and *Yick Wo*, and even through the 1950s in *Brown v. Board of Education*, the Supreme Court never alluded to any particular standard of review, much less to a standard called "strict scrutiny." Rather, in those cases, the Court was invalidating racial classifications as inconsistent with the general command of the Equal Protection Clause. It was not until well into the twentieth century that the Court began to articulate the strict scrutiny standard. This section examines the strict scrutiny standard in cases involving suspect classifications, beginning with the two cases that laid the groundwork in this area-- *United States v. Carolene Products Co.* and *Korematsu v. United States*.

United States v. Carolene Products Co.
304 U.S. 144 (1938)

Mr. Justice STONE delivered the opinion of the Court.

The question for decision is whether the 'Filled Milk Act' of Congress, which prohibits the shipment in interstate commerce of skimmed milk compounded with any fat or oil other than milk fat so as to resemble milk or cream, transcends the power of Congress to regulate interstate commerce or infringes the Fifth Amendment.

[Carolene Products was indicted for violating the act by the shipment in interstate commerce of certain packages of 'Milnut,' a compound of condensed skimmed milk and coconut oil made in imitation of condensed milk or cream. The Court determined that Congress' power to regulate commerce included the power to exclude from commerce articles that it reasonably believed were injurious to the public health.]

Second. The prohibition of shipment of appellee's product in interstate commerce does not infringe the Fifth Amendment.

There is no need to consider it [the statutory characterization of filled milk as injurious to health and as a fraud upon the public] here as more than a declaration of the legislative findings deemed to support and justify the action taken as a constitutional exertion of the legislative power, aiding informed judicial review, as do the reports of legislative committees, by revealing the rationale of the legislation. Even in the absence of such aids, the existence of facts supporting the legislative judgment is to be presumed, for regulatory legislation affecting ordinary commercial transactions is not to be pronounced unconstitutional unless in the light of the facts made known or generally assumed it is of such a character as to preclude the assumption that it rests upon some rational basis within the knowledge and experience of the legislators.[FN 4] The present statutory

---

[FN 4] There may be narrower scope for operation of the presumption of constitutionality when legislation appears on its face to be within a specific prohibition of the Constitution, such as those of the first ten Amendments, which are deemed equally specific when held to be embraced within the Fourteenth. See *Stromberg v. California*, 283 U.S. 359, 369, 370; *Lovell v. Griffin*, 303 U.S. 444 (1938).

It is unnecessary to consider now whether legislation which restricts those political processes which can ordinarily be expected to bring about repeal of undesirable legislation, is to be subjected to more exacting judicial scrutiny under the general prohibitions of the Fourteenth Amendment than are most other types of legislation. On restrictions upon the right to vote, see *Nixon v. Herndon*, 273 U.S. 536; *Nixon v. Condon*, 286 U.S. 73; on restraints upon the dissemination of information, see *Near v. Minnesota*, 283 U.S. 697; *Grosjean*

findings affect appellee no more than the reports of the Congressional committees and since in the absence of the statutory findings they would be presumed, their incorporation in the statute is no more prejudicial than surplusage.

Where the existence of a rational basis for legislation whose constitutionality is attacked depends upon facts beyond the sphere of judicial notice, such facts may properly be made the subject of judicial inquiry, *Borden's Farm Products Co. v. Baldwin*, 293 U.S. 194, and the constitutionality of a statute predicated upon the existence of a particular state of facts may be challenged by showing to the court that those facts have ceased to exist. But by their very nature such inquiries, where the legislative judgment is drawn in question, must be restricted to the issue whether any state of facts either known or which could reasonably be assumed affords support for it. Here the demurrer challenges the validity of the statute on its face and it is evident from all the considerations presented to Congress, and those of which we may take judicial notice, that the question is at least debatable whether commerce in filled milk should be left unregulated, or in some measure restricted, or wholly prohibited. As that decision was for Congress, neither the finding of a court arrived at by weighing the evidence, nor the verdict of a jury can be substituted for it.

The prohibition of shipment in interstate commerce of appellee's product, as described in the indictment, is a constitutional exercise of the power to regulate interstate commerce. As the statute is not unconstitutional on its face, the demurrer should have been overruled and the judgment will be *Reversed*.

NOTES

1. Footnote Four of the *Carolene Products* case has been called "the most famous footnote--and perhaps the most famous passage--in all of the American Judiciary's treatment of constitutional law." Dan T. Coenen, *The Future of Footnote Four*, 41 Ga. L Rev. 797, 798 (2007). It is something of an oddity in that one would not expect the Court to announce a major equal protection doctrine in a footnote to a case about mixing skim milk and coconut oil. That, however, is what the Court did, and there is a probable explanation for its decision to do so.

When the *Carolene Products* opinion was written in 1938, the Court "was beginning to dig itself out of the constitutional debris left by its wholesale capitulation to the New Deal a year before." Bruce A. Ackerman, *Beyond Carolene Products*, 98 Harv. L. Rev. 713 (1985). The opinion came just one year after the Court's ruling in *West Coast Hotel Co. v. Parrish*, 300 U.S.

---

v. American Press Co., 297 U.S. 233; *Lovell v. Griffin*, *supra*; on interferences with political organizations, see *Stromberg v. California*, supra, 283 U.S. 359, 369; *Fiske v. Kansas*, 274 U.S. 380; *Whitney v. California*, 274 U.S. 357, 373-378; *Herndon v. Lowry*, 301 U.S. 242; and see Holmes, J., in *Gitlow v. New York*, 268 U.S. 652, 673; as to prohibition of peaceable assembly, see *De Jonge v. Oregon*, 299 U.S. 353, 365.

Nor need we enquire whether similar considerations enter into the review of statutes directed at particular religious, *Pierce v. Society of Sisters*, 268 U.S. 510, or national, *Meyer v. Nebraska*, 262 U.S. 390; *Bartels v. Iowa*, 262 U.S. 404; *Farrington v. Tokushige*, 273 U.S. 284, or racial minorities. *Nixon v. Herndon*, *supra*; *Nixon v. Condon*, *supra*; whether prejudice against discrete and insular minorities may be a special condition, which tends seriously to curtail the operation of those political processes ordinarily to be relied upon to protect minorities, and which may call for a correspondingly more searching judicial inquiry. Compare *McCulloch v. Maryland*, 4 Wheat. 316, 428; *South Carolina State Highway Department v. Barnwell Bros.*, 303 U.S. 177 (1938), note 2, and cases cited.

379 (1937), which overruled *Parrish v. Children's Hospital,* 261 U.S. 525 (1923). *Adkins* was the case that effectively overruled the views associated with *Lochner v. New York,* 198 U.S. 45 (1905). *Lochner* had been understood to stand for the view that state regulation of contracts interfered with the "liberty of contract" that is part of the Due Process Clause, and was therefore beyond the power of the state. In rejecting that view, the *Parrish* Court had adopted an attitude of judicial deference toward legislative judgments.

But if the *Parrish* decision required the Court generally to defer to legislative judgment, did that mean that the Court had to be deferential in all matters? Footnote Four answers that question in the negative. It suggests that the Court should adopt a more demanding scrutiny in cases where prejudice against discrete and insular minorities tends to exclude them from the majoritarian political process. The cleverness of the *Carolene Products* rationale is that it allows the Court to interfere with the democratic process in order to preserve the democratic process.

Footnote Four identified "discrete and insular minorities" as a particular concern to courts. That concern has become one of the factors that courts consider when they determine whether or not a particular group constitutes a suspect class. That issue is examined in Chapter 3.B.2.

Korematsu v. United States
323 U.S. 214 (1944)

Mr. Justice BLACK delivered the opinion of the Court.

The petitioner, an American citizen of Japanese descent, was convicted in a federal district court for remaining in San Leandro, California, a 'Military Area', contrary to Civilian Exclusion Order No. 34 of the Commanding General of the Western Command, U.S. Army, which directed that after May 9, 1942, all persons of Japanese ancestry should be excluded from that area. No question was raised as to petitioner's loyalty to the United States. The Circuit Court of Appeals affirmed, and the importance of the constitutional question involved caused us to grant certiorari.

It should be noted, to begin with, that all legal restrictions which curtail the civil rights of a single racial group are immediately suspect. That is not to say that all such restrictions are unconstitutional. It is to say that courts must subject them to the most rigid scrutiny. Pressing public necessity may sometimes justify the existence of such restrictions; racial antagonism never can.

Exclusion Order No. 34, which the petitioner knowingly and admittedly violated, was one of a number of military orders and proclamations, all of which were substantially based upon Executive Order No. 9066, 7 Fed. Reg.1407. That order, issued after we were at war with Japan, declared that "the successful prosecution of the war requires every possible protection against espionage and against sabotage to national-defense material, national-defense premises, and national-defense utilities."

One of the series of orders and proclamations, a curfew order, which like the exclusion order here was promulgated pursuant to Executive Order 9066, subjected all persons of Japanese ancestry in prescribed West Coast military areas to remain in their residences from 8 p.m. to 6 a.m. As is the case with the exclusion order here, that prior curfew order was designed as a "protection against espionage and against sabotage." In *Kiyoshi Hirabayashi v. United States,* 320 U.S. 81 (1774), we sustained a conviction obtained for violation of the curfew order. The

Hirabayashi conviction and this one thus rest on the same 1942 Congressional Act and the same basic executive and military orders, all of which orders were aimed at the twin dangers of espionage and sabotage.

In the light of the principles we announced in the *Hirabayashi* case, we are unable to conclude that it was beyond the war power of Congress and the Executive to exclude those of Japanese ancestry from the West Coast war area at the time they did. True, exclusion from the area in which one's home is located is a far greater deprivation than constant confinement to the home from 8 p.m. to 6 a.m. Nothing short of apprehension by the proper military authorities of the gravest imminent danger to the public safety can constitutionally justify either. But exclusion from a threatened area, no less than curfew, has a definite and close relationship to the prevention of espionage and sabotage. The military authorities, charged with the primary responsibility of defending our shores, concluded that curfew provided inadequate protection and ordered exclusion. They did so, as pointed out in our *Hirabayashi* opinion, in accordance with Congressional authority to the military to say who should, and who should not, remain in the threatened areas.

In this case the petitioner challenges the assumptions upon which we rested our conclusions in the *Hirabayashi* case. He also urges that by May 1942, when Order No. 34 was promulgated, all danger of Japanese invasion of the West Coast had disappeared. After careful consideration of these contentions we are compelled to reject them.

Here, as in the *Hirabayashi* case, *supra*, 320 U.S. at page 99,

> we cannot reject as unfounded the judgment of the military authorities and of Congress that there were disloyal members of that population, whose number and strength could not be precisely and quickly ascertained. We cannot say that the war-making branches of the Government did not have ground for believing that in a critical hour such persons could not readily be isolated and separately dealt with, and constituted a menace to the national defense and safety, which demanded that prompt and adequate measures be taken to guard against it.

Like curfew, exclusion of those of Japanese origin was deemed necessary because of the presence of an unascertained number of disloyal members of the group, most of whom we have no doubt were loyal to this country. It was because we could not reject the finding of the military authorities that it was impossible to bring about an immediate segregation of the disloyal from the loyal that we sustained the validity of the curfew order as applying to the whole group. In the instant case, temporary exclusion of the entire group was rested by the military on the same ground. The judgment that exclusion of the whole group was for the same reason a military imperative answers the contention that the exclusion was in the nature of group punishment based on antagonism to those of Japanese origin. That there were members of the group who retained loyalties to Japan has been confirmed by investigations made subsequent to the exclusion. Approximately five thousand American citizens of Japanese ancestry refused to swear unqualified allegiance to the United States and to renounce allegiance to the Japanese Emperor, and several thousand evacuees requested repatriation to Japan.

It is said that we are dealing here with the case of imprisonment of a citizen in a concentration camp solely because of his ancestry, without evidence or inquiry concerning his loyalty and good disposition towards the United States. Our task would be simple, our duty clear, were this a case involving the imprisonment of a loyal citizen in a concentration camp because of racial prejudice. Regardless of the true nature of the assembly and relocation centers--and we deem it unjustifiable to call them concentration camps with all the ugly connotations that term implies--we are dealing specifically with nothing but an exclusion order. To cast this case into outlines of racial prejudice, without reference to the real military dangers which were presented, merely confuses the issue. *Korematsu* was not excluded from the Military Area because of hostility to him or his race. He was excluded because we are at war with the Japanese Empire, because the properly constituted military authorities feared an invasion of our West Coast and felt constrained to take proper security measures, because they decided that the military urgency of the situation demanded that all citizens of Japanese ancestry be segregated from the West Coast temporarily, and finally, because Congress, reposing its confidence in this time of war in our military leaders--as inevitably it must--determined that they should have the power to do just this. There was evidence of disloyalty on the part of some, the military authorities considered that the need for action was great, and time was short. We cannot-by availing ourselves of the calm perspective of hindsight-now say that at that time these actions were unjustified.

Affirmed.

NOTES

1. *Korematsu* is a case that appears to espouse two antithetical views. On the one hand, the Court insisted that all racial classifications are suspect and will be strictly scrutinized, and that racial antagonism can never justify racial classifications. Since racial antagonism was a specific problem in *Korematsu*, the Court might have been expected to invalidate the exclusion order, which was directed at all persons of Japanese ancestry. In fact, the Court did exactly the opposite. It adopted an extremely deferential attitude toward the assertions of the military and never asked for evidence that the exclusion order was necessary. Today, *Korematsu* is cited because it identified the necessity of strict scrutiny of racial classifications, but the case is also a cautionary tale about the evils of racial prejudice and the danger of an attitude that is too deferential toward the military in time of war.

2. In the years since *Korematsu*, is has become clear that the alleged factual basis for the exclusion order was entirely illusory. In 1988, Congress passed, and President Reagan signed, The Civil Liberties Act of 1988., Pub L. 100-383. That act provided reparations payments of $20,000 to those who had been interned and also provided that:

> The Congress recognizes that, as described by the Commission on Wartime Relocation and Internment of Civilians, a grave injustice was done to both citizens and permanent resident aliens of Japanese ancestry by the evacuation, relocation, and internment of civilians during World War II. As the Commission documents, these actions were carried out without adequate security reasons and without any acts of espionage or sabotage documented by the Commission, and were motivated largely by racial prejudice, wartime hysteria, and a failure of political leadership. The excluded individuals of Japanese ancestry suffered enormous damages, both material and intangible, and there were incalculable losses in education and job training, all of which resulted in significant human suffering for which appropriate compensation has not been made. For these fundamental violations of the basic civil liberties and constitutional rights of these individuals of Japanese ancestry, the Congress apologizes on behalf of the Nation.

3.   As for Korematsu himself, in 1984 the court granted his petition for a writ of *coram nobis* to vacate his conviction on the grounds of governmental misconduct, *Korematsu v. United States*, 584 F. Supp. 1406 (N.D.Cal.1984), noting:

> *Korematsu* remains on the pages of our legal and political history. As a legal precedent it is now recognized as having very limited application. As historical precedent it stands as a constant caution that in times of war or declared military necessity our institutions must be vigilant in protecting constitutional guarantees. It stands as a caution that in times of distress the shield of military necessity and national security must not be used to protect governmental actions from close scrutiny and accountability. It stands as a caution that in times of international hostility and antagonisms our institutions, legislative, executive and judicial, must be prepared to exercise their authority to protect all citizens from the petty fears and prejudices that are so easily aroused. *Id.* at 1420.

4.   For all of its problems (and they are clearly substantial), *Korematsu* remains important because, along with *Carolene Products*, it is one of the earliest Court statements of the strict scrutiny standard. It does not include all of the language that we have come to cite for that standard-- narrowly tailored to achieve a compelling interest--but *Korematsu* includes the words "suspect," "rigid scrutiny," and "public necessity." It also notes that "racial antagonism" can never justify a governmental classification. Ultimately, however, the *Korematsu* Court talked a good game, but it did not walk the walk.

5.   The Court did not use the strict scrutiny language in relation to racial classifications again until the 1964 case of *McLaughlin v. Florida*, almost twenty years later.

McLaughlin v. Florida
379 U.S. 184 (1964)

Mr. Justice WHITE delivered the opinion of the Court.

At issue in this case is the validity of a conviction under § 798.05 of the Florida statutes, F.S.A., providing that:

> Any negro man and white woman, or any white man and negro woman, who are not married to each other, who shall habitually live in and occupy in the nighttime the same room shall each be punished by imprisonment not exceeding twelve months, or by fine not exceeding five hundred dollars.

Because the section applies only to a white person and a Negro who commit the specified acts and because no couple other than one made up of a white and a Negro is subject to conviction upon proof of the elements comprising the offense it proscribes, we hold § 798.05 invalid as a denial of the equal protection of the laws guaranteed by the Fourteenth Amendment.

I.

It is readily apparent that § 798.05 treats the interracial couple made up of a white person and a Negro differently than it does any other couple. No couple other than a Negro and a white person can be convicted under § 798.05 and no other section proscribes the precise conduct banned by §

798.05. Florida makes no claim to the contrary in this Court. However, all whites and Negroes who engage in the forbidden conduct are covered by the section and each member of the interracial couple is subject to the same penalty.

Normally, the widest discretion is allowed the legislative judgment in determining whether to attack some, rather than all, of the manifestations of the evil aimed at; and normally that judgment is given the benefit of every conceivable circumstance which might suffice to characterize the classification as reasonable rather than arbitrary and invidious. But we deal here with a classification based upon the race of the participants, which must be viewed in light of the historical fact that the central purpose of the Fourteenth Amendment was to eliminate racial discrimination emanating from official sources in the States. This strong policy renders racial classifications 'constitutionally suspect,' *Bolling v. Sharpe*, 347 U.S. 497, 499; and subject to the 'most rigid scrutiny,' *Korematsu v. United States*, 323 U.S. 214, 216; and 'in most circumstances irrelevant' to any constitutionally acceptable legislative purpose, *Kiyoshi Hirabayashi v. United States*, 320 U.S. 81, 100. Thus it is that racial classifications have been held invalid in a variety of contexts. See, e.g., *Tancil v. Woolls* (*Virginia Board of Elections v. Hamm*), 379 U.S. 19 (designation of race in voting and property records); *Anderson v. Martin*, 375 U.S. 399 (designation of race on nomination papers and ballots); *Watson v. City of Memphis*, 373 U.S. 526 (segregation in public parks and playgrounds); *Brown v. Board of Education*, 349 U.S. 294 (segregation in public schools).

We deal here with a racial classification embodied in a criminal statute. In this context, where the power of the State weighs most heavily upon the individual or the group, we must be especially sensitive to the policies of the Equal Protection Clause which, as reflected in congressional enactments dating from 1870, were intended to secure 'the full and equal benefit of all laws and proceedings for the security of persons and property' and to subject all persons 'to like punishment, pains, penalties, taxes, licenses, and exactions of every kind, and to no other.' R.S. § 1977, 42 U.S.C. § 1981 (1958 ed.).

Our inquiry, therefore, is whether there clearly appears in the relevant materials some overriding statutory purpose requiring the proscription of the specified conduct when engaged in by a white person and a Negro, but not otherwise. Without such justification the racial classification contained in § 798.05 is reduced to an invidious discrimination forbidden by the Equal Protection Clause.

II.

There is involved here an exercise of the state police power which trenches upon the constitutionally protected freedom from invidious official discrimination based on race. Such a law, even though enacted pursuant to a valid state interest, bears a heavy burden of justification, as we have said, and will be upheld only if it is necessary, and not merely rationally related, to the accomplishment of a permissible state policy. Those provisions of chapter 798 which are neutral as to race express a general and strong state policy against promiscuous conduct, whether engaged in by those who are married, those who may marry or those who may not. These provisions, if enforced, would reach illicit relations of any kind and in this way protect the integrity of the marriage laws of the State, including what is claimed to be a valid ban on interracial marriage. These same provisions, moreover, punish premarital sexual relations as severely or more severely in some instances than do those provisions which focus on the interracial couple. Florida has offered no argument that the State's policy against interracial marriage cannot be as adequately served by the general, neutral, and existing ban on illicit behavior as by a provision such as § 798.05 which singles out the promiscuous interracial couple for special statutory treatment. In short, it has not been shown that § 798.05 is a necessary adjunct to the State's ban on interracial marriage. We accordingly invalidate § 798.05 without expressing any views about the State's prohibition of interracial marriage, and reverse these convictions.

Reversed.

NOTES

1. At two different points in its opinion the *McLaughlin* Court explained the scrutiny that it employed. Initially, the Court insisted that there must be an "overriding statutory purpose" to justify the racial classification, for "[w]ithout such justification the racial classification contained in § 798.05 is reduced to an invidious discrimination forbidden by the Equal Protection Clause." Later, the Court explained that the law would be upheld "only if it is necessary, and not merely rationally related, to the accomplishment of a permissible state policy." This second phrasing of the test insisted that the classification be "necessary" to its purpose but required that the purpose be only "permissible." No reference was made to its earlier insistence on an "overriding statutory purpose." This is not the exact language of our current strict scrutiny standard, but it contains language that is getting close to it.

2. Three years after *McLaughlin*, in *Loving v. Virginia*, 388 U.S. 1 (1967), the Court invalidated Virginia's law prohibiting interracial marriage. The Court rejected the notion that the equal application of the law to whites and blacks (blacks could not marry whites *and* whites could not marry blacks) could save the statute. The Court then stated:

> Because we reject the notion that the mere 'equal application' of a statute containing racial classifications is enough to remove the classifications from the Fourteenth Amendment's proscription of all invidious racial discriminations, we do not accept the State's contention that these statutes should be upheld if there is any possible basis for concluding that they serve a rational purpose. The mere fact of equal application does not mean that our analysis of these statutes should follow the approach we have taken in cases involving no racial discrimination . . . In these cases, involving distinctions not drawn according to race, the Court has merely asked whether there is any rational foundation for the discriminations, and has deferred to the wisdom of the state legislatures. In the case at bar, however, we deal with statutes containing racial classifications, and the fact of equal application does not immunize the statute from the very heavy burden of justification which the Fourteenth Amendment has traditionally required of state statutes drawn according to race.
>
> Over the years, this Court has consistently repudiated '(d)istinctions between citizens solely because of their ancestry' as being 'odious to a free people whose institutions are founded upon the doctrine of equality.' *Hirabayashi v. United States*, 320 U.S. 81 (1943). At the very least, the Equal Protection Clause demands that racial classifications, especially suspect in criminal statutes, be subjected to the 'most rigid scrutiny,' *Korematsu v. United States*, 323 U.S. 214 (1944), and, if they are ever to be upheld, they must be shown to be necessary to the accomplishment of some permissible state objective, independent of the racial discrimination which it was the object of the

> Fourteenth Amendment to eliminate. Indeed, two members of this Court have already stated that they 'cannot conceive of a valid legislative purpose * * * which makes the color of a person's skin the test of whether his conduct is a criminal offense.' *McLaughlin v. Florida,* supra, 379 U.S. at 198 (Stewart, J., joined by Douglas, J., concurring).
>
> There is patently no legitimate overriding purpose independent of invidious racial discrimination which justifies this classification.

As in *McLaughlin*, the *Loving* Court combines a reference to an "overriding purpose" with a demand that racial classifications be "necessary to the accomplishment of some permissible state objective."

3. Two years later, in *Shapiro v. Thompson*, 394 U.S. 618 (1969) (an equal protection case that involved the implied fundamental right to travel) the Court first used language that we have come to associate with strict scrutiny:

> At the outset, we reject appellants' argument that a mere showing of a rational relationship between the waiting period and these four admittedly permissible state objectives will suffice to justify the classification. See *Lindsley v. Natural Carbonic Gas Co.,* 220 U.S. 61, 78 (1911); *Flemming v. Nestor,* 363 U.S. 603, 611, (1960); *McGowan v. Maryland,* 366 U.S. 420, 426 (1961). The waiting-period provision denies welfare benefits to otherwise eligible applicants solely because they have recently moved into the jurisdiction. But in moving from State to State or to the District of Columbia appellees were exercising a constitutional right, and *any classification which serves to penalize the exercise of that right, unless shown to be necessary to promote a compelling governmental interest, is unconstitutional.* Cf. *Skinner v. Oklahoma,* 316 U.S. 535, 541, 1 (1942); *Korematsu v. United States,* 323 U.S. 214, 216, (1944); *Bates v. Little Rock,* 361 U.S. 516, 524, (1960); *Sherbert v. Verner,* 374 U.S. 398, 406 (1963) (emphasis added).

4. With regard to the strict scrutiny standard as it is applied to racial classifications, the Court's earliest use of the complete "necessary to promote a compelling government interest" language does not appear until 1984, in *Palmore v. Sidoti,* 466 U.S. 429 (1984). In *Sidoti*, the Court reversed a state court judgment that had divested the natural mother of the custody of her infant child because of her remarriage to a person of a different race. In holding that it was inappropriate for the state court to give weight to private racial biases, the Court noted that the standard of review was as follows:

> A core purpose of the Fourteenth Amendment was to do away with all governmentally imposed discrimination based on race. See *Strauder v. West Virginia,* 100 U.S. 303, 307–308, 310 (1880). Classifying persons according to their race is more likely to reflect racial prejudice than legitimate public concerns; the race, not the person, dictates the category. See *Personnel Administrator of Mass. v. Feeney,* 442 U.S. 256, 272 (1979). *Such classifications are subject to the most exacting scrutiny; to pass constitutional muster, they must be justified by a compelling governmental interest and must be "necessary ... to the accomplishment" of their legitimate purpose,* McLaughlin v. Florida, 379 U.S. 184 (1964). See *Loving v. Virginia,* 388 U.S. 1, 11 (1967) (emphasis added).

5. Thus, a strict scrutiny standard with two components seemed to be taking shape: (1) *a compelling purpose* and (2) a *necessary* connection between the classification and that compelling purpose. However, as mentioned above, the standard was applied to First Amendment as well as to equal protection cases. During the 1980s, these First Amendment cases began to alter the exact language of the strict scrutiny standard. For example, in *Consolidated Edison Co. of New York, Inc. v. Public Service*, 447 U.S. 530 (1980) the Court, considering whether a ban on bill inserts violated the First Amendment, used the following test:

> The Commission's ban on bill inserts is not, of course, invalid merely because it imposes a limitation upon speech. See *First National Bank of Boston v. Bellotti*, supra, 435 U.S., at 786. We must consider whether the State can demonstrate that its regulation is constitutionally permissible. The Commission's arguments require us to consider three theories that might justify the state action. We must determine whether the prohibition is (i) a reasonable time, place, or manner restriction, (ii) a permissible subject-matter regulation, or (iii) *a narrowly tailored means of serving a compelling state interest.* Where a government restricts the speech of a private person, the state action may be sustained only if the government can show that the regulation is a *precisely drawn means of serving a compelling state interest.* (emphasis added).

In this way, the language that a classification had to be *necessary* to a compelling interest was transformed into a requirement that it be *narrowly tailored* to a compelling interest. During the 1980s, this linguistic change affected the strict scrutiny standard in equal protection cases as well, in a series of affirmative action cases for which there was no majority opinion. In these cases, the Court also began to insist that a racial classification be *narrowly tailored* rather than *necessary* to a compelling purpose.

In 1980 the Court upheld a federal statute that required that 10% of federal funds granted for local public works projects be set aside for work performed by minority business enterprises. *Fullilove v. Klutznick,* 448 U.S. 448 (1980). There was no majority opinion in the case. Chief Justice Burger announced the judgment of the Court and delivered an opinion, in which Justice White and Justice Powell joined. In that opinion, the Chief Justice stated, "We recognize the need for careful judicial evaluation to assure that any congressional program that employs racial or ethnic criteria to accomplish the objective of remedying the present effects of past discrimination is *narrowly tailored* to the achievement of that goal." *Id.* at 480. Burger's opinion had replaced the requirement that a racial classification be "necessary" to promote a compelling interest with a requirement that the racial classification be "narrowly tailored" to the achievement of its goal. It does not seem that Burger intended any substantive difference between the two formulations, but the "narrowly tailored" language turned out to be fashionable.

Four years later the Court invalidated a provision in a collective bargaining agreement under which the school board had extended preferential protection against layoffs to some minority employees. *Wygant v. Jackson Bd. of Educ.*, 476 U.S. 267 (1986). Once again, there was no majority opinion. Justice POWELL announced the judgment of the Court and delivered an opinion in which Chief Justice Burger and Justice Rehnquist joined, and which Justice O'Connor joined in part. In that opinion, Justice Powell explained what he considered the proper standard of review for racial classifications:

> There are two prongs to this examination. First, any racial classification "must be

justified by a compelling governmental interest." *Palmore v. Sidoti*, 466 U.S. 429, 432, (1984); see *Loving v. Virginia*, supra, 388 U.S., at 11; cf. *Graham v. Richardson*, 403 U.S. 365, 375 (1971) (alienage). Second, the means chosen by the State to effectuate its purpose must be "*narrowly tailored* to the achievement of that goal." *Fullilove*, supra, 448 U.S., at 480. We must decide whether the layoff provision is supported by a compelling state purpose and whether the means chosen to accomplish that purpose are narrowly tailored. (emphasis added).

That same year, in *Local 28 of Sheet Metal Workers' Intern. Ass'n v. E.E.O.C.*, 478 U.S. 421 (1986), the Court upheld a federal district court decision that had, as a remedial measure, ordered a union to end its discriminatory practice and to admit a certain percentage of nonwhites to union membership. In a portion of Justice Brennan's opinion that was supported only by a plurality of the Court, Brennan wrote:

> Petitioners also allege that the membership goal and Fund order contravene the equal protection component of the Due Process Clause of the Fifth Amendment because they deny benefits to white individuals based on race. We have consistently recognized that government bodies constitutionally may adopt racial classifications as a remedy for past discrimination. See *Wygant v. Jackson Board of Education*, 476 U.S. 267 (1986); *Fullilove v. Klutznick*, 448 U.S. 448 (1980); *University of California Regents v. Bakke*, 438 U.S. 265, (1978); *Swann v. Charlotte-Mecklenburg Board of Education*, 402 U.S. 1 (1971). We have not agreed, however, on the proper test to be applied in analyzing the constitutionality of race-conscious remedial measures. . . . We need not resolve this dispute here, since we conclude that the relief ordered in this case passes even the most rigorous test—it *is narrowly tailored to further the Government's compelling interest in remedying past discrimination.* (emphasis added).

Finally, in 1987, in *U.S. v. Paradise*, 480 U.S. 149 (1987), the Court upheld a remedial order in the form of a one-black-for-one-white promotion requirement to be applied as an interim measure to state trooper promotions in the Alabama Department of Public Safety. Once again, there was no majority opinion. Justice Brennan's plurality opinion stated:

> It is now well established that government bodies, including courts, may constitutionally employ racial classifications essential to remedy unlawful treatment of racial or ethnic groups subject to discrimination. See *Sheet Metal Workers v. EEOC*, 478 U.S. 412, 480 (1986), and cases cited therein. See also *Wygant v. Jackson Board of Education*, 476 U.S. 267, 286 (1986) ("The Court is in agreement that ... remedying past or present racial discrimination ... is a sufficiently weighty state interest to warrant the remedial use of a carefully constructed affirmative action program") (O'CONNOR, J., concurring in part and concurring in judgment). But although this Court has consistently held that some elevated level of scrutiny is required when a racial or ethnic distinction is made for remedial purposes, it has yet to reach consensus on the appropriate constitutional analysis. We need not do so in this case, however, because we conclude that the relief ordered survives even strict scrutiny analysis: it is *"narrowly tailored" to serve a "compelling [governmental] purpose."* Id., at 274 (opinion of POWELL, J.).b (emphasis added).

6. By 1987, then, although the terminology preferred to describe the strict scrutiny standard was that the classification had to be "narrowly tailored" to a compelling interest rather than

"necessary" to a compelling interest, that language had not yet been adopted in a majority opinion. It was not until 1993 that the Court adopted in a majority opinion that precise language:

> Classifications of citizens solely on the basis of race "are by their very nature odious to a free people whose institutions are founded upon the doctrine of equality." *Hirabayashi v. United States*, 320 U.S. 81, 100 (1943). Accord, *Loving v. Virginia*, 388 U.S. 1, 11 (1967). They threaten to stigmatize individuals by reason of their membership in a racial group and to incite racial hostility. *Croson*, supra, 488 U.S., at 493, (plurality opinion); *UJO*, supra, 430 U.S., at 173, (Brennan, J., concurring in part) ("[E]ven in the pursuit of remedial objectives, an explicit policy of assignment by race may serve to stimulate our society's latent race consciousness, suggesting the utility and propriety of basing decisions on a factor that ideally bears no relationship to an individual's worth or needs"). *Accordingly, we have held that the Fourteenth Amendment requires state legislation that expressly distinguishes among citizens because of their race to be narrowly tailored to further a compelling governmental interest.* See, e.g., *Wygant v. Jackson Bd. of Ed.*, 476 U.S. 267, 277–278 (plurality opinion); id., (O'CONNOR, J., concurring in part and concurring in judgment). (Emphasis added). *Shaw v. Reno*, 509 U.S. 630 (1993),

It is now clear that this language—*narrowly tailored to further a compelling governmental interest*—is the Court's current view of the proper statement of the strict scrutiny standard.

D. RACIAL SEGREGATION IN SCHOOLS

The Court's 1896 decision in *Plessy v. Ferguson*, 163 U.S. 537 (1896) provided constitutional validation for the doctrine of separate-but-equal. In the fifty-eight years that followed *Plessy*, state-mandated or state-endorsed separation of the races became common in the southern states in schools, parks, swimming pools, restrooms, courtroom seating, and public transportation. Additionally, there was substantial racial segregation by private persons in the management of hotels and restaurants. However, that private conduct, lacking a state actor, was clearly outside the scope of the Equal Protection Clause.

In a series of cases beginning in the late 1930s, the Court began to limit the reach of *Plessy* by focusing on the "equal" part of the doctrine rather than the "separate" part. In *Missouri ex rel. Gaines v. Canada*, 305 U.S. 337 (1938) and in *Sweatt v. Painter*, 339 U.S. 629 (1950), the Court determined that the all-white law schools at University of Missouri and the University of Texas violated the Equal Protection Clause because there was not an "equal" alternative for black students. These cases limited the scope of *Plessy* but left its basic doctrinal holding intact. It was not until 1954, in the case of *Brown v. Board of Education*, that the Court took on *Plessy* unequivocally.

Brown v. Board of Education of Topeka
347 U.S. 483 (1954)

Mr. Chief Justice WARREN delivered the opinion of the Court.

[Cases from the States of Kansas, South Carolina, Virginia, and Delaware were consolidated. The cases involved state statutes or state constitutional provisions that either required or permitted racially segregated public schools.]

In each of the cases, minors of the Negro race, through their legal representatives, seek the aid of the courts in obtaining admission to the public schools of their community on a nonsegregated basis. In each instance, they have been denied admission to schools attended by white children under laws requiring or permitting segregation according to race. This segregation was alleged to deprive the plaintiffs of the equal protection of the laws under the Fourteenth Amendment.

In the first cases in this Court construing the Fourteenth Amendment, decided shortly after its adoption, the Court interpreted it as proscribing all state-imposed discriminations against the Negro race. The doctrine of "separate but equal" did not make its appearance in this court until 1896 in the case of *Plessy v. Ferguson*, involving not education but transportation. American courts have since labored with the doctrine for over half a century. In this Court, there have been six cases involving the 'separate but equal' doctrine in the field of public education. In *Cumming v. Board of Education of Richmond County*, 175 U.S. 528, and *Gong Lum v. Rice*, 275 U.S. 78, the validity of the doctrine itself was not challenged. In more recent cases, all on the graduate school level, inequality was found in that specific benefits enjoyed by white students were denied to Negro students of the same educational qualifications. *State of Missouri ex rel. Gaines v. Canada*, 305 U.S. 337; *Sipuel v. Board of Regents of University of Oklahoma*, 332 U.S. 631; *Sweatt v. Painter*, 339 U.S. 629; *McLaurin v. Oklahoma State Regents*, 339 U.S. 637. In none of these cases was it necessary to re-examine the doctrine to grant relief to the Negro plaintiff. And in *Sweatt v. Painter*, the Court expressly reserved decision on the question whether *Plessy v. Ferguson* should be held inapplicable to public education.

In the instant cases, that question is directly presented. Here, unlike *Sweatt v. Painter*, there are findings below that the Negro and white schools involved have been equalized, or are being equalized, with respect to buildings, curricula, qualifications and salaries of teachers, and other 'tangible' factors. Our decision, therefore, cannot turn on merely a comparison of these tangible factors in the Negro and white schools involved in each of the cases. We must look instead to the effect of segregation itself on public education.

In approaching this problem, we cannot turn the clock back to 1868 when the Amendment was adopted, or even to 1896 when *Plessy v. Ferguson* was written. We must consider public education in the light of its full development and its present place in American life throughout the Nation. Only in this way can it be determined if segregation in public schools deprives these plaintiffs of the equal protection of the laws.

Today, education is perhaps the most important function of state and local governments. Compulsory school attendance laws and the great expenditures for education both demonstrate our recognition of the importance of education to our democratic society. It is required in the performance of our most basic public responsibilities, even service in the armed forces. It is the very foundation of good citizenship. Today it is a principal instrument in awakening the child to cultural values, in preparing him for later professional training, and in helping him to adjust normally to his environment. In these days, it is doubtful that any child may reasonably be expected to succeed in life if he is denied the opportunity of an education. Such an opportunity, where the state has undertaken to provide it, is a right which must be made available to all on equal terms.

We come then to the question presented: Does segregation of children in public schools solely on the basis of race, even though the physical facilities and other 'tangible' factors may be equal, deprive the children of the minority group of equal educational opportunities? We believe that it does.

In *Sweatt v. Painter*, *supra* (339 U.S. 629), in finding that a segregated law school for Negroes could not provide them equal educational opportunities, this Court relied in large part on 'those qualities which are incapable of objective measurement but which make for greatness in a law school.' In *McLaurin v. Oklahoma State Regents*, *supra* (339 U.S. 637), the Court, in requiring that a Negro admitted to a white graduate school be treated like all other students, again resorted to intangible considerations: 'his ability to study, to engage in discussions and exchange views with other students, and, in general, to learn his profession.' Such considerations apply with added force to children in grade and high schools. To separate them from others of similar age and qualifications solely because of their race generates a feeling of inferiority as to their status in the community that may affect their hearts and minds in a way unlikely ever to be undone. The effect of this separation on their educational opportunities was well stated by a finding in the Kansas case by a court which nevertheless felt compelled to rule against the Negro plaintiffs:

> Segregation of white and colored children in public schools has a detrimental effect upon the colored children. The impact is greater when it has the sanction of the law; for the policy of separating the races is usually interpreted as denoting the inferiority of the negro group. A sense of inferiority affects the motivation of a child to learn. Segregation with the sanction of law, therefore, has a tendency to (retard) the educational and mental development of Negro children and to deprive them of some of the benefits they would receive in a racial(ly) integrated school system.

Whatever may have been the extent of psychological knowledge at the time of *Plessy v. Ferguson*, this finding is amply supported by modern authority. Any language in *Plessy v. Ferguson* contrary to this finding is rejected. We conclude that in the field of public education the doctrine of 'separate but equal' has no place. Separate educational facilities are inherently unequal. Therefore, we hold that the plaintiffs and others similarly situated for whom the actions have been brought are, by reason of the segregation complained of, deprived of the equal protection of the laws guaranteed by the Fourteenth Amendment. This disposition makes unnecessary any discussion whether such segregation also violates the Due Process Clause of the Fourteenth Amendment.

NOTES

1. In terms of its impact on American society, *Brown v. Board of Education* is clearly one of the most significant decisions in Supreme Court history. By overturning *Plessy v. Ferguson* and its doctrine of separate but equal, this case marked the beginning of the end for widespread, state-imposed racial segregation in public programs and facilities. *Brown*, however, did not contain a substantial amount of legal analysis. There was no discussion of the standard of review of racial classifications, no attempt to explain the flaw in *Plessy's* distinction between political and civil equality, on the one hand, and social equality, on the other, and no attempt to extend its holding beyond the context of public education. The case seemed to turn not on any substantial constitutional doctrine but on the fact that, for children in racially segregated schools, separation by race "generates a feeling of inferiority as to their status in the community that may affect their

hearts and minds in a way unlikely ever to be undone."

In its original *Brown* decision the Court did not order any particular remedy for the constitutional violation. Instead, it set the case for reargument on its docket during the following term. In *Brown v. Board of Education*, 349 U.S. 294 (1955), the Court considered the proper remedy and concluded:

> While giving weight to these public and private considerations, the courts will require that the defendants make a prompt and reasonable start toward full compliance with our May 17, 1954, ruling. Once such a start has been made, the courts may find that additional time is necessary to carry out the ruling in an effective manner. The burden rests upon the defendants to establish that such time is necessary in the public interest and is consistent with good faith compliance at the earliest practicable date. To that end, the courts may consider problems related to administration, arising from the physical condition of the school plant, the school transportation system, personnel, revision of school districts and attendance areas into compact units to achieve a system of determining admission to the public schools on a nonracial basis, and revision of local laws and regulations which may be necessary in solving the foregoing problems. They will also consider the adequacy of any plans the defendants may propose to meet these problems and to effectuate a transition to a racially nondiscriminatory school system. During this period of transition, the courts will retain jurisdiction of these cases. The judgments below . . . are accordingly reversed and the cases are remanded to the District Courts to take such proceedings and enter such orders and decrees consistent with this opinion as are necessary and proper to admit to public schools on a racially nondiscriminatory basis with all deliberate speed the parties to these cases.

In the years after *Brown*, however, it became clear that the holding in the case would not easily be given effect. In many of the affected states, state and local officials engaged in a campaign of massive resistance to prevent the racial integration of public schools. In 1956, President Eisenhower sent federal troops to Arkansas to enable black students to enter an all-white high school in response to the governor's use of the state's National Guard to prevent their enrollment. Opponents of the *Brown* decision used states' rights arguments to justify their unwillingness to comply with the Supreme Court's *Brown* mandate. The Court answered those arguments in the following case.

Cooper v. Aaron
358 U.S. 1 (1958)

[In the wake of *Brown v. Board of Ed.*, 347 U.S. 483 (1955), the School Board in Little Rock, Arkansas, developed a plan to desegregate its schools with a goal of full integration at the end of five years. At the same time, state officials worked in opposition to desegregation by, for example, amending the State Constitution to oppose "in every Constitutional manner the Unconstitutional desegregation decisions ... of the United States Supreme Court," and by passing a law that would exempt students from compulsory attendance requirements at racially mixed schools. On September 2, 1957, the day before nine black students were to enter Central High School, local school authorities were met with drastic opposing action by the Governor of Arkansas who dispatched units of the Arkansas National Guard to the Central High School grounds and placed the school 'off limits' to black students. On the morning of September 4, 1957, black children attempted to enter the high school but units of the Arkansas National Guard, acting pursuant to the Governor's order, stood shoulder to shoulder at the school grounds and thereby forcibly prevented the nine black students from entering, as they continued to do every school day during the following three weeks. On September 25, the President of the United States dispatched federal troops to Central High School and the black students were admitted. Regular army troops continued at the high school until November 27, 1957. Federalized National Guardsmen who remained throughout the balance of the school year eventually replaced them. Eight of the black students remained in attendance at the school throughout the school year.]

Opinion of the Court by The CHIEF JUSTICE, Mr. Justice BLACK, Mr. Justice FRANKFURTER, Mr. Justice DOUGLAS, Mr. Justice BURTON, Mr. Justice CLARK, Mr. Justice HARLAN, Mr. Justice BRENNAN, and Mr. Justice WHITTAKER.

As this case reaches us it raises questions of the highest importance to the maintenance of our federal system of government. It necessarily involves a claim by the Governor and Legislature of a State that there is no duty on state officials to obey federal court orders resting on this Court's considered interpretation of the United States Constitution. Specifically it involves actions by the Governor and Legislature of Arkansas upon the premise that they are not bound by our holding in *Brown v. Board of Education*, 347 U.S. 483. That holding was that the Fourteenth Amendment forbids States to use their governmental powers to bar children on racial grounds from attending schools where there is state participation through any arrangement, management, funds or property. We are urged to uphold a suspension of the Little Rock School Board's plan to do away with segregated public schools in Little Rock until state laws and efforts to upset and nullify our holding in *Brown v. Board of Education* have been further challenged and tested in the courts. We reject these contentions.

The constitutional rights of respondents are not to be sacrificed or yielded to the violence and disorder which have followed upon the actions of the Governor and Legislature. As this Court said some 41 years ago in a unanimous opinion in a case involving another aspect of racial segregation: 'It is urged that this proposed segregation will promote the public peace by preventing race conflicts. Desirable as this is, and important as is the preservation of the public peace, this aim cannot be accomplished by laws or ordinances which deny rights created or protected by the federal Constitution.' *Buchanan v. Warley*, 245 U.S. 60, 81. Thus law and order are not here to be preserved by depriving the Negro children of their constitutional rights. The record before us clearly establishes that the growth of the Board's difficulties to a magnitude beyond its unaided power to control is the product of state action. Those difficulties, as counsel for the Board forthrightly conceded on the oral argument in this Court, can also be brought under control by state action.

The controlling legal principles are plain. The command of the Fourteenth Amendment is that no 'State' shall deny to any person within its jurisdiction the equal protection of the laws. 'A State acts by its legislative, its executive, or its judicial authorities. It can act in no other way. The constitutional provision, therefore, must mean that no agency of the State, or of the officers or agents by whom its powers are exerted, shall deny to any person within its jurisdiction the equal protection of the laws. Whoever, by virtue of public position under a State government, denies or takes away the equal protection of the laws, violates the constitutional inhibition; and as he acts in the name and for the State, and is clothed with the State's power, his act is that of the State. This must be so, or the constitutional prohibition has no meaning.' *Ex parte Virginia*, 100 U.S. 339, 347. Thus the prohibitions of the Fourteenth Amendment extend to all action of the State denying equal protection of the laws; whatever the agency of the State taking the action, or whatever the guise in which it is taken. In short, the constitutional rights of children not to be discriminated

CHAPTER 2: RACE CLASSIFICATIONS

against in school admission on grounds of race or color declared by this Court in the *Brown* case can neither be nullified openly and directly by state legislators or state executive or judicial officers, nor nullified indirectly by them through evasive schemes for segregation whether attempted 'ingeniously or ingenuously.' *Smith v. Texas*, 311 U.S. 128, 132.

What has been said, in the light of the facts developed, is enough to dispose of the case. However, we should answer the premise of the actions of the Governor and Legislature that they are not bound by our holding in the Brown case. It is necessary only to recall some basic constitutional propositions which are settled doctrine.

Article VI of the Constitution makes the Constitution the 'supreme Law of the Land.' In 1803, Chief Justice Marshall, speaking for a unanimous Court, referring to the Constitution as 'the fundamental and paramount law of the nation,' declared in the notable case of *Marbury v. Madison*, 1 Cranch 137, 177, that 'It is emphatically the province and duty of the judicial department to say what the law is.' This decision declared the basic principle that the federal judiciary is supreme in the exposition of the law of the Constitution, and that principle has ever since been respected by this Court and the Country as a permanent and indispensable feature of our constitutional system. It follows that the interpretation of the Fourteenth Amendment enunciated by this Court in the Brown case is the supreme law of the land, and Art. VI of the Constitution makes it of binding effect on the States 'any Thing in the Constitution or Laws of any State to the Contrary notwithstanding.' Every state legislator and executive and judicial officer is solemnly committed by oath taken pursuant to Art. VI, ¶3 'to support this Constitution.' Chief Justice Taney, speaking for a unanimous Court in 1859, said that this requirement reflected the framers' 'anxiety to preserve it [the Constitution] in full force, in all its powers, and to guard against resistance to or evasion of its authority, on the part of a State.' *Ableman v. Booth*, 21 How. 506, 524.

No state legislator or executive or judicial officer can war against the Constitution without violating his undertaking to support it. Chief Justice Marshall spoke for a unanimous Court in saying that: 'If the legislatures of the several states may, at will, annul the judgments of the courts of the United States, and destroy the rights acquired under those judgments, the constitution itself becomes a solemn mockery.' *United States v. Peters*, 5 Cranch 115. A Governor who asserts a power to nullify a federal court order is similarly restrained. If he had such power, said Chief Justice Hughes, in 1932, also for a unanimous Court, 'it is manifest that the fiat of a state Governor, and not the Constitution of the United States, would be the supreme law of the land; that the restrictions of the Federal Constitution upon the exercise of state power would be but impotent phrases.' *Sterling v. Constantin*, 287 U.S. 378, 397-398.

It is, of course, quite true that the responsibility for public education is primarily the concern of the States, but it is equally true that such responsibilities, like all other state activity, must be exercised consistently with federal constitutional requirements as they apply to state action. The Constitution created a government dedicated to equal justice under law. The Fourteenth Amendment embodied and emphasized that ideal. State support of segregated schools through any arrangement, management, funds, or property cannot be squared with the Amendment's command that no State shall deny to any person within its jurisdiction the equal protection of the laws. The right of a student not to be segregated on racial grounds in schools so maintained is indeed so fundamental and pervasive that it is embraced in the concept of due process of law. *Bolling v. Sharpe*, 347 U.S. 497. The basic decision in *Brown* was unanimously reached by this Court only after the case had been briefed and twice argued and the issues had been given the most serious consideration. Since the first Brown opinion three new Justices have come to the Court. They are at one with the Justices still on the Court who participated in that basic decision as to its correctness, and that decision is now unanimously reaffirmed. The principles announced in that decision and the obedience of the States to them, according to the command of the Constitution, are indispensable for the protection of the freedoms guaranteed by our fundamental charter for all of us. Our constitutional ideal of equal justice under law is thus made a living truth.

NOTES

1. The Court's opinion in *Cooper v. Aaron* was a rousing defense of two basic principles of the American constitution. The first is that the constitution and laws of the United States are the supreme law of the land, notwithstanding any state laws or state constitutional provisions to the contrary. The second, that federal courts in general and the United States Supreme Court in particular, have the final power to determine what the language of the Constitution means. Once these two principles were stated, the result in *Cooper v. Aaron* followed inexorably. The Governor and the state legislature of Arkansas seemed to forget that the states' rights argument on which they relied was soundly defeated on the battlefields of the American Civil War.

Green v. County School Bd. of New Kent County, Va.
391 U.S. 430 (1968)

[New Kent County in Virginia was a rural area with no residential racial segregation but substantial school segregation. Following the decision in *Brown v. Board of Education*, the county maintained its tradition of segregation by assigning students to the school they had attended the previous year. School officials eventually adopted a "freedom of choice" plan, under which each student could choose the school he or she wished to attend.]

Mr. Justice BRENNAN delivered the opinion of the Court.

The question for decision is whether, under all the circumstances here, respondent School Board's adoption of a 'freedom-of-choice' plan which allows a pupil to choose his own public school constitutes adequate compliance with the Board's responsibility 'to achieve a system of determining admission to the public schools on a non-racial basis.' *Brown v. Board of Education of Topeka, Kan.*, 349 U.S. 294, 300-301 (*Brown II*).

The pattern of separate 'white' and 'Negro' schools in the New Kent County school system established under compulsion of state laws is precisely the pattern of segregation to which *Brown I* and *Brown II* were particularly addressed, and which *Brown I* declared unconstitutionally denied Negro school children equal protection of the laws. Racial identification of the system's schools was complete, extending not just to the composition of student bodies at the two schools but to every facet of school operations--faculty, staff, transportation, extracurricular activities and facilities. In short, the State, acting through the local school board and school officials, organized and operated a dual system, part 'white' and part 'Negro.'

It was such dual systems that 14 years ago *Brown I* held unconstitutional and a year later *Brown II* held must be abolished; school boards operating such school systems were required by Brown II 'to effectuate a transition to a racially nondiscriminatory school system.' 349 U.S., at 301. It is of course true that for the time immediately after *Brown II* the concern was with making an initial break in a long-established pattern of excluding Negro children from schools attended by white children. The principal focus was on obtaining for those Negro children courageous enough to break with tradition a place in the 'white' schools. See, e.g., *Cooper v. Aaron*, 358 U.S. 1. Under *Brown II* that immediate goal was only the first step, however. The transition to a unitary, nonracial system of public education was and is the ultimate end to be brought about; it was because of the 'complexities arising from the transition to a system of public education freed of racial discrimination' that we provided for 'all deliberate speed' in the implementation of the principles of Brown I. 349 U.S., at 299-301,. Thus we recognized the task would necessarily involve solution of 'varied local school problems.' In referring to the 'personal interest of the plaintiffs in admission to public schools as soon as practicable on a nondiscriminatory basis,' we also noted that '(t)o effectuate this interest may call for elimination of a variety of obstacles in making the transition.' Yet we emphasized that the constitutional rights of Negro children required school officials to bear the burden of establishing that additional time to carry out the ruling in an effective manner 'is necessary in the public interest and is consistent with good faith compliance at the earliest practicable date.'

It is against this background that 13 years after *Brown II* commanded the abolition of dual systems we must measure the effectiveness of respondent School Board's 'freedom-of-choice' plan to achieve that end. The School Board contends that it has fully discharged its obligation by adopting a plan by which every student, regardless of race, may 'freely' choose the school he will attend. The Board attempts to cast the issue in its broadest form by arguing that its 'freedom-of-choice' plan may be faulted only by reading the Fourteenth Amendment as universally requiring 'compulsory integration,' a reading it insists the wording of the Amendment will not support. But that argument ignores the thrust of *Brown II*. In the light of the command of that case, what is involved here is the question whether the Board has achieved the 'racially nondiscriminatory school system' *Brown II* held must be effectuated in order to remedy the established unconstitutional deficiencies of its segregated system. In the context of the state-imposed segregated pattern of long standing, the fact that in 1965 the Board opened the doors of the former 'white' school to Negro children and of the 'Negro' school to white children merely begins, not ends, our inquiry whether the Board has taken steps adequate to abolish its dual, segregated system. *Brown II* was a call for the dismantling of well-entrenched dual systems tempered by an awareness that complex and multifaceted problems would arise which would require time and flexibility for a successful resolution. School boards such as the respondent then operating state-compelled dual systems were nevertheless clearly charged with the affirmative duty to take whatever steps might be necessary to convert to a unitary system in which racial discrimination would be eliminated root and branch. The constitutional rights of Negro school children articulated in *Brown I* permit no less than this; and it was to this end that *Brown II* commanded school boards to bend their efforts.

In determining whether respondent School Board met that command by adopting its 'freedom-of-choice' plan, it is relevant that this first step did not come until some 11 years after *Brown I* was decided and 10 years after *Brown II* directed the making of a 'prompt and reasonable start.' This deliberate perpetuation of the unconstitutional dual system can only have compounded the harm of such a system. Such delays are no longer tolerable, for 'the governing constitutional principles no longer bear the imprint of newly enunciated doctrine.' Moreover, a plan that at this late date fails to provide meaningful assurance of prompt and effective disestablishment of a dual system is also intolerable. 'The time for mere 'deliberate speed' has run out.' The burden on a school board today is to come forward with a plan that promises realistically to work, and promises realistically to work now.

The New Kent School Board's 'freedom-of-choice' plan cannot be accepted as a sufficient step to 'effectuate a transition' to a unitary system. In three years of operation not a single white child has chosen to attend Watkins school and although 115 Negro children enrolled in New Kent school in 1967 (up from 35 in 1965 and 111 in 1966) 85% of the Negro children in the system still attend the all-Negro Watkins school. In other words, the school system remains a dual system. Rather than further the dismantling of the dual system, the plan has operated simply to burden children and their parents with a responsibility which *Brown II* placed squarely on the School Board. The Board must be required to formulate a new plan and, in light of other courses which appear open to the Board, such as zoning, fashion steps which promise realistically to convert promptly to a system without a 'white' school and a 'Negro' school, but just schools.

The judgment of the Court of Appeals is vacated insofar as it affirmed the District Court and the case is remanded to the District Court for further proceedings consistent with this opinion. It is so ordered.

NOTES

1. By the time the Court decided *Green* in 1968, fifteen years had passed since the second *Brown* decision ordered federal courts to proceed "with all deliberate speed" in fashioning appropriate remedies. The schools in New Kent County, like many throughout the south, remained substantially segregated. School officials defended the situation on the ground that each student had the freedom to choose his or her school. According to this line of thinking, if the freedom of choice plan resulted in segregated schools, it was the fault of the students and parents, not of the school board.

The *Green* Court pointedly rejected this view. New Kent County operated a state compelled "dual system," with identifiably white and black schools. This was precisely the kind of system that *Brown* found unconstitutional. In this context, the school board was charged with "the affirmative duty to take whatever steps might be necessary to convert to a unitary system in which racial discrimination would be eliminated root and branch."

In New Kent County, the Court noted, where no residential segregation existed, a unitary, nonracial school system could be brought about with a minimum of administrative difficulty by using geographical attendance zones. That solution, however, would not work in school districts with substantial residential segregation. In the next case, the Court considered the limits of a district court's powers in ordering remedies that would adequately address constitutional violations where redrawing attendance zones would not be adequate.

Swann v. Charlotte-Mecklenburg Bd. of Ed.
402 U.S. 1 (1971)

[The Charlotte-Mecklenburg school system, the forty-third largest in the Nation, encompassed the city of Charlotte and surrounding Mecklenburg County, North Carolina. During the 1968-1969 school year, the system served more than 84,000 pupils in 107 schools. Approximately 71% of the pupils were white and 29% black. Almost all of the black students attended schools within the city of Charlotte. Two-thirds of these attended schools that were either totally black or more than 99% black. As part of continuing litigation concerning the desegregation of the school system that began in 1965, two remedial plans were before the court. The first relied for the most part on redrawing school district lines, while the second required, in addition to redrawn district lines, substantial transportation of students to reduce segregation.]

Mr. Chief Justice BURGER delivered the opinion for a unanimous Court.

We granted certiorari in this case to review important issues as to the duties of school authorities and the scope of powers of federal courts under this Court's mandates to eliminate racially separate public schools established and maintained by state action. *Brown v. Board of Education*, 347 U.S. 483 (1954) (*Brown I*).

III

The objective today remains to eliminate from the public schools all vestiges of state-imposed segregation. Segregation was the evil struck down by *Brown I* as contrary to the equal protection guarantees of the Constitution. That was the violation sought to be corrected by the remedial measures of *Brown II*. That was the basis for the holding in *Green* that school authorities are 'clearly charged with the affirmative duty to take whatever steps might be necessary to convert to a unitary system in which racial discrimination would be eliminated root and branch.' 391 U.S., at 437-438.

If school authorities fail in their affirmative obligations under these holdings, judicial authority may be invoked. Once a right and a violation have been shown, the scope of a district court's equitable powers to remedy past wrongs is broad, for breadth and flexibility are inherent in equitable remedies. The task is to correct, by a balancing of the individual and collective interests, the condition that offends the Constitution.

School authorities are traditionally charged with broad power to formulate and implement educational policy and might well conclude, for example, that in order to prepare students to live in a pluralistic society each school should have a prescribed ratio of Negro to white students reflecting the proportion for the district as a whole. To do this as an educational policy is within the broad discretionary powers of school authorities; absent a finding of a constitutional violation, however, that would not be within the authority of a federal court. As with any equity case, the nature of the violation determines the scope of the remedy. In default by the school authorities of their obligation to proffer acceptable remedies, a district court has broad power to fashion a remedy that will assure a unitary school system.

V

The central issue in this case is that of student assignment, and there are essentially four problem areas:

(1) to what extent racial balance or racial quotas may be used as an implement in a remedial order to correct a previously segregated system;

(2) whether every all-Negro and all-white school must be eliminated as an indispensable part of a remedial process of desegregation;

(3) what the limits are, if any, on the rearrangement of school districts and attendance zones, as a remedial measure; and

(4) what the limits are, if any, on the use of transportation facilities to correct state-enforced racial school segregation.

(1) Racial Balances or Racial Quotas.

The constant theme and thrust of every holding from *Brown I* to date is that state-enforced separation of races in public schools is discrimination that violates the Equal Protection Clause. The remedy commanded was to dismantle dual school systems.

We are concerned in these cases with the elimination of the discrimination inherent in the dual school systems, not with myriad factors of human existence which can cause discrimination in a multitude of ways on racial, religious, or ethnic grounds. The target of the cases from *Brown I* to the present was the dual school system. The elimination of racial discrimination in public schools is a large task and one that should not be retarded by efforts to achieve broader purposes lying beyond the jurisdiction of school authorities. One vehicle can carry only a limited amount of baggage. It would not serve the important objective of *Brown I* to seek to use school desegregation cases for purposes beyond their scope, although desegregation of schools ultimately will have impact on other forms of discrimination.

Our objective in dealing with the issues presented by these cases is to see that school authorities exclude no pupil of a racial minority from any school, directly or indirectly, on account of race; it does not and cannot embrace all the problems of racial prejudice, even when those problems contribute to disproportionate racial concentrations in some schools.

In this case it is urged that the District Court has imposed a racial balance requirement of 71%-29% on individual schools. The District Judge went on to acknowledge that variation 'from that norm may be unavoidable.' This contains intimations that the 'norm' is a fixed mathematical racial balance reflecting the pupil constituency of the system. If we were to read the holding of the District Court to require, as a matter of substantive constitutional right, any particular degree of racial balance or mixing, that approach would be disapproved and we would be obliged to reverse. The constitutional command to desegregate schools does not mean that every school in every community must always reflect the racial composition of the school system as a whole.

[The Court then found that "the use made of mathematical ratios was no more than a starting point in the process of shaping a remedy, rather than an inflexible requirement.," and that the district court decree "was within its discretionary powers, as an equitable remedy for the particular circumstances."]

(2) One-race Schools.

The record in this case reveals the familiar phenomenon that in metropolitan areas minority groups are often found concentrated in one part of the city. In some circumstances certain schools may remain all or largely of one race until new schools can be provided or neighborhood patterns change. Schools all or predominantly of one race in a district of mixed population will require close scrutiny to determine that school assignments are not part of state-enforced segregation.

In light of the above, it should be clear that the existence of some small number of one-race, or virtually one-race, schools within a district is not in and of itself the mark of a system that still practices segregation by law. The district judge or school authorities should make every effort to achieve the greatest possible degree of actual desegregation and will thus necessarily be concerned with the elimination of one-race schools. No per se rule can adequately embrace all the difficulties of reconciling the competing interests involved; but in a system with a history of segregation the need for remedial criteria of sufficient specificity to assure a school authority's compliance with its constitutional duty warrants a presumption against schools that are substantially disproportionate in their racial composition. Where the school authority's proposed plan for conversion from a dual to a unitary system contemplates the continued existence of some schools that are all or predominantly of one race, they have the burden of showing that such school assignments are genuinely nondiscriminatory. The court should scrutinize such schools, and the burden upon the school authorities will be to satisfy the court that their racial composition is not the result of present or past discriminatory action on their part.

(3) Remedial Altering of Attendance Zones.

The maps submitted in these cases graphically demonstrate that one of the principal tools employed by school planners and by courts to break up the dual school system has been a frank-- and sometimes drastic--gerrymandering of school districts and attendance zones. An additional step was pairing, 'clustering,' or 'grouping' of schools with attendance assignments made deliberately to accomplish the transfer of Negro students out of formerly segregated Negro schools and transfer of white students to formerly all-Negro schools. More often than not, these zones are neither compact nor contiguous; indeed they may be on opposite ends of the city. As an interim corrective measure, this cannot be said to be beyond the broad remedial powers of a court.

Absent a constitutional violation there would be no basis for judicially ordering assignment of students on a racial basis. All things being equal, with no history of discrimination, it might well be desirable to assign pupils to schools nearest their homes. But all things are not equal in a system that has been deliberately constructed and maintained to enforce racial segregation. The remedy for such segregation may be administratively awkward, inconvenient, and even bizarre in some situations and may impose burdens on some; but all awkwardness and inconvenience cannot be avoided in the interim period when remedial adjustments are being made to eliminate the dual school systems.

We hold that the pairing and grouping of noncontiguous school zones is a permissible tool and such action is to be considered in light of the objectives sought.

(4) Transportation of Students.

The scope of permissible transportation of students as an implement of a remedial decree has never been defined by this Court and by the very nature of the problem it cannot be defined with precision. No rigid guidelines as to student transportation can be given for application to the infinite variety of problems presented in thousands of situations. Bus transportation has been an integral part of the public education system for years, and was perhaps the single most important factor in the transition from the one-room schoolhouse to the consolidated school. Eighteen million of the Nation's public school children, approximately 39% were transported to their schools by bus in 1969-1970 in all parts of the country.

[T]he remedial techniques used in the District Court's order were within that court's power to provide equitable relief; implementation of the decree is well within the capacity of the school authority.

The decree provided that the buses used to implement the plan would operate on direct routes. Students would be picked up at schools near their homes and transported to the schools they were to attend. The trips for elementary school pupils average about seven miles and the District Court found that they would take 'not over 35 minutes at the most.' This system compares favorably with the transportation plan previously operated in Charlotte under which each day 26,600 students on all grade levels were transported an average of 15 miles one way for an average trip requiring over an hour. In these circumstances, we find no basis for holding that the local school authorities may not be required to employ bus transportation as one tool of school desegregation. Desegregation plans cannot be limited to the walk-in school.

An objection to transportation of students may have validity when the time or distance of travel is so great as to either risk the health of the children or significantly impinge on the educational process. District courts must weigh the soundness of any transportation plan in light of what is said in subdivisions (1), (2), and (3) above. It hardly needs stating that the limits on time of travel will vary with many factors, but probably with none more than the age of the students. The reconciliation of competing values in a desegregation case is, of course, a difficult task with many sensitive facets but fundamentally no more so than remedial measures courts of equity have traditionally employed.

Judgment of Court of Appeals affirmed in part; order of District Court *affirmed*.

NOTES

1. The *Swann* opinion set forth important guidelines on scope and limits of remedies in school desegregation cases. The general principle was that "the nature of the violation determines the scope of the remedy." Where school authorities had been unwilling to address unconstitutional segregation in their schools, however, "judicial authority may be invoked. Once a right and a violation have been shown, the scope of a district court's equitable powers to remedy past wrongs is broad, for breadth and flexibility are inherent in equitable remedies." Specifically, the *Swann* Court endorsed the following remedial principles:

(a) District courts can use mathematical ratios, that is, they may prescribe required percentages for black and white students, as a starting point but not as an inflexible requirement.

(b) The existence of some small number of one-race, or virtually one-race, schools within a district is not in and of itself the mark of a system that still practices segregation by law.

(c) District courts can alter attendance zones in order to eliminate the vestiges of a dual system.

(d) District courts can order school districts to employ bus transportation as one tool of school desegregation since desegregation plans cannot be limited to the walk-in school.

2. Up through the *Swann* decision in 1971, all of the school segregation cases that made their way to the Supreme Court originated in the southern states where law had mandated segregated schools. In those cases, the question was not whether there was a constitutional violation but rather what was the appropriate remedy. Outside of the south, however, there was also substantial racial segregation in public schools. This segregation resulted not from state law but from a host of factors including residential segregation, site location of schools, and school attendance zones. It

was not until 1973, in the following case, that the Court addressed the constitutionality of school segregation in these non-southern cities.

Keyes v. School Dist. No. 1, Denver, Colo.
413 U.S. 189 (1973)

Mr. Justice BRENNAN delivered the opinion of the Court.

This school desegregation case concerns the Denver, Colorado, school system. That system has never been operated under a constitutional or statutory provision that mandated or permitted racial segregation in public education. Rather, the gravamen of this action, brought in June 1969 in the District Court for the District of Colorado by parents of Denver schoolchildren, is that respondent School Board alone, by use of various techniques such as the manipulation of student attendance zones, school site selection and a neighborhood school policy, created or maintained racially or ethnically (or both racially and ethnically) segregated schools throughout the school district, entitling petitioners to a decree directing desegregation of the entire school district.

II

In our view, the only other question that requires our decision at this time is ... whether the District Court and the Court of Appeals applied an incorrect legal standard in addressing petitioners' contention that respondent School Board engaged in an unconstitutional policy of deliberate segregation in the core city schools. Our conclusion is that those courts did not apply the correct standard in addressing that contention.

Petitioners apparently concede for the purposes of this case that in the case of a school system like Denver's, where no statutory dual system has ever existed, plaintiffs must prove not only that segregated schooling exists but also that it was brought about or maintained by intentional state action. Petitioners proved that for almost a decade after 1960 respondent School Board had engaged in an unconstitutional policy of deliberate racial segregation in the Park Hill schools. Indeed, the District Court found that '(b)etween 1960 and 1969 the Board's policies with respect to these northeast Denver schools show an undeviating purpose to isolate Negro students' in segregated schools 'while preserving the Anglo character of (other) schools.' In addition, there was uncontroverted evidence that teachers and staff had for years been assigned on the basis of a minority teacher to a minority school throughout the school system. Respondent argues, however, that a finding of state-imposed segregation as to a substantial portion of the school system can be viewed in isolation from the rest of the district, and that even if state-imposed segregation does exist in a substantial part of the Denver school system, it does not follow that the District Court could predicate on that fact a finding that the entire school system is a dual system. We do not agree. We have never suggested that plaintiffs in school desegregation cases must bear the burden of proving the elements of de jure segregation as to each and every school or each and every student within the school system. Rather, we have held that where plaintiffs prove that a current condition of segregated schooling exists within a school district where a dual system was compelled or authorized by statute at the time of our decision in *Brown v. Board of Education*, 347 U.S. 483 (1954) (*Brown I*), the State automatically assumes an affirmative duty 'to effectuate a transition to a racially nondiscriminatory school system,' *Brown v. Board of Education*, 349 U.S. 294, 301 (1955) (*Brown II*), that is, to eliminate from the public schools within their school system 'all vestiges of state-imposed segregation.' *Swann v. Charlotte-Mecklenburg Board of Education*,

402 U.S. 1, 15 (1971).

This is not a case, however, where a statutory dual system has ever existed. Nevertheless, where plaintiffs prove that the school authorities have carried out a systematic program of segregation affecting a substantial portion of the students, schools, teachers, and facilities within the school system, it is only common sense to conclude that there exists a predicate for a finding of the existence of a dual school system. Several considerations support this conclusion. First, it is obvious that a practice of concentrating Negroes in certain schools by structuring attendance zones or designating 'feeder' schools on the basis of race has the reciprocal effect of keeping other nearby schools predominantly white. Similarly, the practice of building a school to a certain size and in a certain location, 'with conscious knowledge that it would be a segregated school,' 303 F. Supp., at 285, has a substantial reciprocal effect on the racial composition of other nearby schools. So also, the use of mobile classrooms, the drafting of student transfer policies, the transportation of students, and the assignment of faculty and staff, on racially identifiable bases, have the clear effect of earmarking schools according to their racial composition, and this, in turn, together with the elements of student assignment and school construction, may have a profound reciprocal effect on the racial composition of residential neighborhoods within a metropolitan area, thereby causing further racial concentration within the schools. In short, common sense dictates the conclusion that racially inspired school board actions have an impact beyond the particular schools that are the subjects of those actions.

Applying these principles in the special context of school desegregation cases, we hold that a finding of intentionally segregative school board actions in a meaningful portion of a school system, as in this case, creates a presumption that other segregated schooling within the system is not adventitious. It establishes, in other words, a prima facie case of unlawful segregative design on the part of school authorities, and shifts to those authorities the burden of proving that other segregated schools within the system are not also the result of intentionally segregative actions. This is true even if it is determined that different areas of the school district should be viewed independently of each other because, even in that situation, there is high probability that where school authorities have effectuated an intentionally segregative policy in a meaningful portion of the school system, similar impermissible considerations have motivated their actions in other areas of the system. We emphasize that the differentiating factor between de jure segregation and so-called de facto segregation to which we referred in *Swann* is purpose or intent to segregate. Where school authorities have been found to have practiced purposeful segregation in part of a school system, they may be expected to oppose system-wide desegregation, as did the respondents in this case, on the ground that their purposefully segregative actions were isolated and individual events, thus leaving plaintiffs with the burden of proving otherwise. But at that point where an intentionally segregative policy is practiced in a meaningful or significant segment of a school system, as in this case, the school authorities cannot be heard to argue that plaintiffs have proved only 'isolated and individual' unlawfully segregative actions. In that circumstance, it is both fair and reasonable to require that the school authorities bear the burden of showing that their actions as to other segregated schools within the system were not also motivated by segregative intent.

The respondent School Board invoked at trial its 'neighborhood school policy' as explaining racial and ethnic concentrations within the core city schools, arguing that since the core city area population had long been Negro and Hispano, the concentrations were necessarily the result of residential patterns and not of purposefully segregative policies. We have no occasion to consider in this case whether a 'neighborhood school policy' of itself will justify racial or ethnic concentrations in the absence of a finding that school authorities have committed acts constituting de jure segregation. It is enough that we hold that the mere assertion of such a policy is not dispositive where, as in this case, the school authorities have been found to have practiced de jure segregation in a meaningful portion of the school system by techniques that indicate that the 'neighborhood school' concept has not been maintained free of manipulation.

Thus, respondent School Board having been found to have practiced deliberate racial segregation in schools attended by over one-third of the Negro school population, that crucial finding establishes a prima facie case of intentional segregation in the core city schools. In such case, respondent's neighborhood school policy is not to be determinative 'simply because it appears to be neutral.'

The judgment of the Court of Appeals is modified to vacate instead of reverse the parts of the Final Decree that concern the core city schools, and the case is remanded to the District Court for further proceedings consistent with this opinion. It is so ordered.

NOTES

1. In *Keyes*, the Court anticipated by three years its holding in *Washington v. Davis*, (see Section E, *infra*) that governmental action that is (1) racially neutral on its face but (2) has a racially disproportionate impact, is not a racial classification subject to strict scrutiny unless a racially discriminatory purpose is also involved. Thus, in Denver, Colorado, a school district where racial segregation had never been mandated by law, the mere fact that a particular school was all-white or all-black did not establish a constitutional violation. The Court explained that "the differentiating factor between de jure segregation and so-called de facto segregation to which we referred in *Swann* is purpose or intent to segregate." In terms of the burdens that plaintiffs would face, the Court explained:

> [W]e hold that a finding of intentionally segregative school board actions in a meaningful portion of a school system, as in this case, creates a presumption that other segregated schooling within the system is not adventitious. It establishes, in other words, a prima facie case of unlawful segregative design on the part of school authorities, and shifts to those authorities the burden of proving that other segregated schools within the system are not also the result of intentionally segregative actions.

The *Keyes* Court identified the kinds of school board decisions that could be used to create a racially segregated school system, including decisions about where to build zones and how to draw attendance zones. When school boards had used these techniques over a number of years to create identifiably black and white schools, the board could not use its neighborhood school policy as a defense.

A year after *Keyes*, the Court considered another school segregation case arising from a northern city, this one from Detroit. The Court in *Swann* had authorized lower courts to use powerful remedies for school segregation, including the redrawing of attendance zones and the busing of students. The *Swann* case, however, had arisen in North Carolina, a state with a long history of government at the county (rather than city or town) level. Thus, in *Swann*, because the school system included both the city of Charlotte and its surrounding suburbs, the Court's remedy readily included both the city and suburbs. In northern states, however, local government was more commonly based at the city and town level and a city and its suburbs typically had separate school systems. Because a high percentage of minorities lived within city limits, it was more difficult for a federal district court to craft an effective desegregation plan if the plan was limited to the city school system. Could a judge extend a desegregation remedy beyond city limits to include the suburbs? This was the question the Court took up in the next case.

Milliken v. Bradley
418 U.S. 717 (1974)

Mr. Chief Justice BURGER delivered the opinion of the Court.

We granted certiorari in these consolidated cases to determine whether a federal court may impose a multidistrict, areawide remedy to a single-district de jure segregation problem absent any finding that the other included school districts have failed to operate unitary school systems within their districts, absent any claim or finding that the boundary lines of any affected school district were established with the purpose of fostering racial segregation in public schools, absent any finding that the included districts committed acts which effected segregation within the other districts, and absent a meaningful opportunity for the included neighboring school districts to present evidence or be heard on the propriety of a multidistrict remedy or on the question of constitutional violations by those neighboring districts.

II

[The Court here summarized some of its earlier cases.] Proceeding from these basic principles, we first note that in the District Court the complainants sought a remedy aimed at the condition alleged to offend the Constitution--the segregation within the Detroit City School District. The court acted on this theory of the case and in its initial ruling on the 'Desegregation Area' stated:

> The task before this court, therefore, is now, and . . . has always been, now to desegregate the Detroit public schools. 345 F. Supp., at 921.

Thereafter, however, the District Court abruptly rejected the proposed Detroit-only plans on the ground that 'while (they) would provide a racial mix more in keeping with the Black-White proportions of the student population (they) would accentuate the racial identifiability of the (Detroit) district as a Black school system, and would not accomplish desegregation.' '(T)he racial composition of the student body is such,' said the court, 'that the plan's implementation would clearly make the entire Detroit public school system racially identifiable,' 'leav(ing) many of its schools 75 to 90 per cent Black.' Consequently, the court reasoned, it was imperative to 'look beyond the limits of the Detroit school district for a solution to the problem of segregation in the Detroit public schools . . .' since '(s)chool district lines are simply matters of political convenience and may not be used to deny constitutional rights.' Accordingly, the District Court proceeded to redefine the relevant area to include areas of predominantly white pupil population in order to ensure that 'upon implementation, no school, grade or classroom (would be) substantially disproportionate to the overall pupil racial composition' of the entire metropolitan area.

While specifically acknowledging that the District Court's findings of a condition of segregation were limited to Detroit, the Court of Appeals approved the use of a metropolitan remedy largely on the grounds that it is

CHAPTER 2: RACE CLASSIFICATIONS

impossible to declare 'clearly erroneous' the District Judge's conclusion that any Detroit only segregation plan will lead directly to a single segregated Detroit school district overwhelmingly black in all of its schools, surrounded by a ring of suburbs and suburban school districts overwhelmingly white in composition in a State in which the racial composition is 87 per cent white and 13 per cent black. 484 F.2d, at 249.

Viewing the record as a whole, it seems clear that the District Court and the Court of Appeals shifted the primary focus from a Detroit remedy to the metropolitan area only because of their conclusion that total desegregation of Detroit would not produce the racial balance which they perceived as desirable. Both courts proceeded on an assumption that the Detroit schools could not be truly desegregated - in their view of what constituted desegregation--unless the racial composition of the student body of each school substantially reflected the racial composition of the population of the metropolitan area as a whole. The metropolitan area was then defined as Detroit plus 53 of the outlying school districts.

In *Swann*, which arose in the context of a single independent school district, the Court held:

> f we were to read the holding of the District Court to require, as a matter of substantive constitutional right, any particular degree of racial balance or mixing, that approach would be disapproved and we would be obliged to reverse. 402 U.S., at 24.

The clear import of this language from *Swann* is that desegregation, in the sense of dismantling a dual school system, does not require any particular racial balance in each 'school, grade or classroom.' See *Spencer v. Kugler*, 404 U.S. 1027 (1972).

Here the District Court's approach to what constituted 'actual desegregation' raises the fundamental question, not presented in *Swann*, as to the circumstances in which a federal court may order desegregation relief that embraces more than a single school district. The court's analytical starting point was its conclusion that school district lines are no more than arbitrary lines on a map drawn 'for political convenience.' Boundary lines may be bridged where there has been a constitutional violation calling for interdistrict relief, but the notion that school district lines may be casually ignored or treated as a mere administrative convenience is contrary to the history of public education in our country. No single tradition in public education is more deeply rooted than local control over the operation of schools; local autonomy has long been thought essential both to the maintenance of community concern and support for public schools and to quality of the educational process. See *Wright v. Council of the City of Emporia*, 407 U.S., at 469. Thus, in *San Antonio Independent School District v. Rodriguez*, 411 U.S. 1, 50 (1973), we observed that local control over the educational process affords citizens an opportunity to participate in decision-making, permits the structuring of school programs to fit local needs, and encourages 'experimentation, innovation, and a healthy competition for educational excellence.'

The Michigan educational structure involved in this case, in common with most States, provides for a large measure of local control, and a review of the scope and character of these local powers indicates the extent to which the interdistrict remedy approved by the two courts could disrupt and alter the structure of public education in Michigan. The metropolitan remedy would require, in effect, consolidation of 54 independent school districts historically administered as separate units into a vast new super school district. Entirely apart from the logistical and other serious problems attending large-scale transportation of students, the consolidation would give rise to an array of other problems in financing and operating this new school system.

Of course, no state law is above the Constitution. School district lines and the present laws with respect to local control, are not sacrosanct and if they conflict with the Fourteenth Amendment federal courts have a duty to prescribe appropriate remedies. But our prior holdings have been confined to violations and remedies within a single school district. We therefore turn to address, for the first time, the validity of a remedy mandating cross-district or interdistrict consolidation to remedy a condition of segregation found to exist in only one district.

The controlling principle consistently expounded in our holdings is that the scope of the remedy is determined by the nature and extent of the constitutional violation. *Swann*, 402 U.S., at 16. Before the boundaries of separate and autonomous school districts may be set aside by consolidating the separate units for remedial purposes or by imposing a cross-district remedy, it must first be shown that there has been a constitutional violation within one district that produces a significant segregative effect in another district. Specifically, it must be shown that racially discriminatory acts of the state or local school districts, or of a single school district have been a substantial cause of interdistrict segregation. Thus an interdistrict remedy might be in order where the racially discriminatory acts of one or more school districts caused racial segregation in an adjacent district, or where district lines have been deliberately drawn on the basis of race. In such circumstances an interdistrict remedy would be appropriate to eliminate the interdistrict segregation directly caused by the constitutional violation. Conversely, without an interdistrict violation and interdistrict effect, there is no constitutional wrong calling for an interdistrict remedy.

The record before us, voluminous as it is, contains evidence of de jure segregated conditions only in the Detroit schools; indeed, that was the theory on which the litigation was initially based and on which the District Court took evidence. With no showing of significant violation by the 53 outlying school districts and no evidence of any interdistrict violation or effect, the court went beyond the original theory of the case as framed by the pleadings and mandated a metropolitan area remedy. To approve the remedy ordered by the court would impose on the outlying districts, not shown to have committed any constitutional violation, a wholly impermissible remedy based on a standard not hinted at in *Brown I* and *II* or any holding of this Court.

The constitutional right of the Negro respondents residing in Detroit is to attend a unitary school system in that district. Unless petitioners drew the district lines in a discriminatory fashion, or arranged for white students residing in the Detroit district to attend schools in Oakland and Macomb Counties, they were under no constitutional duty to make provisions for Negro students to do so. The view of the dissenters, that the existence of a dual system in Detroit can be made the basis for a decree requiring cross-district transportation of pupils, cannot be supported on the grounds that it represents merely the devising of a suitably flexible remedy for the violation of rights already established by our prior decisions. It can be supported only by drastic expansion of the constitutional right itself, an expansion without any support in either constitutional principle or precedent.

Reversed and *remanded.*

NOTES

1.   The basic principle announced in *Milliken* was that "the scope of the remedy is determined by the nature and extent of the constitutional violation." At the conceptual level, this principle

makes perfect sense, for in constitutional law, as in all other areas of law, the remedy is determined by the violation of the right. In the context of racially segregated schools, however, this statement of the principle was virtually certain to frustrate any attempt to desegregate urban schools in cities with a high minority population. In Detroit, for example, the Court conceded that, without an interdistrict remedy, many of the Detroit schools would be 75% to 90% black. The Court noted the historic importance associated with the idea of local control of schools, but it made no mention of the fact that an historical accident—that in most northern cities, local government was established at the city and town level rather than the county level--would leave most northern cities with racially segregated schools and no constitutional remedy.

The Court in *Brown* overruled *Plessy's* doctrine of "separate but equal." But *Milliken*, coupled with the Supreme Court's 1973 case, *San Antonio School District v. Rodriguez*, 411 U.S. 1 (1973) (see Chap. 8.F. *infra*), effectively endorsed a system that was separate *and* unequal. In *Milliken*, the Court determined that racial segregated school systems did not violate the Constitution so long as the segregation was bounded by city boundaries. In *Rodriguez*, the Court ruled that the existence of vast differentials in wealth and spending power between urban and suburban school districts did not violate the Constitution. Taken together, the two cases seemed to endorse the principle that school districts could be racially and financially unequal.

Parents Involved in Community Schools v. Seattle School Dist. No. 1
551 U.S. 701 (2007)

[The case itself is printed in Sec. F of this chapter, on affirmative action. What follows here is a partial summary and commentary.]

In 2007, the Court considered two consolidated cases from public school systems in which school officials had voluntarily adopted race-conscious attendance rules in order to promote racial integration within the school system. The 5 to 4 decision that invalidated those plans included a fierce disagreement on the meaning and legacy of *Brown v. Board of Education*. The dissenters, who would have approved of the voluntary race-conscious action to promote integration, cited the following language from the Court's earlier opinion in *Swann*:

> School authorities are traditionally charged with broad power to formulate and implement educational policy and might well conclude, for example, that in order to prepare students to live in a pluralistic society each school should have a prescribed ratio of Negro to white students reflecting the proportion for the district as a whole. To do this as an educational policy is within the broad discretionary powers of school authorities. 402 U.S., at 16.

This quotation supports the view that the evil that *Brown* addressed was racial segregation in schools. In order to address this evil, then, schools could take voluntary steps to eliminate racial segregation or they could wait to be ordered to do so by a federal court. Under this view of *Brown*, the school districts and the courts each have a role to play in accomplishing the goal of eliminating segregation.

The *Parents Involved* majority, however, had a very different view of the legacy of *Brown*. To the majority, the problem in *Brown* was not racial segregation, but rather the use of race as a classificatory tool. In support of this view, the majority cited the words of Robert Carter, the plaintiff's attorney in *Brown*, who said at oral argument in the case, "We have one fundamental contention which we will seek to develop in the course of this argument, and that contention is that no State has any authority under the equal-protection clause of the Fourteenth Amendment to use race as a factor in affording educational opportunities among its citizens." *Parents Involved*, 551 U.S. at 747. The *Parents* majority insisted that this language did not differentiate between a racial classification designed to produce a racially segregated school and a racial classification designed to produce a racially integrated school:

> What do the racial classifications do in these cases, if not determine admission to a public school on a racial basis? Before *Brown*, schoolchildren were told where they could and could not go to school based on the color of their skin. The school districts in these cases have not carried the heavy burden of demonstrating that we should allow this once again—even for very different reasons. For schools that never segregated on the basis of race, such as Seattle, or that have removed the vestiges of past segregation, such as Jefferson County, the way "to achieve a system of determining admission to the public schools on a nonracial basis," *Brown II*, 349 U.S., at 300–301, is to stop assigning students on a racial basis. The way to stop discrimination on the basis of race is to stop discriminating on the basis of race. *Parents Involved*, 551 U.S. at 747-48.

There has been much criticism of the majority's use of the *Brown* holding and Attorney Carter's language. As for the logic of the majority's argument, it takes the *Brown* language out of context: "That Mr. Carter thought racial classifications were impermissible to segregate schools does not mean that he thought they could not be used to integrate schools. That question was not before the Court in Brown and Mr. Carter did not address it." Joel K. Goldstein, *Not Hearing History: A Critique of Chief Justice Roberts's Reinterpretation of Brown*, 69 Ohio State L.J 791 (2008).

Those in the NAACP who had prepared the plaintiff's argument in *Brown*, including Robert Carter himself, strongly disagreed with the *Parents Involved* majority:

> Surviving members of the NAACP's legal team responded with outrage, accusing the Chief Justice of misrepresenting their position to further an agenda with which they deeply disagree. The Chief Justice's reading of Brown was "preposterous"; it stood the NAACP's "argument on its head"; it was "dirty pool." Christopher W. Schmidt, *Brown and the Colorblind Constitution*, 94 Cornell Law. R. 203 (2008).

E. THE REQUIREMENT OF RACIALLY DISCRIMINATORY PURPOSE

The standard racial classification that requires strict scrutiny is explicit. For example, a requirement that only white persons can serve on a jury, or that all those of Japanese ancestry must go to an internment camp, requires strict scrutiny, and "No inquiry into legislative purpose is necessary when the racial classification appears on the face of the statute." *Shaw v. Reno*, 509 U.S. 630, 642 (1993). Explicit racial classifications by government actors, once common in America, are now rare outside the context of affirmative action. Explicit governmental racial discrimination that would disadvantage minorities are almost unheard of today.

What is still common, however, are governmental actions, racially neutral on their face, that have a disproportionately negative effect on racial minorities. As long ago as the Court's opinion in *Yick Wo v. Hopkins*, 118 U.S. 356 (1886), the Court saw that a racially neutral rule (requiring a permit to operate a laundry in a wooden building) could be used to discriminate against a particular racial or national group (all Chinese applicants were denied permits and almost all white applicants were granted permits). The *Yick Wo* opinion did not include any great discussion of the difference between discriminatory purpose and discriminatory effect, but it invalidated a rule where the only evidence of its racial design was in its racial effect.

Ninety years after *Yick Wo*, the Court in the following case formalized a rule about the necessity of proving a racially discriminatory purpose in a situation where there is no explicit racial classification.

Washington v. Davis
426 U.S. 229 (1976)

[Black police officers challenged the hiring and promotion practices of the Metropolitan Police Department for the District of Columbia, with specific emphasis on "Test 21," a test designed by the Civil Service Commission to evaluate verbal ability, vocabulary, and reading comprehension. The test had a racially disproportionate impact--a higher percentage of black applicants failed the test than did white applicants. There was, however, no evidence that that test had been adopted with a purpose to exclude black applicants from the District police force.]

Mr. Justice WHITE delivered the opinion of the Court.

This case involves the validity of a qualifying test administered to applicants for positions as police officers in the District of Columbia Metropolitan Police Department. The test was sustained by the District Court but invalidated by the Court of Appeals. We are in agreement with the District Court and hence reverse the judgment of the Court of Appeals.

II

Because the Court of Appeals erroneously applied the legal standards applicable to Title VII cases in resolving the constitutional issue before it, we reverse its judgment in respondents' favor. As the Court of Appeals understood Title VII, employees or applicants proceeding under it need not concern themselves with the employer's possibly discriminatory purpose but instead may focus solely on the racially differential impact of the challenged hiring or promotion practices. This is not the constitutional rule. We have never held that the constitutional standard for adjudicating claims of invidious racial discrimination is identical to the standards applicable under Title VII, and we decline to do so today.

The central purpose of the Equal Protection Clause of the Fourteenth Amendment is the prevention of official conduct discriminating on the basis of race. It is also true that the Due Process Clause of the Fifth Amendment contains an equal protection component prohibiting the United States from invidiously discriminating between individuals or groups. *Bolling v. Sharpe*, 347 U.S. 497 (1954). But our cases have not embraced the proposition that a law or other official act, without regard to whether it reflects a racially discriminatory purpose, is unconstitutional solely because it has a racially disproportionate impact.

This is not to say that the necessary discriminatory racial purpose must be express or appear on the face of the statute, or that a law's disproportionate impact is irrelevant in cases involving

Constitution-based claims of racial discrimination. A statute, otherwise neutral on its face, must not be applied so as invidiously to discriminate on the basis of race. *Yick Wo v. Hopkins*, 118 U.S. 356 (1886). It is also clear from the cases dealing with racial discrimination in the selection of juries that the systematic exclusion of Negroes is itself such an "unequal application of the law . . . as to show intentional discrimination." *Akins v. Texas, supra*, 325 U.S., at 404. A prima facie case of discriminatory purpose may be proved as well by the absence of Negroes on a particular jury combined with the failure of the jury commissioners to be informed of eligible Negro jurors in a community, *Hill v. Texas*, 316 U.S. 400, 404 (1942), or with racially non-neutral selection procedures, *Alexander v. Louisiana, supra*. With a prima facie case made out, "the burden of proof shifts to the State to rebut the presumption of unconstitutional action by showing that permissible racially neutral selection criteria and procedures have produced the monochromatic result." *Alexander, supra*, 405 U.S., at 632.

Necessarily, an invidious discriminatory purpose may often be inferred from the totality of the relevant facts, including the fact, if it is true, that the law bears more heavily on one race than another. It is also not infrequently true that the discriminatory impact in the jury cases for example, the total or seriously disproportionate exclusion of Negroes from jury venires may for all practical purposes demonstrate unconstitutionality because in various circumstances the discrimination is very difficult to explain on nonracial grounds. Nevertheless, we have not held that a law, neutral on its face and serving ends otherwise within the power of government to pursue, is invalid under the Equal Protection Clause simply because it may affect a greater proportion of one race than of another. Disproportionate impact is not irrelevant, but it is not the sole touchstone of an invidious racial discrimination forbidden by the Constitution. Standing alone, it does not trigger the rule, *McLaughlin v. Florida*, 379 U.S. 184 (1964), that racial classifications are to be subjected to the strictest scrutiny and are justifiable only by the weightiest of considerations.

As an initial matter, we have difficulty understanding how a law establishing a racially neutral qualification for employment is nevertheless racially discriminatory and denies "any person . . . equal protection of the laws" simply because a greater proportion of Negroes fail to qualify than members of other racial or ethnic groups. Had respondents, along with all others who had failed Test 21, whether white or black, brought an action claiming that the test denied each of them equal protection of the laws as compared with those who had passed with high enough scores to qualify them as police recruits, it is most unlikely that their challenge would have been sustained. Test 21, which is administered generally to prospective Government employees, concededly seeks to ascertain whether those who take it have acquired a particular level of verbal skill; and it is untenable that the Constitution prevents the Government from seeking modestly to upgrade the communicative abilities of its employees rather than to be satisfied with some lower level of competence, particularly where the job requires special ability to communicate orally and in writing. Respondents, as Negroes, could no more successfully claim that the test denied them equal protection than could white applicants who also failed. The conclusion would not be different in the face of proof that more Negroes than whites had been disqualified by Test 21. That other Negroes also failed to score well would, alone, not demonstrate that respondents individually were being denied equal protection of the laws by the application of an otherwise valid qualifying test being administered to prospective police recruits.

Nor on the facts of the case before us would the disproportionate impact of Test 21 warrant the conclusion that it is a purposeful device to discriminate against Negroes and hence an infringement of the constitutional rights of respondents as well as other black applicants. As we have said, the test is neutral on its face and rationally may be said to serve a purpose the

Government is constitutionally empowered to pursue. Even agreeing with the District Court that the differential racial effect of Test 21 called for further inquiry, we think the District Court correctly held that the affirmative efforts of the Metropolitan Police Department to recruit black officers, the changing racial composition of the recruit classes and of the force in general, and the relationship of the test to the training program negated any inference that the Department discriminated on the basis of race or that "a police officer qualifies on the color of his skin rather than ability."

Under Title VII, Congress provided that when hiring and promotion practices disqualifying substantially disproportionate numbers of blacks are challenged, discriminatory purpose need not be proved, and that it is an insufficient response to demonstrate some rational basis for the challenged practices. It is necessary, in addition, that they be "validated" in terms of job performance in any one of several ways, perhaps by ascertaining the minimum skill, ability, or potential necessary for the position at issue and determining whether the qualifying tests are appropriate for the selection of qualified applicants for the job in question. However this process proceeds, it involves a more probing judicial review of, and less deference to, the seemingly reasonable acts of administrators and executives than is appropriate under the Constitution where special racial impact, without discriminatory purpose, is claimed. We are not disposed to adopt this more rigorous standard for the purposes of applying the Fifth and the Fourteenth Amendments in cases such as this.

A rule that a statute designed to serve neutral ends is nevertheless invalid, absent compelling justification, if in practice it benefits or burdens one race more than another would be far-reaching and would raise serious questions about, and perhaps invalidate, a whole range of tax, welfare, public service, regulatory, and licensing statutes that may be more burdensome to the poor and to the average black than to the more affluent white. Given that rule, such consequences would perhaps be likely to follow. However, in our view, extension of the rule beyond those areas where it is already applicable by reason of statute, such as in the field of public employment, should await legislative prescription.

As we have indicated, it was error to direct summary judgment for respondents based on the Fifth Amendment. The judgment of the Court of Appeals accordingly is reversed. *So ordered.*

NOTES

1.   The problem that the Court addressed in *Washington v. Davis* was really one of proof. There was no question that the decisions made by governmental officials in the District of Columbia adversely affected black applicants for positions in the police department. But the decision did not involve an *explicit* racial classification so the question was whether an *implicit* racial classification, that is, one that *resulted* from the government action, would trigger strict scrutiny of its own accord. The logic behind this view is that the results speak for themselves—a test that excludes black applicants disproportionately in relation to white applicants is a racially discriminatory test.

The Court rejected this interpretation of the Constitution. The Court of Appeals in the case had applied to the constitutional issue the burden-shifting principle that was the standard method of proving racial discrimination under Title VII. Title VII is a federal statute that prohibits racial discrimination in employment. To make a prima facie case under Title VII, a plaintiff need only show that a particular employment practice has a racially discriminatory effect. Once that showing has been made, the burden shifts to the employer to introduce evidence that the practice was adopted for a legitimate, non-racial reason. In the context of a challenge to an employment test, the employer would have to show that the test was "validated,"—that successful performance on the test correlated with successful performance on the job.

The Title VII burden-shifting standard recognizes that it is difficult to prove motivation, particularly if an actor knows in advance that he should hide any inappropriate motives. The Title VII test still requires that a plaintiff prove racial discrimination, but it throws onto the employer the burden of disproving inappropriate motivation. When the Court rejected this standard for claims under the Equal Protection Clause, it left on the plaintiff the entire burden of proving something that is very difficult to prove—why the defendant acted in a way that produced a racially disproportionate impact.

The Court did concede that evidence of racially disproportionate impact was not irrelevant but, unless the impact was so stark as to leave no alternative explanation of an outcome, it was only a starting point. There is some precedent where the Court found disproportionate impact so stark it left no question that the a racially discriminatory purpose was at work:

(1) *Yick Wo v. Hopkins*, 118 U.S. 356 (1886) (invalidating under the Equal Protection Clause a city ordinance that required a permit to operate a laundry in a wooden building. The ordinance itself created no racial classification but every white person who applied received a permit, save one, while every application from a person of Chinese descent was denied);

(2) *Guinn v. United States*, 238 U.S. 347 (1915) (invalidating under the Fifteenth Amendment an Oklahoma statute that imposed a literacy test to qualify for voting, but then exempted from that test all those who had been eligible to vote on or before January 1, 1866 and their lineal descendants. The effect of the statute was that all black persons were subject to the literacy test and the only people exempt from it were white);

(3) *Gomillion v. Lightfoot*, 364 U.S. 339 (1960) (invalidating under the Fifteenth Amendment an Alabama statute that altered the shape of the city of Tuskegee from a square to an uncouth twenty-eight-sided figure where the inevitable effect of these redrawn boundaries was to remove from the city all save four or five of its 400 black voters while not removing a single white voter).

In most cases of racially discriminatory impact, however, it is not possible to prove discriminatory purpose, even where it is statistically clear that race played an important role in a governmental decision. The next three cases show how difficult the Court has made it to prove discriminatory purpose on the basis of discriminatory effect.

Village of Arlington Heights v. Metropolitan Housing Development Corp.
429 U.S. 252 (1977)

Mr. Justice POWELL delivered the opinion of the Court.

In 1971 respondent Metropolitan Housing Development Corporation (MHDC) applied to petitioner, the Village of Arlington Heights, Ill., for the rezoning of a 15-acre parcel from single-family to multiple-family classification. Using federal financial assistance, MHDC planned to build 190 clustered townhouse units for low- and moderate-income tenants. The Village denied the rezoning request. MHDC, joined by other plaintiffs alleged that the denial was racially discriminatory and that it violated, *inter alia*, the Fourteenth Amendment.

III

Our decision last Term in *Washington v. Davis*, 426 U.S. 229 (1976), made it clear that official action will not be held unconstitutional solely because it results in a racially disproportionate impact. "Disproportionate impact is not irrelevant, but it is not the sole touchstone of an invidious racial discrimination." *Id.*, at 242. Proof of racially discriminatory intent or purpose is required to show a violation of the Equal Protection Clause. Although some contrary indications may be drawn from some of our cases, the holding in *Davis* reaffirmed a principle well established in a variety of contexts. E.g., *Keyes v. School Dist. No. 1, Denver, Colo.*, 413 U.S. 189, 208 (1973) (schools); *Wright v. Rockefeller*, 376 U.S. 52, 56-57 (1964) (election districting); *Akins v. Texas*, 325 U.S. 398, 403-404 (1945) (jury selection).

Davis does not require a plaintiff to prove that the challenged action rested solely on racially discriminatory purposes. Rarely can it be said that a legislature or administrative body operating under a broad mandate made a decision motivated solely by a single concern, or even that a particular purpose was the "dominant" or "primary" one. In fact, it is because legislators and administrators are properly concerned with balancing numerous competing considerations that courts refrain from reviewing the merits of their decisions, absent a showing of arbitrariness or irrationality. But racial discrimination is not just another competing consideration. When there is a proof that a discriminatory purpose has been a motivating factor in the decision, this judicial deference is no longer justified.

Determining whether invidious discriminatory purpose was a motivating factor demands a sensitive inquiry into such circumstantial and direct evidence of intent as may be available. The impact of the official action whether it "bears more heavily on one race than another," *Washington v. Davis, supra*, 426 U.S., at 242, may provide an important starting point. Sometimes a clear pattern, unexplainable on grounds other than race, emerges from the effect of the state action even when the governing legislation appears neutral on its face. *Yick Wo v. Hopkins*, 118 U.S. 356 (1886); *Guinn v. United States*, 238 U.S. 347 (1915); *Lane v. Wilson*, 307 U.S. 268 (1939); *Gomillion v. Lightfoot*, 364 U.S. 339 (1960). The evidentiary inquiry is then relatively easy. But such cases are rare. Absent a pattern as stark as that in *Gomillion* or *Yick Wo*, impact alone is not determinative, and the Court must look to other evidence.

The historical background of the decision is one evidentiary source, particularly if it reveals a series of official actions taken for invidious purposes. See *Lane v. Wilson, supra*; *Griffin v. School Board*, 377 U.S. 218 (1964); *Davis v. Schnell*, 81 F. Supp. 872 (S.D.Ala.), *aff'd* per curiam (1949); *cf. Keyes v. School Dist. No. 1, Denver, Colo., supra*, 413 U.S., at 207. The specific sequence of events leading up the challenged decision also may shed some light on the decisionmaker's purposes. *Reitman v. Mulkey*, 387 U.S. 369, 373-376 (1967); *Grosjean v. American Press Co.*, 297 U.S. 233, 250 (1936). For example, if the property involved here always had been zoned R-5 [higher density housing] but suddenly was changed to R-3 [single-family homes] when the town learned of MHDC's plans to erect integrated housing, we would have a far different case. Departures from the normal procedural sequence also might afford evidence that improper purposes are playing a role. Substantive departures too may be relevant, particularly if the factors usually considered important by the decisionmaker strongly favor a decision contrary to the one reached.

The legislative or administrative history may be highly relevant, especially where there are contemporary statements by members of the decisionmaking body, minutes of its meetings, or reports. In some extraordinary instances the members might be called to the stand at trial to testify concerning the purpose of the official action, although even then such testimony frequently will be barred by privilege. See *Tenney v. Brandhove*, 341 U.S. 367 (1951); *United States v. Nixon*, 418 U.S. 683, 705 (1974); 8 J. Wigmore, Evidence § 2371 (McNaughton rev.ed. 1961).

The foregoing summary identifies, without purporting to be exhaustive, subjects of proper inquiry in determining whether racially discriminatory intent existed. With these in mind, we now address the case before us.

IV

The impact of the Village's decision does arguably bear more heavily on racial minorities. Minorities constitute 18% of the Chicago area population, and 40% of the income groups said to be eligible for Lincoln Green. But there is little about the sequence of events leading up to the decision that would spark suspicion. The area around the Viatorian property has been zoned R-3 since 1959, the year when Arlington Heights first adopted a zoning map. Single-family homes surround the 80-acre site, and the Village is undeniably committed to single-family homes as its dominant residential land use. The rezoning request progressed according to the usual procedures. The Plan Commission even scheduled two additional hearings, at least in part to accommodate MHDC and permit it to supplement its presentation with answers to questions generated at the first hearing.

The statements by the Plan Commission and Village Board members, as reflected in the official minutes, focused almost exclusively on the zoning aspects of the MHDC petition, and the zoning factors on which they relied are not novel criteria in the Village's rezoning decisions. There is no reason to doubt that there has been reliance by some neighboring property owners on the maintenance of single-family zoning in the vicinity. The Village originally adopted its buffer policy long before MHDC entered the picture and has applied the policy too consistently for us to infer discriminatory purpose from its application in this case. Finally, MHDC called one member of the Village Board to the stand at trial. Nothing in her testimony supports an inference of invidious purpose.

In sum, the evidence does not warrant overturning the concurrent findings of both courts below. Respondents simply failed to carry their burden of proving that discriminatory purpose was a motivating factor in the Village's decision. This conclusion ends the constitutional inquiry. The court of Appeals' further finding that the Village's decision carried a discriminatory "ultimate effect" is without independent constitutional significance.

Reversed and *remanded*.

NOTES

1. Once the Court determined, in *Washington v. Davis*, that the constitutional standard was

discriminatory *purpose*, it had to deal with the fact that, in today's world, there will almost never be direct evidence of a racially discriminatory purpose. What this means is that, even if one were to assume as a fact that the Village of Arlington Heights refused to rezone *because* the Village wanted to keep blacks out, it would be very unlikely that the Village government would announce that "We are refusing to rezone in order to keep black people out of the village." Racial discrimination is far more sophisticated than that. A government authority that has racist motives will almost always cloak that motivation with a fig leaf of respectability. Thus, if a court is ever to find evidence of racially discriminatory purpose, it will have to look at circumstantial evidence.

The *Arlington Heights* Court noted that the first bit of circumstantial evidence of purpose was discriminatory effect, that is, where "the impact of the official action . . . 'bears more heavily on one race than another.'" But this evidence provides only a starting point, and "[a]bsent a pattern as stark as that in *Gomillion* or *Yick Wo*, impact alone is not determinative, and the Court must look to other evidence." What other evidence will be relevant? The Court mentioned the following:

(1) the historical background of the decision;
(2) the specific sequence of events leading up the challenged decision;
(3) departures from the normal procedural sequence;
(4) substantive departures, where, for example, the factors usually considered important by the decisionmaker strongly favor a decision contrary to the one reached;
(5) the legislative or administrative history.

Notwithstanding all of this evidence that the *Arlington Heights* Court suggested would be relevant, it is rarely sufficient to prove discriminatory purpose.

Personnel Adm'r of Massachusetts v. Feeney
442 U.S. 256 (1979)

[This case involved a challenge to a Massachusetts statute that gave a preference to veterans in state hiring. 98% of those benefited by the preference were male. The plaintiffs claimed that a preference that worked to benefit so many men and so few women was a gender classification. This case is reported at greater length in the Chapter 3 on Gender Classifications, *see* Ch. 3.D. 4. The portion of the case included here is the Court's description of what is required to prove discriminatory purpose.]

III

The appellee's ultimate argument rests upon the presumption, common to the criminal and civil law, that a person intends the natural and foreseeable consequences of his voluntary actions.

"Discriminatory purpose," however, implies more than intent as volition or intent as awareness of consequences. See *United Jewish Organizations v. Carey*, 430 U.S. 144, 179. It implies that the decisionmaker, in this case a state legislature, selected or reaffirmed a particular course of action at least in part "because of," not merely "in spite of," its adverse effects upon an identifiable group. Yet, nothing in the record demonstrates that this preference for veterans was originally devised or subsequently re-enacted because it would accomplish the collateral goal of keeping women in a stereotypic and predefined place in the Massachusetts Civil Service.

[The Court then determined that the veterans' preference was not a gender classification.]

NOTES

1. *Feeney* involved an alleged gender classification rather than an alleged racial classification, but the constitutional issue is the same—to what extent does an adverse impact, in this case on females, constitute purposeful discrimination. The discriminatory effect in *Feeney* was extremely robust—those benefited by the challenged statute were more than 98% male, and the legislature could not have been unaware of that fact. But the *Feeney* rejected "the presumption, common to the criminal and civil law, that a person intends the natural and foreseeable consequences of his voluntary actions." The Court conceded that the Massachusetts legislature had "intended" to prefer veterans and that "it cannot seriously be argued that the Legislature of Massachusetts could have been unaware that most veterans are men. It would thus be disingenuous to say that the adverse consequences of this legislation for women were unintended, in the sense that they were not volitional or in the sense that they were not foreseeable." But that was not what matter constitutionally. According to the Court:

> Discriminatory purpose, however, implies more than intent as volition or intent as awareness of consequences . . . It implies that the decisionmaker, in this case a state legislature, selected or reaffirmed a particular course of action at least in part "because of," not merely "in spite of," its adverse effects upon an identifiable group.

The Court's "because of" not merely "in spite of" standard would mean that statistical correlation would rarely be sufficient to prove discriminatory purpose. If a statute that is designed to benefit a population that is more than 98% male is not a gender classification, then there will be very, very few discriminatory purposes proven by evidence of discriminatory effect. The next case illustrates how difficult is to prove purpose from effect.

McCleskey v. Kemp
481 U.S. 279 (1987)

[Warren McCleskey, a black man, was convicted of armed robbery and murder in a Georgia state court. The victim was a white police officer. The jury imposed the death penalty. On appeal, McCleskey argued that the capital sentencing process in Georgia was racially discriminatory. As proof of racial bias in the capital sentencing process, McCleskey introduced the "Baldus Study," a statistical analysis of murder conviction sentencing in Georgia. Even after taking account of 230 variables that could have explained the disparities on nonracial grounds, the Baldus study concluded that defendants charged with killing white victims were 4.3 times as likely to receive a death sentence as defendants charged with killing black victims and that black defendants were 1.1 times as likely to receive a death sentence as other defendants. Thus, the Baldus study indicated that black defendants who kill white victims had the greatest likelihood of receiving the death penalty.]

Justice POWELL delivered the opinion of the Court.

McCleskey's first claim is that the Georgia capital punishment statute violates the Equal Protection Clause of the Fourteenth Amendment. He argues that race has infected the administration of Georgia's statute in two ways: persons who murder whites are more likely to be sentenced to death than persons who murder blacks, and black murderers are more likely to be sentenced to death than white murderers. As a black defendant who killed a white victim, McCleskey claims that the Baldus study demonstrates that he was discriminated against because of his race and because of the race of his victim. In its broadest form, McCleskey's claim of discrimination extends to every actor in the Georgia capital sentencing process, from the prosecutor who sought the death penalty and the jury that imposed the sentence, to the State itself that enacted the capital punishment statute and allows it to remain in effect despite its allegedly discriminatory application. We agree with the Court of Appeals, and every other court that has considered such a challenge, that this claim must fail.

A

Our analysis begins with the basic principle that a defendant who alleges an equal protection violation has the burden of proving "the existence of purposeful discrimination." *Whitus v. Georgia,* 385 U.S. 545, 550 (1967). A corollary to this principle is that a criminal defendant must prove that the purposeful discrimination "had a discriminatory effect" on him. *Wayte v. United States,* 470 U.S. 598, 608 (1985). Thus, to prevail under the Equal Protection Clause, McCleskey must prove that the decisionmakers in *his* case acted with discriminatory purpose. He offers no evidence specific to his own case that would support an inference that racial considerations played a part in his sentence. Instead, he relies solely on the Baldus study. McCleskey argues that the Baldus study compels an inference that his sentence rests on purposeful discrimination. McCleskey's claim that these statistics are sufficient proof of discrimination, without regard to the facts of a particular case, would extend to all capital cases in Georgia, at least where the victim was white and the defendant is black.

The Court has accepted statistics as proof of intent to discriminate in certain limited contexts. First, this Court has accepted statistical disparities as proof of an equal protection violation in the selection of the jury venire in a particular district. Although statistical proof normally must present a "stark" pattern to be accepted as the sole proof of discriminatory intent under the Constitution, *Arlington Heights v. Metropolitan Housing Dev. Corp.,* 429 U.S. 252, 266 (1977), "[b]ecause of the nature of the jury-selection task, ... we have permitted a finding of constitutional violation even when the statistical pattern does not approach [such] extremes." *Id.,* at 266, n. 13. Second, this Court has accepted statistics in the form of multiple-regression analysis to prove statutory violations under Title VII of the Civil Rights Act of 1964. *Bazemore v. Friday,* 478 U.S. 385, 400-401 (1986) (opinion of BRENNAN, J., concurring in part).

But the nature of the capital sentencing decision, and the relationship of the statistics to that decision, are fundamentally different from the corresponding elements in the venire-selection or Title VII cases. Most importantly, each particular decision to impose the death penalty is made by a petit jury selected from a properly constituted venire. Each jury is unique in its composition, and the Constitution requires that its decision rest on consideration of innumerable factors that vary according to the characteristics of the individual defendant and the facts of the particular capital offense. Thus, the application of an inference drawn from the general statistics to a specific decision in a trial and sentencing simply is not comparable to the application of an inference drawn from general statistics to a specific venire-selection or Title VII case. In those cases, the statistics relate to fewer entities, and fewer variables are relevant to the challenged decisions.

Another important difference between the cases in which we have accepted statistics as proof of discriminatory intent and this case is that, in the venire-selection and Title VII contexts, the decisionmaker has an opportunity to explain the statistical disparity. Here, the State has no practical opportunity to rebut the Baldus study. "[C]ontrolling considerations of ... public policy," *McDonald v. Pless,* 238 U.S. 264, 267 (1915), dictate that jurors "cannot be called ... to testify to the motives and influences that led to their verdict." *Chicago, B. & Q.R. Co. v. Babcock,* 204 U.S. 585, 593 (1907). Similarly, the policy considerations behind a prosecutor's traditionally "wide discretion" suggest the impropriety of our requiring prosecutors to defend their decisions to seek death penalties, "often years after they were made." Moreover, absent far stronger proof, it is unnecessary to seek such a rebuttal, because a legitimate and unchallenged explanation for the decision is apparent from the record: McCleskey committed an act for which the United States Constitution and Georgia laws permit imposition of the death penalty.

Finally, McCleskey's statistical proffer must be viewed in the context of his challenge. McCleskey challenges decisions at the heart of the State's criminal justice system. "[O]ne of society's most basic tasks is that of protecting the lives of its citizens and one of the most basic ways in which it achieves the task is through criminal laws against murder." *Gregg v. Georgia,* 428 U.S. 153, 226 (1976) (WHITE, J., concurring). Implementation of these laws necessarily requires discretionary judgments. Because discretion is essential to the criminal justice process, we would demand exceptionally clear proof before we would infer that the discretion has been abused. The unique nature of the decisions at issue in this case also counsels against adopting such an inference from the disparities indicated by the Baldus study. Accordingly, we hold that the Baldus study is clearly insufficient to support an inference that any of the decisionmakers in McCleskey's case acted with discriminatory purpose.

B

McCleskey also suggests that the Baldus study proves that the State as a whole has acted with a discriminatory purpose. He appears to argue that the State has violated the Equal Protection Clause by adopting the capital punishment statute and allowing it to remain in force despite its allegedly discriminatory application. But "'[d]iscriminatory purpose' ... implies more than intent as volition or intent as awareness of consequences. It implies that the decisionmaker, in this case a state legislature, selected or reaffirmed a particular course of action at least in part 'because of,' not merely 'in spite of,' its adverse effects upon an identifiable group." *Personnel Administrator of Massachusetts v. Feeney,* 442 U.S. 256, 279 (1979. For this claim to prevail, McCleskey would have to prove that the Georgia Legislature enacted or maintained the death penalty statute *because of* an anticipated racially discriminatory effect. In *Gregg v. Georgia, supra,* this Court found that the Georgia capital sentencing system could operate in a fair and neutral manner. There was no evidence then, and there is none now, that the Georgia Legislature enacted the capital punishment statute to further a racially discriminatory purpose.

Nor has McCleskey demonstrated that the legislature maintains the capital punishment statute because of the racially disproportionate impact suggested by the Baldus study. As legislatures necessarily have wide discretion in the choice of criminal laws and penalties, and as there were legitimate reasons for the Georgia Legislature to adopt and maintain capital punishment, we will not infer a discriminatory purpose on the part of the State of Georgia. Accordingly, we reject McCleskey's equal protection claims.

Justice BRENNAN, with whom Justice MARSHALL joins, and with whom Justice BLACKMUN and Justice STEVENS join in all but Part I, dissenting.

At some point in this case, Warren McCleskey doubtless asked his lawyer whether a jury was likely to sentence him to die. A candid reply to this question would have been disturbing. First, counsel would have to tell McCleskey that few of the details of the crime or of McCleskey's past criminal conduct were more important than the fact that his victim was white. Furthermore, counsel would feel bound to tell McCleskey that defendants charged with killing white victims in Georgia are 4.3 times as likely to be sentenced to death as defendants charged with killing blacks. In addition, frankness would compel the disclosure that it was more likely than not that the race of McCleskey's victim would determine whether he received a death sentence: 6 of every 11 defendants convicted of killing a white person would not have received the death penalty if their victims had been black while, among defendants with aggravating and mitigating factors comparable to McCleskey's, 20 of every 34 would not have been sentenced to die if their victims had been black. Finally, the assessment would not be complete without the information that cases involving black defendants and white victims are more likely to result in a death sentence than cases featuring any other racial combination of defendant and victim. The story could be told in a variety of ways, but McCleskey could not fail to grasp its essential narrative line: there was a significant chance that race would play a prominent role in determining if he lived or died.

The Baldus study indicates that, after taking into account some 230 nonracial factors that might legitimately influence a sentencer, the jury *more likely than not* would have spared McCleskey's life had his victim been black.

C

Evaluation of McCleskey's evidence cannot rest solely on the numbers themselves. We must also ask whether the conclusion suggested by those numbers is consonant with our understanding of history and human experience. Georgia's legacy of a race-conscious criminal justice system, as well as this Court's own recognition of the persistent danger that racial attitudes may affect criminal proceedings, indicates that McCleskey's claim is not a fanciful product of mere statistical artifice.

For many years, Georgia operated openly and formally precisely the type of dual system the evidence shows is still effectively in place. The criminal law expressly differentiated between crimes committed by and against blacks and whites, distinctions whose lineage traced back to the time of slavery. During the colonial period, black slaves who killed whites in Georgia, regardless of whether in self-defense or in defense of another, were automatically executed. A. Higginbotham, In the Matter of Color: Race in the American Legal Process 256 (1978). In more recent times, some 40 years ago, Gunnar Myrdal's epochal study of American race relations produced findings mirroring McCleskey's evidence.

This historical review of Georgia criminal law is not intended as a bill of indictment calling the State to account for past transgressions. Citation of past practices does not justify the automatic condemnation of current ones. But it would be unrealistic to ignore the influence of history in assessing the plausible implications of McCleskey's evidence. "[A]mericans share a historical experience that has resulted in individuals within the culture ubiquitously attaching a significance to race that is irrational and often outside their awareness." Lawrence, The Id, The Ego, and Equal Protection: Reckoning With Unconscious Racism, 39 Stan. L. Rev. 327 (1987).

NOTES

1. Why was Warren McCleskey sentenced to the death penalty? According to the five-person majority, it was because he committed a crime for which the penalty is death. According to the four-person dissent, because he was black and had killed a white man — "the jury more likely than not would have spared McCleskey's life had his victim been black." The dissent noted that McCleskey's death sentence was imposed by a state with a long history in which "[t]he criminal law expressly differentiated between crimes committed by and against blacks and whites, distinctions whose lineage traced back to the time of slavery." None of this was relevant or persuasive to the majority, which insisted that McCleskey would have to prove that his conviction was because of, and not in spite of, his race and the race of his victim. The Baldus study clearly showed that race was a factor, and probably a significant factor in decisions to impose capital punishment, but that evidence was not sufficient to satisfy the high bar established by the majority for proof of discriminatory purpose.

What was going on in jury rooms in the state of Georgia? Why did race seem to be such an important factor even if it could not be proven that the death penalty was imposed as a result of discriminatory purpose? The dissent cited a law review article, Charles R. Lawrence III, *The Id, The Ego, and Equal Protection: Reckoning With Unconscious Racism*, 39 Stan. L. Rev. 327 (1987). This is an influential article, the eighth most-cited law review article of all time. *See* Fred R. Shapiro and Michelle Pearse, *Most-Cited Law Review Articles of All Time*, 110 Michigan L. Rev. 1483 (2012). In it, Lawrence argues that the Court's reasoning in *Washington v. Davis* creates a false dichotomy under which facially neutral government actions are either (1) intentionally discriminatory and therefore unconstitutional, or (2) unintentionally discriminatory and therefore constitutional. This division ignores the fact that in America, with its long history of slavery, racial segregation, and racial discrimination, "a large part of the behavior that produces racial discrimination is influenced by unconscious racial motivation. *Id.* at 322. For Lawrence, "A crucial factor in the process that produces unconscious racism is the tacitly transmitted cultural stereotype. If an individual has never known a black doctor or lawyer or is exposed to blacks only through a mass media where they are portrayed in the stereotyped roles of comedian, criminal, musician, or athlete, he is likely to deduce that blacks as a group are naturally inclined toward certain behavior and unfit for certain roles." *Id.* at 343. In America today, where explicit racism is widely viewed as wrong and culturally unacceptable, a person will not typically be aware of the influence of racist stereotypes, and thus, a search of "purposeful" or "intentional" racial discrimination will come up empty.

Lawrence notes that in the *Arlington Heights* case, the denial of the zoning variance had a cultural meaning that demeaned blacks, since there was a long history of residential segregation, statutorily mandated housing segregation, and restrictive covenants that prohibited the sale of property to black people. In *Washington v. Davis*, Lawrence noted the presence of two relevant cultural stereotypes—that blacks were not to hold positions of authority (e.g. police officer), and that, due to racial inferiority, blacks were less likely to perform well on an exam testing proficiency in verbal and written language skills. Evidence that these stereotypes underlay the exclusion of black applicants from the police force might help show that the use of an exam that had a foreseeably discriminatory effect was in fact a racist decision. Since the Court, however, insisted on evidence of discriminatory purpose, none of this evidence would be relevant.

There is another, surprising effect of the Court's insistence on proof of discriminatory purpose. When taken together with the Court's holding in affirmative action cases that *all* racial classifications receive strict scrutiny, (*see* Sec. F, *infra*), the intent standard seems to turn the purpose of the Equal Protection Clause on its head. The overriding purpose of the Equal Protection Clause, as the Court noted in *Strauder*, was to protect the newly freed slaves from the oppressions of those who had formerly exercised unlimited dominion over them. Yet it is hard to see that purpose at work in recent court decisions. Professor David Kairys explains:

> Taken together, the Court's race decisions over the past few decades make it quite easy for white plaintiffs to establish a claim of reverse discrimination to invalidate good faith legislative and executive efforts aimed at achieving meaningful equality, but near impossible for minority plaintiffs to establish a claim of discrimination, even under circumstances closely resembling traditional discrimination against minorities or pre-Brown segregation. The Court has essentially established two distinct sets of rules, assumptions, and approaches--one characterized by insensitivity to race and the other by hypersensitivity to race. Which applies in particular circumstances depends on whether whites or minorities are claiming discrimination. The result of this retrenchment is that over the last few decades almost all of the winning plaintiffs in equal protection race cases before the Supreme Court have been white. David Kairys, *Unconscious Racism*, 83 Temple L. Rev. 857 (2011).

F. AFFIRMATIVE ACTION

For most of American history the purpose of the government's race-conscious decisions was virtually always to discriminate against racial minorities. It was in this context of invidious racial discrimination that the rules about strict scrutiny of racial classifications developed, and it was in this context that the claim was made that our Constitution ought to be colorblind. Things began to change in the 1970s when government actors began to take race-conscious action to *benefit* rather than to *harm* racial minorities. Although the reasons for such programs were not always formally identified, surely a large measure of justification was America's long history of racial discrimination. Racially-imposed slavery existed for more than two hundred years and state-imposed racial segregation and discrimination was common for an additional one hundred years. The effects of that long-standing discrimination would not simply disappear as soon as states stopped actively discriminating. Evidence of current effects of past racial discrimination in America was widespread, and Justice Brennan's concurring and dissenting opinion in the *Bakke* case set forth some of it in the context of admission to the California Medical School at Davis:

> From the inception of our national life, Negroes have been subjected to unique legal disabilities impairing access to equal educational opportunity. Under slavery, penal sanctions were imposed upon anyone attempting to educate Negroes. After enactment of the Fourteenth Amendment the States continued to deny Negroes equal educational opportunity, enforcing a strict policy of segregation that itself stamped Negroes as inferior, *Brown I*, that relegated minorities to inferior educational institutions, and that denied them intercourse in the mainstream of professional life necessary to advancement. Segregation was not limited to public facilities, moreover, but was enforced by criminal penalties against private action as well. Thus, as late as 1908, this Court enforced a state criminal conviction against a private college for teaching Negroes together with whites.
>
> *Green v. County School Board*, 391 U.S. 430 (1968), gave explicit recognition to the fact that the habit of discrimination and the cultural tradition of race prejudice cultivated by

centuries of legal slavery and segregation were not immediately dissipated when *Brown I*, announced the constitutional principle that equal educational opportunity and participation in all aspects of American life could not be denied on the basis of race. Rather, massive official and private resistance prevented, and to a lesser extent still prevents, attainment of equal opportunity in education at all levels and in the professions. The generation of minority students applying to Davis Medical School since it opened in 1968—most of whom were born before or about the time *Brown I* was decided—clearly have been victims of this discrimination. Judicial decrees recognizing discrimination in public education in California testify to the fact of widespread discrimination suffered by California-born minority applicants; many minority group members living in California, moreover, were born and reared in school districts in Southern States segregated by law. Since separation of school-children by race "generates a feeling of inferiority as to their status in the community that may affect their hearts and minds in a way unlikely ever to be undone," *Brown I*, supra, 347 U.S., at 494, the conclusion is inescapable that applicants to medical school must be few indeed who endured the effects of de jure segregation, the resistance to *Brown I*, or the equally debilitating pervasive private discrimination fostered by our long history of official discrimination, cf. *Reitman v. Mulkey*, 387 U.S. 369 (1967), and yet come to the starting line with an education equal to whites. *Bakke*, 438 U.S. at 371 (Brennan, J., concurring an dissenting).

It is likely that the goal of remedying the effects of past discrimination was a substantial factor in the Davis Medical School's decision to give minorities special consideration in the admissions process.

As it turned out, however, remedying the effects of past societal discrimination, absent an appropriate judicial, legislative, or administrative finding of a past violation of a constitutional or statutory violation, would be insufficient to justify race-conscious government action. In what came to be called "affirmative action," the Court adopted a very demanding standard of justification. In the following case, the Supreme Court began the process of developing a standard of review for race-conscious decisions that would benefit minorities.

Regents of University of California v. Bakke
438 U.S. 265 (1978)

[The admissions committee of the Medical School at the University of California at Davis adopted a policy that set aside sixteen of one hundred seats in the first year class for minority students. Alan Bakke, a white applicant who was rejected, filed suit alleging that this affirmative action program for minorities violated the Equal Protection Clause. There was no majority opinion for the Supreme Court. Justice Powell wrote an opinion in which no other Justice joined. Powell's opinion, however, was widely viewed as stating the rule of the case. This focus on Powell's opinion followed from the fact that he joined with one group of four Justices (the Stevens group) in providing five votes for the view that the existing program at the medical school, which set aside a certain number of seats for minorities, violated Title VI of the Civil Rights Act. In addition, Powell joined with another group of four Justices (the Brennan group) in providing five votes for the position that it was appropriate for the medical school to take race into account as a factor in admissions process. In the years following *Bakke*, there was some dispute in the lower courts as to the proper weight that should be given to Powell's opinion, but this dispute became moot when a majority of the Court in *Grutter v. Bollinger*, 539 U.S. 306 (2003) adopted Powell's view. What follows here is Justice Powell's view of when it is appropriate for a university to take race into account in the admissions process.]

Mr. Justice POWELL announced the judgment of the Court.

Petitioner does not deny that decisions based on race or ethnic origin by faculties and administrations of state universities are reviewable under the Fourteenth Amendment. For his part, respondent does not argue that all racial or ethnic classifications are *per se* invalid. The parties do disagree as to the level of judicial scrutiny to be applied to the special admissions program. Petitioner argues that the court below erred in applying strict scrutiny, as this inexact term has been applied in our cases. That level of review, petitioner asserts, should be reserved for classifications that disadvantage "discrete and insular minorities." See *United States v. Carolene Products Co.,* 304 U.S. 144, 152 n. 4 (1938). Respondent, on the other hand, contends that the California court correctly rejected the notion that the degree of judicial scrutiny accorded a particular racial or ethnic classification hinges upon membership in a discrete and insular minority and duly recognized that the "rights established [by the Fourteenth Amendment] are personal rights." *Shelley v. Kraemer,* 334 U.S. 1, 22 (1948).

En route to this crucial battle over the scope of judicial review, the parties fight a sharp preliminary action over the proper characterization of the special admissions program. Petitioner prefers to view it as establishing a "goal" of minority representation in the Medical School. Respondent, echoing the courts below, labels it a racial quota.

This semantic distinction is beside the point: The special admissions program is undeniably a classification based on race and ethnic background. To the extent that there existed a pool of at least minimally qualified minority applicants to fill the 16 special admissions seats, white applicants could compete only for 84 seats in the entering class, rather than the 100 open to minority applicants. Whether this limitation is described as a quota or a goal, it is a line drawn on the basis of race and ethnic status.

The guarantees of the Fourteenth Amendment extend to all persons. Its language is explicit: "No State shall . . . deny to any person within its jurisdiction the equal protection of the laws." It is settled beyond question that the "rights created by the first section of the Fourteenth Amendment are, by its terms, guaranteed to the individual. The rights established are personal rights." *Shelley v. Kraemer,* 335 U.S. 1, 22 (1948). The guarantee of equal protection cannot mean one thing when applied to one individual and something else when applied to a person of another color. If both are not accorded the same protection, then it is not equal.

Nevertheless, petitioner argues that the court below erred in applying strict scrutiny to the special admissions program because white males, such as respondent, are not a "discrete and insular minority" requiring extraordinary protection from the majoritarian political process. *Carolene Products Co., supra,* 304 U.S., at 152–153 n. 4. This rationale, however, has never been invoked in our decisions as a prerequisite to subjecting racial or ethnic distinctions to strict scrutiny. Nor has this Court held that discreteness and insularity constitute necessary preconditions to a holding that a particular classification is invidious. These characteristics may be relevant in deciding whether or not to add new types of classifications to the list of "suspect" categories or whether a particular classification survives close examination. See, *e. g., Massachusetts Board of Retirement v. Murgia,* 427 U.S. 307, 313 (1976) (age); *San Antonio Independent School Dist. v. Rodriquez,* 411 U.S. 1, 28 (1973) (wealth); *Graham v. Richardson,* 403 U.S. 365, 372 (1971) (aliens). Racial and ethnic classifications, however, are subject to stringent examination without regard to these additional characteristics. We declared as much in the first cases explicitly to recognize racial distinctions as suspect:

> Distinctions between citizens solely because of their ancestry are by their very nature odious to a free people whose institutions are founded upon the doctrine of equality. *Hirabayashi*, 320 U.S., at 100.

> [A]ll legal restrictions which curtail the civil rights of a single racial group are immediately suspect. That is not to say that all such restrictions are unconstitutional. It is to say that courts must subject them to the most rigid scrutiny. *Korematsu*, 323 U.S., at 216.

The Court has never questioned the validity of those pronouncements. Racial and ethnic distinctions of any sort are inherently suspect and thus call for the most exacting judicial examination.

B

This perception of racial and ethnic distinctions is rooted in our Nation's constitutional and demographic history. The Court's initial view of the Fourteenth Amendment was that its "one pervading purpose" was "the freedom of the slave race, the security and firm establishment of that freedom, and the protection of the newly-made freeman and citizen from the oppressions of those who had formerly exercised dominion over him." *Slaughter-House Cases*, 16 Wall. 36, 71 (1873). The Equal Protection Clause, however, was "[v]irtually strangled in infancy by post-civil-war judicial reactionism." It was relegated to decades of relative desuetude while the Due Process Clause of the Fourteenth Amendment, after a short germinal period, flourished as a cornerstone in the Court's defense of property and liberty of contract. In that cause, the Fourteenth Amendment's "one pervading purpose" was displaced. See, *e. g., Plessy v. Ferguson*, 163 U.S. 537 (1896). It was only as the era of substantive due process came to a close that the Equal Protection Clause began to attain a genuine measure of vitality, see, *e. g., United States v. Carolene Products*, 304 U.S. 144 (1938).

By that time it was no longer possible to peg the guarantees of the Fourteenth Amendment to the struggle for equality of one racial minority. During the dormancy of the Equal Protection Clause, the United States had become a Nation of minorities. Each had to struggle — and to some extent struggles still — to overcome the prejudices not of a monolithic majority, but of a "majority" composed of various minority groups of whom it was said — perhaps unfairly in many cases — that a shared characteristic was a willingness to disadvantage other groups. As the Nation filled with the stock of many lands, the reach of the Clause was gradually extended to all ethnic groups seeking protection from official discrimination. See *Strauder v. West Virginia*, 100 U.S. 303 (1880) (Celtic Irishmen) (dictum); *Yick Wo v. Hopkins*, 118 U.S. 356 (1886) (Chinese); *Truax v. Raich*, 239 U.S. 33, 41 (1915) (Austrian resident aliens); *Korematsu, supra* (Japanese); *Hernandez v. Texas*, 347 U.S. 475 (1954) (Mexican-Americans). The guarantees of equal protection, said the Court in *Yick Wo*, "are universal in their application, to all persons within the territorial jurisdiction, without regard to any differences of race, of color, or of nationality; and the equal protection of the laws is a pledge of the protection of equal laws." 118 U.S., at 369.

Although many of the Framers of the Fourteenth Amendment conceived of its primary function as bridging the vast distance between members of the Negro race and the white "majority," *Slaughter-House Cases, supra,* the Amendment itself was framed in universal terms, without reference to color, ethnic origin, or condition of prior servitude. As this Court recently remarked in interpreting the 1866 Civil Rights Act to extend to claims of racial discrimination against white persons, "the 39th Congress was intent upon establishing in the federal law a broader principle than would have been necessary simply to meet the particular and immediate plight of the newly freed Negro slaves." *McDonald v. Santa Fe Trail Transportation Co.,* 427 U.S. 273, 296 (1976). And that legislation was specifically broadened in 1870 to ensure that "all persons," not merely "citizens," would enjoy equal rights under the law. See *Runyon v. McCrary,* 427 U.S. 160, 192–202 (1976) (WHITE, J., dissenting). Indeed, it is not unlikely that among the Framers were many who would have applauded a reading of the Equal Protection Clause that states a principle of universal application and is responsive to the racial, ethnic, and cultural diversity of the Nation.

Over the past 30 years, this Court has embarked upon the crucial mission of interpreting the Equal Protection Clause with the view of assuring to all persons "the protection of equal laws," *Yick Wo, supra,* in a Nation confronting a legacy of slavery and racial discrimination. Because the landmark decisions in this area arose in response to the continued exclusion of Negroes from the mainstream of American society, they could be characterized as involving discrimination by the "majority" white race against the Negro minority. But they need not be read as depending upon that characterization for their results. It suffices to say that "[o]ver the years, this Court has consistently repudiated '[d]istinctions between citizens solely because of their ancestry' as being 'odious to a free people whose institutions are founded upon the doctrine of equality.'" *Loving v. Virginia,* 388 U.S. 1, 11 (1967), quoting *Hirabayashi,* 320 U.S., at 100.

Petitioner urges us to adopt for the first time a more restrictive view of the Equal Protection Clause and hold that discrimination against members of the white "majority" cannot be suspect if its purpose can be characterized as "benign." The clock of our liberties, however, cannot be turned back to 1868. *Brown v. Board of Education, supra,* 347 U.S., at 492; accord, *Loving v. Virginia, supra,* 388 U.S., at 9. It is far too late to argue that the guarantee of equal protection to *all* persons permits the recognition of special wards entitled to a degree of protection greater than that accorded others. "The Fourteenth Amendment is not directed solely against discrimination due to a 'two-class theory'—that is, based upon differences between 'white' and Negro." *Hernandez,* 347 U.S., at 478.

Once the artificial line of a "two-class theory" of the Fourteenth Amendment is put aside, the difficulties entailed in varying the level of judicial review according to a perceived "preferred" status of a particular racial or ethnic minority are intractable. The concepts of "majority" and "minority" necessarily reflect temporary arrangements and political judgments. As observed above, the white "majority" itself is composed of various minority groups, most of which can lay claim to a history of prior discrimination at the hands of the State and private individuals. Not all of these groups can receive preferential treatment and corresponding judicial tolerance of distinctions drawn in terms of race and nationality, for then the only "majority" left would be a new minority of white Anglo-Saxon Protestants. There is no principled basis for deciding which groups would merit "heightened judicial solicitude" and which would not. Courts would be asked to evaluate the extent of the prejudice and consequent harm suffered by various minority groups. Those whose societal injury is thought to exceed some arbitrary level of tolerability then would be entitled to preferential classifications at the expense of individuals belonging to other groups. Those classifications would be free from exacting judicial scrutiny. As these preferences began to have their desired effect, and the consequences of past discrimination were undone, new judicial rankings would be necessary. The kind of variable sociological and political analysis necessary to produce such rankings simply does not lie within the judicial competence—even if they otherwise were politically feasible and socially desirable.

Moreover, there are serious problems of justice connected with the idea of preference itself. First, it may not always be clear that a so-called preference is in fact benign. Courts may be asked to validate burdens imposed upon individual members of a particular group in order to advance the group's general interest. See *United Jewish Organizations v. Carey,* 430 U.S., at 172–173. (BRENNAN, J., concurring in part). Nothing in the Constitution supports the notion that individuals may be asked to suffer otherwise impermissible burdens in order to enhance the societal standing of their ethnic groups. Second, preferential programs may only reinforce common stereotypes holding that certain groups are unable to achieve success without special protection based on a factor having no relationship to individual worth. See *DeFunis v. Odegaard,* 416 U.S. 312, 343 (1974) (Douglas, J., dissenting). Third, there is a measure of inequity in forcing innocent persons in respondent's position to bear the burdens of redressing grievances not of their making.

By hitching the meaning of the Equal Protection Clause to these transitory considerations, we would be holding, as a constitutional principle, that judicial scrutiny of classifications touching on racial and ethnic background may vary with the ebb and flow of political forces. Disparate constitutional tolerance of such classifications well may serve to exacerbate racial and ethnic antagonisms rather than alleviate them. *United Jewish Organizations, supra,* 430 U.S., at 173–174 (BRENNAN, J., concurring in part). Also, the mutability of a constitutional principle, based upon shifting political and social judgments, undermines the chances for consistent application of the Constitution from one generation to the next, a critical feature of its coherent interpretation. *Pollock v. Farmers' Loan & Trust Co.,* 157 U.S. 429, 650–651 (1895) (White, J., dissenting). In expounding the Constitution, the Court's role is to discern "principles sufficiently absolute to give them roots throughout the community and continuity over significant periods of time, and to lift them above the level of the pragmatic political judgments of a particular time and place." A. Cox, The Role of the Supreme Court in American Government 114 (1976).

If it is the individual who is entitled to judicial protection against classifications based upon his racial or ethnic background because such distinctions impinge upon personal rights, rather than the individual only because of his membership in a particular group, then constitutional standards may be applied consistently. Political judgments regarding the necessity for the particular classification may be weighed in the constitutional balance, *Korematsu v. United States,* 323 U.S. 214 (1944), but the standard of justification will remain constant. This is as it should be, since those political judgments are the product of rough compromise struck by contending groups within the democratic process. When they touch upon an individual's race or ethnic background, he is entitled to a judicial determination that the burden he is asked to bear on that basis is precisely tailored to serve a compelling governmental interest. The Constitution guarantees that right to every person regardless of his background. *Shelley v. Kraemer,* 334 U.S., at 22; *Missouri ex rel. Gaines v. Canada,* 305 U.S., at 351.

IV

We have held that in "order to justify the use of a suspect classification, a State must show that its purpose or interest is both constitutionally permissible and substantial, and that its use of the classification is 'necessary . . . to the accomplishment' of its purpose or the safeguarding of its interest." *In re Griffiths,* 413 U.S. 717, 721–722 (1973); *Loving v. Virginia,* 388 U.S., at 11;

McLaughlin v. Florida, 379 U.S. 184, 196 (1964). The special admissions program purports to serve the purposes of: (i) "reducing the historic deficit of traditionally disfavored minorities in medical schools and in the medical profession," (ii) countering the effects of societal discrimination; (iii) increasing the number of physicians who will practice in communities currently underserved; and (iv) obtaining the educational benefits that flow from an ethnically diverse student body. It is necessary to decide which, if any, of these purposes is substantial enough to support the use of a suspect classification.

A

If petitioner's purpose is to assure within its student body some specified percentage of a particular group merely because of its race or ethnic origin, such a preferential purpose must be rejected not as insubstantial but as facially invalid. Preferring members of any one group for no reason other than race or ethnic origin is discrimination for its own sake. This the Constitution forbids. *E. g., Loving v. Virginia, supra*, 388 U.S., at 11; *McLaughlin v. Florida, supra*, 379 U.S., at 196 (1954).

B

The State certainly has a legitimate and substantial interest in ameliorating, or eliminating where feasible, the disabling effects of identified discrimination. The line of school desegregation cases, commencing with *Brown*, attests to the importance of this state goal and the commitment of the judiciary to affirm all lawful means toward its attainment. In the school cases, the States were required by court order to redress the wrongs worked by specific instances of racial discrimination. That goal was far more focused than the remedying of the effects of "societal discrimination," an amorphous concept of injury that may be ageless in its reach into the past.

We have never approved a classification that aids persons perceived as members of relatively victimized groups at the expense of other innocent individuals in the absence of judicial, legislative, or administrative findings of constitutional or statutory violations. After such findings have been made, the governmental interest in preferring members of the injured groups at the expense of others is substantial, since the legal rights of the victims must be vindicated. In such a case, the extent of the injury and the consequent remedy will have been judicially, legislatively, or administratively defined. Also, the remedial action usually remains subject to continuing oversight to assure that it will work the least harm possible to other innocent persons competing for the benefit. Without such findings of constitutional or statutory violations, it cannot be said that the government has any greater interest in helping one individual than in refraining from harming another. Thus, the government has no compelling justification for inflicting such harm.

Petitioner does not purport to have made, and is in no position to make, such findings. Its broad mission is education, not the formulation of any legislative policy or the adjudication of particular claims of illegality. For reasons similar to those stated in Part III of this opinion, isolated segments of our vast governmental structures are not competent to make those decisions, at least in the absence of legislative mandates and legislatively determined criteria. Before relying upon these sorts of findings in establishing a racial classification, a governmental body must have the authority and capability to establish, in the record, that the classification is responsive to identified discrimination. Lacking this capability, petitioner has not carried its burden of justification on this issue.

Hence, the purpose of helping certain groups whom the faculty of the Davis Medical School perceived as victims of "societal discrimination" does not justify a classification that imposes disadvantages upon persons like respondent, who bear no responsibility for whatever harm the beneficiaries of the special admissions program are thought to have suffered. To hold otherwise would be to convert a remedy heretofore reserved for violations of legal rights into a privilege that all institutions throughout the Nation could grant at their pleasure to whatever groups are perceived as victims of societal discrimination. That is a step we have never approved.

C

Petitioner identifies, as another purpose of its program, improving the delivery of health-care services to communities currently underserved. It may be assumed that in some situations a State's interest in facilitating the health care of its citizens is sufficiently compelling to support the use of a suspect classification. But there is virtually no evidence in the record indicating that petitioner's special admissions program is either needed or geared to promote that goal.

D

The fourth goal asserted by petitioner is the attainment of a diverse student body. This clearly is a constitutionally permissible goal for an institution of higher education. Academic freedom, though not a specifically enumerated constitutional right, long has been viewed as a special concern of the First Amendment. The freedom of a university to make its own judgments as to education includes the selection of its student body. Mr. Justice Frankfurter summarized the "four essential freedoms" that constitute academic freedom:

> It is the business of a university to provide that atmosphere which is most conducive to speculation, experiment and creation. It is an atmosphere in which there prevail "the four essential freedoms" of a university—to determine for itself on academic grounds who may teach, what may be taught, how it shall be taught, and who may be admitted to study. *Sweezy v. New Hampshire*, 354 U.S. 234, 263 (1957) (concurring in result).

The atmosphere of "speculation, experiment and creation"—so essential to the quality of higher education—is widely believed to be promoted by a diverse student body. As the Court noted in *Keyishian*, it is not too much to say that the "nation's future depends upon leaders trained through wide exposure" to the ideas and mores of students as diverse as this Nation of many peoples.

Thus, in arguing that its universities must be accorded the right to select those students who will contribute the most to the "robust exchange of ideas," petitioner invokes a countervailing constitutional interest, that of the First Amendment. In this light, petitioner must be viewed as seeking to achieve a goal that is of paramount importance in the fulfillment of its mission.

Ethnic diversity, however, is only one element in a range of factors a university properly may consider in attaining the goal of a heterogeneous student body. Although a university must have wide discretion in making the sensitive judgments as to who should be admitted, constitutional limitations protecting individual rights may not be disregarded. Respondent urges—and the courts below have held—that petitioner's dual admissions program is a racial classification that impermissibly infringes his rights under the Fourteenth Amendment. As the interest of diversity is compelling in the context of a university's admissions program, the question remains whether the program's racial classification is necessary to promote this interest.

V

It may be assumed that the reservation of a specified number of seats in each class for individuals from the preferred ethnic groups would contribute to the attainment of considerable ethnic diversity in the student body. But petitioner's argument that this is the only effective means of serving the interest of diversity is seriously flawed. In a most fundamental sense the argument misconceives the nature of the state interest that would justify consideration of race or ethnic background. It is not an interest in simple ethnic diversity, in which a specified percentage of the student body is in effect guaranteed to be members of selected ethnic groups, with the remaining percentage an undifferentiated aggregation of students. The diversity that furthers a compelling state interest encompasses a far broader array of qualifications and characteristics of which racial or ethnic origin is but a single though important element. Petitioner's special admissions program, focused *solely* on ethnic diversity, would hinder rather than further attainment of genuine diversity.

Nor would the state interest in genuine diversity be served by expanding petitioner's two-track system into a multitrack program with a prescribed number of seats set aside for each identifiable category of applicants. Indeed, it is inconceivable that a university would thus pursue the logic of petitioner's two-track program to the illogical end of insulating each category of applicants with certain desired qualifications from competition with all other applicants.

The experience of other university admissions programs, which take race into account in achieving the educational diversity valued by the First Amendment, demonstrates that the assignment of a fixed number of places to a minority group is not a necessary means toward that end. An illuminating example is found in the Harvard College program:

"In recent years Harvard College has expanded the concept of diversity to include students from disadvantaged economic, racial and ethnic groups. Harvard College now recruits not only Californians or Louisianans but also blacks and Chicanos and other minority students ...

> In practice, this new definition of diversity has meant that race has been a factor in some admission decisions. When the Committee on Admissions reviews the large middle group of applicants who are 'admissible' and deemed capable of doing good work in their courses, the race of an applicant may tip the balance in his favor just as geographic origin or a life spent on a farm may tip the balance in other candidates' cases. A farm boy from Idaho can bring something to Harvard College that a Bostonian cannot offer. Similarly, a black student can usually bring something that a white person cannot offer ...

> In Harvard College admissions the Committee has not set target-quotas for the number of blacks, or of musicians, football players, physicists or Californians to be admitted in a given year.... But that awareness [of the necessity of including more than a token number of black students] does not mean that the Committee sets a minimum number of blacks or of people from west of the Mississippi who are to be admitted. It means only that in choosing among thousands of applicants who are not only 'admissible' academically but have other strong qualities, the Committee, with a number of criteria in mind, pays some attention to distribution among many types and categories of students. App. to Brief for Columbia University, Harvard University, Stanford University, and the

University of Pennsylvania, as *Amici Curiae* 2–3.

In such an admissions program, race or ethnic background may be deemed a "plus" in a particular applicant's file, yet it does not insulate the individual from comparison with all other candidates for the available seats. The file of a particular black applicant may be examined for his potential contribution to diversity without the factor of race being decisive when compared, for example, with that of an applicant identified as an Italian-American if the latter is thought to exhibit qualities more likely to promote beneficial educational pluralism. Such qualities could include exceptional personal talents, unique work or service experience, leadership potential, maturity, demonstrated compassion, a history of overcoming disadvantage, ability to communicate with the poor, or other qualifications deemed important. In short, an admissions program operated in this way is flexible enough to consider all pertinent elements of diversity in light of the particular qualifications of each applicant, and to place them on the same footing for consideration, although not necessarily according them the same weight. Indeed, the weight attributed to particular quality may vary from year to year depending upon the "mix" both of the student body and the applicants for the incoming class.

B

The fatal flaw in petitioner's preferential program is its disregard of individual rights as guaranteed by the Fourteenth Amendment. *Shelley v. Kraemer*, 334 U.S., at 22. Such rights are not absolute. But when a State's distribution of benefits or imposition of burdens hinges on ancestry or the color of a person's skin, that individual is entitled to a demonstration that the challenged classification is necessary to promote a substantial state interest. Petitioner has failed to carry this burden. For this reason, that portion of the California court's judgment holding petitioner's special admissions program invalid under the Fourteenth Amendment must be affirmed.

C

In enjoining petitioner from ever considering the race of any applicant, however, the courts below failed to recognize that the State has a substantial interest that legitimately may be served by a properly devised admissions program involving the competitive consideration of race and ethnic origin. For this reason, so much of the California court's judgment as enjoins petitioner from any consideration of the race of any applicant must be reversed.

VI

With respect to respondent's entitlement to an injunction directing his admission to the Medical School, petitioner has conceded that it could not carry its burden of proving that, but for the existence of its unlawful special admissions program, respondent still would not have been admitted. Hence, respondent is entitled to the injunction, and that portion of the judgment must be *affirmed*.

NOTES

1. Justice Powell's *Bakke* opinion, although joined by no other Justice, established three basic principles that have become part of the foundation of the Supreme Court's rules on affirmative action. The first is that *all* racial classifications, whether invidious or remedial, are suspicious and

will receive the same level of strict scrutiny. The second is that it is not permissible to use race-conscious decisions to rectify the present effects of past societal discrimination. The third is that, absent the rather unlikely circumstance in which an institution will identify itself as an unlawful actor, the only purpose that universities may pursue when they make race-conscious decisions is the promotion of diversity. None of these three principles necessarily followed from the Supreme Court's pre-*Bakke* precedents.

Powell's first claim, that all racial classifications are equally suspect, flies in the face of the Court's earlier decisions in *Strauder* and *Carolene Products*. The *Strauder* Court held that the *one pervading purpose* of the Equal Protection Clause was the freedom of the slave race and the protection of the newly made freeman from oppression. Clearly, that view of the Equal Protection Clause would prohibit racial classifications that discriminated *against* racial minorities, but would not address the racial classifications designed to *benefit* minorities. Further, the famous Footnote 4 of the *Carolene Products* case spoke about heightened scrutiny of classifications that disadvantaged a discrete and insular minority. White males, like Alan Bakke, are not members of a group that is a discrete and insular minority. Notwithstanding these precedents, however, Justice Powell purported to find in the Supreme Court precedents support for his conclusion that all racial classifications were equally objectionable.

Powell's second basic principle was that addressing the effects of societal discrimination was not a compelling purpose that would justify race-conscious classifications. A government institution could only use race in a remedial way if there had been a prior administrative, judicial, or legislative finding of a statutory or constitutional violation. Justice Brennan disagreed:

> Davis' articulated purpose of remedying the effects of past societal discrimination is, under our cases, sufficiently important to justify the use of race-conscious admissions programs where there is a sound basis for concluding that minority underrepresentation is substantial and chronic, and that the handicap of past discrimination is impeding access of minorities to the Medical School.
>
> Properly construed, therefore, our prior cases unequivocally show that a state government may adopt race-conscious programs if the purpose of such programs is to remove the disparate racial impact its actions might otherwise have and if there is reason to believe that the disparate impact is itself the product of past discrimination, whether its own or that of society at large. There is no question that Davis' program is valid under this test.
>
> Davis clearly could conclude that the serious and persistent underrepresentation of minorities in medicine depicted by these statistics is the result of handicaps under which minority applicants labor as a consequence of a background of deliberate, purposeful discrimination against minorities in education and in society generally, as well as in the medical profession. *Bakke*, 432 U.S. at 362 (Brennan, J., concurring and dissenting).

The effect of Powell's view was that it would be very rare for a governmental actor, acting of its own accord, to take race-conscious action to address the effects of societal discrimination. Thus, the remedial use of race was limited to situations where there had been either (1) a legislative finding of past discrimination, *see e.g., Fullilove v. Klutznick,* 448 U.S. 448 (1980) (upholding a federal statute requiring a 10% set aside for minority business enterprises after Congress had made legislative findings of statutory violations); (2) a judicial finding of past discrimination, *see e.g., Local 28 of Sheet Metal Workers' Intern. Ass'n v. E.E.O.C.*, 478 U.S. 421 (1986), (upholding a federal district court decision that had, as a remedial measure, ordered a union to end its discriminatory practice and to admit a certain percentage of nonwhites to union membership; or (3) an administrative finding of past discrimination, *see e.g., id.* at 427 (noting the decision of the New York State Commission for Human Rights determining that petitioners had excluded blacks from the union and the apprenticeship program in violation of state law).

Powell's limitation on the remedial use of race left one compelling interest open to universities--the achievement of a diverse student body. Although diversity may be a very important aspect of university education, an exclusive focus on diversity as justification to make race-based admission decisions would preclude arguments about basic fairness and the recognition of the handicaps that black Americans labor against.

For more than fifteen years after *Powell's* opinion in *Bakke* (not until 1995), the Supreme Court did not issue an affirmative action opinion that was joined by a majority of the court. This meant that, for a long time, it was difficult to divine where exactly the law of affirmative action stood. In the following case from 1989, again without a majority opinion, the Court discusses the power of a local government to take race-conscious action to address discrimination in the local construction industry.

City of Richmond v. J.A. Croson Co.
488 U.S. 469 (1989)

Justice O'CONNOR announced the judgment of the Court and delivered the opinion of the Court with respect to Parts I, III-B, and IV, an opinion with respect to Part II, in which THE CHIEF JUSTICE and Justice WHITE join, and an opinion with respect to Parts III-A and V, in which THE CHIEF JUSTICE, Justice WHITE, and Justice KENNEDY join.

In this case, we confront once again the tension between the Fourteenth Amendment's guarantee of equal treatment to all citizens, and the use of race-based measures to ameliorate the effects of past discrimination on the opportunities enjoyed by members of minority groups in our society. In *Fullilove v. Klutznick*, 448 U.S. 448 (1980), we held that a congressional program requiring that 10% of certain federal construction grants be awarded to minority contractors did not violate the equal protection principles embodied in the Due Process Clause of the Fifth Amendment. Relying largely on our decision in *Fullilove*, some lower federal courts have applied a similar standard of review in assessing the constitutionality of state and local minority set-aside provisions under the Equal Protection Clause of the Fourteenth Amendment. We noted probable jurisdiction in this case to consider the applicability of our decision in *Wygant* (476 U.S. 267 (1986)), to a minority set-aside program adopted by the city of Richmond, Virginia.

I

On April 11, 1983, the Richmond City Council adopted the Minority Business Utilization Plan (the Plan). The Plan required prime contractors to whom the city awarded construction contracts to subcontract at least 30% of the dollar amount of the contract to one or more Minority Business Enterprises (MBE's). The Plan defined an MBE as "[a] business at least fifty-one (51) percent of which is owned and controlled ... by minority group members." "Minority group members" were defined as "[c]itizens of the United States who are Blacks, Spanish-speaking, Orientals, Indians, Eskimos, or Aleuts."

II

The parties and their supporting amici fight an initial battle over the scope of the city's power to adopt legislation designed to address the effects of past discrimination. Relying on our decision in *Wygant*, appellee argues that the city must limit any race-based remedial efforts to eradicating the effects of its own prior discrimination. This is essentially the position taken by the Court of Appeals below. Appellant argues that our decision in *Fullilove* is controlling, and that as a result the city of Richmond enjoys sweeping legislative power to define and attack the effects of prior discrimination in its local construction industry. We find that neither of these two rather stark alternatives can withstand analysis.

[The Court here summarized Chief Justice Burger's opinion in *Fullilove,* with particular emphasis on the fact that the Court was there reviewing an act of Congress.]

What appellant ignores is that Congress, unlike any State or political subdivision, has a specific constitutional mandate to enforce the dictates of the Fourteenth Amendment. The power to "enforce" may at times also include the power to define situations which Congress determines threaten principles of equality and to adopt prophylactic rules to deal with those situations. See *Katzenbach v. Morgan*, 384 U.S., at 651 ("Correctly viewed, § 5 is a positive grant of legislative power authorizing Congress to exercise its discretion in determining whether and what legislation is needed to secure the guarantees of the Fourteenth Amendment"). See also *South Carolina v. Katzenbach*, 383 U.S. 301, 326 (1966) (similar interpretation of congressional power under § 2 of the Fifteenth Amendment). The Civil War Amendments themselves worked a dramatic change in the balance between congressional and state power over matters of race. Speaking of the Thirteenth and Fourteenth Amendments in *Ex parte Virginia*, 100 U.S. 339, 345 (1880), the Court stated: "They were intended to be, what they really are, limitations of the powers of the States and enlargements of the power of Congress."

That Congress may identify and redress the effects of society-wide discrimination does not mean that, a fortiori, the States and their political subdivisions are free to decide that such remedies are appropriate. Section 1 of the Fourteenth Amendment is an explicit constraint on state power, and the States must undertake any remedial efforts in accordance with that provision. To hold otherwise would be to cede control over the content of the Equal Protection Clause to the 50 state legislatures and their myriad political subdivisions.

It would seem equally clear, however, that a state or local subdivision (if delegated the authority from the State) has the authority to eradicate the effects of private discrimination within its own legislative jurisdiction. This authority must, of course, be exercised within the constraints of § 1 of the Fourteenth Amendment. Our decision in *Wygant* is not to the contrary. *Wygant* addressed the constitutionality of the use of racial quotas by local school authorities pursuant to an agreement reached with the local teachers' union. It was in the context of addressing the school board's power to adopt a race-based layoff program affecting its own work force that the *Wygant* plurality indicated that the Equal Protection Clause required "some showing of prior discrimination by the governmental unit involved." *Wygant,* 476 U.S., at 274. As a matter of state law, the city of Richmond has legislative authority over its procurement policies, and can use its spending powers to remedy private discrimination, if it identifies that discrimination with the particularity required by the Fourteenth Amendment. To this extent, on the question of the city's competence, the Court of Appeals erred in following *Wygant* by rote in a case involving a state entity which has state-law authority to address discriminatory practices within local commerce under its jurisdiction.

Thus, if the city could show that it had essentially become a "passive participant" in a system of racial exclusion practiced by elements of the local construction industry, we think it clear that the city could take affirmative steps to dismantle such a system. It is beyond dispute that any public entity, state or federal, has a compelling interest in assuring that public dollars, drawn from the tax contributions of all citizens, do not serve to finance the evil of private prejudice. Cf. Norwood v. Harrison, 413 U.S. 455, 465 (1973) ("Racial discrimination in state-operated schools is barred by the Constitution and [i]t is also axiomatic that a state may not induce, encourage or promote private persons to accomplish what it is constitutionally forbidden to accomplish").

III

A

The Equal Protection Clause of the Fourteenth Amendment provides that "[n]o State shall ... deny to any person within its jurisdiction the equal protection of the laws." (Emphasis added.) As this Court has noted in the past, the "rights created by the first section of the Fourteenth Amendment are, by its terms, guaranteed to the individual. The rights established are personal rights." Shelley v. Kraemer, 334 U.S. 1, 22 (1948). The Richmond Plan denies certain citizens the opportunity to compete for a fixed percentage of public contracts based solely upon their race. To whatever racial group these citizens belong, their "personal rights" to be treated with equal dignity and respect are implicated by a rigid rule erecting race as the sole criterion in an aspect of public decisionmaking.

Absent searching judicial inquiry into the justification for such race-based measures, there is simply no way of determining what classifications are "benign" or "remedial" and what classifications are in fact motivated by illegitimate notions of racial inferiority or simple racial politics. Indeed, the purpose of strict scrutiny is to "smoke out" illegitimate uses of race by assuring that the legislative body is pursuing a goal important enough to warrant use of a highly suspect tool. The test also ensures that the means chosen "fit" this compelling goal so closely that there is little or no possibility that the motive for the classification was illegitimate racial prejudice or stereotype.

B

We think it clear that the factual predicate offered in support of the Richmond Plan suffers from the same two defects identified as fatal in *Wygant*. The District Court found the city council's "findings sufficient to ensure that, in adopting the Plan, it was remedying the present effects of past discrimination in the construction industry." Like the "role model" theory employed in *Wygant*, a generalized assertion that there has been past discrimination in an entire industry provides no guidance for a legislative body to determine the precise scope of the injury it seeks to remedy. It "has no logical stopping point." *Wygant, supra,* at 275 (plurality opinion). "Relief" for such an ill-defined wrong could extend until the percentage of public contracts awarded to MBE's in Richmond mirrored the percentage of minorities in the population as a whole.

Appellant argues that it is attempting to remedy various forms of past discrimination that are alleged to be responsible for the small number of minority businesses in the local contracting industry. Among these the city cites the exclusion of blacks from skilled construction trade unions and training programs. This past discrimination has prevented them "from following the traditional path from laborer to entrepreneur." The city also lists a host of nonracial factors which would seem to face a member of any racial group attempting to establish a new business enterprise, such as deficiencies in working capital, inability to meet bonding requirements, unfamiliarity with bidding procedures, and disability caused by an inadequate track record.

While there is no doubt that the sorry history of both private and public discrimination in this country has contributed to a lack of opportunities for black entrepreneurs, this observation, standing alone, cannot justify a rigid racial quota in the awarding of public contracts in Richmond, Virginia. Like the claim that discrimination in primary and secondary schooling justifies a rigid racial preference in medical school admissions, an amorphous claim that there has been past discrimination in a particular industry cannot justify the use of an unyielding racial quota.

It is sheer speculation how many minority firms there would be in Richmond absent past societal discrimination, just as it was sheer speculation how many minority medical students would have been admitted to the medical school at Davis absent past discrimination in educational opportunities. Defining these sorts of injuries as "identified discrimination" would give local governments license to create a patchwork of racial preferences based on statistical generalizations about any particular field of endeavor. These defects are readily apparent in this case. The 30% quota cannot in any realistic sense be tied to any injury suffered by anyone. The District Court relied upon five predicate "facts" in reaching its conclusion that there was an adequate basis for the 30% quota: (1) the ordinance declares itself to be remedial; (2) several proponents of the measure stated their views that there had been past discrimination in the construction industry; (3) minority businesses received 0.67% of prime contracts from the city while minorities constituted 50% of the city's population; (4) there were very few minority contractors in local and state contractors' associations; and (5) in 1977, Congress made a determination that the effects of past discrimination had stifled minority participation in the construction industry nationally.

None of these "findings," singly or together, provide the city of Richmond with a "strong basis in evidence for its conclusion that remedial action was necessary." *Wygant*, 476 U.S., at 277, (plurality opinion). There is nothing approaching a prima facie case of a constitutional or statutory violation by anyone in the Richmond construction industry. The District Court accorded great weight to the fact that the city council designated the Plan as "remedial." But the mere recitation of a "benign" or legitimate purpose for a racial classification is entitled to little or no weight. Racial classifications are suspect, and that means that simple legislative assurances of good intention cannot suffice.

The District Court also relied on the highly conclusionary statement of a proponent of the Plan that there was racial discrimination in the construction industry "in this area, and the State, and around the nation." It also noted that the city manager had related his view that racial discrimination still plagued the construction industry in his home city of Pittsburgh. These statements are of little probative value in establishing identified discrimination in the Richmond construction industry. The factfinding process of legislative bodies is generally entitled to a presumption of regularity and deferential review by the judiciary. See *Williamson v. Lee Optical of Oklahoma, Inc.*, 348 U.S. 483, 488-489 (1955). But when a legislative body chooses to employ a suspect classification, it cannot rest upon a generalized assertion as to the classification's relevance to its goals. See *McLaughlin v. Florida*, 379 U.S. 184, 190-192 (1964). A governmental actor cannot render race a legitimate proxy for a particular condition merely by declaring that the condition exists. The history of racial classifications in this country suggests that blind judicial deference to legislative or executive pronouncements of necessity has no place in equal protection analysis.

Reliance on the disparity between the number of prime contracts awarded to minority firms and the minority population of the city of Richmond is similarly misplaced. There is no doubt that "[w]here gross statistical disparities can be shown, they alone in a proper case may constitute prima facie proof of a pattern or practice of discrimination" under Title VII. *Hazelwood School Dist. v. United States*, 433 U.S. 299, 307-308 (1977). But it is equally clear that "[w]hen special qualifications are required to fill particular jobs, comparisons to the general population (rather than to the smaller group of individuals who possess the necessary qualifications) may have little probative value." See also *Mayor of Philadelphia v. Educational Equality League*, 415 U.S. 605, 620 (1974) ("[T]his is not a case in which it can be assumed that all citizens are fungible for purposes of determining whether members of a particular class have been unlawfully excluded").

In sum, none of the evidence presented by the city points to any identified discrimination in the Richmond construction industry. We, therefore, hold that the city has failed to demonstrate a compelling interest in apportioning public contracting opportunities on the basis of race. To accept Richmond's claim that past societal discrimination alone can serve as the basis for rigid racial preferences would be to open the door to competing claims for "remedial relief" for every disadvantaged group. The dream of a Nation of equal citizens in a society where race is irrelevant to personal opportunity and achievement would be lost in a mosaic of shifting preferences based on inherently unmeasurable claims of past wrongs. "Courts would be asked to evaluate the extent of the prejudice and consequent harm suffered by various minority groups. Those whose societal injury is thought to exceed some arbitrary level of tolerability then would be entitled to preferential classifications. . . ." *Bakke*, 438 U.S., at 296-297 (Powell, J.). We think such a result would be contrary to both the letter and spirit of a constitutional provision whose central command is equality.

V

Nothing we say today precludes a state or local entity from taking action to rectify the effects of identified discrimination within its jurisdiction. If the city of Richmond had evidence before it that nonminority contractors were systematically excluding minority businesses from subcontracting opportunities it could take action to end the discriminatory exclusion. Where there is a significant statistical disparity between the number of qualified minority contractors willing and able to perform a particular service and the number of such contractors actually engaged by the locality or the locality's prime contractors, an inference of discriminatory exclusion could arise. See *Bazemore v. Friday*, 478 U.S., at 398; *Teamsters v. United States*, 431 U.S., at 337-339. Under such circumstances, the city could act to dismantle the closed business system by taking appropriate measures against those who discriminate on the basis of race or other illegitimate criteria. *See, e.g., New York State Club Assn. v. New York City*, 487 U.S. 1, 10-11, 13-14 (1988). In the extreme case, some form of narrowly tailored racial preference might be necessary to break down patterns of deliberate exclusion.

Proper findings in this regard are necessary to define both the scope of the injury and the extent of the remedy necessary to cure its effects. Such findings also serve to assure all citizens that the deviation from the norm of equal treatment of all racial and ethnic groups is a temporary matter, a measure taken in the service of the goal of equality itself. Absent such findings, there is a danger that a racial classification is merely the product of unthinking stereotypes or a form of racial politics. Because the city of Richmond has failed to identify the need for remedial action in the awarding of its public construction contracts, its treatment of its citizens on a racial basis violates the dictates of the Equal Protection Clause. Accordingly, the judgment of the Court of Appeals for the Fourth Circuit is

Affirmed.

NOTES

1. The *Croson* Court, again without a majority opinion, attempted to explain when it was permissible for a governmental entity to use race-conscious measures to address past racial discrimination. In doing so, the Court had to distinguish its earlier holding in *Fullilove* with its later holding in *Wygant*. In *Fullilove*, the Court had approved a set aside for minority business enterprises based on a broad "legislative" finding by Congress that there had been substantial racial discrimination in the national construction industry. In *Wygant*, the Court had insisted that a race-conscious remedial measure adopted by a local government was inappropriate absent "some showing of prior discrimination by the governmental unit involved." The Court explained that, although the Fourteenth Amendment gives the federal government broader power to redress racial discrimination, the *Wygant* standard was too narrow. The city of Richmond did not have to base its remedial program only on *its own* past discriminatory acts, but could act if "it had essentially become a 'passive participant' in a system of racial exclusion practiced by elements of the local construction industry."

It was, however, essential that the city make findings of constitutional or statutory violations in which it had become a passive participant—"Proper findings in this regard are necessary to define both the scope of the injury and the extent of the remedy necessary to cure its effects." This the city had not done and thus its minority set-aside program was unconstitutional. The *Croson* case illustrates why it is unlikely that local governments will ague that an affirmative action program is justified to remedy past racial discrimination, even in a locality with a long history of racial discrimination. First, it is against a locality's interest to identify itself as a prior discriminator, with all the possible legal and social consequences that might follow from such an admission. Second, a local government would need to create an appropriate "fact-finding" body with the authority and the competence to make judicial-like "findings" of past violations. That is something that is very unlikely to happen.

2. From 1978, the year of the *Bakke* decision, until 1995, the year of the *Adarand* decision that follows, none of the Supreme Court affirmative action cases contained a majority opinion. That meant that it was continually necessary to add up the number of Justices who concurred in a particular opinion and try to determine the holding of the case. This led to a large amount of uncertainty with regard to affirmative action programs. Because *Adarand* was the first opinion with which a majority of the Justices agreed to significant portions, the decision put an end to a great deal of uncertainty. Most important was their agreement on strict scrutiny as the proper the proper standard of review for all race-conscious government action, including affirmative action. That portion of the opinion follows.

Adarand Constructors, Inc. v. Pena
515 U.S. 200 (1995)

[A division of the United States Department of Transportation awarded the Colorado Mountain Gravel & Construction Company a prime highway construction project. Because the contract terms promised additional compensation if the company hired subcontractors certified as controlled by "socially and economically disadvantaged individuals," the guardrail work was assigned to Gonzales, who was certified as disadvantaged, rather than to Adarand Construction, which was not certified but which did submit the lowest project bid. Adarand filed suit alleging the selection process violated its right to equal protection under the Fifth Amendment.]

Justice O'CONNOR announced the judgment of the Court and delivered an opinion with respect to Parts I, II, III-A, III-B, III-D, and IV, which is for the Court except insofar as it might be inconsistent with the views expressed in Justice SCALIA's concurrence, and an opinion with respect to Part III-C in which Justice KENNEDY joins.

III

Adarand's claim arises under the Fifth Amendment to the Constitution, which provides that "No person shall ... be deprived of life, liberty, or property, without due process of law." Although this Court has always understood that Clause to provide some measure of protection against arbitrary treatment by the Federal Government, it is not as explicit a guarantee of equal treatment as the Fourteenth Amendment, which provides that "No State shall ... deny to any person within its jurisdiction the equal protection of the laws" (emphasis added). Our cases have accorded varying degrees of significance to the difference in the language of those two Clauses. We think it necessary to revisit the issue here.

A

Through the 1940's, this Court had routinely taken the view in non-race-related cases that, "[u]nlike the Fourteenth Amendment, the Fifth contains no equal protection clause and it provides no guaranty against discriminatory legislation by Congress." *Detroit Bank v. United States*, 317 U.S. 329, 337 (1943); see also, e.g., *Helvering v. Lerner Stores Corp.*, 314 U.S. 463 (1941); *LaBelle Iron Works v. United States*, 256 U.S. 377, 392 (1921) ("Reference is made to cases decided under the equal protection clause of the Fourteenth Amendment ...; but clearly they are not in point. The Fifth Amendment has no equal protection clause"). When the Court first faced a Fifth Amendment equal protection challenge to a federal racial classification, it adopted a similar approach, with most unfortunate results. In *Hirabayashi v. United States*, 320 U.S. 81 (1943), the Court considered a curfew applicable only to persons of Japanese ancestry. The Court observed- correctly-that "[d]istinctions between citizens solely because of their ancestry are by their very nature odious to a free people whose institutions are founded upon the doctrine of equality," and that "racial discriminations are in most circumstances irrelevant and therefore prohibited." *Id.*, at 100. But it also cited *Detroit Bank* for the proposition that the Fifth Amendment "restrains only such discriminatory legislation by Congress as amounts to a denial of due process," 320 U.S., at 100, and upheld the curfew because "circumstances within the knowledge of those charged with the responsibility for maintaining the national defense afforded a rational basis for the decision which they made." *Id.*, at 102.

Eighteen months later, the Court again approved wartime measures directed at persons of

Japanese ancestry. *Korematsu v. United States*, 323 U.S. 214 (1944), concerned an order that completely excluded such persons from particular areas. The Court did not address the view, expressed in cases like *Hirabayashi* and *Detroit Bank*, that the Federal Government's obligation to provide equal protection differs significantly from that of the States. Instead, it began by noting that "all legal restrictions which curtail the civil rights of a single racial group are immediately suspect ... [and] courts must subject them to the most rigid scrutiny." 323 U.S., at 216. That promising dictum might be read to undermine the view that the Federal Government is under a lesser obligation to avoid injurious racial classifications than are the States. *Cf. id.,* at 234-235 (Murphy, J., dissenting) ("[T]he order deprives all those within its scope of the equal protection of the laws as guaranteed by the Fifth Amendment"). But in spite of the "most rigid scrutiny" standard it had just set forth, the Court then inexplicably relied on "the principles we announced in the *Hirabayashi* case," id., at 217, to conclude that, although "exclusion from the area in which one's home is located is a far greater deprivation than constant confinement to the home from 8 p.m. to 6 a.m.," the racially discriminatory order was nonetheless within the Federal Government's power.

In *Bolling v. Sharpe*, 347 U.S. 497 (1954), the Court for the first time explicitly questioned the existence of any difference between the obligations of the Federal Government and the States to avoid racial classifications. *Bolling* did note that "[t]he 'equal protection of the laws' is a more explicit safeguard of prohibited unfairness than 'due process of law,' " But *Bolling* then concluded that, "[i]n view of [the] decision that the Constitution prohibits the states from maintaining racially segregated public schools, it would be unthinkable that the same Constitution would impose a lesser duty on the Federal Government."

Later cases in contexts other than school desegregation did not distinguish between the duties of the States and the Federal Government to avoid racial classifications. (citing *McLaughlin v. Florida,* 379 U.S. 184 (1964)).

Cases decided after *McLaughlin* continued to treat the equal protection obligations imposed by the Fifth and the Fourteenth Amendments as indistinguishable; one commentator observed that "[i]n case after case, fifth amendment equal protection problems are discussed on the assumption that fourteenth amendment precedents are controlling." Karst, *The Fifth Amendment's Guarantee of Equal Protection*, 55 N.C. L. Rev. 541, 554 (1977). *Loving v. Virginia,* 388 U.S. 1 (1967), which struck down a race-based state law, cited *Korematsu* for the proposition that "the Equal Protection Clause demands that racial classifications ... be subjected to the 'most rigid scrutiny.'" 388 U.S., at 11. The various opinions in *Frontiero v. Richardson*, 411 U.S. 677 (1973), which concerned sex discrimination by the Federal Government, took their equal protection standard of review from *Reed v. Reed,* 404 U.S. 71 (1971), a case that invalidated sex discrimination by a State, without mentioning any possibility of a difference between the standards applicable to state and federal action. Thus, in 1975, the Court stated explicitly that "[t]his Court's approach to Fifth Amendment equal protection claims has always been precisely the same as to equal protection claims under the Fourteenth Amendment." *Weinberger v. Wiesenfeld,* 420 U.S. 636, 638, n. 2; see also *Buckley v. Valeo,* 424 U.S. 1, 93 (1976) ("Equal protection analysis in the Fifth Amendment area is the same as that under the Fourteenth Amendment"); *United States v. Paradise*, 480 U.S. 149, 166, n. 16 (1987) (plurality opinion of Brennan, J.) ("[T]he reach of the equal protection guarantee of the Fifth Amendment is coextensive with that of the Fourteenth"). We do not understand a few contrary suggestions appearing in cases in which we found special deference to the political branches of the Federal Government to be appropriate, e.g., *Hampton v. Mow Sun Wong,* 426 U.S. 88, 100, 101-102, n. 21 (1976) (federal power over immigration), to detract from this general rule.

B

Most of the cases discussed above involved classifications burdening groups that have suffered discrimination in our society. In 1978, the Court confronted the question whether race-based governmental action designed to benefit such groups should also be subject to "the most rigid scrutiny." [The Court here discussed *Bakke, Fullilove, Wygant*, and *Croson*.]

Despite lingering uncertainty in the details, however, the Court's cases through *Croson* had established three general propositions with respect to governmental racial classifications. First, skepticism: "'Any preference based on racial or ethnic criteria must necessarily receive a most searching examination,'" *Wygant*, 476 U.S., at 273 (plurality opinion of Powell, J.); *Fullilove*, 448 U.S., at 491 (opinion of Burger, C.J.); see also id., at 523 (Stewart, J., dissenting) ("[A]ny official action that treats a person differently on account of his race or ethnic origin is inherently suspect"); *McLaughlin*, 379 U.S., at 192 ("[R]acial classifications [are] 'constitutionally suspect'"); *Hirabayashi*, 320 U.S., at 100 ("Distinctions between citizens solely because of their ancestry are by their very nature odious to a free people"). Second, consistency: "[T]he standard of review under the Equal Protection Clause is not dependent on the race of those burdened or benefited by a particular classification," *Croson*, 488 U.S., at 494 (plurality opinion); id., at 520 (SCALIA, J., concurring in judgment); see also *Bakke*, 438 U.S., at 289-290 (opinion of Powell, J.), i.e., all racial classifications reviewable under the Equal Protection Clause must be strictly scrutinized. And third, congruence: "Equal protection analysis in the Fifth Amendment area is the same as that under the Fourteenth Amendment," *Buckley v. Valeo*, 424 U.S., at 93; see also Weinberger v. Wiesenfeld, 420 U.S., at 638, n. 2; *Bolling v. Sharpe*, 347 U.S., at 500. Taken together, these three propositions lead to the conclusion that any person, of whatever race, has the right to demand that any governmental actor subject to the Constitution justify any racial classification subjecting that person to unequal treatment under the strictest judicial scrutiny.

[The Court here briefly discussed and repudiated its earlier opinion *Metro Broadcasting, Inc. v. FCC*, 497 U.S. 547 (1990), a case that involved a Fifth Amendment challenge to two race-based policies of the Federal Communications Commission (FCC). In *Metro Broadcasting*, the Court had applied intermediate scrutiny to an affirmative action program created by the federal government.]

The three propositions undermined by *Metro Broadcasting* all derive from the basic principle that the Fifth and Fourteenth Amendments to the Constitution protect persons, not groups. It follows from that principle that all governmental action based on race-a group classification long recognized as "in most circumstances irrelevant and therefore prohibited," *Hirabayashi*, 320 U.S., at 100--should be subjected to detailed judicial inquiry to ensure that the personal right to equal protection of the laws has not been infringed. These ideas have long been central to this Court's understanding of equal protection, and holding "benign" state and federal racial classifications to different standards does not square with them. "[A] free people whose institutions are founded upon the doctrine of equality," ibid., should tolerate no retreat from the principle that government may treat people differently because of their race only for the most compelling reasons. Accordingly, we hold today that all racial classifications, imposed by whatever federal, state, or local governmental actor, must be analyzed by a reviewing court under strict scrutiny. In other words, such classifications are constitutional only if they are narrowly tailored measures that further compelling governmental interests. To the extent that *Metro Broadcasting* is inconsistent with that holding, it is overruled.

IV

Because our decision today alters the playing field in some important respects, we think it best to remand the case to the lower courts for further consideration in light of the principles we have announced. Accordingly, the judgment of the Court of Appeals is vacated, and the case is remanded for further proceedings consistent with this opinion.

It is so ordered.

NOTES

1. With its majority decision, the Court finally gave definitive answers to three overlapping questions: (1) are all racial classifications equally suspicious? (2) does the race of the person disadvantaged by a racial classification affect the standard of review? and (3) does the same standard of review apply to racial classifications made by federal and state governments? In answering these questions, the Court gave an extremely detailed review of its precedents on discrimination by federal and state actors, and ultimately answered the questions by reference to three broad principles: skepticism, consistency, and congruence.

The skepticism principle meant that *all* racial classifications are equally suspect. The consistency principle meant that the same standard of review would be applied whether a white or black person was disadvantaged or benefited. The congruence principle meant that the equal protection standard under the Fourteenth Amendment (and thus applied to the states) was exactly the same as the equal protection standard implied in the Fifth Amendment (and thus applied against the federal government). What followed from these three principles was the Court's holding:

> that all racial classifications, imposed by whatever federal, state, or local governmental actor, must be analyzed by a reviewing court under strict scrutiny. In other words, such classifications are constitutional only if they are narrowly tailored measures that further compelling governmental interests.

Pena introduced a certain amount of clarity into the law of affirmative action, particularly with regard to the use of race in the remedial context. But there still was substantial disagreement in the lower courts as to whether or not diversity was a compelling interest and what weight should be given to Justice Powell's solitary opinion from *Bakke*. Those issues became clearer in 2003 when the Court decided *Grutter v. Bollinger*, the next case.

Grutter v. Bollinger
539 U.S. 306 (2003)

[The University of Michigan Law School had crafted an admission policy that was consistent with the demands of Justice Powell's opinion in *Bakke*. The plan identified students with "a strong likelihood of succeeding in the practice of law and contributing in diverse ways to the well-being of others." Although the school's written policy recognized the many possible bases for diversity admissions, it emphasized racial and ethnic diversity with a focus on "African-Americans, Hispanics and Native Americans" who might not otherwise be admitted to the school in significant numbers. No quota was set, but the admission staff was directed to consider race or ethnicity as a factor among all other factors, and to be mindful that a "critical mass" of minority students should be offered admission. Barbara Grutter was a white applicant denied admission. She claimed that the law school's admissions practices violated the Equal Protection Clause.]

Justice O'CONNOR delivered the opinion of the Court.

II

A

We last addressed the use of race in public higher education over 25 years ago. In the landmark *Bakke* case, we reviewed a racial set-aside program that reserved 16 out of 100 seats in a medical school class for members of certain minority groups. The decision produced six separate opinions, none of which commanded a majority of the Court. Four Justices would have upheld the program against all attack on the ground that the government can use race to "remedy disadvantages cast on minorities by past racial prejudice." Four other Justices avoided the constitutional question altogether and struck down the program on statutory grounds. Justice Powell provided a fifth vote not only for invalidating the set-aside program, but also for reversing the state court's injunction against any use of race whatsoever. The only holding for the Court in *Bakke* was that a "State has a substantial interest that legitimately may be served by a properly devised admissions program involving the competitive consideration of race and ethnic origin." Thus, we reversed that part of the lower court's judgment that enjoined the university "from any consideration of the race of any applicant."

Since this Court's splintered decision in *Bakke*, Justice Powell's opinion announcing the judgment of the Court has served as the touchstone for constitutional analysis of race-conscious admissions policies. Public and private universities across the Nation have modeled their own admissions programs on Justice Powell's views on permissible race-conscious policies. We therefore discuss Justice Powell's opinion in some detail. [The Court here summarized Justice Powell's opinion in *Bakke*.]

In the wake of our fractured decision in *Bakke,* courts have struggled to discern whether Justice Powell's diversity rationale, set forth in part of the opinion joined by no other Justice, is nonetheless binding precedent under [*Marks v. United States,* 430 U.S. 188 (1977)]. In that case, we explained that "[w]hen a fragmented Court decides a case and no single rationale explaining the result enjoys the assent of five Justices, the holding of the Court may be viewed as that position taken by those Members who concurred in the judgments on the narrowest grounds." 430 U.S., at 193. As the divergent opinions of the lower courts demonstrate, however, "[t]his test is more easily stated than applied to the various opinions supporting the result in *[Bakke].*" *Nichols v. United States,* 511 U.S. 738, 745-746 (1994). Compare, *e.g., Johnson v. Board of Regents of Univ. of Ga.,* 263 F.3d 1234 (C.A.11 2001) (Justice Powell's diversity rationale was not the holding of the Court); *Hopwood v. Texas,* 236 F.3d 256, 274-275 (C.A.5 2000) *(Hopwood II)* (same); *Hopwood I,* 78 F.3d 932 (C.A.5 1996) (same), with *Smith v. University of Wash. Law School,* 233 F.3d, at 1199 (Justice Powell's opinion, including the diversity rationale, is controlling under *Marks*).

We do not find it necessary to decide whether Justice Powell's opinion is binding under *Marks.* It does not seem "useful to pursue the *Marks* inquiry to the utmost logical possibility when it has so obviously baffled and divided the lower courts that have considered it." *Nichols v. United States, supra,* at 745-746. More important, for the reasons set out below, today we endorse Justice Powell's view that student body diversity is a compelling state interest that can justify the use of race in university admissions.

B

The Equal Protection Clause provides that no State shall "deny to any person within its jurisdiction the equal protection of the laws." Because the Fourteenth Amendment "protect[s] *persons,* not *groups,*" all "governmental action based on race--a *group* classification long recognized as in most circumstances irrelevant and therefore prohibited--should be subjected to detailed judicial inquiry to ensure that the *personal* right to equal protection of the laws has not been infringed." *Adarand Constructors, Inc. v. Peña,* 515 U.S. 200, 227 (1995). We are a "free people whose institutions are founded upon the doctrine of equality." *Loving v. Virginia,* 388 U.S. 1, 11 (1967). It follows from that principle that "government may treat people differently because of their race only for the most compelling reasons." *Adarand Constructors, Inc. v. Peña,* 515 U.S., at 227.

We have held that all racial classifications imposed by government "must be analyzed by a reviewing court under strict scrutiny." This means that such classifications are constitutional only if they are narrowly tailored to further compelling governmental interests. "Absent searching judicial inquiry into the justification for such race-based measures," we have no way to determine what "classifications are 'benign' or 'remedial' and what classifications are in fact motivated by illegitimate notions of racial inferiority or simple racial politics." *Richmond v. J.A. Croson Co.,* 488 U.S. 469, 493 (1989) (plurality opinion). We apply strict scrutiny to all racial classifications to "'smoke out' illegitimate uses of race by assuring that [government] is pursuing a goal important enough to warrant use of a highly suspect tool."

Strict scrutiny is not "strict in theory, but fatal in fact." *Adarand Constructors, Inc. v. Peña, supra,* at 237. Although all governmental uses of race are subject to strict scrutiny, not all are invalidated by it. As we have explained, "whenever the government treats any person unequally because of his or her race, that person has suffered an injury that falls squarely within the language and spirit of the Constitution's guarantee of equal protection." 515 U.S., at 229-230. But that observation "says nothing about the ultimate validity of any particular law; that determination is the job of the court applying strict scrutiny." When race-based action is necessary to further a compelling governmental interest, such action does not violate the constitutional guarantee of equal protection so long as the narrow-tailoring requirement is also satisfied.

Context matters when reviewing race-based governmental action under the Equal Protection Clause. See *Gomillion v. Lightfoot,* 364 U.S. 339, 343-344 (1960) (admonishing that, "in dealing with claims under broad provisions of the Constitution, which derive content by an interpretive process of inclusion and exclusion, it is imperative that generalizations, based on and qualified by the concrete situations that gave rise to them, must not be applied out of context in disregard of variant controlling facts"). In *Adarand Constructors, Inc. v. Peña,* we made clear that strict scrutiny must take " 'relevant differences' into account." 515 U.S., at 228. Indeed, as we explained, that is its "fundamental purpose." Not every decision influenced by race is equally objectionable, and strict scrutiny is designed to provide a framework for carefully examining the importance and the sincerity of the reasons advanced by the governmental decisionmaker for the use of race in that particular context.

III

A

With these principles in mind, we turn to the question whether the Law School's use of race is justified by a compelling state interest. Before this Court, as they have throughout this litigation, respondents assert only one justification for their use of race in the admissions process: obtaining "the educational benefits that flow from a diverse student body." In other words, the Law School asks us to recognize, in the context of higher education, a compelling state interest in student body diversity.

We first wish to dispel the notion that the Law School's argument has been foreclosed, either expressly or implicitly, by our affirmative-action cases decided since *Bakke.* It is true that some language in those opinions might be read to suggest that remedying past discrimination is the only permissible justification for race-based governmental action. See, *e.g., Richmond v. J.A. Croson Co., supra,* at 493 (plurality opinion) (stating that unless classifications based on race are "strictly reserved for remedial settings, they may in fact promote notions of racial inferiority and lead to a politics of racial hostility"). But we have never held that the only governmental use of race that can survive strict scrutiny is remedying past discrimination. Nor, since *Bakke,* have we directly addressed the use of race in the context of public higher education. Today, we hold that the Law School has a compelling interest in attaining a diverse student body.

The Law School's educational judgment that such diversity is essential to its educational mission is one to which we defer. The Law School's assessment that diversity will, in fact, yield educational benefits is substantiated by respondents and their *amici.* Our scrutiny of the interest asserted by the Law School is no less strict for taking into account complex educational judgments in an area that lies primarily within the expertise of the university. Our holding today is in keeping with our tradition of giving a degree of deference to a university's academic decisions, within constitutionally prescribed limits. See *Regents of Univ. of Mich. v. Ewing,* 474 U.S. 214, 225 (1985); *Board of Curators of Univ. of Mo. v. Horowitz,* 435 U.S. 78, 96, n. 6 (1978); *Bakke,* 438 U.S., at 319, n. 53 (opinion of Powell, J.).

We have long recognized that, given the important purpose of public education and the expansive freedoms of speech and thought associated with the university environment, universities occupy a special niche in our constitutional tradition. In announcing the principle of student body diversity as a compelling state interest, Justice Powell invoked our cases recognizing a constitutional dimension, grounded in the First Amendment, of educational autonomy: "The freedom of a university to make its own judgments as to education includes the selection of its student body." *Bakke, supra,* at 312. From this premise, Justice Powell reasoned that by claiming "the right to select those students who will contribute the most to the 'robust exchange of ideas,'" a university "seek[s] to achieve a goal that is of paramount importance in the fulfillment of its mission." 438 U.S., at 313, (quoting *Keyishian v. Board of Regents of Univ. of State of N. Y., supra,* at 603). Our conclusion that the Law School has a compelling interest in a diverse student body is informed by our view that attaining a diverse student body is at the heart of the Law School's proper institutional mission, and that "good faith" on the part of a university is "presumed" absent "a showing to the contrary." 438 U.S., at 318-319.

As part of its goal of "assembling a class that is both exceptionally academically qualified and broadly diverse," the Law School seeks to "enroll a 'critical mass' of minority students." The Law School's interest is not simply "to assure within its student body some specified percentage of a particular group merely because of its race or ethnic origin." *Bakke,* 438 U.S., at 307 (opinion of Powell, J.). That would amount to outright racial balancing, which is patently unconstitutional. *Ibid.; Freeman v. Pitts,* 503 U.S. 467, 494 (1992) ("Racial balance is not to be achieved for its own sake"); *Richmond v. J.A. Croson Co.,* 488 U.S., at 507. Rather, the Law School's concept of critical mass is defined by reference to the educational benefits that diversity is designed to produce.

These benefits are substantial. As the District Court emphasized, the Law School's admissions policy promotes "cross-racial understanding," helps to break down racial stereotypes, and "enables [students] to better understand persons of different races. These benefits are "important and laudable," because "classroom discussion is livelier, more spirited, and simply more enlightening and interesting" when the students have "the greatest possible variety of backgrounds."

The Law School's claim of a compelling interest is further bolstered by its *amici,* who point to the educational benefits that flow from student body diversity. In addition to the expert studies and reports entered into evidence at trial, numerous studies show that student body diversity promotes learning outcomes, and "better prepares students for an increasingly diverse workforce and society, and better prepares them as professionals."

These benefits are not theoretical but real, as major American businesses have made clear that the skills needed in today's increasingly global marketplace can only be developed through exposure to widely diverse people, cultures, ideas, and viewpoints. What is more, high-ranking retired officers and civilian leaders of the United States military assert that, "[b]ased on [their] decades of experience," a "highly qualified, racially diverse officer corps ... is essential to the military's ability to fulfill its principle mission to provide national security." The primary sources for the Nation's officer corps are the service academies and the Reserve Officers Training Corps (ROTC), the latter comprising students already admitted to participating colleges and universities. At present, "the military cannot achieve an officer corps that is *both* highly qualified *and* racially diverse unless the service academies and the ROTC used limited race-conscious recruiting and admissions policies." To fulfill its mission, the military "must be selective in admissions for training and education for the officer corps, *and* it must train and educate a highly qualified, racially diverse officer corps in a racially diverse educational setting." We agree that "[i]t requires only a small step from this analysis to conclude that our country's other most selective institutions must remain both diverse and selective."

We have repeatedly acknowledged the overriding importance of preparing students for work and citizenship, describing education as pivotal to "sustaining our political and cultural heritage" with a fundamental role in maintaining the fabric of society. *Plyler v. Doe,* 457 U.S. 202, 221 (1982). This Court has long recognized that "education ... is the very foundation of good citizenship." *Brown v. Board of Education,* 347 U.S. 483, 493 (1954). For this reason, the diffusion of knowledge and opportunity through public institutions of higher education must be accessible to all individuals regardless of race or ethnicity. The United States, as *amicus curiae,* affirms that "[e]nsuring that public institutions are open and available to all segments of American society, including people of all races and ethnicities, represents a paramount government objective." And, "[n]owhere is the importance of such openness more acute than in the context of higher education." Effective participation by members of all racial and ethnic groups in the civic life of our Nation is essential if the dream of one Nation, indivisible, is to be realized.

B

Even in the limited circumstances when drawing racial distinctions is permissible to further a compelling state interest, government is still "constrained in how it may pursue that end: [T]he means chosen to accomplish the [government's] asserted purpose must be specifically and narrowly framed to accomplish that purpose." *Shaw v. Hunt,* 517 U.S. 899, 908 (1996). The purpose of the narrow tailoring requirement is to ensure that "the means chosen 'fit' th[e] compelling goal so closely that there is little or no possibility that the motive for the classification was illegitimate racial prejudice or stereotype." *Richmond v. J.A. Croson Co.,* 488 U.S., at 493 (plurality opinion).

Since *Bakke,* we have had no occasion to define the contours of the narrow-tailoring inquiry with respect to race-conscious university admissions programs. That inquiry must be calibrated to fit the distinct issues raised by the use of race to achieve student body diversity in public higher education. Contrary to Justice KENNEDY's assertions, we do not "abando[n] strict scrutiny." Rather, as we have already explained we adhere to *Adarand's* teaching that the very purpose of strict scrutiny is to take such "relevant differences into account."

To be narrowly tailored, a race-conscious admissions program cannot use a quota system--it cannot "insulat[e] each category of applicants with certain desired qualifications from competition with all other applicants." *Bakke,* 438 U.S., at 315 (opinion of Powell, J.). Instead, a university may consider race or ethnicity only as a "'plus' in a particular applicant's file," without "insulat[ing] the individual from comparison with all other candidates for the available seats." *Id.,* at 317. In other words, an admissions program must be "flexible enough to consider all pertinent elements of diversity in light of the particular qualifications of each applicant, and to place them on the same footing for consideration, although not necessarily according them the same weight." *Ibid.*

We find that the Law School's admissions program bears the hallmarks of a narrowly tailored plan. As Justice Powell made clear in *Bakke,* truly individualized consideration demands that race be used in a flexible, nonmechanical way. It follows from this mandate that universities cannot establish quotas for members of certain racial groups or put members of those groups on separate admissions tracks. See *id.,* at 315-316. Nor can universities insulate applicants who belong to certain racial or ethnic groups from the competition for admission. Universities can, however, consider race or ethnicity more flexibly as a "plus" factor in the context of individualized consideration of each and every applicant.

We are satisfied that the Law School's admissions program, like the Harvard plan described by Justice Powell, does not operate as a quota. Properly understood, a "quota" is a program in which a certain fixed number or proportion of opportunities are "reserved exclusively for certain minority groups." *Richmond v. J.A. Croson Co., supra,* at 496 (plurality opinion). Quotas "'impose a fixed number or percentage which must be attained, or which cannot be exceeded,'" *Sheet Metal Workers v. EEOC,* 478 U.S. 421, 495 (1986) (O'CONNOR, J., concurring in part and dissenting in part), and "insulate the individual from comparison with all other candidates for the available seats," *Bakke, supra,* at 317 (opinion of Powell, J.). In contrast, "a permissible goal ... require[s] only a good-faith effort ... to come within a range demarcated by the goal itself," *Sheet Metal Workers v. EEOC, supra,* at 495, and permits consideration of race as a "plus" factor in any given case while still ensuring that each candidate "compete[s] with all other qualified applicants," *Johnson v. Transportation Agency, Santa Clara Cty.,* 480 U.S. 616, 638 (1987).

Justice Powell's distinction between the medical school's rigid 16-seat quota and Harvard's flexible use of race as a "plus" factor is instructive. Harvard certainly had minimum *goals* for minority enrollment, even if it had no specific number firmly in mind. See *Bakke, supra,* at 323 (opinion of Powell, J.) ("10 or 20 black students could not begin to bring to their classmates and to each other the variety of points of view, backgrounds and experiences of blacks in the United States"). What is more, Justice Powell flatly rejected the argument that Harvard's program was "the functional equivalent of a quota" merely because it had some "'plus'" for race, or gave greater "weight" to race than to some other factors, in order to achieve student body diversity. 438 U.S., at 317-318.

The Law School's goal of attaining a critical mass of underrepresented minority students does not transform its program into a quota. As the Harvard plan described by Justice Powell recognized, there is of course "some relationship between numbers and achieving the benefits to be derived from a diverse student body, and between numbers and providing a reasonable environment for those students admitted." "[S]ome attention to numbers," without more, does not transform a flexible admissions system into a rigid quota. Nor, as Justice KENNEDY posits, does the Law School's consultation of the "daily reports," which keep track of the racial and ethnic composition of the class (as well as of residency and gender), "sugges[t] there was no further attempt at individual review save for race itself" during the final stages of the admissions process. To the contrary, the Law School's admissions officers testified without contradiction that they never gave race any more or less weight based on the information contained in these reports. Moreover, as Justice KENNEDY concedes, between 1993 and 1998, the number of African-American, Latino, and Native-American students in each class at the Law School varied from 13.5 to 20.1 percent, a range inconsistent with a quota.

That a race-conscious admissions program does not operate as a quota does not, by itself, satisfy the requirement of individualized consideration. When using race as a "plus" factor in university admissions, a university's admissions program must remain flexible enough to ensure that each applicant is evaluated as an individual and not in a way that makes an applicant's race or ethnicity the defining feature of his or her application. The importance of this individualized consideration in the context of a race-conscious admissions program is paramount. See *Bakke,* 438 U.S., at 318, n. 52 (opinion of Powell, J.) (identifying the "denial ... of th[e] right to individualized consideration" as the "principal evil" of the medical school's admissions program).

Here, the Law School engages in a highly individualized, holistic review of each applicant's file, giving serious consideration to all the ways an applicant might contribute to a diverse educational environment. The Law School affords this individualized consideration to applicants of all races. There is no policy, either *de jure* or *de facto,* of automatic acceptance or rejection based on any single "soft" variable. Unlike the program at issue in *Gratz v. Bollinger*, 539 U.S. 244, the Law School awards no mechanical, predetermined diversity "bonuses" based on race or ethnicity. See *post*, 539 U.S., at 271-272 (distinguishing a race-conscious admissions program that automatically awards 20 points based on race from the Harvard plan, which considered race but "did not contemplate that any single characteristic automatically ensured a specific and identifiable contribution to a university's diversity"). Like the Harvard plan, the Law School's admissions policy "is flexible enough to consider all pertinent elements of diversity in light of the particular qualifications of each applicant, and to place them on the same footing for consideration, although not necessarily according them the same weight." *Bakke, supra,* at 317 (opinion of Powell, J.).

We also find that, like the Harvard plan Justice Powell referenced in *Bakke,* the Law School's race-conscious admissions program adequately ensures that all factors that may contribute to student body diversity are meaningfully considered alongside race in admissions decisions. With respect to the use of race itself, all underrepresented minority students admitted by the Law School have been deemed qualified. By virtue of our Nation's struggle with racial inequality, such students are both likely to have experiences of particular importance to the Law School's mission, and less likely to be admitted in meaningful numbers on criteria that ignore those experiences.

The Law School does not, however, limit in any way the broad range of qualities and experiences that may be considered valuable contributions to student body diversity. To the contrary, the 1992 policy makes clear "[t]here are many possible bases for diversity admissions," and provides examples of admittees who have lived or traveled widely abroad, are fluent in several languages, have overcome personal adversity and family hardship, have exceptional records of extensive community service, and have had successful careers in other fields. The Law School seriously considers each "applicant's promise of making a notable contribution to the class by way of a particular strength, attainment, or characteristic--*e.g.,* an unusual intellectual achievement, employment experience, nonacademic performance, or personal background." All applicants have the opportunity to highlight their own potential diversity contributions through the submission of a personal statement, letters of recommendation, and an essay describing the ways in which the applicant will contribute to the life and diversity of the Law School.

What is more, the Law School actually gives substantial weight to diversity factors besides race. The Law School frequently accepts nonminority applicants with grades and test scores lower than underrepresented minority applicants (and other nonminority applicants) who are rejected. This shows that the Law School seriously weighs many other diversity factors besides race that can make a real and dispositive difference for nonminority applicants as well. By this flexible approach, the Law School sufficiently takes into account, in practice as well as in theory, a wide variety of characteristics besides race and ethnicity that contribute to a diverse student body. Justice KENNEDY speculates that "race is likely outcome determinative for many members of minority groups" who do not fall within the upper range of LSAT scores and grades. (Dissenting opinion). But the same could be said of the Harvard plan discussed approvingly by Justice Powell in *Bakke,* and indeed of any plan that uses race as one of many factors. See 438 U.S., at 316 ("'When the Committee on Admissions reviews the large middle group of applicants who are "admissible" and deemed capable of doing good work in their courses, the race of an applicant may tip the balance in his favor'").

We acknowledge that "there are serious problems of justice connected with the idea of preference itself." *Bakke,* 438 U.S., at 298 (opinion of Powell, J.). Narrow tailoring, therefore, requires that a race-conscious admissions program not unduly harm members of any racial group.

Even remedial race-based governmental action generally "remains subject to continuing oversight to assure that it will work the least harm possible to other innocent persons competing for the benefit." *Id.,* at 308. To be narrowly tailored, a race-conscious admissions program must not "unduly burden individuals who are not members of the favored racial and ethnic groups." *Metro Broadcasting, Inc. v. FCC,* 497 U.S. 547, 630 (1990) (O'CONNOR, J., dissenting).

We are satisfied that the Law School's admissions program does not. Because the Law School considers "all pertinent elements of diversity," it can (and does) select nonminority applicants who have greater potential to enhance student body diversity over underrepresented minority applicants. See *Bakke, supra,* at 317 (opinion of Powell, J.). As Justice Powell recognized in *Bakke,* so long as a race-conscious admissions program uses race as a "plus" factor in the context of individualized consideration, a rejected applicant

> will not have been foreclosed from all consideration for that seat simply because he was not the right color or had the wrong surname. . . . His qualifications would have been weighed fairly and competitively, and he would have no basis to complain of unequal treatment under the Fourteenth Amendment. 438 U.S., at 318.

We agree that, in the context of its individualized inquiry into the possible diversity contributions of all applicants, the Law School's race-conscious admissions program does not unduly harm nonminority applicants.

We are mindful, however, that "[a] core purpose of the Fourteenth Amendment was to do away with all governmentally imposed discrimination based on race." *Palmore v. Sidoti,* 466 U.S. 429, 432 (1984). Accordingly, race-conscious admissions policies must be limited in time. This requirement reflects that racial classifications, however compelling their goals, are potentially so dangerous that they may be employed no more broadly than the interest demands. Enshrining a permanent justification for racial preferences would offend this fundamental equal protection principle. We see no reason to exempt race-conscious admissions programs from the requirement that all governmental use of race must have a logical end point. The Law School, too, concedes that all "race-conscious programs must have reasonable durational limits."

We take the Law School at its word that it would "like nothing better than to find a race-neutral admissions formula" and will terminate its race-conscious admissions program as soon as practicable. It has been 25 years since Justice Powell first approved the use of race to further an interest in student body diversity in the context of public higher education. Since that time, the number of minority applicants with high grades and test scores has indeed increased. We expect that 25 years from now, the use of racial preferences will no longer be necessary to further the interest approved today.

IV

In summary, the Equal Protection Clause does not prohibit the Law School's narrowly tailored use of race in admissions decisions to further a compelling interest in obtaining the educational benefits that flow from a diverse student body. Consequently, petitioner's statutory claims based on Title VI and 42 U.S.C. § 1981 also fail. See *Bakke, supra,* at 287 (opinion of Powell, J.) ("Title VI ... proscribe[s] only those racial classifications that would violate the Equal Protection Clause or the Fifth Amendment"); *General Building Contractors Assn., Inc. v. Pennsylvania,* 458 U.S. 375, 389-391 (1982) (the prohibition against discrimination in § 1981 is co-extensive with the Equal Protection Clause). The judgment of the Court of Appeals for the Sixth Circuit, accordingly, is affirmed.

It is so ordered.

NOTES

1. The majority opinion in *Grutter* put an end to what appeared to be an unresolvable disagreement on the effect of Justice Powell's opinion in *Bakke*. It turns out that Justice Powell was prescient and, although it took twenty-five years, the Court eventually adopted his views. Specifically, the Court first held that the Law School had a compelling interest in attaining a diverse student body. In terms of the educational value of diversity, the Court said that it would defer to the university's educational judgment that such diversity is essential to its educational mission. The Court conceded that the benefits of diversity are substantial—promoting cross-racial understanding, breaking break down racial stereotypes, enabling students to better understand persons of different races, and creating classrooms that are livelier, more spirited, and simply more enlightening and interesting.

With regard to the second part of the strict scrutiny test—narrow tailoring—the Court insisted that all candidates had to be part of the same pool, without insulating any individual from comparison with all other candidates for the available seats. The Court found that the University of Michigan program was narrowly tailored in that the Law School engaged in a highly individualized, holistic review of each applicant's file, giving serious consideration to all the ways an applicant might contribute to a diverse educational environment. In terms of diversity, the Court noted that the university did not limit itself to seeking racial diversity only, which would be a prohibited purpose, but in fact identified many possible bases for diversity--having lived or traveled abroad, being fluent in foreign languages, having overcome personal adversity or family hardship, having a record of community service or a successful career, an unusual intellectual achievement, employment experience, nonacademic performance, or personal background. Finally, the admissions program did not unduly burden innocent parties since it considered all pertinent elements of diversity and would sometimes favor select nonminority applicants who have greater potential to enhance student body diversity over underrepresented minority applicants. All in all, the Michigan law school program satisfied the test of being narrowly tailored to the achievement of a compelling interest.

2. Since the *Grutter* Court approved the law school's program promoting diversity and since, as noted above, universities are unlikely to voluntarily adopt a race conscious admissions program to address their own past discrimination, universities that want to take race into account must do so only in the context of a broader program to achieve various kinds of diversity. For example, the University of Maryland, as of 2012, identifies the following factors that it will consider in order to produce a diverse class:

> High School Achievement, Extracurricular Activities, Grades in Academic Subjects, Special Talents or Skills, Progression of Performance, Community Involvement, Breadth of Life Experiences, Community Service, Geographic Origin, Demonstrated Leadership, Gender, Learning Differences, SAT I or ACT Scores, Quality of Coursework, Work Experience, Residency Status, Recognition of Special Achievements, Race, Extenuating Circumstances, Ethnicity, Socio-Economic Background, Family Educational Background, Written Expression of Ideas, Academic Endeavors Outside of the

Classroom, Rank in Class, English as a Second Language, Language Spoken at Home. *See http://www.admissions.umd.edu/requirements/AdmissionReviewFactors.php#*

In this extensive list, race and ethnicity are only two of twenty-six factors, and they are somewhat hidden in the middle of the list. It seems that university administrators have taken the *Grutter* holding to heart.

3. On the same day that the Court approved the University of Michigan Law School's race-conscious admission program, it invalidated the University of Michigan's undergraduate race-conscious admissions program. The factual differences in the two programs, and the reason why that led to a different constitutional result, are explained in the next case.

Gratz v. Bollinger
539 U.S. 244 (2003)

[In making admissions decisions, the undergraduate admissions office at the University of Michigan used a selection index on which an applicant could score a maximum of 150 points. Each application received points based on high school grade point average, standardized test scores, academic quality of an applicant's high school, strength or weakness of high school curriculum, in-state residency, alumni relationship, personal essay, and personal achievement or leadership. Of particular significance, an applicant was entitled to 20 points based upon his or her membership in an underrepresented racial or ethnic minority group, which was defined as including African-Americans, Hispanics, and Native Americans. Barbara Gratz, a white applicant denied admission, claimed that this admissions preference violated the Equal Protection Clause.]

Chief Justice REHNQUIST delivered the opinion of the Court.

[The Court initially summarized the requirement that the consideration of race in admissions must be narrowly tailored to achieve a compelling purpose.]

The current LSA [College of Literature, Science, and Arts] policy does not provide such individualized consideration. The LSA's policy automatically distributes 20 points to every single applicant from an "underrepresented minority" group, as defined by the University. The only consideration that accompanies this distribution of points is a factual review of an application to determine whether an individual is a member of one of these minority groups. Moreover, unlike Justice Powell's example, where the race of a "particular black applicant" could be considered without being decisive, see *Bakke,* 438 U.S., at 317, the LSA's automatic distribution of 20 points has the effect of making "the factor of race ... decisive" for virtually every minimally qualified underrepresented minority applicant.

Respondents contend that "[t]he volume of applications and the presentation of applicant information make it impractical for [LSA] to use the ... admissions system" upheld by the Court today in *Grutter*. But the fact that the implementation of a program capable of providing individualized consideration might present administrative challenges does not render constitutional an otherwise problematic system. See *J.A. Croson Co.,* 488 U.S., at 508 (citing *Frontiero v. Richardson,* 411 U.S. 677, 690 (1973) (plurality opinion of Brennan, J.) (rejecting "'administrative convenience'" as a determinant of constitutionality in the face of a suspect classification)). Nothing in Justice Powell's opinion in *Bakke* signaled that a university may employ whatever means it desires to achieve the stated goal of diversity without regard to the limits imposed by our strict scrutiny analysis.

We conclude, therefore, that because the University's use of race in its current freshman admissions policy is not narrowly tailored to achieve respondents' asserted compelling interest in diversity, the admissions policy violates the Equal Protection Clause of the Fourteenth Amendment. Accordingly, we reverse that portion of the District Court's decision granting respondents summary judgment with respect to liability and remand the case for proceedings consistent with this opinion.

It is so ordered.

NOTES

1. The problem in the *Gratz* case was that the advantage given to minority students was a purely mathematical calculation—an additional 20 points on the admissions scale. This kind of measurement was too similar to the mathematical calculation that had been prohibited in *Bakke*, in which the medical school had set aside 16 seats for minorities. It also failed *Grutter's* "individual consideration" test.

2. The *Bakke*, *Grutter*, and *Gratz* cases all arose in university settings. To what extent were those precedents relevant to voluntary actions by local school boards that made race-conscious decisions in order to limit racial segregation in public schools? The Court took up that question in the next case.

Parents Involved in Community Schools v. Seattle School Dist. No. 1
551 U.S. 701 (2007)

Chief Justice ROBERTS announced the judgment of the Court, and delivered the opinion of the Court with respect to Parts I, II, III–A, and III–C, and an opinion with respect to Parts III–B and IV, in which Justices SCALIA, THOMAS, and ALITO join.

The school districts in these cases voluntarily adopted student assignment plans that rely upon race to determine which public schools certain children may attend. The Seattle school district classifies children as white or nonwhite; the Jefferson County school district as black or "other." In Seattle, this racial classification is used to allocate slots in oversubscribed high schools. In Jefferson County, it is used to make certain elementary school assignments and to rule on transfer requests. In each case, the school district relies upon an individual student's race in assigning that student to a particular school, so that the racial balance at the school falls within a predetermined range based on the racial composition of the school district as a whole. Parents of students denied assignment to particular schools under these plans solely because of their race brought suit, contending that allocating children to different public schools on the basis of race violated the Fourteenth Amendment guarantee of equal protection. The Courts of Appeals below upheld the plans. We granted certiorari, and now reverse.

I

Both cases present the same underlying legal question—whether a public school that had not operated legally segregated schools or has been found to be unitary may choose to classify students by race and rely upon that classification in making school assignments.

III

A

It is well established that when the government distributes burdens or benefits on the basis of individual racial classifications, that action is reviewed under strict scrutiny. *Johnson v. California,* 543 U.S. 499, 505–506 (2005); *Grutter v. Bollinger,* 539 U.S. 306, 326 (2003); *Adarand,* 515 U.S. 200, 224 (1995). As the Court recently reaffirmed, "'racial classifications are simply too pernicious to permit any but the most exact connection between justification and classification.' " *Gratz v. Bollinger,* 539 U.S. 244, 270 (2003) (quoting *Fullilove v. Klutznick,* 448 U.S. 448, 537 (1980) (STEVENS, J., dissenting); brackets omitted). In order to satisfy this searching standard of review, the school districts must demonstrate that the use of individual racial classifications in the assignment plans here under review is "narrowly tailored" to achieve a "compelling" government interest. *Adarand, supra,* at 227.

Without attempting in these cases to set forth all the interests a school district might assert, it suffices to note that our prior cases, in evaluating the use of racial classifications in the school context, have recognized two interests that qualify as compelling. The first is the compelling interest of remedying the effects of past intentional discrimination. See *Freeman v. Pitts,* 503 U.S. 467, 494 (1992). Yet the Seattle public schools have not shown that they were ever segregated by law, and were not subject to court-ordered desegregation decrees. The Jefferson County public schools were previously segregated by law and were subject to a desegregation decree entered in 1975. In 2000, the District Court that entered that decree dissolved it, finding that Jefferson County had "eliminated the vestiges associated with the former policy of segregation and its pernicious effects," and thus had achieved "unitary" status. Jefferson County accordingly does not rely upon an interest in remedying the effects of past intentional discrimination in defending its present use of race in assigning students.

Nor could it. We have emphasized that the harm being remedied by mandatory desegregation plans is the harm that is traceable to segregation, and that "the Constitution is not violated by racial imbalance in the schools, without more." *Milliken v. Bradley,* 433 U.S. 267, 280, n. 14 (1977). Once Jefferson County achieved unitary status, it had remedied the constitutional wrong that allowed race-based assignments. Any continued use of race must be justified on some other basis.

The second government interest we have recognized as compelling for purposes of strict scrutiny is the interest in diversity in higher education upheld in *Grutter,* 539 U.S., at 328. The specific interest found compelling in *Grutter* was student body diversity "in the context of higher education." The diversity interest was not focused on race alone but encompassed "all factors that may contribute to student body diversity." We described the various types of diversity that the law school sought:

> [The law school's] policy makes clear there are many possible bases for diversity admissions, and provides examples of admittees who have lived or traveled widely abroad, are fluent in several languages, have overcome personal adversity and family hardship, have exceptional records of extensive community service, and have had

successful careers in other fields.

The Court quoted the articulation of diversity from Justice Powell's opinion in *Regents of the University of California v. Bakke,* 438 U.S. 265 (1978), noting that "it is not an interest in simple ethnic diversity, in which a specified percentage of the student body is in effect guaranteed to be members of selected ethnic groups, that can justify the use of race." *Grutter, supra,* at 324–325. Instead, what was upheld in *Grutter* was consideration of "a far broader array of qualifications and characteristics of which racial or ethnic origin is but a single though important element." 539 U.S., at 325.

The entire gist of the analysis in *Grutter* was that the admissions program at issue there focused on each applicant as an individual, and not simply as a member of a particular racial group. The classification of applicants by race upheld in *Grutter* was only as part of a "highly individualized, holistic review," 539 U.S., at 337. As the Court explained, "[t]he importance of this individualized consideration in the context of a race-conscious admissions program is paramount." The point of the narrow tailoring analysis in which the *Grutter* Court engaged was to ensure that the use of racial classifications was indeed part of a broader assessment of diversity, and not simply an effort to achieve racial balance, which the Court explained would be "patently unconstitutional." *Id.* at 330.

In the present cases, by contrast, race is not considered as part of a broader effort to achieve "exposure to widely diverse people, cultures, ideas, and viewpoints"; race, for some students, is determinative standing alone. The districts argue that other factors, such as student preferences, affect assignment decisions under their plans, but under each plan when race comes into play, it is decisive by itself. It is not simply one factor weighed with others in reaching a decision, as in *Grutter*; it is *the* factor. Like the University of Michigan undergraduate plan struck down in *Gratz,* 539 U.S., at 275, the plans here "do not provide for a meaningful individualized review of applicants" but instead rely on racial classifications in a "nonindividualized, mechanical" way. *Id.* at 276, 280 (O'Connor, J., concurring).

Even when it comes to race, the plans here employ only a limited notion of diversity, viewing race exclusively in white/nonwhite terms in Seattle and black/"other" terms in Jefferson County. But see *Metro Broadcasting, Inc. v. FCC,* 497 U.S. 547, 610 (1990) (O'Connor, J., dissenting) ("We are a Nation not of black and white alone, but one teeming with divergent communities knitted together by various traditions and carried forth, above all, by individuals"). The Seattle "Board Statement Reaffirming Diversity Rationale" speaks of the "inherent educational value" in "[p]roviding students the opportunity to attend schools with diverse student enrollment," But under the Seattle plan, a school with 50 percent Asian–American students and 50 percent white students but no African-American, Native-American, or Latino students would qualify as balanced, while a school with 30 percent Asian-American, 25 percent African-American, 25 percent Latino, and 20 percent white students would not. It is hard to understand how a plan that could allow these results can be viewed as being concerned with achieving enrollment that is "'broadly diverse.'"

In upholding the admissions plan in *Grutter,* though, this Court relied upon considerations unique to institutions of higher education, noting that in light of "the expansive freedoms of speech and thought associated with the university environment, universities occupy a special niche in our constitutional tradition." 539 U.S., at 329. See also *Bakke, supra,* at 312, 313 (opinion of Powell, J.). The Court explained that "[c]ontext matters" in applying strict scrutiny, and repeatedly noted that it was addressing the use of race "in the context of higher education." *Grutter, supra,* at 327, 328, 334. The Court in *Grutter* expressly articulated key limitations on its holding—defining a specific type of broad-based diversity and noting the unique context of higher education—but these limitations were largely disregarded by the lower courts in extending *Grutter* to uphold race-based assignments in elementary and secondary schools. The present cases are not governed by *Grutter.*

B

Perhaps recognizing that reliance on *Grutter* cannot sustain their plans, both school districts assert additional interests, distinct from the interest upheld in *Grutter,* to justify their race-based assignments. In briefing and argument before this Court, Seattle contends that its use of race helps to reduce racial concentration in schools and to ensure that racially concentrated housing patterns do not prevent nonwhite students from having access to the most desirable schools. Jefferson County has articulated a similar goal, phrasing its interest in terms of educating its students "in a racially integrated environment." Each school district argues that educational and broader socialization benefits flow from a racially diverse learning environment, and each contends that because the diversity they seek is racial diversity—not the broader diversity at issue in *Grutter*—it makes sense to promote that interest directly by relying on race alone.

The parties and their *amici* dispute whether racial diversity in schools in fact has a marked impact on test scores and other objective yardsticks or achieves intangible socialization benefits. The debate is not one we need to resolve, however, because it is clear that the racial classifications employed by the districts are not narrowly tailored to the goal of achieving the educational and social benefits asserted to flow from racial diversity. In design and operation, the plans are directed only to racial balance, pure and simple, an objective this Court has repeatedly condemned as illegitimate.

The plans are tied to each district's specific racial demographics, rather than to any pedagogic concept of the level of diversity needed to obtain the asserted educational benefits. In Seattle ... the benefits of racial diversity require enrollment of at least 31 percent white students; in Jefferson County, at least 50 percent. There must be at least 15 percent nonwhite students under Jefferson County's plan; in Seattle, more than three times that figure. This comparison makes clear that the racial demographics in each district—whatever they happen to be—drive the required "diversity" numbers. The plans here are not tailored to achieving a degree of diversity necessary to realize the asserted educational benefits; instead the plans are tailored, in the words of Seattle's Manager of Enrollment Planning, Technical Support, and Demographics, to "the goal established by the school board of attaining a level of diversity within the schools that approximates the district's overall demographics."

The districts offer no evidence that the level of racial diversity necessary to achieve the asserted educational benefits happens to coincide with the racial demographics of the respective school districts—or rather the white/nonwhite or black/"other" balance of the districts, since that is the only diversity addressed by the plans. When asked for "a range of percentage that would be diverse," however, Seattle's expert said it was important to have "sufficient numbers so as to avoid students feeling any kind of specter of exceptionality." The district did not attempt to defend the proposition that anything outside its range posed the "specter of exceptionality." Nor did it demonstrate in any way how the educational and social benefits of racial diversity or avoidance of racial isolation are more likely to be achieved at a school that is 50 percent white and 50 percent

Asian-American, which would qualify as diverse under Seattle's plan, than at a school that is 30 percent Asian-American, 25 percent African-American, 25 percent Latino, and 20 percent white, which under Seattle's definition would be racially concentrated.

In *Grutter,* the number of minority students the school sought to admit was an undefined "meaningful number" necessary to achieve a genuinely diverse student body. 539 U.S., at 316, 335–336. Although the matter was the subject of disagreement on the Court, see *id.* at 346–347 (SCALIA, J., concurring in part and dissenting in part); *id.,* at 382–383 (Rehnquist, C. J., dissenting); *id.* at 388–392 (KENNEDY, J., dissenting), the majority concluded that the law school did not count back from its applicant pool to arrive at the "meaningful number" it regarded as necessary to diversify its student body. *Id.* at 335–336. Here the racial balance the districts seek is a defined range set solely by reference to the demographics of the respective school districts.

This working backward to achieve a particular type of racial balance, rather than working forward from some demonstration of the level of diversity that provides the purported benefits, is a fatal flaw under our existing precedent. We have many times over reaffirmed that "[r]acial balance is not to be achieved for its own sake." *Freeman,* 503 U.S., at 494. See also *Richmond v. J.A. Croson Co.,* 488 U.S. 469, 507 (1989); *Bakke,* 438 U.S., at 307 (opinion of Powell, J.) ("If petitioner's purpose is to assure within its student body some specified percentage of a particular group merely because of its race or ethnic origin, such a preferential purpose must be rejected ... as facially invalid"). *Grutter* itself reiterated that "outright racial balancing" is "patently unconstitutional." 539 U.S., at 330.

Accepting racial balancing as a compelling state interest would justify the imposition of racial proportionality throughout American society, contrary to our repeated recognition that "[a]t the heart of the Constitution's guarantee of equal protection lies the simple command that the Government must treat citizens as individuals, not as simply components of a racial, religious, sexual or national class." *Miller v. Johnson,* 515 U.S. 900, 911 (1995) (quoting *Metro Broadcasting,* 497 U.S., at 602 (O'Connor, J., dissenting). Allowing racial balancing as a compelling end in itself would "effectively assur[e] that race will always be relevant in American life, and that the 'ultimate goal' of 'eliminating entirely from governmental decisionmaking such irrelevant factors as a human being's race' will never be achieved." *Croson, supra,* at 495 (plurality opinion of O'Connor, J.) (quoting *Wygant v. Jackson Bd. of Ed.,* 476 U.S. 267 (1986) (STEVENS, J., dissenting), in turn quoting *Fullilove,* 448 U.S., at 547 (STEVENS, J., dissenting)). An interest "linked to nothing other than proportional representation of various races ... would support indefinite use of racial classifications, employed first to obtain the appropriate mixture of racial views and then to ensure that the [program] continues to reflect that mixture." *Metro Broadcasting, supra,* at 614 (O'Connor, J., dissenting).

The validity of our concern that racial balancing has "no logical stopping point," *Croson, supra,* at 498 (quoting *Wygant, supra,* at 275 (plurality opinion); see also *Grutter, supra,* at 343, is demonstrated here by the degree to which the districts tie their racial guidelines to their demographics. As the districts' demographics shift, so too will their definition of racial diversity.

The principle that racial balancing is not permitted is one of substance, not semantics. Racial balancing is not transformed from "patently unconstitutional" to a compelling state interest simply by relabeling it "racial diversity." While the school districts use various verbal formulations to describe the interest they seek to promote—racial diversity, avoidance of racial isolation, racial integration—they offer no definition of the interest that suggests it differs from racial balance.

Jefferson County phrases its interest as "racial integration," but integration certainly does not require the sort of racial proportionality reflected in its plan. Even in the context of mandatory desegregation, we have stressed that racial proportionality is not required, see *Milliken*, 433 U.S., at 280, n. 14 ("[A desegregation] order contemplating the substantive constitutional right [to a] particular degree of racial balance or mixing is ... infirm as a matter of law); *Swann v. Charlotte–Mecklenburg Bd. of Ed.*, 402 U.S. 1, 24 (1971) ("The constitutional command to desegregate schools does not mean that every school in every community must always reflect the racial composition of the school system as a whole"), and here Jefferson County has already been found to have eliminated the vestiges of its prior segregated school system.

The en banc Ninth Circuit declared that "when a racially diverse school system is the goal (or racial concentration or isolation is the problem), there is no more effective means than a consideration of race to achieve the solution." *Parents Involved VII, supra*, at 1191. For the foregoing reasons, this conclusory argument cannot sustain the plans. However closely related race-based assignments may be to achieving racial balance, that itself cannot be the goal, whether labeled "racial diversity" or anything else. To the extent the objective is sufficient diversity so that students see fellow students as individuals rather than solely as members of a racial group, using means that treat students solely as members of a racial group is fundamentally at cross-purposes with that end.

C

The districts assert, as they must, that the way in which they have employed individual racial classifications is necessary to achieve their stated ends. The minimal effect these classifications have on student assignments, however, suggests that other means would be effective. [The Court here noted here that the racial classifications used by the two school districts had only a minimal effect on the assignment of students and this limited effect cast doubt on the necessity of using racial classifications. The Court also mentioned that the school districts had not shown that they considered methods other than explicit racial classifications to achieve their stated goals.]

IV

The parties and their *amici* debate which side is more faithful to the heritage of *Brown*, but the position of the plaintiffs in *Brown* was spelled out in their brief and could not have been clearer: "[T]he Fourteenth Amendment prevents states from according differential treatment to American children on the basis of their color or race." Brief for Appellants in Nos. 1, 2, and 4 and for Respondents in No. 10 on Reargument in *Brown I*, O.T.1953, p. 15 (Summary of Argument). What do the racial classifications at issue here do, if not accord differential treatment on the basis of race? As counsel who appeared before this Court for the plaintiffs in *Brown* put it: "We have one fundamental contention which we will seek to develop in the course of this argument, and that contention is that no State has any authority under the equal-protection clause of the Fourteenth Amendment to use race as a factor in affording educational opportunities among its citizens." Tr. of Oral Arg. in *Brown I*, O. T. 1953, No. 8, p. 7 (Robert L. Carter, Dec. 9, 1952). There is no ambiguity in that statement. And it was that position that prevailed in this Court, which emphasized in its remedial opinion that what was "[a]t stake is the personal interest of the plaintiffs in admission to public schools as soon as practicable *on a nondiscriminatory basis*," and what was required was "determining admission to the public schools *on a nonracial basis*." *Brown II, supra*, at 300–301 (emphasis added). What do the racial classifications do in these cases, if not determine admission to a public school on a racial basis?

Before *Brown*, schoolchildren were told where they could and could not go to school based on the color of their skin. The school districts in these cases have not carried the heavy burden of demonstrating that we should allow this once again—even for very different reasons. For schools that never segregated on the basis of race, such as Seattle, or that have removed the vestiges of past segregation, such as Jefferson County, the way "to achieve a system of determining admission to the public schools on a nonracial basis," *Brown II*, 349 U.S., at 300–301, is to stop assigning students on a racial basis. The way to stop discrimination on the basis of race is to stop discriminating on the basis of race.

The judgments of the Courts of Appeals for the Sixth and Ninth Circuits are reversed, and the cases are remanded for further proceedings. *It is so ordered.*

Justice BREYER, with whom Justice STEVENS, Justice SOUTER, and Justice GINSBURG join, dissenting.

II

The Legal Standard

A longstanding and unbroken line of legal authority tells us that the Equal Protection Clause permits local school boards to use race-conscious criteria to achieve positive race-related goals, even when the Constitution does not compel it. Because of its importance, I shall repeat what this Court said about the matter in *Swann*. Chief Justice Burger, on behalf of a unanimous Court in a case of exceptional importance, wrote:

> "School authorities are traditionally charged with broad power to formulate and implement educational policy and might well conclude, for example, that in order to prepare students to live in a pluralistic society each school should have a prescribed ratio of Negro to white students reflecting the proportion for the district as a whole. To do this as an educational policy is within the broad discretionary powers of school authorities." 402 U.S., at 16.

The statement was not a technical holding in the case. But the Court set forth in *Swann* a basic principle of constitutional law—a principle of law that has found "wide acceptance in the legal culture." Thus, in *North Carolina Bd. of Ed. v. Swann*, 402 U.S. 43, 45, (1971), this Court, citing *Swann*, restated the point. "[S]chool authorities," the Court said, "have wide discretion in formulating school policy, and ... as a matter of educational policy school authorities may well conclude that some kind of racial balance in the schools is desirable quite apart from any constitutional requirements." Then–Justice Rehnquist echoed this view in *Bustop, Inc. v. Los Angeles Bd. of Ed.*, 439 U.S. 1380, 1383, (1978) (opinion in chambers), making clear that he too believed that *Swann*'s statement reflected settled law: "While I have the gravest doubts that [a state supreme court] was *required* by the United States Constitution to take the [desegregation] action that it has taken in this case, I have very little doubt that it was *permitted* by that Constitution to take such action." (Emphasis in original.)

These statements nowhere suggest that this freedom is limited to school districts where court-ordered desegregation measures are also in effect. Indeed, in *McDaniel*, a case decided the same day as *Swann*, a group of parents challenged a race-conscious student assignment plan that the Clarke County School Board had *voluntarily* adopted as a remedy without a court order (though under federal agency pressure—pressure Seattle also encountered). The plan required that each elementary school in the district maintain 20% to 40% enrollment of African-American students, corresponding to the racial composition of the district. See *Barresi v. Browne,* 226 Ga. 456, 456–459, 175 S.E.2d 649, 650–651 (1970). This Court upheld the plan, see *McDaniel,* 402 U.S., at 41, rejecting the parents' argument that "a person may not be *included* or *excluded* solely because he is a Negro or because he is white."

A

Compelling Interest

The principal interest advanced in these cases to justify the use of race-based criteria goes by various names. Sometimes a court refers to it as an interest in achieving racial "diversity." Other times a court, like the plurality here, refers to it as an interest in racial "balancing." I have used more general terms to signify that interest, describing it, for example, as an interest in promoting or preserving greater racial "integration" of public schools. By this term, I mean the school districts' interest in eliminating school-by-school racial isolation and increasing the degree to which racial mixture characterizes each of the district's schools and each individual student's public school experience.

Regardless of its name, however, the interest at stake possesses three essential elements. First, there is a historical and remedial element: an interest in setting right the consequences of prior conditions of segregation. This refers back to a time when public schools were highly segregated, often as a result of legal or administrative policies that facilitated racial segregation in public schools. It is an interest in continuing to combat the remnants of segregation caused in whole or in part by these school-related policies, which have often affected not only schools, but also housing patterns, employment practices, economic conditions, and social attitudes. It is an interest in maintaining hard-won gains. And it has its roots in preventing what gradually may become the *de facto* resegregation of America's public schools

Second, there is an educational element: an interest in overcoming the adverse educational effects produced by and associated with highly segregated schools. Cf. *Grutter,* 539 U.S., at 345 (GINSBURG, J., concurring). Studies suggest that children taken from those schools and placed in integrated settings often show positive academic gains. Other studies reach different conclusions. But the evidence supporting an educational interest in racially integrated schools is well established and strong enough to permit a democratically elected school board reasonably to determine that this interest is a compelling one.

Third, there is a democratic element: an interest in producing an educational environment that reflects the "pluralistic society" in which our children will live. *Swann,* 402 U.S. It is an interest in helping our children learn to work and play together with children of different racial backgrounds. It is an interest in teaching children to engage in the kind of cooperation among Americans of all races that is necessary to make a land of three hundred million people one Nation.

The compelling interest at issue here, then, includes an effort to eradicate the remnants, not of general "societal discrimination," *ante,* at 2758 (plurality opinion), but of primary and secondary school segregation, see *supra,* at 2803, 2807; it includes an effort to create school environments that provide better educational opportunities for all children; it includes an effort to help create citizens better prepared to know, to understand, and to work with people of all races and backgrounds, thereby furthering the kind of democratic government our Constitution foresees. If an educational interest that combines these three elements is not "compelling," what is?

NOTES

1. The *Parents Involved* case either limited *Grutter*, or alternatively, brought to the surface limits that were already implicit in *Grutter*. First, *Parents Involved* made clear that the diversity rationale in *Grutter* is limited to the context of higher education, given the considerations unique to universities and the expansive freedoms of speech and thought associated with the university environment. By comparison, it seems, there are no expansive freedoms of speech and thought that would make diversity compelling in primary or secondary public schools. Second, *Parents Involved* contrasts the diversity that was approved in *Grutter*—a desire to bring together students of many different backgrounds and talents, of which race was only one consideration—with the diversity that was the goal in *Parents Involved*—racial diversity alone.

The most extreme language in the *Parents Involved* opinion appeared in Section III.B, which did not command five votes and was therefore not the opinion of the Court. In that section, the Court identified the purpose of the plans as "racial balanc[ing], pure and simple, an objective this Court has repeatedly condemned." The plurality then continued:

> The principle that racial balancing is not permitted is one of substance, not semantics. Racial balancing is not transformed from "patently unconstitutional" to a compelling state interest simply by relabeling it "racial diversity." While the school districts use various verbal formulations to describe the interest they seek to promote—racial diversity, avoidance of racial isolation, racial integration—they offer no definition of the interest that suggests it differs from racial balance.

The plurality here treated an attempt by a school board to promote integration in public schools as the equivalent of prohibited racial balancing. This demonization of integration as a goal is relatively new, for there was a time when racial integration was viewed as a positive social good. See *e.g., King v. Harris*, 464 F. Supp. 827, 837 (E.D.N.Y. 1979) ("It is now well settled that HUD has an affirmative duty to promote racial integration through its housing policy.").

Justice Kennedy, who provided the fifth vote for the majority, did not join Section III.B. and he explained why:

> My views do not allow me to join the balance of the opinion by THE CHIEF JUSTICE, which seems to me to be inconsistent in both its approach and its implications with the history, meaning, and reach of the Equal Protection Clause . . .
>
> This is by way of preface to my respectful submission that parts of the opinion by THE CHIEF JUSTICE imply an all-too-unyielding insistence that race cannot be a factor in instances when, in my view, it may be taken into account. The plurality opinion is too dismissive of the legitimate interest government has in ensuring all people have equal opportunity regardless of their race. The plurality's postulate that "[t]he way to stop discrimination on the basis of race is to stop discriminating on the basis of race," is not sufficient to decide these cases. Fifty years of experience since *Brown v. Board of*

Education, 347 U.S. 483 (1954), should teach us that the problem before us defies so easy a solution. School districts can seek to reach *Brown's* objective of equal educational opportunity. The plurality opinion is at least open to the interpretation that the Constitution requires school districts to ignore the problem of de facto resegregation in schooling. I cannot endorse that conclusion. To the extent the plurality opinion suggests the Constitution mandates that state and local school authorities must accept the status quo of racial isolation in schools, it is, in my view, profoundly mistaken.

In the administration of public schools by the state and local authorities it is permissible to consider the racial makeup of schools and to adopt general policies to encourage a diverse student body, one aspect of which is its racial composition. *Cf. Grutter v. Bollinger*, 539 U.S. 306 (2003) (KENNEDY, J., dissenting). If school authorities are concerned that the student-body compositions of certain schools interfere with the objective of offering an equal educational opportunity to all of their students, they are free to devise race-conscious measures to address the problem in a general way and without treating each student in different fashion solely on the basis of a systematic, individual typing by race.

School boards may pursue the goal of bringing together students of diverse backgrounds and races through other means, including strategic site selection of new schools; drawing attendance zones with general recognition of the demographics of neighborhoods; allocating resources for special programs; recruiting students and faculty in a targeted fashion; and tracking enrollments, performance, and other statistics by race. These mechanisms are race conscious but do not lead to different treatment based on a classification that tells each student he or she is to be defined by race, so it is unlikely any of them would demand strict scrutiny to be found permissible.

2. Justice Breyer, writing for the four dissenting judges, thought that the plurality had misread *Brown* and its progeny. Breyer quoted the language of the majority in *Swann*:

> School authorities are traditionally charged with broad power to formulate and implement educational policy and might well conclude, for example, that in order to prepare students to live in a pluralistic society each school should have a prescribed ratio of Negro to white students reflecting the proportion for the district as a whole. To do this as an educational policy is within the broad discretionary powers of school authorities. 402 U.S., at 16.

Breyer thought that, in reviewing the actions of school boards, the terminology should not decide the case, whether the purpose was called "racial diversity," "racial balancing," "racial integration," or "eliminating racial isolation." Whatever it is called, Breyer stated that the interest at stake possesses three essential elements: (1) a historical and remedial element: an interest in setting right the consequences of prior conditions of segregation; (2) an educational element: an interest in overcoming the adverse educational effects produced by and associated with highly segregated schools; and (3) a democratic element: an interest in producing an educational environment that reflects the "pluralistic society" in which our children will live. Breyer thought that the interests of the school boards in *Parents Involved* possessed all three.

3. In *Ricci v. DeStefano*, 557 U.S. 557 (2009), the Court held that the city of New Haven violated Title VII of the Civil Rights Act of 1964 when it refused to certify the results of

promotion exams for firefighters because almost all of the successful test takers were white. The city's justification for its behavior was that it wanted to avoid disparate impact liability under Title VII, that is, its use of the exam results would have had a disproportionately adverse impact on minority applicants and thus would constitute a prima facie case of discrimination. The Court rejected that defense because the city did not have a strong basis in the evidence to believe that it could not have justified the disparate impact. This meant that the city's attempt to address a prima facie case of disparate impact was in fact a disparate treatment violation--the city had intentionally discriminated, against white test takers, on the basis of race.

Ricci was not an equal protection case, but there is an equal protection issue lurking in its background. As Justice Scalia, concurring, explained:

> I join the Court's opinion in full, but write separately to observe that its resolution of this dispute merely postpones the evil day on which the Court will have to confront the question: Whether, or to what extent, are the disparate-impact provisions of Title VII of the Civil Rights Act of 1964 consistent with the Constitution's guarantee of equal protection? . . . But if the Federal Government is prohibited from discriminating on the basis of race, *Bolling v. Sharpe*, 347 U.S. 497 (1954), then surely it is also prohibited from enacting laws mandating that third parties— e.g., employers, whether private, State, or municipal—discriminate on the basis of race. See *Buchanan v. Warley*, 245 U.S. 60 (1917). As the facts of these cases illustrate, Title VII's disparate-impact provisions place a racial thumb on the scales, often requiring employers to evaluate the racial outcomes of their policies, and to make decisions based on (because of) those racial outcomes. That type of racial decisionmaking is, as the Court explains, discriminatory. *Ricci*, 557 U.S. at 594 (Scalia, J., concurring).

Even though New Haven's action was race neutral on its face—refusing to give effect to an employment exam, its purpose was racial—to ensure a sufficient number of minority firefighters. Justice Scalia suggested that this kind of race-neutral yet race-conscious decision may be as objectionable as any other race-neutral decision that is adopted *because of* its discriminatory effect. For a thorough discussion of this issue, see Michelle Adams, *Is Integration a Discriminatory Purpose?* 96 Iowa L. Rev. 837 (2011).

4. In 1996, the United States Court of Appeals for the Fifth Circuit, in a pre-*Grutter* ruling, struck down the use of race-based criteria in admissions at the University of Texas. *Hopwood v. Texas*, 78 F.3d 932 (5th Cir. 1996). In response, the Texas Legislature enacted the Top Ten Percent Law, which automatically admitted Texas high school seniors in the top ten percent of their public high school class to any Texas state university. Although the Ten Percent law is racially neutral, it had the effect of increasing minority enrollment at Texas universities. Because substantial racial segregation exists in Texas public high schools, all top students at predominantly segregated high schools will likely be minorities. The ten percent rule would probably be of questionable constitutional validity under Justice Scalia's view in the preceding paragraph, but that issue has not been litigated.

In *Fisher v. University of Texas*, 631 F.3d 213 (5th Cir. 2011), a different aspect of the University of Texas admissions plan was challenged by a white applicant who was rejected by the University of Texas at Austin. After the Supreme Court's 2003 decision in *Grutter*, the university adopted a policy that, in conjunction with the ten percent rule, attempted to achieve a diverse class. Race was one of many factors the school would consider. The court of appeals upheld the policy as narrowly tailored to achieve a compelling interest, notwithstanding an argument that the program's real goal was racial balancing and that, given the ten percent plan, additional consideration of race in admissions process was unnecessary and not narrowly tailored to its goal. The Supreme Court has granted certiorari, 132 S. Ct. 1536 (2012), and may use the case as an opportunity to revisit its rules on affirmative action.

G. WHAT IS A RACIAL CLASSIFICATION? WHAT IS A NATIONAL ORIGIN CLASSIFICATION?

Since classifications based on race will be strictly scrutinized and usually invalidated, it is important to be able to identify a "race classification." That kind of identification is easy enough in very mainstream cases, but can be close to impossible at the margins. The concept of race is very inexact and confusing.

During the nineteenth century and well into the twentieth, courts were quite comfortable with dividing humans into different races. One of the standard divisions held that humans could be divided into three races—the Caucasoid, the Mongoloid, and the Negroid. These three races could be correlated with geography—European, Asian, and African, or with color—white, yellow, and black. There was not always agreement, however, on the number of races. For example, a trial judge in Virginia as late as 1967 thought that there were five, rather than three, races:

> Almighty God created the races white, black, yellow, malay and red, and he placed them on separate continents. And but for the interference with his arrangement there would be no cause for such marriages. The fact that he separated the races shows that he did not intend for the races to mix. *Loving v. Virginia*, 388 U.S. 1 (1967).

No matter the disagreements over the number of races, there was no dispute about the hierarchy of races, with whites at the top and others unmistakably at the bottom. Thus, for example, the Court in the *Dred Scott* case justified its conclusion that slaves could not be citizens with the following assertions about racial inferiority:

> They had for more than a century before been regarded as beings of an inferior order, and altogether unfit to associate with the white race, either in social or political relations; and so far inferior, that they had no rights which the white man was bound to respect; and that the negro might justly and lawfully be reduced to slavery for his benefit. He was bought and sold, and treated as an ordinary article of merchandise and traffic, whenever a profit could be made by it. This opinion was at that time fixed and universal in the civilized portion of the white race. It was regarded as an axiom in morals as well as in politics, which no one thought of disputing, or supposed to be open to dispute; and men in every grade and position in society daily and habitually acted upon it in their private pursuits, as well as in matters of public concern, without doubting for a moment the correctness of this opinion. *Dred Scott v. Standford*, 60 U.S. 394, 407 (1856).

In recent years, the idea that racial classifications are a social construct, neither scientific nor genetic, has become much more widely accepted. The Court adopted this view when it said:

> Many modern biologists and anthropologists, however, criticize racial classifications as arbitrary and of little use in understanding the variability of human beings. It is said that

genetically homogeneous populations do not exist and traits are not discontinuous between populations; therefore, a population can only be described in terms of relative frequencies of various traits. Clear-cut categories do not exist. The particular traits which have generally been chosen to characterize races have been criticized as having little biological significance. It has been found that differences between individuals of the same race are often greater than the differences between the "average" individuals of different races. These observations and others have led some, but not all, scientists to conclude that racial classifications are for the most part sociopolitical, rather than biological, in nature. *Saint Francis College v. Al-Khazraji*, 481 U.S. 604, 610, n.4 (1987).

A recent review of two books in *American Science* concurred:

The consensus among Western researchers today is that human races are sociocultural constructs. Still, the concept of human race as an objective biological reality persists in science and in society. It is high time that policy makers, educators and those in the medical-industrial complex rid themselves of the misconception of race as type or as genetic population. Jan Sapp, *Race Finished*, American Scientist, March-April, 2012.

There are dissenting views that insist that race is still relevant as a biological construct. Thus, for example, DNA evidence has been used forensically to identify suspects by race. *See generally* Christian B. Sundquist, *The Meaning of Race in the DNA Era: Science, History, and the Law*, 27 Temple J. S. L.T. & E. 231(2008).

Whether or not race is biologically based or a social construct, a determination of race is still important when race is used to ascertain eligibility for the benefits of affirmative action, and the Supreme Court has used a casual definition of race in such cases. The Court has noted that, at the time of the adoption of the Equal Protection Clause, the term "race" encompassed ethnicity. *Saint Francis College v. Al-Khazraji*, 481 U.S. 604 (1987). Thus, it was not surprising that in *Yick Wo v. Hopkins*, 118 U.S. 356 (1886), one of the earliest equal protection cases, the Court treated discrimination against Chinese persons as racial discrimination. The Court also spoke of discrimination against persons of Japanese descent as racial discrimination in *Korematsu v. United States*, 323 U.S. 214 (1944). In 1956, in *Hernandez v. Texas*, 347 U.S. 475 (1954), the Court identified persons of Mexican descent as a clearly identifiable class. The *Hernandez* Court noted that the Equal Protection Clause does not articulate a limited two-class theory (black and white), but that "community prejudices are not static, and from time to time other differences from the community norm may define other groups which need the same protection."

It is not always clear, however, whether discrimination against a particular ethnic group will be treated as the equivalent of a racial classification. In *United States v. Biaggi*, 673 F. Supp. 96, 101(E.D. Ny. 1987), the court identified Italian-Americans as a "cognizable racial group," but the court in *United States v. Sgro*, 816 F. 2d 30 (1st Cir. 1987) found otherwise. In *Murchu v. United States*, 926 F.2d 50 (1st Cir. 1991), the court found that Irish-Americans did not constitute a cognizable racial group, given "the complete absence of any allegations or evidence that Americans of Irish ancestry—even if otherwise a cognizable group-were being subject to unequal treatment by their fellow Americans . . . and hence needed protection from community prejudices."

CHAPTER 3

GENDER CLASSIFICATIONS

A. Traditional Thinking

For a long time in this country, it was commonplace to ascribe different social and familial roles to men and women, that is, men and women were assigned to "separate spheres." For women, the predominant roles were those of wife and mother, while for men it was thought that the proper roles were those in the marketplace, in government, and in the world of ideas. Of course, men were husbands and fathers too, but these familial roles for men were not thought of as interfering with their public roles. Even in earlier centuries, of course, this description of separate male and female roles was a gross generalization, belied by the actual experiences of many men and women. One could cite, for example, the heroic pioneer families who crossed the wilderness and eked out a living in a hostile environment, with no strong sense of assigning particular tasks on the basis of gender. The description of the separate spheres for men and women did, however, have some basis in fact.

Throughout the nineteenth and for most of the twentieth centuries, the American legal system was untroubled by the different roles assigned to men and women, and legal rules typically gave effect to those roles. Women challenging those roles in court did not succeed. During the period from 1872 through 1961, the Supreme Court decided four cases that challenged gender-role stereotyping, and all four challenges failed.

In 1872, the Court decided *Bradwell v. Illinois,* 82 U.S. 130 (1872), a case in which Myra Bradwell was denied admission to the Illinois bar because she was a woman. The Court determined that the right to practice law was not protected by the privileges or immunities clause of the Fourteenth Amendment and therefore affirmed Bradwell's exclusion from the bar, without explicitly considering the gender issue. Justice Bradley, however, in his concurring opinion, spoke quite explicitly about the gender differences that justified the exclusion of women from the practice of law. Bradley stated:

> It certainly cannot be affirmed, as an historical fact, that this [the right to engage in a profession] has ever been established as one of the fundamental privileges and immunities of the sex. On the contrary, the civil law, as well as nature herself, has always recognized a wide difference in the respective spheres and destinies of man and woman. Man is, or should be, woman's protector and defender. The natural and proper timidity

and delicacy which belongs to the female sex evidently unfits it for many of the occupations of civil life. The constitution of the family organization, which is founded in the divine ordinance, as well as in the nature of things, indicates the domestic sphere as that which properly belongs to the domain and functions of womanhood. The harmony, not to say identity, of interest and views which belong, or should belong, to the family institution is repugnant to the idea of a woman adopting a distinct and independent career from that of her husband. So firmly fixed was this sentiment in the founders of the common law that it became a maxim of that system of jurisprudence that a woman had no legal existence separate from her husband, who was regarded as her head and representative in the social state; and, notwithstanding some recent modifications of this civil status, many of the special rules of law flowing from and dependent upon this cardinal principle still exist in full force in most States. One of these is that a married woman is incapable, without her husband's consent, of making contracts which shall be binding on her or him. This very incapacity was one circumstance which the Supreme Court of Illinois deemed important in rendering a married woman incompetent fully to perform the duties and trusts that belong to the office of an attorney and counsellor.

It is true that many women are unmarried and not affected by any of the duties, complications, and incapacities arising out of the married state, but these are exceptions to the general rule. The paramount destiny and mission of woman are to fulfill the noble and benign offices of wife and mother. This is the law of the Creator. And the rules of civil society must be adapted to the general constitution of things, and cannot be based upon exceptional cases. *Bradley v. Illinois*, 83 U.S. at 141-42.

In 1908, at a time when the Court was invalidating state laws that regulated the working hours and conditions as an improper restraint on liberty, *see Lochner v. New York*, 198 U.S. 45 (1905), it upheld in, *Muller v. Oregon*, 208 U.S. 412 (1908), a state law that limited employment by women to ten hours of work per day. The Court explained:

That woman's physical structure and the performance of maternal functions place her at a disadvantage in the struggle for subsistence is obvious. This is especially true when the burdens of motherhood are upon her. Even when they are not, by abundant testimony of the medical fraternity continuance for a long time on her feet at work, repeating this from day to day, tends to injurious effects upon the body, and, as healthy mothers are essential to vigorous offspring, the physical well-being of woman becomes an object of public interest and care in order to preserve the strength and vigor of the race . . .

Differentiated by these matters from the other sex, she is properly placed in a class by herself, and legislation designed for her protection may be sustained, even when like legislation is not necessary for men, and could not be sustained. It is impossible to close one's eyes to the fact that she still looks to her brother and depends upon him . . .

The two sexes differ in structure of body, in the functions to be performed by each, in the amount of physical strength, in the capacity for long continued labor, particularly when done standing, the influence of vigorous health upon the future well-being of the race, the self-reliance which enables one to assert full rights, and in the capacity to maintain the struggle for subsistence. This difference justifies a difference in legislation, and upholds that which is designed to compensate for some of the burdens which rest upon her.

In 1948, in *Goesaert v. Cleary*, 335 U.S. 464 (1948), the Court upheld a state law that prohibited women from working as bartenders unless the woman was the wife or daughter of a male owner. Justice Frankfurter, writing for the Court, did not appear to take the equal protection challenge very seriously, citing the "historic calling" of "the alewife, sprightly and ribald, in Shakespeare." Frankfurter indicated that the state could "deny to all women opportunities for bartending," and that the legislature was free to devise preventative measures to address the moral and social problems that arise from bartending by women. "Since the line [drawn by the legislature] is not without a basis in reason, we cannot give ear to the suggestion that the real impulse behind this legislation was an unchivalrous desire of male bartenders to try to monopolize the calling."

Finally, in 1961, in *Hoyt v. Florida*, 368 U.S. 57 (1961), the Court upheld a system of jury selection in which men were called automatically but women were called only if they had taken the affirmative step of registering to be in the jury pool. This system resulted in a pool of jurors that was almost entirely male. The Court was not troubled by this exclusion of women in that it was consistent with the social roles assigned to the sexes:

> In neither respect can we conclude that Florida's statute is not 'based on some reasonable classification,' and that it is thus infected with unconstitutionality. Despite the enlightened emancipation of women from the restrictions and protections of bygone years, and their entry into many parts of community life formerly considered to be reserved to men, woman is still regarded as the center of home and family life. We cannot say that it is constitutionally impermissible for a State, acting in pursuit of the general welfare, to conclude that a woman should be relieved from the civic duty of jury service unless she herself determines that such service is consistent with her own special responsibilities.

It was not until 1971 that the Court would begin to take claims of gender discrimination seriously. In that year, in *Reed v. Reed*, the Court for the first time invalidated a gender classification.

A NOTE ON TERMINOLOGY

When there is discussion about laws that treat men and women differently, the terms "sex classification" and "gender classification" are both in common use. Not everyone considers the terms to be interchangeable. Mary Ann C. Case writes:

> As most feminist theorists use the terminology, "sex" refers to the anatomical and physiological distinctions between men and women; "gender," by contrast, is used to refer to the cultural overlay on those anatomical and physiological distinctions. While it is a sex distinction that men can grow beards and women typically cannot, it is a gender distinction that women wear dresses in this society and men typically do not. Mary Ann C. Case, *Disaggregating Gender from Sex and Sexual Orientation: The Effeminate Man in the Law and Feminist Jurisprudence*, 105 Yale L.J. 1, 10-11 (1995).

Courts do not, however, follow this suggested usage and in fact use the terms "sex" and "gender" interchangeably. Thus, for example, in *Nguyen v. I.N.S*, 533 U.S. 53 (2001), a case that involved a statute that treated mothers and fathers differently, the five-person majority repeatedly described the issue as one of a "gender classification" while the four person dissent described it as a "sex classification."

B. THE ROAD TO INTERMEDIATE SCRUTINY: 1971-1976

1. *THE SUPREME COURT PRECEDENTS*

Reed v. Reed
404 U.S. 71 (1971)

[Richard Lynn Reed was a minor child whose adoptive parents were separated at the time of his death. Both parents petitioned the court to be appointed administer of their son's estate, which had a total value of less than $1,000. The Idaho Probate court recognized that both applicants were equally entitled to act as administrator according to Idaho Code § 15-312, which identified members of the class of individuals entitled to administer the estate of someone who dies intestate. The Court made no judgment regarding capability. The father was appointed based on the application of § 15-314 of the Idaho Code, which specified that "of several persons claiming and equally entitled (under § 15-312) to administer, males must be preferred to females." The mother, Sally Reed, appealed on constitutional grounds, alleging a violation of the Equal Protection Clause of the Fourteenth Amendment.]

Mr. Chief Justice BURGER delivered the opinion for a unanimous Court:

Having examined the record and considered the briefs and oral arguments of the parties, we have concluded that the arbitrary preference established in favor of males by the Idaho Code cannot stand in the face of the Fourteenth Amendment's command that no State deny the equal protection of the laws to any person within its jurisdiction.

Idaho does not, of course, deny letters of administration to women altogether. Indeed, under [the statute], a woman whose spouse dies intestate has a preference over a son, father, brother, or any other male relative of the decedent. Moreover, we can judicially notice that in this country, presumably due to the greater longevity of women, a large proportion of estates, both intestate and under wills of decedents, are administered by surviving widows.

[The challenged statute] is restricted in its operation to those situations where competing applications for letters of administration have been filed by both male and female members of the same entitlement class. In such situations, [the statute] provides that different treatment be accorded to the applicants on the basis of their sex; it thus establishes a classification subject to scrutiny under the Equal Protection Clause.

In applying that clause, this Court has consistently recognized that the Fourteenth Amendment does not deny to States the power to treat different classes of persons in different ways. The Equal Protection Clause of that amendment does, however, deny to States the power to legislate that different treatment be accorded to persons placed by a statute into different classes on the basis of criteria wholly unrelated to the objective of that statute. A classification 'must be reasonable, not arbitrary, and must rest upon some ground of difference having a fair and substantial relation to the object of the legislation, so that all persons similarly circumstanced shall be treated alike.' *Royster Guano Co. v. Virginia*, 253 U.S. 412, 415 (1920). The question presented by this case, then, is whether a difference in the sex of competing applicants for letters of administration bears a rational relationship to a state objective that is sought to be advanced by the operation of [the statutory provisions].

In upholding the latter section, the Idaho Supreme Court concluded that its objective was to eliminate one area of controversy when two or more persons, equally entitled under [the statute], seek letters of administration and thereby present the probate court 'with the issue of which one should be named.' The court also concluded that where such persons are not of the same sex, the elimination of females from consideration 'is neither an illogical nor arbitrary method devised by the legislature to resolve an issue that would otherwise require a hearing as to the relative merits of the two or more petitioning relatives.'

Clearly the objective of reducing the workload on probate courts by eliminating one class of contests is not without some legitimacy. The crucial question, however, is whether [the statute] advances that objective in a manner consistent with the command of the Equal Protection Clause. We hold that it does not. To give a mandatory preference to members of either sex over members of the other, merely to accomplish the elimination of hearings on the merits, is to make the very kind of arbitrary legislative choice forbidden by the Equal Protection Clause of the Fourteenth Amendment; and whatever may be said as to the positive values of avoiding intrafamily controversy, the choice in this context may not lawfully be mandated solely on the basis of sex.

The objective of [the statute] clearly is to establish degrees of entitlement of various classes of persons in accordance with their varying degrees and kinds of relationship to the intestate. Regardless of their sex, persons within any one of the enumerated classes of that section are similarly situated with respect to that objective. By providing dissimilar treatment for men and women who are thus similarly situated, the challenged section violates the Equal Protection Clause.

The judgment of the Idaho Supreme Court is reversed and the case remanded for further proceedings not inconsistent with this opinion.

NOTES

1. *Reed* is significant in that it is the first case in which the Court invalidated a gender classification under the Equal Protection Clause. The *Reed* Court, however, did not announce any higher standard of review but rather purported to follow the traditional rational basis test, that is, whether the gender classification "bears a rational relationship to a state objective that is sought to be advanced by the operation of [the statute]." The preference for men over women in the choice of administrator was arbitrary, according to the Court, and did not even meet the rational basis standard. Of course, this more demanding version of rational basis review is not the same as the traditional very deferential version. If the Court had been inclined to uphold the statute under rational basis review, it would have been an easy task. As to the purpose of the law, the *Reed* Court suggested that it was administrative convenience--simply the desire to avoid a hearing on the merits of who would be a better administrator. Two years later, however, in *Frontiero v. Richardson*, the Court would look back on *Reed* and suggest that the real purpose of the statute was to identify those "conversant with business affairs" and thus more qualified to administer an

estate. In relation to this purpose (and under rational basis review, there need be no evidence of purpose), men and women were not similarly situated, since, particularly in 1971, men were far more likely than women to have business experience.

The fact that it was rational to distinguish between men and women in this context demonstrates the inadequacy of traditional rational basis review in relation to gender classifications. To the extent that women had less business experience than men, that difference was in a large measure the result of discrimination against women in the work place and of stereotypical views about the proper roles of men and women. In that situation, a mere rationality standard would tend to give effect to, endorse, and thereby lock in the gender inequalities that currently existed. The *Reed* Court avoided this problem by applying a heightened form of rationality review: the Court considered only one legislative purpose (administrative convenience) and then found that men and women were similarly situated in relation to that purpose. That method resolved the *Reed* case adequately, but did not provide a strong foundation for the future, in that the Court might return to the deferential version of rational basis review at any time. Two years later, in *Frontiero v. Richardson*, a plurality of the Court determined that gender classifications should be subject to strict scrutiny.

Frontiero v. Richardson
411 U.S. 677 (1973)

[A federal statute provided certain medical, dental, and housing benefits to the spouses of military personnel. The benefits were granted automatically to a serviceman's wife, but a servicewoman was required to demonstrate that her husband was in fact dependent on her for over half of his support. Plaintiff Sharon Frontiero's husband was a full-time student receiving veteran's benefits totaling almost 60% of his individual living expenses and thus not eligible for the spousal dependency benefit. Frontiero argued that the requirement placed a dual burden on female members of the armed forces. Procedurally, an additional showing was required of women but not men before a benefit would be conferred. Substantively, servicemen were granted an economic benefit that was not granted to similarly situated servicewomen. The Court considered whether that difference in treatment violated the Due Process Clause of the Fifth Amendment.]

Mr. Justice BRENNAN announced the judgment of the Court in an opinion in which Mr. Justice DOUGLAS, Mr. Justice WHITE, and Mr. Justice MARSHALL join.

At the outset, appellants contend that classifications based upon sex, like classifications based upon race, alienage, and national origin, are inherently suspect and must therefore be subjected to close judicial scrutiny. We agree and, indeed, find at least implicit support for such an approach in our unanimous decision only last Term in *Reed v. Reed*, 404 U.S. 71 (1971).

[The Court noted that the *Reed* opinion had departed from the traditional rational basis standard and that that departure was "clearly justified."]

There can be no doubt that our Nation has had a long and unfortunate history of sex discrimination. Traditionally, such discrimination was rationalized by an attitude of 'romantic paternalism', which, in practical effect, put women, not on a pedestal, but in a cage. Indeed, this paternalistic attitude became so firmly rooted in our national consciousness that, 100 years ago, a distinguished Member of this Court was able to proclaim:

Man is, or should be, women's protector and defender. The natural and proper timidity and delicacy which belongs to the female sex evidently unfits it for many of the occupations of civil life. The constitution of the family organization, which is founded in the divine ordinance, as well as in the nature of things, indicates the domestic sphere as that which properly belongs to the domain and functions of womanhood. The harmony, not to say identity, of interests and views which belong, or should belong, to the family institution is repugnant to the idea of a woman adopting a distinct and independent career from that of her husband . . .

The paramount destiny and mission of woman are to fulfill the noble and benign offices of wife and mother. This is the law of the Creator.' *Bradwell v. State of Illinois*, 16 Wall. 130, 141 (1873) (Bradley, J., concurring).

As a result of notions such as these, our statute books gradually became laden with gross, stereotyped distinctions between the sexes and, indeed, throughout much of the 19th century the position of women in our society was, in many respects, comparable to that of blacks under the pre-Civil War slave codes. Neither slaves nor women could hold office, serve on juries, or bring suit in their own names, and married women traditionally were denied the legal capacity to hold or convey property or to serve as legal guardians of their own children. And although blacks were guaranteed the right to vote in 1870, women were denied even that right - which is itself 'preservative of other basic civil and political rights' - until adoption of the Nineteenth Amendment half a century later.

It is true, of course, that the position of women in America has improved markedly in recent decades. Nevertheless, it can hardly be doubted that, in part because of the high visibility of the sex characteristic, women still face pervasive, although at times more subtle, discrimination in our educational institutions, in the job market and, perhaps most conspicuously, in the political arena.[FN17]

Moreover, since sex, like race and national origin, is an immutable characteristic determined solely by the accident of birth, the imposition of special disabilities upon the members of a particular sex because of their sex would seem to violate 'the basic concept of our system that legal burdens should bear some relationship to individual responsibility . . .' *Weber v. Aetna Casualty & Surety Co.*, 406 U.S. 164, 175 (1972). And what differentiates sex from such non-suspect statuses as intelligence or physical disability, and aligns it with the recognized suspect criteria, is that the sex characteristic frequently bears no relation to ability to perform or contribute to society. As a result, statutory distinctions between the sexes often have the effect of invidiously relegating the entire class of females to inferior legal status without regard to the actual capabilities of its individual members.

We might also note that, over the past decade, Congress has itself manifested an increasing sensitivity to sex-based classifications. In Tit. VII of the Civil Rights Act of 1964, for example,

---

[FN17] It is true, of course, that when viewed in the abstract, women do not constitute a small and powerless minority. Nevertheless, in part because of past discrimination, women are vastly underrepresented in this Nation's decisionmaking councils. There has never been a female President, nor a female member of this Court. Not a single woman presently sits in the United States Senate, and only 14 women hold seats in the House of Representatives. And, as appellants point out, this underrepresentation is present throughout all levels of our State and Federal Government. See Joint Reply Brief of Appellants and American Civil Liberties Union (Amicus Curiae) 9.

Congress expressly declared that no employer, labor union, or other organization subject to the provisions of the Act shall discriminate against any individual on the basis of 'race, color, religion, sex, or national origin.' Similarly, the Equal Pay Act of 1963 provides that no employer covered by the Act 'shall discriminate . . . between employees on the basis of sex.' And s 1 of the Equal Rights Amendment, passed by Congress on March 22, 1972, and submitted to the legislatures of the States for ratification, declares that '(e)quality of rights under the law shall not be denied or abridged by the United States or by any State on account of sex.' Thus, Congress itself has concluded that classifications based upon sex are inherently invidious, and this conclusion of a coequal branch of Government is not without significance to the question presently under consideration.

With these considerations in mind, we can only conclude that classifications based upon sex, like classifications based upon race, alienage, or national origin, are inherently suspect, and must therefore be subjected to strict judicial scrutiny. Applying the analysis mandated by that stricter standard of review, it is clear that the statutory scheme now before us is constitutionally invalid.

III

The sole basis of the classification established in the challenged statutes is the sex of the individuals involved. Thus, under [the challenged statute], a female member of the uniformed services seeking to obtain housing and medical benefits for her spouse must prove his dependency in fact, whereas no such burden is imposed upon male members. In addition, the statutes operate so as to deny benefits to a female member, such as appellant Sharron Frontiero, who provides less than one-half of her spouse's support, while at the same time granting such benefits to a male member who likewise provides less than one-half of his spouse's support. Thus, to this extent at least, it may fairly be said that these statutes command 'dissimilar treatment for men and women who are . . . similarly situated.' *Reed v. Reed*, 404 U.S., at 77.

Moreover, the Government concedes that the differential treatment accorded men and women under these statutes serves no purpose other than mere 'administrative convenience.' In essence, the Government maintains that, as an empirical matter, wives in our society frequently are dependent upon their husbands, while husbands rarely are dependent upon their wives. Thus, the Government argues that Congress might reasonably have concluded that it would be both cheaper and easier simply conclusively to presume that wives of male members are financially dependent upon their husbands, while burdening female members with the task of establishing dependency in fact.

The Government offers no concrete evidence, however, tending to support its view that such differential treatment in fact saves the Government any money. In order to satisfy the demands of strict judicial scrutiny, the Government must demonstrate, for example, that it is actually cheaper to grant increased benefits with respect to all male members, than it is to determine which male members are in fact entitled to such benefits and to grant increased benefits only to those members whose wives actually meet the dependency requirement. Here, however, there is substantial evidence that, if put to the test, many of the wives of male members would fail to qualify for benefits. And in light of the fact that the dependency determination with respect to the husbands of female members is presently made solely on the basis of affidavits rather than through the more costly hearing process, the Government's explanation of the statutory scheme is, to say the least, questionable.

In any case, our prior decisions make clear that, although efficacious administration of governmental programs is not without some importance, 'the Constitution recognizes higher values than speed and efficiency.' *Stanley v. Illinois*, 405 U.S. 645, 656 (1972). And when we enter the realm of 'strict judicial scrutiny,' there can be no doubt that 'administrative convenience' is not a shibboleth, the mere recitation of which dictates constitutionality. On the contrary, any statutory scheme which draws a sharp line between the sexes, solely for the purpose of achieving administrative convenience, necessarily commands 'dissimilar treatment for men and women who are . . . similarly situated,' and therefore involves the 'very kind of arbitrary legislative choice forbidden by the (Constitution) . . .' *Reed v. Reed*, 404 U.S., at 77. We therefore conclude that, by according differential treatment to male and female members of the uniformed services for the sole purpose of achieving administrative convenience, the challenged statutes violate the Due Process Clause of the Fifth Amendment insofar as they require a female member to prove the dependency of her husband. *Reversed.*

NOTES

1. It is important to note that the lead opinion in the *Frontiero* case was for a plurality, not a majority, of the Court. Four Justices were of the view that classifications based on sex were as suspect as those based on race, and should thus be subject to strict scrutiny. This was a position that never gained a fifth vote. *Craig v. Boren*, the next case in this chapter, rejected strict scrutiny for gender classifications but created a new, third tier of review—intermediate scrutiny.

2. If the Court had applied traditional rational basis scrutiny to the gender classification in *Frontiero*, the classification would have easily survived. As the Court noted, the challenged classification was based on an assumption that wives were very likely to be financially dependent on their husbands but husbands were very unlikely to be financially dependent on their wives. In relation, therefore, to a purpose of providing support for *dependent* spouses, men and women were not similarly situated. As in *Reed*, however, the accuracy of the generalization embedded in the law—that wives are dependent on their husbands—was in large measure the result of past gender discrimination and gender stereotyping. Something more than rational basis review was necessary to smoke out the impermissible gender discrimination and stereotyping.

3. The *Frontiero* plurality suggested that gender classifications were as impermissible as race classifications and therefore subject to the most demanding form of review—strict scrutiny. In explaining why gender classifications were suspect, the Court identified a number of factors that were relevant: a history of discrimination against women, the relevance of the sex characteristic, immutability, political power, status as a discrete and insular minority, stereotypes about the roles of women, the visibility of the sex trait. These factors are considered in more detail in this chapter *infra*, in Section B.2.

4. In 1971 in *Reed v. Reed*, the Court had applied rational basis review to invalidate a gender classification. In 1973, a plurality of the Court had used strict scrutiny to invalidate a gender classification. It was not until 1976, in *Craig v. Boren* (*see infra*) that the Court would fix permanently on an intermediate standard of review for gender classifications. Between 1973 and 1976, the Court continued to invalidate gender classifications, without deciding exactly what the standard of review was. These cases included:

(a) *Weinberger v. Wiesenfeld*, 420 U.S 636 (1975)

The Court reviewed a provision of the Social Security Act under which the surviving widow of a covered worker received benefits but not a surviving widower. The Court described this distinction as based on an "archaic and overbroad generalization" that "male workers' earnings are vital to the support of their families, while the earnings of female wage earners do not significantly contribute to their families' support." The Court conceded that there was empirical support for the notion that men are more likely than women to be the primary supporters of their families, but this generalization did not suffice to denigrate the importance of the earnings of women who do work and who do contribute significantly to the support of their families. The gender-based distinction was "entirely irrational."

(b) *Stanton v. Stanton*, 421 U.S. 7 (1975)

The Court reviewed a Utah statute under which females would reach the age of majority at 18 but males at 21. Without determining whether heightened scrutiny was necessary, the Court noted:

> Notwithstanding the 'old notions' to which the Utah court referred, we perceive nothing rational in the distinction drawn by [the statute] which, when related to the divorce decree, results in [liability for support for a daughter only to age 18 but for a son to age 21]. This imposes 'criteria wholly unrelated to the objective of that statute.' A child, male or female, is still a child. No longer is the female destined solely for the home and the rearing of the family, and only the male for the marketplace and the world of ideas. Women's activities and responsibilities are increasing and expanding. Coeducation is a fact, not a rarity. The presence of women in business, in the professions, in government and, indeed, in all walks of life where education is a desirable, if not always a necessary, antecedent is apparent and a proper subject of judicial notice. If a specified age of minority is required for the boy in order to assure him parental support while he attains his education and training, so, too, is it for the girl. To distinguish between the two on educational grounds is to be self-serving: if the female is not to be supported so long as the male, she hardly can be expected to attend school as long as he does, and bringing her education to an end earlier coincides with the role-typing society has long imposed.
>
> We therefore conclude that under any test—compelling state interest, or rational basis, or something in between—[the statute], in the context of child support, does not survive an equal protection attack. In that context, no valid distinction between male and female may be drawn.

Craig v. Boren
429 U.S. 190 (1976)

[In Oklahoma, the sale of beer that contained 3.2% alcohol was permitted to females who were 18 or older. Males, however, were restricted from purchasing this "near beer" until the age of 21. The statute was purportedly enacted to enhance traffic safety.]

Mr. Justice BRENNAN delivered the opinion of the Court.

The interaction of two sections of an Oklahoma statute prohibits the sale of "nonintoxicating" 3.2% beer to males under the age of 21 and to females under the age of 18. The question to be decided is whether such a gender-based differential constitutes a denial to males 18-20 years of age of the equal protection of the laws in violation of the Fourteenth Amendment.

A

Analysis may appropriately begin with the reminder that *Reed* emphasized that statutory classifications that distinguish between males and females are "subject to scrutiny under the Equal Protection Clause." 404 U.S. at 75. To withstand constitutional challenge, previous cases establish that classifications by gender must serve important governmental objectives and must be substantially related to achievement of those objectives. Thus, in *Reed*, the objectives of "reducing the workload on probate courts," and "avoiding intrafamily controversy," were deemed of insufficient importance to sustain use of an overt gender criterion in the appointment of administrators of intestate decedents' estates. Decisions following Reed similarly have rejected administrative ease and convenience as sufficiently important objectives to justify gender-based classifications. *See, e.g., Stanley v. Illinois*, 405 U.S. 645, 656 (1972); *Frontiero v. Richardson*, 411 U.S. 677, 690 (1973); *cf. Schlesinger v. Ballard*, 419 U.S. 498, 506-507 (1975). And only two Terms ago, *Stanton v. Stanton*, 421 U.S. 7 (1975), expressly stating that *Reed v. Reed* was "controlling," 421 U.S., at 13, held that *Reed* required invalidation of a Utah differential age-of-majority statute, notwithstanding the statute's coincidence with and furtherance of the State's purpose of fostering "old notions" of role typing and preparing boys for their expected performance in the economic and political worlds.

Reed v. Reed has also provided the underpinning for decisions that have invalidated statutes employing gender as an inaccurate proxy for other, more germane bases of classification. Hence, "archaic and overbroad" generalizations, *Schlesinger v. Ballard, supra*, 419 U.S. at 508, concerning the financial position of servicewomen, *Frontiero v. Richardson, supra*, 411 U.S. at 689, and working women, *Weinberger v. Wiesenfeld*, 420 U.S. 636, 643 (1975), could not justify use of a gender line in determining eligibility for certain governmental entitlements. Similarly, increasingly outdated misconceptions concerning the role of females in the home rather than in the "marketplace and world of ideas" were rejected as loose-fitting characterizations incapable of supporting state statutory schemes that were premised upon their accuracy. *Stanton v. Stanton, supra*. In light of the weak congruence between gender and the characteristic or trait that gender purported to represent, it was necessary that the legislatures choose either to realign their substantive laws in a gender-neutral fashion, or to adopt procedures for identifying those instances where the sex-centered generalization actually comported with fact.

In this case, too, "*Reed*, we feel is controlling . . ." *Stanton v. Stanton, supra*, 421 U.S. at 13. We turn then to the question whether, under Reed, the difference between males and females with respect to the purchase of 3.2% beer warrants the differential in age drawn by the Oklahoma statute. We conclude that it does not.

B

The District Court recognized that *Reed v. Reed* was controlling. In applying the teachings of that case, the court found the requisite important governmental objective in the traffic-safety goal proffered by the Oklahoma Attorney General. It then concluded that the statistics introduced by the appellees established that the gender-based distinction was substantially related to achievement of that goal.

C

We accept for purposes of discussion the District Court's identification of the objective underlying §§ 241 and 245 as the enhancement of traffic safety. Clearly, the protection of public health and safety represents an important function of state and local governments. However, appellees' statistics in our view cannot support the conclusion that the gender-based distinction closely serves to achieve that objective and therefore the distinction cannot under *Reed* withstand equal protection challenge.

The appellees introduced a variety of statistical surveys. First, an analysis of arrest statistics for 1973 demonstrated that 18-20-year-old male arrests for "driving under the influence" and "drunkenness" substantially exceeded female arrests for that same age period. Similarly, youths aged 17-21 were found to be overrepresented among those killed or injured in traffic accidents, with males again numerically exceeding females in this regard. Third, a random roadside survey in Oklahoma City revealed that young males were more inclined to drive and drink beer than were their female counterparts. Fourth, Federal Bureau of Investigation nationwide statistics exhibited a notable increase in arrests for "driving under the influence." Finally, statistical evidence gathered in other jurisdictions, particularly Minnesota and Michigan, was offered to corroborate Oklahoma's experience by indicating the pervasiveness of youthful participation in motor vehicle accidents following the imbibing of alcohol. Conceding that "the case is not free from doubt," the District Court nonetheless concluded that this statistical showing substantiated "a rational basis for the legislative judgment underlying the challenged classification."

Even were this statistical evidence accepted as accurate, it nevertheless offers only a weak answer to the equal protection question presented here. The most focused and relevant of the statistical surveys, arrests of 18-20-year-olds for alcohol-related driving offenses, exemplifies the ultimate unpersuasiveness of this evidentiary record. Viewed in terms of the correlation between sex and the actual activity that Oklahoma seeks to regulate driving while under the influence of alcohol the statistics broadly establish that .18% of females and 2% of males in that age group were arrested for that offense. While such a disparity is not trivial in a statistical sense, it hardly can form the basis for employment of a gender line as a classifying device. Certainly if maleness is to serve as a proxy for drinking and driving, a correlation of 2% must be considered an unduly tenuous "fit." Indeed, prior cases have consistently rejected the use of sex as a decisionmaking factor even though the statutes in question certainly rested on far more predictive empirical relationships than this.

Moreover, the statistics exhibit a variety of other shortcomings that seriously impugn their value to equal protection analysis. Setting aside the obvious methodological problems, the surveys do not adequately justify the salient features of Oklahoma's gender-based traffic-safety law. None purports to measure the use and dangerousness of 3.2% beer as opposed to alcohol generally, a detail that is of particular importance since, in light of its low alcohol level, Oklahoma apparently considers the 3.2% beverage to be "nonintoxicating." Moreover, many of the studies, while graphically documenting the unfortunate increase in driving while under the influence of alcohol, make no effort to relate their findings to age-sex differentials as involved here. Indeed, the only survey that explicitly centered its attention upon young drivers and their use of beer albeit apparently not of the diluted 3.2% variety reached results that hardly can be viewed as impressive in justifying either a gender or age classification.

There is no reason to belabor this line of analysis. It is unrealistic to expect either members of the judiciary or state officials to be well versed in the rigors of experimental or statistical technique. But this merely illustrates that proving broad sociological propositions by statistics is a dubious business, and one that inevitably is in tension with the normative philosophy that underlies the Equal Protection Clause. Suffice to say that the showing offered by the appellees does not satisfy us that sex represents a legitimate, accurate proxy for the regulation of drinking and driving. In fact, when it is further recognized that Oklahoma's statute prohibits only the selling of 3.2% beer to young males and not their drinking the beverage once acquired (even after purchase by their 18-20-year-old female companions), the relationship between gender and traffic safety becomes far too tenuous to satisfy Reed's requirement that the gender-based difference be substantially related to achievement of the statutory objective.

We hold, therefore, that under Reed, Oklahoma's 3.2% beer statute invidiously discriminates against males 18-20 years of age.

We conclude that the gender-based differential contained in [the Oklahoma statute] constitutes a denial of the equal protection of the laws to males aged 18-20 and reverse the judgment of the District Court. [The Court also noted in a footnote that "Insofar as *Goesart v. Cleary*, 335 U.S. 464 (1948), may be inconsistent, that decision is disapproved."].

Mr. Justice STEVENS, concurring.

There is only one Equal Protection Clause. It requires every State to govern impartially. It does not direct the courts to apply one standard of review in some cases and a different standard in other cases. Whatever criticism may be leveled at a judicial opinion implying that there are at least three such standards applies with the same force to a double standard.

I am inclined to believe that what has become known as the two-tiered analysis of equal protection claims does not describe a completely logical method of deciding cases, but rather is a method the Court has employed to explain decisions that actually apply a single standard in a reasonably consistent fashion. I also suspect that a careful explanation of the reasons motivating particular decisions may contribute more to an identification of that standard than an attempt to articulate it in all-encompassing terms. It may therefore be appropriate for me to state the principal reasons which persuaded me to join the Court's opinion.

In this case, the classification is not as obnoxious as some the Court has condemned, nor as inoffensive as some the Court has accepted. It is objectionable because it is based on an accident of birth, because it is a mere remnant of the now almost universally rejected tradition of discriminating against males in this age bracket, and because, to the extent it reflects any physical difference between males and females, it is actually perverse. The question then is whether the traffic safety justification put forward by the State is sufficient to make an otherwise offensive classification acceptable.

The classification is not totally irrational. For the evidence does indicate that there are more males than females in this age bracket who drive and also more who drink. Nevertheless, there are several reasons why I regard the justification as unacceptable. It is difficult to believe that the statute was actually intended to cope with the problem of traffic safety, since it has only a minimal effect on access to a not very intoxicating beverage and does not prohibit its consumption. Moreover, the empirical data submitted by the State accentuate the unfairness of treating all 18-21-year-old males as inferior to their female counterparts. The legislation imposes a restraint on

100% of the males in the class allegedly because about 2% of them have probably violated one or more laws relating to the consumption of alcoholic beverages. It is unlikely that this law will have a significant deterrent effect either on that 2% or on the law-abiding 98%. But even assuming some such slight benefit, it does not seem to me that an insult to all of the young men of the State can be justified by visiting the sins of the 2% on the 98%.

Mr. Justice REHNQUIST, dissenting.

The Court's disposition of this case is objectionable on two grounds. First is its conclusion that men challenging a gender-based statute which treats them less favorably than women may invoke a more stringent standard of judicial review than pertains to most other types of classifications. Second is the Court's enunciation of this standard, without citation to any source, as being that "classifications by gender must serve important governmental objectives and must be substantially related to achievement of those objectives." The only redeeming feature of the Court's opinion, to my mind, is that it apparently signals a retreat by those who joined the plurality opinion in *Frontiero v. Richardson*, 411 U.S. 677 (1973), from their view that sex is a "suspect" classification for purposes of equal protection analysis.

I

The Court's conclusion that a law which treats males less favorably than females "must serve important governmental objectives and must be substantially related to achievement of those objectives" apparently comes out of thin air. The Equal Protection Clause contains no such language, and none of our previous cases adopt that standard. I would think we have had enough difficulty with the two standards of review which our cases have recognized the norm of "rational basis," and the "compelling state interest" required where a "suspect classification" is involved so as to counsel weightily against the insertion of still another "standard" between those two. How is this Court to divine what objectives are important? How is it to determine whether a particular law is "substantially" related to the achievement of such objective, rather than related in some other way to its achievement? Both of the phrases used are so diaphanous and elastic as to invite subjective judicial preferences or prejudices relating to particular types of legislation, masquerading as judgments whether such legislation is directed at "important" objectives or, whether the relationship to those objectives is "substantial" enough.

NOTES

1. The Court's assertion that "previous cases establish that classifications by gender must serve important governmental objectives and must be substantially related to achievement of those objectives," is certainly debatable if not disingenuous. Although previous cases had indeed invalidated gender classifications and had used standards of review that were something more than rational basis review, no equal protection case before *Craig* had ever applied a standard that required either a "substantial relation" or an "important governmental objective." As Justice Rehnquist correctly pointed out in dissent, this standard is "without citation to any source" and "apparently comes out of thin air." How important is an "important" objective? How substantial does a "substantial relation" have to be? The Court has never really given an adequate answer to these questions but one thing is clear: this level of scrutiny is "intermediate," that is, somewhere between the extreme deference of rational basis review and the extreme necessity of strict scrutiny. This means, first, that the purpose for which the law is intended must be more significant

than a purpose that is merely permissible, but not as significant as a purpose that is compelling. In relation to the required correlation between the classification and purpose, the correlation must be closer than a mere rational relationship, but not as close as a "narrowly tailored" or "necessary" relationship.

2. With *Craig v. Boren*, the Court had now completed what has come to be called the "three tiers of scrutiny"—rational basis for most classifications, strict scrutiny for racial classifications (and in a few other situations), and intermediate scrutiny for gender classifications (and in a few other situations). Not surprisingly, intermediate scrutiny produces intermediate results. Unlike rational basis review, it invalidates a substantial number of challenged classifications. Unlike strict scrutiny, it is not almost invariably fatal. This is probably a very appropriate level of scrutiny for gender classifications. Given that many gender classifications are the result of discrimination and stereotyping, it is good to have a standard of review sufficiently robust to uncover those factors. On the other hand, given that there are many gender classifications that are widely acceptable to most people (*e.g.*, separate sports programs for males and females and disability leave for women only following childbirth), it is good to have a standard of review sufficiently tolerant that it can account for and not prohibit these differences. Intermediate scrutiny provides that level of review.

2. *WHAT FACTORS MAKE A CLASSIFICATION SUSPECT?*

When the Court was going about the business of invalidating racial classifications in the nineteenth century, *e.g., Strauder v. West Virginia*, and *Yick Wo v. Hopkins*, or when it was holding that racial segregation in public education was inherently unequal, *Brown v. Board of Education*, it did not need to develop a theory about racial classifications being inherently suspect. The Court could simply hold that racial classifications are the very type of discrimination that the Equal Protection Clause was designed to prohibit.

When, however, in 1973 a plurality of the Court determined that sex was a suspect classification that would receive heightened scrutiny, that plurality needed to explain what it was that made a class suspect. The *Frontiero* Court did this by identifying a series of factors that, taken together, made sex a suspect classification. The Court's choice to identify certain "factors" as relevant to this determination has been much discussed and criticized. This section examines those factors.

Depending on the method of counting, there are at least four factors that make a classification suspect, and possibly as many as seven. They are: relevance, a history of discrimination, immutability, political powerlessness, being a discrete and insular minority, visibility, and stereotyping.

(1) *Relevance.* One of the most important factors identified by the *Frontiero* plurality was the *relevance* of the trait. Unlike intelligence or physical disability, "the sex characteristic frequently bears no relation to ability to perform or contribute to society." The Court in *Cleburne*, 473 U.S. 432, 440 (1985) would later explain why the irrelevance of a classification makes the classification suspect: "These factors [race, alienage, and national origin] are so seldom relevant to the achievement of any legitimate state interest that laws grounded in such considerations are deemed to reflect prejudice and antipathy--a view that those in the burdened class are not as worthy or deserving as others." In a sense, then, a finding that a trait is not relevant creates a

presumption that the government has disadvantaged those with the trait for an impermissible purpose, a mere desire to treat those with that trait as less worthy.

The irrelevance of the sex characteristic can be readily contrasted with disability and age classifications, which the Court has found to be non-suspect. With regard to the mentally retarded, the Court noted, "those who are mentally retarded have a reduced ability to cope with and function in the everyday world." With regard to the elderly, the Court has noted, "physical ability generally declines with age." *Murgia*, 427 U.S. 307, 315 (1976). Thus, classifications that take mental ability or age into account will not be considered suspect because those classifications are relevant to the purpose of the laws that affect them.

The "bears no relation" test on its face appears to ask whether the challenged trait bears any relation *in general* to a person's ability to perform or contribute to society *generally*. In *Windsor v. United States*, 699 F.3d 169 (2d Cir. 2012), those defending the federal Defense of Marriage Act argued that the "bears no relation" question should be asked in relation to the specific purpose of the statute that created the classification rather than in relation to one's general ability to perform. This meant that the proper question would have been whether sexual orientation bears a relation to procreation and the raising of children. The *Windsor* court rejected this limiting interpretation, determining that there was "no precedential application of that standard to support its interpretation, and it is inconsistent with actual cases."

(2) *A history of discrimination*. A second factor that led the *Frontiero* plurality to treat gender as a quasi-suspect class was that "[t]here can be no doubt that our Nation has had a long and unfortunate history of sex discrimination." The Court's first examples of this history—inability to hold office, serve on juries, bring suit in their own names, and, for married women, the lack of capacity to hold or convey property or to serve as legal guardians of their own children—were all *government-imposed* forms of discrimination, given effect through the legal system. The Court then also noted that "women still face pervasive, although at times more subtle, discrimination in our educational institutions, in the job market and, perhaps most conspicuously, in the political arena.

A history of discrimination against a particular group is a relevant factor in according that group heightened scrutiny because it suggests that the group's current disadvantages are the result of past discrimination rather than a thoughtful pursuit of a public purpose. The *Frontiero* Court expressly made the comparison between the history of discrimination against women and the history of discrimination against blacks.

In identifying a history of discrimination that would make a class suspect, other courts have also considered evidence of private as well as governmental discrimination. In *Kerrigan v. Commissioner of Public Health*, 289 Conn. 135 (2008), as part of its finding that gays were a quasi-suspect class, the court included all of the following as evidence of a history of discrimination: hate crimes, taunting, employment discrimination, moral and religious disapproval, and classification as deviants.

In terms of the kind of discrimination that would make a class suspect, Marcy Strauss asks, "'The Court has not . . . defined what quantum, kind or how recent past discrimination is required.' Nor has the Court clarified the requisite historical period. In other words, how much time is necessary to establish a history of discrimination? What happens when a relatively new group with minimal history seeks suspect status (e.g., transgendered individuals)?" Marcy Strauss,

Reevaluating Suspect Classifications, 35 Seattle U. L. Rev. 135, 151 (2011) (citing J. Harvie Wilkinson, *The Supreme Court, the Equal Protection Clause and the Three Faces of Constitutional Equality*, 61 Va. L. Rev. 945 (1975)).

(3) *Immutability*. According to the *Frontiero* plurality, "since sex, like race and national origin, is an *immutable* characteristic determined solely by the accident of birth, the imposition of special disabilities upon the members of a particular sex because of their sex would seem to violate 'the basic concept of our system that legal burdens should bear some relationship to individual responsibility,'" citing *Weber v. Aetna Casualty & Surety Co.*, 406 U.S. 164, 175 (1972). The Court's brief description of immutability suggests why immutability makes a class suspect. Since an immutable trait is an "accident of birth," the person who has that trait did not choose to have it, and thus, it is unfair to impose a disadvantage on a person on the basis of a trait over which he has no control.

What does "immutable" mean? Its literal meaning is that the thing "cannot be changed," but this is too limiting a definition, because even traits like race and gender are not literally unchangeable. An alternative explanation that has been used by a number of courts is that the trait is central to one's identity: "Because a person's sexual orientation is so integral an aspect of one's identity, it is not appropriate to require a person to repudiate or change his or her sexual orientation in order to avoid discriminatory treatment." *In re Marriage Cases*, 43 Cal.4th 757, 842 (2008). Michael A. Helfand argues that the immutability test really should turn on whether the trait was chosen. "[T]he immutability inquiry in the equal protection context is not concerned with whether an individual can exit the classification in question, but whether or not the individual chose to enter the classification." Michael A. Helfand, *The Usual Suspect Classifications: Criminals, Aliens, and the Future of Same-Sex Marriage*, 12 U. Penn. J. Const. L. 1, 39 (2009).

Kenji Yoshino argues that the immutability factor needs to be retired in that it has an assimilationist bias: "By withholding protection from these classifications [whose defining traits can be altered or concealed], the judiciary is subtly encouraging groups comprised by such classifications to assimilate by changing or hiding their defining characteristic. This is an assimilationist bias in equal protection." Kenji Yoshino, *Assimilationist Bias in Equal Protection: The Visibility Presumption and the Case of "Don't Ask, Don't Tell,"* 108 Yale L. J. 485 (1998).

(4) *Political Powerlessness*. The *Frontiero* plurality spoke of a pervasive, if sometimes subtle, discrimination against women in the political arena. While conceding that "women do not constitute a small and powerless minority," the court noted that "women are vastly underrepresented in this Nation's decisionmaking councils. There has never been a female President, nor a female member of this Court. Not a single woman presently sits in the United States Senate, and only 14 women hold seats in the House of Representatives. And, as appellants point out, this underrepresentation is present throughout all levels of our State and Federal Government."

This reference to being a powerless minority is an obvious allusion to the famous Footnote 4 of United *States v. Carolene Products Co.*, 304 U.S. 144 (1938), in which the Court suggested that "prejudice against discrete and insular minorities may be a special condition, which tends seriously to curtail the operation of those political processes ordinarily to be relied upon to protect minorities, and which may call for a correspondingly more searching judicial inquiry." The *Carolene Products* footnote actually makes reference to several factors: (1) discrete and insular minority, (2) political powerlessness, and (3) prejudice. It is not uncommon for courts today to summarize all of these factors under the category of "political powerlessness." *See Kerrigan v. Commissioner of Public Health*, 289 Conn. 135 (2008); *Windsor v. United States*, 699 F.3d 169 (2d Cir. 2012).

 Kenji Yoshino proposes a refined analysis of political powerlessness:

> Currently, the Court has proffered three tests for political powerlessness. In *United States v. Carolene Products*, the Court asked whether groups were "discrete and insular minorities." In *Frontiero*, a plurality of the Court looked to whether a group was underrepresented in the "[n]ation's decisionmaking councils." And in *Cleburne*, the Court examined whether the group was unable "to attract the attention of the lawmakers." Kenji Yoshino, *Assimilationist Bias in Equal Protection: The Visibility Presumption and the Case of "Don't Ask, Don't Tell,"* 108 Yale L. J. 485, 565 (1998).

Yoshino argues that the current "political powerlessness" standard is applied inconsistently and is too coarse to be used effectively. *Id.*

 Marcy Strauss notes the contradictions in the "political powerlessness" argument:

> While the Court in *Cleburne* held that rational basis review was justified since the legislative response to the mentally disabled "negates any claim that the mentally retarded are politically powerless in the sense that they have no ability to attract the attention of the lawmakers," the Court in *Frontiero* used the existence of laws against sex discrimination to reach precisely the opposite conclusion. Marcy Strauss, *Reevaluating Suspect Classifications*, 35 Seattle U. L. Rev. 135, 158 (2011).

(5) *Discrete and Insular Minority*. This factor substantially overlaps with the "politically powerless" standard and is also derived from the *Carolene Products* Footnote 4. The discrete and insular factor is considered to be important because it is likely that a discrete and insular minority will be excluded from the majoritarian political process and thus will need the help of the courts to level the political playing field.

 Bruce Ackerman has written a critique of the idea that discrete and insular minorities are in need of special protection from the courts. Bruce A. Ackerman, *Beyond Carolene Products*, 98 Harv. L. Rev. 713 (1985). He first attempts to define the terms. Ackerman identifies a minority as "discrete" when "its members are marked out in ways that make it relatively easy for others to identify them." *Id.* at 729. A minority is "insular" when there is "a tendency of group members to interact with great frequency in a variety of social contexts." *Id.* at 726. Of these groups Ackerman says:

> *Carolene* is utterly wrongheaded in its diagnosis. Other things being equal, 'discreteness and insularity' will normally be a source of enormous bargaining advantage, not disadvantage, for a group engaged in pluralist American politics. Except for special cases, the concerns that underlie *Carolene* should lead judges to protect groups that possess the opposite characteristics from the ones *Carolene* emphasizes—groups that are 'anonymous and diffuse' rather than 'discrete and insular.' It is these groups that both political science and American history indicate are systematically disadvantaged in a pluralist democracy. *Id.* at 723-24.

(6) *Visibility*. The *Frontiero* plurality noted that "in part because of the high *visibility* of the sex characteristic, women still face pervasive, although at times more subtle, discrimination in our educational institutions, in the job market and, perhaps most conspicuously, in the political arena." The visibility factor seems to one of the less important factors and it is frequently ignored in court opinions. But it still carries some weight. The underlying idea is that, when a trait is visible, like race or gender, it will be easier for those inclined to discriminate to carry out their discriminatory actions. On the other hand, according to this view, it is more difficult for a discriminator to discriminate on the basis of a trait that can be hidden, like sexual orientation, and therefore, classifications based on sexual orientation would be less likely to be considered suspect.

Kenji Yoshino has criticized this use of the visibility factor since it creates an assimilationist bias in equal protection law. Yoshino identifies three different kinds of assimilationist bias—converting (where the group is forced to change the trait that defines it), passing (where the group is forced to hide its identity), and covering (where the group is permitted to retain its identity as long as it mutes the difference between itself and the mainstream). *Yoshino*, 108 Yale L. J. at 500. Yoshino, who thinks the visibility factor (along with the immutability factor) should be retired, argues:

> [T]he visibility presumption, like the immutability presumption, is deeply flawed. There is no innate connection between visibility and political powerlessness, nor is there an innate connection between invisibility and political power. Rather, the net effects of visibility will depend on context, sometimes disempowering a group and sometimes empowering it. *Id.* at 537.

(7) *Stereotype*. The *Frontiero* plurality noted that, traditionally, gender discrimination was rationalized by an attitude of romantic paternalism about the proper roles of women in society—principally the roles of wife and mother—and, as a result, "our statute books gradually became laden with gross, *stereotyped* distinctions between the sexes." According to this view, the existence of a stereotype about a particular group should make the classification suspect. Stereotypes are generalizations about groups that are either based on a false generalization, *e.g.,* women are bad drivers, or based on an accurate generalization that is perceived to be unfair because it is inaccurate as to particular members of the class. Thus, the generalization that most women cannot meet the demanding physical standards at VMI is accurate as a generalization but inaccurate as to some individual women. The Court in the *VMI* case found this kind of generalization to be an unacceptable gender stereotype. On the other hand, when the courts are applying the rational basis standard of review, they are quite accepting of this kind of generalization, even if it is unfair to individual members of the class. In the *Murgia* case, for example, the Court approved a law that was based on the generalization that older people are less fit, even though this generalization was clearly not true of the individual older plaintiff in the case.

When courts cite a list of factors that makes a classification suspect, they often ignore the stereotype factor, but it is still cited on occasion, particularly in cases on gender discrimination. Mary Ann Case has argued that the notion of gender stereotypes can explain all of the Supreme Court's gender cases. When a law distinguishes between males and females, we can determine the outcome of the case by simply asking, "Does the sex-respecting rule rely on a stereotype?" Mary Ann Case, *"The Very Stereotype the Law Condemns": Constitutional Sex Discrimination Law as a Quest For Perfect Proxies*, 85 Corn. L. Rev. 1447 (2000). Case argues that, to survive equal protection review, a gender classification must embody a perfect proxy: the generalization "must be true of either all women or no women or all men or no men; there must be a zero or a hundred on one side of the sex equation or the other." *Id.* at 1449-50.

For a recent defense of the anti-stereotyping principle, *see* Cary Franklin, *The Anti-Stereotyping Principle in Constitutional Sex Discrimination Law*, 85 N.Y.U. L. Rev. 83 (2010). Franklin argues that the anti-stereotyping principle, initially advanced by Ruth Bader Ginsburg in the 1970s, is better suited to guide courts than an anti-classification principle or an anti-subordination principle. Under the anti-stereotyping principle, "the state could not act in ways that reflected or reinforced traditional conceptions of men's and women's roles." *Id.* at 88.

For a recent critique of the anti-stereotyping principle, *see* Meredith M Render, *Gender Rules*, 22 Yale J. Law & Fem. 133 (2010). Render argues that, in common understanding, a stereotype is a generalization that is applied unfairly. Since, however, it is difficult to delimit the type of unfairness that transforms a garden-variety generalization into a stereotype, "the concept of 'stereotype' begins to seem like an empty idea." *Id.* at 144.

(8) *How Do the Factors Work Together?* Having identified a list of factors that it considers in determining whether a class is suspect, the Court has been unclear and inconsistent in its use of the factors. How many factors do you need? Are any factors essential? According to Marcy Strauss:

> The Court has never described how the factors exist in relation to each other, explained which factors are to be given priority, or clarified how much weight to assign any particular factor. . . . Without more guidance, courts are left performing a mushy, gestalt-type analysis. Presumably, the more factors satisfied the merrier. Beyond that, it is unclear how the factors interplay. Marcy Strauss, *Reevaluating Suspect Classifications*, 35 Seattle U. L. Rev. 135, 168 (2011).

(9) *Suspect Class or Suspect Classification?* Is the Court concerned with a suspect class or a suspect classification? To the extent that heightened scrutiny focuses on discrete and insular minorities, a history of discrimination against a particular group, and political powerlessness, the focus seems to be the fact of a particular group's being a suspect class. This kind of focus emphasizes the anti-subordination principle. But the Court has not used suspect class analysis solely to protect suspect classes. According to Darren Lenard Hutchinson:

> Although the Court has relied upon the *Carolene Products* "suspect class" doctrine as a justification for rejecting or questioning the legislative process, in recent case law, the Court has applied heightened scrutiny "symmetrically." In other words, once a subordinate class successfully establishes that the discrimination it faces warrants exacting judicial scrutiny, the Court applies heightened scrutiny symmetrically and extends judicial solicitude to any individual who encounters discrimination based on the "same" trait as members of the subordinate class. The Court's doctrine shifts from one that protects suspect "classes" to one that presumes the unconstitutionality of certain suspect "classifications." Thus, while blacks or women might constitute suspect classes due to their socially disadvantaged statuses, whites and men receive heightened scrutiny when they challenge laws that classify on the basis of race or gender. Darren Lenard Hutchinson, *"Unexplainable on Grounds Other than Race": The Inversion of Privilege and Subordination in Equal Protection Jurisprudence*, 2003 U. Ill. L. Rev. 615, 638-39 (2003).

C. PROHIBITED GENDER CLASSIFICATIONS

In the years after *Craig v. Boren*, the Court decided a number of cases in which it used intermediate scrutiny to invalidate gender classifications, typically because the classifications involved were based on stereotypes or on insufficiently accurate generalizations about men and women. These cases included:

1. *IN THE CALCULATION OF SOCIAL SECURITY BENEFITS*

In *Califano v. Goldfarb*, 430 U.S. 199 (1977), a plurality of the Court invalidated a provision of the Social Security Act under which a surviving widow of a covered worker would automatically be entitled to survivors' benefits, but a surviving widower would receive such benefits only if he had been receiving at least one-half of his support from his deceased wife. Quoting the intermediate scrutiny standard articulated in *Craig v. Boren* and noting that gender classifications "have frequently been revealed on analysis to rest only upon 'old notions' and 'archaic and overbroad' generalizations," the court concluded that:

> The differential treatment of nondependent widows and widowers results not . . . from a deliberate congressional intention to remedy the arguably greater needs of the former, but rather from an intention to aid the dependent spouses of deceased wage earners, coupled with a presumption that wives are usually dependent. This presents precisely the situation faced in *Frontiero* and *Wiesenfeld*. The only conceivable justification for writing the presumption of wives' dependency into the statute is the assumption, not verified by the government in *Frontiero* or here, but based simply on 'archaic and overbroad' generalizations that it would save the Government time, money, and effort simply to pay benefits to all widows, rather than to require proof of dependency of both sexes. We [hold] that such assumptions do not suffice to justify a gender-based discrimination in the distribution of employment related benefits.

2. *IN THE AWARD OF ALIMONY*

In *Orr v. Orr*, 440 U.S. 268 (1979), the Court, using intermediate scrutiny, invalidated a state statute under which husbands, but not wives, could be required to pay alimony on divorce. The Court rejected the first of the statutory purposes advanced by the state: the state's preference for, and statutory reinforcement of, an allocation of family responsibilities under which the wife plays a dependent role. The Court rejected this purpose since the old notion that "generally it is the man's primary responsibility to provide a home and its essentials" can no longer justify a statute that discriminates on the basis of gender. The Court conceded that the second and third purposes advanced by the state—providing help for needy spouses and compensating women for past discrimination in marriage that had left women less able to fend for themselves in the working world following divorce—were "important" purposes as required by intermediate scrutiny. The question was whether or not the gender classification in the alimony statute was substantially related to these purposes. The Court determined that they were not.

> Legislative classifications which distribute benefits and burdens on the basis of gender carry the inherent risk of reinforcing the stereotypes about the "proper place" of women and their need for special protection. Thus, even statutes purportedly designed to

compensate for and ameliorate the effects of past discrimination must be carefully tailored. Where, as here, the State's compensatory and ameliorative purposes are as well served by a gender-neutral classification as one that gender classifies and therefore carries with it the baggage of sexual stereotypes, the State cannot be permitted to classify on the basis of sex.

3. *IN THE REQUIRED PARENTAL CONSENT FOR ADOPTION*

In *Caban v. Mohammed*, 441 U.S. 380 (1979), the Court invalidated a statute under which the adoption of a child born out of wedlock required the consent of the mother, but not of the father. The state argued that this distinction was justified, in part, "by a fundamental difference between maternal and paternal relations—that 'a natural mother, absent special circumstances, bears a closer relationship with her child . . . than a father does.'" The Court rejected the validity of this assertion:

Contrary to appellees' argument and to the apparent presumption underlying [the statute], maternal and paternal roles are not invariably different in importance. Even if unwed mothers as a class were closer than unwed fathers to their newborn infants, this generalization concerning parent-child relations would become less acceptable as a basis for legislative distinctions as the age of the child increased. . . . We reject, therefore, the claim that the broad, gender-based distinction of [the statute] is required by any universal difference between maternal and paternal relations at every phase of a child's development.

4. *IN THE RIGHT TO CONTROL THE DISPOSITION OF REAL PROPERTY*

In *Kirchberg v. Feenstra*, 450 U.S. 455 (1981), the Court invalidated a statute under which the husband was "head and master" of property jointly owned with his wife. The state had advanced only one justification for the statutory distinction—"one of the two spouses has to be designated as the manager of the community." Even if that were an important interest, the gender classification was not substantially related to it in that the wife as well as the husband could be designated as the sole manager of the property. In this situation, the state's choice of the husband over the wife "clearly embodies the type of express gender-based discrimination that we have found unconstitutional."

5. *ALL-FEMALE UNIVERSITY PROGRAMS*

Mississippi University for Women v. Hogan
458 U.S. 718 (1982)

[The state of Mississippi had, for almost 100 years, operated the Mississippi University for Women (MUW), a school exclusively for women. Joe Hogan, a male, applied and was rejected. Hogan claimed the admissions policy of MUW's School of Nursing violated the Equal Protection Clause of the Fourteenth Amendment.]

Justice O'CONNOR delivered the opinion of the Court.

This case presents the narrow issue of whether a state statute that excludes males from enrolling in a state-supported professional nursing school violates the Equal Protection Clause of the Fourteenth Amendment.

We begin our analysis aided by several firmly established principles. Because the challenged policy expressly discriminates among applicants on the basis of gender, it is subject to scrutiny under the Equal Protection Clause of the Fourteenth Amendment. *Reed v. Reed*, 404 U.S. 71, 75 (1971). That this statutory policy discriminates against males rather than against females does not exempt it from scrutiny or reduce the standard of review. *Caban v. Mohammed*, 441 U.S. 380, 394 (1979); *Orr v. Orr*, 440 U.S. 268, 279 (1979). Our decisions also establish that the party seeking to uphold a statute that classifies individuals on the basis of their gender must carry the burden of showing an "exceedingly persuasive justification" for the classification. *Kirchberg v. Feenstra*, 450 U.S. 455, 461 (1981); *Personnel Administrator of Mass. v. Feeney*, 442 U.S. 256 (1979). The burden is met only by showing at least that the classification serves "important governmental objectives and that the discriminatory means employed" are "substantially related to the achievement of those objectives." *Wengler v. Druggists Mutual Ins. Co.*, 446 U.S. 142 (1980).

Thus, we apply the test previously relied upon by the Court to measure the constitutionality of gender-based discrimination. Because we conclude that the challenged statutory classification is not substantially related to an important objective, we need not decide whether classifications based upon gender are inherently suspect. Although the test for determining the validity of a gender-based classification is straightforward, it must be applied free of fixed notions concerning the roles and abilities of males and females. Care must be taken in ascertaining whether the statutory objective itself reflects archaic and stereotypic notions. Thus, if the statutory objective is to exclude or "protect" members of one gender because they are presumed to suffer from an inherent handicap or to be innately inferior, the objective itself is illegitimate. See *Frontiero v. Richardson*, 411 U.S. 677, 684-685 (1973) (plurality opinion). If the State's objective is legitimate and important, we next determine whether the requisite direct, substantial relationship between objective and means is present. The purpose of requiring that close relationship is to assure that the validity of a classification is determined through reasoned analysis rather than through the mechanical application of traditional, often inaccurate, assumptions about the proper roles of men and women.

The need for the requirement is amply revealed by reference to the broad range of statutes already invalidated by this Court, statutes that relied upon the simplistic, outdated assumption that gender could be used as a "proxy for other, more germane bases of classification," *Craig v. Boren*, 429 U.S. 190, 198 (1976), to establish a link between objective and classification. Applying this framework, we now analyze the arguments advanced by the State to justify its refusal to allow males to enroll for credit in MUW's School of Nursing.

The State's primary justification for maintaining the single-sex admissions policy of MUW's School of Nursing is that it compensates for discrimination against women and, therefore, constitutes educational affirmative action. As applied to the School of Nursing, we find the State's argument unpersuasive.

In limited circumstances, a gender-based classification favoring one sex can be justified if it intentionally and directly assists members of the sex that is disproportionately burdened. See *Schlesinger v. Ballard*, 419 U.S. 498 (1975). However, we consistently have emphasized that "the mere recitation of a benign, compensatory purpose is not an automatic shield which protects against any inquiry into the actual purposes underlying a statutory scheme." *Weinberger v. Wiesenfeld*, 420 U.S. 636, 648 (1975). The same searching analysis must be made, regardless of whether the State's objective is to eliminate family controversy, *Reed v. Reed*, 404 U.S. 71 (1971), to achieve administrative efficiency, *Frontiero v. Richardson*, 411 U.S. 677 (1973), or to balance the burdens borne by males and females.

It is readily apparent that a State can evoke a compensatory purpose to justify an otherwise discriminatory classification only if members of the gender benefited by the classification actually suffer a disadvantage related to the classification. We considered such a situation in *Califano v. Webster*, 430 U.S. 313 (1977), which involved a challenge to a statutory classification that allowed women to eliminate more low-earning years than men for purposes of computing Social Security retirement benefits. Although the effect of the classification was to allow women higher monthly benefits than were available to men with the same earning history, we upheld the statutory scheme, noting that it took into account that women "as such have been unfairly hindered from earning as much as men" and "work[ed] directly to remedy" the resulting economic disparity.

In sharp contrast, Mississippi has made no showing that women lacked opportunities to obtain training in the field of nursing or to attain positions of leadership in that field when the MUW School of Nursing opened its door or that women currently are deprived of such opportunities. In fact, in 1970, the year before the School of Nursing's first class enrolled, women earned 94 percent of the nursing baccalaureate degrees conferred in Mississippi and 98.6 percent of the degrees earned nationwide. That year was not an aberration; one decade earlier, women had earned all the nursing degrees conferred in Mississippi and 98.9 percent of the degrees conferred nationwide. As one would expect, the labor force reflects the same predominance of women in nursing. When MUW's School of Nursing began operation, nearly 98 percent of all employed registered nurses were female.

Rather than compensate for discriminatory barriers faced by women, MUW's policy of excluding males from admission to the School of Nursing tends to perpetuate the stereotyped view of nursing as an exclusively woman's job. By assuring that Mississippi allots more openings in its state-supported nursing schools to women than it does to men, MUW's admissions policy lends credibility to the old view that women, not men, should become nurses, and makes the assumption that nursing is a field for women a self-fulfilling prophecy. See *Stanton v. Stanton*, 421 U.S. 7 (1975). Thus, we conclude that, although the State recited a "benign, compensatory purpose," it failed to establish that the alleged objective is the actual purpose underlying the discriminatory classification.

The policy is invalid also because it fails the second part of the equal protection test, for the State has made no showing that the gender-based classification is substantially and directly related to its proposed compensatory objective. To the contrary, MUW's policy of permitting men to attend classes as auditors fatally undermines its claim that women, at least those in the School of Nursing, are adversely affected by the presence of men. MUW permits men who audit to participate fully in classes. Additionally, both men and women take part in continuing education courses offered by the School of Nursing, in which regular nursing students also can enroll. The uncontroverted record reveals that admitting men to nursing classes does not affect teaching style, that the presence of men in the classroom would not affect the performance of the female nursing students, and that men in coeducational nursing schools do not dominate the classroom. In sum, the record in this case is flatly inconsistent with the claim that excluding men from the School of Nursing is necessary to reach any of MUW's educational goals.

CHAPTER 3: GENDER CLASSIFICATIONS   179

Thus, considering both the asserted interest and the relationship between the interest and the methods used by the State, we conclude that the State has fallen far short of establishing the "exceedingly persuasive justification" needed to sustain the gender-based classification. Accordingly, we hold that MUW's policy of denying males the right to enroll for credit in its School of Nursing violates the Equal Protection Clause of the Fourteenth Amendment.

NOTES

1. The *Hogan* Court broke down the different elements of the "substantially related to an important interest" test and, in doing so, demonstrated that it was a test quite a bit more demanding than rational basis review. With regard to the issue of which party has the burden of proving what, the Court stated that "the party seeking to uphold a statute that classifies individuals on the basis of their gender must carry the burden of showing an 'exceedingly persuasive justification' for the classification." This contrasts with rational basis review where there need not be any evidence of the purpose, and where "those attacking the rationality of the legislative classification have the burden 'to negative every conceivable basis which might support it.'"

2. With regard to the importance of the purpose, the Court ruled out any classification that reflected archaic or stereotypical notions about the roles of women, including the notion that women are innately inferior. With regard to the substantial relationship that was required between classification and purpose, the Court noted that this connection would require "reasoned analysis" and would rule out "the mechanical application of traditional, often inaccurate, assumptions about the proper roles of men and women." In light of this requirement, the Court insisted that "the mere recitation of a benign, compensatory purpose is not an automatic shield which protects against any inquiry into the actual purposes underlying a statutory scheme." Ultimately, the problem for MUW was that, by limiting its nursing program to women, the school was giving effect to, and thereby endorsing, the stereotype that nursing is a woman's profession. That is not a permissible purpose.

6. *EXCLUDING WOMEN FROM THE JURY*

J.E.B. v. Alabama
511 U.S. 127 (1994)

[In a jury trial to determine paternity and child support, the State used peremptory strikes almost exclusively to remove male jurors from the panel. Although petitioner J.E.B. responded by using peremptory strikes to remove female jurors, the final panel was entirely female. J.E.B. argued that the State's use of its challenges to remove male jurors based on gender alone was a violation of the Equal Protection Clause.]

Justice BLACKMUN delivered the opinion of the Court.

In *Batson v. Kentucky,* 476 U.S. 79 (1986), this Court held that the Equal Protection Clause of the Fourteenth Amendment governs the exercise of peremptory challenges by a prosecutor in a criminal trial. The Court explained that although a defendant has "no right to a 'petit jury composed in whole or in part of persons of his own race,'" the "defendant does have the right to be tried by a jury whose members are selected pursuant to nondiscriminatory criteria." Since

Batson, we have reaffirmed repeatedly our commitment to jury selection procedures that are fair and nondiscriminatory. We have recognized that whether the trial is criminal or civil, potential jurors, as well as litigants, have an equal protection right to jury selection procedures that are free from state-sponsored group stereotypes rooted in, and reflective of, historical prejudice.

Although premised on equal protection principles that apply equally to gender discrimination, all our recent cases defining the scope of *Batson* involved alleged racial discrimination in the exercise of peremptory challenges. Today we are faced with the question whether the Equal Protection Clause forbids intentional discrimination on the basis of gender, just as it prohibits discrimination on the basis of race. We hold that gender, like race, is an unconstitutional proxy for juror competence and impartiality. Today we reaffirm what, by now, should be axiomatic: Intentional discrimination on the basis of gender by state actors violates the Equal Protection Clause, particularly where, as here, the discrimination serves to ratify and perpetuate invidious, archaic, and overbroad stereotypes about the relative abilities of men and women.

II

Discrimination on the basis of gender in the exercise of peremptory challenges is a relatively recent phenomenon. Gender-based peremptory strikes were hardly practicable during most of our country's existence, since, until the 20th century, women were completely excluded from jury service. So well entrenched was this exclusion of women that in 1880 this Court, while finding that the exclusion of African-American men from juries violated the Fourteenth Amendment, expressed no doubt that a State "may confine the selection [of jurors] to males." *Strauder v. West Virginia,* 100 U.S., at 310.

Many States continued to exclude women from jury service well into the present century, despite the fact that women attained suffrage upon ratification of the Nineteenth Amendment in 1920. States that did permit women to serve on juries often erected other barriers, such as registration requirements and automatic exemptions, designed to deter women from exercising their right to jury service.

The prohibition of women on juries was derived from the English common law which, according to Blackstone, rightfully excluded women from juries under "the doctrine of *propter defectum sexus,* literally, the 'defect of sex.'" *United States v. De Gross,* 960 F.2d 1433, 1438 (CA9 1992) (en banc), quoting 2 W. Blackstone, Commentaries. In this country, supporters of the exclusion of women from juries tended to couch their objections in terms of the ostensible need to protect women from the ugliness and depravity of trials. Women were thought to be too fragile and virginal to withstand the polluted courtroom atmosphere. See *Bailey v. State,* 215 Ark. 53, 61 (1949) ("Criminal court trials often involve testimony of the foulest kind, and they sometimes require consideration of indecent conduct, the use of filthy and loathsome words, references to intimate sex relationships, and other elements that would prove humiliating, embarrassing and degrading to a lady"); *In re Goodell,* 39 Wis. 232, 245-246 (1875) (endorsing statutory ineligibility of women for admission to the bar because "[r]everence for all womanhood would suffer in the public spectacle of women ... so engaged").

This Court in *Ballard v. United States,* 329 U.S. 187 (1946), first questioned the fundamental fairness of denying women the right to serve on juries. Relying on its supervisory powers over the federal courts, it held that women may not be excluded from the venire in federal trials in States where women were eligible for jury service under local law. In response to the argument that women have no superior or unique perspective, such that defendants are denied a fair trial by virtue of their exclusion from jury panels, the Court explained:

> It is said ... that an all male panel drawn from the various groups within a community will be as truly representative as if women were included. The thought is that the factors which tend to influence the action of women are the same as those which influence the action of men-personality, background, economic status--and not sex. Yet it is not enough to say that women when sitting as jurors neither act nor tend to act as a class. Men likewise do not act like a class. . .The truth is that the two sexes are not fungible; a community made up exclusively of one is different from a community composed of both; the subtle interplay of influence one on the other is among the imponderables. To insulate the courtroom from either may not in a given case make an iota of difference. Yet a flavor, a distinct quality is lost if either sex is excluded. *Id.* at 193-194.

Fifteen years later, however, the Court still was unwilling to translate its appreciation for the value of women's contribution to civic life into an enforceable right to equal treatment under state laws governing jury service. In *Hoyt v. Florida,* 368 U.S., at 61, the Court found it reasonable, "[d]espite the enlightened emancipation of women," to exempt women from mandatory jury service by statute, allowing women to serve on juries only if they volunteered to serve. The Court justified the differential exemption policy on the ground that women, unlike men, occupied a unique position "as the center of home and family life." *Id.* at 62.

In 1975, the Court finally repudiated the reasoning of *Hoyt* and struck down, under the Sixth Amendment, an affirmative registration statute nearly identical to the one at issue in *Hoyt.* See *Taylor v. Louisiana,* 419 U.S. 522, (1975).We explained: "Restricting jury service to only special groups or excluding identifiable segments playing major roles in the community cannot be squared with the constitutional concept of jury trial." The diverse and representative character of the jury must be maintained "'partly as assurance of a diffused impartiality and partly because sharing in the administration of justice is a phase of civic responsibility.'"

III

Taylor relied on Sixth Amendment principles, but the opinion's approach is consistent with the heightened equal protection scrutiny afforded gender-based classifications. Since *Reed v. Reed,* 404 U.S. 71 (1971), this Court consistently has subjected gender-based classifications to heightened scrutiny in recognition of the real danger that government policies that professedly are based on reasonable considerations in fact may be reflective of "archaic and overbroad" generalizations about gender, see *Schlesinger v. Ballard,* 419 U.S. 498, 506-507 (1975), or based on "outdated misconceptions concerning the role of females in the home rather than in the 'marketplace and world of ideas.'" *Craig v. Boren,* 429 U.S. 190, 198-199 (1976). See also *Cleburne v. Cleburne Living Center, Inc.,* 473 U.S. 432, 441 (1985) (differential treatment of the sexes "very likely reflect[s] outmoded notions of the relative capabilities of men and women").

Despite the heightened scrutiny afforded distinctions based on gender, respondent argues that gender discrimination in the selection of the petit jury should be permitted, though discrimination on the basis of race is not. Respondent suggests that "gender discrimination in this country . . . has never reached the level of discrimination" against African-Americans, and therefore gender discrimination, unlike racial discrimination, is tolerable in the courtroom.

While the prejudicial attitudes toward women in this country have not been identical to those held toward racial minorities, the similarities between the experiences of racial minorities and women, in some contexts, "overpower those differences." Note, Beyond *Batson:* Eliminating Gender-Based Peremptory Challenges, 105 Harv. L. Rev. 1920, 1921 1992). As a plurality of this Court observed in *Frontiero v. Richardson,* 411 U.S., at 685:

> [T]hroughout much of the 19th century the position of women in our society was, in many respects, comparable to that of blacks under the pre-Civil War slave codes. Neither slaves nor women could hold office, serve on juries, or bring suit in their own names, and married women traditionally were denied the legal capacity to hold or convey property or to serve as legal guardians of their own children . . . And although blacks were guaranteed the right to vote in 1870, women were denied even that right-which is itself 'preservative of other basic civil and political rights'--until adoption of the Nineteenth Amendment half a century later.

Certainly, with respect to jury service, African-Americans and women share a history of total exclusion, a history which came to an end for women many years after the embarrassing chapter in our history came to an end for African-Americans.

We need not determine, however, whether women or racial minorities have suffered more at the hands of discriminatory state actors during the decades of our Nation's history. It is necessary only to acknowledge that "our Nation has had a long and unfortunate history of sex discrimination," *id.* at 684, a history which warrants the heightened scrutiny we afford all gender-based classifications today. Under our equal protection jurisprudence, gender-based classifications require "an exceedingly persuasive justification" in order to survive constitutional scrutiny. See *Personnel Administrator of Mass. v. Feeney,* 442 U.S. 256, 273 (1979). See also *Mississippi Univ. for Women v. Hogan,* 458 U.S. 718, 724 (1982). Thus, the only question is whether discrimination on the basis of gender in jury selection substantially furthers the State's legitimate interest in achieving a fair and impartial trial. In making this assessment, we do not weigh the value of peremptory challenges as an institution against our asserted commitment to eradicate invidious discrimination from the courtroom. Instead, we consider whether peremptory challenges based on gender stereotypes provide substantial aid to a litigant's effort to secure a fair and impartial jury.

What respondent fails to recognize is that the only legitimate interest it could possibly have in the exercise of its peremptory challenges is securing a fair and impartial jury. See *Edmonson v. Leesville Concrete Co.,* 500 U.S. 614, 620 (1991) ("[The] sole purpose [of the peremptory challenge] is to permit litigants to assist the government in the selection of an impartial trier of fact"). This interest does not change with the parties or the causes. The State's interest in *every* trial is to see that the proceedings are carried out in a fair, impartial, and nondiscriminatory manner.

Far from proffering an exceptionally persuasive justification for its gender-based peremptory challenges, respondent maintains that its decision to strike virtually all the males from the jury in this case "may reasonably have been based upon the perception, supported by history, that men otherwise totally qualified to serve upon a jury in any case might be more sympathetic and receptive to the arguments of a man alleged in a paternity action to be the father of an out-of-wedlock child, while women equally qualified to serve upon a jury might be more sympathetic and receptive to the arguments of the complaining witness who bore the child."

We shall not accept as a defense to gender-based peremptory challenges "the very stereotype the law condemns." *Powers v. Ohio,* 499 U.S., at 410. Respondent's rationale, not unlike those regularly expressed for gender-based strikes, is reminiscent of the arguments advanced to justify the total exclusion of women from juries. Respondent offers virtually no support for the conclusion that gender alone is an accurate predictor of juror's attitudes; yet it urges this Court to condone the same stereotypes that justified the wholesale exclusion of women from juries and the ballot box. Respondent seems to assume that gross generalizations that would be deemed impermissible if made on the basis of race are somehow permissible when made on the basis of gender.

Discrimination in jury selection, whether based on race or on gender, causes harm to the litigants, the community, and the individual jurors who are wrongfully excluded from participation in the judicial process. The litigants are harmed by the risk that the prejudice that motivated the discriminatory selection of the jury will infect the entire proceedings. See *Edmonson,* 500 U.S., at 628 (discrimination in the courtroom "raises serious questions as to the fairness of the proceedings conducted there"). The community is harmed by the State's participation in the perpetuation of invidious group stereotypes and the inevitable loss of confidence in our judicial system that state-sanctioned discrimination in the courtroom engenders.

When state actors exercise peremptory challenges in reliance on gender stereotypes, they ratify and reinforce prejudicial views of the relative abilities of men and women. Because these stereotypes have wreaked injustice in so many other spheres of our country's public life, active discrimination by litigants on the basis of gender during jury selection "invites cynicism respecting the jury's neutrality and its obligation to adhere to the law." *Powers v. Ohio,* 499 U.S., at 412. The potential for cynicism is particularly acute in cases where gender-related issues are prominent, such as cases involving rape, sexual harassment, or paternity. Discriminatory use of peremptory challenges may create the impression that the judicial system has acquiesced in suppressing full participation by one gender or that the "deck has been stacked" in favor of one side. See *id.* at 413 ("The verdict will not be accepted or understood [as fair] if the jury is chosen by unlawful means at the outset").

In recent cases we have emphasized that individual jurors themselves have a right to nondiscriminatory jury selection procedures ... All persons, when granted the opportunity to serve on a jury, have the right not to be excluded summarily because of discriminatory and stereotypical presumptions that reflect and reinforce patterns of historical discrimination. Striking individual jurors on the assumption that they hold particular views simply because of their gender is "practically a brand upon them, affixed by the law, an assertion of their inferiority." *Strauder v. West Virginia,* 100 U.S. at 308 (1880). It denigrates the dignity of the excluded juror, and, for a woman, reinvokes a history of exclusion from political participation. The message it sends to all those in the courtroom, and all those who may later learn of the discriminatory act, is that certain individuals, for no reason other than gender, are presumed unqualified by state actors to decide important questions upon which reasonable persons could disagree. Our conclusion that litigants may not strike potential jurors solely on the basis of gender does not imply the elimination of all peremptory challenges. Neither does it conflict with a State's legitimate interest in using such challenges in its effort to secure a fair and impartial jury. Parties still may remove jurors who they feel might be less acceptable than others on the panel; gender simply may not serve as a proxy for bias. Parties may also exercise their peremptory challenges to remove from the venire any group or class of individuals normally subject to "rational basis" review. Even strikes based on characteristics that are disproportionately associated with one gender could be appropriate, absent a showing of pretext.

If conducted properly, *voir dire* can inform litigants about potential jurors, making reliance upon stereotypical and pejorative notions about a particular gender or race both unnecessary and unwise. *Voir dire* provides a means of discovering actual or implied bias and a firmer basis upon which the parties may exercise their peremptory challenges intelligently. The experience in the many jurisdictions that have barred gender-based challenges belies the claim that litigants and trial courts are incapable of complying with a rule barring strikes based on gender. As with race-based *Batson* claims, a party alleging gender discrimination must make a prima facie showing of intentional discrimination before the party exercising the challenge is required to explain the basis for the strike. When an explanation is required, it need not rise to the level of a "for cause" challenge; rather, it merely must be based on a juror characteristic other than gender, and the proffered explanation may not be pretextual.

V

Equal opportunity to participate in the fair administration of justice is fundamental to our democratic system. It not only furthers the goals of the jury system. It reaffirms the promise of equality under the law--that all citizens, regardless of race, ethnicity, or gender, have the chance to take part directly in our democracy. *Powers v. Ohio,* 499 U.S., at 407 ("Indeed, with the exception of voting, for most citizens the honor and privilege of jury duty is their most significant opportunity to participate in the democratic process"). When persons are excluded from participation in our democratic processes solely because of race or gender, this promise of equality dims, and the integrity of our judicial system is jeopardized.

The judgment of the Court of Civil Appeals of Alabama is reversed, and the case is remanded to that court for further proceedings not inconsistent with this opinion. *It is so ordered.*

NOTES

1. In extending the reach of *Batson v. Kentucky,* the Court had to address the argument that the exclusion of women from a jury was not as offensive as exclusion on the basis of race. The Court noted that although "the prejudicial attitudes toward women in this country have not been identical to those held toward racial minorities, the similarities between the experiences of racial minorities and women, in some contexts, 'overpower those differences.'"

2. The Court in *J.E.B.* noted that the only legitimate interest the state might have in limiting the membership of juries was the selection of a fair and impartial jury. Yet, the state's justification for the excluding men from the jury was nothing more than the repetition of a stereotype—that male jurors would be more sympathetic to the alleged father in a paternity action while female jurors would tend to be sympathetic to the mother who had made the complaint.

7. *ALL-MALE UNIVERSITY PROGRAMS*

United States v. Virginia
518 U.S. 515 (1996)

[For over 150 years, the Virginia Military Institute (VMI) provided a public education to young men. VMI provided its students with a challenging training program, designed to instill in its graduates physical and mental discipline and to provide students with a heightened awareness of their own capacity to endure stress. VMI did not accept women on the ground that women were not suitable for this kind of adversative method of education.]

Justice GINSBURG delivered the opinion of the Court.

Virginia's public institutions of higher learning include an incomparable military college, Virginia Military Institute (VMI). The United States maintains that the Constitution's equal protection guarantee precludes Virginia from reserving exclusively to men the unique educational opportunities VMI affords. We agree.

I

Founded in 1839, VMI is today the sole single-sex school among Virginia's 15 public institutions of higher learning. VMI's distinctive mission is to produce "citizen-soldiers," men prepared for leadership in civilian life and in military service. VMI pursues this mission through pervasive training of a kind not available anywhere else in Virginia. Assigning prime place to character development, VMI uses an "adversative method" modeled on English public schools and once characteristic of military instruction. VMI constantly endeavors to instill physical and mental discipline in its cadets and impart to them a strong moral code. The school's graduates leave VMI with heightened comprehension of their capacity to deal with duress and stress, and a large sense of accomplishment for completing the hazardous course.

VMI has notably succeeded in its mission to produce leaders; among its alumni are military generals, Members of Congress, and business executives. The school's alumni overwhelmingly perceive that their VMI training helped them to realize their personal goals. VMI's endowment reflects the loyalty of its graduates; VMI has the largest per-student endowment of all public undergraduate institutions in the Nation.

Neither the goal of producing citizen-soldiers nor VMI's implementing methodology is inherently unsuitable to women. And the school's impressive record in producing leaders has made admission desirable to some women. Nevertheless, Virginia has elected to preserve exclusively for men the advantages and opportunities a VMI education affords.

III

The cross-petitions in this suit present two ultimate issues. First, does Virginia's exclusion of women from the educational opportunities provided by VMI--extraordinary opportunities for military training and civilian leadership development--deny to women "capable of all of the individual activities required of VMI cadets," the equal protection of the laws guaranteed by the Fourteenth Amendment? Second, if VMI's "unique" situation,--as Virginia's sole single-sex public institution of higher education--offends the Constitution's equal protection principle, what is the remedial requirement?

IV

We note, once again, the core instruction of this Court's pathmarking decisions in *J.E.B. v. Alabama,* 511 U.S. 127 (1994), and *Mississippi Univ. for Women,* 458 U.S., at 724. Parties who seek to defend gender-based government action must demonstrate an "exceedingly persuasive justification" for that action.

Today's skeptical scrutiny of official action denying rights or opportunities based on sex responds to volumes of history. As a plurality of this Court acknowledged a generation ago, "our Nation has had a long and unfortunate history of sex discrimination." *Frontiero v. Richardson,* 411 U.S. 677, 684 (1973). Through a century plus three decades and more of that history, women did not count among voters composing "We the People"; not until 1920 did women gain a constitutional right to the franchise. And for a half century thereafter, it remained the prevailing doctrine that government, both federal and state, could withhold from women opportunities accorded men so long as any "basis in reason" could be conceived for the discrimination. See, *e.g., Goesaert v. Cleary,* 335 U.S. 464, 467 (1948)

In 1971, for the first time in our Nation's history, this Court ruled in favor of a woman who complained that her State had denied her the equal protection of its laws. *Reed v. Reed,* 404 U.S. 71, 73 (holding unconstitutional Idaho Code prescription that, among "several persons claiming and equally entitled to administer [a decedent's estate], males must be preferred to females"). Since *Reed,* the Court has repeatedly recognized that neither federal nor state government acts compatibly with the equal protection principle when a law or official policy denies to women, simply because they are women, full citizenship stature--equal opportunity to aspire, achieve, participate in and contribute to society based on their individual talents and capacities. See, *e.g., Kirchberg v. Feenstra,* 450 U.S. 455, 462-463 (1981) (affirming invalidity of Louisiana law that made husband "head and master" of property jointly owned with his wife, giving him unilateral right to dispose of such property without his wife's consent); *Stanton v. Stanton,* 421 U.S. 7 (1975) (invalidating Utah requirement that parents support boys until age 21, girls only until age 18).

Without equating gender classifications, for all purposes, to classifications based on race or national origin, the Court, in post-*Reed* decisions, has carefully inspected official action that closes a door or denies opportunity to women (or to men). See *J.E.B.,* 511 U.S., at 152 (KENNEDY, J., concurring in judgment) (case law evolving since 1971 "reveal[s] a strong presumption that gender classifications are invalid"). To summarize the Court's current directions for cases of official classification based on gender: Focusing on the differential treatment for denial of opportunity for which relief is sought, the reviewing court must determine whether the proffered justification is "exceedingly persuasive." The burden of justification is demanding and it rests entirely on the State. See *Mississippi Univ. for Women,* 458 U.S., at 724. The State must show "at least that the [challenged] classification serves 'important governmental objectives and that the discriminatory means employed' are 'substantially related to the achievement of those objectives.'" *Ibid.* (quoting *Wengler v. Druggists Mut. Ins. Co.,* 446 U.S. 142, 150(1980)). The justification must be genuine, not hypothesized or invented *post hoc* in response to litigation. And it must not rely on overbroad generalizations about the different talents, capacities, or preferences of males and females. See *Weinberger v. Wiesenfeld,* 420 U.S. 636, 643, 648 (1975); *Califano v. Goldfarb,* 430 U.S. 199, 223-224 (1977) (STEVENS, J., concurring in judgment).

The heightened review standard our precedent establishes does not make sex a proscribed classification. Supposed "inherent differences" are no longer accepted as a ground for race or national origin classifications. See *Loving v. Virginia,* 388 U.S. 1 (1967). Physical differences between men and women, however, are enduring: "[T]he two sexes are not fungible; a community made up exclusively of one [sex] is different from a community composed of both." *Ballard v. United States,* 329 U.S. 187, 193 (1946).

"Inherent differences" between men and women, we have come to appreciate, remain cause for celebration, but not for denigration of the members of either sex or for artificial constraints on an individual's opportunity. Sex classifications may be used to compensate women "for particular economic disabilities [they have] suffered," *Califano v. Webster,* 430 U.S. 313, 320 (1977) *(per curiam),* to "promot[e] equal employment opportunity," see *California Fed. Sav. & Loan Assn. v. Guerra,* 479 U.S. 272, 289 (1987), to advance full development of the talent and capacities of our Nation's people. But such classifications may not be used, as they once were, see *Goesaert,* 335 U.S., at 467, to create or perpetuate the legal, social, and economic inferiority of women.

Measuring the record in this case against the review standard just described, we conclude that Virginia has shown no "exceedingly persuasive justification" for excluding all women from the citizen-soldier training afforded by VMI. We therefore affirm the Fourth Circuit's initial judgment, which held that Virginia had violated the Fourteenth Amendment's Equal Protection Clause. Because the remedy proffered by Virginia--the Mary Baldwin VWIL program-does not cure the constitutional violation, *i.e.,* it does not provide equal opportunity, we reverse the Fourth Circuit's final judgment in this case.

V

The Fourth Circuit initially held that Virginia had advanced no state policy by which it could justify, under equal protection principles, its determination "to afford VMI's unique type of program to men and not to women." Virginia challenges that "liability" ruling and asserts two justifications in defense of VMI's exclusion of women. First, the Commonwealth contends, "single-sex education provides important educational benefits," and the option of single-sex education contributes to "diversity in educational approaches," Second, the Commonwealth argues, "the unique VMI method of character development and leadership training," the school's adversative approach, would have to be modified were VMI to admit women. We consider these two justifications in turn.

A

Single-sex education affords pedagogical benefits to at least some students, Virginia emphasizes, and that reality is uncontested in this litigation. Similarly, it is not disputed that diversity among public educational institutions can serve the public good. But Virginia has not shown that VMI was established, or has been maintained, with a view to diversifying, by its categorical exclusion of women, educational opportunities within the Commonwealth. In cases of this genre, our precedent instructs that "benign" justifications proffered in defense of categorical exclusions will not be accepted automatically; a tenable justification must describe actual state purposes, not rationalizations for actions in fact differently grounded. See *Wiesenfeld,* 420 U.S., at 648, and n. 16 ("mere recitation of a benign [or] compensatory purpose" does not block "inquiry into the actual purposes" of government-maintained gender-based classifications); *Goldfarb,* 430 U.S., at 212-213 (rejecting government-proffered purposes after "inquiry into the actual purposes.").

Mississippi Univ. for Women is immediately in point. There the State asserted, in justification of its exclusion of men from a nursing school, that it was engaging in "educational affirmative action" by "compensat[ing] for discrimination against women." Undertaking a "searching analysis," the Court found no close resemblance between "the alleged objective" and "the actual purpose underlying the discriminatory classification." Pursuing a similar inquiry here, we reach the same conclusion.

Neither recent nor distant history bears out Virginia's alleged pursuit of diversity through single-sex educational options. In 1839, when the Commonwealth established VMI, a range of educational opportunities for men and women was scarcely contemplated. Higher education at the time was considered dangerous for women; reflecting widely held views about women's proper place, the Nation's first universities and colleges--for example, Harvard in Massachusetts, William and Mary in Virginia--admitted only men. VMI was not at all novel in this respect: In admitting no women, VMI followed the lead of the Commonwealth's flagship school, the University of Virginia, founded in 1819.

"[N]o struggle for the admission of women to a state university," a historian has recounted, "was longer drawn out, or developed more bitterness, than that at the University of Virginia." 2 T. Woody, A History of Women's Education in the United States 254 (1929) (History of Women's Education). In 1879, the State Senate resolved to look into the possibility of higher education for women, recognizing that Virginia "'has never, at any period of her history,' "provided for the higher education of her daughters, though she "'has liberally provided for the higher education of her sons.'" Despite this recognition, no new opportunities were instantly open to women.

Virginia eventually provided for several women's seminaries and colleges. Farmville Female Seminary became a public institution in 1884. Two women's schools, Mary Washington College and James Madison University, were founded in 1908; another, Radford University, was founded in 1910. By the mid-1970's, all four schools had become coeducational.

Debate concerning women's admission as undergraduates at the main university continued well past the century's midpoint. Familiar arguments were rehearsed. If women were admitted, it was feared, they "would encroach on the rights of men; there would be new problems of government, perhaps scandals; the old honor system would have to be changed; standards would be lowered to those of other coeducational schools; and the glorious reputation of the university, as a school for men, would be trailed in the dust."

Ultimately, in 1970, "the most prestigious institution of higher education in Virginia," the University of Virginia, introduced coeducation and, in 1972, began to admit women on an equal basis with men. See *Kirstein v. Rector and Visitors of Univ. of Virginia,* 309 F. Supp. 184, 186 (E.D.Va.1970). A three-judge Federal District Court confirmed: "Virginia may not now deny to women, on the basis of sex, educational opportunities at the Charlottesville campus that are not afforded in other institutions operated by the [S]tate."

Virginia describes the current absence of public single-sex higher education for women as "an historical anomaly." But the historical record indicates action more deliberate than anomalous: First, protection of women against higher education; next, schools for women far from equal in resources and stature to schools for men; finally, conversion of the separate schools to coeducation. The state legislature, prior to the advent of this controversy, had repealed "[a]ll Virginia statutes requiring individual institutions to admit only men or women." And in 1990, an official commission, "legislatively established to chart the future goals of higher education in Virginia," reaffirmed the policy "'of affording broad access' "while maintaining" 'autonomy and diversity.'" 976 F.2d, at 898-899 (quoting Report of the Virginia Commission on the University of the 21st Century). Significantly, the commission reported: "'Because colleges and universities provide opportunities for students to develop values and learn from role models, it is extremely important that they deal with faculty, staff, and students without regard to sex, race, or ethnic origin.'"

This statement, the Court of Appeals observed, "is the only explicit one that we have found in the record in which the Commonwealth has expressed itself with respect to gender distinctions."

In sum, we find no persuasive evidence in this record that VMI's male-only admission policy "is in furtherance of a state policy of 'diversity.'" No such policy, the Fourth Circuit observed, can be discerned from the movement of all other public colleges and universities in Virginia away from single-sex education. That court also questioned "how one institution with autonomy, but with no authority over any other state institution, can give effect to a state policy of diversity among institutions." A purpose genuinely to advance an array of educational options, as the Court of Appeals recognized, is not served by VMI's historic and constant plan-a plan to "affor[d] a unique educational benefit only to males." However "liberally" this plan serves the Commonwealth's sons, it makes no provision whatever for her daughters. That is not *equal* protection.

B

Virginia next argues that VMI's adversative method of training provides educational benefits that cannot be made available, unmodified, to women. Alterations to accommodate women would necessarily be "radical," so "drastic," Virginia asserts, as to transform, indeed "destroy," VMI's program. Neither sex would be favored by the transformation, Virginia maintains: Men would be deprived of the unique opportunity currently available to them; women would not gain that opportunity because their participation would "eliminat[e] the very aspects of [the] program that distinguish [VMI] from ... other institutions of higher education in Virginia."

The District Court forecast from expert witness testimony, and the Court of Appeals accepted, that coeducation would materially affect "at least these three aspects of VMI's program-physical training, the absence of privacy, and the adversative approach." And it is uncontested that women's admission would require accommodations, primarily in arranging housing assignments and physical training programs for female cadets. It is also undisputed, however, that "the VMI methodology could be used to educate women." The District Court even allowed that some women may prefer it to the methodology a women's college might pursue. "[S]ome women, at least, would want to attend [VMI] if they had the opportunity," the District Court recognized, and "some women," the expert testimony established, "are capable of all of the individual activities required of VMI cadets," The parties, furthermore, agree that "*some* women can meet the physical standards [VMI] now impose[s] on men." In sum, as the Court of Appeals stated, "neither the goal of producing citizen soldiers," VMI's *raison d'être,* "nor VMI's implementing methodology is inherently unsuitable to women."

In support of its initial judgment for Virginia, a judgment rejecting all equal protection objections presented by the United States, the District Court made "findings" on "gender-based developmental differences." These "findings" restate the opinions of Virginia's expert witnesses, opinions about typically male or typically female "tendencies." For example, "[m]ales tend to need an atmosphere of adversativeness," while "[f]emales tend to thrive in a cooperative atmosphere." "I'm not saying that some women don't do well under [the] adversative model," VMI's expert on educational institutions testified, "undoubtedly there are some [women] who do"; but educational experiences must be designed "around the rule," this expert maintained, and not "around the exception."

The United States does not challenge any expert witness estimation on average capacities or preferences of men and women. Instead, the United States emphasizes that time and again since this Court's turning point decision in *Reed v. Reed,* 404 U.S. 71 (1971), we have cautioned reviewing courts to take a "hard look" at generalizations or "tendencies" of the kind pressed by Virginia, and relied upon by the District Court State actors controlling gates to opportunity, we have instructed, may not exclude qualified individuals based on "fixed notions concerning the roles and abilities of males and females." *Mississippi Univ. for Women,* 458 U.S., at 725; see *J.E.B.,* 511 U.S., at 139, n. 11 (equal protection principles, as applied to gender classifications, mean state actors may not rely on "overbroad" generalizations to make "judgments about people that are likely to ... perpetuate historical patterns of discrimination").

It may be assumed, for purposes of this decision, that most women would not choose VMI's adversative method. As Fourth Circuit Judge Motz observed, however, in her dissent from the Court of Appeals' denial of rehearing en banc, it is also probable that "many men would not want to be educated in such an environment." (On that point, even our dissenting colleague might agree.) Education, to be sure, is not a "one size fits all" business. The issue, however, is not whether "women-or men-should be forced to attend VMI"; rather, the question is whether the Commonwealth can constitutionally deny to women who have the will and capacity, the training and attendant opportunities that VMI uniquely affords.

The notion that admission of women would downgrade VMI's stature, destroy the adversative system and, with it, even the school, is a judgment hardly proved, a prediction hardly different from other "self-fulfilling prophec[ies]," see *Mississippi Univ. for Women,* 458 U.S., at 730, once routinely used to deny rights or opportunities. When women first sought admission to the bar and access to legal education, concerns of the same order were expressed. For example, in 1876, the Court of Common Pleas of Hennepin County, Minnesota, explained why women were thought ineligible for the practice of law. Women train and educate the young, the court said, which "forbids that they shall bestow that time (early and late) and labor, so essential in attaining to the eminence to which the true lawyer should ever aspire. It cannot therefore be said that the opposition of courts to the admission of females to practice ... is to any extent the outgrowth of ... 'old fogyism[.]' ... [I]t arises rather from a comprehension of the magnitude of the responsibilities connected with the successful practice of law, and a desire to *grade up* the profession." In re Application of Martha Angle Dorsett to Be Admitted to Practice as Attorney and Counselor at Law (Minn. C.P. Hennepin Cty., 1876), in The Syllabi, Oct. 21, 1876, pp. 5, 6 (emphasis added).

A like fear, according to a 1925 report, accounted for Columbia Law School's resistance to women's admission, although "[t]he faculty ... never maintained that women could not master legal learning. . . . No, its argument has been ... more practical. If women were admitted to the Columbia Law School, [the faculty] said, then the choicer, more manly and red-blooded graduates of our great universities would go to the Harvard Law School!" The Nation, Feb. 18, 1925, p. 173.

Medical faculties similarly resisted men and women as partners in the study of medicine. See R. Morantz-Sanchez, Sympathy and Science: Women Physicians in American Medicine 51-54, 250 (1985); see also M. Walsh, "Doctors Wanted: No Women Need Apply" 121-122 (1977) (quoting E. Clarke, Medical Education of Women, 4 Boston Med. & Surg. J. 345, 346 (1869) ("'God forbid that I should ever see men and women aiding each other to display with the scalpel the secrets of the reproductive system ...' ")); More recently, women seeking careers in policing encountered resistance based on fears that their presence would "undermine male solidarity," see F. Heidensohn, Women in Control? 201 (1992); deprive male partners of adequate assistance, see *id.* at 184-185; and lead to sexual misconduct, see C. Milton et al., Women in Policing 32-33 (1974). Field studies did not confirm these fears. See Heidensohn, *supra,* at 92-93; P. Bloch & D. Anderson, Policewomen on Patrol: Final Report (1974).

Women's successful entry into the federal military academies, and their participation in the Nation's military forces, indicate that Virginia's fears for the future of VMI may not be solidly grounded. The Commonwealth's justification for excluding all women from "citizen-soldier" training for which some are qualified, in any event, cannot rank as "exceedingly persuasive," as we have explained and applied that standard.

Virginia and VMI trained their argument on "means" rather than "end," and thus misperceived our precedent. Single-sex education at VMI serves an "important governmental objective," they maintained, and exclusion of women is not only "substantially related," it is essential to that objective. By this notably circular argument, the "straightforward" test *Mississippi Univ. for Women* described, see 458 U.S., at 724-725, was bent and bowed.

The Commonwealth's misunderstanding and, in turn, the District Court's, is apparent from VMI's mission: to produce "citizen-soldiers," individuals "'imbued with love of learning, confident in the functions and attitudes of leadership, possessing a high sense of public service, advocates of the American democracy and free enterprise system, and ready ... to defend their country in time of national peril.'"

Surely that goal is great enough to accommodate women, who today count as citizens in our American democracy equal in stature to men. Just as surely, the Commonwealth's great goal is not substantially advanced by women's categorical exclusion, in total disregard of their individual merit, from the Commonwealth's premier "citizen-soldier" corps. Virginia, in sum, "has fallen far short of establishing the 'exceedingly persuasive justification,'" *Mississippi Univ. for Women,* 458 U.S., at 731, that must be the solid base for any gender-defined classification.

VI

In the second phase of the litigation, Virginia presented its remedial plan-maintain VMI as a male-only college and create VWIL as a separate program for women. The plan met District Court approval. The Fourth Circuit, in turn, deferentially reviewed the Commonwealth's proposal and decided that the two single-sex programs directly served Virginia's reasserted purposes: single-gender education, and "achieving the results of an adversarial method in a military environment." Inspecting the VMI and VWIL educational programs to determine whether they "afford[ed] to both genders benefits comparable in substance, [if] not in form and detail," the Court of Appeals concluded that Virginia had arranged for men and women opportunities "sufficiently comparable" to survive equal protection evaluation. The United States challenges this "remedial" ruling as pervasively misguided.

A

A remedial decree, this Court has said, must closely fit the constitutional violation; it must be shaped to place persons unconstitutionally denied an opportunity or advantage in "the position they would have occupied in the absence of [discrimination]." See *Milliken v. Bradley,* 433 U.S.

267 (1977) The constitutional violation in this suit is the categorical exclusion of women from an extraordinary educational opportunity afforded men. A proper remedy for an unconstitutional exclusion, we have explained, aims to "eliminate [so far as possible] the discriminatory effects of the past" and to "bar like discrimination in the future." *Louisiana v. United States,* 380 U.S. 145, 154 (1965).

Virginia chose not to eliminate, but to leave untouched, VMI's exclusionary policy. For women only, however, Virginia proposed a separate program, different in kind from VMI and unequal in tangible and intangible facilities. Having violated the Constitution's equal protection requirement, Virginia was obliged to show that its remedial proposal "directly address[ed] and relate[d] to" the violation, see *Milliken,* 433 U.S., at 282, *i.e.,* the equal protection denied to women ready, willing, and able to benefit from educational opportunities of the kind VMI offers. Virginia described VWIL as a "parallel program," and asserted that VWIL shares VMI's mission of producing "citizen-soldiers" and VMI's goals of providing "education, military training, mental and physical discipline, character ... and leadership development." If the VWIL program could not "eliminate the discriminatory effects of the past," could it at least "bar like discrimination in the future"? A comparison of the programs said to be "parallel" informs our answer. In exposing the character of, and differences in, the VMI and VWIL programs, we recapitulate facts earlier presented.

VWIL affords women no opportunity to experience the rigorous military training for which VMI is famed. Instead, the VWIL program "deemphasize[s]" military education, and uses a "cooperative method" of education "which reinforces self-esteem." VWIL students participate in ROTC and a "largely ceremonial" Virginia Corps of Cadets, but Virginia deliberately did not make VWIL a military institute. The VWIL House is not a military-style residence and VWIL students need not live together throughout the 4-year program, eat meals together, or wear uniforms during the schoolday. VWIL students thus do not experience the "barracks" life "crucial to the VMI experience," the spartan living arrangements designed to foster an "egalitarian ethic." "[T]he most important aspects of the VMI educational experience occur in the barracks," the District Court found, yet Virginia deemed that core experience nonessential, indeed inappropriate, for training its female citizen-soldiers.

VWIL students receive their "leadership training" in seminars, externships, and speaker series, episodes and encounters lacking the "[p]hysical rigor, mental stress, ... minute regulation of behavior, and indoctrination in desirable values" made hallmarks of VMI's citizen-soldier training. Kept away from the pressures, hazards, and psychological bonding characteristic of VMI's adversative training, VWIL students will not know the "feeling of tremendous accomplishment" commonly experienced by VMI's successful cadets.

Virginia maintains that these methodological differences are "justified pedagogically," based on "important differences between men and women in learning and developmental needs," "psychological and sociological differences" Virginia describes as "real" and "not stereotypes." The Task Force charged with developing the leadership program for women, drawn from the staff and faculty at Mary Baldwin College, "determined that a military model and, especially VMI's adversative method, would be wholly inappropriate for educating and training *most women.*" See also 44 F.3d, at 1233-1234 (noting Task Force conclusion that, while "some women would be suited to and interested in [a VMI-style experience]," VMI's adversative method "would not be effective for *women as a group*" (emphasis added)). The Commonwealth embraced the Task Force view, as did expert witnesses who testified for Virginia.

As earlier stated, generalizations about "the way women are," estimates of what is appropriate for *most women,* no longer justify denying opportunity to women whose talent and capacity place them outside the average description. Notably, Virginia never asserted that VMI's method of education suits *most men.* It is also revealing that Virginia accounted for its failure to make the VWIL experience "the entirely militaristic experience of VMI" on the ground that VWIL "is planned for women who do not necessarily expect to pursue military careers." By that reasoning, VMI's "entirely militaristic" program would be inappropriate for men in general or *as a group,* for "[o]nly about 15% of VMI cadets enter career military service."

In contrast to the generalizations about women on which Virginia rests, we note again these dispositive realities: VMI's "implementing methodology" is not "inherently unsuitable to women," "some women ... do well under [the] adversative model," "some women, at least, would want to attend [VMI] if they had the opportunity," "some women are capable of all of the individual activities required of VMI cadets," and "can meet the physical standards [VMI] now impose[s] on men," It is on behalf of these women that the United States has instituted this suit, and it is for them that a remedy must be crafted, a remedy that will end their exclusion from a state-supplied educational opportunity for which they are fit, a decree that will "bar like discrimination in the future." *Louisiana,* 380 U.S., at 154.

B

In myriad respects other than military training, VWIL does not qualify as VMI's equal. VWIL's student body, faculty, course offerings, and facilities hardly match VMI's. Nor can the VWIL graduate anticipate the benefits associated with VMI's 157-year history, the school's prestige, and its influential alumni network.

Mary Baldwin College, whose degree VWIL students will gain, enrolls first-year women with an average combined SAT score about 100 points lower than the average score for VMI freshmen. The Mary Baldwin faculty holds "significantly fewer Ph.D.'s," and receives substantially lower salaries than the faculty at VMI.

Mary Baldwin does not offer a VWIL student the range of curricular choices available to a VMI cadet. VMI awards baccalaureate degrees in liberal arts, biology, chemistry, civil engineering, electrical and computer engineering, and mechanical engineering. VWIL students attend a school that "does not have a math and science focus," they cannot take at Mary Baldwin any courses in engineering or the advanced math and physics courses VMI offers,

For physical training, Mary Baldwin has "two multi-purpose fields" and "[o]ne gymnasium." VMI has "an NCAA competition level indoor track and field facility; a number of multi-purpose fields; baseball, soccer and lacrosse fields; an obstacle course; large boxing, wrestling and martial arts facilities; an 11-laps-to-the-mile indoor running course; an indoor pool; indoor and outdoor rifle ranges; and a football stadium that also contains a practice field and outdoor track."

Although Virginia has represented that it will provide equal financial support for in-state VWIL students and VMI cadets, and the VMI Foundation has agreed to endow VWIL with $5.4625 million, the difference between the two schools' financial reserves is pronounced. Mary Baldwin's endowment, currently about $19 million, will gain an additional $35 million based on future commitments; VMI's current endowment, $131 million--the largest public college per-student endowment in the Nation--will gain $220 million.

The VWIL student does not graduate with the advantage of a VMI degree. Her diploma does not unite her with the legions of VMI "graduates [who] have distinguished themselves" in military and civilian life. "[VMI] alumni are exceptionally close to the school," and that closeness accounts, in part, for VMI's success in attracting applicants. A VWIL graduate cannot assume that the "network of business owners, corporations, VMI graduates and non-graduate employers ... interested in hiring VMI graduates," will be equally responsive to her search for employment.

Virginia, in sum, while maintaining VMI for men only, has failed to provide any "comparable single-gender women's institution." Instead, the Commonwealth has created a VWIL program fairly appraised as a "pale shadow" of VMI in terms of the range of curricular choices and faculty stature, funding, prestige, alumni support and influence.

Virginia's VWIL solution is reminiscent of the remedy Texas proposed 50 years ago, in response to a state trial court's 1946 ruling that, given the equal protection guarantee, African-Americans could not be denied a legal education at a state facility. See *Sweatt v. Painter,* 339 U.S. 629, (1950). Reluctant to admit African-Americans to its flagship University of Texas Law School, the State set up a separate school for Heman Sweatt and other black law students. As originally opened, the new school had no independent faculty or library, and it lacked accreditation. Nevertheless, the state trial and appellate courts were satisfied that the new school offered Sweatt opportunities for the study of law "substantially equivalent to those offered by the State to white students at the University of Texas."

Before this Court considered the case, the new school had gained "a faculty of five full-time professors; a student body of 23; a library of some 16,500 volumes serviced by a full-time staff; a practice court and legal aid association; and one alumnus who ha[d] become a member of the Texas Bar." This Court contrasted resources at the new school with those at the school from which Sweatt had been excluded. The University of Texas Law School had a full-time faculty of 16, a student body of 850, a library containing over 65,000 volumes, scholarship funds, a law review, and moot court facilities.

More important than the tangible features, the Court emphasized, are "those qualities which are incapable of objective measurement but which make for greatness" in a school, including "reputation of the faculty, experience of the administration, position and influence of the alumni, standing in the community, traditions and prestige." Facing the marked differences reported in the *Sweatt* opinion, the Court unanimously ruled that Texas had not shown "substantial equality in the [separate] educational opportunities" the State offered. Accordingly, the Court held, the Equal Protection Clause required Texas to admit African-Americans to the University of Texas Law School. In line with *Sweatt,* we rule here that Virginia has not shown substantial equality in the separate educational opportunities the Commonwealth supports at VWIL and VMI.

VII

A generation ago, "the authorities controlling Virginia higher education," despite long established tradition, agreed "to innovate and favorably entertain[ed] the [then] relatively new idea that there must be no discrimination by sex in offering educational opportunity." Commencing in 1970, Virginia opened to women "educational opportunities at the Charlottesville campus that [were] not afforded in other [state-operated] institutions." A federal court approved the Commonwealth's innovation, emphasizing that the University of Virginia "offer[ed] courses of instruction ... not available elsewhere." The court further noted: "[T]here exists at Charlottesville a 'prestige' factor [not paralleled in] other Virginia educational institutions."

VMI, too, offers an educational opportunity no other Virginia institution provides, and the school's "prestige"-associated with its success in developing "citizen-soldiers"--is unequaled. Virginia has closed this facility to its daughters and, instead, has devised for them a "parallel program," with a faculty less impressively credentialed and less well paid, more limited course offerings, fewer opportunities for military training and for scientific specialization. VMI, beyond question, "possesses to a far greater degree" than the VWIL program "those qualities which are incapable of objective measurement but which make for greatness in a ... school," including "position and influence of the alumni, standing in the community, traditions and prestige." Women seeking and fit for a VMI-quality education cannot be offered anything less, under the Commonwealth's obligation to afford them genuinely equal protection.

A prime part of the history of our Constitution, historian Richard Morris recounted, is the story of the extension of constitutional rights and protections to people once ignored or excluded. VMI's story continued as our comprehension of "We the People" expanded. There is no reason to believe that the admission of women capable of all the activities required of VMI cadets would destroy the Institute rather than enhance its capacity to serve the "more perfect Union."

* * *

For the reasons stated, the initial judgment of the Court of Appeals, is affirmed, the final judgment of the Court of Appeals, is reversed, and the case is remanded for further proceedings consistent with this opinion. *It is so ordered.*

NOTES

1. The Court in the *VMI* case could have simply treated the case as controlled by *Mississippi University for Women v. Hogan, i.e.*, that VMI was almost the exact mirror image of the situation at MUW—the one school based on the impermissible stereotype that nursing is a woman's profession and the other school based on the impermissible stereotype that military service is a man's profession. It should be noted that both stereotypes were substantially accurate, in that, at the time of the decisions, 98% of nurses were women and 85% of military personal were male. This type of statistical accuracy would have been a more than sufficient defense to the constitutional challenges if the Court had been applying rational basis review. The Court, however, in Justice Ginsburg's majority opinion, used the case to explicate the substantial scrutiny standard at great length, and to demonstrate that it was a very demanding standard.

2. As for the intermediate standard itself, the *VMI* Court made very clear the differences between that standard and the much more deferential rational basis standard. While rational basis analysis allowed courts to hypothesize governmental purposes, intermediate scrutiny would require evidence of genuine, actual purpose. While under the rational basis standard, "those attacking the rationality of the legislative classification have the burden 'to negative every conceivable basis which might support it,'" under intermediate scrutiny, the burden of justification rested entirely on the State, that is, the state not only had to prove that the law served an important purpose but also that the gender classification was substantially related to that purpose. And, as the Court noted, this required of the state an "exceedingly persuasive justification."

3. The Court conceded that physical differences between the sexes were enduring and these differences would in some cases justify different treatment for men and women but the Court also noted that the state would not be allowed to rely on overbroad generalizations about the different talents, capacities, or preferences of males and females. In particular, the Court noted that, under the intermediate scrutiny standard, the Court would look at the way a generalization about women as a class had the effect of artificially constraining an *individual* woman's opportunity and whether such individual opportunity was limited by overbroad generalizations about the different talents, capacities, or preferences of men and women.

4. One of the claims that the VMI defendants had made to justify the all-male character of the school was that the separation of men and women was based on the different learning styles of men and women. Men, it was claimed, are suited for an adversative, in-your-face, confrontational style of learning, while women are more suited for gentler, more cooperative style of learning. The VMI defendants even cited the work of Carol Gilligan, who had written how women approach ethical issues differently from men, as justification for the exclusion of women from VMI. An amicus brief filed with the Court by American Association of University Professors, including Carol Gilligan, responded:

> Gilligan's research and theories were used to support the claim that an educational program geared specifically to meet men's developmental and educational needs is effective and provides unique benefits for both the men who attend and for society at large, and that introducing women into this kind of setting would be counterproductive for women and would deprive men of an unique and valuable opportunity. However, nothing in Gilligan's work provides support for these propositions. . . . The testimony in this case misconstrues the purpose and import of Gilligan's work, in particular her acclaimed book, In a Different Voice: Psychological Theory and Women's Development (1982). Brief Amici Curiae in Support of Petitioner by the American Association of University Professors, at 23-24.

Nor was Justice Ginsburg persuaded by this argument, which was effectively a generalization about women that may have had an underlying factual basis but had become an unacceptable stereotype. Justice Ginsburg conceded that few women would want to attend VMI or be suited for its program; but few men would be interested in the VMI program either. And, it turns out, *some* women would prefer VMI's adversative educational method and would want to attend that institution, *some* women are capable of all the activities required of VMI cadets, and *some* women could meet the physical standards currently imposed on men. VMI could not use broad generalizations about women to exclude from its program those women to whom the generalization did not apply.

5. With regard to the purposes that VMI set forth in defense of its single-sex program, the Court conceded that diversity in higher education was a public good. However, after considering both historical and current evidence, the Court concluded that diversity of educational opportunity was in no way the purpose of the VMI program. Especially significant was the fact that because there were no other single-sex public institutions in Virginia at that time, only males were given the option of single-sex education. Another defense VMI relied on was the argument that the admission of women would destroy the very nature of the VMI program in that the program would have to be modified to such an extent that it would no longer be recognizable. The Court identified this argument as "circular," confusing means and ends. In effect, VMI argued that they had to keep their program all-male because, if they didn't, it won't be all male. The Court rejected this version of intermediate scrutiny as "bent and bowed."

D. PERMITTED GENDER CLASSIFICATIONS

The cases in the previous section make clear that intermediate scrutiny is a demanding standard that sees through stereotypes about proper roles for men and women. It is a standard that will invalidate a substantial proportion of gender classifications. But intermediate scrutiny is not strict scrutiny, and a certain percentage of gender classifications will survive review, that is, the Court will find that the gender classification is substantially related to an important governmental interest. This section examines these cases.

1. *BASED ON GENUINE BIOLOGICAL DIFFERENCES BETWEEN THE SEXES*

Michael M. v. Superior Court of Sonoma County
450 U.S. 464 (1981)

[Petitioner Michael M., age 17 ½, was charged with statutory rape under § 261.5 of the California Penal Code. Evidence showed that he had met a 16 ½ year old girl who was intoxicated and that he had intercourse with her after he struck her face for resisting his advances. Michael alleged that the law under which he was convicted violated the equal protection clause of the Fourteenth Amendment because only men could be criminally liable for sexual intercourse under the statute.]

Justice REHNQUIST announced the judgment of the Court and delivered an opinion, in which THE CHIEF JUSTICE, Justice STEWART, and Justice POWELL joined.

The question presented in this case is whether California's "statutory rape" law violates the Equal Protection Clause of the Fourteenth Amendment. Section 261.5 defines unlawful sexual intercourse as "an act of sexual intercourse accomplished with a female not the wife of the perpetrator, where the female is under the age of 18 years." The statute thus makes men alone criminally liable for the act of sexual intercourse.

As is evident from our opinions, the Court has had some difficulty in agreeing upon the proper approach and analysis in cases involving challenges to gender-based classifications. The issues posed by such challenges range from issues of standing, see *Orr v. Orr*, 440 U.S. 268 (1979), to the appropriate standard of judicial review for the substantive classification. Unlike the California Supreme Court, we have not held that gender-based classifications are "inherently suspect" and thus we do not apply so-called "strict scrutiny" to those classifications. See *Stanton v. Stanton*, 421 U.S. 7 (1975). Our cases have held, however, that the traditional minimum rationality test takes on a somewhat "sharper focus" when gender-based classifications are challenged. See *Craig v. Boren*, 429 U.S. 190, 210 n.* (1976) (POWELL, J., concurring). In *Reed v. Reed*, 404 U.S. 71 (1971), for example, the Court stated that a gender-based classification will be upheld if it bears a "fair and substantial relationship" to legitimate state ends, while in *Craig v. Boren, supra*, 429 U.S. at 197, the Court restated the test to require the classification to bear a "substantial relationship" to "important governmental objectives."

Underlying these decisions is the principle that a legislature may not "make overbroad generalizations based on sex which are entirely unrelated to any differences between men and women or which demean the ability or social status of the affected class." *Parham v. Hughes*, 441

U.S. 347, 354 (1979) (plurality opinion of STEWART, J.). But because the Equal Protection Clause does not "demand that a statute necessarily apply equally to all persons" or require "'things which are different in fact ... to be treated in law as though they were the same,' this Court has consistently upheld statutes where the gender classification is not invidious, but rather realistically reflects the fact that the sexes are not similarly situated in certain circumstances. *Parham v. Hughes, supra; Califano v. Webster*, 430 U.S. 313 (1977); *Schlesinger v. Ballard*, 419 U.S. 498 (1975); *Kahn v. Shevin*, 416 U.S. 351 (1974). As the Court has stated, a legislature may "provide for the special problems of women." *Weinberger v. Wiesenfeld*, 420 U.S. 636, 653 (1975).

Applying those principles to this case, the fact that the California Legislature criminalized the act of illicit sexual intercourse with a minor female is a sure indication of its intent or purpose to discourage that conduct. Precisely why the legislature desired that result is of course somewhat less clear. This Court has long recognized that "[i]nquiries into congressional motives or purposes are a hazardous matter," *United States v. O'Brien*, 391 U.S. 367, 383-384 (1968); *Palmer v. Thompson*, 403 U.S. 217, 224 (1971), and the search for the "actual" or "primary" purpose of a statute is likely to be elusive. *Arlington Heights v. Metropolitan Housing Dev. Corp.*, 429 U.S. 252, 265 (1977); *McGinnis v. Royster*, 410 U.S. 263, 276-277 (1973). Here, for example, the individual legislators may have voted for the statute for a variety of reasons. Some legislators may have been concerned about preventing teenage pregnancies, others about protecting young females from physical injury or from the loss of "chastity," and still others about promoting various religious and moral attitudes towards premarital sex.

The justification for the statute offered by the State, and accepted by the Supreme Court of California, is that the legislature sought to prevent illegitimate teenage pregnancies. That finding, of course, is entitled to great deference. *Reitman v. Mulkey*, 387 U.S. 369, 373-374 (1967). And although our cases establish that the State's asserted reason for the enactment of a statute may be rejected, if it "could not have been a goal of the legislation," *Weinberger v. Wiesenfeld, supra*, 420 U.S. at 648, n. 16, this is not such a case.

We are satisfied not only that the prevention of illegitimate pregnancy is at least one of the "purposes" of the statute, but also that the State has a strong interest in preventing such pregnancy. At the risk of stating the obvious, teenage pregnancies, which have increased dramatically over the last two decades, have significant social, medical, and economic consequences for both the mother and her child, and the State. Of particular concern to the State is that approximately half of all teenage pregnancies end in abortion. And of those children who are born, their illegitimacy makes them likely candidates to become wards of the State.

Subsequent to the decision below, the California Legislature considered and rejected proposals to render [the challenged statute] gender neutral, thereby ratifying the judgment of the California Supreme Court. That is enough to answer petitioner's contention that the statute was the "'accidental by-product of a traditional way of thinking about females.'" Certainly this decision of the California Legislature is as good a source as is this Court in deciding what is "current" and what is "outmoded" in the perception of women.

We need not be medical doctors to discern that young men and young women are not similarly situated with respect to the problems and the risks of sexual intercourse. Only women may become pregnant, and they suffer disproportionately the profound physical, emotional and psychological consequences of sexual activity. The statute at issue here protects women from sexual intercourse at an age when those consequences are particularly severe.

The question thus boils down to whether a State may attack the problem of sexual intercourse and teenage pregnancy directly by prohibiting a male from having sexual intercourse with a minor female. We hold that such a statute is sufficiently related to the State's objectives to pass constitutional muster.

Because virtually all of the significant harmful and inescapably identifiable consequences of teenage pregnancy fall on the young female, a legislature acts well within its authority when it elects to punish only the participant who, by nature, suffers few of the consequences of his conduct. It is hardly unreasonable for a legislature acting to protect minor females to exclude them from punishment. Moreover, the risk of pregnancy itself constitutes a substantial deterrence to young females. No similar natural sanctions deter males. A criminal sanction imposed solely on males thus serves to roughly "equalize" the deterrents on the sexes.

We are unable to accept petitioner's contention that the statute is impermissibly underinclusive and must, in order to pass judicial scrutiny, be *broadened* so as to hold the female as criminally liable as the male. It is argued that this statute is not *necessary* to deter teenage pregnancy because a gender-neutral statute, where both male and female would be subject to prosecution, would serve that goal equally well. The relevant inquiry, however, is not whether the statute is drawn as precisely as it might have been, but whether the line chosen by the California Legislature is within constitutional limitations. *Kahn v. Shevin*, 416 U.S., at 356 n. 10.

In any event, we cannot say that a gender-neutral statute would be as effective as the statute California has chosen to enact. The State persuasively contends that a gender-neutral statute would frustrate its interest in effective enforcement. Its view is that a female is surely less likely to report violations of the statute if she herself would be subject to criminal prosecution. In an area already fraught with prosecutorial difficulties, we decline to hold that the Equal Protection Clause requires a legislature to enact a statute so broad that it may well be incapable of enforcement.

We similarly reject petitioner's argument that [the statute] is impermissibly overbroad because it makes unlawful sexual intercourse with prepubescent females, who are, by definition, incapable of becoming pregnant. Quite apart from the fact that the statute could well be justified on the grounds that very young females are particularly susceptible to physical injury from sexual intercourse, see *Rundlett v. Oliver*, 607 F.2d 495 (CA1 1979), it is ludicrous to suggest that the Constitution requires the California Legislature to limit the scope of its rape statute to older teenagers and exclude young girls.

There remains only petitioner's contention that the statute is unconstitutional as it is applied to him because he, like Sharon, was under 18 at the time of sexual intercourse. Petitioner argues that the statute is flawed because it presumes that as between two persons under 18, the male is the culpable aggressor. We find petitioner's contentions unpersuasive. Contrary to his assertions, the statute does not rest on the assumption that males are generally the aggressors. It is instead an attempt by a legislature to prevent illegitimate teenage pregnancy by providing an additional deterrent for men. The age of the man is irrelevant since young men are as capable as older men of inflicting the harm sought to be prevented.

In upholding the California statute we also recognize that this is not a case where a statute is being challenged on the grounds that it "invidiously discriminates" against females. To the contrary, the statute places a burden on males which is not shared by females. But we find nothing to suggest that men, because of past discrimination or peculiar disadvantages, are in need of the special solicitude of the courts. Nor is this a case where the gender classification is made "solely for ... administrative convenience," as in *Frontiero v. Richardson*, 411 U.S. 677, 690 (1973) (emphasis omitted), or rests on "the baggage of sexual stereotypes" as in *Orr v. Orr*, 440 U.S., at 283. As we have held, the statute instead reasonably reflects the fact that the consequences of sexual intercourse and pregnancy fall more heavily on the female than on the male.

Accordingly, the judgment of the California Supreme Court is *Affirmed*.

[Justice Brennan, dissenting, insisted that the actual purpose of the statute was not to prevent teenage pregnancy, but rather to protect young women because their chastity was considered particularly precious and they were thus uniquely in need of the State's protection.]

NOTES

1. The standard of scrutiny in *Michael M.* —decided one year before *Hogan* and fifteen years before *VMI*, —is not nearly as demanding a standard as that in the later cases. While the Court in *Hogan* and *VMI* had insisted that the burden was entirely on the state to prove the actual, not hypothesized, purpose of the statute, the *Michael M.* Court was far more deferential. The Court conceded that it was not clear why the legislature had adopted the statute but was not troubled by that lack of information because, contrary to the Court in *Hogan* and *VMI*, inquiry into legislative motive and purpose is a "hazardous matter" and the search for actual purpose was likely to be "elusive." Thus, the Court accepted at face value the state's claim that the purpose of the law was to prevent teenage pregnancies. Justice Brennan, in dissent, was far more skeptical, suspecting that the actual purpose of the law was to give effect to a very traditional stereotype about men and women in relation to sex—that men are by nature sexual aggressors and that women are in need of special protection to preserve their chastity, something which is apparently not important for men to preserve.

2. Once the Court determined that the purpose of the law was to prevent teenage pregnancy, the gendered nature of the law seemed to make more sense, since only women get pregnant. This genuine biological difference between men and women is an appropriate justification for some different treatment of men and women, *e.g.*, disability leave for women after pregnancy, but it is not clear that genuine biological differences were really at work in *Michael M.* It is quite possible, and in fact not uncommon in other states, to draw up a statute on statutory rape that is gender-neutral, *i.e.*, one that would hold both parties criminally liable. But the Court insisted that "necessity" was not the test, and the fact that the California legislature could have achieved its purpose in gender-neutral fashion did not mean that the statue failed the intermediate scrutiny test.

3. The Court's explication of the details of intermediate scrutiny has advanced considerably since the *Michael M.* case in 1981, particularly as articulated by Justice Ginsburg in *VMI*. Therefore, it seems that the Court's rather casual approach to intermediate scrutiny should not be given too much weight. However, the Court's determination that genuine biological differences are an appropriate reason to treat men and women differently is still very much the rule, as the next two cases demonstrate.

4. In *California Federal Savings & Loan Association v Guerra*, 479 U.S. 272 (1987), the Court considered a California statute that required employers to provide female employees an unpaid pregnancy disability leave of up to four months. This was not an equal protection case; rather the

question before the Court was whether the California state statute was preempted by a federal statute—Title VII of the Civil Rights Act of 1964 which prohibited discrimination on the basis of sex and, as amended, prohibited discrimination on the basis of pregnancy. The Court determined that the federal statute had been primarily concerned with discrimination *against* pregnant women, not with discrimination that *benefited* those women, and that therefore the federal law did not preempt the state law. In making this determination, the Court noted that the purpose of the California statute was to promote equal employment opportunity. If employers were required to reinstate women after a reasonable pregnancy disability leave, women would not lose their jobs on account of pregnancy disability. The Court explained that by taking pregnancy into account, the statute allowed women, as well as men, to have families without losing their jobs.

The Court's analysis of the pregnancy leave statute, although made under a federal statute, is quite relevant to a consideration of pregnancy and the Equal Protection Clause. It is undoubtedly true that only women can become pregnant and that this genuine biological difference is a proper ground for treating men and women differently. But the *Guerra* case also demonstrates the difficulty in confining the boundaries of appropriately different treatment. Thus, for example, the statute identified the leave as a disability leave, one related to the physical disability that follows childbirth. There is no question that leave associated with physical disability following childbirth is substantially related to the important governmental interest, identified by the *Guerra* Court as providing equal employment opportunity. The Court, however, did not question whether or not the four-month term of the leave raised questions about whether its purpose was actually to provide for disability. Since, for many women, particularly those who have had uncomplicated deliveries, the period of physical disability is far shorter than four months, a skeptic might think that the statute was a disguised maternity leave statute, the actual purpose of which was to give mothers time to be at home with their newborn children. Having a parent home with a newborn is, of course, a commendable purpose, but since the statute limited that benefit to mothers, it also suggests a very traditional kind of stereotyping—the view that the mother's role is more important to the child than is the father's role. This very stereotype was condemned by the Court as unconstitutional in *Caban v. Mohammed*, 441 U.S. 380 (1979).

There is another physiological difference between men and women that might have justified the four-month leave for mothers, *i.e.*, if it had been identified as a breastfeeding leave. Only women can breast feed and breastfeeding is highly recommended for newborns. But the state had never identified breastfeeding as a purpose of the statute, new mothers were not required to breastfeed in order to take advantage of the statute, and under intermediate scrutiny, the state has the burden of proving the actual purpose of the statute.

Nguyen v. INS
533 U.S. 53 (2001)

[Taun Ahn Nguyen was born in 1960 to unwed parents in Saigon, Vietnam. His mother was Vietnamese and his father an American citizen. When his parents' relationship ended, Nguyen continued to reside with his father, first in Vietnam and then, after age six, in Texas, where his father raised him. When he was twenty-two, Nguyen pleaded guilty to two counts of sexually assaulting a child and was sentenced to eight years in prison on each count. Three years later, the United States Immigration and Naturalization Services (INS) commenced deportation proceedings against Nguyen.

Nguyen could not have been deported had he been a citizen. He challenged the federal law that set forth different requirements for children born abroad to unmarried parents, depending on the gender of the citizen parent. If Nguyen's mother had been the citizen parent, he would have automatically become a citizen so long as his mother had been physically present in the United States or one of its possessions for a continuous period of one year. Since, however, Nguyen's father was the citizen parent, the law provided that, while he was under eighteen, he had to be (1) legitimated under the law of his residence or domicile, (2) acknowledged by his father under oath, or (3) adjudicated to be the child by a competent court. None of these requirements had been satisfied in Nguyen's case.]

Justice KENNEDY delivered the opinion of the Court.

Title 8 U.S.C. §1409 governs the acquisition of United States citizenship by persons born to one United States citizen parent and one noncitizen parent when the parents are unmarried and the child is born outside of the United States or its possessions. The statute imposes different requirements for the child's acquisition of citizenship depending upon whether the citizen parent is the mother or the father. The question before us is whether the statutory distinction is consistent with the equal protection guarantee embedded in the Due Process Clause of the Fifth Amendment.

We hold that §1409(a) is consistent with the constitutional guarantee of equal protection.

III

For a gender-based classification to withstand equal protection scrutiny, it must be established "'at least that the [challenged] classification serves "important governmental objectives and that the discriminatory means employed" are "substantially related to the achievement of those objectives."' " *United States v. Virginia*, 518 U.S. 515, 533 (1996) (quoting *Mississippi Univ. for Women v. Hogan*, 458 U.S. 718, 724 (1982), in turn quoting *Wengler v. Druggists Mut. Ins. Co.*, 446 U.S. 142, 150(1980)). For reasons to follow, we conclude §1409 satisfies this standard.

The statutory distinction relevant in this case, then, is that §1409(a)(4) requires one of three affirmative steps to be taken if the citizen parent is the father, but not if the citizen parent is the mother: legitimation; a declaration of paternity under oath by the father; or a court order of paternity. Congress' decision to impose requirements on unmarried fathers that differ from those on unmarried mothers is based on the significant difference between their respective relationships to the potential citizen at the time of birth. Specifically, the imposition of the requirement for a paternal relationship, but not a maternal one, is justified by two important governmental objectives. We discuss each in turn.

A

The first governmental interest to be served is the importance of assuring that a biological parent-child relationship exists. In the case of the mother, the relation is verifiable from the birth itself. The mother's status is documented in most instances by the birth certificate or hospital records and the witnesses who attest to her having given birth.

In the case of the father, the uncontestable fact is that he need not be present at the birth. If he is present, furthermore, that circumstance is not incontrovertible proof of fatherhood. See *Lehr v.*

Robertson, 463 U.S. 248, 260, n. 16 (1983) ("'The mother carries and bears the child, and in this sense her parental relationship is clear. The validity of the father's parental claims must be gauged by other measures'" (quoting *Caban v. Mohammed,* 441 U.S. 380, 397 (1979) (Stewart, J., dissenting))); *Trimble v. Gordon,* 430 U.S. 762, 770 (1977) ("The more serious problems of proving paternity might justify a more demanding standard for illegitimate children claiming under their fathers' estates than that required ... under their mothers' estates ..."). Fathers and mothers are not similarly situated with regard to the proof of biological parenthood. The imposition of a different set of rules for making that legal determination with respect to fathers and mothers is neither surprising nor troublesome from a constitutional perspective. Cf. *Cleburne v. Cleburne Living Center, Inc.,* 473 U.S. 432, 439 (1985) (explaining that the Equal Protection Clause "is essentially a direction that all persons similarly situated should be treated alike"); *F.S. Royster Guano Co. v. Virginia,* 253 U.S. 412, 415 (1920). Section 1409(a)(4)'s provision of three options for a father seeking to establish paternity-legitimation, paternity oath, and court order of paternity-is designed to ensure an acceptable documentation of paternity.

Petitioners argue that the requirement of §1409(a)(1), that a father provide clear and convincing evidence of parentage, is sufficient to achieve the end of establishing paternity, given the sophistication of modern DNA tests. Section 1409(a)(1) does not actually mandate a DNA test, however. The Constitution, moreover, does not require that Congress elect one particular mechanism from among many possible methods of establishing paternity, even if that mechanism arguably might be the most scientifically advanced method. With respect to DNA testing, the expense, reliability, and availability of such testing in various parts of the world may have been of particular concern to Congress. The requirement of §1409(a)(4) represents a reasonable conclusion by the legislature that the satisfaction of one of several alternatives will suffice to establish the blood link between father and child required as a predicate to the child's acquisition of citizenship. Cf. *Lehr, supra,* at 267-268 (upholding New York statutory requirement that gave mothers of children born out of wedlock notice of an adoption hearing, but only extended that right to fathers who mailed a postcard to a "putative fathers registry"). Given the proof of motherhood that is inherent in birth itself, it is unremarkable that Congress did not require the same affirmative steps of mothers.

Finally, to require Congress to speak without reference to the gender of the parent with regard to its objective of ensuring a blood tie between parent and child would be to insist on a hollow neutrality. As Justice STEVENS pointed out in *Miller,* Congress could have required both mothers and fathers to prove parenthood within 30 days or, for that matter, 18 years, of the child's birth. 523 U.S., at 436. Given that the mother is always present at birth, but that the father need not be, the facially neutral rule would sometimes require fathers to take additional affirmative steps which would not be required of mothers, whose names will appear on the birth certificate as a result of their presence at the birth, and who will have the benefit of witnesses to the birth to call upon. The issue is not the use of gender specific terms instead of neutral ones. Just as neutral terms can mask discrimination that is unlawful, gender specific terms can mark a permissible distinction. The equal protection question is whether the distinction is lawful. Here, the use of gender specific terms takes into account a biological difference between the parents. The differential treatment is inherent in a sensible statutory scheme, given the unique relationship of the mother to the event of birth.

B

1

The second important governmental interest furthered in a substantial manner by §1409(a)(4) is the determination to ensure that the child and the citizen parent have some demonstrated opportunity or potential to develop not just a relationship that is recognized, as a formal matter, by the law, but one that consists of the real, everyday ties that provide a connection between child and citizen parent and, in turn, the United States. In the case of a citizen mother and a child born overseas, the opportunity for a meaningful relationship between citizen parent and child inheres in the very event of birth, an event so often critical to our constitutional and statutory understandings of citizenship. The mother knows that the child is in being and is hers and has an initial point of contact with him. There is at least an opportunity for mother and child to develop a real, meaningful relationship.

The same opportunity does not result from the event of birth, as a matter of biological inevitability, in the case of the unwed father. Given the 9-month interval between conception and birth, it is not always certain that a father will know that a child was conceived, nor is it always clear that even the mother will be sure of the father's identity. This fact takes on particular significance in the case of a child born overseas and out of wedlock. One concern in this context has always been with young people, men for the most part, who are on duty with the Armed Forces in foreign countries.

When we turn to the conditions which prevail today, we find that the passage of time has produced additional and even more substantial grounds to justify the statutory distinction. The ease of travel and the willingness of Americans to visit foreign countries have resulted in numbers of trips abroad that must be of real concern when we contemplate the prospect of accepting petitioners' argument, which would mandate, contrary to Congress' wishes, citizenship by male parentage subject to no condition save the father's previous length of residence in this country.

Principles of equal protection do not require Congress to ignore this reality. To the contrary, these facts demonstrate the critical importance of the Government's interest in ensuring some opportunity for a tie between citizen father and foreign born child which is a reasonable substitute for the opportunity manifest between mother and child at the time of birth. Indeed, especially in light of the number of Americans who take short sojourns abroad, the prospect that a father might not even know of the conception is a realistic possibility. Even if a father knows of the fact of conception, moreover, it does not follow that he will be present at the birth of the child. Thus, unlike the case of the mother, there is no assurance that the father and his biological child will ever meet. Without an initial point of contact with the child by a father who knows the child is his own, there is no opportunity for father and child to begin a relationship. Section 1409 takes the unremarkable step of ensuring that such an opportunity, inherent in the event of birth as to the mother-child relationship, exists between father and child before citizenship is conferred upon the latter.

The importance of the governmental interest at issue here is too profound to be satisfied merely by conducting a DNA test. The fact of paternity can be established even without the father's knowledge, not to say his presence. Paternity can be established by taking DNA samples even from a few strands of hair, years after the birth. See Federal Judicial Center, Reference Manual on Scientific Evidence 497 (2d ed.2000). Yet scientific proof of biological paternity does nothing, by itself, to ensure contact between father and child during the child's minority.

Congress is well within its authority in refusing, absent proof of at least the opportunity for the development of a relationship between citizen parent and child, to commit this country to embracing a child as a citizen entitled as of birth to the full protection of the United States, to the absolute right to enter its borders, and to full participation in the political process. If citizenship is to be conferred by the unwitting means petitioners urge, so that its acquisition abroad bears little relation to the realities of the child's own ties and allegiances, it is for Congress, not this Court, to make that determination. Congress has not taken that path but has instead chosen, by means of § 1409, to ensure in the case of father and child the opportunity for a relationship to develop, an opportunity which the event of birth itself provides for the mother and child. It should be unobjectionable for Congress to require some evidence of a minimal opportunity for the development of a relationship with the child in terms the male can fulfill.

While the INS' brief contains statements indicating the governmental interest we here describe, see Brief for Respondent 38, 41, it suggests other interests as well. Statements from the INS' brief are not conclusive as to the objects of the statute, however, as we are concerned with the objectives of Congress, not those of the INS. We ascertain the purpose of a statute by drawing logical conclusions from its text, structure, and operation.

Petitioners and their *amici* argue in addition that, rather than fulfilling an important governmental interest, § 1409 merely embodies a gender-based stereotype. Although the above discussion should illustrate that, contrary to petitioners' assertions, § 1409 addresses an undeniable difference in the circumstance of the parents at the time a child is born, it should be noted, furthermore, that the difference does not result from some stereotype, defined as a frame of mind resulting from irrational or uncritical analysis. There is nothing irrational or improper in the recognition that at the moment of birth--a critical event in the statutory scheme and in the whole tradition of citizenship law--the mother's knowledge of the child and the fact of parenthood have been established in a way not guaranteed in the case of the unwed father. This is not a stereotype. See *Virginia,* 518 U.S., at 533 ("The heightened review standard our precedent establishes does not make sex a proscribed classification . . . Physical differences between men and women ... are enduring").

Having concluded that facilitation of a relationship between parent and child is an important governmental interest, the question remains whether the means Congress chose to further its objective-the imposition of certain additional requirements upon an unwed father-substantially relate to that end. Under this test, the means Congress adopted must be sustained.

First, it should be unsurprising that Congress decided to require that an opportunity for a parent--child relationship occur during the formative years of the child's minority. In furtherance of the desire to ensure some tie between this country and one who seeks citizenship, various other statutory provisions concerning citizenship and naturalization require some act linking the child to the United States to occur before the child reaches 18 years of age. See, *e.g.,* 8 U.S.C. §1431 (child born abroad to one citizen parent and one noncitizen parent shall become a citizen if, *inter alia,* the noncitizen parent is naturalized before the child reaches 18 years of age and the child begins to reside in the United States before he or she turns 18); §1432 (imposing same conditions in the case of a child born abroad to two alien parents who are naturalized).

Second, petitioners argue that §1409(a)(4) is not effective. In particular, petitioners assert that, although a mother will know of her child's birth, "knowledge that one is a parent, no matter how it is acquired, does not guarantee a relationship with one's child." They thus maintain that the imposition of the additional requirements of §1409(a)(4) only on the children of citizen fathers must reflect a stereotype that women are more likely than men to actually establish a relationship with their children.

This line of argument misconceives the nature of both the governmental interest at issue and the manner in which we examine statutes alleged to violate equal protection. As to the former, Congress would of course be entitled to advance the interest of ensuring an actual, meaningful relationship in every case before citizenship is conferred. Or Congress could excuse compliance with the formal requirements when an actual father-child relationship is proved. It did neither here, perhaps because of the subjectivity, intrusiveness, and difficulties of proof that might attend an inquiry into any particular bond or tie. Instead, Congress enacted an easily administered scheme to promote the different but still substantial interest of ensuring at least an opportunity for a parent-child relationship to develop. Petitioners' argument confuses the means and ends of the equal protection inquiry; §1409(a)(4) should not be invalidated because Congress elected to advance an interest that is less demanding to satisfy than some other alternative.

Even if one conceives of the interest Congress pursues as the establishment of a real, practical relationship of considerable substance between parent and child in every case, as opposed simply to ensuring the potential for the relationship to begin, petitioners' misconception of the nature of the equal protection inquiry is fatal to their argument. A statute meets the equal protection standard we here apply so long as it is "'substantially related to the achievement of'" the governmental objective in question. *Virginia, supra,* at 533 (quoting *Hogan,* 458 U.S., at 724, in turn quoting *Wengler,* 446 U.S., at 150). It is almost axiomatic that a policy which seeks to foster the opportunity for meaningful parent-child bonds to develop has a close and substantial bearing on the governmental interest in the actual formation of that bond. None of our gender-based classification equal protection cases have required that the statute under consideration must be capable of achieving its ultimate objective in every instance.

In this difficult context of conferring citizenship on vast numbers of persons, the means adopted by Congress are in substantial furtherance of important governmental objectives. The fit between the means and the important end is "exceedingly persuasive." See *Virginia, supra,* at 533. We have explained that an "exceedingly persuasive justification" is established "by showing at least that the classification serves 'important governmental objectives and that the discriminatory means employed' are 'substantially related to the achievement of those objectives.'" *Hogan, supra,* at 724 (citations omitted). Section 1409 meets this standard.

V

To fail to acknowledge even our most basic biological differences--such as the fact that a mother must be present at birth but the father need not be--risks making the guarantee of equal protection superficial, and so disserving it. Mechanistic classification of all our differences as stereotypes would operate to obscure those misconceptions and prejudices that are real. The distinction embodied in the statutory scheme here at issue is not marked by misconception and prejudice, nor does it show disrespect for either class. The difference between men and women in relation to the birth process is a real one, and the principle of equal protection does not forbid Congress to address the problem at hand in a manner specific to each gender.

The judgment of the Court of Appeals is *Affirmed.*

NOTES

1. The majority opinion in *Nguyen* purported to apply intermediate scrutiny—that the gender classification be substantially related to an important governmental interest. But the majority's understanding of intermediate scrutiny was far less demanding than the "exceedingly persuasive justification" that the Court had demanded in the *VMI* case. Justice O'Connor, joined by Justices Souter, Ginsburg, and Breyer, in strongly-worded dissent, noted that "While the Court invokes heightened scrutiny, the manner in which it explains and applies this standard is a stranger to our precedents." As O'Connor explained, previous gender cases had shown a suspicion of gender classifications, even when they accurately reflected the way most men or women behave and even when they enjoyed empirical support, since such classifications were used to deny individuals opportunity. According to O'Connor, the majority opinion departed from the accepted version of intermediate scrutiny in three ways. First:

> In the first sentence of its equal protection analysis, the majority glosses over the crucial matter of the burden of justification . . . ("For a gender-based classification to withstand equal protection scrutiny, it must be established . . ."); . . . In other circumstances, the Court's use of an impersonal construction might represent a mere elision of what we have stated expressly in our prior cases. Here, however, the elision presages some of the larger failings of the opinion.

> For example, the majority hypothesizes about the interests served by the statute and fails adequately to inquire into the actual purposes of [the statute].

The majority's use of the passive voice—"it must be established" was not simply a grammatical accident, but effectively overruled the Court's admonition in *VMI* that the burden was entirely on the state to identify the purpose of the law. As a result, the *Nguyen* majority was able to identify two purposes—assuring a biological parent/child relationship and assuring an actual parent/child relationship—without providing any evidentiary support for those assertions. As the majority explained, "We ascertain the purpose of a statute by drawing logical conclusions from its text, structure, and operation."

Secondly, according to the O'Connor, the *Nguyen* majority also failed to "explain adequately the importance of the interests that it claims to be served by the provision," but simply asserted that they were important.

Finally, and perhaps most importantly, the majority "casually dismisse[d] the relevance of available sex-neutral alternatives," for "[t]he virtual certainty of a biological link that modern DNA testing affords reinforces the sufficiency of [the statute]. Under strict scrutiny, the availability of alternative means to achieve the state's goals is likely to be fatal to a statutory classification. Under rational basis review, "[t]he fact that other means are better suited to the achievement of governmental ends therefore is of no moment." But "because we require a much tighter fit between means and ends under heightened scrutiny, the availability of sex-neutral alternatives to a sex-based classification is often highly probative of the validity of the classification." Justice O'Connor then cited., *Wengler,* 446 U.S., at 151, *Orr v. Orr,* 440 U.S. 268, 281 (1979), and *Wiesenfeld,* 420 U.S., at 653, wherein the availability of alternative means was part of the Court's determination that intermediate scrutiny had not been satisfied.

In *Nguyen*, the ready availability of an alternative, non-gendered means to achieve the state's goal--DNA evidence--called into question the connection between gender and purpose. Even more so when the alternative method was likely to be *better* suited to achieve the state's goal. The majority had placed great weight on the biological fact that, since mothers give birth, the mother would always be present at birth but the father would not, and had used this difference to justify the gender difference in the statute. But Justice O'Connor pointed out that the fallacy of this claim:

> While it is doubtless true that a mother's blood relation to a child is uniquely "verifiable from the birth itself" to those present at birth, . . . the majority has not shown that a mother's birth relation is uniquely verifiable *by the INS,* much less that any greater verifiability warrants a sex-based, rather than a sex-neutral, statute.

Justice O'Connor concluded:

> No one should mistake the majority's analysis for a careful application of this Court's equal protection jurisprudence concerning sex-based classifications. Today's decision instead represents a deviation from a line of cases in which we have vigilantly applied heightened scrutiny to such classifications to determine whether a constitutional violation has occurred. I trust that the depth and vitality of these precedents will ensure that today's error remains an aberration. I respectfully dissent.

2. *TO REMEDY THE EFFECTS OF PAST DISCRIMINATION AGAINST WOMEN*

Kahn v. Shevin
416 U.S. 351 (1974)

[Florida law provided a property tax exemption to widows, but not to widowers. When the appellant Kahn applied for and was denied the exemption after the death of his wife, he filed suit, alleging that term "widow," a gender-based designation, is a discriminatory classification that is in violation of the Equal Protection Clause of the Fourteenth Amendment.]

Mr. Justice DOUGLAS delivered the opinion of the Court.

There can be no dispute that the financial difficulties confronting the lone woman in Florida or in any other State exceed those facing the man. Whether from overt discrimination or from the socialization process of a male-dominated culture, the job market is inhospitable to the woman seeking any but the lowest paid jobs. There are, of course, efforts under way to remedy this situation. On the federal level, Title VII of the Civil Rights Act of 1964 prohibits covered employers and labor unions from discrimination on the basis of sex. But firmly entrenched practices are resistant to such pressures, and, indeed, data compiled by the Women's Bureau of the United States Department of Labor show that in 1972 a woman working full time had a median income which was only 57.9% of the median for males--a figure actually six points lower than had been achieved in 1955. The disparity is likely to be exacerbated for the widow. While the widower can usually continue in the occupation which preceded his spouse's death, in many cases the widow will find herself suddenly forced into a job market with which she is unfamiliar, and in

CHAPTER 3: GENDER CLASSIFICATIONS

which, because of her former economic dependency, she will have fewer skills to offer.

There can be no doubt, therefore, that Florida's differing treatment of widows and widowers "rest(s) upon some ground of difference having a fair and substantial relation to the object of the legislation." *Reed v. Reed*, 404 U.S. 71, 76, quoting *Royster Guano Co. v. Virginia*, 253 U.S. 412, 415.

This is not a case like *Frontiero v. Richardson*, 411 U.S. 677, where the Government denied its female employees both substantive and procedural benefits granted males 'solely . . . for administrative convenience.' We deal here with a state tax law reasonably designed to further the state policy of cushioning the financial impact of spousal loss upon the sex for which that loss imposes a disproportionately heavy burden. We have long held that '(w)here taxation is concerned and no specific federal right, apart from equal protection, is imperiled, the States have large leeway in making classifications and drawing lines which in their judgment produce reasonable systems of taxation.' *Lehnhausen v. Lake Shore Auto Parts Co.*, 410 U.S. 356, 359. A state tax law is not arbitrary although it 'discriminate(s) in favor of a certain class . . . if the discrimination is founded upon a reasonable distinction, or difference in state policy,' not in conflict with the Federal Constitution. *Allied Stores v. Bowers*, 358 U.S. 522, 528. This principle has weathered nearly a century of Supreme Court adjudication and it applies here as well. The statute before us is well within those limits.

Affirmed.

NOTES

1. The topic of affirmative action usually arises in the context of racial classifications, but as *Kahn* demonstrates, there are also instances of gender classifications adopted to benefit, rather than harm, women. The Court decided *Kahn* in 1974, before it had adopted the intermediate scrutiny standard, and it is not clear from the opinion what standard is being used. The Court cited both *Reed* and *Frontiero* but did not appear to adopt a standard of review from either case. The Court upheld the statute on the ground that "the States have large leeway in making classifications and drawing lines which in their judgment produce reasonable systems of taxation," a standard that looks very much like rational basis review.

Califano v. Webster
430 U.S. 313 (1977)

[Social security benefits are determined based on a calculation that includes average annual earnings. For women, this average was calculated based on the highest annual salaries earned by age 62, but for men the average was based on the highest annual salaries earned by age 65. Because women were allowed to exclude three additional lower-earning yearly salaries, the average monthly wage calculation for women was slightly higher than that for men. This corresponded to a higher post-retirement benefit determination. Appellant argued that the outcome of this methodology, where post-retirement benefits would differ based on gender when annual earnings were identical, was irrational and in violation of the Due Process Clause of the Fifth Amendment.]

PER CURIAM.

To withstand scrutiny under the equal protection component of the Fifth Amendment's Due Process Clause, 'classifications by gender must serve important governmental objectives and must be substantially related to achievement of those objectives.' *Craig v. Boren*, 429 U.S. 190, 197 (1976). Reduction of the disparity in economic condition between men and women caused by the long history of discrimination against women has been recognized as such an important governmental objective. *Schlesinger v. Ballard*, 419 U.S. 498 (1975); *Kahn v. Shevin*, 416 U.S. 351 (1974). But 'the mere recitation of a benign, compensatory purpose is not an automatic shield which protects against any inquiry into the actual purposes underlying a statutory scheme.' *Weinberger v. Wiesenfeld*, 420 U.S. 636, 648 (1975). Accordingly, we have rejected attempts to justify gender classifications as compensation for past discrimination against women when the classifications in fact penalized women wage earners, *Califano v. Goldfarb*, 430 U.S. 199, 209 n. 8 (1977); *Weinberger v. Wiesenfeld*, *supra*, at 645, or when the statutory structure and its legislative history revealed that the classification was not enacted as compensation for past discrimination. *Califano v. Goldfarb*, supra, at 212-216; *Weinberger v. Wiesenfeld*, *supra*, at 648.

The statutory scheme involved here is more analogous to those upheld in *Kahn* and *Ballard* than to those struck down in *Wiesenfeld* and *Goldfarb*. The more favorable treatment of the female wage earner enacted here was not a result of 'archaic and overbroad generalizations' about women, *Schlesinger v. Ballard*, *supra*, at 508, or of 'the role-typing society has long imposed' upon women, *Stanton v. Stanton*, 421 U.S. 7, 15 (1975), such as casual assumptions that women are 'the weaker sex' or are more likely to be child-rearers or dependents. Cf. *Califano v. Goldfarb*, *supra*; *Weinberger v. Wiesenfeld*, *supra*. Rather, 'the only discernible purpose of (§215's more favorable treatment is) the permissible one of redressing our society's longstanding disparate treatment of women.' *Califano v. Goldfarb*, *supra*, at 209 n. 8.

The challenged statute operated directly to compensate women for past economic discrimination. Retirement benefits under the Act are based on past earnings. But as we have recognized: 'Whether from over discrimination or from the socialization process of a male-dominated culture, the job market is inhospitable to the woman seeking any but the lowest paid jobs.' *Kahn v. Shevin*, 416 U.S., at 353. Thus, allowing women, who as such have been unfairly hindered from earning as much as men, to eliminate additional low-earning years from the calculation of their retirement benefits works directly to remedy some part of the effect of past discrimination.

The legislative history of [the statute] also reveals that Congress directly addressed the justification for differing treatment of men and women in the former version of that section and purposely enacted the more favorable treatment for female wage earners to compensate for past employment discrimination against women. Before 1956, the sexes were treated equally by [the statute]; the computation it required turned on the attainment of 'retirement age,' which was then defined as 65 for both sexes. In 1956, however, retirement age was redefined as 62 for women and 65 for men, thereby changing the calculation. A House Report emphasizes that this reduction in the retirement age for women was purposely made to remedy discrimination against women in the job market:

> Your committee believes that the age of eligibility should be reduced to 62 for women workers. . . . A recent study by the United States Employment Service in the Department of Labor showed that age limits are applied more frequently to job openings for women

than for men and that the age limits applied are lower. H.R.Rep. No. 1189, 84th Cong., 1st Sess., 7 (1955).

Thus, the legislative history is clear that the differing treatment of men and women in former § 215(b)(3) was not 'the accidental byproduct of a traditional way of thinking about females,' *Califano v. Goldfarb*, 430 U.S., at 223, but rather was deliberately enacted to compensate for particular economic disabilities suffered by women.

Reversed.

NOTES

1. The Court in *Webster* makes clear that it is using intermediate scrutiny, that the "[r]eduction of the disparity in economic condition between men and women caused by the long history of discrimination against women has been recognized as such an important governmental objective," and that it is clear from the legislative history that this remedial purpose is in fact the legislative objective. The Court notes, citing previous cases, that "the mere recitation of a benign, compensatory purpose is not an automatic shield which protects against any inquiry into the actual purposes underlying a statutory scheme."

3. ***JUSTIFIED BY A BROADER AND UNCHALLENGED GENDER-BASED DIFFERENCE***

Schlesinger v. Ballard
419 U.S. 498 (1975)

Mr. Justice STEWART delivered the opinion of the Court.

Appellee Robert C. Ballard is a lieutenant in the United States Navy. After more than nine years of active service as a commissioned officer, he failed, for a second time, to be selected for promotion to the grade of lieutenant commander, and was therefore subject to mandatory discharge under 10 U.S.C. § 6382(a). He brought suit in federal court claiming that if he had been a woman officer, he would have been subject to a different separation statute, 10 U.S.C. § 6401, under which he would have been entitled to 13 years of commissioned service before a mandatory discharge for want of promotion. He claimed that the application of § 6382 to him, when compared with the treatment of women officers subject to § 6401, was an unconstitutional discrimination based on sex in violation of the Due Process Clause of the Fifth Amendment.

II

It is against this background that we must decide whether, agreeably to the Due Process Clause of the Fifth Amendment, the Congress may accord to women naval officers a 13-year tenure of commissioned service under § 6401 before mandatory discharge for want of promotion, while requiring under § 6382(a) the mandatory discharge of male lieutenants who have been twice passed over for promotion but who, like Ballard, may have had less than 13 years of commissioned service. In arguing that Congress has acted unconstitutionally, appellee relies primarily upon the Court's recent decisions in *Frontiero v. Richardson*, 411 U.S. 677, and *Reed v. Reed*, 404 U.S. 71. [The Court here discussed the *Frontiero* and *Reed* cases.]

In both *Reed* and *Frontiero* the challenged classifications based on sex were premised on overbroad generalizations that could not be tolerated under the Constitution. In *Reed*, the assumption underlying the Idaho statute was that men would generally be better estate administrators than women. In *Frontiero*, the assumption underlying the Federal Armed Services benefit statutes was that female spouses of servicemen would normally be dependent upon their husbands, while male spouses of servicewomen would not.

In contrast, the different treatment of men and women naval officers under §§ 6382 and 6401 reflects, not archaic and overbroad generalizations, but, instead, the demonstrable fact that male and female line officers in the Navy are not similarly situated with respect to opportunities for professional service. Appellee has not challenged the current restrictions on women officers' participation in combat and in most sea duty. Specifically 'women may not be assigned to duty in aircraft that are engaged in combat missions nor may they be assigned to duty on vessels of the Navy other than hospital ships and transports.' Thus, in competing for promotion, female lieutenants will not generally have compiled records of seagoing service comparable to those of male lieutenants. In enacting and retaining [the statute], Congress may thus quite rationally have believed that women line officers had less opportunity for promotion than did their male counterparts, and that a longer period of tenure for women officers would, therefore, be consistent with the goal to provide women officers with 'fair and equitable career advancement programs.' H.R.Rep. No. 216, *supra*, at 5.

The complete rationality of this legislative classification is underscored by the fact that in corps where male and female lieutenants are similarly situated, Congress has not differentiated between them with respect to tenure. Thus women staff officers not appointed under § 5590 are subject to the same mandatory attrition rule of § 6382(a) as are male officers. These include officers in the Medical, Dental, Judge Advocate General's, and Medical Service Corps. Conversely, active male lieutenants who are members of the Nurse Corps, like female lieutenants in that Corps, are within the ambit of 10 U.S.C. § 6396(c), which contains a 13-year tenure provision like § 6401.

In both *Reed* and *Frontiero* the reason asserted to justify the challenged gender-based classifications was administrative convenience, and that alone. Here, on the contrary, the operation of the statutes in question results in a flow of promotions commensurate with the Navy's current needs and serves to motivate qualified commissioned officers to so conduct themselves that they may realistically look forward to higher levels of command. This Court has recognized that 'it is the primary business of armies and navies to fight or be ready to fight wars should the occasion arise.' *U.S. ex rel. Toth v. Quarles*, 350 U.S. 11, 17. The responsibility for determining how best our Armed Forces shall attend to that business rests with Congress, see U.S.Const., Art. I, § 8, cls. 12-14, and with the President. See U.S.Const., Art. II, § 2, cl. 1. We cannot say that, in exercising its broad constitutional power here, Congress has violated the Due Process Clause of the Fifth Amendment.

The judgment is *reversed*.

NOTES

1. The different treatment of men and women in terms of the years until forced separation from the military certainly has the look of discrimination, but it turns out not to be unconstitutional

discrimination. The Court explains this by saying that the discrimination in years of service is justified by a larger, unchallenged gender discrimination—the exclusion of women from combat and most forms of sea duty, a classification that was not challenged by the plaintiffs in the case. Given the deference the Court gives to the military, it is unlikely that the Court would find the exclusion of women from combat roles to be unconstitutional. It is clear, however, that, as a matter of military policy rather than judicial edict, the number of combat roles from which women are excluded has been continuously diminishing. *See infra*, Sec. E.3.

In addition, the *Ballard* Court, deciding the case before *Craig v. Boren*, used a very deferential standard of review—that "Congress *may thus quite rationally have believed* that women line officers had less opportunity for promotion than did their male counterparts, and that a longer period of tenure for women officers would, therefore, be consistent with the goal to provide women officers with "fair and equitable career advancement programs."

Rostker v. Goldberg
453 U.S. 57 (1981)

[The Military Selective Service Act (MSSA) empowered the President to require male citizens ages 18 to 26 to register. The purpose of this registration was to facilitate possible conscription for training and service in the United States Armed Forces should a draft be necessary at some point in the future. In a lawsuit from 1971 that had lain dormant for lack of justiciability while draft registration was suspended, several men had challenged the facial validity of the MSSA, alleging unlawful gender discrimination. In 1980, the court certified a plaintiff class of males who were registered, subject to registration, or liable for training and service in the U.S. Armed Forces, and the suit was allowed to proceed.]

Justice REHNQUIST delivered the opinion of the Court.

The question presented is whether the Military Selective Service Act violates the Fifth Amendment to the United States Constitution in authorizing the President to require the registration of males and not females.

II

Whenever called upon to judge the constitutionality of an Act of Congress--"the gravest and most delicate duty that this Court is called upon to perform," *Blodgett v. Holden*, 275 U.S. 142, 148 (1927) (Holmes, J.)--the Court accords "great weight to the decisions of Congress." *Columbia Broadcasting System, Inc. v. Democratic National Committee*, 412 U.S. 94, 102 (1973). The Congress is a coequal branch of government whose Members take the same oath we do to uphold the Constitution of the United States. As Justice Frankfurter noted in *Joint Anti-Fascist Refugee Committee v. McGrath*, 341 U.S. 123, 164 (1951) (concurring opinion), we must have "due regard to the fact that this Court is not exercising a primary judgment but is sitting in judgment upon those who also have taken the oath to observe the Constitution and who have the responsibility for carrying on government." The customary deference accorded the judgments of Congress is certainly appropriate when, as here, Congress specifically considered the question of the Act's constitutionality.

This is not, however, merely a case involving the customary deference accorded congressional decisions. The case arises in the context of Congress' authority over national defense and military affairs, and perhaps in no other area has the Court accorded Congress greater deference. In rejecting the registration of women, Congress explicitly relied upon its constitutional powers under Art. I, § 8, cls. 12-14. The "specific findings" section of the Report of the Senate Armed Services Committee, later adopted by both Houses of Congress, began by stating:

> Article I, section 8 of the Constitution commits exclusively to the Congress the powers to raise and support armies, provide and maintain a Navy, and make rules for Government and regulation of the land and naval forces, and pursuant to these powers it lies within the discretion of the Congress to determine the occasions for expansion of our Armed Forces, and the means best suited to such expansion should it prove necessary. S.Rep.No.96-826, *supra*, at 160.

This Court has consistently recognized Congress' "broad constitutional power" to raise and regulate armies and navies, *Schlesinger v. Ballard*, 419 U.S. 498, 510 (1975). As the Court noted in considering a challenge to the selective service laws: "The constitutional power of Congress to raise and support armies and to make all laws necessary and proper to that end is broad and sweeping." *United States v. O'Brien*, 391 U.S. 367, 377 (1968).

Not only is the scope of Congress' constitutional power in this area broad, but the lack of competence on the part of the courts is marked. In *Gilligan v. Morgan*, 413 U.S. 1, 10 (1973), the Court noted:

> [I]t is difficult to conceive of an area of governmental activity in which the courts have less competence. The complex, subtle, and professional decisions as to the composition, training, equipping, and control of a military force are essentially professional military judgments, subject *always* to civilian control of the Legislative and Executive Branches. [The Court discussed *Schlesinger v. Ballard*.]

None of this is to say that Congress is free to disregard the Constitution when it acts in the area of military affairs. In that area, as any other, Congress remains subject to the limitations of the Due Process Clause, see *Ex parte Milligan*, 4 Wall. 2 (1866); *Hamilton v. Kentucky Distilleries & Warehouse Co.*, 251 U.S. 146, 156 (1919), but the tests and limitations to be applied may differ because of the military context. We of course do not abdicate our ultimate responsibility to decide the constitutional question, but simply recognize that the Constitution itself requires such deference to congressional choice. In deciding the question before us we must be particularly careful not to substitute our judgment of what is desirable for that of Congress, or our own evaluation of evidence for a reasonable evaluation by the Legislative Branch.

The Solicitor General argues, largely on the basis of the foregoing cases emphasizing the deference due Congress in the area of military affairs and national security, that this Court should scrutinize the MSSA only to determine if the distinction drawn between men and women bears a rational relation to some legitimate Government purpose, see *U.S. Railroad Retirement Bd. v. Fritz*, 449 U.S. 166 (1980), and should not examine the Act under the heightened scrutiny with which we have approached gender-based discrimination, see *Michael M. v. Superior Court of Sonoma County*, 450 U.S. 464 (1981); *Craig v. Boren*, 429 U.S. 190 (1976); *Reed v. Reed, supra*. We do not think that the substantive guarantee of due process or certainty in the law will be advanced by any further "refinement" in the applicable tests as suggested by the Government. Announced degrees of "deference" to legislative judgments, just as levels of "scrutiny" which this

CHAPTER 3: GENDER CLASSIFICATIONS 215

Court announces that it applies to particular classifications made by a legislative body, may all too readily become facile abstractions used to justify a result. In this case the courts are called upon to decide whether Congress, acting under an explicit constitutional grant of authority, has by that action transgressed an explicit guarantee of individual rights which limits the authority so conferred. Simply labeling the legislative decision "military" on the one hand or "gender-based" on the other does not automatically guide a court to the correct constitutional result.

No one could deny that under the test of *Craig v. Boren, supra*, the Government's interest in raising and supporting armies is an "important governmental interest." Congress and its Committees carefully considered and debated two alternative means of furthering that interest: the first was to register only males for potential conscription, and the other was to register both sexes. Congress chose the former alternative. When that decision is challenged on equal protection grounds, the question a court must decide is not which alternative it would have chosen, had it been the primary decisionmaker, but whether that chosen by Congress denies equal protection of the laws.

III

This case is quite different from several of the gender-based discrimination cases we have considered in that, despite appellees' assertions, Congress did not act "unthinkingly" or "reflexively and not for any considered reason." The question of registering women for the draft not only received considerable national attention and was the subject of wide-ranging public debate, but also was extensively considered by Congress in hearings, floor debate, and in committee.

The MSSA established a plan for maintaining "adequate armed strength ... to insure the security of [the] Nation." 50 U.S.C.App. § 451(b). Registration is the first step "in a united and continuous process designed to raise an army speedily and efficiently," *Falbo v. United States*, 320 U.S. 549, 553 (1944), and Congress provided for the reactivation of registration in order to "provid[e] the means for the early delivery of inductees in an emergency."

Congress determined that any future draft, which would be facilitated by the registration scheme, would be characterized by a need for combat troops. The Senate Report explained, in a specific finding later adopted by both Houses, that "[i]f mobilization were to be ordered in a wartime scenario, the primary manpower need would be for combat replacements." As Senator Jepsen put it, "the shortage would be in the combat arms. That is why you have drafts." Congress' determination that the need would be for combat troops if a draft took place was sufficiently supported by testimony adduced at the hearings so that the courts are not free to make their own judgment on the question. The purpose of registration, therefore, was to prepare for a draft *of combat troops*.

Women as a group, however, unlike men as a group, are not eligible for combat. The restrictions on the participation of women in combat in the Navy and Air Force are statutory. Under 10 U.S.C. § 6015 (1976 ed., Supp. III), "women may not be assigned to duty on vessels or in aircraft that are engaged in combat missions," and under 10 U.S.C. § 8549 female members of the Air Force "may not be assigned to duty in aircraft engaged in combat missions." The Army and Marine Corps preclude the use of women in combat as a matter of established policy. See App. 86, 34, 58. Congress specifically recognized and endorsed the exclusion of women from combat in exempting women from registration. In the words of the Senate Report:

The principle that women should not intentionally and routinely engage in combat is fundamental, and enjoys wide support among our people. It is universally supported by military leaders who have testified before the Committee ... Current law and policy exclude women from being assigned to combat in our military forces, and the Committee reaffirms this policy.

The existence of the combat restrictions clearly indicates the basis for Congress' decision to exempt women from registration. The purpose of registration was to prepare for a draft of combat troops. Since women are excluded from combat, Congress concluded that they would not be needed in the event of a draft, and therefore decided not to register them.

Congress' decision to authorize the registration of only men, therefore, does not violate the Due Process Clause. The exemption of women from registration is not only sufficiently but also closely related to Congress' purpose in authorizing registration. See *Michael M.*, 450 U.S., at 472-473; *Craig v. Boren*, 429 U.S. 190 (1976); *Reed v. Reed*, 404 U.S. 71 (1971). The fact that congress and the Executive have decided that women should not serve in combat fully justifies Congress in not authorizing their registration, since the purpose of registration is to develop a pool of potential combat troops. As was the case in *Schlesinger v. Ballard, supra*, "the gender classification is not invidious, but rather realistically reflects the fact that the sexes are not similarly situated" in this case. *Michael M., supra*, at 469. The Constitution requires that Congress treat similarly situated persons similarly, not that it engage in gestures of superficial equality.

In light of the foregoing, we conclude that Congress acted well within its constitutional authority when it authorized the registration of men, and not women, under the Military Selective Service Act. The decision of the District Court holding otherwise is accordingly *Reversed*.

NOTES

1. Although *Rostker* was decided five years after the Court had settled on intermediate scrutiny for gender classifications, and the classification at issue in *Rostker* was undeniably a gender classification, the Court did not apply intermediate scrutiny. The Court insisted that deference was due to the registration statute because (1) it had been enacted by Congress (rather than federal agency or a state legislature), and Congress specifically considered the question of the Act's constitutionality; and (2) it involved national defense and military affairs, an area in which the Court accorded Congress greatest deference. In addressing the intersection of a gender classification, which would require heightened scrutiny, and a Congressional act affecting the military, which would require deference, the Court rejected the idea that the law will be advanced by any further refinement in the applicable tests as suggested by the Government. "Announced degrees of 'deference' to legislative judgments, just as levels of 'scrutiny' which this Court announces that it applies to particular classifications made by a legislative body, may all too readily become facile abstractions used to justify a result."

Having rejected the choice of using a facile abstraction to decide the case, the Court, without a clear statement of the level of scrutiny, upheld the statute, finding that "[t]he exemption of women from registration is not only sufficiently but also closely related to Congress' purpose in authorizing registration." As in *Scheslinger*, the Court justified the exclusion of women from draft registration by the exclusion of women from combat, without considering the constitutionality of that second exclusion.

4. CLASSIFICATIONS THAT ARE TREATED AS IF THEY ARE NOT GENDER CLASSIFICATIONS

Geduldig v. Aiello
417 U.S. 484 (1974)

[California administered an employment disability insurance program, funded from mandatory contributions of covered employees. It covered physical or mental illness but excluded from coverage any disability "caused by or arising in connection with pregnancy."]
Mr. Justice STEWART delivered the opinion of the Court.

We cannot agree that the exclusion of this disability from coverage amounts to invidious discrimination under the Equal Protection Clause. California does not discriminate with respect to the persons or groups which are eligible for disability insurance protection under the program. The classification challenged in this case relates to the asserted underinclusiveness of the set of risks that the State has selected insure. Although California has created a program to insure most risks of employment disability, it has not chosen to insure all such risks, and this decision is reflected in the level of annual contributions exacted from participating employees. This Court has held that, consistently with the Equal Protection Clause, a State 'may take one step at a time, addressing itself to the phase of the problem which seems most acute to the legislative mind . . . The legislature may select one phase of one field and apply a remedy there, neglecting the others. . . .' *Williamson v. Lee Optical of Oklahoma Inc.*, 348 U.S. 483, 489 (1955); *Jefferson v. Hackney*, 406 U.S. 535 (1972). Particularly with respect to social welfare programs, so long as the line drawn by the State is rationally supportable, the courts will not interpose their judgment as to the appropriate stopping point. '(T)he Equal Protection Clause does not require that a State must choose between attacking every aspect of a problem or not attacking the problem at all.' *Dandridge v. Williams*, 397 U.S. 471, 486—487 (1970).

The District Court suggested that moderate alterations in what it regarded as 'variables' of the disability insurance program could be made to accommodate the substantial expense required to include normal pregnancy within the program's protection. The same can be said, however, with respect to the other expensive class of disabilities that are excluded from coverage—short-term disabilities. If the Equal Protection Clause were thought to compel disability payments for normal pregnancy, it is hard to perceive why it would not also compel payments for short-term disabilities suffered by participating employees.

It is evident that a totally comprehensive program would be substantially more costly than the present program and would inevitably require state subsidy, a higher rate of employee contribution, a lower scale of benefits for those suffering insured disabilities, or some combination of these measures. There is nothing in the Constitution, however, that requires the State to subordinate or compromise its legitimate interests solely to create a more comprehensive social insurance program than it already has.

The State has a legitimate interest in maintaining the self-supporting nature of its insurance program. Similarly, it has an interest in distributing the available resources in such a way as to keep benefit payments at an adequate level for disabilities that are covered, rather than to cover all disabilities inadequately. Finally, California has a legitimate concern in maintaining the contribution rate at a level that will not unduly burden participating employees, particularly low-income employees who may be most in need of the disability insurance.

These policies provide an objective and wholly noninvidious basis for the State's decision not to create a more comprehensive insurance program than it has. There is no evidence in the record that the selection of the risks insured by the program worked to discriminate against any definable group or class in terms of the aggregate risk protection derived by that group or class from the program.[FN20] There is no risk from which men are protected and women are not. Likewise, there is no risk from which women are protected and men are not.

The appellee simply contends that, although she has received insurance protection equivalent to that provided all other participating employees, she has suffered discrimination because she encountered a risk that was outside the program's protection. For the reasons we have stated, we hold that this contention is not a valid one under the Equal Protection Clause of the Fourteenth Amendment.

The stay heretofore issued by the Court is vacated, and the judgment of the District Court is *reversed*.

NOTES

1. Is the Court being serious when it says that "[t]here is no risk from which men are protected and women are not. Likewise, there is no risk from which women are protected and men are not," or when it says that "[t]he program divides potential recipients into two groups—pregnant women and nonpregnant persons"? Isn't this the same Court that would justify a statutory rape law that only men could violate on the ground that "only women can get pregnant"?

When the Court made the same kind of assertions in interpreting a federal civil rights statute, *see*, *General Elec. Co. v. Gilbert,* 429 U.S. 125 (1976) (ruling that discrimination on the basis of pregnancy was not sex discrimination under Title VII), Congress overruled the Court in the Pregnancy Discrimination Act of 1978, which specifies that sex discrimination includes discrimination on the basis of pregnancy. Of course, Congress cannot overrule the Supreme Court on matters of constitutional law, so *Geduldig* is still the law of the land.

[FN20] The dissenting opinion to the contrary, this case is thus a far cry from cases like *Reed v. Reed,* 404 U.S. 71 (1971), and *Frontiero v. Richardson,* 411 U.S. 677 (1973), involving discrimination based upon gender as such. The California insurance program does not exclude anyone from benefit eligibility because of gender but merely removes one physical condition—pregnancy—from the list of compensable disabilities. While it is true that only women can become pregnant, it does not follow that every legislative classification concerning pregnancy is a sex-based classification like those considered in *Reed, supra,* and *Frontiero, supra.* Normal pregnancy is an objectively identifiable physical condition with unique characteristics. Absent a showing that distinctions involving pregnancy are mere pretexts designed to effect an invidious discrimination against the members of one sex or the other, lawmakers are constitutionally free to include or exclude pregnancy from the coverage of legislation such as this on any reasonable basis, just as with respect to any other physical condition. The lack of identity between the excluded disability and gender as such under this insurance program becomes clear upon the most cursory analysis. The program divides potential recipients into two groups—pregnant women and nonpregnant persons. While the first group is exclusively female, the second includes members of both sexes. The fiscal and actuarial benefits of the program thus accrue to members of both sexes.

Personnel Adm'r of Massachusetts v. Feeney
442 U.S. 256 (1979)

Mr. Justice STEWART delivered the opinion of the Court.

This case presents a challenge to the constitutionality of the Massachusetts veterans' preference statute, Mass.Gen.Laws Ann., ch. 31, § 23, on the ground that it discriminates against women in violation of the Equal Protection Clause of the Fourteenth Amendment. Under ch. 31, § 23, all veterans who qualify for state civil service positions must be considered for appointment ahead of any qualifying nonveterans. The preference operates overwhelmingly to the advantage of males.

The appellee Helen B. Feeney is not a veteran. She brought this action pursuant to 42 U.S.C. § 1983, alleging that the absolute preference formula established in ch. 31, § 23, inevitably operates to exclude women from consideration for the best Massachusetts civil service jobs and thus unconstitutionally denies them the equal protection of the laws.

The veterans' hiring preference in Massachusetts, as in other jurisdictions, has traditionally been justified as a measure designed to reward veterans for the sacrifice of military service, to ease the transition from military to civilian life, to encourage patriotic service, and to attract loyal and well-disciplined people to civil service occupations. See, *e.g., Hutcheson v. Director of Civil Service*, 361 Mass. 480 (1972).

When this litigation was commenced, over 98% of the veterans in Massachusetts were male; only 1.8% were female. At the outset of this litigation appellants conceded that for "many of the permanent positions for which males and females have competed" the veterans' preference has "resulted in a substantially greater proportion of female eligibles than male eligibles" not being certified for consideration. The impact of the veterans' preference law upon the public employment opportunities of women has thus been severe. This impact lies at the heart of the appellee's federal constitutional claim.

The equal protection guarantee of the Fourteenth Amendment does not take from the States all power of classification. *Massachusetts Bd. of Retirement v. Murgia*, 427 U.S. 307, 314. Most laws classify, and many affect certain groups unevenly, even though the law itself treats them no differently from all other members of the class described by the law. When the basic classification is rationally based, uneven effects upon particular groups within a class are ordinarily of no constitutional concern. *New York City Transit Authority v. Beazer*, 440 U.S. 568. The calculus of effects, the manner in which a particular law reverberates in a society, is a legislative and not a judicial responsibility. *Dandridge v. Williams*, 397 U.S. 471; *San Antonio School Dist. v. Rodriguez*, 411 U.S. 1. In assessing an equal protection challenge, a court is called upon only to measure the basic validity of the legislative classification. *Barrett v. Indiana*, 229 U.S. 26, 29-30; *Railway Express Agency v. New York*, 336 U.S. 106. When some other independent right is not at stake, see, *e. g., Shapiro v. Thompson,* 394 U.S. 618, and when there is no "reason to infer antipathy," *Vance v. Bradley*, 440 U.S. 93, 97, it is presumed that "even improvident decisions will eventually be rectified by the democratic process . . . ."

Certain classifications, however, in themselves supply a reason to infer antipathy. Race is the paradigm. A racial classification, regardless of purported motivation, is presumptively invalid and can be upheld only upon an extraordinary justification. *Brown v. Board of Education*, 347 U.S.

483; *McLaughlin v. Florida*, 379 U.S. 184. This rule applies as well to a classification that is ostensibly neutral but is an obvious pretext for racial discrimination. *Yick Wo v. Hopkins*, 118 U.S. 356. But, as was made clear in *Washington v. Davis*, 426 U.S. 229, and *Arlington Heights v. Metropolitan Housing Dev. Corp.*, 429 U.S. 252, even if a neutral law has a disproportionately adverse effect upon a racial minority, it is unconstitutional under the Equal Protection Clause only if that impact can be traced to a discriminatory purpose.

Classifications based upon gender, not unlike those based upon race, have traditionally been the touchstone for pervasive and often subtle discrimination. *Caban v. Mohammed*, 441 U.S. 380, 398. This Court's recent cases teach that such classifications must bear a close and substantial relationship to important governmental objectives, *Craig v. Boren*, 429 U.S. 190, 197, and are in many settings unconstitutional. Although public employment is not a constitutional right, *Massachusetts Bd. of Retirement v. Murgia, supra*, and the States have wide discretion in framing employee qualifications, see, *e. g., New York City Transit Authority v. Beazer, supra*, these precedents dictate that any state law overtly or covertly designed to prefer males over females in public employment would require an exceedingly persuasive justification to withstand a constitutional challenge under the Equal Protection Clause of the Fourteenth Amendment.

III

A

The question whether ch. 31, § 23, establishes a classification that is overtly or covertly based upon gender must first be considered. The appellee has conceded that ch. 31, § 23, is neutral on its face. She has also acknowledged that state hiring preferences for veterans are not *per se* invalid, for she has limited her challenge to the absolute lifetime preference that Massachusetts provides to veterans. The District Court made two central findings that are relevant here: first, that ch. 31, § 23, serves legitimate and worthy purposes; second, that the absolute preference was not established for the purpose of discriminating against women. The appellee has thus acknowledged and the District Court has thus found that the distinction between veterans and nonveterans drawn by ch. 31, § 23, is not a pretext for gender discrimination. The appellee's concession and the District Court's finding are clearly correct.

If the impact of this statute could not be plausibly explained on a neutral ground, impact itself would signal that the real classification made by the law was in fact not neutral. See *Washington v. Davis*, 426 U.S., at 242; *Arlington Heights v. Metropolitan Housing Dev. Corp., supra*, 429 U.S., at 266. But there can be but one answer to the question whether this veteran preference excludes significant numbers of women from preferred state jobs because they are women or because they are nonveterans. Apart from the facts that the definition of "veterans" in the statute has always been neutral as to gender and that Massachusetts has consistently defined veteran status in a way that has been inclusive of women who have served in the military, this is not a law that can plausibly be explained only as a gender-based classification. Indeed, it is not a law that can rationally be explained on that ground. Veteran status is not uniquely male. Although few women benefit from the preference the nonveteran class is not substantially all female. To the contrary, significant numbers of nonveterans are men, and all nonveterans-male as well as female- are placed at a disadvantage. Too many men are affected by ch. 31, § 23, to permit the inference that the statute is but a pretext for preferring men over women.

Moreover, as the District Court implicitly found, the purposes of the statute provide the surest explanation for its impact. Just as there are cases in which impact alone can unmask an invidious classification, cf. *Yick Wo v. Hopkins,* 118 U.S. 356, there are others, in which-notwithstanding impact-the legitimate noninvidious purposes of a law cannot be missed. This is one. The distinction made by ch. 31, § 23, is, as it seems to be, quite simply between veterans and nonveterans, not between men and women.

B

The dispositive question, then, is whether the appellee has shown that a gender-based discriminatory purpose has, at least in some measure, shaped the Massachusetts veterans' preference legislation.

The contention that this veterans' preference is "inherently nonneutral" or "gender-biased" presumes that the State, by favoring veterans, intentionally incorporated into its public employment policies the panoply of sex-based and assertedly discriminatory federal laws that have prevented all but a handful of women from becoming veterans. There are two serious difficulties with this argument. First, it is wholly at odds with the District Court's central finding that Massachusetts has not offered a preference to veterans for the purpose of discriminating against women. Second, it cannot be reconciled with the assumption made by both the appellee and the District Court that a more limiting hiring preference for veterans could be sustained. Taken together, these difficulties are fatal.

To the extent that the status of veteran is one that few women have been enabled to achieve, every hiring preference for veterans, however, modest or extreme, is inherently gender-biased. If Massachusetts by offering such a preference can be said intentionally to have incorporated into its state employment policies the historical gender-based federal military personnel practices, the degree of the preference would or should make no constitutional difference. Invidious discrimination does not become less so because the discrimination accomplished is of a lesser magnitude. Discriminatory intent is simply not amenable to calibration. It either is a factor that has influenced the legislative choice or it is not. The District Court's conclusion that the absolute veterans' preference was not originally enacted or subsequently reaffirmed for the purpose of giving an advantage to males as such necessarily compels the conclusion that the State is intended nothing more than to prefer "veterans." Given this finding, simple logic suggests that an intent to exclude women from significant public jobs was not at work in this law. To reason that it was, by describing the preference as "inherently nonneutral" or "gender-biased," is merely to restate the fact of impact, not to answer the question of intent.

To be sure, this case is unusual in that it involves a law that by design is not neutral. The law overtly prefers veterans as such. As opposed to the written test at issue in *Davis,* it does not purport to define a job-related characteristic. To the contrary, it confers upon a specifically described group-perceived to be particularly deserving-a competitive headstart. But the District Court found, and the appellee has not disputed, that this legislative choice was legitimate. The basic distinction between veterans and nonveterans, having been found not gender-based, and the goals of the preference having been found worthy, ch. 31 must be analyzed as is any other neutral law that casts a greater burden upon women as a group than upon men as a group. The enlistment policies of the Armed Services may well have discrimination on the basis of sex. See *Frontiero v. Richardson,* 411 U.S. 677; cf. *Schlesinger v. Ballard,* 419 U.S. 498. But the history of discrimination against women in the military is not on trial in this case.

2

The appellee's ultimate argument rests upon the presumption, common to the criminal and civil law, that a person intends the natural and foreseeable consequences of his voluntary actions. Her position was well stated in the concurring opinion in the District Court:

> Conceding . . . that the goal here was to benefit the veteran, there is no reason to absolve the legislature from awareness that the means chosen to achieve this goal would freeze women out of all those state jobs actively sought by men. To be sure, the legislature did not wish to harm women. But the cutting-off of women's opportunities was an inevitable concomitant of the chosen scheme-as inevitable as the proposition that if tails is up, heads must be down. Where a law's consequences are *that* inevitable, can they meaningfully be described as unintended?

This rhetorical question implies that a negative answer is obvious, but it is not. The decision to grant a preference to veterans was of course "intentional." So, necessarily, did an adverse impact upon nonveterans follow from that decision. And it cannot seriously be argued that the Legislature of Massachusetts could have been unaware that most veterans are men. It would thus be disingenuous to say that the adverse consequences of this legislation for women were unintended, in the sense that they were not volitional or in the sense that they were not foreseeable.

"Discriminatory purpose," however, implies more than intent as volition or intent as awareness of consequences. See *United Jewish Organizations v. Carey,* 430 U.S. 144, 179. It implies that the decisionmaker, in this case a state legislature, selected or reaffirmed a particular course of action at least in part "because of," not merely "in spite of," its adverse effects upon an identifiable group. Yet, nothing in the record demonstrates that this preference for veterans was originally devised or subsequently re-enacted because it would accomplish the collateral goal of keeping women in a stereotypic and predefined place in the Massachusetts Civil Service.

To the contrary, the statutory history shows that the benefit of the preference was consistently offered to "any person" who was a veteran. That benefit has been extended to women under a very broad statutory definition of the term veteran. The preference formula itself, which is the focal point of this challenge, was first adopted--so it appears from this record-out of a perceived need to help a small group of older Civil War veterans. It has since been reaffirmed and extended only to cover new veterans. When the totality of legislative actions establishing and extending the Massachusetts veterans' preference are considered, see *Washington v. Davis,* 426 U.S., at 242, the law remains what it purports to be: a preference for veterans of either sex over nonveterans of either sex, not for men over women.

IV

Veterans' hiring preferences represent an awkward--and, many argue, unfair--exception to the widely shared view that merit and merit alone should prevail in the employment policies of government. After a war, such laws have been enacted virtually without opposition. During peacetime, they inevitable have come to be viewed in many quarters as undemocratic and unwise. Absolute and permanent preferences, as the troubled history of this law demonstrates, have always been subject to the objection that they give the veteran more than a square deal. But the Fourteenth Amendment "cannot be made a refuge from ill-advised . . . laws." *District of Columbia v. Brooke,*

214 U.S. 138, 150. The substantial edge granted to veterans by ch. 31, § 23, may reflect unwise policy. The appellee, however, has simply failed to demonstrate that the law in any way reflects a purpose to discriminate on the basis of sex.

The judgment is reversed, and the case is remanded for further proceedings consistent with this opinion. *It is so ordered.*

NOTES

1. Notwithstanding the fact that more than 98% of the persons benefitted by the Massachusetts statute were male, and notwithstanding the fact that this was clearly a foreseeable result of the statute's preference for veterans, the Court insists that the distinction made by the statute is "quite simply between veterans and nonveterans, not between men and women." The Court conceded that "[t]o the extent that the status of veteran is one that few women have been enabled to achieve, every hiring preference for veterans, however, modest or extreme, is inherently gender-biased." But that did not make it a gender classification. Although the decision to grant a preference to veterans was of course "intentional," it did not create a gender classification since "'Discriminatory purpose'. . . implies more than intent as volition or intent as awareness of consequences . . . It implies that the decisionmaker, in this case a state legislature, selected or reaffirmed a particular course of action at least in part "because of," not merely "in spite of," its adverse effects upon an identifiable group."

E. CURRENT ISSUES OF GENDER EQUALITY

Notwithstanding the existence of heightened scrutiny of gender classifications, there continue to be a number of gender distinctions that are commonly made in America by government entities. The gender classifications addressed in this section have not been the subject of a Supreme Court opinion so their ultimate constitutionality is not certain. It is possible, however, to apply existing Supreme Court precedents to analogous factual contexts. In addition, there are lower court opinions on point. This section will examine gender classifications in sports programs, pupil assignment in public schools, the exclusion of women from combat roles in the military, and gender segregation in prisons.

1. *GENDER CLASSIFICATIONS IN GOVERNMENT-RUN SPORTS PROGRAMS*

Probably the most ubiquitous, most visible, and yet rarely challenged, gender classification is the division of most sport programs by gender. Most sports programs are segregated by gender at the youth level, in high school, and in college. Thus we have separate boys' and girls' soccer programs, separate boys' and girls' basketball programs, separate boys' baseball and girls' softball programs, and football for boys and field hockey for girls. Although there is the occasional legal case of the girl who wants to play football, *e.g., Force by Force v. Pierce City School District*, 570 F Supp. 1020 (W.D. Mo. 1983), or the boy who wants to play field hockey, *see* Adam S. Darowski, *For Kenny, Who Wanted to Play Women's Field Hockey*, 12 Duke J. Gender L. & Pol'y 153 (2005), the general idea that males and females should have separate sports programs is not seriously challenged. Since many of the entities that run youth, high school, and college sports are state actors, there is clearly an equal protection issue here.

There are very good practical and common-sense reasons to separate males and females on the playing fields. Donna Lopiano, formerly the chief executive officer of the Women's Sports Foundation, has explained how the inherent biological differences between the sexes justify gender-segregated sports programs:

> Sport is basically a strength, speed and reaction time activity involving propelling a mass through space or overcoming the resistance of a mass. Physiologically and anatomically you cannot compare highly skilled male and female athletes on these parameters because of the inherent biological differences between the sexes. Men are stronger, faster, have better reaction time and more muscle tissue per unit of body mass. That is why athletic teams and competition are sex separate. Women compete against women and men compete against men. Women excel in balance, accuracy and fine motor skill activities while men excel in strength, speed and gross motor skills. *Ass'n for Intercollegiate Athletics for Women v. Nat'l Collegiate Athletic Ass'n*, 558 F. Supp. 487, 496 (D.D.C. 1983), aff'd, 735 F.2d 577 (D.C. Cir. 1984).

In addition, males have a higher level of testosterone than females and this affects athletic performance. The New York Times noted that testosterone "affects everything from muscle size and strength to the size of the heart to the amount of oxygen-carrying blood cells in the body to the percentage of fat on an athlete's body. Every one of those effects gives men a performance advantage." Gina Kolata, Men, Women and Speed. 2 Words: Got Testosterone?, N.Y. Times, Aug. 22, 2008, at D1. Thus, the decision to have males and females compete separately in sports seems to be both prudent in terms of avoiding injury and fair in terms of providing equal athletic opportunity to women.

The equal protection implications of these differences, however, are not so obvious. When Justice O'Connor wrote the majority opinion in *United States v. Virginia*, 518 U.S. 515 (1996), her explanation for why VMI's all-male student body violated the Equal Protection Clause included language that makes it very difficult to justify separating males and females in sports. Justice O'Connor's opinion conceded that the generalization at work at VMI was probably accurate—very few women would want to come to VMI and very few women could succeed at VMI. But that was not was mattered. Justice O'Connor focused on (1) the unfairness of a rule that overlooked the *individual* talents and capacities of those who wanted to attend VMI; (2) "artificial constraints on an *individual's* opportunity;" (3) the exclusion of "qualified *individuals* based on 'fixed notions concerning the roles and abilities of males and females;'" and (4) the denial of opportunity to "women who have the will and capacity." Justice O'Connor explained that the case did not turn on generalizations about the average physical capacities of men and women but on the capabilities of a very few women: "*some women* ... do well under [the] adversative model," "*some women*, at least, would want to attend [VMI] if they had the opportunity," "*some women* are capable of all of the individual activities required of VMI cadets," and "can meet the physical standards [VMI] now impose[s] on men," "It is on behalf of *these women* that the United States has instituted this suit, and it is for them that a remedy must be crafted."

Notably, this very critique of the VMI program appears to be equally applicable to gender segregation of sports programs. Such separation of males and females makes sense as a general matter, but it ignores the situations of individual women to whom the generalization does not apply--those women who could compete successfully with men in athletics. Why should a generalization about women as a class prevent an individual woman from being judged in a tryout on the basis of her individual ability?

The courts do not generally put sports programs to this kind of demanding test. Rather more common is the example of *O'Connor v. Board of Education of School District 23*, 545 F. Supp. 376 (N.D. Ill. 1982), in which a federal district court considered the claim of an outstanding young female basketball player who wanted to play in the boys' league but was forced to play with the girls. The court succinctly identified the dilemma: "Karen O'Connor is an extraordinarily gifted basketball player. She is also female. Therein lies the problem."

The school board in the case did not dispute Karen's claim that "only participation on the boys' team will provide her with a level of competition suited to her level of skills." On the other hand, the plaintiffs conceded that the separation of boys and girls in the basketball program was substantially related to the important goal of maximizing the participation of both sexes in interscholastic sports "[s]ince boys, on the whole, are substantially better basketball players than are girls." The issue, then, was "whether the defendants' policies need to be justified only in terms of differences between the sexes as a whole or whether they must also be justified as applied to Karen's particular case." The district court then noted Supreme Court precedents that suggested that, given "the treacherous nature of generalizations about the sexes, it might be inappropriate to apply the generalization without regard for the individual case." Ultimately, however, the district court decided to make use of such a treacherous generalization, since it adopted the view set forth in Justice Stevens' earlier opinion denying a stay in the case: "If the classification is reasonable in substantially all of its applications, I do not believe that the general rule can be said to be unconstitutional simply because it appears arbitrary in an individual case." The district court then granted the school district's motion for summary judgment, and Karen O'Connor was left to play basketball in the girls' league. This result is inconsistent with Justice O'Connor's view of equal protection in the *VMI* case, and yet it the likely justification for the continued very common practice of segregating males and females in sport.

2. GENDER-SEGREGATED PUBLIC SCHOOL CLASSROOMS

Single-sex education was common in American universities well into the 1960s but a significant percentage of single-sex institutions of higher education became co-educational during that decade. At the high school level, many private and Catholic high schools were single-sex but it was a very rare public school that was single-sex. Public schools like Boston Latin School (for boys) and Girls Latin School (for girls) were the exception.

The Supreme Court's twin decisions in *Mississippi University for Women v. Hogan*, 458 U.S. 718 (1982), and *United States v. Virginia*, 518 U.S. 515 (1996), effectively put an end to single-sex education by public entities at the university level. The *VMI* case did not categorically rule out the possibility that a public single-sex university could satisfy the demands of the Equal Protection Clause. Justice O'Connor's majority opinion, however, set a standard so high that it made it unlikely that a university could be so devoted to single-sex education that it would spend the resources in what would likely be a vain attempt to create single-sex schools that addressed the individual talents and capacities of their students, as O'Connor's opinion demanded.

At the primary and secondary level, there were few single-sex public schools until 2006, when the Department of Education under President George W. Bush published new regulations interpreting Title IX, a federal statute that forbids sex discrimination in programs that receive federal funds. 34 C.F.R. § 106.34 (see 71 Fed. Reg. 62,530, 62,534-62,535 (Oct. 25, 2006). These regulations authorized public schools to provide single-sex schools and single-sex classrooms under certain conditions, provided that enrollment in the single-sex program was voluntary. The American Civil Liberties Union estimates that since 2006, more than 500 schools have adopted some form of single-sex instruction. *See* Preliminary Findings of ACLU: "Teach Kids, Not Stereotypes" Campaign (August 20, 2012).

Single-sex education raises both educational and legal issues. There is substantial disagreement in educational circles over the value of single-sex education. Proponents of single-sex education point to studies that show better learning outcomes, less distraction, more effective teaching, and a higher level of student satisfaction in single-sex environments. *See generally* National Association for Single Sex Public Education Website. On the other hand, the journal *Science* published a study of single-sex education that concluded that the movement towards single-sex education "is deeply misguided, and often justified by weak, cherry-picked, or misconstrued scientific claims rather than by valid scientific evidence . . . [and] there is no well-designed research showing that single-sex (SS) education improves students' academic performance, but there is evidence that sex segregation increases gender stereotyping and legitimizes institutional sexism." Diane Halpern et al., The Pseudoscience of Single-Sex Schooling, 333 Science 1706, 1707 (2011).

As a matter of constitutional law, single-sex public schools or single-sex classrooms within a public school must meet the test of being substantially related to an important governmental interest, and they may not be designed in a manner that gives effect to stereotypes about the proper roles of males and females. In recent litigation over single-sex education, courts have considered whether programs complied with the Department of Education's Title IX regulations, but have not decided whether or not the programs violate the Equal Protection Clause. *See Doe v. Wood County Bd. of Educ.*, --- F.Supp.2d ---- (S.D. W.Va. 2012) (single-sex classrooms likely to violate voluntariness requirement of Title IX regulations but not deciding equal protection issue); *A.N.A. ex rel. S.F.A. v. Breckinridge County Bd. of Educ.*, 833 F.Supp.2d 673 (W.D.Ky.,2011) (plaintiffs lacked standing to challenge single-sex program); *Doe ex rel. Doe v. Vermilion Parish School Bd.*, 421 Fed.Appx. 366 (5th Cir. 2011) (expressing no view on whether Title IX regulations violated the Equal Protection Clause and finding issues of legality of same-sex program substantially moot).

3. *MILITARY COMBAT EXCLUSION*

Women have long been excluded from combat positions in the United States military but this changed in January, 2013. On January 23, 2013, the New York Times reported:

> Defense Secretary Leon E. Panetta is lifting the military's official ban on women in combat, which will open up hundreds of thousands of additional front-line jobs to them, senior defense officials said Wednesday. The groundbreaking decision overturns a 1994 Pentagon rule that restricts women from artillery, armor, infantry and other such combat roles, even though in reality women have frequently found themselves in combat in Iraq and Afghanistan; according to the Pentagon, hundreds of thousands of women have

deployed in those conflicts. As of last year, more than 800 women had been wounded in the two wars and more than 130 had died. N.Y. Times. January 23, 2013.

This voluntary decision by the Pentagon made moot a law suit that had been filed in federal district court in California on November 27, 2012, challenging the exclusion of women from combat as a violation of the Equal Protection Clause. *Hegar et al. v. Panetta,* D.D.Cal (11/17/2012)

In light of these recent events, the analysis of the constitutionality of the exclusion of women from combat is something of an academic, rather than real-world, exercise. That being said, it may still be helpful to review two conflicting lines of precedents that the federal court might have used to evaluate the combat exclusion.

On the one hand, the Supreme Court precedents on judicial review of military policy have been extremely deferential to the military, even when the Court has purported to be applying a heightened level of scrutiny. Thus, in *Korematsu v. United States*, 323 U.S. 214 (1944), the Court upheld the military's exclusion of Japanese-Americans, even though it purported to be applying strict scrutiny. In *Rostker v. Goldberg,* 453 U.S. 57 (1981), the Court upheld the military's male-only draft, even though it purported to be applying intermediate scrutiny. The simple fact is that the Supreme Court has not shown itself willing to apply the same constitutional rules to the military that it applies to other government entities. If the Court had applied this kind of scrutiny to the exclusion of women from combat, it is very likely that the exclusion would have been upheld.

On the other hand, the Court's opinion in *United States v. Virginia*,518 U.S. 515 (1996), suggests a very different kind of analysis. If the Court were willing to apply to the combat exclusion the same kind of scrutiny it applied to the exclusion of female cadets, , it is hard to imagine that the combat exclusion would survive.As Justice O'Connor explained in that case, the government cannot focus on generalizations about the average physical capacities of men and women. However, "some women ... do well under [the] adversative model," "some women, at least, would want to attend [VMI] if they had the opportunity," "some women are capable of all of the individual activities required of VMI cadets," and "can meet the physical standards [VMI] now impose[s] on men," "It is on behalf of these women that the United States has instituted this suit, and it is for them that a remedy must be crafted."

4. *GENDER SEGREGATION IN PRISONS*

Prisons in American are segregated by gender. This has not been thought to raise a constitutional issue. As one court noted, "As an initial matter, we note that the segregation of inmates by sex is unquestionably constitutional." *Women Prisoners of District of Columbia Dept. of Corrections v. District of Columbia*, 93 F.3d 910 (D.C. Cir. 1996). In cases where plaintiffs challenge certain aspects of gender-segregated prisons, plaintiffs usually assume that the overall structure of the prison system is acceptable but challenge certain consequences that follow gender segregation.

In *Pitts v. Thornburgh*, 866 F.2d 1450 (D.C. Cir.1989), the plaintiffs complained that the prison that housed female prisoners for the District of Columbia was much farther away from the District than was the prison that housed male prisoners. The court applied intermediate scrutiny and determined that the separate, geographically distant, prisons satisfied that standard. The court concluded that the government interest in minimizing overcrowding in its correctional facilities was an important interest and then determined that the gender classification was substantially related to it:

> Our inquiry into the relation between the classification under challenge and the government interest advanced to justify it begins by noting a pervasive characteristic of American prisons, namely, the separation of inmates on the basis of gender. The classification at issue obviously responds directly to this common characteristic of correctional institutions, a characteristic found in both the federal and District prison systems. This fact strongly suggests that the location policy does not "employ[ ] gender as an inaccurate proxy for other, more germane bases of classification," which is the central concern of equal protection principles in this context.
>
> Importantly, appellants do not quarrel with the federal prison system's establishment of facilities restricted to a single sex. Nor do appellants attack the gender-based segregation within the few federal facilities that incarcerate both men and women. Similarly, appellants do not challenge the District's policy of segregating its facilities according to gender. Their challenge is much more narrowly focused on the physical location of the gender-separated facilities. We therefore assume for purposes of our analysis that these general, widespread practices in American prison systems do not run afoul of constitutional commands.

In *Women Prisoners of District of Columbia Dept. of Corrections v. District of Columbia*, 93 F.3d 910 (D.C. Cir. 1996), plaintiffs complained that women in the female prison benefited from fewer programs than men did in their male prison. The court rejected the equal protection claim on the ground that women prisoners were not similarly situated with male prisoners in that women were far more likely than men to be single-parent primary caretakers, much less likely to be serving sentences for violent crimes, and more likely to be housed in small prison facilities. As a result, the court found that the District did not have to provide exactly the same programs to men and women in separate prison facilities.

As with other gender classifications discussed in this section, there appear to be very good pragmatic and commonsense reasons to separate men and women in prison. Concerns about safety and privacy are certainly important governmental interests. Yet it is difficult, as a matter of constitutional law, to identify anything that is inherently "male" or "female" about serving time in prison that would make a gender classification substantially related to those concerns. This is not a case where the biological differences between the genders support a gender separation. Courts, however, are very unlikely to use the Equal Protection Clause to invalidate our current system of gender segregation in prisons.

CHAPTER 4

CLASSIFICATIONS DISADVANTAGING NONMARITAL CHILDREN

A. THE COMMON LAW RULES THAT DISADVANTAGED NONMARITAL CHILDREN

The common law treated children born to unmarried parents as inferior to and less worthy than children born to married parents. First was the matter of terminology. The common law identified children born of unmarried parents as "bastards," a term that, although for most part eliminated from our modern legal vocabulary, still retains its meaning as a slang term to describe an obnoxious or despicable person. Second were the substantive differences. Blackstone notes that a bastard was a "filius nullius," a son of nobody, and could inherit nothing. Blackstone, Vol. I, *Commentaries on the Laws of England*, 458. In addition, the common law in several American states well into the twentieth century was that a nonmarital child had no right of support from his father. *E.g. Baston v. Sears*, 15 Ohio St. 2d 166, 239 NE. 2d 62 (1968). In addition, most statutory programs that provided benefits for dependents, including Social Security and workers compensation, treated nonmarital children less favorably than marital children. Finally, statutory causes of action like wrongful death actions only benefited marital children.

Until 1968, the Supreme Court had not identified any constitutional problem with this legal regime that formally disadvantaged nonmarital children. That began to change with the Courts decision in *Levy v. Louisiana*.

B. THE COURT'S UNCERTAIN MOVEMENT TOWARD INTERMEDIATE SCRUTINY OF CLASSIFICATIONS DISADVANTAGING NONMARITAL CHILDREN

1. THE COURT INVALIDATES CERTAIN CLASSIFICATIONS USING RATIONAL BASIS REVIEW

Levy v. Louisiana
391 U.S. 68 (1968)

[Louise Levy was unmarried when she gave birth to each of the five children she raised. When she died, her children brought a wrongful death action against their mother's doctor and insurance company to recover damages for their loss and for their mother's pain and suffering. The children's lawsuit was dismissed and their right to recover was barred by a trial court that interpreted the word "child" under La. Civ.Code Ann. Art. 2315 to mean "legitimate child."]

Mr. Justice DOUGLAS delivered the opinion of the Court.

We start from the premise that illegitimate children are not 'nonpersons.' They are humans, live, and have their being. They are clearly 'persons' within the meaning of the Equal Protection Clause of the Fourteenth Amendment.

While a State has broad power when it comes to making classifications (*Ferguson v. Skrupa*, 372 U.S. 726, 732), it may not draw a line which constitutes an invidious discrimination against a particular class. See *Skinner v. State of Oklahoma*, 316 U.S. 535, 541-542. Though the test has been variously stated, the end result is whether the line drawn is a rational one. See *Morey v. Doud*, 354 U.S. 457, 465-466.

In applying the Equal Protection Clause to social and economic legislation, we give great latitude to the legislature in making classifications. *Williamson v. Lee Optical*, 348 U.S. 483, 489. Even so, would a corporation, which is a 'person,' for certain purposes, within the meaning of the Equal Protection Clause (*Pembina Consol. Silver Mining & Milling Co. v. Pennsylvania*, 125 U.S. 181, 188) be required to forgo recovery for wrongs done its interests because its incorporators were all bastards? However that might be, we have been extremely sensitive when it comes to basic civil rights (*Skinner v. State of Oklahoma, supra*, 316 U.S., at 541; *Harper v. Virginia State Board of Elections*, 383 U.S. 663, 669-670) and have not hesitated to strike down an invidious classification even though it had history and tradition on its side. (*Brown v. Board of Education*, 347 U.S. 483; *Harper v. Virginia State Board of Elections, supra*, 383 U.S. at 669.) The rights asserted here involve the intimate, familial relationship between a child and his own mother. When the child's claim of damage for loss of his mother is in issue, why, in terms of 'equal protection,' should the tortfeasors go free merely because the child is illegitimate? Why should the illegitimate child be denied rights merely because of his birth out of wedlock? He certainly is subject to all the responsibilities of a citizen, including the payment of taxes and conscription under the Selective Service Act. How under our constitutional regime can he be denied correlative rights which other citizens enjoy?

Legitimacy or illegitimacy of birth has no relation to the nature of the wrong allegedly inflicted on the mother. These children, though illegitimate, were dependent on her; she cared for them and nurtured them; they were indeed hers in the biological and in the spiritual sense; in her death they suffered wrong in the sense that any dependent would.

We conclude that it is invidious to discriminate against them when no action, conduct, or demeanor of theirs is possibly relevant to the harm that was done the mother.

Reversed.

NOTES

1. *Levy* is the first case in which the Supreme Court invalidated a classification that disadvantaged nonmarital children and it was a harbinger of things to come. The case was decided eight years before the Court created the intermediate scrutiny standard in *Craig v. Boren*, so the Court did not have that standard available to it. The Court stated that "[t]hough the test has been variously stated, the end result is whether the line drawn is a rational one," but the Court certainly did not apply the deference that is usually associated with that rationality standard. There is language in the *Levy* opinion that suggests the Court is not, in fact, applying rational basis review. The Court stated that it had been "extremely sensitive when it comes to basic civil rights," citing *Skinner v. Oklahoma, Harper v. Virginia State Board of Elections*, and *Brown v Board of Education*, all of which had applied heightened scrutiny. The Court also described the rights asserted as "involv[ing] the intimate, familial relationship between a child and his own mother," a right that the Court had also treated as fundamental in cases such as *Meyer v. Nebraska*. Thus, *Levy* was certainly not a run-of-the-mill rational basis case.

2. *Levy* also identifies the problem with the common law rules that disadvantaged nonmarital children—"Legitimacy or illegitimacy of birth has no relation to the nature of the wrong allegedly inflicted on the mother." The wrong allegedly inflicted on the mother was her death caused by the negligence of another. But the harm to the children, her dependents, was the loss of support that followed. The children's status as illegitimate under state law bore no relation either to the wrong inflicted on the mother or to the harm suffered by the children.

3. *A Note on Terminology*. In accordance with the custom of the day and with the statutory language, the *Levy* Court identifies the injured parties as "illegitimate" children. This terminology is a step up from the common law term—bastard—but it is still a derogatory and judgmental term, since "illegitimate" literally means "unlawful." The term itself first assumes that sexual relations outside of marriage are somehow unlawful, and second it visits this wrong of the parent on the child. Today, a far more common, and morally neutral, way to describe children whose parents are not married is "nonmarital" children.

Glona v. American Guarantee & Liability Insurance Co.
391 U.S. 73 (1968)

[*Glona* was a companion case decided the same day as *Levy*, and it involved a kind of mirror image fact pattern—a *mother* was suing for the wrongful death of *her child*, but the claim was disallowed because the child was illegitimate.]

Yet we see no possible rational basis for assuming that if the natural mother is allowed recovery for the wrongful death of her illegitimate child, the cause of illegitimacy will be served. It would, indeed, be farfetched to assume that women have illegitimate children so that they can be compensated in damages for their death. A law which creates an open season on illegitimates in the area of automobile accidents gives a windfall to tortfeasors. But it hardly has a causal connection with the 'sin,' which is, we are told, the historic reason for the creation of the disability.

NOTES

1. The *Glona* Court is clearing applying the rational basis standard, although not the deferential version of it. The Court notes the absence of causation between the denial of a wrongful death remedy and the presumed desire to prevent the "sin" of extramarital sexual relations.

Weber v. Aetna Cas. & Sur. Co.
406 U.S. 164 (1972)

[At the time of his death from a work-related injury, Henry Clyde Stokes was married to Adlay Jones Stokes, who had been committed to a mental hospital. He lived with his pregnant girlfriend, Willie May Weber, and their illegitimate child, along with the four children from his marriage. A second child was born posthumously to Stokes and Weber. Because Louisiana state law prohibited Stokes, who was not divorced, from acknowledging a child born out of wedlock, he was unable to formally acknowledge paternity of his children with Weber.

After Stokes' death, his four legitimate children filed a workmen's compensation claim. Weber joined the suit and filed a claim on behalf of her two illegitimate children. When, in a separate action, the four legitimate children received a settlement from a third party in excess of workmen's compensation benefits, the trial court ruled that the settlement extinguished all parties' right to settle under workmen's compensation. The two illegitimate offspring, who did not share in that settlement, would receive nothing.]

Mr. Justice POWELL delivered the opinion of the Court.

The question before us, on writ of certiorari to the Supreme Court of Louisiana, concerns the right of dependent unacknowledged, illegitimate children to recover under Louisiana workmen's compensation laws benefits for the death of their natural father on an equal footing with his dependent legitimate children. We hold that Louisiana's denial of equal recovery rights to dependent unacknowledged illegitimates violates the Equal Protection Clause of the Fourteenth Amendment. *Levy v. Louisiana*, 391 U.S. 68 (1968); *Glona v. American Guarantee & Liability Insurance Co.*, 391 U.S. 73 (1968).

I

For purposes of recovery under workmen's compensation, Louisiana law defines children to include 'only legitimate children, stepchildren, posthumous children, adopted children, and illegitimate children acknowledged under the provisions of Civil Code Articles 203, 204, and 205.' Thus, legitimate children and acknowledged illegitimates may recover on an equal basis. Unacknowledged illegitimate children, however, are relegated to the lesser status of 'other dependents' under § 1232(8) of the workmen's compensation statute and may recover only if there are not enough surviving dependents in the preceding classifications to exhaust the maximum allowable benefits. Both the Louisiana Court of Appeal and a divided Louisiana Supreme Court

CHAPTER 4: CLASSIFICATIONS DISADVANTAGING NONMARITAL CHILDREN

sustained these statutes over petitioner's constitutional objections, holding that our decision in *Levy, supra*, was not controlling.

We disagree. In *Levy*, the Court held invalid as denying equal protection of the laws, a Louisiana statute which barred an illegitimate child from recovering for the wrongful death of its mother when such recoveries by legitimate children were authorized. The Court there decided that the fact of a child's birth out of wedlock bore no reasonable relation to the purpose of wrongful-death statutes which compensate children for the death of a mother.

The court below sought to distinguish *Levy* as involving a statute which absolutely excluded all illegitimates from recovery, whereas in the compensation statute in the instant case acknowledged illegitimates may recover equally with legitimate children and 'the unacknowledged illegitimate child is not denied a right to recover compensation, he being merely relegated to a less favorable position as are other dependent relatives such as parents . . .' *Stokes v. Aetna Casualty & Surety Co.*, 257 La. 424, 433-434 (1970). The Louisiana Supreme Court likewise characterized *Levy* as a tort action where the tortfeasor escaped liability on the fortuity of the potential claimant's illegitimacy, whereas in the present action full compensation was rendered, and 'no tort feasor goes free because of the law.'

We do not think *Levy* can be disposed of by such finely carved distinctions. The Court in *Levy* was not so much concerned with the tortfeasor going free as with the equality of treatment under the statutory recovery scheme. Here, as in *Levy*, there is impermissible discrimination. An unacknowledged illegitimate child may suffer as much from the loss of a parent as a child born within wedlock or an illegitimate later acknowledged. So far as this record shows, the dependency and natural affinity of the unacknowledged illegitimate children for their father were as great as those of the four legitimate children whom Louisiana law has allowed to recover. The legitimate children and the illegitimate children all lived in the home of the deceased and were equally dependent upon him for maintenance and support. It is inappropriate, therefore, for the court below to talk of relegating the unacknowledged illegitimates 'to a less favorable position as are other dependent relatives such as parents.' The unacknowledged illegitimates are not a parent or some 'other dependent relative'; in this case they are dependent children, and as such are entitled to rights granted other dependent children.

Respondents contend that our recent ruling in *Labine v. Vincent*, 401 U.S. 532 (1971), controls this case. In *Labine*, the Court upheld, against constitutional objections, Louisiana intestacy laws which had barred an acknowledged illegitimate child from sharing equally with legitimate children in her father's estate. That decision reflected, in major part, the traditional deference to a State's prerogative to regulate the disposition at death of property within its borders. *Id.*, at 538. The Court has long afforded broad scope to state discretion in this area. Yet the substantial state interest in providing for 'the stability of . . . land titles and in the prompt and definitive determination of the valid ownership of property left by decedents,' *Labine v. Vincent*, 229 So.2d 449, 452 (La.App.1969), is absent in the case at hand.

Moreover, in *Labine* the intestate, unlike deceased in the present action, might easily have modified his daughter's disfavored position. As the Court there remarked:

> Ezra Vincent could have left one-third of his property to his illegitimate daughter had he bothered to follow the simple formalities of executing a will. He could, of course, have legitimated the child by marrying her mother in which case the child could have inherited

his property either by intestate succession or by will as any other legitimate child. *Labine, supra*, 401 U.S., at 539.

Such options, however, were not realistically open to Henry Stokes. Under Louisiana law he could not have acknowledged his illegitimate children even had he desired to do so. The burdens of illegitimacy, already weighty, become doubly so when neither parent nor child can legally lighten them.

Both the statute in *Levy* and the statute in the present case involve state-created compensation schemes, designed to provide close relatives and dependents of a deceased a means of recovery for his often abrupt and accidental death. Both wrongful-death statutes and workmen's compensation codes represent outgrowths and modifications of our basic tort law. The former alleviated the harsh common-law rule under which 'no person could inherit the personal right of another to recover for tortious injuries to his body'; the latter removed difficult obstacles to recovery in work-related injuries by offering a more certain, though generally less remunerative, compensation. In the instant case, the recovery sought under the workmen's compensation statute was in lieu of an action under the identical death statute which was at issue in *Levy*. Given the similarities in the origins and purposes of these two statutes, and the similarity of Louisiana's pattern of discrimination in recovery rights, it would require a disregard of precedent and the principles of stare decisis to hold that *Levy* did not control the facts of the case before us. It makes no difference that illegitimates are not so absolutely or broadly barred here as in *Levy*; the discrimination remains apparent.

II

Having determined that *Levy* is the applicable precedent we briefly reaffirm here the reasoning which produced that result. The tests to determine the validity of state statutes under the Equal Protection Clause have been variously expressed, but this Court requires, at a minimum, that a statutory classification bear some rational relationship to a legitimate state purpose. *Morey v. Doud*, 354 U.S. 457 (1957); *Williamson v. Lee Optical Co.*, 348 U.S. 483 (1955); *Gulf, Colorado and Santa Fe R. Co. v. Ellis*, 165 U.S. 150 (1897); *Yick Wo v. Hopkins*, 118 U.S. 356 (1886). Though the latitude given state economic and social regulation is necessarily broad, when state statutory classifications approach sensitive and fundamental personal rights, this Court exercises a stricter scrutiny, *Brown v. Board of Education*, 347 U.S. 483 (1954); *Harper v. Virginia State Board of Elections*, 383 U.S. 663 (1966). The essential inquiry in all the foregoing cases is, however, inevitably a dual one: What legitimate state interest does the classification promote? What fundamental personal rights might the classification endanger?

The Louisiana Supreme Court emphasized strongly the State's interest in protecting 'legitimate family relationships,' 257 La., at 433, and the regulation and protection of the family unit have indeed been a venerable state concern. We do not question the importance of that interest; what we do question is how the challenged statute will promote it. As was said in *Glona*:

> (W)e see no possible rational basis . . . for assuming that if the natural mother is allowed recovery for the wrongful death of her illegitimate child, the cause of illegitimacy will be served. It would, indeed, be farfetched to assume that women have illegitimate children so that they can be compensated in damages for their death. *Glona v. American Guarantee & Liability Insurance Co., supra*, 391 U.S., at 75.

Nor can it be thought here that persons will shun illicit relations because the offspring may not one day reap the benefits of workmen's compensation.

It may perhaps be said that statutory distinctions between the legitimate and illegitimate reflect closer family relationships in that the illegitimate is more often not under care in the home of the father nor even supported by him. The illegitimate, so this argument runs, may thus be made less eligible for the statutory recoveries and inheritances reserved for those more likely to be within the ambit of familial care and affection. Whatever the merits elsewhere of this contention, it is not compelling in a statutory compensation scheme where dependency on the deceased is a prerequisite to anyone's recovery, and where the acknowledgment so necessary to equal recovery rights may be unlikely to occur or legally impossible to effectuate even where the illegitimate child may be nourished and loved.

Finally, we are mindful that States have frequently drawn arbitrary lines in workmen's compensation and wrongful-death statutes to facilitate potentially difficult problems of proof. Nothing in our decision would impose on state court systems a greater burden in this regard. By limiting recovery to dependents of the deceased, Louisiana substantially lessens the possible problems of locating illegitimate children and of determining uncertain claims of parenthood. Our decision fully respects Louisiana's choice on this matter. It will not expand claimants for workmen's compensation beyond those in a direct blood and dependency relationship with the deceased and it avoids altogether diffuse questions of affection and affinity which pose difficult probative problems. Our ruling requires equality of treatment between two classes of persons the genuineness of whose claims the State might in any event be required to determine.

The state interest in legitimate family relationships is not served by the statute; the state interest in minimizing problems of proof is not significantly disturbed by our decision. The inferior classification of dependent unacknowledged illegitimates bears, in this instance, no significant relationship to those recognized purposes of recovery which workmen's compensation statutes commendably serve.

The status of illegitimacy has expressed through the ages society's condemnation of irresponsible liaisons beyond the bonds of marriage. But visiting this condemnation on the head of an infant is illogical and unjust. Moreover, imposing disabilities on the illegitimate child is contrary to the basic concept of our system that legal burdens should bear some relationship to individual responsibility or wrongdoing. Obviously, no child is responsible for his birth and penalizing the illegitimate child is an ineffectual--as well as an unjust-way of deterring the parent. Courts are powerless to prevent the social opprobrium suffered by these hapless children, but the Equal Protection Clause does enable us to strike down discriminatory laws relating to status of birth where-as in this case-the classification is justified by no legitimate state interest, compelling or otherwise.

Reversed and *remanded.*

NOTES

1. The *Weber* Court identifies the problem as "equality of treatment under the statutory recovery scheme," and as "impermissible discrimination." The illegitimate children suffered just as much a loss as the legitimate children. They had the same natural affinity and were just as

dependent on their father as were the legitimate children. Therefore, the Court concluded that they were entitled to the same rights granted to the other dependent children. The fact that their father was not married to their mother was not relevant to a statutory scheme that provided support to the surviving children of deceased wage earners.

2. As for the standard of review, the Court noted that "[t]he tests to determine the validity of state statutes under the Equal Protection Clause have been variously expressed, but this Court requires, at a minimum, that a statutory classification bear some rational relationship to a legitimate state purpose." The Court noted that the Court exercises a stricter scrutiny "when state statutory classifications approach sensitive and fundamental personal rights," but did not indicate that this was such a case. The Court identified the state interest as "the regulation and protection of the family unit," and conceded that this was an important interest, but was not at all convinced that the statutory classification treating legitimate and illegitimate children differently would promote that interest. It is not plausible to believe that "persons will shun illicit relations because the offspring may not one day reap the benefits of workmen's compensation." Thus, the statutory classification was not related to the stated purpose of the law.

3. At the end of the opinion, the Court spoke to what was really going on in the statute—it was designed neither to protect the family unit nor to deal with problems of proof of parenthood. Rather, it was an expression of condemnation of the conduct of the illegitimate child's parents:

> The status of illegitimacy has expressed through the ages society's condemnation of irresponsible liaisons beyond the bonds of marriage. But visiting this condemnation on the head of an infant is illogical and unjust Moreover, imposing disabilities on the illegitimate child is contrary to the basic concept of our system that legal burdens should bear some relationship to individual responsibility or wrongdoing. Obviously, no child is responsible for his birth and penalizing the illegitimate child is an ineffectual-as well as an unjust-way of deterring the parent.

The Court in this statement assumes, without deciding, that the state does have the authority to condemn irresponsible liaisons beyond the boundaries of marriage. We know since *Lawrence v. Texas*, 539 U.S. 558 (2003), that this is not true. *See, infra*, Ch. 7. But even conceding the legitimacy of this objective in a case that preceded *Lawrence* by forty years, the state cannot pursue that objective by punishing the children who resulted from that relationship.

Gomez v. Perez
409 U.S. 535 (1973)

[A mother filed a petition seeking support from the alleged father of her minor child. After a hearing, the state trial judge found that defendant was indeed the biological father of the child, and that the child needed the support and maintenance of her father. Because, however, the child was illegitimate, the court concluded that, under state law, there was no legal obligation to support the child.]

PER CURIAM.

The issue presented by this appeal is whether the laws of Texas may constitutionally grant legitimate children a judicially enforceable right to support from their natural fathers and at the same time deny that right to illegitimate children.

In Texas, both at common law and under the statutes of the State, the natural father has a continuing and primary duty to support his legitimate children. That duty extends even beyond dissolution of the marriage, and is enforceable on the child's behalf in civil proceedings and, further, is the subject of criminal sanctions. The duty to support exists despite the fact that the father may not have custody of the child. The Court of Civil Appeals has held in this case that nowhere in this elaborate statutory scheme does the State recognize any enforceable duty on the part of the biological father to support his illegitimate children and that, absent a statutory duty to support, the controlling law is the Texas common-law rule that illegitimate children, unlike legitimate children, have no legal right to support from their fathers. See also *Home of the Holy Infancy v. Kaska*, 397 S.W.2d 208 (Tex.1965); *Lane v. Phillips*, supra, at 243, 6 S.W., at 611; *Bjorgo v. Bjorgo*, 391 S.W.2d 528 (Tex.Civ.App.1965). It is also true that fathers may set up illegitimacy as a defense to prosecutions for criminal nonsupport of their children.

We have held that under the Equal Protection Clause of the Fourteenth Amendment a State may not create a right of action in favor of children for the wrongful death of a parent and exclude illegitimate children from the benefit of such a right. *Levy v. Louisiana*, 391 U.S. 68 (1968). Similarly, we have held that illegitimate children may not be excluded from sharing equally with other children in the recovery of workmen's compensation benefits for the death of their parent. *Weber v. Aetna Casualty & Surety Co.*, 406 U.S. 164 (1972). Under these decisions, a State may not invidiously discriminate against illegitimate children by denying them substantial benefits accorded children generally. We therefore hold that once a State posits a judicially enforceable right on behalf of children to needed support from their natural fathers there is no constitutionally sufficient justification for denying such an essential right to a child simply because its natural father has not married its mother. For a State to do so is 'illogical and unjust.' We recognize the lurking problems with respect to proof of paternity. Those problems are not to be lightly brushed aside, but neither can they be made into an impenetrable barrier that works to shield otherwise invidious discrimination.

The judgment is reversed and the case remanded for further proceedings not inconsistent with this opinion.

2. *THE COURT UPHOLDS CERTAIN CLASSIFICATIONS USING SOMETHING LIKE RATIONAL BASIS REVIEW*

In light of the four cases on illegitimacy in the previous section, (*Levy, Glona, Weber*, and *Gomez*), all decided between 1968 and 1973, one might have predicted that all classifications based on illegitimacy were likely to violate the Equal Protection Clause. There was, however, another set of illegitimacy cases that upheld distinctions between marital and nonmarital children. This section considers these cases.

Labine v. Vincent
401 U.S. 532 (1971)

[Rita Vincent was born to Lou Bertha Patterson and Ezra Vincent, who were not married. Shortly after her birth, her parents jointly executed an acknowledgment that Ezra Vincent was the natural father of Rita Vincent. Under state law, the acknowledgment gave Vincent the right to claim support from her father and his heirs and the right to be a beneficiary if named in her father's will, but not a right to inherit from his estate. When Vincent was six years old, her father died intestate and, although he had no other direct descendants, his collateral heirs claimed his estate as their own. As her guardian, Vincent's mother filed suit on her behalf challenging as unconstitutional the Louisiana law that prevented her from inheriting her father's estate as a legitimate heir would.]

Mr. Justice BLACK delivered the opinion of the Court.

In this Court appellant argues that Louisiana's statutory scheme for intestate succession that bars this illegitimate child from sharing in her father's estate constitutes an invidious discrimination against illegitimate children that cannot stand under the Due Process and Equal Protection Clauses of the Constitution. Much reliance is placed upon the Court's decisions in *Levy v. Louisiana*, 391 U.S. 68 (1968), and *Glona v. American Guarantee & Liability Insurance Co.*, 391 U.S. 73 (1968). For the reasons set out below, we find appellant's reliance on those cases misplaced, and we decline to extend the rationale of those cases where it does not apply. Accordingly, we affirm the decision below.

In *Levy* the Court held that Louisiana could not consistently with the Equal Protection Clause bar an illegitimate child from recovering for the wrongful death of its mother when such recoveries by legitimate children were authorized. The cause of action alleged in *Levy* was in tort. It was undisputed that Louisiana had created a statutory tort and had provided for the survival of the deceased's cause of action, so that a large class of persons injured by the tort could recover damages in compensation for their injury. Under those circumstances the Court held that the State could not totally exclude from the class of potential plaintiffs illegitimate children who were unquestionably injured by the tort that took their mother's life. *Levy* did not say and cannot fairly be read to say that a State can never treat an illegitimate child differently from legitimate offspring.[FN 6]

The people of Louisiana, through their legislature have carefully regulated many of the property rights incident to family life. Louisiana law prescribes certain formalities requisite to the contracting of marriage. Once marriage is contracted there, husbands have obligations to their wives. Fathers have obligations to their children. Should the children prosper while the parents fall upon hard times, children have a statutory obligation to support their parents. To further strengthen and preserve family ties, Louisiana regulates the disposition of property upon the death of a family man. The surviving spouse is entitled to an interest in the deceased spouse's estate. Legitimate children have a right of forced heirship in their father's estate and can even retrieve property transferred by their father during his lifetime in reduction of their rightful interests.

[FN 6] Nor is *Glona v. American Guarantee & Liability Insurance Co.*, 391 U.S. 73 (1968), analogous to this case. In *Glona* the majority relied on Louisiana's 'curious course' of sanctions against illegitimacy to demonstrate that there was no 'rational basis' for prohibiting a mother from recovering for the wrongful death of her son. Even if we were to apply the 'rational basis' test to the Louisiana intestate succession statute, that statute clearly has a rational basis in view of Louisiana's interest in promoting family life and of directing the disposition of property left within the State.

Louisiana also has a complex set of rules regarding the rights of illegitimate children. Children born out of wedlock and who are never acknowledged by their parents apparently have no right to take property by intestate succession from their father's estate. In some instances, their father may not even bequeath property to them by will. Illegitimate children acknowledged by their fathers are 'natural children.' Natural children can take from their father by intestate succession 'to the exclusion only of the State.' They may be bequeathed property by their father only to the extent of either one-third or one-fourth of his estate and then only if their father is not survived by legitimate children or their heirs. Finally, children born out of wedlock can be legitimated or adopted, in which case they may take by intestate succession or by will as any other child.

These rules for intestate succession may or may not reflect the intent of particular parents. Many will think that it is unfortunate that the rules are so rigid. Others will think differently. But the choices reflected by the intestate succession statute are choices which it is within the power of the State to make. The Federal Constitution does not give this Court the power to overturn the State's choice under the guise of constitutional interpretation because the Justices of this Court believe that they can provide better rules. Of course, it may be said that the rules adopted by the Louisiana Legislature 'discriminate' against illegitimates. But the rules also discriminate against collateral relations, as opposed to ascendants, and against ascendants, as opposed to descendants. Other rules determining property rights based on family status also 'discriminate' in favor of wives and against 'concubines.' The dissent attempts to distinguish these other 'discriminations' on the ground that they have a biological or social basis. There is no biological difference between a wife and a concubine nor does the Constitution require that there be such a difference before the State may assert its power to protect the wife and her children against the claims of a concubine and her children. The social difference between a wife and a concubine is analogous to the difference between a legitimate and an illegitimate child. One set of relationships is socially sanctioned, legally recognized, and gives rise to various rights and duties. The other set of relationships is illicit and beyond the recognition of the law. Similarly, the State does not need biological or social reasons for distinguishing between ascendants and descendants. Some of these discriminatory choices are perhaps more closely connected to our conceptions of social justice or the ways in which most dying men wish to dispose of their property than the Louisiana rules governing illegitimate children. It may be possible that some of these choices are more 'rational' than the choices inherent in Louisiana's categories of illegitimates. But the power to make rules to establish, protect, and strengthen family life as well as to regulate the disposition of property left in Louisiana by a man dying there is committed by the Constitution of the United States and the people of Louisiana to the legislature of that State. Absent a specific constitutional guarantee, it is for that legislature, not the life-tenured judges of this Court, to select from among possible laws. We cannot say that Louisiana's policy provides a perfect or even a desirable solution or the one we would have provided for the problem of the property rights of illegitimate children. Neither can we say that Louisiana does not have the power to make laws for distribution of property left within the State.

We emphasize that this is not a case, like *Levy*, where the State has created an insurmountable barrier to this illegitimate child. There is not the slightest suggestion in this case that Louisiana has barred this illegitimate from inheriting from her father. Ezra Vincent could have left one-third of his property to his illegitimate daughter had he bothered to follow the simple formalities of executing a will. He could, of course, have legitimated the child by marrying her mother in which case the child could have inherited his property either by intestate succession or by will as any other legitimate child. Finally, he could have awarded his child the benefit of Louisiana's intestate succession statute on the same terms as legitimate children simply by stating in his acknowledgment of paternity his desire to legitimate the little girl. See *Bergeron v. Miller*, 230 So.2d 417 (La.App.1970).

In short, we conclude that in the circumstances presented in this case, there is nothing in the vague generalities of the Equal Protection and Due Process Clauses which empowers this Court to nullify the deliberate choices of the elected representatives of the people of Louisiana.

Affirmed.

Mr. Justice BRENNAN, with whom Mr. Justice DOUGLAS, Mr. Justice WHITE, and Mr. Justice MARSHALL join, dissenting.

In my view, Louisiana's intestate succession laws, insofar as they treat illegitimate children whose fathers have publicly acknowledged them differently from legitimate children, plainly violate the Equal Protection Clause of the Fourteenth Amendment. The Court today effectively concedes this, and to reach its result, resorts to the startling measure of simply excluding such illegitimate children from the protection of the Clause, in order to uphold the untenable and discredited moral prejudice of bygone centuries which vindictively punished not only the illegitimates' parents, but also the hapless, and innocent, children. Based upon such a premise, today's decision cannot even pretend to be a principled decision. This is surprising from Justices who have heretofore so vigorously decried decisionmaking rested upon personal predilections, to borrow the Court's words, of 'life-tenured judges of this Court.' I respectfully dissent.

NOTES

1. Coming after *Levy* and *Glona*, *Labine* is a surprising case. *Labine* holds that Louisiana can exclude the acknowledged illegitimate child from the father's intestate estate. In *Levy*, the Court had called into question the relevance of the marital status of a child's parents: "Legitimacy or illegitimacy of birth has no relation to the nature of the wrong allegedly inflicted on the mother." But, looking back, the *Labine* Court says that "*Levy* did not say and cannot fairly be read to say that a State can never treat an illegitimate child differently from legitimate offspring." *Labine* effectively reintroduces and endorses the relevance of the parents' marriage. And since no one contested the child's paternity claim, the case is clearly not about the problem of proof. Rather the *Labine* Court forthrightly proclaims that it is constitutionally acceptable to discriminate against illegitimates:

> Of course, it may be said that the rules adopted by the Louisiana Legislature 'discriminate' against illegitimates. But the rules also discriminate against collateral relations, as opposed to ascendants, and against ascendants, as opposed to descendants. Other rules determining property rights based on family status also 'discriminate' in favor of wives and against 'concubines.'. . . The social difference between a wife and a concubine is analogous to the difference between a legitimate and an illegitimate child. One set of relationships is socially sanctioned, legally recognized, and gives rise to various rights and duties. The other set of relationships is illicit and beyond the recognition of the law.

For the *Labine* Court, discrimination against illegitimates is a rational discrimination, justified by the state's "interest in promoting family life and of directing the disposition of property left within the State."

The majority opinion in *Labine* purports to give effect to a formal distinction adopted by state law, in order to promote family life and to direct the disposition of property on death. But, according to the dissenters, the majority was upholding "the untenable and discredited moral prejudice of bygone centuries which vindictively punished not only the illegitimates' parents, but also the hapless, and innocent, children." As subsequent cases would indicate, the dissenters had the better argument. In *Trimble v. Gordon*, 430 U.S. 762 (1977), the Court would subsequently say that "*Labine v. Vincent* is difficult to place in the pattern of this Court's equal protection decisions, and subsequent cases have limited its force as a precedent."

Mathews v. Lucas
427 U.S. 495 (1976)

[Robert Cuffee and Belmira Lucas, who were not married, had two children together. After living together for eighteen years, the couple separated and, two years later, Cuffee died. On behalf of their children, who were ages eight and fifteen at the time of their father's death, Lucas applied for surviving children's benefits under the Social Security Act. Although an administrative hearing established paternity, the application was nonetheless rejected because there had been no formal acknowledgement or judicial ruling of paternity during Cuffee's lifetime. In addition, the children were not living with their father and they did not demonstrate that he provided them with financial support at the time of his death.]

Mr. Justice BLACKMUN delivered the opinion of the Court.

This case presents the issue of the constitutionality, under the Due Process Clause of the Fifth Amendment, of those provisions of the Social Security Act that condition the eligibility of certain illegitimate children for a surviving child's insurance benefits upon a showing that the deceased wage earner was the claimant child's parent and, at the time of his death, was living with the child or was contributing to his support.

II

In operative terms, the [Social Security] Act provides that an unmarried son or daughter of an individual, who died fully or currently insured under the Act, may apply for and be entitled to a survivor's benefit, if the applicant is under 18 years of age at the time of application (or is a full-time student and under 22 years of age) and was dependent, within the meaning of the statute, at the time of the parent's death. A child is considered dependent for this purpose if the insured father was living with or contributing to the child's support at the time of death. Certain children, however, are relieved of the burden of such individualized proof of dependency. Unless the child has been adopted by some other individual, a child who is legitimate, or a child who would be entitled to inherit personal property from the insured parent's estate under the applicable state intestacy law, is considered to have been dependent at the time of the parent's death. Even lacking this relationship under state law, a child, unless adopted by some other individual, is entitled to a presumption of dependency if the decedent, before death, (a) had gone through a marriage ceremony with the other parent, resulting in a purported marriage between them which, but for a nonobvious legal defect, would have been valid, or (b) in writing had acknowledged the child to be his, or (c) had been decreed by a court to be the child's father, or (d) had been ordered by a court to support the child because the child was his.

III

The Secretary [of the Social Security Administration] does not disagree that the Lucas children and others similarly circumstanced are treated differently, as a class, from those children legitimate and illegitimate who are relieved by statutory presumption of any requirement of proving actual dependency at the time of death through cohabitation or contribution: for children in the advantage classes may be statutorily entitled to benefits even if they have never been dependent upon the father through whom they claim. Statutory classifications, of course, are not Per se unconstitutional; the matter depends upon the character of the discrimination and its relation to legitimate legislative aims. "The essential inquiry . . . is . . . inevitably a dual one: What legitimate (governmental) interest does the classification promote? What fundamental personal rights might the classification endanger?" *Weber v. Aetna Casualty & Surety Co.*, 406 U.S. 164, 173 (1972).

It is true, of course, that the legal status of illegitimacy, however defined, is, like race or national origin, a characteristic determined by causes not within the control of the illegitimate individual, and it bears no relation to the individual's ability to participate in and contribute to society. The Court recognized in *Weber* that visiting condemnation upon the child in order to express society's disapproval of the parents' liaisons

> is illogical and unjust. Moreover, imposing disabilities on the illegitimate child is contrary to the basic concept of our system that legal burdens should bear some relationship to individual responsibility or wrongdoing. Obviously, no child is responsible for his birth and penalizing the illegitimate child is an ineffectual as well as an unjust way of deterring the parent. 406 U.S., at 175.

But where the law is arbitrary in such a way, we have had no difficulty in finding the discrimination impermissible on less demanding standards than those advocated here. *New Jersey Welfare Rights Org. v. Cahill*, 411 U.S. 619 (1973); *Richardson v. Davis*, 409 U.S. 1069 (1972); *Richardson v. Griffin*, 409 U.S. 1069 (1972); *Weber, supra*; *Levy v. Louisiana*, 391 U.S. 68 (1968). And such irrationality in some classifications does not in itself demonstrate that other, possibly rational, distinctions made in part on the basis of legitimacy are inherently untenable. Moreover, while the law has long placed the illegitimate child in an inferior position relative to the legitimate in certain circumstances, particularly in regard to obligations of support or other aspects of family law, see generally, *e. g.*, H. Krause, *Illegitimacy: Law and Social Policy* 21-42 (1971); Gray & Rudovsky, *The Court Acknowledges the Illegitimate: Levy v. Louisiana and Glona v. American Guarantee & Liability Insurance Co.*, 118 U.Pa.L.Rev. 1, 19-38 (1969), perhaps in part because the roots of the discrimination rest in the conduct of the parents rather than the child, and perhaps in part because illegitimacy does not carry an obvious badge, as race or sex do, this discrimination against illegitimates has never approached the severity or pervasiveness of the historic legal and political discrimination against women and Negroes. See *Frontiero v. Richardson*, 411 U.S. 677, 684-686 (1973) (plurality opinion).

We therefore adhere to our earlier view, see *Labine v. Vincent*, 401 U.S. 532 (1971), that the Act's discrimination between individuals on the basis of their legitimacy does not "command extraordinary protection from the majoritarian political process," *San Antonio School Dist. v. Rodriguez*, 411 U.S. 1, 28 (1973), which our most exacting scrutiny would entail. See *Jimenez,*

417 U.S., at 631-634, *Weber*, 406 U.S., at 173.

IV

Relying on *Weber*, the Court, in *Gomez v. Perez*, 409 U.S. 535, 538 (1973), held that "once a State posits a judicially enforceable right on behalf of children to needed support from their natural fathers there is no constitutionally sufficient justification for denying such an essential right to a child simply because its natural father has not married its mother." The same principle, which we adhere to now, applies when the judicially enforceable right to needed support lies against the Government rather than a natural father. See *New Jersey Welfare Rights Org. v. Cahill*, *supra*.

Consistent with our decisions, the Secretary explains the design of the statutory scheme assailed here as a program to provide for all children of deceased insureds who can demonstrate their "need" in terms of dependency at the times of the insureds' deaths. *Cf. Jimenez*, 417 U.S., at 634. He authenticates this description by reference to the explicit language of the Act specifying that the applicant child's classification as legitimate, or acknowledged, etc., is ultimately relevant only to the determination of dependency, and by reference to legislative history indicating that the statute was not a general welfare provision for legitimate or otherwise "approved" children of deceased insureds, but was intended just "to replace the support lost by a child when his father . . . dies . . . ."

Taking this explanation at face value, we think it clear that conditioning entitlement upon dependency at the time of death is not impermissibly discriminatory in providing only for those children for whom the loss of the parent is an immediate source of the need. *Cf. Geduldig v. Aiello*, 417 U.S. 484, 492-497 (1974); *Jefferson v. Hackney*, 406 U.S. 535 (1972); *Richardson v. Belcher*, 404 U.S. 78 (1971). See also *Weber*, 406 U.S., at 174-175.

But appellees contend that the actual design of the statute belies the Secretary's description, and that the statute was intended to provide support for insured decedents' children generally, if they had a "legitimate" claim to support, without regard to actual dependency at death; in any case, they assert, the statute's matrix of classifications bears no adequate relationship to actual dependency at death. Since such dependency does not justify the statute's discriminations, appellees argue, those classifications must fall under *Gomez v. Perez*, *supra*. These assertions are in effect one and the same. The basis for appellees' argument is the obvious fact that each of the presumptions of dependency renders the class of befit-recipients incrementally overinclusive, in the sense that some children within each class of presumptive dependents are automatically entitled to benefits under the statute although they could not in fact prove their economic dependence upon insured wage earners at the time of death. We conclude that the statutory classifications are permissible, however, because they are reasonably related to the likelihood of dependency at death.

A

Congress' purpose in adopting the statutory presumptions of dependency was obviously to serve administrative convenience. While Congress was unwilling to assume that every child of a deceased insured was dependent at the time of death, by presuming dependency on the basis of relatively readily documented facts, such as legitimate birth, or existence of a support order or paternity decree, which could be relied upon to indicate the likelihood of continued actual dependency, Congress was able to avoid the burden and expense of specific case-by-case determination in the large number of cases where dependency is objectively probable. Such presumptions in aid of administrative functions, though they may approximate, rather than precisely mirror, the results that case-by-case adjudication would show, are permissible under the Fifth Amendment, so long as that lack of precise equivalence does not exceed the bounds of substantiality tolerated by the applicable level of scrutiny. See *Weinberger v. Salfi*, 422 U.S. 749, 772.

In cases of strictest scrutiny, such approximations must be supported at least by a showing that the Government's dollar "lost" to overincluded benefit recipients is returned by a dollar "saved" in administrative expense avoided. *Frontiero v. Richardson*, 411 U.S., at 689 (plurality opinion). Under the standard of review appropriate here, however, the materiality of the relation between the statutory classifications and the likelihood of dependency they assertedly reflect need not be "'scientifically substantiated.'" *James v. Strange*, 407 U.S. 128, 133 (1972), quoting *Roth v. United States*, 354 U.S. 476, 501 (1957) (opinion of Harlan, J.). Nor, in any case, do we believe that Congress is required in this realm of less than strictest scrutiny to weigh the burdens of administrative inquiry solely in terms of dollars ultimately "spent," ignoring the relative amounts devoted to administrative rather than welfare uses. *Cf. Weinberger v. Salfi*, 422 U.S., at 784. Finally, while the scrutiny by which their showing is to be judged is not a toothless one, *e.g., Jimenez v. Weinberger*, 417 U.S. 628 (1974); *Frontiero v. Richardson*, 411 U.S., at 691 (Stewart, J., concurring in judgment, Powell, J., concurring in judgment); *Reed v. Reed*, 404 U.S. 71 (1971), the burden remains upon the appellees to demonstrate the insubstantiality of that relation. See *Lindsley v. Natural Carbonic Gas Co.*, 220 U.S. 61, 78-79 (1911); *cf. United States v. Gainey*, 380 U.S. 63, 67 (1965).

B

Applying these principles, we think that the statutory classifications challenged here are justified as reasonable empirical judgments that are consistent with a design to qualify entitlement to benefits upon a child's dependency at the time of the parent's death. To begin with, we note that the statutory scheme is significantly different from the provisions confronted in cases in which the Court has invalidated legislative discriminations among children on the basis of legitimacy. See *Gomez v. Perez*, 409 U.S. 535 (1973); *New Jersey Welfare Rights Org. v. Cahill*, 411 U.S. 619 (1973); *Weber v. Aetna Casualty & Surety Co.*, 406 U.S. 164 (1972); *Levy v. Louisiana*, 391 U.S. 68 (1968). These differences render those cases of little assistance to appellees. It could not have been fairly argued, with respect to any of the statutes struck down in those cases, that the legitimacy of the child was simply taken as an indication of dependency, or of some other valid ground of qualification. Under all but one of the statutes, not only was the legitimate child automatically entitled to benefits, but an illegitimate child was denied benefits solely and finally on the basis of illegitimacy, and regardless of any demonstration of dependency or other legitimate factor. In *Weber v. Aetna Casualty & Surety Co., supra*, the sole partial exception, the statutory scheme provided for a child's equal recovery under a workmen's compensation plan in the event of the death of the father, not only if the child was dependent, but also only if the dependent child was legitimate. 406 U.S., at 173-174, and n. 12. *Jimenez v. Weinberger, supra*, invalidating discrimination among afterborn illegitimate children as to entitlement to a child's disability benefits under the Social Security Act, is similarly distinguishable. Under the somewhat related statutory matrix considered there, legitimate children and those capable of inheriting personal property under state intestacy law, and those illegitimate solely on account of a nonobvious defect in their parents' marriage, were eligible for benefits, even if they were born after the onset of the father's disability. Other (illegitimate) afterborn children were conclusively denied any benefits, regardless of any showing of dependency. The Court held the discrimination among illegitimate afterborn children impermissible, rejecting the Secretary's claim that the classification was based upon considerations regarding trustworthy proof of dependency, because it could not accept the assertion:

> (T)he blanket and conclusive exclusion of appellants' subclass of illegitimates is reasonably related to the prevention of spurious claims (of dependency). Assuming that the appellants are in fact dependent on the claimant (father), it would not serve the purposes of the Act to conclusively deny them an opportunity to establish their dependency and their right to insurance benefits. 417 U.S., at 636.

Hence, it was held that

> to conclusively deny one subclass benefits presumptively available to the other denies the former the equal protection of the laws guaranteed by the due process provision of the Fifth Amendment. *Id.* at 637.

But this conclusiveness in denying benefits to some classes of afterborn illegitimate children, which belied the asserted legislative reliance on dependency in *Jimenez*, is absent here, for, as we have noted, any otherwise eligible child may qualify for survivorship benefits by showing contribution to support or cohabitation, at the time of death. *Cf. Vlandis v. Kline*, 412 U.S. 441, 452-453, n. 9 (1973), distinguishing *Starns v. Malkerson*, 326 F. Supp. 234 (Minn.1970), summarily aff'd, 401 U.S. 985 (1971).

   It is, of course, not enough simply that any child of a deceased insured is eligible for benefits upon some showing dependency. In *Frontiero v. Richardson, supra,* we found it impermissible to qualify the entitlement to dependent's benefits of a married woman in the uniformed services upon an individualized showing of her husband's actual dependence upon her for more than half his income, when no such showing of actual dependency was required of a married man in the uniformed services to obtain dependent's benefits on account of his wife. The invalidity of that gender-based discrimination rested upon the "overbroad" assumption, *Schlesinger v. Ballard*, 419 U.S. 498, 508 (1975), underlying the discrimination "that male workers' earnings are vital to the support of their families, while the earnings of female wage-earners do not significantly contribute to their families' support." *Weinberger v. Wiesenfeld*, 420 U.S., at 643; see *Frontiero*, 411 U.S., at 689 n. 23. Here, by contrast, the statute does not broadly discriminate between legitimates and illegitimates without more, but is carefully tuned to alternative considerations. The presumption of dependency is withheld only in the absence of any significant indication of the likelihood of actual dependency. Moreover, we cannot say that the factors that give rise to a presumption of dependency lack any substantial relation to the likelihood of actual dependency. Rather, we agree with the assessment of the three-judge court as it originally ruled in *Norton v. Weinberger*, 364 F. Supp. 1117, 1128 (Md.1973):

> (I)t is clearly rational to presume the overwhelming number of legitimate children are actually dependent upon their parents for support. Likewise . . . the children of an invalid marriage . . . would typically live in the wage earner's home or be supported by him. . . . When an order of support is entered by a court, it is reasonable to assume compliance occurred. A paternity decree, while not necessarily ordering support, would almost as strongly suggest support was subsequently obtained. Conceding that a written acknowledgment lacks the imprimatur of a judicial proceeding, it too establishes the basis

for a rational presumption. Men do not customarily affirm in writing their responsibility for an illegitimate child unless the child is theirs and a man who has acknowledged a child is more likely to provide it support than one who does not.

Similarly, we think, where state intestacy law provides that a child may take personal property from a father's estate, it may reasonably be thought that the child will more likely be dependent during the parent's life and at his death. For in its embodiment of the popular view within the jurisdiction of how a parent would have his property devolve among his children in the event of death, without specific directions, such legislation also reflects to some degree the popular conception within the jurisdiction of the felt parental obligation to such an "illegitimate" child in other circumstances, and thus something of the likelihood of actual parental support during, as well as after, life.

To be sure, none of these statutory criteria compels the extension of a presumption of dependency. But the constitutional question is not whether such a presumption is required, but whether it is permitted. Nor, in ratifying these statutory classifications, is our role to hypothesize independently on the desirability or feasibility of any possible alternative basis for presumption. These matters of practical judgment and empirical calculation are for Congress. Drawing upon its own practical experience, Congress has tailored statutory classifications in accord with its calculations of the likelihood of actual support suggested by a narrow set of objective and apparently reasonable indicators. Our role is simply to determine whether Congress' assumptions are so inconsistent or insubstantial as not to be reasonably supportive of its conclusions that individualized factual inquiry in order to isolate each nondependent child in a given class of cases is unwarranted as an administrative exercise. In the end, the precise accuracy of Congress' calculations is not a matter of specialized judicial competence; and we have no basis to question their detail beyond the evident consistency and substantiality. *Cf. United States v. Gainey*, 380 U.S. 63 at 67. We cannot say that these expectations are unfounded, or so indiscriminate as to render the statute's classifications baseless. We conclude, in short, that, in failing to extend any presumption of dependency to appellees and others like them, the Act does not impermissibly discriminate against them as compared with legitimate children or those illegitimate children who are statutorily deemed dependent.

Reversed.

NOTES

1.   *Mathews* is not nearly as surprising a case is *Labine v. Vincent*. *Labine* appeared to suggest that the state could treat nonmarital children as less worthy than marital children since marital children have a relationship with that parents that "is socially sanctioned, legally recognized, and gives rise to various rights and duties," while the relationship of nonmarital children with their parents is "illicit and beyond the recognition of the law." *Mathews*, on the other hand, is ostensibly more about administrative convenience in terms of establishing proof of parenthood. The rule in *Mathews* is concerned with identifying children who were dependent on a parent at the time of the parent's death. Instead of requiring every claimant to prove financial dependency, the statute creates a series of statutory presumptions of dependency. The first presumption is that all legitimate children are considered to be dependent. Illegitimate children also benefit from certain presumptions of dependency—if they are entitled to inherit under state law, if the parents went through a marriage ceremony, if there was a written acknowledgment of parenthood, if a court had

decreed parenthood, or if a court had ordered support payments. Even if an illegitimate child does not benefit from any of these presumptions, that child could still qualify for benefits if he or she proved that he or she was in fact dependent on the now deceased parent. Given this wide array of methods to qualify for benefits, the Court did not consider the distinction between marital and nonmarital children to be an inappropriate discrimination.

2.   Because the *Mathews* case was decided after *Frontiero v. Richardson* but before *Craig v. Boren*, the Court had the benefit of *Frontiero's* discussion of the factors that would make a classification suspect but it did not have a standard of intermediate scrutiny on which to rely. But for the first time in a case involving nonmarital children, the Court did make reference to some of the *Frontiero* factors. Of the factors mentioned in *Frontiero*, the *Mathews* Court mentioned four. First, with regard to immutability, the Court noted that "the legal status of illegitimacy, however defined, is, like race or national origin, a characteristic determined by causes not within the control of the illegitimate individual" Second, the Court noted that illegitimacy "bears no relation to the individual's ability to participate in and contribute to society." To this point, illegitimate children satisfied two of the criteria. In terms of a third criterion, however--a history of discrimination--the Court said "this discrimination against illegitimates has never approached the severity or pervasiveness of the historic legal and political discrimination against women and Negroes." Fourth, with regard to prejudice against a discrete and insular minority, the Court concluded, "the Act's discrimination between individuals on the basis of their legitimacy does not "command extraordinary protection from the majoritarian political process . . . which our most exacting scrutiny would entail." The *Mathews* Court did not mention the two other *Frontiero* factors—whether the trait was highly visible and whether it invoked a stereotype. As a result, the Court spoke of the proper standard as one of arbitrariness and irrationality and determined that the challenged statute met this standard—"We conclude that the statutory classifications are permissible, however, because they are reasonably related to the likelihood of dependency at death."

3.   Between *Mathews* and *Lalli v. Lalli*, (the next case in this section) the Court decided *Trimble v. Gordon*, 430 U.S. 762 (1977). That case involved the constitutionality of a section of the Illinois Probate Act in which illegitimate children were not allowed to inherit from their fathers. The *Trimble* Court first noted that the proper standard of review was something more than traditional rational basis review but something less than strict scrutiny:

> Appellants urge us to hold that classifications based on illegitimacy are "suspect," so that any justifications must survive "strict scrutiny." We considered and rejected a similar argument last Term in *Mathews v. Lucas*, 427 U.S. 495 (1976). As we recognized in *Lucas*, illegitimacy is analogous in many respects to the personal characteristics that have been held to be suspect when used as the basis of statutory differentiations. We nevertheless concluded that the analogy was not sufficient to require "our most exacting scrutiny." Despite the conclusion that classifications based on illegitimacy fall in a "realm of less than strictest scrutiny," *Lucas* also establishes that the scrutiny "is not a toothless one," a proposition clearly demonstrated by our previous decisions in this area.

The state had asserted that the purpose of the challenged statute was the promotion of legitimate family relationships. The *Trimble* Court conceded that "the family unit [is] perhaps the most fundamental social institution of our society." The problem was not with the purpose but with the relationship between classification and purpose since "a State may [not] attempt to influence the actions of men and women by imposing sanctions on the children born of their illegitimate relationships."

A second justification for the challenged statute was the problem of proving paternity, which the Court conceded "might justify a more demanding standard for illegitimate children claiming under their fathers' estates than that required either for illegitimate children claiming under their mothers' estates or for legitimate children generally." But here again, the Court noted that "[d]ifficulties of proving paternity in some situations do not justify the total statutory disinheritance of illegitimate children whose fathers die intestate." Under the actual facts of *Trimble*, it was undisputed that the claimant was in fact the child of the decedent.

Lalli v. Lalli

439 U.S. 259 (1978)

[After Mario Lalli's death, Robert Lalli petitioned New York's Surrogate's Court on behalf of himself and his sister Maureen, claiming to be Mario's nonmarital children. As proof that Mario had openly acknowledged paternity, Robert offered both a notarized statement in which Mario referred to Robert as his son and sworn affidavits that Mario had acknowledged Robert as his son. Under New York State law, however, in order for an illegitimate child to inherit, a court of competent jurisdiction must have made an order of filiation declaring paternity during the lifetime of the father.]

Mr. Justice POWELL announced the judgment of the Court and delivered an opinion, in which THE CHIEF JUSTICE and Mr. Justice STEWART join.

This case presents a challenge to the constitutionality of § 4-1.2 of New York's Estates, Powers, and Trusts Law, which requires illegitimate children who would inherit from their fathers by intestate succession to provide a particular form of proof of paternity. Legitimate children are not subject to the same requirement.

II

We begin our analysis with *Trimble*. At issue in that case was the constitutionality of an Illinois statute providing that a child born out of wedlock could inherit from his intestate father only if the father had "acknowledged" the child and the child had been legitimated by the intermarriage of the parents. The appellant in *Trimble* was a child born out of wedlock whose father had neither acknowledged her nor married her mother. He had, however, been found to be her father in a judicial decree ordering him to contribute to her support. When the father died intestate, the child was excluded as a distributee because the statutory requirements for inheritance had not been met.

We concluded that the Illinois statute discriminated against illegitimate children in a manner prohibited by the Equal Protection Clause. Although, as decided in *Mathews v. Lucas*, 427 U.S. 495, 506 (1976), and reaffirmed in *Trimble, supra*, 430 U.S., at 767, classifications based on illegitimacy are not subject to "strict scrutiny," they nevertheless are invalid under the Fourteenth Amendment if they are not substantially related to permissible state interests. Upon examination, we found that the Illinois law failed that test.

III

The New York statute, enacted in 1965, was intended to soften the rigors of previous law which permitted illegitimate children to inherit only from their mothers. By lifting the absolute bar to paternal inheritance, § 4-1.2 tended to achieve its desired effect. As in *Trimble*, however, the question before us is whether the remaining statutory obstacles to inheritance by illegitimate children can be squared with the Equal Protection Clause.

A

At the outset we observe that § 4-1.2 is different in important respects from the statutory provision overturned in *Trimble*. The Illinois statute required, in addition to the father's acknowledgment of paternity, the legitimation of the child through the intermarriage of the parents as an absolute precondition to inheritance. This combination of requirements eliminated "the possibility of a middle ground between the extremes of complete exclusion and case-by-case determination of paternity." *Trimble*, 430 U.S., at 770-771. As illustrated by the facts in *Trimble*, even a judicial declaration of paternity was insufficient to permit inheritance.

Under § 4-1.2, by contrast, the marital status of the parents is irrelevant. The single requirement at issue here is an evidentiary one--that the paternity of the father be declared in a judicial proceeding sometime before his death. The child need not have been legitimated in order to inherit from his father. Had the appellant in *Trimble* been governed by § 4-1.2, she would have been a distributee of her father's estate.

A related difference between the two provisions pertains to the state interests said to be served by them. The Illinois law was defended, in part, as a means of encouraging legitimate family relationships. No such justification has been offered in support of § 4-1.2. The Court of Appeals disclaimed that the purpose of the statute, "even in small part, was to discourage illegitimacy, to mold human conduct or to set societal norms." *In re Lalli, supra,* 43 N.Y.2d, at 70. The absence in § 4-1.2 of any requirement that the parents intermarry or otherwise legitimate a child born out of wedlock and our review of the legislative history of the statute, *infra,* at 525-526, confirm this view.

Our inquiry, therefore, is focused narrowly. We are asked to decide whether the discrete procedural demands that § 4-1.2 places on illegitimate children bear an evident and substantial relation to the particular state interests this statute is designed to serve.

B

The primary state goal underlying the challenged aspects of § 4-1.2 is to provide for the just and orderly disposition of property at death. We long have recognized that this is an area with which the States have an interest of considerable magnitude. *Trimble, supra,* 430 U.S., at 771; *Weber v. Aetna Casualty & Surety Co.,* 406 U.S., at 170; *Labine v. Vincent,* 401 U.S., at 538.

This interest is directly implicated in paternal inheritance by illegitimate children because of the peculiar problems of proof that are involved. Establishing maternity is seldom difficult. As one New York Surrogate's Court has observed: "[T]he birth of the child is a recorded or registered event usually taking place in the presence of others. In most cases the child remains with the mother and for a time is necessarily reared by her. That the child is the child of a particular woman is rarely difficult to prove." *In re Ortiz,* 60 Misc.2d 756, 761 (1969). Proof of paternity, by contrast, frequently is difficult when the father is not part of a formal family unit. "The putative father often goes his way unconscious of the birth of a child. Even if conscious, he is very often totally unconcerned because of the absence of any ties to the mother. Indeed the mother may not know *who* is responsible for her pregnancy."

Thus, a number of problems arise that counsel against treating illegitimate children identically to all other heirs of an intestate father. These were the subject of a comprehensive study by the Temporary State Commission on the Modernization, Revision and Simplification of the Law of Estates. This group, known as the Bennett Commission, consisted of individuals experienced in the practical problems of estate administration. The Commission issued its report and recommendations to the legislature in 1965. The statute now codified as § 4-1.2 was included.

Although the overarching purpose of the proposed statute was "to alleviate the plight of the illegitimate child," Commission Report 37, the Bennett Commission considered it necessary to impose the strictures of § 4-1.2 in order to mitigate serious difficulties in the administration of the estates of both testate and intestate decedents:

> An illegitimate, if made an unconditional distributee in intestacy, must be served with process in the estate of his parent... How does one cite and serve an illegitimate of whose existence neither family nor personal representative may be aware? And of greatest concern, how achieve finality of decree in *any* estate when there always exists the possibility however remote of a secret illegitimate lurking in the buried past of a parent or an ancestor of a class of beneficiaries? Finality in decree is essential in the Surrogates' Courts since title to real property passes under such decree. 85 Misc.2d, at 859.

> Even where an individual claiming to be the illegitimate child of a deceased man makes himself known, the difficulties facing an estate are likely to persist. Because of the particular problems of proof, spurious claims may be difficult to expose. The Bennett Commission therefore sought to protect "innocent adults and those rightfully interested in their estates from fraudulent claims of heirship and harassing litigation instituted by those seeking to establish themselves as illegitimate heirs." Commission Report 265.

C

As the State's interests are substantial, we now consider the means adopted by New York to further these interests. In order to avoid the problems described above, the Commission recommended a requirement designed to ensure the accurate resolution of claims of paternity and to minimize the potential for disruption of estate administration. Accuracy is enhanced by placing paternity disputes in a judicial forum during the lifetime of the father. As the New York Court of Appeals observed in its first opinion in this case, the "availability [of the putative father] should be a substantial factor contributing to the reliability of the fact-finding process." *In re Lalli,* 38 N.Y.2d, at 82. In addition, requiring that the order be issued during the father's lifetime permits a man to defend his reputation against "unjust accusations in paternity claims," which was a secondary purpose of § 4-1.2. Commission Report 266.

The administration of an estate will be facilitated, and the possibility of delay and uncertainty minimized, where the entitlement of an illegitimate child to notice and participation is a matter of judicial record before the administration commences. Fraudulent assertions of paternity will be much less likely to succeed, or even to arise, where the proof is put before a court of law at a time when the putative father is available to respond, rather than first brought to light when the distribution of the assets of an estate is in the offing.

Appellant contends that § 4-1.2, like the statute at issue in *Trimble*, excludes "significant categories of illegitimate children" who could be allowed to inherit "without jeopardizing the orderly settlement" of their intestate fathers' estates. *Trimble*, 430 U.S., at 771. He urges that those in his position-"known" illegitimate children who, despite the absence of an order of filiation obtained during their fathers' lifetimes, can present convincing proof of paternity--cannot rationally be denied inheritance as they pose none of the risks § 4-1.2 was intended to minimize.

We do not question that there will be some illegitimate children who would be able to establish their relationship to their deceased fathers without serious disruption of the administration of estates and that, as applied to such individuals, § 4-1.2 appears to operate unfairly. But few statutory classifications are entirely free from the criticism that they sometimes produce inequitable results. Our inquiry under the Equal Protection Clause does not focus on the abstract "fairness" of a state law, but on whether the statute's relation to the state interests it is intended to promote is so tenuous that it lacks the rationality contemplated by the Fourteenth Amendment.

The Illinois statute in *Trimble* was constitutionally unacceptable because it effected a total statutory disinheritance of children born out of wedlock who were not legitimated by the subsequent marriage of their parents. The reach of the statute was far in excess of its justifiable purposes. Section 4-1.2 does not share this defect. Inheritance is barred only where there has been a failure to secure evidence of paternity during the father's lifetime in the manner prescribed by the State. This is not a requirement that inevitably disqualifies an unnecessarily large number of children born out of wedlock.

The New York courts have interpreted § 4-1.2 liberally and in such a way as to enhance its utility to both father and child without sacrificing its strength as a procedural prophylactic. For example, a father of illegitimate children who is willing to acknowledge paternity can waive his defenses in a paternity proceeding, or even institute such a proceeding himself. In addition, the courts have excused "technical" failures by illegitimate children to comply with the statute in order to prevent unnecessary injustice. *E. g., In re Niles*, 53 A.D.2d 983 (1976), appeal denied, 40 N.Y.2d 809 (1977) (filiation order may be signed *nunc pro tunc* to relate back to period prior to father's death when court's factual finding of paternity had been made); *In re Kennedy*, 89 Misc.2d 551, 554 (Surr.Ct.1977) (judicial support order treated as "tantamount to an order of filiation," even though paternity was not specifically declared therein).

As the history of § 4-1.2 clearly illustrates, the New York Legislature desired to "grant to illegitimates *in so far as practicable* rights of inheritance on a par with those enjoyed by legitimate children," Commission Report 265 (emphasis added), while protecting the important state interests we have described. Section 4-1.2 represents a carefully considered legislative judgment as to how this balance best could be achieved.

Even if, as Mr. Justice BRENNAN believes, § 4-1.2 could have been written somewhat more equitably, it is not the function of a court "to hypothesize independently on the desirability or feasibility of any possible alternative[s]" to the statutory scheme formulated by New York.

Mathews v. Lucas, 427 U.S., at 515. "These matters of practical judgment and empirical calculation are for [the State]. . . . In the end, the precise accuracy of [the State's] calculations is not a matter of specialized judicial competence; and we have no basis to question their detail beyond the evident consistency and substantiality."

We conclude that the requirement imposed by § 4-1.2 on illegitimate children who would inherit from their fathers is substantially related to the important state interests the statute is intended to promote. We therefore find no violation of the Equal Protection Clause.

The judgment of the New York Court of Appeals is *affirmed.*

NOTES

1. The sequence of *Labine-Trimble-Lalli*, which seem to contradict each other, and the fact that the *Lalli* Court did not have a majority opinion, show that the Court in the 1970's had not yet established an agreed standard of review for illegitimacy classifications, nor had it determined what kind of illegitimacy classifications would survive constitutional scrutiny. The *Lalli* Court for the first time suggested that it would apply a formal level of heightened scrutiny to illegitimacy classifications—"classifications based on illegitimacy are not subject to 'strict scrutiny,' they nevertheless are invalid under the Fourteenth Amendment if they are not substantially related to permissible state interests." This is a hybrid standard. The reference to a "substantial relationship" is the language of intermediate scrutiny while the reference to "permissible state interests" is the language of rational basis review.

2. The *Lalli* Court was careful to note the purpose of the challenged statute was *not* "even in small part ... to discourage illegitimacy, to mold human conduct or to set societal norms." Rather, the purpose of the rule was to address "the peculiar problems of proof" that are involved in paternal inheritance by illegitimate children. As the Court noted, "[e]stablishing maternity is seldom difficult," but "[p]roof of paternity, by contrast, frequently is difficult when the father is not part of a formal family unit." The procedure required by the challenged statute—a judicial determination during the father's life—was sufficiently related to the purpose of proving paternity. At the very end of its decision, the *Lalli* Court once again cited a hybrid standard of review. The Court stated that the test was both (1) that the statute's relationship to its purpose must not be "so tenuous that it lacks the *rationality* contemplated by the Fourteenth Amendment," and (2) that the statutory requirement must be "substantially related to the important state interests the statute is intended to promote."

3. ***The Court Adopts Intermediate Scrutiny for Classifications That Disadvantage Nonmarital Children***

During the 1980's the Court decided three cases that each dealt with statutes that limited the time during which a nonmarital child could bring a paternity or support action against his or her father. The time limits in the three cases were one year (*Mills v. Habluetzel*), two years (*Picket v. Brown*), and six years (*Clark v. Jeter*). The Court invalidated all three statutes of limitation and, by the time of *Clark v. Jeter,* formally adopted an intermediate standard or review for classifications that disadvantage nonmarital children.

Mills v. Habluetzel
456 U.S. 91 (1982)

[A Texas mother filed suit to establish the paternity of her baby nineteen months after giving birth out of wedlock. However, a Texas statute required that paternity be established within twelve months of an illegitimate child's birth. The mother argued that this burden on her child violated the Equal Protection Clause.]

Justice REHNQUIST delivered the opinion of the Court.

This Court has held that once a State posits a judicially enforceable right of children to support from their natural fathers, the Equal Protection Clause of the Fourteenth Amendment prohibits the State from denying that same right to illegitimate children. *Gomez v. Perez*, 409 U.S. 535 (1973). In this case we are required to determine the extent to which the right of illegitimate children recognized in *Gomez* may be circumscribed by a State's interest in avoiding the prosecution of stale or fraudulent claims.

III

Our decision in *Gomez* held that "a State may not invidiously discriminate against illegitimate children by denying them substantial benefits accorded children generally." 409 U.S., at 538. Specifically, we held that a State which grants an opportunity for legitimate children to obtain paternal support must also grant that opportunity to illegitimate children. If *Gomez* and the equal protection principles which underlie it are to have any meaning, it is clear that the support opportunity provided by the State to illegitimate children must be more than illusory. The period for asserting the right to support must be sufficiently long to permit those who normally have an interest in such children to bring an action on their behalf despite the difficult personal, family, and financial circumstances that often surround the birth of a child outside of wedlock. It would hardly satisfy the demands of equal protection and the holding of *Gomez* to remove an "impenetrable barrier" to support, only to replace it with an opportunity so truncated that few could utilize it effectively.

The fact that Texas must provide illegitimate children with a bona fide opportunity to obtain paternal support does not mean, however, that it must adopt procedures for illegitimate children that are coterminous with those accorded legitimate children. Paternal support suits on behalf of illegitimate children contain an element that such suits for legitimate children do not contain: proof of paternity. Such proof is often sketchy and strongly contested, frequently turning upon conflicting testimony from only two witnesses. Indeed, the problems of proving paternity have been recognized repeatedly by this Court. *Parham v. Hughes*, 441 U.S. 347, 357 (1979); *Lalli v. Lalli*, 439 U.S. 259, 269 (1978); *Trimble v. Gordon*, 430 U.S. 762 (1977); *Gomez v. Perez*, 409 U.S., at 538.[FN4]

[FN4] We previously have recognized that blood tests are highly probative in proving paternity, *Little v. Streater*, 452 U.S. 1, 6-8 (1981), but disagree with appellant's contention that their existence negates the State's interest in avoiding the prosecution of stale or fraudulent claims.

Traditional blood tests do not prove paternity. They prove nonpaternity, excluding from the class of possible fathers a high percentage of the general male population. H. Krause, Illegitimacy: Law and Social

This interest is particularly real under Texas procedures. Texas law requires that putative fathers submit to blood tests. Refusal to submit to the tests may result in a citation for contempt, and may be introduced to the jury as evidence that the putative father has not been biologically excluded from the class of possible fathers. The results of the blood tests are introduced at a pretrial conference held for the purpose of dismissing the complaint if the father has been excluded by the tests from the class of possible fathers. Thus, the only paternity cases which actually go to trial in Texas are those in which the putative father has refused to submit to blood tests or has not been excluded by their results, cases in which conventional types of evidence are of paramount importance.

Therefore, in support suits by illegitimate children more than in support suits by legitimate children, the State has an interest in preventing the prosecution of stale or fraudulent claims, and may impose greater restrictions on the former than it imposes on the latter. Such restrictions will survive equal protection scrutiny to the extent they are substantially related to a legitimate state interest. See *Lalli v. Lalli, supra*, 439 U.S., at 265; *Trimble v. Gordon, supra*, 430 U.S., at 767; *Mathews v. Lucas*, 427 U.S. 495, 510 (1976). The State's interest in avoiding the litigation of stale or fraudulent claims will justify those periods of limitation that are sufficiently long to present a real threat of loss or diminution of evidence, or an increased vulnerability to fraudulent claims.

The equal protection analysis in this case, therefore, focuses on two related requirements. First, the period for obtaining support granted by Texas to illegitimate children must be sufficiently long in duration to present a reasonable opportunity for those with an interest in such children to assert claims on their behalf. Second, any time limitation placed on that opportunity must be substantially related to the State's interest in avoiding the litigation of stale or fraudulent claims. Applying these two requirements to the one-year right granted by Texas, we find a denial of equal protection.

By granting illegitimate children only one year in which to establish paternity, Texas has failed to provide them with an adequate opportunity to obtain support. Paternity suits in Texas "may be brought by any person with an interest in the child," but during the child's early years will often be brought by the mother. It requires little experience to appreciate the obstacles to such suits that confront unwed mothers during the child's first year. Financial difficulties caused by childbirth expenses or a birth-related loss of income, continuing affection for the child's father, a desire to avoid disapproval of family and community, or the emotional strain and confusion that often attend the birth of an illegitimate child all encumber a mother's filing of a paternity suit within 12 months of birth. Even if the mother seeks public financial assistance and assigns the child's support claim to the State, it is not improbable that 12 months would elapse without the

---

Policy 123-136 (1971). Thus the fact that a certain male is not excluded by these tests does not prove that he is the child's natural father, only that he is a member of the limited class of possible fathers. More recent developments in the field of blood testing have sought not only to "prove nonpaternity" but also to predict paternity with a high degree of probability. See *Terasaki*, Resolution by HLA Testing of 1000 Paternity Cases Not Excluded by ABO Testing, 16 *J.Fam.L.* 543 (1978). The proper evidentiary weight to be given to these techniques is still a matter of academic dispute. See, *e.g., Jaffee*, Comment on the Judicial Use of HLA Paternity Test Results and Other Statistical Evidence: Response to *Terasaki*, 17 *J.Fam.L.* 457 (1979). Whatever evidentiary rule the courts of a particular State choose to follow, if the blood test evidence does not exclude a certain male, he must thereafter turn to more conventional forms of proof-evidence of lack of access to the mother, his own testimony, the testimony of others-to prove that, although not excluded by the blood test, he is not in fact the child's father. As to this latter form of proof, the State clearly has an interest in litigating claims while the evidence is relatively fresh.

filing of a claim. Several months could pass before a mother finds the need to seek such assistance, takes steps to obtain it, and is willing to join the State in litigation against the natural father. A sense of the inadequacy of this one-year period is accentuated by a realization that failure to file within 12 months "results in illegitimates being forever barred from the right to sue their natural father for child support," *In re Miller*, 605 S.W.2d, at 334, while legitimate children may seek such support at any time until the age of 18.

Moreover, this unrealistically short time limitation is not substantially related to the State's interest in avoiding the prosecution of stale or fraudulent claims. In *Gomez* we recognized that the problems of proof in paternity suits "are not to be lightly brushed aside," but held that such problems do not justify a complete denial of support rights to illegitimate children. 409 U.S. at 538. Neither do they justify a period of limitation which so restricts those rights as effectively to extinguish them. We can conceive of no evidence essential to paternity suits that invariably will be lost in only one year, nor is it evident that the passage of 12 months will appreciably increase the likelihood of fraudulent claims.

Accordingly, we conclude that the one-year period for establishing paternity denies illegitimate children in Texas the equal protection of law. The judgment of the Texas Court of Civil Appeals is reversed, and the case is remanded for further proceedings not inconsistent with this opinion.

NOTES

1. In terms of the appropriate standard of review, the *Mills* Court continued to follow the hybrid measure set forth earlier. Restrictions on nonmarital children will survive equal protection scrutiny to the extent they are "substantially related to a legitimate state interest." The Court found that the state had a legitimate interest: the "interest in avoiding the litigation of stale or fraudulent claims," which would justify those periods of limitation that are "sufficiently long to present a real threat of loss or diminution of evidence, or an increased vulnerability to fraudulent claims." This standard resulted in a two-part test of statutes of limitation:

> First, the period for obtaining support granted by Texas to illegitimate children must be sufficiently long in duration to present a reasonable opportunity for those with an interest in such children to assert claims on their behalf. Second, any time limitation placed on that opportunity must be substantially related to the State's interest in avoiding the litigation of stale or fraudulent claims.

The Court determined that the one-year statute of limitations did not meet this standard.

2. Although the *Mills* Court invalidated the different treatment of marital and nonmarital children in terms of the time within which a support action could be brought, it made clear that the rule it was adopting would not necessarily invalidate all distinctions between marital and nonmarital children. The Court insisted, "The fact that Texas must provide illegitimate children with a bona fide opportunity to obtain paternal support does not mean, however, that it must adopt procedures for illegitimate children that are coterminous with those accorded legitimate children." The difference between the two groups was proof of paternity, and therefore, the state could impose greater restrictions on illegitimate children bringing support suits than it imposed on such suits brought by legitimate children.

Pickett v. Brown
462 U.S. 1 (1983)

[When her son was ten years old, Frances Annette Pickett filed an action to establish that Braxton Brown was his father, thereby laying the foundation for the court to order support payments. Brown, who never acknowledged paternity of or provided financial support to the child, moved to have the suit dismissed pursuant to a Tennessee statute that required that paternity be established within the first two years of a child's birth. The mother challenged the constitutionality of the limitations period.]

Justice BRENNAN delivered the opinion of the Court.

This case requires us to decide the constitutionality of a provision of a Tennessee statute that imposes a two-year limitations period on paternity and child support actions brought on behalf of certain illegitimate children.

I

Under Tennessee law both fathers and mothers are responsible for the support of their minor children. This duty of support is enforceable throughout the child's minority. Tennessee law also makes the father of a child born out of wedlock responsible for "the necessary support and education of the child." Enforcement of this obligation depends on the establishment of paternity. Tennessee Code Ann. § 36-224(1) (1977) provides for the filing of a petition which can lead both to the establishment of paternity and to enforcement of the father's duty of support. With a few exceptions, however, the petition must be filed within two years of the child's birth.

II

We have considered on several occasions during the past 15 years the constitutional validity of statutory classifications based on illegitimacy. See, *e.g., Mills v. Habluetzel, supra; United States v. Clark,* 445 U.S. 23 (1980); *Lalli v. Lalli,* 439 U.S. 259 (1978); *Trimble v. Gordon,* 430 U.S. 762 (1977); *Mathews v. Lucas,* 427 U.S. 495 (1976); *Jiminez v. Weinberger,* 417 U.S. 628 (1974); *New Jersey Welfare Rights Org. v. Cahill,* 411 U.S. 619 (1973); *Gomez v. Perez,* 409 U.S. 535 (1973); *Weber v. Aetna Casualty & Surety Co.,* 406 U.S. 164 (1972); *Glona v. American Guarantee Co.,* 391 U.S. 73 (1968); *Levy v. Louisiana,* 391 U.S. 68 (1968). In several of these cases, we have held the classifications invalid. See, *e.g., Mills v. Habluetzel, supra; Trimble v. Gordon, supra; Jiminez v. Weinberger, supra; New Jersey Welfare Rights Org. v. Cahill, supra; Gomez v. Perez, supra; Weber v. Aetna Casualty & Surety Co., supra; Glona v. American Guarantee Co., supra; Levy v. Louisiana, supra.* Our consideration of these cases has been animated by a special concern for discrimination against illegitimate children. As the Court stated in Weber:

> The status of illegitimacy has expressed through the ages society's condemnation of irresponsible liaisons beyond the bonds of marriage. But visiting this condemnation on the head of an infant is illogical and unjust. Moreover, imposing disabilities on the illegitimate child is contrary to the basic concept of our system that legal burdens should bear some relationship to individual responsibility or wrongdoing. Obviously, no child is responsible for his birth and penalizing the illegitimate child is an ineffectual-as well as

an unjust-way of deterring the parent. Courts are powerless to prevent the social opprobrium suffered by these hapless children, but the Equal Protection Clause does enable us to strike down discriminatory laws relating to status of birth where-as in this case-the classification is justified by no legitimate state interest, compelling or otherwise. 406 U.S. at 175-176 (footnotes omitted).

In view of the history of treating illegitimate children less favorably than legitimate ones, we have subjected statutory classifications based on illegitimacy to a heightened level of scrutiny. Although we have held that classifications based on illegitimacy are not "suspect," or subject to "our most exacting scrutiny," *Trimble v. Gordon,* 430 U.S., at 767; *Mathews v. Lucas,* 427 U.S., at 506, the scrutiny applied to them "is not a toothless one. . . ." *Id.* at 510. In *United States v. Clark, supra,* we stated that "a classification based on illegitimacy is unconstitutional unless it bears 'an evident and substantial relation to the particular ... interests [the] statute is designed to serve.'" 445 U.S., at 27. See also *Lalli v. Lalli,* 439 U.S., at 265 (plurality opinion) ("classifications based on illegitimacy ... are invalid under the Fourteenth Amendment if they are not substantially related to permissible state interests"). We applied a similar standard of review to a classification based on illegitimacy last Term in *Mills v. Habluetzel,* 456 U.S. 91 (1982). We stated that restrictions on support suits by illegitimate children "will survive equal protection scrutiny to the extent they are substantially related to a legitimate state interest." *Id.* at 99.

[The Court here discussed *Gomez* and *Mills.*]

III

Much of what was said in the opinions in *Mills* is relevant here, and the principles discussed in *Mills* require us to invalidate this limitations period on equal protection grounds.

Although Tennessee grants illegitimate children a right to paternal support, and provides a mechanism for enforcing that right, the imposition of a two-year period within which a paternity suit must be brought, restricts the right of certain illegitimate children to paternal support in a way that the identical right of legitimate children is not restricted. In this respect, some illegitimate children in Tennessee are treated differently from, and less favorably than, legitimate children.

Under *Mills,* the first question is whether the two-year limitations period is sufficiently long to provide a reasonable opportunity to those with an interest in illegitimate children to bring suit on their behalf. The statute creates exceptions to the limitations period if the father has provided support for the child or has acknowledged his paternity in writing. The statute also allows suit to be brought by the State or by any person at any time prior to a child's eighteenth birthday if the child is, or is liable to become, a public charge. This addresses Justice O'CONNOR's point in *Mills* that a State has a strong interest in preventing increases in its welfare rolls. For the illegitimate child whose claim is not covered by one of the exceptions in the statute, however, the two-year limitations period severely restricts his right to paternal support. The obstacles to filing a paternity and child support suit within a year after the child's birth, which the Court discussed in *Mills, see id.* at 100, are likely to persist during the child's second year as well. The mother may experience financial difficulties caused not only by the child's birth, but also by a loss of income attributable to the need to care for the child. Moreover, "continuing affection for the child's father, a desire to avoid disapproval of family and community, or the emotional strain and confusion that often attend the birth of an illegitimate child," 456 U.S., at 100, may inhibit a mother from filing a paternity suit on behalf of the child within two years after the child's birth. Justice O'CONNOR suggested in *Mills* that the emotional strain experienced by a mother and her desire to avoid family or community disapproval "may continue years after the child is born." These considerations compel a conclusion that the two-year limitations period does not provide illegitimate children with "an adequate opportunity to obtain support."

The second inquiry under *Mills* is whether the time limitation placed on an illegitimate child's right to obtain support is substantially related to the State's interest in avoiding the litigation of stale or fraudulent claims. In this case, it is clear that the two-year limitations period governing paternity and support suits brought on behalf of certain illegitimate children does not satisfy this test.

First, a two-year limitations period is only a small improvement in degree over the one-year period at issue in *Mills*. It, too, amounts to a restriction effectively extinguishing the support rights of illegitimate children that cannot be justified by the problems of proof surrounding paternity actions. As was the case in *Mills*, "[w]e can conceive of no evidence essential to paternity suits that will be lost in only [two years], nor is it evident that the passage of [24] months will appreciably increase the likelihood of fraudulent claims."

Second, the provisions of [the challenged statute] undermine the State's argument that the limitations period is substantially related to its interest in avoiding the litigation of stale or fraudulent claims. As noted, [the statute] establishes an exception to the statute of limitations for illegitimate children who are, or are likely to become, public charges. Paternity and support suits may be brought on behalf of these children by the State or by any person at any time prior to the child's eighteenth birthday. The State argues that this distinction between illegitimate children receiving public assistance and those who are not is justified by the State's interest in protecting public revenue. Putting aside the question of whether this interest can justify such radically different treatment of two groups of illegitimate children, the State's argument does not address the different treatment accorded illegitimate children who are not receiving public assistance and legitimate children. This difference in treatment is allegedly justified by the State's interest in preventing the litigation of stale or fraudulent claims. But as the exception for children receiving public assistance demonstrates, the State perceives no prohibitive problem in litigating paternity claims throughout a child's minority. There is no apparent reason why claims filed on behalf of illegitimate children who are receiving public assistance when they are more than two years old would not be just as stale, or as vulnerable to fraud, as claims filed on behalf of illegitimate children who are not public charges at the same age. The exception in the statute, therefore, seriously undermines the State's argument that the different treatment accorded legitimate and illegitimate children is substantially related to the legitimate state interest in preventing the prosecution of stale or fraudulent claims and compels a conclusion that the two-year limitations period is not substantially related to a legitimate state interest.

Third, Tennessee tolls most actions during a child's minority. In *Parlato v. Howe*, 470 F. Supp. 996 (ED Tenn.1979), the court stated that "[t]he legal disability statute represents a long-standing policy of the State of Tennessee to protect potential causes of action by minors during the period of their minority." In view of this policy, the court held that a statute imposing a limitations period on medical malpractice actions "was not intended to interfere with the operation of the legal disability statute." *Id.* at 998. Accord, *Braden v. Yoder*, 592 S.W.2d 896 (Tenn.App.1979). Many civil actions are fraught with problems of proof, but Tennessee has chosen to overlook these problems in most instances in favor of protecting the interests of minors. In paternity and child support actions brought on behalf of certain illegitimate children, however, the State instead has chosen to focus on the problems of proof and to impose on these suits a short limitations period.

Although the Tennessee Supreme Court stated that the inapplicability of the tolling provision to paternity actions did not "alone" require invalidation of the limitations period, 638 S.W.2d, at 380, it is clear that this factor, when considered in combination with others already discussed, may lead one "to question whether the burden placed on illegitimates is designed to advance permissible state interests." 456 U.S., at 105 (O'CONNOR, J., concurring).

It is not critical to this argument that the right to file a paternity action generally is given to the mother. It is the child's interests that are at stake. The father's duty of support is owed to the child, not to the mother. Moreover, it is the child who has an interest in establishing a relationship to his father. This reality is reflected in the provision of [the statute] that allows the child to bring suit if the mother is dead or disabled. Cf. S.Rep. No. 93-1356, p. 52 (1974) U.S.Code Cong. & Admin. News 1974, p. 8133 ("[T]he interest primarily at stake in [a] paternity action [is] that of the child"). Restrictive periods of limitation, therefore, necessarily affect the interests of the child and their validity must be assessed in that light.

Finally, the relationship between a statute of limitations and the State's interest in preventing the litigation of stale or fraudulent paternity claims has become more attenuated as scientific advances in blood testing have alleviated the problems of proof surrounding paternity actions. As Justice O'CONNOR pointed out in *Mills,* these advances have "dramatically reduc[ed] the possibility that a defendant will be falsely accused of being the illegitimate child's father." *Id.* at 104, n. 2 (concurring opinion). Although Tennessee permits the introduction of blood test results only in cases "where definite exclusion [of paternity] is established," it is noteworthy that blood tests currently can achieve a "mean probability of exclusion [of] at least ... 90 percent . . ." Miale, Jennings, Rettberg, Sell & Krause, Joint AMA-ABA Guidelines: Present Status of Serologic Testing in Problems of Disputed Parentage, 10 Family L.Q. 247, 256 (1976). In *Mills,* the Court rejected the argument that recent advances in blood testing negated the State's interest in avoiding the prosecution of stale or fraudulent claims. 456 U.S. at 98, n. 4. It is not inconsistent with this view, however, to suggest that advances in blood testing render more attenuated the relationship between a statute of limitations and the State's interest in preventing the prosecution of stale or fraudulent paternity claims. This is an appropriate consideration in determining whether a period of limitations governing paternity actions brought on behalf of illegitimate children is substantially related to a legitimate state interest.

IV

The two-year limitations period established by Tenn. Code Ann. § 36-224(2) does not provide certain illegitimate children with an adequate opportunity to obtain support and is not substantially related to the legitimate state interest in preventing the litigation of stale or fraudulent claims. It therefore denies certain illegitimate children the equal protection of the laws guaranteed by the Fourteenth Amendment. Accordingly, the judgment of the Tennessee Supreme Court is reversed and the case is remanded for proceedings not inconsistent with this opinion.

It is so ordered.

NOTES

1. The *Pickett* Court continues to cite a hybrid standard of review: restrictions on support suits by illegitimate children "will survive equal protection scrutiny to the extent they are substantially

related to a legitimate state interest." For the first time, however, the Court mentions that "scientific advances in blood testing have alleviated the problems of proof surrounding paternity actions." The Court, writing its opinion in 1983, noted that "blood tests currently can achieve a 'mean probability of exclusion [of] at least ... 90 percent. . . .'" As will be seen in Section 5, *infra*, current DNA tests can determine paternity with nearly 100% accuracy. Thus, concerns about the problems of proof of paternity and the prosecution of stale or fraudulent claims are far less valid.

Clark v. Jeter
486 U.S. 456 (1988)

[Tiffany Jeter was born out of wedlock in 1973. Ten years later her mother, Cherlyn Clark, filed a support order on behalf of her daughter. Under Pennsylvania law, illegitimate children were required to establish paternity within six years of birth. Genetic testing established that there was a 99.3% probability that Gene Jeter was Tiffany's father and, when support was denied, her mother raised a constitutional challenge to the statute on Fourteenth Amendment and Due Process grounds.]

Justice O'CONNOR delivered the opinion of the Court.

Under Pennsylvania law, an illegitimate child must prove paternity before seeking support from his or her father, and a suit to establish paternity ordinarily must be brought within six years of an illegitimate child's birth. By contrast, a legitimate child may seek support from his or her parents at any time. We granted certiorari to consider the constitutionality of this legislative scheme.

II

In considering whether state legislation violates the Equal Protection Clause of the Fourteenth Amendment, we apply different levels of scrutiny to different types of classifications. At a minimum, a statutory classification must be rationally related to a legitimate governmental purpose. *San Antonio Independent School Dist. v. Rodriguez*, 411 U.S. 1, 17 (1973); Cf. *Lyng v. Automobile Workers*, 485 U.S. 360, 370 (1988). Classifications based on race or national origin, e.g., *Loving v. Virginia*, 388 U.S. 1, 11 (1967), and classifications affecting fundamental rights, e.g., *Harper v. Virginia Bd. of Elections*, 383 U.S. 663, 672 (1966), are given the most exacting scrutiny. Between these extremes of rational basis review and strict scrutiny lies a level of intermediate scrutiny, which generally has been applied to discriminatory classifications based on sex or illegitimacy. See, e.g., *Mississippi University for Women v. Hogan*, 458 U.S. 718, 723-724, and n. 9 (1982); *Mills v. Habluetzel*, 456 U.S. 91, 99 (1982); *Craig v. Boren*, 429 U.S. 190, 197 (1976); *Mathews v. Lucas*, 427 U.S. 495, 505-506 (1976).

To withstand intermediate scrutiny, a statutory classification must be substantially related to an important governmental objective. Consequently we have invalidated classifications that burden illegitimate children for the sake of punishing the illicit relations of their parents, because "visiting this condemnation on the head of an infant is illogical and unjust." *Weber v. Aetna Casualty & Surety Co.*, 406 U.S. 164, 175 (1972). Yet, in the seminal case concerning the child's right to support, this Court acknowledged that it might be appropriate to treat illegitimate children differently in the support context because of "lurking problems with respect to proof of paternity." *Gomez v. Perez*, 409 U.S. 535, 538 (1973).

This Court has developed a particular framework for evaluating equal protection challenges to statutes of limitations that apply to suits to establish paternity, and thereby limit the ability of illegitimate children to obtain support.

> First, the period for obtaining support ... must be sufficiently long in duration to present a reasonable opportunity for those with an interest in such children to assert claims on their behalf. Second, any time limitation placed on that opportunity must be substantially related to the State's interest in avoiding the litigation of stale or fraudulent claims. *Mills v. Habluetzel,* 456 U.S., at 99-100.

[The Court here discussed *Mills v. Habluetzel* and *Pickett v. Brown.*]

In light of this authority, we conclude that Pennsylvania's 6-year statute of limitations violates the Equal Protection Clause. Even six years does not necessarily provide a reasonable opportunity to assert a claim on behalf of an illegitimate child. "The unwillingness of the mother to file a paternity action on behalf of her child, which could stem from her relationship with the natural father or ... from the emotional strain of having an illegitimate child, or even from the desire to avoid community and family disapproval, may continue years after the child is born. The problem may be exacerbated if, as often happens, the mother herself is a minor." *Mills, supra,* at 105, n. 4. Not all of these difficulties are likely to abate in six years. A mother might realize only belatedly "a loss of income attributable to the need to care for the child," *Pickett, supra,* 462 U.S. at 12. Furthermore, financial difficulties are likely to increase as the child matures and incurs expenses for clothing, school, and medical care. See, *e.g., Moore v. McNamara,* 40 Conn.Supp. 6, 11, 12 (1984) (invalidating a 3-year statute of limitations). Thus it is questionable whether a State acts reasonably when it requires most paternity and support actions to be brought within six years of an illegitimate child's birth.

We do not rest our decision on this ground, however, for it is not entirely evident that six years would necessarily be an unreasonable limitations period for child support actions involving illegitimate children. We are, however, confident that the 6-year statute of limitations is not substantially related to Pennsylvania's interest in avoiding the litigation of stale or fraudulent claims. In a number of circumstances, Pennsylvania permits the issue of paternity to be litigated more than six years after the birth of an illegitimate child. The statute itself permits a suit to be brought more than six years after the child's birth if it is brought within two years of a support payment made by the father. And in other types of suits, Pennsylvania places no limits on when the issue of paternity may be litigated. For example, the intestacy statute, 20 Pa. Cons. Stat. § 2107(3) (1982), permits a child born out of wedlock to establish paternity as long as "there is clear and convincing evidence that the man was the father of the child." Likewise, no statute of limitations applies to a father's action to establish paternity. *In re Mengel,* 287 Pa.Super. 186 (1981). Recently, the Pennsylvania Legislature enacted a statute that tolls most other civil actions during a child's minority. 42 Pa. Cons. Stat. § 5533(b) (Supp.1987). In *Pickett* and *Mills,* similar tolling statutes cast doubt on the State's purported interest in avoiding the litigation of stale or fraudulent claims. 462 U.S., at 15-16; 456 U.S., at 104-105. Pennsylvania's tolling statute has the same implications here.

A more recent indication that Pennsylvania does not consider proof problems insurmountable is the enactment by the Pennsylvania Legislature in 1985 of an 18-year statute of limitations for paternity and support actions. 23 Pa. Cons. Stat. § 4343(b) (1985). To be sure the legislature did not act spontaneously, but rather under the threat of losing some federal funds. Nevertheless, the new statute is a tacit concession that proof problems are not overwhelming. The legislative history of the federal Child Support Enforcement Amendments explains why Congress thought such statutes of limitations are reasonable. Congress adverted to the problem of stale and fraudulent claims, but recognized that increasingly sophisticated tests for genetic markers permit the exclusion of over 99% of those who might be accused of paternity, regardless of the age of the child. H.R.Rep. No. 98-527, p. 38 (1983). This scientific evidence is available throughout the child's minority, and it is an additional reason to doubt that Pennsylvania had a substantial reason for limiting the time within which paternity and support actions could be brought.

We conclude that the Pennsylvania statute does not withstand heightened scrutiny under the Equal Protection Clause. We therefore find it unnecessary to reach Clark's due process claim. The judgment of the Superior Court is reversed, and the case is remanded for further proceedings not inconsistent with this opinion.

It is so ordered.

NOTES

1. Twenty years after it first invalidated a classification disadvantaging nonmarital children in *Levy v. Louisiana*, the Court in *Clark v. Jeter* finally declared in a formal way that nonmarital children are a quasi-suspect class and that classifications disadvantaging them should receive intermediate scrutiny. The Court said:

> Between these extremes of rational basis review and strict scrutiny lies a level of intermediate scrutiny, which generally has been applied to discriminatory classifications based on sex or illegitimacy. See, *e.g., Mississippi University for Women v. Hogan*, 458 U.S. 718, 723-724, and n. 9 (1982); *Mills v. Habluetzel*, 456 U.S. 91, 99 (1982); *Craig v. Boren*, 429 U.S. 190, 197 (1976); *Mathews v. Lucas*, 427 U.S. 495, 505-506 (1976). . . . To withstand intermediate scrutiny, a statutory classification must be substantially related to an important governmental objective.

The Court's list of citations supporting its assertion is slightly disingenuous. Of the four cases cited, two involved gender discrimination, not discrimination against nonmarital children. The other two cited cases did involve discrimination against nonmarital children, but neither one applied the full-blown version of intermediate scrutiny. It was not until *Clark v. Jeter* in 1988 that the Court formally adopted the intermediate scrutiny standard for nonmarital children.

4. *SHOULD NONMARITAL CHILDREN BE CONSIDERED A QUASI-SUSPECT CLASS?*

The time frame from when the Supreme Court first invalidated a gender classification (1971) to when a plurality of the Court declared gender a suspect classification (1973) to when the Court invented intermediate scrutiny (1976) was a period of only five years. On the other hand, with regard to classifications disadvantaging nonmarital children, the period of time from when the first invalidated an illegitimacy classification (1968) until it formally applied intermediate scrutiny to nonmarital children (1988), was twenty years. In a sense, the Court backed into intermediate scrutiny. One of the effects of this long-term, informal development of intermediate scrutiny of illegitimacy is that there is no analogous case to *Frontiero v. Richardson*, where the Court focused on the factors that would make a classification suspect and then applied each of them to gender. When the Court finally applied intermediate scrutiny to illegitimacy classifications in *Clark v. Jeter*, it claimed that it had been doing so for a long time, and therefore, did not need to justify that level of review by reference to certain factors.

Mathews v. Lucas comes closest to considering the factors that would make the status of nonmarital children quasi-suspect. There, the Court alluded to four of the *Frontiero* factors (see, *supra*, at IV.B.2.b.) but then, using a rational basis standard, upheld the statute. If one applies the *Frontiero* factors, should nonmarital children be a quasi-suspect class? Consider each of the factors:

(1) *A history of discrimination.* There is no question that there is a long and substantial history of legal and social discrimination against nonmarital children. A nonmarital child had no right to paternal support, could not inherit from his or her father, and could not qualify as a dependent child under government benefit programs or as a surviving dependent under certain statutory causes of action.

(2) *Stereotype.* This is probably the least important factor and there may be no strong stereotype associated with nonmarital status in general, but some politicians have equated that status with dependency on government benefit programs or part of a failed family structure.

(3) *Highly visible trait.* Clearly, the nonmarital status of one's parents is not at all a visible trait.

(4) *Discrete and insular minority that needs protection from the majoritarian political process.* Nonmarital children in general are not a discrete and insular group and there is no history of excluding them from the political process, either in terms of right to vote or in the ability to run for political office.

(5) *Immutable characteristic.* To the extent immutable refers to the fact that a characteristic is determined solely by the accident of birth, nonmarital status clearly is immutable. Further, to the extent that disadvantaging those with this trait is "inconsistent with the basic legal concept that 'legal burdens should bear some relationship to individual responsibility,'" then it is immutable. If, however, "immutable" means "cannot be changed," then the trait does not clearly satisfy the criterion since, in many states, a nonmarital child can be legitimated, although usually only with the father's consent.

(6) *Bears no relation to ability to perform or contribute to society.* Unlike age or mental capacity, the marital status of one's parents bears no relation to an individual's abilities.

Thus, nonmarital children clearly satisfy two of the *Frontiero* factors: a history of discrimination and that the trait bears no relation to ability to perform or contribute to society. There is some less solid support for two more of the factors: stereotype and immutable characteristic. And there is no evidence at all for two of the factors: highly visible trait and discrete and insular minority. If one compares these factors as applied to nonmarital children on the one hand and gay men and women on the other, it seems far more likely that gay men and women should be considered a quasi-suspect class. On this point, *see* Ch.VI.B.

5. DOES THE AVAILABILITY OF RELIABLE DNA EVIDENCE ELIMINATE THE FINAL REMAINING JUSTIFICATION FOR TREATING NONMARITAL CHILDREN DIFFERENTLY?

The Supreme Court's cases on nonmarital children make clear that a state may not treat marital and nonmarital children differently in order to condemn or punish the extra-marital relations of their parents. That purpose itself is impermissible, and the means—punishing the children—are not rationally related to it. The Court has, however, approved an alternative justification for classifications regarding nonmarital children—rules designed to deal with the problem of proof of paternity.

The common law background of this problem is relevant to the law today. Before the modern age, it was not possible to know with certainty who was the father of a child. While the mother would always be present at a birth, that was not necessarily the case for the father, and there was no blood-typing or DNA testing to provide conclusive proof of fatherhood. In a world where proof of paternity could never be conclusive, the common law adopted a presumption that a child born to married parents was the child of the husband. *See*, Michael H. v. Gerald D., 491 U.S. 110, 124-25 (1989). This presumption was so strong that it could not be rebutted even with evidence of blood test that showed a 98.07% probability that another man was the father. *Id.* The advantage of this presumption of legitimacy was that marital children did not have to provide any additional proof to inherit property, demand parental support, or to benefit from statutes that protected dependent children.

For nonmarital children, on the other hand, there was no presumption of paternity. Without highly reliable evidence such as the modern day DNA test, at common law these children had a difficult burden in proving paternity. Addressing this problem was, according to the Court, a permissible state interest.

In recent years, there has been an increasing use of DNA evidence to prove paternity. In 1983, in *Pickett v. Brown*, the Court conceded that "it is noteworthy that blood tests currently can achieve a "mean probability of exclusion [of] at least ... 90 percent." In 1988, in *Clark v. Jeter*, the Court referred to blood tests, "which showed a 99.3% probability" of paternity. According to an article published in 1993, the results of DNA tests, when combined with other genetic marking tests, produce a probability of paternity of 99.999999%. E. Donald Shapiro *et al*, *The DNA Paternity Test: Legislating the Future Paternity Action*, 7 J. L. 4 Health 1 (1993). In light of the availability of this highly probative evidence, it seems that "the problem of proof of paternity" is no longer a sound reason for legislatures to treat nonmarital children differently from marital children.

That being said, there is still a Supreme Court precedent that suggests that legislatures need not make use of the best available evidence in identifying paternity. In *Nguyen v. I.N.S.*, 533 U.S. 53 (2001), the Court considered an INS citizenship rule that granted or denied citizenship to children born outside the United States depending on whether their citizen-parent was the mother or the father. The Court treated the case as one of gender discrimination. *See*, *supra*, Chapter 3.D.. The INS rule also treated nonmarital children differently from marital children so the Court could have also analyzed the challenged statue under its reasoning in cases on nonmarital children. The Court's comments on DNA evidence are telling. In relation to the statutory purpose of assuring that a biological parent-child relationship exists between the child and his father, the Court noted that the statute provided three options to prove paternity (involving a legitimation process, acknowledgment, or a court order).

Petitioners argue that the requirement of [the statute], that a father provide clear and convincing evidence of parentage, is sufficient to achieve the end of establishing paternity, given the sophistication of modern DNA tests. [The statute] does not actually mandate a DNA test, however. The Constitution, moreover, does not require that Congress elect one particular mechanism from among many possible methods of establishing paternity, even if that mechanism arguably might be the most scientifically advanced method. With respect to DNA testing, the expense, reliability, and availability of such testing in various parts of the world may have been of particular concern to Congress . . . The requirement of [the statute] represents a reasonable conclusion by the legislature that the satisfaction of one of several alternatives will suffice to establish the blood link between father and child required as a predicate to the child's acquisition of citizenship.

6. *IS THE BATTLE OVER—ARE NONMARITAL CHILDREN NOW THE EQUALS OF MARITAL CHILDREN?*

One way to view the law of nonmarital children, as it has unfolded from the common law rules through the Supreme Court's decisions from 1968 through 1988, is to see it as a progression forward—from a period where the legal system treated nonmarital children as inferior and less worthy, to a period where the Supreme Court, in fits and starts and over time, came to view the different treatment of nonmarital children as invidious discrimination, to the final point where the Court determined that laws discriminating against nonmarital children were sufficiently suspect that it would apply intermediate scrutiny. In this telling, the battle has apparently been won and there is no more work to do. Certainly, there is substantial truth in this version of the story—there are few legal rules today that formally disadvantage nonmarital children.

There is, however, another version of the story that needs to be told. Several recent law review articles have called into question the claim that discrimination against nonmarital children is a thing of the past. In *Illegitimate Harm: Law, Stigma, and Discrimination Against Nonmarital Children*, 63 Fla. L. Rev. 345 (2011), Professor Solangel Maldonado states, "Although many individuals believe that the legal disadvantages attached to 'illegitimate' status have disappeared in the last forty years ... the law continues to discriminate against nonmarital children in a number of areas, including intestate succession, citizenship, and child support. Societal biases against nonmarital children also remain." She notes that both the law and societal biases continue to harm nonmarital children. Government initiatives to promote marriage have the effect of stigmatizing nonmarital children. Thus, the welfare reform law of 1996 provides that "[m]arriage is the foundation of a successful society" and "is an essential institution of a successful society which promotes the interests of children." *Id.* at 381. Among the purposes of the Act are "[to] prevent and reduce the incidence of out-of-wedlock pregnancies," and "[to] encourage the formation and maintenance of two-parent families." *Id.* at 381-82. The goals of the statute "clearly signal that the government believes that nonmarital childbearing is undesirable and should be strongly discouraged." *Id.* at 384.

A Symposium at American University in 2012, entitled, *"The New 'Illegitimacy': Revisiting Why Parentage Should Not Depend on Marriage*, produced a series of articles that identified the continuing problems faced by families without married parents. Among these were Susan Frelich Appleton, *Illegitimacy and Sex, Old and New*, 20 Am. U. J. Gender Soc. Pol'y & L. 347 (2012) (arguing that "modern doctrines of parentage expose family law's continuing interest in regulating sex even more than equalizing children and privatizing dependency."); Melissa Murray, *What's So*

New About the New Illegitimacy?, 20 Am. U. J. Gender Soc. Pol'y & L. 387 (2012) (calling into question the narrative of a progression from common law condemnation to modern day acceptance of nonmarital children and noting that one part of the same-sex marriage argument effectively concedes the preference for a marital family unit); and Cynthia G. Bowman, *The New Illegitimacy: Children of Cohabiting Couples and Stepchildren,* 20 Am. U. J. Gender Soc. Pol'y & L. 437 (2012) (noting continued distinctions between marital and nonmarital children in the areas of inheritance, government benefits when a parent dies, Social Security, workers' compensation, and tort claims against third parties).

CHAPTER 5

CLASSIFICATIONS THAT DISADVANTAGE ALIENS

A. THE LEGAL TRADITION OF TREATING ALIENS DIFFERENTLY FROM CITIZENS

It is part of the inherent power of sovereignty that a state will grant certain rights and benefits to those to whom it accords the status of "citizen," a status that is granted or withheld according to the laws of the state. One who is not a citizen is an "alien," one who is "other." In the United States, one is a citizen by birth or naturalization. Under the Fourteenth Amendment, "All persons born or naturalized in the United States, and subject to the jurisdiction thereof, are citizens of the United States and of the State wherein they reside." Article I, Section 8 provides that Congress has the power "[t]o establish an uniform rule of naturalization." Congress by statute has established the rules for citizenship by naturalization.

Once it is determined that one is a citizen of the United States, certain rights are associated with that status. Generally, only citizens vote, serve on juries, hold elective office, and possess a United States passport. With regard to employment and the receipt of certain government benefits, citizens have some advantages over noncitizens. The exact dividing line between appropriate and inappropriate line drawing between citizens and aliens in these two areas is the principal subject of this chapter. The early Supreme Court precedents in this area produced results that in some cases approved laws disadvantaging aliens and in some cases disapproved them. Thus, the Court approved state laws that prohibited aliens from owning land, *e.g.*, *Terrace v. Thompson*, 263 U.S. 197 (1923), that prohibited aliens from owning firearms for hunting, *Patsone v. Com. of Pennsylvania*, 232 U.S. 138 (1914), and that prohibited aliens from working on public works projects, *People v Crane*, 214 N.Y. 154 (1915), *aff'd*, 239 U.S. 195 (1915).

One of the justifications for treating aliens differently from citizens was the "special public interest doctrine," which was explained and justified by Justice Cardozo in *People v. Crane:*

> To disqualify aliens is discrimination indeed, but not arbitrary discrimination, for the principle of exclusion is the restriction of the resources of the state to the advancement and profit of the members of the state. Ungenerous and unwise such discrimination may be. It is not for that reason unlawful. The state in determining what use shall be made of its own moneys, may legitimately consult the welfare of its own citizens, rather than that of aliens. Whatever is a privilege, rather than a right, may be made dependent upon

citizenship. In its war against poverty, the state is not required to dedicate its own resources to citizens and aliens alike. 214 N.Y., at 161, 164.

On the other hand, on occasion the Court found laws disadvantaging aliens to be unconstitutional. Thus, in *Truax v. Raich*, 239 U.S. 33 (1915), the Court invalidated an Arizona statute under which private employers of more than five workers were required to employ at least 80% citizens. The Court explained that, unlike the public works employment in *Crane*, the discrimination defined by the act did not pertain to the regulation or distribution of the public domain, or of the common property or resources of the people of the state, but was rather directed at ordinary private enterprise. The Court concluded that "[i]t requires no argument to show that the right to work for a living in the common occupations of the community is of the very essence of the personal freedom and opportunity that it was the purpose of the Amendment to secure."

Although the dividing line between permissible and impermissible alienage classifications was not entirely clear, it seemed that the state had a greater leeway to exclude aliens, under the "special public interest doctrine," when dealing with matters in the public sphere than it did in private matters, such as employment contracts. In 1948, however, in *Takahashi v. Fish and Game Commission*, 334 U.S. 410 1948), the Court called into question the "special public interest doctrine." In that case, the Court invalidated a California statute that excluded aliens from commercial fishing. California claimed that it owned the fish within three miles of its coast as a trustee for all California citizens. Therefore, California claimed that it had the power to bar aliens from fishing in the three-mile belt as a means of conserving the supply of fish.

The Court found that the 'special public interest' on which California relied did not provide support for the state ban on commercial fishing by aliens. "To whatever extent the fish in the three-mile belt off California may be 'capable of ownership' by California, we think that 'ownership' is inadequate to justify California in excluding any or all aliens who are lawful residents of the State from making a living by fishing in the ocean off its shores while permitting all others to do so."

For the next twenty-three years, the Supreme Court made no attempt to explain the exact contours of the "special public interest doctrine" or the limits on state classifications of aliens. Then in 1973, in *Graham v. Richardson*, the Court began a new era in its treatment of aliens under the Equal Protection Clause, identifying aliens for the first time as a suspect class.

B. STRICT SCRUTINY OF ALIENAGE CLASSIFICATIONS BY STATE GOVERNMENTS

1. SHOULD ALIENS BE CONSIDERED A SUSPECT CLASS?

Graham v. Richardson
403 U.S. 365 (1971)

[Two cases, from Arizona and Pennsylvania, were consolidated. In each case, the claimant for welfare under the state's general assistance program would have been eligible if she had been a citizen but was denied because she was an alien. The Court considered the claim that these denials of welfare benefits constituted a denial of equal protection.]

Mr. Justice BLACKMUN delivered the opinion of the Court.

These are welfare cases. They provide yet another aspect of the widening litigation in this area. The issue here is whether the Equal Protection Clause of the Fourteenth Amendment prevents a State from conditioning welfare benefits either (a) upon the beneficiary's possession of United States citizenship, or (b) if the beneficiary is an alien, upon his having resided in this country for a specified number of years.

II

The appellants argue initially that the States, consistent with the Equal Protection Clause, may favor United States citizens over aliens in the distribution of welfare benefits. It is said that this distinction involves no 'invidious discrimination' such as was condemned in *King v. Smith*, 392 U.S. 309 (1968), for the State is not discriminating with respect to race or nationality.

The Fourteenth Amendment provides, '(N)or shall any State deprive any person of life, liberty, or property, without due process of law; nor deny to any person within its jurisdiction the equal protection of the laws.' It has long been settled, and it is not disputed here, that the term 'person' in this context encompasses lawfully admitted resident aliens as well as citizens of the United States and entitles both citizens and aliens to the equal protection of the laws of the State in which they reside. *Yick Wo v. Hopkins*, 118 U.S. 356, 369 (1886); *Truax v. Raich*, 239 U.S. 33, *Takahashi v. Fish & Game Comm'n*, 334 U.S., at 420. Nor is it disputed that the Arizona and Pennsylvania statutes in question create two classes of needy persons, indistinguishable except with respect to whether they are or are not citizens of this country. Otherwise qualified United States citizens living in Arizona are entitled to federally funded categorical assistance benefits without regard to length of national residency, but aliens must have lived in this country for 15 years in order to qualify for aid. United States citizens living in Pennsylvania, unable to meet the requirements for federally funded benefits, may be eligible for state-supported general assistance, but resident aliens as a class are precluded from that assistance.

Under traditional equal protection principles, a State retains broad discretion to classify as long as its classification has a reasonable basis. *Lindsley v. Natural Carbonic Gas Co.*, 220 U.S. 61, 78 (1911). This is so in 'the area of economics and social welfare.' *Dandridge v. Williams*, 397 U.S. 471, 485 (1970). But the Court's decisions have established that classifications based on alienage, like those based on nationality or race are inherently suspect and subject to close judicial scrutiny. Aliens as a class are a prime example of a 'discrete and insular' minority (see *United States v. Carolene Products Co.*, 304 U.S. 144, 152-153, n. 4 (1938)) for whom such heightened judicial solicitude is appropriate. Accordingly, it was said in *Takahashi*, 334 U.S., at 420, that 'the power of a state to apply its laws exclusively to its alien inhabitants as a class is confined within narrow limits.'

Arizona and Pennsylvania seek to justify their restrictions on the eligibility of aliens for public assistance solely on the basis of a State's 'special public interest' in favoring its own citizens over aliens in the distribution of limited resources such as welfare benefits. It is true that this Court on occasion has upheld state statutes that treat citizens and noncitizens differently, the ground for distinction having been that such laws were necessary to protect special interests of the State or its citizens. Thus, in *Truax v. Raich*, 239 U.S. 33 (1915), the Court, in striking down an Arizona statute restricting the employment of aliens, emphasized that '(t)he discrimination defined by the act does not pertain to the regulation or distribution of the public domain, or of the common property or resources of the people of the state, the enjoyment of which may be limited to its citizens as against both aliens and the citizens of other states.' 239 U.S., at 39-40. And in *Crane v. New York*, 239 U.S. 195 (1915), the Court affirmed the judgment in *People v. Crane*, 214 N.Y. 154 (1915), upholding a New York statute prohibiting the employment of aliens on public works projects. [The Court here quoted Justice Cardozo in *Crane*.]

On the same theory, the Court has upheld statutes that, in the absence of overriding treaties, limit the right of noncitizens to engage in exploitation of a State's natural resources, restrict the devolution of real property to aliens, or deny to aliens the right to acquire and own land.

Takahashi v. Fish & Game Comm'n, 334 U.S. 410 (1948), however, cast doubt on the continuing validity of the special public-interest doctrine in all contexts. There the Court held that California's purported ownership of fish in the ocean off its shores was not such a special public interest as would justify prohibiting aliens from making a living by fishing in those waters while permitting all others to do so. It was said:

> The Fourteenth Amendment and the laws adopted under its authority thus embody a general policy that all persons lawfully in this country shall abide 'in any state' on an equality of legal privileges with all citizens under nondiscriminatory laws. 334 U.S. at 420.

Whatever may be the contemporary vitality of the special public-interest doctrine in other contexts after *Takahashi*, we conclude that a State's desire to preserve limited welfare benefits for its own citizens is inadequate to justify Pennsylvania's making noncitizens ineligible for public assistance, and Arizona's restricting benefits to citizens and longtime resident aliens. First, the special public interest doctrine was heavily grounded on the notion that '(w)hatever is a privilege, rather than a right, may be made dependent upon citizenship.' *People v. Crane*, 214 N.Y., at 164. But this Court now has rejected the concept that constitutional rights turn upon whether a governmental benefit is characterized as a 'right' or as a 'privilege.' Second, as the Court recognized in *Shapiro*:

> (A) State has a valid interest in preserving the fiscal integrity of its programs. It may legitimately attempt to limit its expenditures, whether for public assistance, public education, or any other program. But a State may not accomplish such a purpose by invidious distinctions between classes of its citizens. The saving of welfare costs cannot justify an otherwise invidious classification. 394 U.S. at 633.

Since an alien as well as a citizen is a 'person' for equal protection purposes, a concern for fiscal integrity is no more compelling a justification for the questioned classification in these cases than it was in *Shapiro*.

Appellants, however, would narrow the application of *Shapiro* to citizens by arguing that the right to travel, relied upon in that decision, extends only to citizens and not to aliens. While many of the Court's opinions do speak in terms of the right of 'citizens' to travel, the source of the constitutional right to travel has never been ascribed to any particular constitutional provision. See *Shapiro v. Thompson*, 394 U.S., at 630 n. 8; *United States v. Guest*, 383 U.S. 745, 757-758 (1966). The Court has never decided whether the right applies specifically to aliens, and it is unnecessary to reach that question here. It is enough to say that the classification involved in Shapiro was subjected to strict scrutiny under the compelling state interest test, not because it was based on any suspect criterion such as race, nationality, or alienage, but because it impinged upon the fundamental right of interstate movement. As was said there, 'The waiting-period provision denies welfare benefits to otherwise eligible applicants solely because they have recently moved into the jurisdiction. But in moving from State to State or to the District of Columbia appellees were exercising a constitutional right, and any classification which serves to penalize the exercise of that right, unless shown to be necessary to promote a compelling governmental interest, is unconstitutional.' 394 U.S. at 634. The classifications involved in the instant cases, on the other hand, are inherently suspect and are therefore subject to strict judicial scrutiny whether or not a fundamental right is impaired. Appellants' attempted reliance on *Dandridge v. Williams*, 397 U.S. 471 (1970), is also misplaced, since the classification involved in that case (family size) neither impinged upon a fundamental constitutional right nor employed an inherently suspect criterion.

We agree with the three-judge court in the Pennsylvania case that the 'justification of limiting expenses is particularly inappropriate and unreasonable when the discriminated class consists of aliens. Aliens like citizens pay taxes and may be called into the armed forces. Unlike the short-term residents in *Shapiro*, aliens may live within a state for many years, work in the state and contribute to the economic growth of the state.' 321 F. Supp., at 253. There can be no 'special public interest' in tax revenues to which aliens have contributed on an equal basis with the residents of the State.

Accordingly, we hold that a state statute that denies welfare benefits to resident aliens and one that denies them to aliens who have not resided in the United States for a specified number of years violate the Equal Protection Clause.

III

An additional reason why the state statutes at issue in these cases do not withstand constitutional scrutiny emerges from the area of federal-state relations. The National Government has 'broad constitutional powers in determining what aliens shall be admitted to the United States, the period they may remain, regulation of their conduct before naturalization, and the terms and conditions of their naturalization.' *Takahashi v. Fish & Game Comm'n*, 334 U.S., at 419. State laws that restrict the eligibility of aliens for welfare benefits merely because of their alienage conflict with these overriding national policies in an area constitutionally entrusted to the Federal Government.

The judgments appealed from are *affirmed*.

NOTES

1.   There are certain provisions of the Constitution that protect citizens only. Thus, Article IV, Sec. 2 provides that "The Citizens of each state shall be entitled to all privileges and immunities of Citizens in the several States." The Fifteenth Amendment provides that "The right of citizens of the United States to vote shall not be denied or abridged . . . on account of race, color, or previous condition of servitude." It is clear that aliens cannot claim the benefit of these sections of the Constitution. On the other hand, the Equal Protection Clause protects "persons," and the *Graham* Court affirms that "that the term 'person' . . . encompasses lawfully admitted resident aliens as well as citizens of the United States and entitles both citizens and aliens to the equal protection of the laws of the State in which they reside."

2. Having determined that the Equal Protection Clause protects aliens, the Court then turned to the level of scrutiny that was appropriate for alienage classifications. The Court declared that its decisions "have established that classifications based on alienage, like those based on nationality or race are inherently suspect and subject to close judicial scrutiny. Aliens as a class are a prime example of a 'discrete and insular' minority (see *United States v. Carolene Products Co.*, 304 U.S. 144, 152-153, n. 4 (1938)) for whom such heightened judicial solicitude is appropriate." Accordingly, it was said in *Takahashi*, 334 U.S., at 420, that "the power of a state to apply its laws exclusively to its alien inhabitants as a class is confined within narrow limits."

This is a strikingly inadequate explanation of the decision to consider alienage classifications to be the constitutional equivalent of racial classifications. The Court claimed that its "decisions have established that classifications based on alienage" are inherently suspect, but the Court cited no case to support that claim, nor could it. The Court referred to the *Carolene Products* footnote, and described aliens as "a prime example of a 'discrete and insular' minority," when they clearly are not. "Discrete" and "insular," both have the meaning of separate, distinct, or isolated. Unlike persons of a particular national origin, like the Irish or Italians, aliens do not tend to stand out visibly or to form societies together so that they would be publicly identified as "alien." It is true that aliens are excluded from the majoritarian political process in that they cannot vote, but that is the only criterion for being a suspect class that aliens meet. In declaring that aliens are a suspect class, the *Graham* Court made no reference to most of the factors that have come to be associated with heightened scrutiny--immutability, a history of discrimination, visibility, stereotypes, and whether the trait bears a relation to ability to perform or contribute to society. In fact, aliens would not score particularly well on the suspect class meter as measured by these factors. While there is a history of discrimination against aliens, that history substantially overlaps with discrimination against certain national origin groups, who happen to have been recent immigrants. The trait is not visible, is not subject to any pervading stereotypes, is not immutable, and, in relation to certain rights of citizens such as the right to vote, hold elective office, and to serve on juries, it *does* bear a relation to ability to contribute to society. Overall, it is hard to justify the Court's conclusion that aliens are a suspect class.

As the cases in the rest of this chapter will demonstrate, the Court has dealt with the problem of justifying the treatment of aliens as a suspect class, not by changing its mind about that categorization, aliens being a suspect class, but by creating two very significant exceptions to the rule that alienage classifications should receive strict scrutiny. One of these exceptions is suggested by the Court's alternative holding near the end of the *Graham* case, based on federalism considerations. The National Government has 'broad constitutional powers in determining what aliens shall be admitted to the United States, the period they may remain, regulation of their conduct before naturalization, and the terms and conditions of their naturalization. . . . State laws that restrict the eligibility of aliens for welfare benefits merely because of their alienage conflict with these overriding national policies in an area constitutionally entrusted to the Federal Government."

3. The Court applied *Graham*, and invalidated an alienage classification, in the following cases:

- *In re Griffiths*, 413 U.S. 717 (1973) (invalidating a Connecticut rule that required attorneys to be citizens):

    The Court has consistently emphasized that a State which adopts a suspect classification 'bears a heavy burden of justification,' *McLaughlin v. Florida*, 379 U.S. 184, 196 (1964), a burden which, though variously formulated, requires the State to meet certain standards of proof. In order to justify the use of a suspect classification, a State must show that its purpose or interest is both constitutionally permissible and substantial, and that its use of the classification is 'necessary . . . to the accomplishment' of its purpose or the safeguarding of its interest.

It in no way denigrates a lawyer's high responsibilities to observe that the powers 'to sign writs and subpoenas, take recognizances, (and) administer oaths' hardly involve matters of state policy or acts of such unique responsibility as to entrust them only to citizens. Nor do we think that the practice of law offers meaningful opportunities adversely to affect the interest of the United States. Certainly the Committee has failed to show the relevance of citizenship to any likelihood that a lawyer will fail to protect faithfully the interest of his clients.

- *Examining Board v. Flores de Otero*, 426 U.S. 572 (1976) (invalidating a Puerto Rican statute that required civil engineers to be citizens):

  In examining the validity of Puerto Rico's virtually complete ban on the private practice of civil engineering by aliens, we apply the standards of our recent decisions in *Graham v. Richardson*, 403 U.S. 365 (1971); *Sugarman v. Dougall*, 413 U.S. 634 (1973); and *In re Griffiths*, 413 U.S. 717 (1973). These cases establish that state classifications based on alienage are subject to "strict judicial scrutiny." *Graham v. Richardson*, 403 U.S., at 376. Statutes containing classifications of this kind will be upheld only if the State or Territory imposing them is able to satisfy the burden of demonstrating "that its purpose or interest is both constitutionally permissible and substantial, and that its use of the classification is 'necessary . . . to the accomplishment' of its purpose or the safeguarding of its interest." *In re Griffiths*, 413 U.S., at 721-722. These principles are applicable to the Puerto Rico statute now under consideration. . . . Official discrimination against lawfully admitted aliens traditionally has taken several forms. Aliens have been prohibited from enjoying public resources or receiving public benefits on the same basis as citizens. See *Graham v. Richardson, supra*; *Takahashi v. Fish & Game Comm'n.*, Aliens have been excluded from public employment. *Sugarman v. Dougall, supra*. And aliens have been restricted from engaging in private enterprises and occupations that are otherwise lawful. See *In re Griffiths, supra*; *Truax v. Raich, supra*; *Yick Wo v. Hopkins*, 118 U.S. 356 (1886). The present Puerto Rico statute, of course, falls into the last category. It is with respect to this kind of discrimination that the States have had the greatest difficulty in persuading this Court that their interests are substantial and constitutionally permissible, and that the discrimination is necessary for the safeguarding of those interests."

- *Nyquist v. Mauclet*, 432 U.S. 1 (1977) (invalidating a New York statute that barred certain resident aliens from state financial assistance for higher education).

2. *THE POLITICAL FUNCTION EXCEPTION TO STRICT SCRUTINY OF ALIENAGE CLASSIFICATIONS*

Sugarman v. Dougall
413 U.S. 634 (1973)

[Four registered aliens were discharged from civil service jobs by the city of New York in accordance with § 53(1) of the New York Civil Service Law, which provided that no person was eligible for appointment for any position in the competitive class unless he was a citizen of the United States. The named defendants, who were from Guyana, El Salvador and the Dominican Republic, worked in various personnel, human resources, staff development and administrative positions. They instituted a class action challenge to the validity of the law, seeking a declaration that it was in violation of the Fourteenth Amendment.]

Mr. Justice BLACKMUN delivered the opinion of the Court.

As is so often the case, it is important at the outset to define the precise and narrow issue that is here presented. The Court is faced only with the question whether New York's flat statutory prohibition against the employment of aliens in the competitive classified civil service is constitutionally valid. The Court is not asked to decide whether a particular alien, any more than a particular citizen, may be refused employment or discharged on an individual basis for whatever legitimate reason the State might possess.

Neither is the Court reviewing a legislative scheme that bars some or all aliens from closely defined and limited classes of public employment on a uniform and consistent basis. The New York scheme, instead, is indiscriminate. The general standard is enunciated in the State's Constitution, Art. V, § 6, and is to the effect that appointments and promotions in the civil service 'shall be made according to merit and fitness to be ascertained, as far as practicable, by examination which, as far as practicable, shall be competitive.' In line with this rather flexible constitutional measure, the classified service is divided by statute into four classes. The first is the exempt class. It includes, generally, the higher offices in the state executive departments, certain municipal officers, certain judicial employees, and positions for which a competitive or noncompetitive examination may be found to be impracticable. The exempt class contains no citizenship restriction whatsoever. The second is the noncompetitive class. This includes positions, not otherwise classified, for which a noncompetitive examination would be practicable. There is no citizenship requirement. The third is the labor class. This includes unskilled laborers holding positions for which competitive examinations would be impracticable. No alienage exclusion is imposed. The fourth is the competitive class with which we are here concerned. This includes all positions for which it is practicable to determine merit and fitness by a competitive examination. Only citizens of the United States may hold positions in this class. The limits of these several classes, particularly the competitive class from which the appellees were deemed to be disqualified, are not readily defined. It would appear, however, that, consistent with the broad scope of the cited constitutional provision, the competitive class reaches various positions in nearly the full range of work tasks, that is, all the way from the menial to the policy making.

Apart from the classified civil service, New York has an unclassified service. This includes, among others, all elective offices, offices filled by legislative appointment, employees of the legislature, various offices filled by the Governor, and teachers. No citizenship requirement is present there.

Other constitutional and statutory citizenship requirements round out the New York scheme. The constitution of the State provides that voters, Art. II, § 1, members of the legislature, Art. III, § 7, the Governor and Lieutenant-Governor, Art. IV, § 2, and the Comptroller and Attorney-General, Art. V, § 1, are to be United States citizens. And Public Officers Law § 3 requires that any person holding 'a civil office' be a citizen of the United States. A 'civil office' is apparently one that 'possesses any of the attributes of a public officer or . . . involve(s) some portion of the sovereign (sic) power.' 1967 Op.N.Y.Atty.Gen. 60; *New York Post Corp. v. Moses*, 12 A.D.2d 243, 250, 95, rev'd on other grounds, 10 N.Y.2d 199 (1961).

We thus have constitutional provisions and a number of statutes that, together, constitute New York's scheme for the exclusion of aliens from public employment. The present case concerns only § 53 of the Civil Service Law. The section's constitutionality, however, is to be judged in the context of the State's broad statutory framework and the justifications the State presents.

III

It is established, of course, that an alien is entitled to the shelter of the Equal Protection Clause. *Graham v. Richardson*, 403 U.S. 365, 371; *Truax v. Raich*, 239 U.S. 33, 39 (1915); *Wong Wing v. United States*, 163 U.S. 228, 238 (1896); *Yick Wo v. Hopkins*, 118 U.S. 356, 369 (1886). This protection extends, specifically, in the words of Mr. Justice Hughes, to aliens who 'work for a living in the common occupations of the community.' *Truax v. Raich*, 239 U.S., at 41.

A. Appellants argue, however, that § 53 does not violate the equal protection guarantee of the Fourteenth Amendment because the statute 'establishes a generic classification reflecting the special requirements of public employment in the career civil service.' The distinction drawn between the citizen and the alien, it is said, 'rests on the fundamental concept of identity between a government and the members, or citizens, of the state.' The civil servant 'participates directly in the formulation and execution of government policy,' and thus must be free of competing obligations to another power. The State's interest in having an employee of undivided loyalty is substantial, for obligations attendant upon foreign citizenship 'might impair the exercise of his judgment or jeopardize public confidence in his objectivity.' Emphasis is placed on our decision in *United Public Workers v. Mitchell*, 330 U.S. 75 (1947), upholding the Hatch Act and its proscription of political activity by certain public employees, and it is said that the public employer 'has broad discretion to establish qualifications for its employees related to the integrity and efficiency of the operations of government.'

It is at once apparent, however, that appellants' asserted justification proves both too much and too little. As the above outline of the New York scheme reveals, the State's broad prohibition of the employment of aliens applies to many positions with respect to which the State's proffered justification has little, if any, relationship. At the same time, the prohibition has no application at all to positions that would seem naturally to fall within the State's asserted purpose. Our standard of review of statutes that treat aliens differently from citizens requires a greater degree of precision.

In *Graham v. Richardson*, 403 U.S., at 372, we observed that aliens as a class 'are a prima example of a 'discrete and insular' minority (see *United States v. Carolene Products Co.*, 304 U.S. 144, 152-153, n. 4 (1938)),' and that classifications based on alienage are 'subject to close judicial scrutiny.' And as long as a quarter century ago we held that the State's power 'to apply its laws exclusively to its alien inhabitants as a class is confined within narrow limits.' *Takahashi v. Fish Comm'n*, 334 U.S., at 420. We therefore look to the substantiality of the State's interest in enforcing the statute in question, and to the narrowness of the limits within which the discrimination is confined.

Applying this standard to New York's purpose in confining civil servants in the competitive class to those persons who have no ties of citizenship elsewhere, § 53 does not withstand the necessary close scrutiny. We recognize a State's interest in establishing its own form of government, and in limiting participation in that government to those who are within 'the basic conception of a political community.' *Dunn v. Blumstein*, 405 U.S. 330, 344 (1972). We recognize, too, the State's broad power to define its political community. But in seeking to achieve this substantial purpose, with discrimination against aliens, the means the State employs must be precisely drawn in light of the acknowledged purpose.

Section 53 is neither narrowly confined nor precise in its application. Its imposed ineligibility may apply to the 'sanitation man, class B,' *Perotta v. Gregory*, 4 Misc.2d 769, 158 N.Y.S.2d 221 (1957), to the typist, and to the office worker, as well as to the person who directly participates in the formulation and execution of important state policy. The citizenship restriction sweeps indiscriminately. Viewing the entire constitutional and statutory framework in the light of the State's asserted interest, the great breadth of the requirement is even more evident. Sections 35 and 41 of the Civil Service Law, relating generally to persons holding elective and high appointive offices, contain no citizenship restrictions. Indeed, even § 53 permits an alien to hold a classified civil service position under certain circumstances. In view of the breadth and imprecision of § 53 in the context of the State's interest, we conclude that the statute does not withstand close judicial scrutiny.

B.   Appellants further contend, however, that the State's legitimate interest is greater than simply limiting to citizens those high public offices that have to do with the formulation and execution of state policy. Understandably relying on this Court's decisions in *Crane v. New York*, 239 U.S. 195 (1915), *Heim v. McCall*, 239 U.S. 175 (1915), and *Ohio ex rel. Clarke v. Deckebach*, 274 U.S. 392 (1927), appellants argue that a State constitutionally may confine public employment to citizens. Mr. Justice (then Judge) Cardozo accepted this 'special public interest' argument because of the State's concern with 'the restriction of the resources of the state to the advancement and profit of the members of the state.' *People v. Crane*, 214 N.Y. 154, 161 aff'd, 239 U.S. 195 (1915). We rejected that approach, however, in the context of public assistance in *Graham*, where it was observed that 'the special public interest doctrine was heavily grounded on the notion that '(w)hatever is a privilege, rather than a right, may be made dependent upon citizenship.' *People v. Crane* . . . . But this Court now has rejected the concept that constitutional rights turn upon whether a governmental benefit is characterized as a 'right' or as a 'privilege."' 403 U.S., at 374.

Appellants argue that our rejection of the special-public-interest doctrine in a public assistance case does not require its rejection here. That the doctrine has particular applicability with regard to public employment is demonstrated, according to appellants, by the decisions in *Crane* and *Heim* that upheld, under Fourteenth Amendment challenge, those provisions of the New York Labor Law that confined employment on public works to citizens of the United States.

We perceive no basis for holding the special-public-interest doctrine inapplicable in *Graham* and yet applicable and controlling here. A resident alien may reside lawfully in New York for a long period of time. He must pay taxes. And he is subject to service in this country's Armed

Forces. 50 U.S.C.App. § 454(a). The doctrine, rooted as it is in the concepts of privilege and of the desirability of confining the use of public resources, has no applicability in this case. To the extent that *Crane*, *Heim*, and *Clarke* intimate otherwise, they were weakened by the decisions in *Takahashi* and *Graham*, and are not to be considered as controlling here.

C. We hold that § 53, which denies all aliens the right to hold positions in New York's classified competitive civil service, violates the Fourteenth Amendment's equal protection guarantee.

IV

While we rule that § 53 is unconstitutional, we do not hold that, on the basis of an individualized determination, an alien may not be refused, or discharged from, public employment, even on the basis of noncitizenship, if the refusal to hire, or the discharge, rests on legitimate state interests that relate to qualifications for a particular position or to the characteristics of the employee. We hold only that a flat ban on the employment of aliens in positions that have little, if any relation to a State's legitimate interest, cannot withstand scrutiny under the Fourteenth Amendment.

Neither do we hold that a State may not, in an appropriately defined class of positions, require citizenship as a qualification for office. Just as 'the Framers of the Constitution intended the States to keep for themselves, as provided in the Tenth Amendment, the power to regulate elections,' *Oregon v. Mitchell*, 400 U.S. 112 (opinion of Black, J.); see *id.*, at 201 (opinion of Harlan, J.), and *id.*, at 293-294 (opinion of Stewart, J.), '(e)ach State has the power to prescribe the qualifications of its officers and the manner in which they shall be chosen.' *Boyd v. Thayer*, 143 U.S. 135, 161 (1892). Such power inheres in the State by virtue of its obligation, already noted above, 'to preserve the basic conception of a political community.' *Dunn v. Blumstein*, 405 U.S., at 344. And this power and responsibility of the State applies, not only to the qualifications of voters, but also to persons holding state elective or important nonelective executive, legislative, and judicial positions, for officers who participate directly in the formulation, execution, or review of broad public policy perform functions that go to the heart of representative government. There, as Judge Lumbard phrased it in his separate concurrence, is 'where citizenship bears some rational relationship to the special demands of the particular position.' 339 F. Supp., at 911.

We have held, of course, that such state action, particularly with respect to voter qualifications is not wholly immune from scrutiny under the Equal Protection Clause. See, for example, *Kramer v. Union School District*, 395 U.S. 621 (1969). But our scrutiny will not be so demanding where we deal with matters resting firmly within a State's constitutional prerogatives. This is no more than a recognition of a State's historical power to exclude aliens from participation in its democratic political institutions, *Pope v. Williams*, 193 U.S., at 632-634; *Boyd v. Thayer*, 143 U.S., at 161, and a recognition of a State's constitutional responsibility for the establishment and operation of its own government, as well as the qualifications of an appropriately designated class of public office holders. U.S.Const. Art. IV, § 4; U.S.Const. Amdt. X; *Luther v. Borden*, *supra*; see *In re Duncan*, 139 U.S. 449, 461 (1891). This Court has never held that aliens have a constitutional right to vote or to hold high public office under the Equal Protection Clause. Indeed, implicit in many of this Court's voting rights decisions is the notion that citizenship is a permissible criterion for limiting such rights. A restriction on the employment of noncitizens, narrowly confined, could have particular relevance to this important state responsibility, for alienage itself is a factor that reasonably could be employed in defining 'political community.'

The judgment of the District Court is *affirmed*.

NOTES

1. The *Sugarman* Court both invalidated the blunderbuss New York statute, which excluded aliens from government positions great and small, and also first spoke of the "political function" exception to the rule of strict scrutiny of alienage classifications. As to the problems with the statute itself, the Court noted that it "is neither narrowly confined nor precise in its application. Its imposed ineligibility may apply to the 'sanitation man, class B,' . . . to the typist, and to the office worker, as well as to the person who directly participates in the formulation and execution of important state policy. The citizenship restriction sweeps indiscriminately." Since the Court was applying some version of strict scrutiny to the statute, it did not "withstand the necessary close scrutiny."

However, the Court does not end its commentary there. It went on to say:

> We recognize a State's interest in establishing its own form of government, and in limiting participation in that government to those who are within 'the basic conception of a political community.' *Dunn v. Blumstein*, 405 U.S. 330, 344 (1972). In defining its political community, a state has power 'to preserve the basic conception of a political community.' *Dunn v. Blumstein*, 405 U.S., at 344. And this power and responsibility of the State applies, not only to the qualifications of voters, but also to persons holding state elective or important nonelective executive, legislative, and judicial positions, for officers who participate directly in the formulation, execution, or review of broad public policy functions that go to the heart of representative government. There, as Judge Lumbard phrased it in his separate concurrence, is "where citizenship bears some rational relationship to the special demands of the particular position."

This exemption from strict scrutiny of state employment decisions for "officers who participate directly in the formulation, execution, or review of broad public policy" is dictum in *Sugarman*, since it is unnecessary to the result in the case and the Court has no occasion to apply it to the statute it was considering. But that language is the basis of the Court's "public function exception" that it applied in subsequent cases.

2. In *Foley v. Connelie*, 435 U.S. 291 (1978), the Court considered a challenge to a New York statute that required state police officers to be citizens. The Court determined that it would not apply strict scrutiny and upheld the statute. The Court explained why strict scrutiny was not appropriate:

> It would be inappropriate, however, to require every statutory exclusion of aliens to clear the high hurdle of "strict scrutiny," because to do so would "obliterate all the distinctions between citizens and aliens, and thus depreciate the historic values of citizenship.". . . The act of becoming a citizen is more than a ritual with no content beyond the fanfare of ceremony. A new citizen has become a member of a Nation, part of a people distinct from others. . . . The individual, at that point, belongs to the polity and is entitled to participate in the processes of democratic decisionmaking. Accordingly, we have recognized "a State's historical power to exclude aliens from participation in its democratic political institutions," part of the sovereign's obligation "'to preserve the basic conception of a political community.'"

The Court then explained the proper standard of review of state statutes that dealt with matters firmly within a State's constitutional prerogatives: "The State need only justify its classification by a showing of some rational relationship between the interest sought to be protected and the limiting classification." The Court summarized its alienage decisions as follows: "The essence of our holdings to date is that although we extend to aliens the right to education and public welfare, along with the ability to earn a livelihood and engage in licensed professions, the right to govern is reserved to citizens."

Next, the Court applied the test to the position of police officer:

> A discussion of the police function is essentially a description of one of the basic functions of government, especially in a complex modern society where police presence is pervasive. The police function fulfills a most fundamental obligation of government to its constituency. Police officers in the ranks do not formulate policy, per se, but they are clothed with authority to exercise an almost infinite variety of discretionary powers.... Police officers very clearly fall within the category of "important non-elective ... officers who participate directly in THE ... EXECUTION ... of broad public policy." ... In the enforcement and execution of the laws the police function is one where citizenship bears a rational relationship to the special demands of the particular position. A State may, therefore, consonant with the Constitution, confine the performance of this important public responsibility to citizens of the United States.

3. In *Ambach v. Norwick*, 441 U.S. 68 (1979), the Court considered a challenge to a New York statute that required public school teachers to be citizens. Once again, the Court applied rational basis review and upheld the statute:

> In determining whether, for purposes of equal protection analysis, teaching in public schools constitutes a governmental function, we look to the role of public education and to the degree of responsibility and discretion teachers possess in fulfilling that role.... Each of these considerations supports the conclusion that public school teachers may be regarded as performing a task "that go[es] to the heart of representative government."

> Within the public school system, teachers play a critical part in developing students' attitude toward government and understanding of the role of citizens in our society. Alone among employees of the system, teachers are in direct, day-to-day contact with students both in the classrooms and in the other varied activities of a modern school. In shaping the students' experience to achieve educational goals, teachers by necessity have wide discretion over the way the course material is communicated to students. They are responsible for presenting and explaining the subject matter in a way that is both comprehensible and inspiring. No amount of standardization of teaching materials or lesson plans can eliminate the personal qualities a teacher brings to bear in achieving these goals. Further, a teacher serves as a role model for his students, exerting a subtle but important influence over their perceptions and values. Thus, through both the presentation of course materials and the example he sets, a teacher has an opportunity to influence the attitudes of students toward government, the political process, and a citizen's social responsibilities. This influence is crucial to the continued good health of a democracy.

Furthermore, it is clear that all public school teachers, and not just those responsible for teaching the courses most directly related to government, history, and civic duties, should help fulfill the broader function of the public school system. Teachers, regardless of their specialty, may be called upon to teach other subjects, including those expressly dedicated to political and social subjects. More importantly, a State properly may regard all teachers as having an obligation to promote civic virtues and understanding in their classes, regardless of the subject taught. Certainly a State also may take account of a teacher's function as an example for students, which exists independently of particular classroom subjects. In light of the foregoing considerations, we think it clear that public school teachers come well within the "governmental function" principle recognized in *Sugarman* and *Foley*. Accordingly, the Constitution requires only that a citizenship requirement applicable to teaching in the public schools bear a rational relationship to a legitimate state interest.

4. In *Cabell v. Chavez-Salido*, 454 U.S. 432 (1982), the Court upheld California statutory provisions that required probation officers to be citizens. The Court explained:

> The cases through *Graham* dealt for the most part with attempts by the States to retain certain economic benefits exclusively for citizens. Since *Graham,* the Court has confronted claims distinguishing between the economic and sovereign functions of government. This distinction has been supported by the argument that although citizenship is not a relevant ground for the distribution of economic benefits, it is a relevant ground for determining membership in the political community . . .
>
> While not retreating from the position that restrictions on lawfully resident aliens that primarily affect economic interests are subject to heightened judicial scrutiny . . . we have concluded that strict scrutiny is out of place when the restriction primarily serves a political function.
>
> The exclusion of aliens from basic governmental processes is not a deficiency in the democratic system but a necessary consequence of the community's process of political self-definition. Self-government, whether direct or through representatives, begins by defining the scope of the community of the governed and thus of the governors as well: Aliens are by definition those outside of this community. Judicial incursions in this area may interfere with those aspects of democratic self-government that are most essential to it. This distinction between the economic and political functions of government has, therefore, replaced the old public/private distinction. Although this distinction rests on firmer foundations than the old public/private distinction, it may be difficult to apply in particular cases.
>
> We need not hold that the District Court was wrong in concluding that citizenship may not be required of toll-service employees, cemetery sextons, and inspectors to hold that the District Court was wrong in striking down the statute on its face. The District Court assumed that if the statute was overinclusive at all, it could not stand. This is not the proper standard. Rather, the inquiry is whether the restriction reaches so far and is so broad and haphazard as to belie the State's claim that it is only attempting to ensure that an important function of government be in the hands of those having the "fundamental legal bond of citizenship." *Ambach v. Norwick*, 441 U.S., at 75. Under this standard, the classifications used need not be precise; there need only be a substantial fit. Our

examination of the California scheme convinces us that it is sufficiently tailored to withstand a facial challenge.

Looking at the functions of California probation officers, we conclude that they, like the state troopers involved in *Foley*, sufficiently partake of the sovereign's power to exercise coercive force over the individual that they may be limited to citizens. Although the range of individuals over whom probation officers exercise supervisory authority is limited, the powers of the probation officer are broad with respect to those over whom they exercise that authority. The probation officer has the power both to arrest, and to release those over whom he has jurisdiction. He has the power and the responsibility to supervise probationers and insure that all the conditions of probation are met and that the probationer accomplishes a successful reintegration into the community. In carrying out these responsibilities the probation officer necessarily has a great deal of discretion that, just like that of the police officer and the teacher, must be exercised, in the first instance, without direct supervision.

Bernal v. Fainter
467 U.S. 216 (1984)

[Petitioner, a native of Mexico and resident alien of Texas, applied to become a notary public as part of his work as a paralegal assisting migrant farm workers. His application was denied based on a Texas statute that required a notary public to be a citizen of the United States.]

Justice MARSHALL delivered the opinion of the Court.

The question posed by this case is whether a statute of the State of Texas violates the Equal Protection Clause of the Fourteenth Amendment of the United States Constitution by denying aliens the opportunity to become notaries public. The Court of Appeals for the Fifth Circuit held that the statute does not offend the Equal Protection Clause. We granted certiorari, 464 U.S. 1007 (1983), and now reverse.

II

As a general matter, a state law that discriminates on the basis of alienage can be sustained only if it can withstand strict judicial scrutiny. In order to withstand strict scrutiny, the law must advance a compelling state interest by the least restrictive means available. Applying this principle, we have invalidated an array of state statutes that denied aliens the right to pursue various occupations. In *Sugarman v. Dougall*, 413 U.S. 634 (1973), we struck down a state statute barring aliens from employment in permanent positions in the competitive class of the state civil service. In *In re Griffiths*, 413 U.S. 717 (1973), we nullified a state law excluding aliens from eligibility for membership in the State Bar. And in *Examining Board v. Flores de Otero*, 426 U.S. 572 (1976), we voided a state law that excluded aliens from the practice of civil engineering.

We have, however, developed a narrow exception to the rule that discrimination based on alienage triggers strict scrutiny. This exception has been labeled the "political function" exception and applies to laws that exclude aliens from positions intimately related to the process of democratic self-government. The contours of the "political function" exception are outlined by our prior decisions.

The rationale behind the political-function exception is that within broad boundaries a State may establish its own form of government and limit the right to govern to those who are full-fledged members of the political community. Some public positions are so closely bound up with the formulation and implementation of self-government that the State is permitted to exclude from those positions persons outside the political community, hence persons who have not become part of the process of democratic self-determination.

> The exclusion of aliens from basic governmental processes is not a deficiency in the democratic system but a necessary consequence of the community's process of political self-definition. Self-government, whether direct or through representatives, begins by defining the scope of the community of the governed and thus of the governors as well: Aliens are by definition those outside of this community. *Id.* at 439–440.

We have therefore lowered our standard of review when evaluating the validity of exclusions that entrust only to citizens important elective and nonelective positions whose operations "go to the heart of representative government." *Sugarman v. Dougall, supra*, 413 U.S., at 647. "While not retreating from the position that restrictions on lawfully resident aliens that primarily affect economic interests are subject to heightened judicial scrutiny ... we have concluded that strict scrutiny is out of place when the restriction primarily serves a political function. . . ." *Cabell v. Chavez–Salido, supra*, 454 U.S., at 439.

To determine whether a restriction based on alienage fits within the narrow political-function exception, we devised in Cabell a two-part test.

> First, the specificity of the classification will be examined: a classification that is substantially overinclusive or underinclusive tends to undercut the governmental claim that the classification serves legitimate political ends. . . . Second, even if the classification is sufficiently tailored, it may be applied in the particular case only to 'persons holding state elective or important nonelective executive, legislative, and judicial positions,' those officers who 'participate directly in the formulation, execution, or review of broad public policy' and hence 'perform functions that go to the heart of representative government.' 454 U.S., at 440 (quoting *Sugarman v. Dougall, supra*, 413 U.S., at 647).[FN 7]

III

We now turn to Article 5949(2) to determine whether it satisfies the *Cabell* test. The statute provides that "[t]o be eligible for appointment as a Notary Public, a person shall be a resident citizen of the United States and of this state ..." Unlike the statute invalidated in *Sugarman*, Article 5949(2) does not indiscriminately sweep within its ambit a wide range of offices and occupations but specifies only one particular post with respect to which the State asserts a right to exclude aliens. Clearly, then, the statute is not overinclusive; it applies narrowly to only one category of persons: those wishing to obtain appointments as notaries. Less clear is whether Article 5949(2) is fatally underinclusive. Texas does not require court reporters to be United States citizens even

---

[FN 7] We emphasize, as we have in the past, that the political-function exception must be narrowly construed; otherwise the exception will swallow the rule and depreciate the significance that should attach to the designation of a group as a "discrete and insular" minority for whom heightened judicial solicitude is appropriate. See *Nyquist v. Mauclet*, 432 U.S. 1, 11 (1977).

though they perform some of the same services as notaries. Nor does Texas require that its Secretary of State be a citizen, even though he holds the highest appointive position in the State and performs many important functions, including supervision of the licensing of all notaries public. We need not decide this issue, however, because of our decision with respect to the second prong of the *Cabell* test.

In support of the proposition that notaries public fall within that category of officials who perform functions that "go to the heart of representative government," the State emphasizes that notaries are designated as public officers by the Texas Constitution. Texas maintains that this designation indicates that the State views notaries as important officials occupying posts central to the State's definition of itself as a political community. This Court, however, has never deemed the source of a position—whether it derives from a State's statute or its Constitution—as the dispositive factor in determining whether a State may entrust the position only to citizens. Rather, this Court has always looked to the actual function of the position as the dispositive factor. The focus of our inquiry has been whether a position was such that the officeholder would necessarily exercise broad discretionary power over the formulation or execution of public policies importantly affecting the citizen population—power of the sort that a self-governing community could properly entrust only to full-fledged members of that community. As the Court noted in Cabell, in determining whether the function of a particular position brings the position within the narrow ambit of the exception, "the Court will look to the importance of the function as a factor giving substance to the concept of democratic self-government." 454 U.S. at 441, n. 7.

The State maintains that even if the actual function of a post is the touchstone of a proper analysis, Texas notaries public should still be classified among those positions from which aliens can properly be excluded because the duties of Texas notaries entail the performance of functions sufficiently consequential to be deemed "political." The Court of Appeals ably articulated this argument:

> With the power to acknowledge instruments such as wills and deeds and leases and mortgages; to take out-of-court depositions; to administer oaths; and the discretion to refuse to perform any of the foregoing acts, notaries public in Texas are involved in countless matters of importance to the day-to-day functioning of state government. The Texas political community depends upon the notary public to insure that those persons executing documents are accurately identified, to refuse to certify any identification that is false or uncertain, and to insist that oaths are properly and accurately administered. Land titles and property succession depend upon the care and integrity of the notary public, as well as the familiarity of the notary with the community, to verify the authenticity of the execution of the documents. 710 F.2d. at 194.

We recognize the critical need for a notary's duties to be carried out correctly and with integrity. But a notary's duties, important as they are, hardly implicate responsibilities that go to the heart of representative government. Rather, these duties are essentially clerical and ministerial. In contrast to state troopers, *Foley v. Connelie*, 435 U.S. 291 (1978), notaries do not routinely exercise the State's monopoly of legitimate coercive force. Nor do notaries routinely exercise the wide discretion typically enjoyed by public school teachers when they present materials that educate youth respecting the information and values necessary for the maintenance of a democratic political system. See *Ambach v. Norwick*, 441 U.S., at 77. To be sure, considerable damage could result from the negligent or dishonest performance of a notary's duties. But the same could be said for the duties performed by cashiers, building inspectors, the janitors who clean up the offices of public officials, and numerous other categories of personnel upon whom we depend for careful, honest service. What distinguishes such personnel from those to whom the political-function exception is properly applied is that the latter are invested either with policymaking responsibility or broad discretion in the execution of public policy that requires the routine exercise of authority over individuals. Neither of these characteristics pertains to the functions performed by Texas notaries.

The inappropriateness of applying the political-function exception to Texas notaries is further underlined by our decision in *In re Griffiths*, 413 U.S. 634 (1973), in which we subjected to strict scrutiny a Connecticut statute that prohibited noncitizens from becoming members of the State Bar. Along with the usual powers and privileges accorded to members of the bar, Connecticut gave to members of its Bar additional authority that encompasses the very duties performed by Texas notaries—authority to "'sign writs and subpoenas, take recognizances, administer oaths and take depositions and acknowledgements of deeds.'" *Id.* at 723 (quoting Connecticut statute). In striking down Connecticut's citizenship requirement, we concluded that "[i]t in no way denigrates a lawyer's high responsibilities to observe that [these duties] hardly involve matters of state policy or acts of such unique responsibility as to entrust them only to citizens." *Id.* at 724. If it is improper to apply the political-function exception to a citizenship requirement governing eligibility for membership in a state bar, it would be anomalous to apply the exception to the citizenship requirement that governs eligibility to become a Texas notary. We conclude, then, that the "political function" exception is inapplicable to Article 5949(2) and that the statute is therefore subject to strict judicial scrutiny.

IV

To satisfy strict scrutiny, the State must show that Article 5949(2) furthers a compelling state interest by the least restrictive means practically available. Respondents maintain that Article 5949(2) serves its "legitimate concern that notaries be reasonably familiar with state law and institutions" and "that notaries may be called upon years later to testify to acts they have performed." However, both of these asserted justifications utterly fail to meet the stringent requirements of strict scrutiny. There is nothing in the record that indicates that resident aliens, as a class, are so incapable of familiarizing themselves with Texas law as to justify the State's absolute and classwide exclusion. The possibility that some resident aliens are unsuitable for the position cannot justify a wholesale ban against all resident aliens. Furthermore, if the State's concern with ensuring a notary's familiarity with state law were truly "compelling," one would expect the State to give some sort of test actually measuring a person's familiarity with the law. The State, however, administers no such test. To become a notary public in Texas, one is merely required to fill out an application that lists one's name and address and that answers four questions pertaining to one's age, citizenship, residency, and criminal record —nothing that reflects the State's asserted interest in insuring that notaries are familiar with Texas law. Similarly inadequate is the State's purported interest in insuring the later availability of notaries' testimony. This justification fails because the State fails to advance a factual showing that the unavailability of notaries' testimony presents a real, as opposed to a merely speculative, problem to the State. Without a factual underpinning, the State's asserted interest lacks the weight we have required of interests properly denominated as compelling.

V

We conclude that Article 5949(2) violates the Fourteenth Amendment of the United States Constitution. Accordingly the judgment of the Court of Appeals is reversed, and the case is remanded for further proceedings consistent with this opinion.

It is so ordered.

NOTES

1. After *Bernal*, we can say that the political function exception to strict scrutiny of alienage classifications applies to police officers, public school teachers, and probation officers, but not to attorneys or notaries public. This is consistent with the Court's description of the exception in *Cabell* that "This distinction between the economic and political functions of government has, therefore, replaced the old public/private distinction." When the government is an actor in the marketplace, it has no special need or any special justification for treating aliens differently from citizens. But when the government is governing, citizenship is an appropriate criterion for participating.

A recent note reviewed the Supreme Court's alienage decisions throughout the twentieth century, both before and after the Court decided in *Graham* that aliens were a suspect class. *See* Michael Cornelius Kelly, *A Wavering Course: United States Supreme Court Treatment of State Laws Regarding Aliens in the Twentieth Century*, 25 Geo. Immigr. L. J. 701 (2011). Kelly finds that the Supreme Court has examined the constitutionality of twenty-eight state or local laws affecting the rights of aliens, and has upheld fourteen and struck down fourteen.

C. THE FEDERAL GOVERNMENT'S POWER TO CLASSIFY ALIENS

Mathews v. Diaz
426 U.S. 67 (1976)

[Appellants were three resident aliens. Each was lawfully admitted to the United States and, after reaching the age of 65, sought to enroll in the Medicare Part B supplemental medical insurance program. They were denied coverage because they did not met the requirements that they be admitted for permanent residence and have also resided in the United States for at least five years.]

Mr. Justice STEVENS delivered the opinion of the Court.

The question presented by the Secretary's appeal is whether Congress may condition an alien's eligibility for participation in a federal medical insurance program on continuous residence in the United States for a five-year period and admission for permanent residence. The District Court held that the first condition was unconstitutional and that it could not be severed from the second. Since we conclude that both conditions are constitutional, we reverse.

II

There are literally millions of aliens within the jurisdiction of the United States. The Fifth Amendment, as well as the Fourteenth Amendment, protects every one of these persons from deprivation of life, liberty, or property without due process of law. *Wong Yang Sung v. McGrath*,

339 U.S. 33, 48-51; *Wong Wing v. United States*, 163 U.S. 228, 238; see *Russian Fleet v. United States*, 282 U.S. 481, 489. Even one whose presence in this country is unlawful, involuntary, or transitory is entitled to that constitutional protection. *Wong Yang Sung, supra* ; *Wong Wing, supra*.

The fact that all persons, aliens and citizens alike, are protected by the Due Process Clause does not lead to the further conclusion that all aliens are entitled to enjoy all the advantages of citizenship or, indeed, to the conclusion that all aliens must be placed in a single homogeneous legal classification. For a host of constitutional and statutory provisions rest on the premise that a legitimate distinction between citizens and aliens may justify attributes and benefits for one class not accorded to the other; and the class of aliens is itself a heterogeneous multitude of persons with a wide-ranging variety of ties to this country.

In the exercise of its broad power over naturalization and immigration, Congress regularly makes rules that would be unacceptable if applied to citizens. The exclusion of aliens and the reservation of the power to deport have no permissible counterpart in the Federal Government's power to regulate the conduct of its own citizenry. The fact that an Act of Congress treats aliens differently from citizens does not in itself imply that such disparate treatment is "invidious."

In particular, the fact that Congress has provided some welfare benefits for citizens does not require it to provide like benefits for all aliens. Neither the overnight visitor, the unfriendly agent of a hostile foreign power, the resident diplomat, nor the illegal entrant, can advance even a colorable constitutional claim to a share in the bounty that a conscientious sovereign makes available to its own citizens and some of its guests. The decision to share that bounty with our guests may take into account the character of the relationship between the alien and this country: Congress may decide that as the alien's tie grows stronger, so does the strength of his claim to an equal share of that munificence.

The real question presented by this case is not whether discrimination between citizens and aliens is permissible; rather, it is whether the statutory discrimination within the class of aliens allowing benefits to some aliens but not to others is permissible. We turn to that question.

III

For reasons long recognized as valid, the responsibility for regulating the relationship between the United States and our alien visitors has been committed to the political branches of the Federal Government. Since decisions in these matters may implicate our relations with foreign powers, and since a wide variety of classifications must be defined in the light of changing political and economic circumstances, such decisions are frequently of a character more appropriate to either the Legislature or the Executive than to the Judiciary. This very case illustrates the need for flexibility in policy choices rather than the rigidity often characteristic of constitutional adjudication. Appellees Diaz and Clara are but two of over 440,000 Cuban refugees who arrived in the United States between 1961 and 1972. And the Cuban parolees are but one of several categories of aliens who have been admitted in order to make a humane response to a natural catastrophe or an international political situation. Any rule of constitutional law that would inhibit the flexibility of the political branches of government to respond to changing world conditions should be adopted only with the greatest caution. The reasons that preclude judicial review of political questions also dictate a narrow standard of review of decisions made by the Congress or the President in the area of immigration and naturalization.

Since it is obvious that Congress has no constitutional duty to provide all aliens with the welfare benefits provided to citizens, the party challenging the constitutionality of the particular line Congress has drawn has the burden of advancing principled reasoning that will at once invalidate that line and yet tolerate a different line separating some aliens from others. In this case the appellees have challenged two requirements first, that the alien be admitted as a permanent resident, and, second, that his residence be of a duration of at least five years. But if these requirements were eliminated, surely Congress would at least require that the alien's entry be lawful; even then, unless mere transients are to be held constitutionally entitled to benefits, some durational requirement would certainly be appropriate. In short, it is unquestionably reasonable for Congress to make an alien's eligibility depend on both the character and the duration of his residence. Since neither requirement is wholly irrational, this case essentially involves nothing more than a claim that it would have been more reasonable for Congress to select somewhat different requirements of the same kind.

We may assume that the five-year line drawn by Congress is longer than necessary to protect the fiscal integrity of the program. We may also assume that unnecessary hardship is incurred by persons just short of qualifying. But it remains true that some line is essential, that any line must produce some harsh and apparently arbitrary consequences, and, of greatest importance, that those who qualify under the test Congress has chosen may reasonably be presumed to have a greater affinity with the United States than those who do not. In short, citizens and those who are most like citizens qualify. Those who are less like citizens do not.

The task of classifying persons for medical benefits, like the task of drawing lines for federal tax purposes, inevitably requires that some persons who have an almost equally strong claim to favored treatment be placed on different sides of the line; the differences between the eligible and the ineligible are differences in degree rather than differences in the character of their respective claims. When this kind of policy choice must be made, we are especially reluctant to question the exercise of congressional judgment. In this case, since appellees have not identified a principled basis for prescribing a different standard than the one selected by Congress, they have, in effect, merely invited us to substitute our judgment for that of Congress in deciding which aliens shall be eligible to participate in the supplementary insurance program on the same conditions as citizens. We decline the invitation.

IV

The cases on which appellees rely are consistent with our conclusion that this statutory classification does not deprive them of liberty or property without due process of law.

Graham v. Richardson, 403 U.S. 365, provides the strongest support for appellees' position. That case holds that state statutes that deny welfare benefits to resident aliens, or to aliens not meeting a requirement of durational residence within the United States, violate the Equal Protection Clause of the Fourteenth Amendment and encroach upon the exclusive federal power over the entrance and residence of aliens. Of course, the latter ground of decision actually supports our holding today that it is the business of the political branches of the Federal Government, rather than that of either the States or the Federal Judiciary, to regulate the conditions of entry and residence of aliens. The equal protection analysis also involves significantly different considerations because it concerns the relationship between aliens and the States rather than between aliens and the Federal Government.

Insofar as state welfare policy is concerned, there is little, if any, basis for treating persons who are citizens of another State differently from persons who are citizens of another country. Both groups are noncitizens as far as the State's interests in administering its welfare programs are concerned. Thus, a division by a State of the category of persons who are not citizens of that State into subcategories of United States citizens and aliens has no apparent justification, whereas, a comparable classification by the Federal Government is a routine and normally legitimate part of its business. Furthermore, whereas the Constitution inhibits every State's power to restrict travel across its own borders, Congress is explicitly empowered to exercise that type of control over travel across the borders of the United States.

Finally, we reject the suggestion that *U. S. Dept. of Agriculture v. Moreno*, 413 U.S. 528, lends relevant support to appellees' claim. No question involving alienage was presented in that case. Rather, we found that the denial of food stamps to households containing unrelated members was not only unsupported by any rational basis but actually was intended to discriminate against certain politically unpopular groups. This case involves no impairment of the freedom of association of either citizens or aliens.

We hold that § 1395o (2)(B) has not deprived appellees of liberty or property without due process of law. The judgment of the District Court is *reversed.*

NOTES

1. The "federal government exception" is the second exception to the Supreme Court's rule that alienage classifications will be strictly scrutinized. The logic of the exception is simple: the federal government is explicitly empowered by the Constitution to regulate naturalization and immigration and, given that broad power, it has the implicit power to impose conditions on those noncitizens it authorizes to enter the country. On the other hand, a person's status as a citizen or alien is simply not relevant to the states, with the exception of those activities that involve the political functioning of the state. Thus, state statutes that classify aliens will be strictly scrutinized while similar federal classifications will receive only a deferential scrutiny.

There are limits to the "federal government exception." Thus, in *Hampton v. Mow Sun Wong*, 426 U.S. 88 (1976), the Court invalidated a rule of the United States Civil Service Commission that excluded all persons except American citizens from employment in most positions of federal service. Even though a branch of the federal government adopted the rule, the Court noted: It is the business of the Civil Service Commission to adopt and enforce regulations which will best promote the efficiency of the federal civil service. That agency has no responsibility for foreign affairs, for treaty negotiations, for establishing immigration quotas or conditions of entry, or for naturalization policies. . . . [Therefore, even] "assuming without deciding that the national interests identified by the petitioners would adequately support an explicit determination by Congress or the President to exclude all noncitizens from the federal service, we conclude that those interests cannot provide an acceptable rationalization for such a determination by the Civil Service Commission. The impact of the rule on the millions of lawfully admitted resident aliens is precisely the same as the aggregate impact of comparable state rules which were invalidated by our decision in *Sugarman*. By broadly denying this class substantial opportunities for employment, the Civil Service Commission rule deprives its members of an aspect of liberty. Since these residents were admitted as a result of decisions made by the Congress and the President, implemented by the Immigration and Naturalization Service acting under the Attorney

General of the United States, due process requires that the decision to impose that deprivation of an important liberty be made either at a comparable level of government or, if it is to be permitted to be made by the Civil Service Commission, that it be justified by reasons which are properly the concern of that agency.

D. RECENT ISSUES ON THE CLASSIFICATIONS OF ALIENS

1. *THE HYBRID STATE/FEDERAL CLASSIFICATION OF ALIENS*

The cases in the previous section make clear that, in limiting the level of welfare benefits available to aliens, state actions will be subject to strict scrutiny but federal actions will be subject only to a rational basis standard. In 1996, however, when Congress enacted the Personal Responsibility and Work Opportunity Reconciliation Act (PRWORA), Pub. L. No 104-193, 110 Stat. 2105, that line became blurred. The Act imposed several limitations on the availability of Medicaid benefits to aliens but gave states the option to offer additional benefits to aliens beyond what the Act required. When some states took advantage of this option by reducing the number of aliens eligible for benefits, the question was raised, was that a state action, subject to strict scrutiny, or a federal action, subject to rational basis review?

In *Soskin v. Reinertson*, 353 F.3d 1242 (10th Cir. 2004), the Court of Appeals for the Tenth Circuit reviewed a Colorado statute that excluded some aliens from Medicaid benefits. The court noted that Congress has extensive powers with respect to aliens and that when Congress exercises these powers to legislate with regard to aliens, the proper standard of judicial review is rational-basis review. The court then determined that the state law reflected a national policy—that "individual aliens not burden the public benefits system"—and so upheld the statute using rational basis review.

On the other hand, in *Aliessa v. Novell*, 96 N.Y.2d 418 (2001), the New York Court of Appeals used strict scrutiny to invalidate a similar New York statute. In response to PRWORA, New York had enacted a statute that terminated Medicaid for certain non-qualified aliens. As the court explained, because PRWORA authorizes each state to deny aliens benefits beyond what the federal law required:

> [I]it is directly in the teeth of *Graham* insofar as it allows the States to "adopt divergent laws on the subject of citizenship requirements for *federally* supported welfare programs." . . . Moreover, [PRWORA] goes significantly beyond what the *Graham* Court declared constitutionally questionable. In the name of national immigration policy, it impermissibly authorizes each State to decide whether to disqualify many otherwise eligible aliens from State Medicaid. Section 122 [the challenged New York state statute] is a product of this authorization. In light of *Graham* and its progeny, [PRWORA] can give section 122 no special insulation from strict scrutiny review. Thus, section 122 must be evaluated as any other State statute that classifies based on alienage. We hold that section 122 violates the Equal Protection Clauses of the United States and New York State Constitutions insofar as it denies State Medicaid to [certain otherwise eligible aliens] and lawfully admitted permanent residents based on their status as aliens.

Professor Juliet P. Stumpf identified the difficulties created by the interaction of PRWORA and the Supreme Court's standards of review for alienage classifications. *See States of Confusion: The Rise of State and Local Power Over Immigration*, 86 N.C.L.Rev. 1557 (2008). Professor Stumpf states that "The PRWORA threw a wrench into this distinction." (referring to the different levels of review for state and federal alienage classifications).

2. THE TREATMENT OF UNDOCUMENTED AND NONIMMIGRANT ALIENS

Undocumented aliens are those who do not have the papers to demonstrate that they are in the United States legally. Nonimmigrant aliens are those who are lawfully in the country, but only temporarily, with no right to remain indefinitely. Undocumented aliens are not considered to be a suspect class. There is a conflict of authority in the federal courts as to whether nonimmigrant aliens are a suspect class.

a. Undocumented Aliens

In *Plyler v. Doe*, 457 U.S. 202 (1982), the Court invalidated a Texas rule that denied free public education to the children of undocumented aliens. *See infra*, Chapter 8. The Court first indicated that "[w]hatever his status under the immigration laws, an alien is surely a "person" in any ordinary sense of that term," and thus could claim the benefit of the Fourteenth Amendment's guarantee of equal protection. The Court went on, however, to state: "We reject the claim that 'illegal aliens' are a 'suspect class.' No case in which we have attempted to define a suspect class has addressed the status of persons unlawfully in our country. Unlike most of the classifications that we have recognized as suspect, entry into this class, by virtue of entry into this country, is the product of voluntary action. Indeed, entry into the class is itself a crime. In addition, it could hardly be suggested that undocumented status is a 'constitutional irrelevancy.'"

b. Nonimmigrant Aliens

Although the Supreme Court has not ruled on the constitutional status of nonimmigrant, legal aliens, there is authority that they are not a suspect class. In *LeClerc v. Webb*, 419 F.3d 405 (5th Cir. 2005), the United States Court of Appeals for the Fifth Circuit upheld, using rational basis review, a Louisiana statute that limited bar membership to aliens who had attained permanent resident status in the United States. The effect of the Louisiana statute was to distinguish between immigrant and nonimmigrant aliens--the nonimmigrant alien being one without an intention to abandon his foreign country residence and whose entry into the United States was for specific and temporary purposes. The court explained: "Based on the aggregate factual and legal distinctions between resident aliens and nonimmigrant aliens, we conclude that although aliens are a suspect class in general, they are not homogeneous and precedent does not support the proposition that nonimmigrant aliens are a suspect class entitled to have state legislative classifications concerning them subjected to strict scrutiny. We decline to extend the Supreme Court's decisions concerning resident aliens to different alien categories when the Court itself has shied away from such expansion." The court then used rational basis review to uphold the statute.

The Court of Appeals for the Second Circuit, however, reached the opposite result. In *Dandamudi v. Tisch*, 686 F.3d 66 (2d Cir. 2012), the court considered a New York statute under which only U.S. Citizens or Legal Permanent Residents ("LPRs") were eligible to obtain a pharmacist's license. The court noted that, under Supreme Court precedent, "statutes that deny opportunities or benefits to aliens are subject to strict scrutiny unless they fall within two narrow exceptions. The first allows states to exclude aliens from certain civic roles that directly affect the political process. The second acknowledges that people who reside in the United States without authorization may be treated differently than those who are here legally." Neither exception applied in *Tisch* and the court was unwilling to create a third exception for nonimmigrant aliens. The court explained:

> Ultimately, for three reasons, we reject the state's argument that this Court should follow the rationale of the Fifth and Sixth Circuits [which had refused to treat nonimmigrant aliens as a suspect class]. First, the Supreme Court's listing in *Graham* of the similarities between citizens and aliens refuted the state's argument that it did have a compelling reason for its law, but this language does not articulate a test for determining when state discrimination against any one subclass of lawful immigrants is subject to strict scrutiny. Second, nonimmigrant aliens are but one subclass of aliens, and the Supreme Court recognizes aliens generally as a discrete and insular minority without significant political clout. Third, even if this Court were to determine that the appropriate level of scrutiny by which to analyze the discrimination should be based on the nonimmigrant aliens' similarity (or proximity) to citizens, we would still apply strict scrutiny in this case because nonimmigrant aliens are sufficiently similar to citizens that discrimination against them in the context presented here must be strictly scrutinized.
>
> Nothing in the Supreme Court's precedent counsels us to "judicially craft[ ] a subset of aliens, scaled by how [we] perceive the aliens' proximity to citizenship." *LeClerc v. Webb*, 444 F.3d 428, 429 (5th Cir.2006) (Higginbotham, J., dissenting from the denial of reh'g en banc).

CHAPTER 6

CLASSIFICATIONS BASED ON SEXUAL ORIENTATION

A. THE LONGSTANDING TRADITION OF TREATING GAY MEN AND WOMEN AS LESS WORTHY

For most of its history, until perhaps the past twenty years, the common law system and its American counterpart very regularly treated gay those with a same-sex orientation as a legal underclass. The conduct that they might engage in was made a crime. They were fired from their jobs without legal recourse. They lost custody of their children. They were not allowed to immigrate into the United States. They were not allowed to serve openly in the military. They could not marry. These rules that treated gay men and women differently were not just of historical interest but were in fact quite widespread well into the 1980's and 1990's. This chapter begins by briefly examining some of the contexts in which gay men and women were penalized.

A NOTE ON TERMINOLOGY

Before moving on to the substantive issues affecting gay men and lesbian women, a brief note on terminology is appropriate. For a long time, the widely-used term for persons involved in same-sex relationships was "homosexual." This term is still widely used by politicians and even in some of the court opinions cited in this chapter that have been decided very recently.

The Gay & Lesbian Alliance Against Defamation (GLAAD), however, counsels against this usage. GLAAD quotes the New York Times Style Guide as follows:

> gay (adj.) is preferred to homosexual in references to social or cultural identity and political or legal issues: gay literature. Use homosexual in specific references to sexual activity and to psychological or clinical orientation. Gay may refer to homosexual men or more generally to homosexual men and women. In specific references to women, lesbian is preferred. When the distinction is useful, write gay men and lesbians. Do not use gay as a singular noun. Gays, a plural noun, may be used only as a last resort, ordinarily in a hard-to-fit headline.
> *http://www.glaad.org/reference/style*

GLAAD adds its own recommendation:

> Please use "gay" or "lesbian" to describe people attracted to members of the same sex. Because of the clinical history of the word "homosexual," it is aggressively used by anti-gay extremists to suggest that gay people are somehow diseased or psychologically/emotionally disordered – notions discredited by the American Psychological Association and the American Psychiatric Association in the 1970s. Please avoid using "homosexual" except in direct quotes. *http://www.glaad.org/reference/offensive*

1. PUBLIC SCHOOL TEACHING

Gaylord v. Tacoma School Dist. No. 10, 88 Wash.2d 286 (1977) is a good example of the old ways. In that case Gaylord, a high school teacher, kept his sexual orientation to himself. The school district first became aware of his sexual orientation when a former high school student told the school's vice-principal he thought Gaylord was a homosexual. When Gaylord was confronted at his home, he admitted that he was gay and attempted unsuccessfully to have the vice-principal drop the matter. Gaylord was discharged from his position on the grounds of immorality.

The Supreme Court of Washington upheld his dismissal. The court explained:

> After Gaylord's homosexual status became publicly known, it would and did impair his teaching efficiency. A teacher's efficiency is determined by his relationship with his students, their parents, the school administration and fellow teachers. If Gaylord had not been discharged after he became known as a homosexual, the result would be fear, confusion, suspicion, parental concern and pressure on the administration by students, parents and other teachers.

Gaylord had been teaching at the school for twelve years and had always been rated as an effective teacher. That performance, however, could not save him. The court explained:

> It is important to remember that Gaylord's homosexual conduct must be considered in the context of his position of teaching high school students. Such students could treat the retention of the high school teacher by the school board as indicating adult approval of his homosexuality. It would be unreasonable to assume as a matter of law a teacher's ability to perform as a teacher required to teach principles of morality is not impaired and creates no danger of encouraging expression of approval and of imitation. Likewise to say that school directors must wait for prior specific overt expression of homosexual conduct before they act to prevent harm from one who chooses to remain 'erotically attracted to a notable degree towards persons of his own sex and is psychologically, if not actually disposed to engage in sexual activity prompted by this attraction' is to ask the school directors to take an unacceptable risk in discharging their fiduciary responsibility of managing the affairs of the school district.

2. IMMIGRATION

In *Boutilier v. Immigration and Naturalization Service*, 387 U.S. 118 (1967), the Court considered a provision of the Immigration and Nationality Act that excluded from admission to the United States persons "afflicted with psychopathic personality." The petitioner in the case had submitted an affidavit in which he admitted to engaging in homosexual relations. Thus, the only issue for the Court was whether the term "psychopathic personality" included homosexuals. The Court held that it did. "The legislative history of the Act indicates beyond a shadow of a doubt that the Congress intended the phrase 'psychopathic personality' to include homosexuals such as petitioner." The Court gave weight to the legislative history of the immigration statute. An earlier version of the bill before Congress had excluded not only "persons with psychopathic personality" but also those "who are homosexuals or sex perverts." Although final version of the bill did not include the latter clause, a Committee reported explained:

> [The provision of the bill] which specifically excluded homosexuals and sex perverts as a separate excludable class does not appear in the instant bill. The Public Health Service has advised that the provision for the exclusion of aliens afflicted with psychopathic personality or a mental defect which appears in the instant bill is sufficiently broad to provide for the exclusion of homosexuals and sex perverts. This change of nomenclature is not to be construed in any way as modifying the intent to exclude all aliens who are sexual deviates.

The Court affirmed the deportation of the petitioner.

3. PARENTING

In *Roe v. Roe*, 324 S.E.2d 691 (1985), the court reviewed a child custody dispute in which the mother asked the court to revoke the father's custody of their child because "it had just come to her attention that the father was living with a man who was his homosexual lover, that the two men occupied the same bed in a bedroom in the house in which the father lived with the child, that the child had reported seeing the two men 'hugging and kissing and sleeping in bed together.'" The Supreme Court of Virginia held that "that such an arrangement is not in the child's best interests and that an award of custody to such a parent constitutes an abuse of judicial discretion." The court explained:

> The father's continuous exposure of the child to his immoral and illicit relationship renders him an unfit and improper custodian as a matter of law . . .
>
> [W]e have no hesitancy in saying that the conditions under which this child must live daily are not only unlawful but also impose an intolerable burden upon her by reason of the social condemnation attached to them, which will inevitably afflict her relationships with her peers and with the community at large. The father's unfitness is manifested by his willingness to impose this burden upon her in exchange for his own gratification.
>
> We conclude that the best interests of the child will only be served by protecting her from the burdens imposed by such behavior, insofar as practicable. In the circumstances of this case, this necessitates not only a change of custody to the mother, but also a cessation of any visitations in the father's home, or in the presence of his homosexual lover, while his present living arrangements continue.

4. SERVICE IN THE MILITARY

Dronenburg v. Zech
741 F.2d 1388 (D.C. Circ., 1984)

[James L. Dronenburg, a Naval officer with nine years of experience as a cryptologist and linguist, had a top security clearance and an unblemished service record. He had earned many citations praising his job performance. At age 27 he was discharged from the Navy after admitting, pursuant to the findings of an investigation, that he was gay and had engaged in homosexual acts on a Naval base in violation of a Navy regulation that stated:

> "[a]ny member [of the Navy] who solicits, attempts, or engages in homosexual acts shall normally be separated from the naval service. The presence of such a member in a military environment seriously impairs combat readiness, efficiency, security and morale."]

BORK, Circuit Judge:

James L. Dronenburg appeals from a district court decision upholding the United States Navy's action administratively discharging him for homosexual conduct. Appellant contends that the Navy's policy of mandatory discharge for homosexual conduct violates his constitutional rights to privacy and equal protection of the laws. The district court granted summary judgment for the Navy, holding that private, consensual, homosexual conduct is not constitutionally protected. We affirm.

III.

Appellant advances two constitutional arguments, a right of privacy and a right to equal protection of the laws. Resolution of the second argument is to some extent dependent upon that of the first. Whether the appellant's asserted constitutional right to privacy is based upon fundamental human rights, substantive due process, the ninth amendment or emanations from the Bill of Rights, if no such right exists, then appellant's right to equal protection is not infringed unless the Navy's policy is not rationally related to a permissible end. *Kelley v. Johnson*, 425 U.S. 238, 247-49 (1976). We think neither right has been violated by the Navy.

A.

[The court here discussed the constitutional right to privacy that arises from the Supreme Court precedents of *Griswold v. Connecticut*, 381 U.S. 479 (1965), *Loving v. Virginia*, 388 U.S. 1 (1967); *Eisenstadt v. Baird*, 405 U.S. 438 (1972); *Roe v. Wade*, 410 U.S. 113 (1973); and *Carey v. Population Services International*, 431 U.S. 678 (1977), and determined that those cases created no general principle that would create a right of privacy that would protect private consensual sexual activity. This issue is discussed *infra*, in this Chapter in Section C. The court distinguished the cases creating a right to privacy with the claim before it as follows:]

In this group of cases, and in those cited in the quoted language from the Court's opinions, we do not find any principle articulated even approaching in breadth that which appellant seeks to have us adopt. The Court has listed as illustrative of the right of privacy such matters as activities relating to marriage, procreation, contraception, family relationships, and child rearing and education. It need hardly be said that none of these covers a right to homosexual conduct.

The question then becomes whether there is a more general principle that explains these cases and is capable of extrapolation to new claims not previously decided by the Supreme Court. It is true that the principle appellant advances would explain all of these cases, but then so would many other, less sweeping principles. The most the Court has said on that topic is that only rights that are "fundamental" or "implicit in the concept of ordered liberty" are included in the right of privacy. These formulations are not particularly helpful to us, however, because they are less prescriptions of a mode of reasoning than they are conclusions about particular rights enunciated. We would find it impossible to conclude that a right to homosexual conduct is "fundamental" or "implicit in the concept of ordered liberty" unless any and all private sexual behavior falls within those categories, a conclusion we are unwilling to draw.

Turning from the decided cases, which we do not think provide even an ambiguous warrant for the constitutional right he seeks, appellant offers arguments based upon a constitutional theory. Though that theory is obviously untenable, it is so often heard that it is worth stating briefly why we reject it.

Appellant denies that morality can ever be the basis for legislation or, more specifically, for a naval regulation, and asserts two reasons why that is so. The first argument is: "if the military can defend its blanket exclusion of homosexuals on the ground that they are offensive to the majority or to the military's view of what is socially acceptable, then no rights are safe from encroachment and no minority is protected against discrimination." Passing the inaccurate characterization of the Navy's position here, it deserves to be said that this argument is completely frivolous. The Constitution has provisions that create specific rights. These protect, among others, racial, ethnic, and religious minorities. If a court refuses to create a new constitutional right to protect homosexual conduct, the court does not thereby destroy established constitutional rights that are solidly based in constitutional text and history.

Appellant goes further, however, and contends that the existence of moral disapproval for certain types of behavior is the very fact that disables government from regulating it. He says that as a matter of general constitutional principle, "it is difficult to understand how an adult's selection of a partner to share sexual intimacy is not immune from burden by the state as an element of constitutionally protected privacy. That the particular choice of partner may be repugnant to the majority argues for its vigilant protection--not its vulnerability to sanction." This theory that majority morality and majority choice is always made presumptively invalid by the Constitution attacks the very predicate of democratic government. When the Constitution does not speak to the contrary, the choices of those put in authority by the electoral process, or those who are accountable to such persons, come before us not as suspect because majoritarian but as conclusively valid for that very reason. We stress, because the possibility of being misunderstood is so great, that this deference to democratic choice does not apply where the Constitution removes the choice from majorities. Appellant's theory would, in fact, destroy the basis for much of the most valued legislation our society has. It would, for example, render legislation about civil rights, worker safety, the preservation of the environment, and much more, unconstitutional. In each of these areas, legislative majorities have made moral choices contrary to the desires of minorities. It is to be doubted that very many laws exist whose ultimate justification does not rest upon the society's morality. For these reasons, appellant's argument will not withstand examination.

We conclude, therefore, that we can find no constitutional right to engage in homosexual conduct and that, as judges, we have no warrant to create one. We need ask, therefore, only whether the Navy's policy is rationally related to a permissible end. *See Kelley v. Johnson,* 425 U.S. 238, 247-49 (1976). We have said that legislation may implement morality. So viewed, this regulation bears a rational relationship to a permissible end. It may be argued, however, that a naval regulation, unlike the act of a legislature, must be rationally related not to morality for its own sake but to some further end which the Navy is entitled to pursue because of the Navy's assigned function. We need not decide that question because, if such a connection is required, this regulation is plainly a rational means of advancing a legitimate, indeed a crucial, interest common to all our armed forces. To ask the question is to answer it. The effects of homosexual conduct within a naval or military unit are almost certain to be harmful to morale and discipline. The Navy is not required to produce social science data or the results of controlled experiments to prove what common sense and common experience demonstrate. This very case illustrates dangers of the sort the Navy is entitled to consider: a 27-year-old petty officer had repeated sexual relations with a 19-year-old seaman recruit. The latter then chose to break off the relationship. Episodes of this sort are certain to be deleterious to morale and discipline, to call into question the even-handedness of superiors' dealings with lower ranks, to make personal dealings uncomfortable where the relationship is sexually ambiguous, to generate dislike and disapproval among many who find homosexuality morally offensive, and, it must be said, given the powers of military superiors over their inferiors, to enhance the possibility of homosexual seduction.

The Navy's policy requiring discharge of those who engage in homosexual conduct serves legitimate state interests which include the maintenance of "discipline, good order and morale[,] ... mutual trust and confidence among service members, ... insur[ing] the integrity of the system of rank and command, ... recruit[ing] and retain[ing] members of the naval service ... and ... prevent[ing] breaches of security." We believe that the policy requiring discharge for homosexual conduct is a rational means of achieving these legitimate interests. *See Beller v. Middendorf,* 632 F.2d 788, 812 (9th Cir.), *cert. denied,* 452 U.S. 905 (1980). The unique needs of the military, "a specialized society separate from civilian society," *Parker v. Levy,* 417 U.S. 733, 743 (1974), justify the Navy's determination that homosexual conduct impairs its capacity to carry out its mission.

Affirmed.

NOTES

1. The court's opinion in *Dronenburg* makes clear that, in relation to classifications that disadvantage gay men, the Due Process Clause will be as relevant as the Equal Protection Clause. The court reviews the Supreme Court precedents in the area of substantive due process, that is, those cases in which the Court interpreted the term "liberty" in the Due Process Clause as imposing not just a procedural, but a substantive, limitation on government action. In particular, the Supreme Court in a serious of cases--*Griswold v. Connecticut,* 381 U.S. 479 (1965); *Loving v. Virginia,* 388 U.S. 1 (1967); *Eisenstadt v. Baird,* 405 U.S. 438 (1972); *Roe v. Wade,* 410 U.S. 113 (1973); and *Carey v. Population Services International,* 431 U.S. 678 (1977)—had identified a fundamental right of privacy that protected from government interference certain private matters affecting marriage, procreation, contraceptives, and abortion. The plaintiffs in *Dronenburg* argued that these cases, taken together, could best be explained as based on a general principle of privacy that precluded government from interfering with private sexual conduct between consenting adults. The *Dronenburg* court was not at all persuaded by that argument. Instead, the court viewed those Supreme Court cases as fact-specific, and limited to traditional notions of marriage and

family. As a result, the regulation at issue did not violate the implied fundamental right of privacy under the Due Process Clause. This left the court with the equal protection issue. Without even considering whether it should apply any heightened scrutiny because gay men might be a suspect class, the court applied a deferential version of rational basis review and concluded that the exclusion of gay men from the military was rationally related not only to the promotion of morality but also to the maintenance of morale in the Navy.

5. CRIMINALIZATION OF SEXUAL ACTIVITY

Bowers v. Hardwick
478 U.S. 186 (1986)

[Michael Hardwick was charged with violating a Georgia sodomy statute by committing that act with another adult male in the bedroom of his own home. The statute defined sodomy as "any sexual act involving the sex organs of one person and the mouth or anus of another." After a preliminary hearing, the District Attorney decided not to present the matter to the grand jury unless further evidence developed. Hardwick then brought suit in the Federal District Court, challenging the constitutionality of the statute insofar as it criminalized consensual sodomy. He asserted that he was a practicing homosexual, that the Georgia sodomy statute, as administered by the defendants, placed him in imminent danger of arrest, and that the statute for several reasons violated the Federal Constitution.]

Justice WHITE delivered the opinion of the Court.

This case does not require a judgment on whether laws against sodomy between consenting adults in general, or between homosexuals in particular, are wise or desirable. It raises no question about the right or propriety of state legislative decisions to repeal their laws that criminalize homosexual sodomy, or of state-court decisions invalidating those laws on state constitutional grounds. The issue presented is whether the Federal Constitution confers a fundamental right upon homosexuals to engage in sodomy and hence invalidates the laws of the many States that still make such conduct illegal and have done so for a very long time. The case also calls for some judgment about the limits of the Court's role in carrying out its constitutional mandate.

We first register our disagreement with the Court of Appeals and with respondent that the Court's prior cases have construed the Constitution to confer a right of privacy that extends to homosexual sodomy and for all intents and purposes have decided this case. The reach of this line of cases was sketched in *Carey v. Population Services International,* 431 U.S. 678, 685 (1977). *Pierce v. Society of Sisters,* 268 U.S. 510 (1925), and *Meyer v. Nebraska,* 262 U.S. 390 (1923), were described as dealing with child rearing and education; *Prince v. Massachusetts,* 321 U.S. 158 (1944), with family relationships; *Skinner v. Oklahoma ex rel. Williamson,* 316 U.S. 535 (1942), with procreation; *Loving v. Virginia,* 388 U.S. 1 (1967), with marriage; *Griswold v. Connecticut, supra,* and *Eisenstadt v. Baird, supra,* with contraception; and *Roe v. Wade,* 410 U.S. 113 (1973), with abortion. The latter three cases were interpreted as construing the Due Process Clause of the Fourteenth Amendment to confer a fundamental individual right to decide whether or not to beget or bear a child. *Carey v. Population Services International, supra,* 431 U.S., at 688-689.

Accepting the decisions in these cases and the above description of them, we think it evident that none of the rights announced in those cases bears any resemblance to the claimed constitutional right of homosexuals to engage in acts of sodomy that is asserted in this case. No connection between family, marriage, or procreation on the one hand and homosexual activity on the other has been demonstrated, either by the Court of Appeals or by respondent. Moreover, any claim that these cases nevertheless stand for the proposition that any kind of private sexual conduct between consenting adults is constitutionally insulated from state proscription is unsupportable. Indeed, the Court's opinion in *Carey* twice asserted that the privacy right, which the *Griswold* line of cases found to be one of the protections provided by the Due Process Clause, did not reach so far. 431 U.S .at 688, n. 5; 694, n. 17.

Precedent aside, however, respondent would have us announce, as the Court of Appeals did, a fundamental right to engage in homosexual sodomy. This we are quite unwilling to do. It is true that despite the language of the Due Process Clauses of the Fifth and Fourteenth Amendments, which appears to focus only on the processes by which life, liberty, or property is taken, the cases are legion in which those Clauses have been interpreted to have substantive content, subsuming rights that to a great extent are immune from federal or state regulation or proscription. Among such cases are those recognizing rights that have little or no textual support in the constitutional language. *Meyer, Prince,* and *Pierce* fall in this category, as do the privacy cases from *Griswold* to *Carey.*

Striving to assure itself and the public that announcing rights not readily identifiable in the Constitution's text involves much more than the imposition of the Justices' own choice of values on the States and the Federal Government, the Court has sought to identify the nature of the rights qualifying for heightened judicial protection. In *Palko v. Connecticut,* 302 U.S. 319, 325, 326 (1937), it was said that this category includes those fundamental liberties that are "implicit in the concept of ordered liberty," such that "neither liberty nor justice would exist if [they] were sacrificed." A different description of fundamental liberties appeared in *Moore v. East Cleveland,* 431 U.S. 494, 503 (1977) (opinion of POWELL, J.), where they are characterized as those liberties that are "deeply rooted in this Nation's history and tradition." *Id.*at 503 (POWELL, J.). See also *Griswold v. Connecticut,* 381 U.S., at 506.

It is obvious to us that neither of these formulations would extend a fundamental right to homosexuals to engage in acts of consensual sodomy. Proscriptions against that conduct have ancient roots. Sodomy was a criminal offense at common law and was forbidden by the laws of the original thirteen States when they ratified the Bill of Rights. In 1868, when the Fourteenth Amendment was ratified, all but 5 of the 37 States in the Union had criminal sodomy laws. In fact, until 1961, all 50 States outlawed sodomy, and today, 24 States and the District of Columbia continue to provide criminal penalties for sodomy performed in private and between consenting adults. Against this background, to claim that a right to engage in such conduct is "deeply rooted in this Nation's history and tradition" or "implicit in the concept of ordered liberty" is, at best, facetious.

Nor are we inclined to take a more expansive view of our authority to discover new fundamental rights imbedded in the Due Process Clause. The Court is most vulnerable and comes nearest to illegitimacy when it deals with judge-made constitutional law having little or no cognizable roots in the language or design of the Constitution. That this is so was painfully demonstrated by the face-off between the Executive and the Court in the 1930's, which resulted in the repudiation of much of the substantive gloss that the Court had placed on the Due Process Clauses of the Fifth and Fourteenth Amendments. There should be, therefore, great resistance to expand the substantive reach of those Clauses, particularly if it requires redefining the category of rights deemed to be fundamental. Otherwise, the Judiciary necessarily takes to itself further authority to govern the country without express constitutional authority. The claimed right pressed on us today falls far short of overcoming this resistance.

Respondent, however, asserts that the result should be different where the homosexual conduct occurs in the privacy of the home. He relies on *Stanley v. Georgia,* 394 U.S. 557 (1969), where the Court held that the First Amendment prevents conviction for possessing and reading obscene material in the privacy of one's home: "If the First Amendment means anything, it means that a State has no business telling a man, sitting alone in his house, what books he may read or what films he may watch."

Stanley did protect conduct that would not have been protected outside the home, and it partially prevented the enforcement of state obscenity laws; but the decision was firmly grounded in the First Amendment. The right pressed upon us here has no similar support in the text of the Constitution, and it does not qualify for recognition under the prevailing principles for construing the Fourteenth Amendment. Its limits are also difficult to discern. Plainly enough, otherwise illegal conduct is not always immunized whenever it occurs in the home. Victimless crimes, such as the possession and use of illegal drugs, do not escape the law where they are committed at home. *Stanley* itself recognized that its holding offered no protection for the possession in the home of drugs, firearms, or stolen goods. And if respondent's submission is limited to the voluntary sexual conduct between consenting adults, it would be difficult, except by fiat, to limit the claimed right to homosexual conduct while leaving exposed to prosecution adultery, incest, and other sexual crimes even though they are committed in the home. We are unwilling to start down that road.

Even if the conduct at issue here is not a fundamental right, respondent asserts that there must be a rational basis for the law and that there is none in this case other than the presumed belief of a majority of the electorate in Georgia that homosexual sodomy is immoral and unacceptable. This is said to be an inadequate rationale to support the law. The law, however, is constantly based on notions of morality, and if all laws representing essentially moral choices are to be invalidated under the Due Process Clause, the courts will be very busy indeed. Even respondent makes no such claim, but insists that majority sentiments about the morality of homosexuality should be declared inadequate. We do not agree, and are unpersuaded that the sodomy laws of some 25 States should be invalidated on this basis.

Accordingly, the judgment of the Court of Appeals is *Reversed.*

NOTES

1. *Bowers* is very likely the low point in the campaign to win equal rights for gay men and women. Not only did the Court reject the argument that Hardwick was engaging in constitutionally protected conduct when he was having consensual sex with another man in his own bedroom, the Court characterized that argument as "facetious," a word that means "frivolous," or "not to be taken seriously." The outcome of the case could be predicted very early in the majority opinion when the majority characterized the issue as whether the constitution created a fundamental right to engage in homosexual sodomy. No matter how hard or how long you look, you will not find any words in the constitution that protect "homosexual sodomy." That made the decision for the majority quite easy.

Of course, no matter how hard you look, you won't find the words "abortion," "contraceptives," or "sterilization" in the Constitution either, and yet, long before *Bowers*, the Court had identified these areas as within the constitutionally protected right of privacy that the state must keep out of without a compelling interest. The *Bowers* majority, however, insisted that all of the Court's substantive due process precedents had involved "family, marriage, or procreation" and that these interests were unconnected with "homosexual activity."

Having decided to apply a rational basis standard of review, the *Bowers* majority determined that the state's criminalization of sodomy was rationally related to the state's legitimate interest in promoting morality. The majoritarian view of morality, as evidenced in the anti-sodomy law, was that sexual relations between same-sex partners were immoral. The *Bowers* majority found no reason to question the equation of same-sex relations with immorality and did not even consider the possibility that the purported promotion of morality was in fact prejudice masquerading as morality.

2. *Bowers* was a due process rather than an equal protection decision but the *Bowers* decision made it much more difficult for gay men and women to prevail in any subsequent equal protection claim. For example, in rejecting a challenge to the Navy's policy of excluding gay persons from military service, the Court of Appeals for the Federal Circuit justified its decision, in part, as follows:

> After *Hardwick* it cannot logically be asserted that discrimination against homosexuals is constitutionally infirm. We agree with the court in *Padula v. Webster* that "there can hardly be more palpable discrimination against a class than making the conduct that defines the class criminal." *Woodward v. United States*, 871 F.2d 1068, 1076 (Fed. Cir 1989), citing *Padula*.

B. CLOSER REVIEW OF SEXUAL ORIENTATION CLASSIFICATIONS IN THE SUPREME COURT

The cases in the preceding section were all relatively modern, decided between 1967 and 1986. Thus, as of 1986, it appeared that the courts were unwilling to use the Equal Protection Clause as a vehicle to intervene in the widespread societal practice of disadvantaging gay men and women. That began to change in the next decade, with the following case.

Romer v. Evans
517 U.S. 620 (1996)

[In *Romer,* the Court considered an amendment to the Colorado constitution that prohibited both state and local governments from enacting statutes, regulations, or ordinances that prohibited discrimination on the basis of "homosexual, lesbian or bisexual orientation." This provision had the double effect of (1) invalidating existing ordinances that prohibited anti-gay discrimination and (2) preventing the adoption of new ordinances that prohibited anti-gay discrimination without re-amending the Colorado constitution. The Court's opinion in *Romer* is set forth in Chapter 1 of this Casebook as an example of heightened rational basis review. The Court could have chosen *Romer* as a vehicle to consider whether gay men and women should be treated as a suspect or quasi-suspect class, but it chose not to follow that path. Instead, the Court invalidated the Colorado constitutional provision using a heightened form of rational basis review, without ever considering the need for a formal level of heightened scrutiny.]

NOTES

1. The techniques of heightened rational basis review that were introduced in Chapter 1 are quite apparent in the Court's *Romer* opinion. First, the Court was unwilling to hypothesize a permissible purpose for the law or give weight to a post hoc rationalization by government attorneys. The Court was unwilling to accept the purported justifications for the law, refused to accept an alleged correlation between the classification in the law and its alleged purpose, and finally, having identified the actual purpose of the amendment, the Court found that purpose to be impermissible. The *Romer* Court stated:

> Laws of the kind now before us raise the inevitable inference that the disadvantage imposed is born of animosity toward the class of persons affected. "[I]f the constitutional conception of 'equal protection of the laws' means anything, it must at the very least mean that a bare ... desire to harm a politically unpopular group cannot constitute a *legitimate* governmental interest." Department of Agriculture v. Moreno, 413 U.S. 528, 534 (1973). Even laws enacted for broad and ambitious purposes often can be explained by reference to legitimate public policies which justify the incidental disadvantages they impose on certain persons. Amendment 2, however, in making a general announcement that gays and lesbians shall not have any particular protections from the law, inflicts on them immediate, continuing, and real injuries that outrun and belie any legitimate justifications that may be claimed for it. . . .

> The primary rationale the State offers for Amendment 2 is respect for other citizens' freedom of association, and in particular the liberties of landlords or employers who have personal or religious objections to homosexuality. Colorado also cites its interest in conserving resources to fight discrimination against other groups. The breadth of the amendment is so far removed from these particular justifications that we find it impossible to credit them. We cannot say that Amendment 2 is directed to any identifiable legitimate purpose or discrete objective. It is a status-based enactment divorced from any factual context from which we could discern a relationship to legitimate state interests; it is a classification of persons undertaken for its own sake, something the Equal Protection Clause does not permit. "[C]lass legislation ... [is] obnoxious to the prohibitions of the Fourteenth Amendment." ...

> We must conclude that Amendment 2 classifies homosexuals not to further a proper legislative end but to make them unequal to everyone else. This Colorado cannot do. A State cannot so deem a class of persons a stranger to its laws. Amendment 2 violates the Equal Protection Clause.

2. *Romer v. Evans* is an important milestone in the law's treatment of sexual orientation as a basis of government classification. Although the Court did not identify gay men and women as a quasi-suspect class, the Court's opinion made clear that discrimination against gay persons for its own sake was no longer constitutionally permissible. Since the Court purported to use rational basis review, its opinion left open the possibility that later courts, in applying that standard, would

use the very deferential version of that standard and thus continue to uphold discriminations on the basis of sexual orientation. That did happen in many cases. Still, the Supreme Court had established a precedent that would allow lower courts to look closely for animosity toward gay men and women and to invalidate statutes on that basis.

3. Even after *Romer*, however, there was still a major obstacle to the law's equal treatment of gay men and women—the Court's 1986 opinion in *Bowers v. Hardwick*. How could an employer's decision not to hire a gay person be wrongful when the conduct that gay persons engaged in was itself illegal? There may have been a logical flaw in this argument, but as long as sodomy statutes could be enforced against gay persons, that differential treatment would be viewed by some as adequate justification for treating gay men and women differently in other areas as well. That argument ended with the next case, *Lawrence v. Texas*.

Lawrence v. Texas
539 U.S. 558 (2003)

Justice KENNEDY delivered the opinion of the Court.

Liberty protects the person from unwarranted government intrusions into a dwelling or other private places. In our tradition the State is not omnipresent in the home. And there are other spheres of our lives and existence, outside the home, where the State should not be a dominant presence. Freedom extends beyond spatial bounds. Liberty presumes an autonomy of self that includes freedom of thought, belief, expression, and certain intimate conduct. The instant case involves liberty of the person both in its spatial and in its more transcendent dimensions.

I

The question before the Court is the validity of a Texas statute making it a crime for two persons of the same sex to engage in certain intimate sexual conduct.

In Houston, Texas, officers of the Harris County Police Department were dispatched to a private residence in response to a reported weapons disturbance. They entered an apartment where one of the petitioners, John Geddes Lawrence, resided. The right of the police to enter does not seem to have been questioned. The officers observed Lawrence and another man, Tyron Garner, engaging in a sexual act. The two petitioners were arrested, held in custody overnight, and charged and convicted before a Justice of the Peace.

The complaints described their crime as "deviate sexual intercourse, namely anal sex, with a member of the same sex (man)." The applicable state law is Tex. Penal Code Ann. § 21.06(a) (2003). It provides: "A person commits an offense if he engages in deviate sexual intercourse with another individual of the same sex." The statute defines "[d]eviate sexual intercourse" as follows:

> (A) any contact between any part of the genitals of one person and the mouth or anus of another person; or
>
> "(B) the penetration of the genitals or the anus of another person with an object. § 21.01(1).

CHAPTER 6: CLASSIFICATIONS BASED ON SEXUAL ORIENTATION

II

We conclude the case should be resolved by determining whether the petitioners were free as adults to engage in the private conduct in the exercise of their liberty under the Due Process Clause of the Fourteenth Amendment to the Constitution. For this inquiry we deem it necessary to reconsider the Court's holding in *Bowers*.

There are broad statements of the substantive reach of liberty under the Due Process Clause in earlier cases, including *Pierce v. Society of Sisters,* 268 U.S. 510 (1925), and *Meyer v. Nebraska,* 262 U.S. 390 (1923); but the most pertinent beginning point is our decision in *Griswold v. Connecticut,* 381 U.S. 479 (1965).

In *Griswold* the Court invalidated a state law prohibiting the use of drugs or devices of contraception and counseling or aiding and abetting the use of contraceptives. The Court described the protected interest as a right to privacy and placed emphasis on the marriage relation and the protected space of the marital bedroom.

After *Griswold* it was established that the right to make certain decisions regarding sexual conduct extends beyond the marital relationship. In *Eisenstadt v. Baird,* 405 U.S. 438 (1972), the Court invalidated a law prohibiting the distribution of contraceptives to unmarried persons. The case was decided under the Equal Protection Clause; but with respect to unmarried persons, the Court went on to state the fundamental proposition that the law impaired the exercise of their personal rights. It quoted from the statement of the Court of Appeals finding the law to be in conflict with fundamental human rights, and it followed with this statement of its own:

> It is true that in *Griswold* the right of privacy in question inhered in the marital relationship.... If the right of privacy means anything, it is the right of the *individual,* married or single, to be free from unwarranted governmental intrusion into matters so fundamentally affecting a person as the decision whether to bear or beget a child.

The opinions in *Griswold* and *Eisenstadt* were part of the background for the decision in *Roe v. Wade,* 410 U.S. 113 (1973). As is well known, the case involved a challenge to the Texas law prohibiting abortions, but the laws of other States were affected as well. Although the Court held the woman's rights were not absolute, her right to elect an abortion did have real and substantial protection as an exercise of her liberty under the Due Process Clause. The Court cited cases that protect spatial freedom and cases that go well beyond it. *Roe* recognized the right of a woman to make certain fundamental decisions affecting her destiny and confirmed once more that the protection of liberty under the Due Process Clause has a substantive dimension of fundamental significance in defining the rights of the person.

In *Carey v. Population Services Int'l,* 431 U.S. 678 (1977), the Court confronted a New York law forbidding sale or distribution of contraceptive devices to persons under 16 years of age. Although there was no single opinion for the Court, the law was invalidated. Both *Eisenstadt* and *Carey,* as well as the holding and rationale in *Roe,* confirmed that the reasoning of *Griswold* could not be confined to the protection of rights of married adults. This was the state of the law with respect to some of the most relevant cases when the Court considered *Bowers v. Hardwick.*

The Court began its substantive discussion in *Bowers* as follows: "The issue presented is whether the Federal Constitution confers a fundamental right upon homosexuals to engage in sodomy and hence invalidates the laws of the many States that still make such conduct illegal and have done so for a very long time." That statement, we now conclude, discloses the Court's own failure to appreciate the extent of the liberty at stake. To say that the issue in *Bowers* was simply the right to engage in certain sexual conduct demeans the claim the individual put forward, just as it would demean a married couple were it to be said marriage is simply about the right to have sexual intercourse. The laws involved in *Bowers* and here are, to be sure, statutes that purport to do no more than prohibit a particular sexual act. Their penalties and purposes, though, have more far-reaching consequences, touching upon the most private human conduct, sexual behavior, and in the most private of places, the home. The statutes do seek to control a personal relationship that, whether or not entitled to formal recognition in the law, is within the liberty of persons to choose without being punished as criminals.

This, as a general rule, should counsel against attempts by the State, or a court, to define the meaning of the relationship or to set its boundaries absent injury to a person or abuse of an institution the law protects. It suffices for us to acknowledge that adults may choose to enter upon this relationship in the confines of their homes and their own private lives and still retain their dignity as free persons. When sexuality finds overt expression in intimate conduct with another person, the conduct can be but one element in a personal bond that is more enduring. The liberty protected by the Constitution allows homosexual persons the right to make this choice.

Having misapprehended the claim of liberty there presented to it, and thus stating the claim to be whether there is a fundamental right to engage in consensual sodomy, the *Bowers* Court said: "Proscriptions against that conduct have ancient roots." In academic writings, and in many of the scholarly *amicus* briefs filed to assist the Court in this case, there are fundamental criticisms of the historical premises relied upon by the majority and concurring opinions in *Bowers*. Brief for Cato Institute as *Amicus Curiae* 16–17; Brief for American Civil Liberties Union et al. as *Amici Curiae* 15–21; Brief for Professors of History et al. as *Amici Curiae* 3–10. We need not enter this debate in the attempt to reach a definitive historical judgment, but the following considerations counsel against adopting the definitive conclusions upon which *Bowers* placed such reliance. At the outset it should be noted that there is no longstanding history in this country of laws directed at homosexual conduct as a distinct matter. Beginning in colonial times there were prohibitions of sodomy derived from the English criminal laws passed in the first instance by the Reformation Parliament of 1533. The English prohibition was understood to include relations between men and women as well as relations between men and men. See, *e.g., King v. Wiseman,* 92 Eng. Rep. 774, 775 (K.B.1718) (interpreting "mankind" in Act of 1533 as including women and girls). Nineteenth-century commentators similarly read American sodomy, buggery, and crime-against-nature statutes as criminalizing certain relations between men and women and between men and men. See, *e.g.,* 2 J. Bishop, Criminal Law § 1028 (1858); 2 J. Chitty, Criminal Law 47–50 (5th Am. ed. 1847); R. Desty, A Compendium of American Criminal Law 143 (1882); J. May, The Law of Crimes § 203 (2d ed. 1893). The absence of legal prohibitions focusing on homosexual conduct may be explained in part by noting that according to some scholars the concept of the homosexual as a distinct category of person did not emerge until the late 19th century. See, e.g., J. Katz, The Invention of Heterosexuality 10 (1995); J. D'Emilio & E. Freedman, Intimate Matters: A History of Sexuality in America 121 (2d ed. 1997) ("The modern terms *homosexuality* and *heterosexuality* do not apply to an era that had not yet articulated these distinctions"). Thus early American sodomy laws were not directed at homosexuals as such but instead sought to prohibit nonprocreative sexual activity more generally. This does not suggest approval of homosexual conduct. It does tend to show that this particular form of conduct was not thought of as a separate category from like conduct between heterosexual persons.

Laws prohibiting sodomy do not seem to have been enforced against consenting adults acting in private. A substantial number of sodomy prosecutions and convictions for which there are surviving records were for predatory acts against those who could not or did not consent, as in the case of a minor or the victim of an assault. As to these, one purpose for the prohibitions was to ensure there would be no lack of coverage if a predator committed a sexual assault that did not constitute rape as defined by the criminal law. Thus the model sodomy indictments presented in a 19th-century treatise, see 2 Chitty, *supra*, at 49, addressed the predatory acts of an adult man against a minor girl or minor boy. Instead of targeting relations between consenting adults in private, 19th-century sodomy prosecutions typically involved relations between men and minor girls or minor boys, relations between adults involving force, relations between adults implicating disparity in status, or relations between men and animals.

To the extent that there were any prosecutions for the acts in question, 19th-century evidence rules imposed a burden that would make a conviction more difficult to obtain even taking into account the problems always inherent in prosecuting consensual acts committed in private. Under then-prevailing standards, a man could not be convicted of sodomy based upon testimony of a consenting partner, because the partner was considered an accomplice. A partner's testimony, however, was admissible if he or she had not consented to the act or was a minor, and therefore incapable of consent. See, *e.g.*, F. Wharton, Criminal Law 443 (2d ed. 1852); 1 F. Wharton, Criminal Law 512 (8th ed. 1880). The rule may explain in part the infrequency of these prosecutions. In all events that infrequency makes it difficult to say that society approved of a rigorous and systematic punishment of the consensual acts committed in private and by adults. The longstanding criminal prohibition of homosexual sodomy upon which the *Bowers* decision placed such reliance is as consistent with a general condemnation of nonprocreative sex as it is with an established tradition of prosecuting acts because of their homosexual character.

The policy of punishing consenting adults for private acts was not much discussed in the early legal literature. We can infer that one reason for this was the very private nature of the conduct. Despite the absence of prosecutions, there may have been periods in which there was public criticism of homosexuals as such and an insistence that the criminal laws be enforced to discourage their practices. But far from possessing "ancient roots," *Bowers,* 478 U.S., at 192, American laws targeting same-sex couples did not develop until the last third of the 20th century. The reported decisions concerning the prosecution of consensual, homosexual sodomy between adults for the years 1880–1995 are not always clear in the details, but a significant number involved conduct in a public place.

It was not until the 1970's that any State singled out same-sex relations for criminal prosecution, and only nine States have done so. Post--*Bowers* even some of these States did not adhere to the policy of suppressing homosexual conduct. Over the course of the last decades, States with same-sex prohibitions have moved toward abolishing them.

In summary, the historical grounds relied upon in *Bowers* are more complex than the majority opinion and the concurring opinion by Chief Justice Burger indicate. Their historical premises are not without doubt and, at the very least, are overstated.

It must be acknowledged, of course, that the Court in *Bowers* was making the broader point that for centuries there have been powerful voices to condemn homosexual conduct as immoral. The condemnation has been shaped by religious beliefs, conceptions of right and acceptable behavior, and respect for the traditional family. For many persons these are not trivial concerns but profound and deep convictions accepted as ethical and moral principles to which they aspire and which thus determine the course of their lives. These considerations do not answer the question before us, however. The issue is whether the majority may use the power of the State to enforce these views on the whole society through operation of the criminal law. "Our obligation is to define the liberty of all, not to mandate our own moral code." *Planned Parenthood of Southeastern Pa. v. Casey,* 505 U.S. 833, 850 (1992).

Chief Justice Burger joined the opinion for the Court in *Bowers* and further explained his views as follows: "Decisions of individuals relating to homosexual conduct have been subject to state intervention throughout the history of Western civilization. Condemnation of those practices is firmly rooted in Judeao–Christian moral and ethical standards." 478 U.S. at 196. As with Justice White's assumptions about history, scholarship casts some doubt on the sweeping nature of the statement by Chief Justice Burger as it pertains to private homosexual conduct between consenting adults. See, *e.g.,* Eskridge, *Hardwick and Historiography,* 1999 U. Ill. L.Rev. 631, 656. In all events we think that our laws and traditions in the past half century are of most relevance here. These references show an emerging awareness that liberty gives substantial protection to adult persons in deciding how to conduct their private lives in matters pertaining to sex. "[H]istory and tradition are the starting point but not in all cases the ending point of the substantive due process inquiry." *County of Sacramento v. Lewis,* 523 U.S. 833, 857 (1998) (KENNEDY, J., concurring).

This emerging recognition should have been apparent when *Bowers* was decided. In 1955 the American Law Institute promulgated the Model Penal Code and made clear that it did not recommend or provide for "criminal penalties for consensual sexual relations conducted in private." ALI, Model Penal Code § 213.2, Comment 2, p. 372 (1980). It justified its decision on three grounds: (1) The prohibitions undermined respect for the law by penalizing conduct many people engaged in; (2) the statutes regulated private conduct not harmful to others; and (3) the laws were arbitrarily enforced and thus invited the danger of blackmail. ALI, Model Penal Code, Commentary 277–280 (Tent. Draft No. 4, 1955). In 1961 Illinois changed its laws to conform to the Model Penal Code. Other States soon followed.

In *Bowers* the Court referred to the fact that before 1961 all 50 States had outlawed sodomy, and that at the time of the Court's decision 24 States and the District of Columbia had sodomy laws. 478 U.S., at 192–193. Justice Powell pointed out that these prohibitions often were being ignored, however. Georgia, for instance, had not sought to enforce its law for decades. *Id.,* at 197–198, n. 2 ("The history of nonenforcement suggests the moribund character today of laws criminalizing this type of private, consensual conduct").

The sweeping references by Chief Justice Burger to the history of Western civilization and to Judeo–Christian moral and ethical standards did not take account of other authorities pointing in an opposite direction. A committee advising the British Parliament recommended in 1957 repeal of laws punishing homosexual conduct. The Wolfenden Report: Report of the Committee on Homosexual Offenses and Prostitution (1963). Parliament enacted the substance of those recommendations 10 years later. Sexual Offences Act 1967, § 1.

Of even more importance, almost five years before *Bowers* was decided the European Court of Human Rights considered a case with parallels to *Bowers* and to today's case. An adult male resident in Northern Ireland alleged he was a practicing homosexual who desired to engage in consensual homosexual conduct. The laws of Northern Ireland forbade him that right. He alleged that he had been questioned, his home had been searched, and he feared criminal prosecution. The court held that the laws proscribing the conduct were invalid under the European Convention on Human Rights. *Dudgeon v. United Kingdom,* 45 Eur. Ct. H.R. (1981) & ¶ 52. Authoritative in all countries that are members of the Council of Europe (21 nations then, 45 nations now), the decision is at odds with the premise in *Bowers* that the claim put forward was insubstantial in our Western civilization.

In our own constitutional system the deficiencies in *Bowers* became even more apparent in the years following its announcement. The 25 States with laws prohibiting the relevant conduct referenced in the *Bowers* decision are reduced now to 13, of which 4 enforce their laws only against homosexual conduct. In those States where sodomy is still proscribed, whether for same-sex or heterosexual conduct, there is a pattern of nonenforcement with respect to consenting adults acting in private. The State of Texas admitted in 1994 that as of that date it had not prosecuted anyone under those circumstances. *State v. Morales,* 869 S.W.2d 941, 943.

Two principal cases decided after *Bowers* cast its holding into even more doubt. In *Planned Parenthood of Southeastern Pa. v. Casey,* 505 U.S. 833 (1992), the Court reaffirmed the substantive force of the liberty protected by the Due Process Clause. The *Casey* decision again confirmed that our laws and tradition afford constitutional protection to personal decisions relating to marriage, procreation, contraception, family relationships, child rearing, and education. In explaining the respect the Constitution demands for the autonomy of the person in making these choices, we stated as follows:

> These matters, involving the most intimate and personal choices a person may make in a lifetime, choices central to personal dignity and autonomy, are central to the liberty protected by the Fourteenth Amendment. At the heart of liberty is the right to define one's own concept of existence, of meaning, of the universe, and of the mystery of human life. Beliefs about these matters could not define the attributes of personhood were they formed under compulsion of the State.

Persons in a homosexual relationship may seek autonomy for these purposes, just as heterosexual persons do. The decision in *Bowers* would deny them this right.

The second post- *Bowers* case of principal relevance is *Romer v. Evans,* 517 U.S. 620 (1996). There the Court struck down class-based legislation directed at homosexuals as a violation of the Equal Protection Clause. *Romer* invalidated an amendment to Colorado's Constitution which named as a solitary class persons who were homosexuals, lesbians, or bisexual either by "orientation, conduct, practices or relationships," *id.,* at 624, and deprived them of protection under state antidiscrimination laws. We concluded that the provision was "born of animosity toward the class of persons affected" and further that it had no rational relation to a legitimate governmental purpose. *Id.* at 634.

As an alternative argument in this case, counsel for the petitioners and some *amici* contend that *Romer* provides the basis for declaring the Texas statute invalid under the Equal Protection Clause. That is a tenable argument, but we conclude the instant case requires us to address whether *Bowers* itself has continuing validity. Were we to hold the statute invalid under the Equal Protection Clause some might question whether a prohibition would be valid if drawn differently, say, to prohibit the conduct both between same-sex and different-sex participants.

Equality of treatment and the due process right to demand respect for conduct protected by the substantive guarantee of liberty are linked in important respects, and a decision on the latter point advances both interests. If protected conduct is made criminal and the law which does so remains unexamined for its substantive validity, its stigma might remain even if it were not enforceable as drawn for equal protection reasons. When homosexual conduct is made criminal by the law of the State, that declaration in and of itself is an invitation to subject homosexual persons to discrimination both in the public and in the private spheres. The central holding of *Bowers* has been brought in question by this case, and it should be addressed. Its continuance as precedent demeans the lives of homosexual persons.

The foundations of *Bowers* have sustained serious erosion from our recent decisions in *Casey* and *Romer*. When our precedent has been thus weakened, criticism from other sources is of greater significance. In the United States criticism of *Bowers* has been substantial and continuing, disapproving of its reasoning in all respects, not just as to its historical assumptions. See, *e.g.,* C. Fried, Order and Law: Arguing the Reagan Revolution—A Firsthand Account 81–84 (1991); R. Posner, Sex and Reason 341–350 (1992). The courts of five different States have declined to follow it in interpreting provisions in their own state constitutions parallel to the Due Process Clause of the Fourteenth Amendment, see *Jegley v. Picado,* 349 Ark. 600 (2002); *Powell v. State,* 270 Ga. 327 (1998); *Gryczan v. State,* 283 Mont. 433 (1997); *Campbell v. Sundquist,* 926 S.W.2d 250 (Tenn.App.1996); *Commonwealth v. Wasson,* 842 S.W.2d 487 (Ky.1992).

To the extent *Bowers* relied on values we share with a wider civilization, it should be noted that the reasoning and holding in *Bowers* have been rejected elsewhere. The European Court of Human Rights has followed not *Bowers* but its own decision in *Dudgeon v. United Kingdom.* See *P.G. & J.H. v. United Kingdom,* App. No. 00044787/98, & ¶ 56 (Eur.Ct.H. R., Sept. 25, 2001); *Modinos v. Cyprus,* 259 Eur. Ct. H.R. (1993); *Norris v. Ireland,* 142 Eur. Ct. H.R. (1988). Other nations, too, have taken action consistent with an affirmation of the protected right of homosexual adults to engage in intimate, consensual conduct. The right the petitioners seek in this case has been accepted as an integral part of human freedom in many other countries. There has been no showing that in this country the governmental interest in circumscribing personal choice is somehow more legitimate or urgent.

The doctrine of *stare decisis* is essential to the respect accorded to the judgments of the Court and to the stability of the law. It is not, however, an inexorable command. *Payne v. Tennessee,* 501 U.S. 808, 828 (1991) ("*Stare decisis* is not an inexorable command; rather, it 'is a principle of policy and not a mechanical formula of adherence to the latest decision'" (quoting *Helvering v. Hallock,* 309 U.S. 106 (1940))). In *Casey* we noted that when a court is asked to overrule a precedent recognizing a constitutional liberty interest, individual or societal reliance on the existence of that liberty cautions with particular strength against reversing course. 505 U.S., at 855–856; see also *id.,* at 844 ("Liberty finds no refuge in a jurisprudence of doubt"). The holding in *Bowers,* however, has not induced detrimental reliance comparable to some instances where recognized individual rights are involved. Indeed, there has been no individual or societal reliance on *Bowers* of the sort that could counsel against overturning its holding once there are compelling reasons to do so. *Bowers* itself causes uncertainty, for the precedents before and after its issuance contradict its central holding.

The rationale of *Bowers* does not withstand careful analysis. In his dissenting opinion in Bowers Justice STEVENS came to these conclusions:

> Our prior cases make two propositions abundantly clear. First, the fact that the governing

majority in a State has traditionally viewed a particular practice as immoral is not a sufficient reason for upholding a law prohibiting the practice; neither history nor tradition could save a law prohibiting miscegenation from constitutional attack. Second, individual decisions by married persons, concerning the intimacies of their physical relationship, even when not intended to produce offspring, are a form of 'liberty' protected by the Due Process Clause of the Fourteenth Amendment. Moreover, this protection extends to intimate choices by unmarried as well as married persons. 478 U.S. at 216.

Justice STEVENS' analysis, in our view, should have been controlling in *Bowers* and should control here.

Bowers was not correct when it was decided, and it is not correct today. It ought not to remain binding precedent. *Bowers v. Hardwick* should be and now is overruled.

The present case does not involve minors. It does not involve persons who might be injured or coerced or who are situated in relationships where consent might not easily be refused. It does not involve public conduct or prostitution. It does not involve whether the government must give formal recognition to any relationship that homosexual persons seek to enter. The case does involve two adults who, with full and mutual consent from each other, engaged in sexual practices common to a homosexual lifestyle. The petitioners are entitled to respect for their private lives. The State cannot demean their existence or control their destiny by making their private sexual conduct a crime. Their right to liberty under the Due Process Clause gives them the full right to engage in their conduct without intervention of the government. "It is a promise of the Constitution that there is a realm of personal liberty which the government may not enter." *Casey, supra,* at 847. The Texas statute furthers no legitimate state interest which can justify its intrusion into the personal and private life of the individual.

Had those who drew and ratified the Due Process Clauses of the Fifth Amendment or the Fourteenth Amendment known the components of liberty in its manifold possibilities, they might have been more specific. They did not presume to have this insight. They knew times can blind us to certain truths and later generations can see that laws once thought necessary and proper in fact serve only to oppress. As the Constitution endures, persons in every generation can invoke its principles in their own search for greater freedom.

The judgment of the Court of Appeals for the Texas Fourteenth District is reversed, and the case is remanded for further proceedings not inconsistent with this opinion.

It is so ordered.

NOTES

1. *Lawrence* is an extremely important case in that it overrules *Bowers* and holds that constitutionally protected liberty includes some measure of private, consensual intimate sexual conduct. The exact holding of the case is difficult to pin down since the majority formulated its description of what is constitutionally protected in several different phrasings, including:

- an autonomy of self that includes freedom of thought, belief, expression, and certain intimate conduct;

- sexuality finding overt expression in intimate conduct with another person;

- individual decisions by married [and unmarried] persons, concerning the intimacies of their physical relationship, even when not intended to produce offspring;

- the petitioners are entitled to respect for their private lives. The State cannot demean their existence or control their destiny by making their private sexual conduct a crime; and

- there is a realm of personal liberty that the government may not enter.

Perhaps we can summarize the interest that *Lawrence* considers to be constitutionally protected to be "private consensual sexual autonomy."

2. The *Lawrence* Court also directly confronted and rejected the claim of the *Bowers* majority that there was a long history and tradition of criminalizing same-sex sexual relations. According to *Lawrence*, "there is no longstanding history in this country of laws directed at homosexual conduct as a distinct matter." To the extent earlier laws criminalized sodomy, that prohibition sought to prohibit nonprocreative sexual activity in general and was thus directed at opposite-sex as well as same-sex relations. Further, laws prohibiting sodomy were not enforced against consenting adults acting in private. They were generally enforced only in cases of nonconsensual activity or activity that took place in a public place. According to *Lawrence*, American laws targeting same-sex couples did not develop until the last third of the 20th century. Thus, according to *Lawrence*, the claim that the criminal prohibition of sodomy had "ancient roots" was simply not true.

3. The *Lawrence* Court also flatly rejected the view in *Bowers* that the promotion of morality is a sufficient state interest to justify the imposition of state intrusion into private consensual conduct—"the fact that the governing majority in a State has traditionally viewed a particular practice as immoral is not a sufficient reason for upholding a law prohibiting the practice; neither history nor tradition could save a law prohibiting miscegenation from constitutional attack."

Courts after *Lawrence* have wrestled with the question of whether the promotion of morality can still be a permissible purpose of a law. Some courts have interpreted this language in Lawrence as meaning that the promotion of morality can never constitute a legitimate purpose to justify a governmental classification. *E.g., Reliable Consultants v. Earle*, 517 F.3d 738 (5th Cir. 2008) (holding that a statute that prohibited the sale of sexual devices violated the constitutional right to engage in private intimate conduct in the home without government intrusion and stating that "These interests in 'public morality' cannot constitutionally sustain the statute after *Lawrence*.")

Other courts read that language more narrowly so that the promotion of morality through legislation, a longstanding practice, remains an appropriate state interest in certain contexts. In terms of the longstanding nature of the practice, a number of Supreme Court cases upheld obscenity statutes. *Barnes v. Glen Theatre, Inc.*, 501 U.S. 560 (1991); *Paris Adult Theatre I v. Slaton*, 413 U.S. 49 (1973); *Roth v. United States*, 354 U.S. 476 (1957). These cases reasoned that protecting "the social interest in order and morality" was a legitimate state interest justifying these statutes. *Roth*, 354 U.S. at 485. In *Williams v. Morgan*, 478 F.3d 1316 (11th Cir. 2007), the Eleventh Circuit upheld a state statute that prohibited the commercial distribution of certain sexual devices. The court distinguished *Lawrence* as follows:

However, while the statute at issue in *Lawrence* criminalized private sexual conduct, the statute at issue in this case forbids public, commercial activity. To the extent *Lawrence* rejects public morality as a legitimate government interest, it invalidates only those laws that target conduct that is both private and non-commercial.

The court upheld the challenged statute because it "target[ed] commerce in sexual devices, an inherently public activity." The court explained further that it did not read *Lawrence* as having "rendered public morality altogether illegitimate as a rational basis." Thus, even after *Lawrence*, the promotion of morality can be a legitimate state interest, at least in the proper context.

4. What standard of review did the *Lawrence* Court apply? Surprisingly, there is not a clear answer to that question. On the one hand, it seems that *Lawrence* must have applied a strict scrutiny standard, since the Court found that the challenged statute interfered with a constitutionally protected liberty interest and the Court cited both *Roe* and *Carey*, cases that insisted that when a legislative enactment infringes on a constitutionally protected liberty, it must be narrowly tailored a compelling interest. On the other hand the *Lawrence* Court never mentioned the "narrowly tailored-compelling interest" test. In fact, at its conclusion, the Court found that "[t]he Texas statute furthers no legitimate state interest which can justify its intrusion into the personal and private life of the individual." This looks like the language of rational basis review. In response to this uncertainty about the standard of review, some courts have determined that adherence to *Lawrence* requires an intermediate level of scrutiny. *See infra* Sec. C.4.

5. Like *Bowers*, *Lawrence* is a due process rather than an equal protection case. It is, however a crucially important precedent for equal protection purposes since it limits a state's ability to single out gay men and women by reference to the sexual conduct they engage in. Justice O'Connor wrote a concurring opinion in *Lawrence* that would have decided the case on equal protection grounds, since it singled out gay persons alone in prohibiting certain personal relationships. The majority's due process holding, however, is broader than O'Connor's equal protection holding in that it completely prohibits states from enacting laws prohibiting private, consensual sexual relationships.

C. WHAT IS THE PROPER STANDARD OF REVIEW OF CLASSIFICATIONS THAT DISADVANTAGE GAY MEN AND WOMEN?

When challenges are made to classifications that disadvantage gay men and women, the first judgment to be made is the proper standard of review. The decision that a court makes at this initial stage of analysis will have a significant, although not conclusive, effect on the outcome of the litigation. Courts have used four different kinds of scrutiny of classifications based on sexual orientation: (1) deferential rational basis review; (2) heightened rational basis review; (3) intermediate scrutiny because gay men and women are a quasi-suspect class; and (4) something like intermediate scrutiny because classifications based on sexual orientation infringe on the implied fundamental right of privacy identified in *Lawrence v. Texas*. This section examines these four standards of review.

1. TRADITIONAL DEFERENTIAL RATIONAL BASIS REVIEW

When a government action is alleged to violate the Equal Protection Clause, the ordinary test it must satisfy is the rational basis standard—the classification must be rationally related to a permissible state interest. This standard is reviewed at some length in Chapter 1, *supra*. The test is usually very deferential because a court will not usually insist on any evidence of the actual purpose of a law nor any evidence that there is an actual connection between the classification and the purpose. When used in this way, the deferential rational basis standard is usually so deferential as to amount to no review at all.

This highly deferential rational basis standard was in fact the standard used, until recently, in almost all cases challenging classifications based on sexual orientation, and, predictably, those challenges failed. *See, e.g., Dronenburg v. Zech*, 741 F.2d 1388 (D.C. Circ., 1984); *Lofton v. Sec. of Dep't of Children & Fam. Servs.*, 358 F.3d 804 (11th Cir.2004); *High Tech Gays v. Def. Indus. Sec. Clearance Office*, 895 F.2d 563 (9th Cir.1990); *Ben–Shalom v. Marsh*, 881 F.2d 454 (7th Cir.1989). Even in recent years, when alternate standards of review of sexual orientation classifications have become more common, the deferential rational basis standard still continues to be used.

For example, in *Citizens for Equal Protection v. Bruning*, 455 F.3d 859 (8th Cir. 2006), the Eighth Circuit considered an amendment to the Nebraska State Constitution that provided that "[o]nly marriage between a man and a woman shall be valid or recognized in Nebraska." The court cited *Heller* and *Beach Communications* for the propositions that "a statutory classification that neither proceeds along suspect lines nor infringes fundamental constitutional rights must be upheld against equal protection challenge if there is any reasonably conceivable state of facts that could provide a rational-basis for the classification," and that the classification was to be afforded "a strong presumption of validity." The State, defending the provision, argued that the government interest that supported this provision was "steering procreation into marriage." The court cited no evidence as to the purpose of the enactment but simply accepted the post-hoc rationalization put forward by the State in defending the case.

The challengers to the law argued that the law did not advance the State's purpose of steering procreation into marriage. As of matter of logic, they argued, keeping gay people out of marriage was not likely to steer heterosexual persons into procreative marriages. But the court was not looking for proof of that correlation. The *Bruning* decision is a classic version of deferential rationality. The court was not concerned with evidence of the actual purpose of the statute, it was not concerned with whether the statutory classification actually advanced a statutory purpose, and it easily rejected the argument that the enactment of the statute was motivated by prejudice against same-sex couples.

Another recent example of this kind of deferential rationality is *In re Kandu*, 315 B.R. 123 (Bankr. W.D. Wash. 2004), in which the Bankruptcy Court upheld the Defense of Marriage Act (DOMA), a federal statute that provides, *inter alia*, that for federal purposes "the word 'marriage' means only a legal union between one man and one woman as husband and wife." In that case, two women who had been legally married in Canada filed a joint bankruptcy petition. The bankruptcy court did not allow the joint filing because the marriage was not recognized under DOMA. The debtors then argued that DOMA was a violation of equal protection. The court, citing both *Heller* and *Beach Communications*, held that the challenger's burden is to "negative every conceivable basis which might support" the statute, whether or not the basis has a foundation in the record." The bankruptcy trustee, defending DOMA, argued that DOMA satisfied the rational-basis test because it "further[ed] the legitimate government interest in encouraging the development of relationships optimal for procreating and raising children." The court cited no evidence that these were the purposes of the statute other than the assertion of the trustee. This is the classic post hoc rationalization of government attorneys that is an acceptable source of purpose only under the deferential version of rational-basis review. The debtors pointed out that the same-sex classification was not well correlated with these purposes. They argued that there were two problems with the procreation and child-rearing justifications: on the one hand, "federal recognition of marriage has never been limited to couples willing or able to conceive and raise children," and on the other hand, "same-sex couples can reproduce with outside assistance." Thus, the statute recognized marriages of couples who could not or would not procreate yet refused to recognize marriages of couples who could and would procreate.

The court rejected those arguments, noting that the trustee need not produce any "evidence to sustain the rationality of a statutory classification" and that "a legislative choice is not subject to courtroom fact-finding and may be based on rational speculation unsupported by evidence or empirical data." The court further found that "the lack of 'scientifically valid studies tending to establish a negative impact on the adjustment of children raised by an intact same-sex couple'" is not a problem in that "it is not incumbent on the government to produce any evidence for the record."

These cases that use the deferential version of rationality review have been the most common form of review of same-sex classifications. They demonstrate that, when a court uses this standard of review, no classification that disadvantages gay men and women will be invalidated.

2. *MORE DEMANDING RATIONAL BASIS REVIEW*

Occasionally, even when applying rational basis review, courts used a heightened version of the doctrine that is not deferential and imposes real constraints on government actors. This version of the doctrine was explored *supra* in Chapter 1. The Supreme Court's decision in *Romer v. Evans*, reprinted in Chapter 1, is an example of this kind of review. In that case, while reviewing a constitutional amendment that denied to gay men and women the basic protections of the legal system, the Court refused to credit the state's alleged purposes—respect for individual religious beliefs and a desire to focus on other forms of discrimination. Instead, the Court looked to the actual purpose of the provision—giving effect to animus against gay men and women—and found it to be an impermissible purpose.

Other more recent lower court cases have followed that model. In *Perry v. Brown*, 681 F.3d 1065 (9th Cir. 2012), the Court of Appeals for the Ninth Circuit invalidated California's Proposition 8, which had amended the California Constitution to provide that "Only marriage between a man and a woman is valid or recognized in California." The court reached this conclusion using the rational basis standard:

> Ordinarily, "if a law neither burdens a fundamental right nor targets a suspect class, we will uphold the legislative classification so long as it bears a rational relation to some legitimate end." *Romer*, 517 U.S. at 631. Such was the case in *Romer*, and it is the case here as well. The end must be one that is legitimate for the *government* to pursue, not just one that would be legitimate for a private actor. *See id.* at 632, 635. The question here, then, is whether California had any more legitimate justification for withdrawing from

gays and lesbians its constitutional protection with respect to the official designation of 'marriage' than Colorado did for withdrawing from that group all protection against discrimination generally.

Proposition 8, like Amendment 2, enacts a "'[d]iscrimination[ ] of an unusual character,' "which requires "'careful consideration to determine whether [it] [is] obnoxious to the' "Constitution. *Id.* at 633 (quoting *Louisville Gas & Elec. Co. v. Coleman,* 277 U.S. 32, 37–38). As in *Romer,* therefore, we must consider whether any *legitimate* state interest constitutes a rational basis for Proposition 8; otherwise, we must infer that it was enacted with only the constitutionally illegitimate basis of "animus toward the class it affects." *Romer,* 517 U.S. at 632.

We first consider four possible reasons offered by Proponents or amici to explain why Proposition 8 might have been enacted: (1) furthering California's interest in childrearing and responsible procreation, (2) proceeding with caution before making significant changes to marriage, (3) protecting religious freedom, and (4) preventing children from being taught about same-sex marriage in schools. To be credited, these rationales "must find some footing in the realities of the subject addressed by the legislation." *Heller v. Doe,* 509 U.S. 312, 321 (1993). They are, conversely, not to be credited if they "could not reasonably be conceived to be true by the governmental decisionmaker." *Vance v. Bradley,* 440 U.S. 93 (1979). Because Proposition 8 did not further any of these interests, we conclude that they cannot have been rational bases for this measure, whether or not they are legitimate state interests.

In *Massachusetts v. U.S. Dept. of Health and Human Services*, 682 F.3d 1(1st Cir. 2012) the Court of Appeals for the First Circuit invalidated Section 3 of DOMA using rational basis review. The court explained:

> Equal protection claims tested by this rational basis standard, famously called by Justice Holmes the "last resort of constitutional argument," *Buck v. Bell*, 274 U.S. 200, 208 (1927), rarely succeed. Courts accept as adequate any plausible factual basis, *Williamson v. Lee Optical of Oklahoma, Inc.,* 348 U.S. 483, 487–88 (1955), without regard to Congress' actual motives. *Beach Commc'ns,* 508 U.S. at 314. Means need not be narrowly drawn to meet—or even be entirely consistent with—the stated legislative ends. *Lee Optical,* 348 U.S. at 487–88. . . .
>
> Under such a rational basis standard, the Gill plaintiffs cannot prevail. Consider only one of the several justifications for DOMA offered by Congress itself, namely, that broadening the definition of marriage will reduce tax revenues and increase social security payments. This is the converse of the very advantages that the Gill plaintiffs are seeking, and Congress could rationally have believed that DOMA would reduce costs, even if newer studies of the actual economic effects of DOMA suggest that it may in fact raise costs for the federal government.
>
> However, that is not the end of the matter. Without relying on suspect classifications, Supreme Court equal protection decisions have both intensified scrutiny of purported justifications where minorities are subject to discrepant treatment and have limited the permissible justifications. And (as we later explain), in areas where state regulation has traditionally governed, the Court may require that the federal government interest in

intervention be shown with special clarity . . . Accordingly, we conclude that the extreme deference accorded to ordinary economic legislation in cases like *Lee Optical* would not be extended to DOMA by the Supreme Court; and without insisting on "compelling" or "important" justifications or "narrow tailoring," the Court would scrutinize with care the purported bases for the legislation. Before providing such scrutiny, a separate element absent in *Moreno, City of Cleburne*, and *Romer*—federalism—must be considered.

The statute, only a few paragraphs in length, is devoid of the express prefatory findings commonly made in major federal laws. Accordingly, in discerning and assessing Congress' basis for DOMA our main resort is the House Committee report and, in lesser measure, to variations of its themes advanced in the briefs before us. The committee report stated:

[T]he Committee briefly discusses four of the governmental interests advanced by this legislation: (1) defending and nurturing the institution of traditional, heterosexual marriage; (2) defending traditional notions of morality; (3) protecting state sovereignty and democratic self-governance; and (4) preserving scarce government resources.

We conclude, without resort to suspect classifications . . . that the rationales offered do not provide adequate support for section 3 of DOMA. Several of the reasons given do not match the statute and several others are diminished by specific holdings in Supreme Court decisions more or less directly on point. If we are right in thinking that disparate impact on minority interests and federalism concerns both require somewhat more in this case than almost automatic deference to Congress' will, this statute fails that test. . . . In reaching our judgment, we do not rely upon the charge that DOMA's hidden but dominant purpose was hostility to homosexuality. . . . Under current Supreme Court authority, Congress' denial of federal benefits to same-sex couples lawfully married in Massachusetts has not been adequately supported by any permissible federal interest.

These cases indicate that the more demanding version of rational basis review is sufficient to invalidate government action that disadvantages gay men and women. The problem is in predicting when a court will apply the more demanding version rather than the more traditional deferential version.

3. *HEIGHTENED SCRUTINY OF SEXUAL ORIENTATION CLASSIFICATIONS BECAUSE GAY MEN AND WOMEN ARE A QUASI-SUSPECT CLASS*

The Supreme Court decided *Romer v. Evans* on the basis of more demanding rationality review and did not even address the issue of whether gay men and women are a quasi-suspect class who should get the benefit of heightened scrutiny. To date, the Supreme Court has still not addressed this issue. In the lower federal courts and state courts, however, there have been a growing number of precedents in recent years.

As far back as 1988, a few federal courts were sympathetic to the argument that gay persons are a suspect class and should benefit from heightened scrutiny. In *Watkins v. U.S. Army*, 847 F.2d 1329 (9th Cir. 1988), a decision of a three-judge panel of the Ninth Circuit found that gay persons were a suspect class. The court therefore applied strict scrutiny to the military's policy of excluding gay persons from the military and found that it violated equal protection. That opinion, however, was withdrawn one year later by the Ninth Circuit judges sitting en banc, 875 F. 2d 699 (9th Cir. 1989), and the case was decided on an alternate, nonconstitutional basis. Thus, the original opinion was the law of the circuit for only one year. Other federal district courts had found gay persons to be a suspect class, but these opinions were reversed on appeal. *E.g., High Tech Gays v. Def. Indus. Sec. Clearance Office,* 895 F.2d 563 (9th Cir.1990); *Ben–Shalom v. Marsh,* 881 F.2d 454 (7th Cir.1989). Thus, as of the beginning of 2012, there were no currently valid federal court decisions holding that gay men and women were a suspect or quasi-suspect class.

State courts, however, interpreting their own state constitutions, were more open to that argument. In 2008, the Supreme Court of Connecticut held that a state law that defined marriage as "the union of one man and one woman" violated the state's equal protection clause. In doing so, the Court used precedents from the United States Supreme Court to justify its finding that gay men and women are a quasi-suspect class and that the marriage statute should receive intermediate scrutiny. The portion of the court's opinion that considers the factors to be considered in determining whether gay persons are a suspect class is exceptionally thoughtful and thorough and that portion of the opinion follows here.

Kerrigan v. Commissioner of Public Health
289 Conn. 135 (2008)
PALMER, J.

Although this court has indicated that a group may be entitled to heightened protection under the state constitution because of its status as a quasi-suspect class, we previously have not articulated the specific criteria to be considered in determining whether recognition as a quasi-suspect class is warranted. The United States Supreme Court, however, consistently has identified two factors that must be met, for purposes of the federal constitution, if a group is to be accorded such status. These two required factors are: (1) the group has suffered a history of invidious discrimination; see *United States v. Virginia,* 518 U.S. 515, 531-32 (1996); *Massachusetts Board of Retirement v. Murgia,* 427 U.S. 307, 313 (1976); and (2) the characteristics that distinguish the group's members bear "no relation to [their] ability to perform or contribute to society." *Frontiero v. Richardson,* 411 U.S. 677, 686 (1973) (plurality opinion); accord *Cleburne v. Cleburne Living Center, Inc., supra,* 473 U.S. at 441; see also *Massachusetts Board of Retirement v. Murgia, supra,* at 313 (heightened scrutiny required when group has "been subjected to unique disabilities on the basis of stereotyped characteristics not truly indicative of [the] abilities [of the group's members]"). The United States Supreme Court also has cited two other considerations that, in a given case, may be relevant in determining whether statutory provisions pertaining to a particular group are subject to heightened scrutiny. These two additional considerations are: (1) the characteristic that defines the members of the class as a discrete group is immutable or otherwise not within their control; see, e.g., *Lyng v. Castillo,* 477 U.S. 635, 638 (1986) (for purposes of suspectness inquiry, relevant consideration is whether members of class "exhibit obvious, immutable, or distinguishing characteristics that define them as a discrete group"); and (2) the group is "a minority or politically powerless." (Internal quotation marks omitted.) *Bowen v. Gilliard,* 483 U.S. 587, 602 (1987); accord *Lyng v. Castillo, supra,* at 638; see also *San Antonio Independent School District v. Rodriguez,* 411 U.S. 1, 28 (1973) (concluding that class comprised of poor families exhibits none of "traditional indicia of suspectness" because class is "not saddled with such disabilities, or subjected to such a history of purposeful unequal treatment, or relegated to such a position of political powerlessness as to command extraordinary protection from the majoritarian political process").

Because of the evident correlation between the indicia of suspectness identified by the United States Supreme Court and the issue of whether a class that has been singled out by the state for unequal treatment is entitled to heightened protection under the federal constitution, we conclude that those factors also are pertinent to the determination of whether a group comprises a quasi-suspect class for purposes of the state constitution. It bears emphasis, however, that the United States Supreme Court has placed far greater weight-indeed, it invariably has placed dispositive weight-on the first two factors, that is, whether the group has been the subject of long-standing and invidious discrimination and whether the group's distinguishing characteristic bears no relation to the ability of the group members to perform or function in society. In circumstances in which a group has been subject to such discrimination and its distinguishing characteristic does not bear any relation to such ability, the court inevitably has employed heightened scrutiny in reviewing statutory classifications targeting those groups.

It is evident, moreover, that immutability and minority status or political powerlessness are subsidiary to the first two primary factors because, as we explain more fully hereinafter, the United States Supreme Court has granted suspect class status to a group whose distinguishing characteristic is not immutable; see *Nyquist v. Mauclet,* 432 U.S. 1, 9 n. 11 (1977) (rejecting immutability requirement in treating group of resident aliens as suspect class despite their ability to opt out of class voluntarily); and has accorded quasi-suspect status to a group that had not been a minority or truly politically powerless. See *Frontiero v. Richardson, supra,* 411 U.S. at 686 n. 17 (plurality opinion) (according women heightened protection despite court's acknowledgment that women "do not constitute a small and powerless minority."

STATUS OF GAY PERSONS AS A QUASI-SUSPECT CLASS

For the reasons that follow, we agree with the plaintiffs' claim that sexual orientation meets all of the requirements of a quasi-suspect classification. Gay persons have been subjected to and stigmatized by a long history of purposeful and invidious discrimination that continues to manifest itself in society. The characteristic that defines the members of this group-attraction to persons of the same sex-bears no logical relationship to their ability to perform in society, either in familial relations or otherwise as productive citizens. Because sexual orientation is such an essential component of personhood, even if there is some possibility that a person's sexual preference can be altered, it would be wholly unacceptable for the state to require anyone to do so. Gay persons also represent a distinct minority of the population. It is true, of course, that gay persons recently have made significant advances in obtaining equal treatment under the law. Nonetheless, we conclude that, as a minority group that continues to suffer the enduring effects of centuries of legally sanctioned discrimination, laws singling them out for disparate treatment are subject to heightened judicial scrutiny to ensure that those laws are not the product of such historical prejudice and stereotyping.

A

History of Discrimination

The defendants do not dispute that gay persons historically have been, and continue to be, the target of purposeful and pernicious discrimination due solely to their sexual orientation. For centuries, the prevailing attitude toward gay persons has been "one of strong disapproval, frequent ostracism, social and legal discrimination, and at times ferocious punishment." R. Posner, Sex and Reason (Harvard University Press 1992) c. 11, p. 291; see also note, "The Constitutional Status of

Sexual Orientation: Homosexuality as a Suspect Classification," 98 Harv. L.Rev. 1285, 1302 (1985) ("It is ... uncontroversial that gays as a group suffer from stigmatization in all spheres of life. The stigma has persisted throughout history, across cultures, and in the United States."). "The American Psychiatric Association [has noted that] ... when compared to other social groups, homosexuals are still among the most stigmatized groups in the nation. Hate crimes are prevalent. Gay persons are still banned from serving openly in the [United States] military service. ... Gay and lesbian adolescents are often taunted and humiliated in their school settings. Many professional persons and employees in all occupations are still fearful of identifying as gay or lesbians in their work settings. . . . In fact, gay persons share a history of persecution comparable to that of blacks and women." *Snetsinger v. Montana University System,* 325 Mont. 148, 163-64 (2004) (Nelson, J., concurring); see also *In re Marriage Cases, supra,* 43 Cal.4th at 841 ("[o]utside of racial and religious minorities, we can think of no group which has suffered such pernicious and sustained hostility . . . as homosexuals"); D. Satcher, Surgeon General, United States Department of Health and Human Services, "The Surgeon General's Call to Action to Promote Sexual Health and Responsible Sexual Behavior" (July 9, 2001) ("[O]ur culture often stigmatizes homosexual behavior, identity and relationships. . . . These anti-homosexual attitudes are associated with psychological distress for homosexual persons and may have a negative impact on mental health, including a greater incidence of depression and suicide, lower self-acceptance and a greater likelihood of hiding sexual orientation...."), available at http://www.surgeongeneral.gov/library/ sexual health/call.htm. Of course, gay persons have been subjected to such severe and sustained discrimination because of our culture's long-standing intolerance of intimate homosexual conduct. As the United States Supreme Court has recognized, "[p]roscriptions against [homosexual sodomy] have ancient roots." *Bowers v. Hardwick,* 478 U.S. 186, 192 (1986), overruled on other grounds by *Lawrence v. Texas,* 539 U.S. 558 (2003); see also *High Tech Gays v. Defense Industrial Security Clearance Office,* 909 F.2d 375, 382 (9th Cir.1990) (Canby, J., dissenting) ("mainstream society has mistreated [homosexuals] for centuries"); *Baker v. Wade,* 769 F.2d 289, 292 (5th Cir.1985) ("the strong objection to homosexual conduct ... has prevailed in Western culture for the past seven centuries"), cert. denied, 478 U.S. 1022 (1986). Much of the condemnation of homosexuality derives from firmly held religious beliefs and moral convictions. See, e.g., *Lawrence v. Texas, supra,* at 571. Until not long ago, gay persons were widely regarded as deviants in need of treatment to deal with their sexual orientation. *See, e.g., Conaway v. Deane,* 401 Md. 219, 283-84 (2007). Moreover, until 2003, when the United States Supreme Court concluded, contrary to its earlier holding in *Bowers* that consensual homosexual conduct is protected under the due process clause of the fourteenth amendment; see *Lawrence v. Texas, supra,* at 578; such conduct carried criminal penalties in over one quarter of the states. *See id.* at 573; see also *Bowers v. Hardwick, supra,* at 193 (observing that "until 1961, all [fifty] [s]tates outlawed sodomy"). Connecticut did not repeal its anti-sodomy law until 1969; Public Acts 1969, No. 828, § 214 (repealing General Statutes [Rev. to 1968] § 53-216); and, as late as 1986, the court in *Bowers* noted that twenty-four states and the District of Columbia "still [made] such conduct illegal and ha[d] done so for a very long time." *Bowers v. Hardwick, supra,* at 190. It therefore is not surprising that no court ever has refused to treat gay persons as a suspect or quasi-suspect class on the ground that they have not suffered a history of invidious discrimination. See E. Gerstmann, The Constitutional Underclass: Gays, Lesbians, and the Failure of Class-Based Equal Protection (University of Chicago Press 1999) c. 4, p. 66.

There is no question, therefore, that gay persons historically have been, and continue to be, the target of purposeful and pernicious discrimination due solely to their sexual orientation. We therefore turn to the second required factor, namely, whether the sexual orientation of gay persons has any bearing on their ability to participate in society.

B

Whether Sexual Orientation Is Related to a Person's Ability to Participate in or Contribute to Society.

The defendants also concede that sexual orientation bears no relation to a person's ability to participate in or contribute to society, a fact that many courts have acknowledged, as well. See, e.g., *Watkins v. United States Army,* 875 F.2d 699, 725 (9th Cir.1989) (Norris, J., concurring in the judgment) ("[s]exual orientation plainly has no relevance to a person's ability to perform or contribute to society" [internal quotation marks omitted]), cert. denied, 498 U.S. 957, 111 S. Ct. 384 (1990); *Equality Foundation of Greater Cincinnati, Inc. v. Cincinnati,* 860 F. Supp. 417, 437 (S.D. Ohio1994) ("[S]exual orientation . . . bears no relation whatsoever to an individual's ability to perform, or to participate in, or contribute to, society.... If homosexuals were afflicted with some sort of impediment to their ability to perform and to contribute to society, the entire phenomenon of 'staying in the [c]loset' and of 'coming out' would not exist; their impediment would betray their status."), *rev'd* on other grounds, 54 F.3d 261 (6th Cir.1995), vacated and remanded, 518 U.S. 1001 (1996); *Conaway v. Deane, supra,* 401 Md. at 282 (gay persons have been subject to unique disabilities unrelated to their ability to contribute to society); *Hernandez v. Robles,* 7 N.Y.3d 338, 388 (2006) (Kaye, C.J., dissenting) ("[o]bviously, sexual orientation is irrelevant to one's ability to perform or contribute"). In this critical respect, gay persons stand in stark contrast to other groups that have been denied suspect or quasi-suspect class recognition, despite a history of discrimination, because the distinguishing characteristics of those groups adversely affect their ability or capacity to perform certain functions or to discharge certain responsibilities in society. See, e.g., *Cleburne v. Cleburne Living Center, Inc., supra,* 473 U.S. at 442 (for purposes of federal constitution, mental retardation is not quasi-suspect classification because, *inter alia,* "it is undeniable ... that those who are mentally retarded have a reduced ability to cope with and function in the everyday world"); *Massachusetts Board of Retirement v. Murgia, supra,* 427 U.S. at 315 (age is not suspect classification because, *inter alia,* "physical ability generally declines with age"); see also *Gregory v. Ashcroft,* 501 U.S. 452, 472 (1991) ("[i]t is an unfortunate fact of life that physical [capacity] and mental capacity sometimes diminish with age").

Unlike the characteristics unique to those groups, however, "homosexuality bears no relation at all to [an] individual's ability to contribute fully to society." L. Tribe, American Constitutional Law (2d Ed. 1988) § 16-33, p. 1616. Indeed, because an individual's homosexual orientation "implies no impairment in judgment, stability, reliability or general social or vocational capabilities"; *Jantz v. Muci,* 759 F.Supp. 1543, 1548 (D.Kan.1991) the observation of the United States Supreme Court that race, alienage and national origin--all suspect classes entitled to the highest level of constitutional protection-"are so seldom relevant to the achievement of any legitimate state interest that laws grounded in such considerations are deemed to reflect prejudice and antipathy"; *Cleburne v. Cleburne Living Center, Inc., supra,* 473 U.S. at 440; is no less applicable to gay persons.

It is highly significant, moreover, that it is the public policy of this state that sexual orientation bears no relation to an individual's ability to raise children; see, e.g., General Statutes § 45a-727 (permitting same sex couples to adopt children); see also General Statutes § 45a-727a (3) (finding of General Assembly that best interests of child are promoted whenever child is part of "loving, supportive and stable family" without reference to sexual preference of parents); to an individual's capacity to enter into relationships analogous to marriage; see General Statutes §§ 46b-38aa through 46b-38pp (granting same sex couples all rights and privileges afforded to opposite sex couples who enter into marriage); and to an individual's ability otherwise to participate fully in every important economic and social institution and activity that the government regulates. See General Statutes §§ 46a-81a through 46a-81n (generally banning sexual orientation discrimination in employment, trade and professional association membership, public accommodations, housing, credit practices, state hiring practices, state licensing practices and in administration of state educational and vocational programs as well as state-administered benefits programs). These statutory provisions constitute an acknowledgment by the state that homosexual orientation is no more relevant to a person's ability to perform and contribute to society than is heterosexual orientation. It therefore is clear that the plaintiffs have satisfied this second and final required prong for determining whether a group is entitled to recognition as a quasi-suspect or suspect class.

C

Immutability of the Group's Distinguishing Characteristic

A third factor that courts have considered in determining whether the members of a class are entitled to heightened protection for equal protection purposes is whether the attribute or characteristic that distinguishes them is immutable or otherwise beyond their control. *See, e.g., Bowen v. Gilliard, supra,* 483 U.S. at 602. Of course, the characteristic that distinguishes gay persons from others and qualifies them for recognition as a distinct and discrete group is the characteristic that historically has resulted in their social and legal ostracism, namely, their attraction to persons of the same sex.

On a number of occasions, in connection with its consideration of a claim that a particular group is entitled to suspect or quasi-suspect class status, the United States Supreme Court has considered whether the group's distinguishing characteristic is immutable. See, e.g., *Mathews v. Lucas, supra,* 427 U.S. at 505 (illegitimacy is "a characteristic determined by causes not within the control of the illegitimate individual"); *Frontiero v. Richardson, supra,* 411 U.S. at 686 (plurality opinion) ("since sex, like race and national origin, is an immutable characteristic determined solely by the accident of birth, the imposition of special disabilities [on] the members of a particular sex because of their sex would seem to violate the basic concept of our system that legal burdens should bear some relationship to individual responsibility"); cf. *Parham v. Hughes,* 441 U.S. 347, 351 (1979) (statute prohibiting father, who has failed to legitimate his illegitimate child, from suing for child's wrongful death does not create inherently suspect class "based [on] certain ... immutable human attributes"); *Johnson v. Robison,* 415 U.S. 361, 375 n. 14 (1974) (conscientious objectors do not constitute suspect class because, inter alia, they lack traditional indicia of suspect class, including "immutable characteristic"). Immutability has been deemed to be a relevant consideration because it "make[s] discrimination more clearly unfair." *High Tech Gays v. Defense Industrial Security Clearance Office, supra,* 909 F.2d at 377 (Canby, J., dissenting). "Immutability may be considered important because it would be pointless to try to deter membership in the immutable group, or because individual group members cannot be blamed for their status, or because immutability heightens the sense of stigma associated with membership...." Note, *supra,* 98 Harv. L.Rev. at 1302-1303. Put differently, "[t]he degree to which an individual controls, or cannot avoid, the acquisition of a defining trait, and the relative ease or difficulty with which a trait can be changed, are relevant to whether a classification is 'suspect' or 'quasi-suspect' because this inquiry is one way of asking whether someone, rather than being victimized, has voluntarily joined a persecuted group and thereby invited the discrimination." *Dean v. District of Columbia,* 653 A.2d 307, 346 (D.C.1995) (Ferren, J., concurring in part and dissenting in part).

A number of courts that have considered this factor have rejected the claim that sexual orientation is an immutable characteristic. Other courts, however, as well as many, if not most, scholarly commentators, have reached a contrary conclusion. Although we do not doubt that sexual orientation--heterosexual or homosexual--is highly resistant to change, it is not necessary for us to decide whether sexual orientation is immutable in the same way and to the same extent that race, national origin and gender are immutable, because, even if it is not, the plaintiffs nonetheless have established that they fully satisfy this consideration.

Sexual intimacy is "a sensitive, key relationship of human existence, central to ... the development of human personality...." *Paris Adult Theatre I v. Slaton,* 413 U.S. 49, 63 (1973). Thus, the United States Supreme Court has recognized that, because "the protected right of homosexual adults to engage in intimate, consensual conduct ... [represents] an integral part of human freedom"; *Lawrence v. Texas, supra,* 539 U.S. at 576-77; individual decisions by consenting adults concerning the intimacies of their physical relationships are entitled to constitutional protection. *See id.* at 578. Indeed, it is indisputable that sexual orientation "forms a significant part of a person's identity." *Able v. United States,* 968 F.Supp. 850, 863 (E.D.N.Y.1997), *rev'd on other grounds,* 155 F.3d 628 (2d Cir.1998); see also L. Tribe, *supra,* § 16-33, at p. 1616 (sexual orientation, whether homosexual or heterosexual, is central to personality of individual). It is equally apparent that, "[b]ecause a person's sexual orientation is so integral an aspect of one's identity, it is not appropriate to require a person to repudiate or change his or her sexual orientation in order to avoid discriminatory treatment." *In re Marriage Cases, supra,* 43 Cal.4th at 842; see also *Hernandez-Montiel v. Immigration & Naturalization Service,* 225 F.3d 1084, 1093 (9th Cir.2000) ("[s]exual orientation and sexual identity ... are so fundamental to one's identity that a person should not be required to abandon them"); *Watkins v. United States Army, supra,* 875 F.2d at 726 (Norris, J., concurring in the judgment) ("Scientific proof aside, it [also] seems appropriate to ask whether heterosexuals feel capable of changing *their* sexual orientation. Would heterosexuals living in a city that passed an ordinance burdening those who engaged in or desired to engage in sex with persons of the *opposite* sex find it easy not only to abstain from heterosexual activity but also to shift the object of their sexual desires to persons of the same sex? ... [T]he possibility of such a difficult and traumatic change does not make sexual orientation 'mutable' for equal protection purposes."); *Jantz v. Muci, supra,* 759 F.Supp. at 1548 ("to discriminate against individuals who accept their given sexual orientation and refuse to alter that orientation to conform to societal norms does significant violence to a central and defining character of those individuals").

In view of the central role that sexual orientation plays in a person's fundamental right to self-determination, we fully agree with the plaintiffs that their sexual orientation represents the kind of distinguishing characteristic that defines them as a discrete group for purposes of determining whether that group should be afforded heightened protection under the equal protection provisions of the state constitution. This prong of the suspectness inquiry surely is satisfied when, as in the present case, the identifying trait is "so central to a person's identity that it would be abhorrent for government to penalize a person for refusing to change [it]. . . ." *Watkins v. United States Army, supra,* 875 F.2d at 726 (Norris, J., concurring in the judgment); see also *Andersen v. King County,* 158 Wash.2d 1, 105 n. 78 (2006) (Bridge, J., concurring in the dissent) ("Courts ... should not conclude that homosexuality is mutable [for purposes of determining whether gay persons are entitled to suspect or quasi-suspect class status] because reasonable minds disagree about the causes of homosexuality or because some religious tenets forbid gay persons from 'acting on' homosexual behavior. Instead, courts should ask whether the characteristic at issue is one *governments* have any business requiring a person to change." [Emphasis in original]). In other words, gay persons, because they are characterized by a "central, defining [trait] of personhood, which may be altered [if at all] only at the expense of significant damage to the individual's sense of self"; *Jantz v. Muci, supra*; are no less entitled to consideration as a suspect or quasi-suspect class than any other group that has been deemed to exhibit an immutable characteristic. See *id.*; see also note, *supra*, 98 Harv. L.Rev. at 1303 (sexual orientation, like race and sex, is "one of only a handful of characteristics that ha[s] such a pervasive and profound impact on the [relevant] aspects of personhood"). To decide otherwise would be to penalize someone for being unable or unwilling to "change ... a central aspect of individual and group identity"; *Watkins v. United States Army, supra*, at 726 (Norris, J., concurring in the judgment); a result repugnant "to the values animating the constitutional ideal of equal protection of the laws." *Id.*

D

Whether the Group Is a Minority or Lacking in Political Power

The final factor that bears consideration is whether the group is "a minority or politically powerless." *Bowen v. Gilliard, supra*, 483 U.S. at 602. We therefore turn to that prong of the test.

1

We commence our analysis by noting that, in previous cases involving groups seeking heightened protection under the federal equal protection clause, the United States Supreme Court described this factor without reference to the minority status of the subject group, focusing instead on the group's lack of political power. See, e.g., *Massachusetts Board of Retirement v. Murgia, supra*, 427 U.S. at 313 (explaining that "a suspect class is one saddled with such disabilities, or subjected to such a history of purposeful unequal treatment, or relegated to such a position of political powerlessness as to command extraordinary protection from the majoritarian political process"; *San Antonio Independent School District v. Rodriguez, supra*, 411 U.S. at 28 (same). In its most recent formulation of the test for determining whether a group is entitled to suspect or quasi-suspect classification, however, the court has indicated that this factor is satisfied upon a showing *either* that the group is a minority *or* that it lacks political power. *Bowen v. Gilliard, supra*, 483 U.S. at 602; *Lyng v. Castillo, supra*, 477 U.S. at 638. Indeed, in characterizing this factor in disjunctive terms, the court cited to *Murgia*; *Bowen v. Gilliard, supra*, at 602-03; *Lyng v. Castillo, supra*, at 638; thereby also indicating that, for purposes of this aspect of the inquiry, the test always has involved a determination of whether the group is a "discrete and insular" minority; *United States v. Carolene Products Co.*, 304 U.S. 144, 152-53 n. 4 (1938); or, if not a true minority; see, e.g., *Frontiero v. Richardson, supra*, 411 U.S. at 686 n. 17 (plurality opinion) (women accorded protected status although not minority); the group nonetheless is lacking in political power. This disjunctive test properly recognizes that a group may warrant heightened protection even though it does not fit the archetype of a discrete and insular minority. The test also properly recognizes that legislation singling out a true minority that meets the first three prongs of the suspectness inquiry must be viewed with skepticism because, under such circumstances, there exists an undue risk that legislation involving the historically disfavored group has been motivated by improper considerations borne of prejudice or animosity.

When this approach is applied to the present case, there is no doubt that gay persons clearly comprise a distinct minority of the population.[FN 30] Consequently, they clearly satisfy the first part

---

[FN 30] It is difficult to discern precisely the percentage of homosexuals in the population. Studies conducted by

of the disjunctive test and, thus, may be deemed to satisfy this prong of the suspectness inquiry on that basis alone.

2

The defendants nevertheless maintain that gay persons should not receive recognition as a quasi-suspect group because they are not politically powerless. In light of this claim, which represents the defendants' primary challenge to the plaintiffs' contention that they are entitled to quasi-suspect class status, and because some courts have applied that component of the suspectness inquiry to deny gay persons protected status even though they represent a minority of the population, we consider the defendants' contention.

In support of their claim, the defendants rely primarily on this state's enactment of the gay rights and civil union laws, which, of course, were designed to provide equal rights for gay persons, and which undoubtedly reflect a measure of political power. The defendants also rely on the fact that several state legislators in Connecticut are openly gay. From the defendants' standpoint, these significant advances undermine the plaintiffs' claim that gay persons are so lacking in political power that they are entitled to heightened judicial protection.

The plaintiffs contend that this test does not require proof that gay persons are wholly lacking in political influence but, rather, that the discrimination to which they have been subjected has been so severe and so persistent that, as with race and sex discrimination, it is not likely to be remedied soon enough merely by resort to the majoritarian political process. In support of their assertion that they do not wield sufficient political power to obviate the need for heightened judicial protection, the plaintiffs note that gay persons are demonstrably less powerful than African-Americans and women, two groups that have been accorded protected status under the federal constitution. As the plaintiffs also emphasize, courts continue to apply heightened scrutiny to statutes that discriminate against women and racial minorities notwithstanding the great strides that both groups have made and continue to make in recent years in terms of their political strength. Indeed, heightened scrutiny is applied to statutes that discriminate against men; see *Craig v. Boren, supra*, 429 U.S. at 197; and against Caucasians. See, e.g., *Richmond v. J.A. Croson Co.*, 488 U.S. 469, 493-96 (1989). Finally, the plaintiffs contend that when African-Americans and women first were recognized as suspect and quasi-suspect classes, respectively, comprehensive legislation barring discrimination against those groups had been in effect for years, and yet the existence of that legislation did not deter the United States Supreme Court from according them

---

Alfred C. Kinsey in the mid-twentieth century indicated that approximately one out of every ten men was gay; A. Kinsey, W. Pomeroy & C. Martin, Sexual Behavior in the Human Male (W.B. Saunders 1948) p. 651; and that lesbians apparently comprised a somewhat smaller percentage of the population. A. Kinsey, W. Pomeroy & C. Martin et al., Sexual Behavior in the Human Female (Indiana University Press Ed. 1998) (1953) p. 474; see also *High Tech Gays v. Defense Industrial Security Clearance Office, supra*, 909 F.2d at 378 (Canby, J., dissenting) (by most estimates, 10 percent of population is homosexual). Although these figures received widespread acceptance for many years, subsequent research suggests that the percentage of homosexuals in the population likely is lower. See, e.g., R. Michael, J. Gagnon & E. Laumann et al., Sex in America: A Definitive Survey (CSG Enterprises, Inc. 1994) c. 9, pp. 174-75 (study finding that 6 percent of men and 4 percent of women were attracted to members of same sex); R. Posner, *supra*, c. 11, at p. 295 (noting that most estimates of percentage of homosexual men in population range from 2 to 5 percent and that estimates of homosexual women in population are lower); cf. *Equality Foundation of Greater Cincinnati, Inc. v. Cincinnati, supra*, 860 F.Supp. at 426 (concluding, after evidentiary hearing, that homosexuals comprise between 5 and 13 percent of population).

protected status. The plaintiffs argue, therefore, that similar legislation protecting gay persons cannot disqualify that group from recognition as a quasi-suspect class. We agree.

We commence our analysis by considering what the term "political powerlessness" actually means for purposes of the suspectness inquiry. Unfortunately, "in most cases the [United States] Supreme Court has no more than made passing reference to the 'political power' factor without actually analyzing it. The defendants are correct, of course, that gay persons are not entirely without political power, both because the legislature has been persuaded of the need for laws prohibiting sexual orientation discrimination and because some gay persons serve openly in public office. We agree with the plaintiffs, however, that they need not demonstrate that gay persons are politically powerless in any literal sense of that term in order to satisfy this component of the suspectness inquiry.

[The court discussed *Frontiero* and the fact that women were not in fact a minority nor politically powerless.]

It is apparent, then, that the political powerlessness aspect of the suspectness inquiry does not require a showing that the group seeking recognition as a protected class is, in fact, without political power ... The term "political powerlessness," therefore, is clearly a misnomer. We apply this facet of the suspectness inquiry not to ascertain whether a group that has suffered invidious discrimination borne of prejudice or bigotry is devoid of political power but, rather, for the purpose of determining whether the group lacks sufficient political strength to bring a prompt end to the prejudice and discrimination through traditional political means. Consequently, a group satisfies the political powerlessness factor if it demonstrates that, because of the pervasive and sustained nature of the discrimination that its members have suffered, there is a risk that that discrimination will not be rectified, sooner rather than later, merely by resort to the democratic process. See *Cleburne v. Cleburne Living Center, Inc., supra*, 473 U.S. at 440. Applying this standard, we have little difficulty in concluding that gay persons are entitled to heightened constitutional protection despite some recent political progress.

That prejudice against gay persons is so widespread and so deep-seated is due, in large measure, to the fact that many people in our state and nation sincerely believe that homosexuality is morally reprehensible. Indeed, homosexuality is contrary to the teachings of more than a few religions. In its amicus brief submitted to this court, the Becket Fund for Religious Liberty, which represents "the interests ... of religious persons and institutions that conscientiously object to treating [same] sex and [opposite] sex unions as moral equivalents," notes that "many religious groups do not accept [a sexual relationship] among same sex couples as a matter of conscience" and that "probably [the] majority ... [of] religious groups ... oppose same sex marriage." As the United States Supreme Court has recognized, "for centuries there have been powerful voices to condemn homosexual conduct as immoral. The condemnation [of homosexuality] has been shaped by religious beliefs, conceptions of right and acceptable behavior, and respect for the traditional family. For many persons these are not trivial concerns but profound and deep convictions accepted as ethical and moral principles to which they aspire and which thus determine the course of their lives." *Lawrence v. Texas, supra*, 539 U.S. at 571. Feelings and beliefs predicated on such profound religious and moral principles are likely to be enduring, and persons and groups adhering to those views undoubtedly will continue to exert influence over public policy makers.

Beyond moral disapprobation, gay persons also face virulent homophobia that rests on nothing more than feelings of revulsion toward gay persons and the intimate sexual conduct with which they are associated. Unfortunately, "[h]omosexuals are hated, quite irrationally, for what they are...." *High Tech Gays v. Defense Industrial Security Clearance Office, supra,* 909 F.2d at 382 (Canby, J., dissenting). Such visceral prejudice is reflected in the large number of hate crimes that are perpetrated against gay persons. The prevalence of such crimes has prompted the legislature to pass hate crime legislation that includes sexual orientation, along with race, religion, ethnicity, disability and gender, as a protected class. The irrational nature of the prejudice directed at gay persons, who "are ridiculed, ostracized, despised, demonized and condemned" merely for being who they are; *Snetsinger v. Montana University System, supra,* 325 Mont. at 160 (Nelson, J., concurring); is entirely different in kind than the prejudice suffered by other groups that previously have been denied suspect or quasi-suspect class status, such as the poor, the mentally disadvantaged and the aged. In fact, the bigotry and hatred that gay persons have faced are akin to, and, in certain respects, perhaps even more severe than, those confronted by some groups that have been accorded heightened judicial protection. See, e.g., *People v. Garcia,* 77 Cal.App.4th 1269, 1279 (2000) (only racial and religious minorities have suffered more intense and deep-seated hostility than homosexuals). This fact provides further reason to doubt that such prejudice soon can be eliminated and underscores the reality that gay persons face unique challenges to their political and social integration.

Insofar as gay persons play a role in the political process, it is apparent that their numbers reflect their status as a small and insular minority. It recently has been noted that, of the more than one-half million people who hold a political office at the local, state and national level, only about 300 are openly gay persons. *Andersen v. King County, supra,* 158 Wash.2d at 105, (Bridge, J., concurring in dissent); see also R. La Corte, "State Legislature Has Second-Largest Gay Caucus in U.S." (January 24, 2008) (putting figure at about 400 openly gay persons). No openly gay person ever has been appointed to a United States Cabinet position or to any federal appeals court. In addition, no openly gay person has served in the United States Senate, and only two currently serve in the United States House of Representatives. Gay persons also lack representation in the highest levels of business, industry and academia. For example, no openly gay person heads a Fortune 500 company; and it has been estimated that there are only fourteen openly gay college and university presidents or chancellors; a number that represents only one half of 1 percent of such positions nationwide.

4

In sum, the relatively modest political influence that gay persons possess is insufficient to rectify the invidious discrimination to which they have been subjected for so long. Like the political gains that women had made prior to their recognition as a quasi-suspect class, the political advances that gay persons have attained afford them inadequate protection, standing alone, in view of the deep-seated and pernicious nature of the prejudice and antipathy that they continue to face. Today, moreover, women have far greater political power than gay persons, yet they continue to be accorded status as a quasi-suspect class. See *Breen v. Carlsbad Municipal Schools, supra,* 138 N.M. at 338 (explaining that intermediate scrutiny is appropriate with respect to discrimination based on sex "even though the darkest period of discrimination may have passed for [the] historically maligned group" and that "[such] scrutiny should still be applied to protect against more subtle forms of unconstitutional discrimination created by unconscious or disguised prejudice"). We conclude, therefore, that, to the extent that gay persons possess some political power, it does not disqualify them from recognition as a quasi-suspect class under the state constitution in view of the pervasive and invidious discrimination to which they historically have been subjected due to an innate personal characteristic that has absolutely no bearing on their ability to perform in or contribute to society.

[The court determined that gay men and women were a quasi-suspect class entitled to intermediate scrutiny. Therefore, Connecticut's prohibition of same-sex marriage did not satisfy the intermediate scrutiny standard.]

Windsor v. United States
699 F.3d 169 (2d Cir. 2012), *cert. granted*, __ U.S. __ (2012)

DENNIS JACOBS, Chief Judge:

Plaintiff Edith Windsor sued as surviving spouse of a same-sex couple that was married in Canada in 2007 and was resident in New York at the time of her spouse's death in 2009. Windsor was denied the benefit of the spousal deduction for federal estate taxes under 26 U.S.C. § 2056(A) solely because Section 3 of the Defense of Marriage Act ("DOMA"), 1 U.S.C. § 7, defines the words "marriage" and "spouse" in federal law in a way that bars the Internal Revenue Service from recognizing Windsor as a spouse or the couple as married. The text of § 3 is as follows:

> In determining the meaning of any Act of Congress, or of any ruling, regulation, or interpretation of the various administrative bureaus and agencies of the United States, the word "marriage" means only a legal union between one man and one woman as husband and wife, the word "spouse" refers only to a person of the opposite sex who is a husband or a wife.

At issue is Windsor's claim for a refund in the amount of $363,053, which turns on the constitutionality of that section of federal law.

[W]e conclude that review of Section 3 of DOMA requires heightened scrutiny. The Supreme Court uses certain factors to decide whether a new classification qualifies as a quasi-suspect class. They include: A) whether the class has been historically "subjected to discrimination," *Bowen v. Gilliard*, 483 U.S. 587, 602 (1987); B) whether the class has a defining characteristic that "frequently bears [a] relation to ability to perform or contribute to society," *Cleburne*, 473 U.S. at 440–41; C) whether the class exhibits "obvious, immutable, or distinguishing characteristics that define them as a discrete group;" *Bowen*, 483 U.S. at 602; and D) whether the class is "a minority or politically powerless." *Id.* Immutability and lack of political power are not strictly necessary factors to identify a suspect class. See *Cleburne*, 473 U.S. at 442 n. 10("'[T]here's not much left of the immutability theory, is there?'") (quoting J. Ely, Democracy and Distrust 150 (1980)); *Cleburne*, 473 U.S. at 472 n. 24(Marshall, J., concurring in part and dissenting in part) ("The 'political powerlessness' of a group may be relevant, but that factor is neither necessary, as the gender cases demonstrate, nor sufficient, as the example of minors illustrates."); *Nyquist v. Mauclet*, 432 U.S. 1, 9 n. 11 (1977) (rejecting the argument that alienage did not deserve strict scrutiny because it was not immutable); see also *Pedersen*, ——— F.Supp.2d at ———, 2012 WL 3113883, at 13; *Golinski*, 824 F.Supp.2d at 983; *Kerrigan v. Comm'r. of Pub. Health*, 289 Conn. 135, 167–68, 957 A.2d 407 (2008). Nevertheless, immutability and political power are indicative, and we consider them here. In this case, all four factors justify heightened scrutiny: A) homosexuals as a group have historically endured persecution and discrimination; B) homosexuality has no relation to aptitude or ability to contribute to society; C) homosexuals are a discernible group with non-obvious distinguishing characteristics, especially in the subset of those who enter same-sex marriages; and D) the class remains a politically weakened minority.

A) History of Discrimination

It is easy to conclude that homosexuals have suffered a history of discrimination. Windsor and several amici labor to establish and document this history, but we think it is not much in debate. Perhaps the most telling proof of animus and discrimination against homosexuals in this country is that, for many years and in many states, homosexual conduct was criminal. These laws had the imprimatur of the Supreme Court. See *Bowers*, 478 U.S. at 196; see also *Lawrence*, 539 U.S. at 578 (noting that such laws "demean[ed] homosexuals'] existence [and] control[led] their destiny").

BLAG [the Bipartisan Legal Advisory Group of the United States House of Representatives that had taken over defense of the statute when the Justice Department declined to defend the statute] argues that discrimination against homosexuals differs from that against racial minorities and women because "homosexuals as a class have never been politically disenfranchised." True, but the difference is not decisive. Citizens born out of wedlock have never been inhibited in voting; yet the Supreme Court has applied intermediate scrutiny in cases of illegitimacy. See generally *Lalli v. Lalli*, 439 U.S. 259 (1978). Second, BLAG argues that, unlike protected classes, homosexuals have not "suffered discrimination for longer than history has been recorded." But whether such discrimination existed in Babylon is neither here nor there. BLAG concedes that homosexuals have endured discrimination in this country since at least the 1920s. Ninety years of discrimination is entirely sufficient to document a "history of discrimination." See *Pedersen*, —— F.Supp.2d at ——, 2012 WL 3113883, at 21 (summarizing that "the majority of cases which have meaningfully considered the question [have] likewise held that homosexuals as a class have experienced a long history of discrimination").

B) Relation to Ability

Also easy to decide in this case is whether the class characteristic "frequently bears [a] relation to ability to perform or contribute to society." Cleburne, 473 U.S. at 440–41; *see Frontiero*, 411 U.S. at 686 ("[W]hat differentiates sex from such non-suspect statuses as intelligence or physical disability, and aligns it with the recognized suspect criteria, is that the sex characteristic frequently bears no relation to ability to perform or contribute to society."). In *Cleburne*, the Supreme Court ruled that heightened scrutiny was inappropriate because "those who are mentally retarded have a reduced ability to cope with and function in the everyday world." 473 U.S. at 442. The Court employed similar reasoning with respect to age classifications, finding that heightened scrutiny was not appropriate for mandatory retirement laws because "physical ability generally declines with age" and such requirements reasonably "serve[d] to remove from ... service those whose fitness for uniformed work presumptively has diminished with age." *Murgia*, 427 U.S. at 316.

There is no such impairment here. There are some distinguishing characteristics, such as age or mental handicap, that may arguably inhibit an individual's ability to contribute to society, at least in some respect. But homosexuality is not one of them. The aversion homosexuals experience has nothing to do with aptitude or performance.

We do not understand BLAG to argue otherwise. Rather, BLAG suggests that the proper consideration is whether "the classification turns on 'distinguishing characteristics relevant to interests the State has the authority to implement,'" quoting *Cleburne*, 473 U.S. at 441. Thus, BLAG urges that same-sex couples have a diminished ability to discharge family roles in procreation and the raising of children. BLAG cites no precedential application of that standard to support its interpretation, and it is inconsistent with actual cases. See, e.g., *Frontiero*, 411 U.S. at 686 (distinguishing that sex, unlike intelligence, has no bearing on one's general ability to contribute to society). In any event, the abilities or inabilities cited by BLAG bear upon whether the law withstands scrutiny (the second step of analysis) rather than upon the level of scrutiny to apply. Cf. *Clark v. Jeter*, 486 U.S. 456, 461 (1988) (defining the test for intermediate scrutiny as whether a classification is "substantially related to an important government interest").

C) Distinguishing Characteristic

We conclude that homosexuality is a sufficiently discernible characteristic to define a discrete minority class. See *Rowland v. Mad River Local School Dist., Montgomery County*, Ohio, 470 U.S. 1009, 1014 (1985) (Brennan, J., dissenting from denial of certiorari) ("[H]omosexuals constitute a significant and insular minority of this country's population.").

This consideration is often couched in terms of "immutability." BLAG and its amici argue that sexual orientation is not necessarily fixed, suggesting that it may change over time, range along a continuum, and overlap (for bisexuals). But the test is broader: whether there are "obvious, immutable, or distinguishing characteristics that define ... a discrete group." See *Bowen*, 483 U.S. at 602 (emphasis added). No "obvious badge" is necessary. See *Mathews v. Lucas*, 427 U.S. 495, 506 (1976). Classifications based on alienage, illegitimacy, and national origin are all subject to heightened scrutiny, *Cleburne*, 473 U.S. at 440–41, even though these characteristics do not declare themselves, and often may be disclosed or suppressed as a matter of preference. What seems to matter is whether the characteristic of the class calls down discrimination when it is manifest.

Thus a person of illegitimate birth may keep that status private, and ensure that no outward sign discloses the status in social settings or in the workplace, or on the subway. But when such a person applies for Social Security benefits on the death of a parent (for example), the illegitimate status becomes manifest. The characteristic is necessarily revealed in order to exercise a legal right. Similarly, sexual preference is necessarily disclosed when two persons of the same sex apply for a marriage license (as they are legally permitted to do in New York), or when a surviving spouse of a same-sex marriage seeks the benefit of the spousal deduction (as Windsor does here).

BLAG argues that a classification based on sexual orientation would be more "amorphous" than discrete. It may be that the category exceeds the number of persons whose sexual orientation is outwardly "obvious, immutable, or distinguishing," and who thereby predictably undergo discrimination. But that is surely also true of illegitimacy and national origin. Again, what matters here is whether the characteristic invites discrimination when it is manifest.

The class affected by Section 3 of DOMA is composed entirely of persons of the same sex who have married each other. Such persons constitute a subset of the larger category of homosexuals; but as counsel for BLAG conceded at argument, there is nothing amorphous, capricious, or tentative about their sexual orientation. Married same-sex couples like Windsor and Spyer are the population most visible to the law, and they are foremost in mind when reviewing DOMA's constitutionality.

We therefore conclude that sexual orientation is a sufficiently distinguishing characteristic to identify the discrete minority class of homosexuals.

D) Political Power

Finally, we consider whether homosexuals are a politically powerless minority. See *Bowen*, 483 U.S. at 602. Without political power, minorities may be unable to protect themselves from discrimination at the hands of the majoritarian political process. We conclude that homosexuals are still significantly encumbered in this respect.

The question is not whether homosexuals have achieved political successes over the years; they clearly have. The question is whether they have the strength to politically protect themselves from wrongful discrimination. When the Supreme Court ruled that sex-based classifications were subject to heightened scrutiny in 1973, the Court acknowledged that women had already achieved major political victories. See *Frontiero*, 411 U.S. at 685. The Nineteenth Amendment had been ratified in 1920, and Title VII had already outlawed sex-based employment. The Court was persuaded nevertheless that women still lacked adequate political power, in part because they were "vastly underrepresented in this Nation's decisionmaking councils," including the presidency, the Supreme Court, and the legislature. *Frontiero*, 411 U.S. at 686 n. 17.

There are parallels between the status of women at the time of *Frontiero* and homosexuals today: their position "has improved markedly in recent decades," but they still "face pervasive, although at times more subtle, discrimination ... in the political arena." *Frontiero*, 411 U.S. at 685–86. It is difficult to say whether homosexuals are "under-represented" in positions of power and authority without knowing their number relative to the heterosexual population. But it is safe to say that the seemingly small number of acknowledged homosexuals so situated is attributable either to a hostility that excludes them or to a hostility that keeps their sexual preference private— which, for our purposes, amounts to much the same thing. Moreover, the same considerations can be expected to suppress some degree of political activity by inhibiting the kind of open association that advances political agendas. See *Rowland*, 470 U.S. at 1014 (Brennan, J., dissenting from denial of certiorari) ("Because of the immediate and severe opprobrium often manifested against homosexuals once so identified publicly, members of this group are particularly powerless to pursue their rights openly in the political arena.").

In sum, homosexuals are not in a position to adequately protect themselves from the discriminatory wishes of the majoritarian public.

Analysis of these four factors supports our conclusion that homosexuals compose a class that is subject to heightened scrutiny. We further conclude that the class is quasi-suspect (rather than suspect) based on the weight of the factors and on analogy to the classifications recognized as suspect and quasi-suspect. While homosexuals have been the target of significant and long-standing discrimination in public and private spheres, this mistreatment "is not sufficient to require 'our most exacting scrutiny.'" *Trimble v. Gordon*, 430 U.S. 762, 767 (1977) (quoting *Mathews v. Lucas*, 427 U.S. 495, 506 (1976)).

[The portion of the court's opinion that applies the intermediate scrutiny standard is reprinted *infra* in this Chapter in Section D.3.]

NOTES

1. In determining what groups constitute a suspect class and should therefore receive strict scrutiny, the Supreme Court has not consistently identified exactly what factors must be present and what weight should be given to the factors considered. In *Frontiero v. Richardson*, the Court made its most substantial statement of the relevant factors. Of those *Frontiero* factors, the *Kerrigan* and *Windsor* courts identified four: (1) a history of discrimination; (2) relevance—whether the trait bears any relation to ability to perform or contribute to society; (3) immutability; and (4) political powerlessness. Two additional factors that the *Frontiero* Court alluded to—visibility and stereotyping—were not mentioned by either the *Kerrigan* or *Windsor* courts.

2. *History of Discrimination.* The question of whether a particular group has suffered a history of discrimination is basically an empirical one. Neither court, however, insisted on primary evidence of this fact, but accepted historical and scholarly opinion as well as previous judicial findings. The *Kerrigan* court noted evidence of strong disapproval, frequent ostracism, social and legal discrimination, ferocious punishment, stigmatization, taunting and humiliation in school settings, condemnation derived from firmly held religious belief, and criminalization of conduct in many states. The *Windsor* court noted that the most telling proof of animus and discrimination against homosexuals in this country was that, for many years and in many states, homosexual conduct was criminal. Both courts found that the first factor was satisfied.

3. *Relevance—does the trait bear any relation to ability to perform or contribute to society?* The *Kerrigan* court emphasized the difference between gay persons and other groups that had been denied suspect or quasi-suspect status. For the other groups—the mentally retarded and the aged—there was a definite connection between that status and ability to perform. The mentally retarded have a reduced ability to cope with and function in the everyday world while, with regard to the elderly, physical ability generally declines with age. In contrast, said the *Kerrigan* court, sexual orientation implies no impairment in judgment, stability, reliability, or general capabilities. In fact, with regard to one of the most important functions connected with marriage—raising children—it was already the public policy of the state of Connecticut that sexual orientation bears no relation to an individual's ability to raise children, since existing state law permitted same-sex couples to adopt children.

The *Windsor* court addressed a slightly different argument with regard to relevance—the argument that the court should consider not whether the trait was relevant in general to ability to perform but rather whether it is relevant to the particular purpose of the statute. By this measure, since the purpose of the statute was to promote procreation and the raising of children, the question would be sexual orientation is relevant to that particular purpose. The *Windsor* court rejected that argument and said that that kind of relevance was part of the application of a particular standard, not a test for initially deciding which standard to apply.

4. *Immutability.* Is sexual orientation immutable? The literal meaning of the word is that something cannot be changed. This has led the argument that if a person's sexual orientation can be changed, then the trait is not immutable and gay persons are not a suspect class. The *Kerrigan* court adopted a much more complex version of the term "immutable." First, the court noted that traits that the Supreme Court has identified as immutable tend to be traits beyond a person's control. To discriminate based on a trait that is beyond a person's control seems both unfair and pointless. Further, even though the *Kerrigan* court conceded that sexual orientation is highly resistant to change, it did not need to decide whether it was as immutable as race or gender. The test of immutability is whether the trait is so central to a person's identity that a person ought not

to be penalized for refusing to change it, or, put another way, whether the trait can be characterized as a central, defining trait of personhood, which may be altered if at all only at the expense of significant damage to the individual's sense of self. The court asked the question—how easy or fair would it be for government to penalize heterosexuals for not changing their sexual orientation?

The *Windsor* court's analysis of immutability focused on whether the characteristic of the class calls down discrimination when it is manifest. The opponents of same-sex marriage had argued that a classification based on sexual orientation would be more amorphous than discrete and thus the category would exceed the number of persons whose sexual orientation is outwardly obvious, immutable, or distinguishing, and who thereby predictably undergo discrimination. But what mattered for the Windsor court was whether the characteristic invited discrimination when it is manifest. On the facts of *Windsor*, the class affected was composed entirely of persons of the same sex who have married each other. Such persons constituted a subset of the larger category of homosexuals but there was nothing amorphous, capricious, or tentative about their sexual orientation.

5. *Politically Powerless.* This final factor is based on the famous Footnote 4 of the *Carolene Products* case, which spoke of special scrutiny of discrimination directed at discrete and insular minorities who have been excluded from the majoritarian political process. Footnote 4 actual identifies *two* factors—minority status and political powerlessness. According to the *Kerrigan* court, these factors are phrased disjunctively, so that one need prove *either* minority status *or* political powerlessness. Gay persons satisfy both tests. With regard to minority status, gay men and women are a distinct minority of the population. With regard to political powerlessness, the court had to deal with the effect of recently enacted legislation that was favorable to gay men and women and the fact that there were several openly gay state legislators. But blacks and women have also been protected by legislation and serve in legislatures and their status as suspect or quasi-suspect is not threatened. For the *Kerrigan* court, the test of political powerlessness was whether the discrimination against a group was so severe that it was "not likely to be remedied soon enough merely by resort to the majoritarian political process." The court found that gay men and women satisfied this standard. The prejudice against gay men and women was not likely to be remedied soon because many of those who would discriminate against gay men and women would not consider that conduct to be evidence of prejudice but rather of a sincere religious belief that homosexuality is morally reprehensible. In addition to moral disapproval, gay men and women also face homophobia that rests on feelings of revulsion. As a result, according to *Kerrigan*, very few gay openly gay men and women hold political office. Thus, gay men and women satisfy the criterion of being politically powerless.

The *Windsor* court explained the "politically powerless" test as whether the group has the strength to politically protect themselves from wrongful discrimination. The court answered yes. Without knowing the exact percentage of the population that is gay, the court concluded that the relatively small number of gay persons in positions of power and authority is attributable either to a hostility that excludes them or to a hostility that keeps their sexual preference private and suppresses the kind of open association that advances political agendas. Gay persons satisfied this standard.

4. HEIGHTENED SCRUTINY OF SEXUAL ORIENTATION CLASSIFICATIONS BECAUSE THEY INFRINGE ON THE FUNDAMENTAL RIGHT OF PRIVACY

An alternative route to heightened scrutiny of sexual orientation classifications focuses not on fact that the adversely affected parties are gay but on the fact that the prohibited conduct is part of the constitutionally protected right of privacy identified in *Lawrence v. Texas*. The next two cases use this reasoning.

Witt v. Department of Air Force
527 F.3d 806 (9th Cir. 2008)

[Major Margaret Witt was, by all accounts, an outstanding Air Force officer and had received numerous medals of commendation. Major Witt was in a long-term relationship with a woman who was unaffiliated with the military. The couple shared a home 250 miles from the base at which Witt was stationed. Witt never discussed or disclosed the relationship to military personnel and no part of the relationship was conducted on the grounds of the Air Force Base. Pursuant to the Don't Ask, Don't Tell policy, however, Witt was suspended from duty pending discharge after her relationship with the civilian woman was disclosed and investigated. Witt sued the Air Force, the Secretary of Defense, the Secretary of the Air Force, and her Air Force commander, alleging that the policy violated substantive due process, the Equal Protection Clause, and procedural due process.]

III

To evaluate Major Witt's substantive due process claim, we first must determine the proper level of scrutiny to apply. In previous cases, we have applied rational basis review to DADT and predecessor policies. *See, e.g., Holmes*, 124 F.3d at 1136; *Philips*, 106 F.3d at 1425-26. However, Major Witt argues that *Lawrence* effectively overruled those cases by establishing a fundamental right to engage in adult consensual sexual acts. The Air Force disagrees. Having carefully considered *Lawrence* and the arguments of the parties, we hold that *Lawrence* requires something more than traditional rational basis review and that remand is therefore appropriate.

A

In *Lawrence*, the Supreme Court struck down a Texas statute that criminalized consensual homosexual sodomy. 539 U.S. at 578. In doing so, it also overruled *Bowers v. Hardwick*, 478 U.S. 186 (1986), a 1986 decision of the Supreme Court that had upheld a Georgia law criminalizing consensual sodomy. The Court in *Lawrence* noted that "broad statements of the substantive reach of liberty under the Due Process Clause" can be found in earlier cases, including *Pierce v. Society of Sisters*, 268 U.S. 510 (1925), *Meyer v. Nebraska*, 262 U.S. 390 (1923), and, most pertinently, in *Griswold v. Connecticut*, 381 U.S. 479 (1965). *Lawrence*, 539 U.S. at 564. "After *Griswold*," the Court wrote, "it was established that the right to make certain decisions regarding sexual conduct extends beyond the marital relationship."

[The Court here quoted the *Lawrence* Court's decision.]

The Supreme Court then provided additional reasons why it was overruling *Bowers*. First, the Court explained, *Bowers* was predicated on the erroneous belief that homosexuality was "subject to state intervention throughout the history of Western civilization." Second, the logic in *Bowers* "demean [ed] the lives of homosexual persons" and had been widely rejected by state courts and international tribunals.

The Supreme Court concluded:

> [Homosexuals'] right to liberty under the Due Process Clause gives them the full right to engage in their conduct without intervention of the government. "It is a promise of the Constitution that there is a realm of personal liberty which the government may not enter." *Planned Parenthood v. Casey,* 505 U.S. 833, 847 (1992). The Texas statute furthers no legitimate state interest which can justify its intrusion into the personal and private life of the individual.

B

Major Witt argues that *Lawrence* recognized a fundamental right to engage in private, consensual, homosexual conduct and therefore requires us to subject DADT to heightened scrutiny. The Air Force argues that *Lawrence* applied only rational basis review, and that the Ninth Circuit's decisions in *Holmes, Philips*, and *Beller* remain binding law on DADT's validity. Because *Lawrence* is, perhaps intentionally so, silent as to the level of scrutiny that it applied, both parties draw upon language from *Lawrence* that supports their views.

Major Witt argues that the "plain language" of *Lawrence* demonstrates that heightened scrutiny is required here. She notes that, in *Lawrence,* the Supreme Court relied on *Griswold,* 381 U.S. 479, *Roe v. Wade,* 410 U.S. 113 (1973), and *Carey v. Population Services International,* 431 U.S. 678 (1977), all of which are fundamental rights cases. She also observes that the language of *Lawrence* emphasizes the importance of the right at issue and refers to "substantial protections" afforded "adult persons in deciding how to conduct their private lives in matters pertaining to sex." "Substantial protections" are not afforded under rational basis review, Major Witt argues, because rational basis review considers only whether the challenged policy is rationally related to a legitimate state interest.

In response, the Air Force argues that the same "plain language" implies only rational basis review. In particular, the Air Force stresses the passage in *Lawrence* that states that the challenged statute "further[ed] no *legitimate state interest* which can justify its intrusion into the personal and private life of the individual," 539 U.S. at 578. According to the Air Force, legitimate interests are the hallmark of rational basis review. The Air Force also notes that *Lawrence* never stated that it was applying anything other than rational basis review, so, the Air Force concludes, it surely was not.

2

The parties urge us to pick through *Lawrence* with a fine-toothed comb and to give credence to the particular turns of phrase used by the Supreme Court that best support their claims. But given the studied limits of the verbal analysis in *Lawrence,* this approach is not conclusive. Nor does a review of our circuit precedent answer the question; as the Court of Appeals for the Armed Forces stated in *Marcum,* 60 M.J. at 204, "[a]lthough particular sentences within the Supreme Court's opinion may be culled in support of the Government's argument, other sentences may be extracted to support Appellant's argument." In these ambiguous circumstances, we analyze *Lawrence* by considering what the Court actually *did,* rather than by dissecting isolated pieces of text. In so doing, we conclude that the Supreme Court applied a heightened level of scrutiny in *Lawrence*.

We cannot reconcile what the Supreme Court did in *Lawrence* with the minimal protections afforded by traditional rational basis review. First, the Court overruled *Bowers,* an earlier case in which the Court had upheld a Georgia sodomy law under rational basis review. If the Court was undertaking rational basis review, then *Bowers* must have been wrong because it failed under that standard; namely, it must have lacked "any reasonably conceivable state of facts that could provide a rational basis for the classification." *FCC v. Beach Commc'ns, Inc.,* 508 U.S. 307, 313 (1993). But the Court's criticism of *Bowers* had nothing to do with the basis for the law; instead, the Court rejected *Bowers* because of the "Court's own failure to appreciate the extent of the liberty at stake." *Lawrence,* 539 U.S. at 567.

The criticism that the Court in *Bowers* had misapprehended "the extent of the liberty at stake" does not sound in rational basis review. Under rational basis review, the Court determines whether governmental action is so arbitrary that a rational basis for the action cannot even be conceived *post hoc.* If the Court was applying that standard-"a paradigm of judicial restraint," *Beach,* 508 U.S. at 3--it had no reason to consider the extent of the liberty involved. Yet it did, ultimately concluding that the ban on homosexual sexual conduct sought to "control a personal relationship that, whether or not entitled to formal recognition in the law, is within the liberty of persons to choose without being punished as criminals." *Lawrence,* 539 U.S. at 567. This is inconsistent with rational basis review.

Second, the cases on which the Supreme Court explicitly based its decision in *Lawrence* are based on heightened scrutiny. As Major Witt pointed out, those cases include *Griswold, Roe,* and *Carey.* Moreover, the Court stated that *Casey,* a post- *Bowers* decision, cast its holding in *Bowers* into doubt. *Lawrence,* 539 U.S.at 573-74. Notably, the Court did not mention or apply the post-*Bowers* case of *Romer v. Evans,* 517 U.S. 620 (1996), in which the Court applied rational basis review to a law concerning homosexuals. Instead, the Court overturned *Bowers* because "[i]ts continuance as precedent demeans the lives of homosexual persons." *Lawrence,* 539 U.S. at 575.

Third, the *Lawrence* Court's rationale for its holding--the inquiry analysis that it was applying-is inconsistent with rational basis review. The Court declared: "The Texas statute furthers no legitimate state interest *which can justify its intrusion into the personal and private life of the individual." Id.* at 578. Were the Court applying rational basis review, it would not identify a legitimate state interest to "justify" the particular intrusion of liberty at issue in *Lawrence;* regardless of the liberty involved, any hypothetical rationale for the law would do.

We therefore conclude that *Lawrence* applied something more than traditional rational basis review. This leaves open the question whether the Court applied strict scrutiny, intermediate scrutiny, or another heightened level of scrutiny. Substantive due process cases typically apply strict scrutiny in the case of a fundamental right and rational basis review in all other cases. When a fundamental right is recognized, substantive due process forbids the infringement of that right "at all, no matter what process is provided, unless the infringement is narrowly tailored to serve a compelling state interest." *Reno v. Flores,* 507 U.S. 292, 301-02 (1993). Few laws survive such scrutiny, and DADT most likely would not.[FN 5] However, we hesitate to apply strict scrutiny when

---

[FN 5] The rationale for DADT is found at 10 U.S.C. § 654(a)(15), which states Congress's finding that:

> The presence in the armed forces of persons who demonstrate a propensity or intent to engage in homosexual acts would create an unacceptable risk to the high standards of morale, good order and

CHAPTER 6: CLASSIFICATIONS BASED ON SEXUAL ORIENTATION

the Supreme Court did not discuss narrow tailoring or a compelling state interest in *Lawrence*, and we do not address the issue here.

Instead, we look to another recent Supreme Court case that applied a heightened level of scrutiny to a substantive due process claim--a scrutiny that resembles and expands upon the analysis performed in *Lawrence*. In *Sell v. United States*, 539 U.S. 166, 179 (2003), the Court considered whether the Constitution permits the government to forcibly administer antipsychotic drugs to a mentally-ill defendant in order to render that defendant competent to stand trial. The Court held that the defendant has a "significant constitutionally protected liberty interest" at stake, so the drugs could be administered forcibly "only if the treatment is medically appropriate, is substantially unlikely to have side effects that may undermine the fairness of the trial, and, taking account of less intrusive alternatives, is necessary significantly to further important governmental trial-related interests."

Although the Court's holding in *Sell* is specific to the context of forcibly administering medication, the scrutiny employed by the Court to reach that holding is instructive. *See Miller v. Gammie*, 335 F.3d 889, 900 (9th Cir.2003) (en banc) (holding that we are bound by the theory or reasoning underlying a Supreme Court case, not just by its holding). The Court recognized a "significant" liberty interest--the interest "in avoiding the unwanted administration of antipsychotic drugs"- and balanced that liberty interest against the "legitimate" and "important" state interest "in providing appropriate medical treatment to reduce the danger that an inmate suffering from a serious mental disorder represents to himself or others." *Sell*, 539 U.S. at 178. To balance those two interests, the Court required the state to justify its intrusion into an individual's recognized liberty interest against forcible medication--just as *Lawrence* determined that the state had failed to "justify its intrusion into the personal and private life of the individual." *Lawrence*, 539 U.S. at 578.

The heightened scrutiny applied in *Sell* consisted of four factors:

First, a court must find that *important* governmental interests are at stake.
Second, the court must conclude that involuntary medication will *significantly further* those concomitant state interests.
Third, the court must conclude that involuntary medication is *necessary* to further those interests. The court must find that any alternative, less intrusive treatments are unlikely to achieve substantially the same results.
Fourth, the court must conclude that administration of the drugs is *medically appropriate*.

The fourth factor is specific to the medical context of *Sell*, but the first three factors apply equally here. We thus take our direction from the Supreme Court and adopt the first three heightened-scrutiny *Sell* factors as the heightened scrutiny balancing analysis required under *Lawrence*. We hold that when the government attempts to intrude upon the personal and private lives of homosexuals, in a manner that implicates the rights identified in *Lawrence*, the government must advance an important governmental interest, the intrusion must significantly further that interest, and the intrusion must be necessary to further that interest. In other words, for the third factor, a less intrusive means must be unlikely to achieve substantially the government's interest. *See also Aptheker v. Sec'y of State*, 378 U.S. 500, 508 (1964) ("Even though the governmental purpose be legitimate and substantial, that purpose cannot be pursued by means that

---

discipline, and unit cohesion that are the essence of military capability.

broadly stifle fundamental personal liberties when the end can be more narrowly achieved." (Internal quotation marks omitted)).

In addition, we hold that this heightened scrutiny analysis is as-applied rather than facial. "This is the preferred course of adjudication since it enables courts to avoid making unnecessarily broad constitutional judgments." *City of Cleburne v. Cleburne Living Ctr. Inc.,* 473 U.S. 432, 447 (1985). In *Cleburne,* the Court employed a "type of 'active' rational basis review," *Pruitt,* 963 F.2d at 1165-66, in requiring the city to justify its zoning ordinance as applied to the specific plaintiffs in that case. And *Sell* required courts to "consider the facts of the individual case in evaluating the Government's interest." 539 U.S. at 180. Under this review, we must determine not whether DADT has some hypothetical, post hoc rationalization in general, but whether a justification exists for the application of the policy as applied to Major Witt. This approach is necessary to give meaning to the Supreme Court's conclusion that "liberty gives substantial protection to adult persons in deciding how to conduct their private lives in matters pertaining to sex." *Lawrence,* 539 U.S. at 572.

Here, applying heightened scrutiny to DADT in light of current Supreme Court precedents, it is clear that the government advances an important governmental interest. DADT concerns the management of the military, and "judicial deference to ... congressional exercise of authority is at its apogee when legislative action under the congressional authority to raise and support armies and make rules and regulations for their governance is challenged." *Rostker v. Goldberg,* 453 U.S. 57, 70 (1981). Notably, "deference does not mean abdication." *Id.* "Congress, of course, is subject to the requirements of the Due Process Clause when legislating in the area of military affairs . . . ." *Weiss v. United States,* 510 U.S. 163, 176 (1994).

However, it is unclear on the record before us whether DADT, as applied to Major Witt, satisfies the second and third factors. The Air Force attempts to justify the policy by relying on congressional findings regarding "unit cohesion" and the like, but that does not go to whether the application of DADT specifically to Major Witt significantly furthers the government's interest and whether less intrusive means would achieve substantially the government's interest.[FN 11] Remand therefore is required for the district court to develop the record on Major Witt's substantive due process claim. Only then can DADT be measured against the appropriate constitutional standard.

V

The issues posed by this case might generate great concern both from those who welcome Major Witt's continued participation in the Air Force and from those who may oppose it. Those issues must be, and have been, addressed in the first instance by leaders of the military community and by those in Congress with law-making responsibilities. All of Congress's laws must abide by the United States Constitution, however. Taking direction from what the Supreme Court decided in *Lawrence* and *Sell,* we hold that DADT, after *Lawrence,* must satisfy an intermediate level of scrutiny under substantive due process, an inquiry that requires facts not present on the record before us.

[FN 11] Indeed, the facts as alleged by Major Witt indicate the contrary. Major Witt was a model officer whose sexual activities hundreds of miles away from base did not affect her unit until the military initiated discharge proceedings under DADT and, even then, it was her suspension pursuant to DADT, not her homosexuality, that damaged unit cohesion.

In light of the foregoing, we **VACATE** and **REMAND** the district court's judgment with regard to Major Witt's substantive due process claim and procedural due process claim, and **AFFIRM** with regard to the equal protection clause claim. The parties shall bear their own costs on appeal.

NOTES

1. The court in *Witt* conceded, as have many others, that the standard of review used by the Supreme Court in *Lawrence* was quite ambiguous — something more than rational basis review and yet not the "narrowly tailored to a compelling interest" test that is emblematic of strict scrutiny. The *Witt* court resolved the problem by using an intermediate scrutiny test that the Supreme Court had used in *Sell v. United States*, 539 U.S. 166 (2003), a substantive due process case about forcibly administering antipsychotic drugs to a mentally-ill defendant in order to render that defendant competent to stand trial. From that *Sell* case, the *Witt* court drew a three-part test that it described as "an intermediate level of scrutiny under substantive due process." The test required that, when it attempts to intrude upon the personal and private lives of homosexuals in a manner that implicates the rights identified in *Lawrence*, "the government must advance an important governmental interest, the intrusion must significantly further that interest, and the intrusion must be necessary to further that interest."

The *Witt* court determined that the DADT policy advanced an important governmental interest—the management of the military. But the record was not at all clear that DADT satisfied the second and third factors. The military's attempt to justify the policy by reference to "unit cohesion" had never been considered in Major Witt's individual case. The court remanded to the district court for findings on those issues.

2. On remand, *Witt v. U.S. Dept. of Air Force*, 739 F.Supp.2d 1308 (W.D. Wash. 2010), the district court determined that application of DADT to Major Witt violated her substantive due process rights. The court determined that its mandate from the Ninth Circuit was to apply the heightened scrutinized test on an as-applied basis rather than facially. The court noted the government's important interests in unit morale, good order, discipline, and cohesion, but determined that application of DADT in Major Witt's case did not further those interests:

> The evidence produced at trial overwhelmingly supports the conclusion that the suspension and discharge of Margaret Witt did not significantly further the important government interest in advancing unit morale and cohesion . . . The evidence before the Court is that Major Margaret Witt was an exemplary officer. She was an effective leader, a caring mentor, a skilled clinician, and an integral member of an effective team. Her loss within the squadron resulted in a diminution of the unit's ability to carry out its mission. Good flight nurses are hard to find. . . The evidence produced at trial overwhelmingly supports the conclusion that the suspension and discharge of Margaret Witt did not significantly further the important government interest in advancing unit morale and cohesion.

3. In *Cook v. Gates*, 528 F.3d 42 (1st Cir. 2008), the United States Court of Appeals for the First Circuit also considered the constitutionality of the military's Don't Ask, Don't Tell policy. The court noted the disagreement among courts and commenters on the proper interpretation of *Lawrence*, with some reading *Lawrence* as applying a rational basis test, some seeing the case as applying strict scrutiny, and a third group viewing the case as applying a balancing test

somewhere between rational basis and strict scrutiny. The *Cook* court concluded that *Lawrence* had in fact protected a liberty interest for adults to engage in private, consensual sexual intimacy, and had applied a balancing of interests. The court determined, however, that it need not apply strict scrutiny's "narrowly tailored to serve a compelling interest" test but rather, would adopt the balancing approach:

> *Lawrence* is, in our view, another in this line of Supreme Court authority that identifies a protected liberty interest and then applies a standard of review that lies between strict scrutiny and rational basis. In invalidating the convictions, the *Lawrence* Court determined that there was no legitimate state interest that was adequate to "justify" the intrusion on liberty worked by the law. 539 U.S. at 578. In other words, *Lawrence* balanced the strength of the state's asserted interest in prohibiting immoral conduct against the degree of intrusion into the petitioners' private sexual life caused by the statute in order to determine whether the law was unconstitutionally applied. See *Casey*, 505 U.S. at 873 ("[N]ot every law which makes a right more difficult to exercise is, ipso facto, an infringement of that right.").

The court then determined, even under this heightened balancing test, that DADT survived scrutiny, both facially and on and as-applied basis:

> The plaintiffs' facial challenge fails. *Lawrence* did not identify a protected liberty interest in all forms and manner of sexual intimacy. *Lawrence* recognized only a narrowly defined liberty interest in adult consensual sexual intimacy in the confines of one's home and one's own private life. *Lawrence,* 539 U.S. at 567. The Court made it abundantly clear that there are many types of sexual activity that are beyond the reach of that opinion. *Id.* at 578. Here, the Act includes such other types of sexual activity. The Act provides for the separation of a service person who engages in a public homosexual act or who coerces another person to engage in a homosexual act. Both of these forms of conduct are expressly excluded from the liberty interest recognized by *Lawrence.*

> The plaintiffs' as-applied challenge, on the other hand, presents a more difficult question. The plaintiffs point out that the Act could apply to some conduct that falls within the zone of protected liberty identified by *Lawrence*. The Act, for example, could cover homosexual conduct occurring off base between two consenting adults in the privacy of their home. . . . Acknowledging the government interest identified in this case, one that our deferential posture requires us to take at face value, as-applied challenges to the Act must fail as well.

> Here . . . there is a detailed legislative record concerning Congress' reasons for passing the Act. This record makes plain that Congress concluded, after considered deliberation, that the Act was necessary to preserve the military's effectiveness as a fighting force, 10 U.S.C. § 654(a)(15), and thus, to ensure national security. This is an exceedingly weighty interest and one that unquestionably surpasses the government interest that was at stake in *Lawrence*. See *Lawrence*, 539 U.S. at 585 (O'Connor, J., concurring).

> Every as-applied challenge brought by a member of the armed forces against the Act, at its core, implicates this interest. Every member of the armed forces has one fact in common—at a moment's notice he or she may be deployed to a combat area. 10 U.S.C. § 654(a)(11). The conditions of service in such an area bring into play the animating

concerns behind the Act, namely, maintaining the morale and unit cohesion that the military deems essential to an effective fighting force. See 10 U.S.C § 654(a)(12), (15). Accordingly, we have no choice but to dismiss the plaintiffs' as-applied challenge.

4. The cases in this section examined the general question of the proper level of scrutiny to be applied to classifications that disadvantage persons on the basis of their sexual orientation. The next section will examine these different standards of review in three important factual contexts.

D. CURRENT ISSUES ON SEXUAL ORIENTATION CLASSIFICATIONS

In recent years, the application of the Equal Protection Clause to sexual orientation discrimination has been principally litigated in three factual contexts: the exclusion of gay persons from the military; state laws that limit marriage to one man and one woman: and the federal Defense of Marriage Act (DOMA), under which the federal government does not recognize same-sex marriages even when they are valid under state law, and which asserts that states need not give full faith and credit to same-sex marriages even when valid in the state in which the marriage took place. This section examines the courts' treatment of sexual orientation classifications in each of these factual contexts.

1. *THE EXCLUSION OF GAY MEN AND WOMEN FROM THE MILITARY*

The United States military's longstanding policy of excluding gay persons from military service has changed over time, but the military consistently refused to allow gay men and women to serve openly in the military. An early version of the policy provided that one "who solicits, attempts or engages in homosexual acts shall normally be separated from the naval service," but discharge was not invariably mandatory. *See Dronenburg v. Zech*, 741 F.2d 1388, 1389 (D.C. Cir. 1984). A subsequent version excluded "a person who has committed homosexual acts or is an admitted homosexual but as to whom there is no evidence that they have engaged in homosexual acts." See *Watkins v. U.S. Army*, 847 F.2d 1329, 1336 (9th Cir. 1988) (citing Army Regulation 601-280), opinion withdrawn on reh'g, 875 F.2d 699 (9th Cir. 1989). The most recent version of the rule, commonly known as the "Don't Ask, Don't Tell" (DADT) policy, provided that a member of the armed forces would be discharged if any one of the following findings were made: (1) "That the member has engaged in, attempted to engage in, or solicited another to engage in a homosexual act or acts;" (2) "That the member has stated that he or she is a homosexual . . . unless there is a further finding...that the member has demonstrated that he or she is not a person who engages in, attempts to engage in, has a propensity to engage in, or intends to engage in homosexual acts;" or (3) "That the member has married or attempted to marry a person known to be of the same biological sex." 10 U.S.C. 654(b) (2006).

In December 2010, Congress ended the policy that prohibited gay men and women from serving in the United States military on the same terms as heterosexual persons. *See* Don't Ask, Don't Tell Repeal Act of 2010. This statutory change effectively ended many years of litigation over the constitutionality of a changing series of military policies that excluded openly gay persons from service. Even though the cases decided under the old policies are now effectively moot, they provide a good example of the direction in which courts were moving in evaluating challenges to laws that classified on the basis of sexual orientation.

For a long time, challenges to the policy of excluding gay persons from the military were reviewed under a deferential rational basis standard and, predictably, failed. *See, e.g., Dronenburg v. Zech*, 741 F.2d 1388 (D.C. Circ., 1984); *High Tech Gays v. Def. Indus. Sec. Clearance Office*, 895 F.2d 563 (9th Cir.1990); *Ben–Shalom v. Marsh*, 881 F.2d 454 (7th Cir.1989). In more recent years, at least two courts have applied an intermediate level of review to the exclusion of gay men and women from the military. *Witt v. Department of Air Force*, 527 F.3d 806 (9th Cir. 2008); *Cook v. Gates*, 528 F.3d 42 (1st Cir. 2008), on the ground that, under *Lawrence v. Texas*, the military's policy interfered with an implied fundamental right. The following case applies that standard to the policy.

Log Cabin Republicans v. United States
716 F.Supp.2d 884 (C.D. Cal. 2010)

[The Log Cabin Republicans [LCR] are a national non-profit organization addressing the interests of Republicans who are gay and lesbian. The organization filed a challenge to "Don't Ask, Don't Tell" (DADT) on behalf of its members in the United States District Court for the Central District of California.]

Plaintiff claims the Don't Ask, Don't Tell Act violates its members' substantive due process rights, identified in *Lawrence* as rights associated with the "autonomy of self that includes freedom of thought, belief, expression, and certain intimate conduct." *Lawrence*, 539 U.S. at 562.

The Act contains a series of findings that mirror the concerns of then-chairman of the Joint Chiefs of Staff Colin Powell's testimony before Congress: "military life is fundamentally different from civilian life;" "[s]uccess in combat requires military units that are characterized by high morale, good order and discipline, and unit cohesion;" and "the presence in the [A]rmed [F]orces of persons who demonstrate a propensity of intent to engage in homosexual acts would create an unacceptable risk to the high standards of morale, good order and discipline and unit cohesion that are the essence of military capability." *See* 10 U.S.C. § 654(a) (1993).

B. The Standard of Review

[The court announced that it was bound by the Ninth Circuit's decision in *Witt v. Department of Air Force*, 527 F.3d 806 (9th Cir.2008), which required that the DADT policy must "[1] advance an important governmental interest, [2] significantly further that interest, and [3] be necessary to further that interest." The court focused on the second and third prongs.]

C. The Act Does Not Significantly Further the Government's Interests in Military Readiness or Unit Cohesion

a. Discharge of Qualified Servicemembers Despite Troop Shortages

[The court here noted that, between 1993 and 2009, the military discharged more than 13,000 men and women under DADT. Starting in 2002, after the U.S. began fighting in Afghanistan, the number of servicemembers discharged under the Act fell sharply, despite the greater raw number of military personnel.]

b. Discharge of Servicemembers with Critically Needed Skills and Training

Among those discharged were many with critically needed skills. According to the Government's own data, many of those discharged pursuant to the Act had education, training, or specialization in so-called "critical skills," including Arabic, Chinese, Farsi, or Korean language fluency; military intelligence; counterterrorism; weapons development; and medicine. Far from furthering the military's readiness, the discharge of these service men and women had a direct and deleterious effect on this governmental interest.

c. The Act's Impact on Military Recruiting

[The court here noted that DADT negatively affected military recruiting in two ways: its existence discouraged those who would otherwise enlist from doing so, and many colleges and universities would not permit military recruiting or Army ROTC programs on campus because the Act's requirements violate their employment nondiscrimination policies.]

[A] 2005 GAO Report estimated that over the ten-year period after enactment of the Act, "it could have cost the [Department of Defense] about $95 million in constant fiscal year 2004 dollars to recruit replacements for service members separated under the policy. Also the Navy, Air Force, and Army estimated that the cost to train replacements for separated service members by occupation was approximately $48.8 million, $16.6 million, and $29.7 million, respectively."

d. Admission of Lesser Qualified Enlistees

Plaintiff introduced evidence that while Defendants continued to enforce the Act by discharging servicemembers under it-albeit in dramatically reduced numbers-after 2001, they also began to admit more convicted felons and misdemeanants into the Armed Forces, by granting so-called "moral waivers" to the against such admissions. . . . In addition to the increased numbers of convicted felons and misdemeanants allowed to join the ranks of the military forces, Professor Frank testified that increased numbers of recruits lacking the required level of education and physical fitness were allowed to enlist because of troop shortages during the years following 2001.

e. Other Effects of the Policy

Dr. Korb testified about other effects the Don't Ask, Don't Tell Act has on military preparedness. He opined that in order for the military to perform its mission successfully, it must mold persons from vastly different backgrounds who join it into a united and task-oriented organization. He described the military as a meritocracy, but testified that the Don't Ask, Don't Tell Act detracts from the merit-based nature of the organization, because discharges under the Act are not based on the servicemember's failure to perform his or her duties properly, or on the effect of the soldier's presence on the unit's morale or cohesion.

f. Decreased and Delayed Discharge of Suspected Violators of the Act

LCR also produced evidence demonstrating that Defendants routinely delayed the discharge of servicemembers suspected of violating the Act's provisions until after they had completed their overseas deployments ... Defendants deployed servicemembers under investigation for violating the Act to combat missions or, if they were already so deployed, delayed the completion of the investigation until the end of the deployment.

This evidence, in particular, directly undermines any contention that the Act furthers the Government's purpose of military readiness, as it shows Defendants continue to deploy gay and lesbian members of the military into combat, waiting until they have returned before resolving the charges arising out of the suspected homosexual conduct. If the warrior's suspected violation of the Act created a threat to military readiness, to unit cohesion, or to any of the other important Government objectives, it follows that Defendants would not deploy him or her to combat before resolving the investigation. It defies logic that the purposes of the Act could be served by suspending the investigation during overseas deployments, only to discharge a servicemember upon his or her return to a non-combat station.

Taken as a whole, the evidence introduced at trial shows that the effect of the Act has been, not to advance the Government's interests of military readiness and unit cohesion, much less to do so significantly, but to harm that interest.

D. The Act is Not Necessary to Advance the Government's Interests

The *Witt* court held that to justify the infringement on the fundamental rights identified in *Lawrence,* a defendant must satisfy both the requirement that the Act "significantly furthers" the Government's interests and the requirement that it is "necessary" to achieve them. To the extent that Defendants have made a distinct argument here that the Act is necessary to achieve the Government's significant interest, they have not met their burden as to this prong of the *Witt* test, either.

2. Defendants' Contention that the Act is Necessary to Protect Unit Cohesion and Privacy

Defendants point to the Act's legislative history and prefatory findings as evidence that the Policy is necessary to protect unit cohesion and heterosexual service members' privacy. In particular, they quote and rely on General Colin Powell's statements in his testimony before Congress in 1993.

General Powell expressed his qualified support for the continued service of gays and lesbians in the Armed Forces and the narrow nature of his concerns. He emphasized his concern that "active military service is not an everyday job in an ordinary workplace.... There is often no escape from the military environment for days, weeks and often months on end. We place unique demands and constraints upon our young men and women not the least of which are bathing and sleeping in close quarters." ("Our concern has not been about homosexuals seducing heterosexuals or heterosexuals attacking homosexuals....").

First, it must be noted that Plaintiff introduced uncontradicted testimony that General Powell has changed his views since 1993 on the necessity of the Policy and agrees with the current Commander-in-Chief that it should be reviewed.

More importantly, however, Plaintiff produced powerful evidence demonstrating that the Act is not necessary in order to further the governmental interest that General Powell expressed, *i.e.,* unit cohesion and particularly the concern that cohesion might be eroded if openly homosexual servicemembers shared close living quarters with heterosexuals.

In summary, Defendants have failed to satisfy their burden under the *Witt* standard. They have not shown the Don't Ask, Don't Tell policy "significantly furthers" the Government's interests nor that it is "necessary" in order to achieve those goals.

The Don't Ask, Don't Tell Act infringes the fundamental rights of United States servicemembers in many ways, some described above. The Act denies homosexuals serving in the Armed Forces the right to enjoy "intimate conduct" in their personal relationships. The Act denies them the right to speak about their loved ones while serving their country in uniform; it punishes them with discharge for writing a personal letter, in a foreign language, to a person of the same sex with whom they shared an intimate relationship before entering military service; it discharges them for including information in a personal communication from which an unauthorized reader might discern their homosexuality. In order to justify the encroachment on these rights, Defendants faced the burden at trial of showing the Don't Ask, Don't Tell Act was necessary to significantly further the Government's important interests in military readiness and unit cohesion. Defendants failed to meet that burden. Thus, Plaintiff is entitled to judgment in its favor on the first claim in its First Amended Complaint for violation of the substantive due process rights guaranteed under the Fifth Amendment.

VI. CONCLUSION

Throughout the consideration and resolution of this controversy, the Court has kept well in mind the overriding principle that "judicial deference to such congressional exercise of authority is at its apogee when legislative action under the congressional authority to raise and support armies and make rules and regulations for their governance is challenged." *Rostker,* 453 U.S. at 70. Nevertheless, as the Supreme Court held in *Rostker,* "deference does not mean abdication." Plaintiff has demonstrated it is entitled to the relief sought on behalf of its members, a judicial declaration that the Don't Ask, Don't Tell Act violates the Fifth and First Amendments, and a permanent injunction barring its enforcement.

IT IS SO ORDERED.

NOTES

1. In *Log Cabin Republicans v. United States*, 658 F.3d 1162 (9th Cir. 2011), the United States Court of Appeals, in light of the repeal of DADT, vacated the above district court decision as moot. The court explained the effect of its decision as follows:

> Because Log Cabin has stated its intention to use the district court's judgment collaterally, we will be clear: It may not. Nor may its members or anyone else. We vacate the district court's judgment, injunction, opinions, orders, and factual findings—indeed, all of its past rulings—to clear the path completely for any future litigation. Those now-void legal rulings and factual findings have no precedential, preclusive, or binding effect. The repeal of Don't Ask, Don't Tell provides Log Cabin with all it sought and may have had standing to obtain.

Notwithstanding this language to the effect that the district court opinion has no precedential value, it is reproduced here because it is a very careful review of the usefulness, effectiveness, and necessity of the Don't Ask, Don't Tell law. The law was neither useful, nor effective, nor necessary.

2. Because the Don't Ask, Don't Tell policy ended more than a year ago, it is possible to evaluate whether the concerns that were expressed by opponents of gay persons in the military—concerns over morale and readiness—were grounded in reality. The evidence suggests that they were not. The New York Times reported:

One Year Later, Military Says Gay Policy Is Working

> It has been exactly a year since "don't ask, don't tell" was repealed, and by most measures the change has been a success. Gay service members say they feel relief they no longer have to live secret lives. Pentagon officials say that recruiting, retention and overall morale have not been affected. None of the dire predictions of opponents, including warnings of a mass exodus of active duty troops, have occurred.
>
> "My view is that the military has kind of moved beyond it," Defense Secretary Leon E. Panetta said in May, eight months after the repeal. Even the Marine Corps, the service most opposed to the change, has fallen in line. "I get in front of the Marines as often as I can, as long as I can get away from Washington, and I'll be honest with you, I don't even get a question," the Marine commandant, James F. Amos, said at the National Press Club last month. "I'm very pleased with how this turned out." N.Y. Times, Sept. 19, 2012, A17.

3. In 1984, Judge Bork, in *Dronenburg v. Zech*, 741 F.2d 1388 (D.C. Circ., 1984) upheld the then existing military policy that excluded gay men and women from the military. Applying a highly deferential version of rational basis review, Judge Bork wrote:

> [T]his regulation is plainly a rational means of advancing a legitimate, indeed a crucial, interest common to all our armed forces. To ask the question is to answer it. The effects of homosexual conduct within a naval or military unit are almost certain to be harmful to morale and discipline. The Navy is not required to produce social science data or the results of controlled experiments to prove what common sense and common experience demonstrate.

Judge Bork was too quick to conclude that "[t]o ask the question is to answer it." Navy petty officer James L. Dronenburg, whose discharge from the Navy was upheld, deserved a better fate.

2. *STATE RULES LIMITING MARRIAGE TO A MAN AND A WOMAN*

A vast majority of American states still preserve the traditional definition of marriage—as between a man and a woman—and thus prohibit same-sex marriage. As of November, 2012, however, nine states have recognized same-sex marriage: three as a result of judicial decision under their state constitutions (Massachusetts, Connecticut, and Iowa), three as a result of legislative enactment (Vermont, New Hampshire, and New York), and three by popular referendum (Maine, Maryland, and Washington). This section examines continuing challenges to state laws that limit marriage to those between a man and a woman in the federal courts under the United States Constitution.

As is the case for all other equal protection challenges to same-sex classifications, a court's choice of a standard of review tends to shape the result. This section examines two cases challenging the exclusion of same-sex couples from marriage. Both arise under the Equal

Protection Clause of the United States Constitution. In the first case, the court uses a very deferential version of rational basis review, while in the second the court uses the more demanding version of that standard.

Citizens for Equal Protection v. Bruning
455 F.3d 859 (8th Cir. 2006)

LOKEN, Chief Judge.

In November 2000, Nebraska voters passed by a large majority a constitutional amendment, codified as Article I, § 29 of the Nebraska Constitution, providing:

> Only marriage between a man and a woman shall be valid or recognized in Nebraska. The uniting of two persons of the same sex in a civil union, domestic partnership, or other similar same-sex relationship shall not be valid or recognized in Nebraska.

Three public interest groups whose members include gay and lesbian citizens of Nebraska commenced this action, alleging that it violated the Equal Protection Clause.

[The Court initially summarized *Romer v. Evans*, 517 U.S. 620 (1996).]

Relying primarily on *Romer*, Appellees argue that § 29 violates the Equal Protection Clause because it raises an insurmountable political barrier to same-sex couples obtaining the many governmental and private sector benefits that are based upon a legally valid marriage relationship. Appellees do not assert a right to marriage or same-sex unions. Rather, they seek "a level playing field, an equal opportunity to convince the people's elected representatives that same-sex relationships deserve legal protection." *Citizens for Equal Protection*, 368 F.Supp.2d at 985 n. 1. The argument turns on the fact that § 29 is an amendment to the Nebraska Constitution. Unlike state-wide legislation restricting marriage to a man and a woman, a constitutional amendment deprives gays and lesbians of "equal footing in the political arena" because state and local government officials now lack the power to address issues of importance to this minority.

As Supreme Court decisions attest, the level of judicial scrutiny to be applied in determining the validity of state legislative and constitutional enactments under the Fourteenth Amendment is a subject of continuing debate and disagreement among the Justices. Though the most relevant precedents are murky, we conclude for a number of reasons that § 29 should receive rational-basis review under the Equal Protection Clause, rather than a heightened level of judicial scrutiny.

If sexual orientation, like race, were a "suspect classification" for purposes of the Equal Protection Clause, then Appellees' focus on the political burden erected by a constitutional amendment would find support in cases like *Reitman v. Mulkey*, 387 U.S. 369 (1967), *Hunter v. Erickson*, 393 U.S. 385 (1969), and *Washington v. Seattle Sch. Dist. No. 1*, 458 U.S. 457 (1982). But the Supreme Court has never ruled that sexual orientation is a suspect classification for equal protection purposes. The Court's general standard is that rational-basis review applies "where individuals in the group affected by a law have distinguishing characteristics relevant to interests the State has the authority to implement." *City of Cleburne v. Cleburne Living Center*, 473 U.S. 432, 441 (1985). As we will explain, that is the case here, and therefore Appellees are not entitled to strict scrutiny review on this ground.

Rational-basis review is highly deferential to the legislature or, in this case, to the electorate that directly adopted § 29 by the initiative process. "In areas of social and economic policy, a statutory classification that neither proceeds along suspect lines nor infringes fundamental constitutional rights must be upheld against equal protection challenge if there is any reasonably conceivable state of facts that could provide a rational-basis for the classification." *F.C.C. v. Beach Communications, Inc.,* 508 U.S. 307, 313 (1993). Thus, the classification created by § 29 and other laws defining marriage as the union between one man and one woman is afforded a "strong presumption of validity." *Heller v. Doe,* 509 U.S. 312, 319 (1993). The Equal Protection Clause "is not a license for courts to judge the wisdom, fairness, or logic of [the voters'] choices." *Beach Communications,* 508 U.S. at 313.

Our rational-basis review begins with an historical fact--the institution of marriage has always been, in our federal system, the predominant concern of state government. The Supreme Court long ago declared, and recently reaffirmed, that a State "has absolute right to prescribe the conditions upon which the marriage relation between its own citizens shall be created, and the causes for which it may be dissolved." *Pennoyer v. Neff,* 95 U.S. 714, 734-35 (1878). This necessarily includes the power to classify those persons who may validly marry. "Surely, for example, a State may legitimately say that no one can marry his or her sibling, that no one can marry who is not at least 14 years old, that no one can marry without first passing an examination for venereal disease, or that no one can marry who has a living husband or wife." *Zablocki v. Redhail,* 434 U.S. 374, 392 (1978) (Stewart, J., concurring). In this constitutional environment, rational-basis review must be particularly deferential.

The State argues that the many laws defining marriage as the union of one man and one woman and extending a variety of benefits to married couples are rationally related to the government interest in "steering procreation into marriage." By affording legal recognition and a basket of rights and benefits to married heterosexual couples, such laws "encourage procreation to take place within the socially recognized unit that is best situated for raising children." The State and its supporting amici cite a host of judicial decisions and secondary authorities recognizing and upholding this rationale. The argument is based in part on the traditional notion that two committed heterosexuals are the optimal partnership for raising children, which modern-day homosexual parents understandably decry. But it is also based on a "responsible procreation" theory that justifies conferring the inducements of marital recognition and benefits on opposite-sex couples, who can otherwise produce children by accident, but not on same-sex couples, who cannot. Whatever our personal views regarding this political and sociological debate, we cannot conclude that the State's justification "lacks a rational relationship to legitimate state interests."

The district court rejected the State's justification as being "at once too broad and too narrow." *Citizens for Equal Protection,* 368 F.Supp.2d at 1002. But under rational-basis review, "Even if the classification ... is to some extent both underinclusive and overinclusive, and hence the line drawn ... imperfect, it is nevertheless the rule that ... perfection is by no means required." *Vance v. Bradley,* 440 U.S. 93, 108 (1979). Legislatures are permitted to use generalizations so long as "the question is at least debatable." *Heller,* 509 U.S. at 326. The package of government benefits and restrictions that accompany the institution of formal marriage serve a variety of other purposes. The legislature-or the people through the initiative process--may rationally choose not to expand in wholesale fashion the groups entitled to those benefits. "We accept such imperfection because it is in turn rationally related to the secondary objective of legislative convenience." *Vance,* 440 U.S. at 109.

Appellees argue that § 29 does not rationally advance this purported state interest because "prohibiting protection for gay people's relationships" does not steer procreation into marriage. This demonstrates, Appellees argue, that § 29's only purpose is to disadvantage gay people. But the argument disregards the expressed intent of traditional marriage laws-to encourage heterosexual couples to bear and raise children in committed marriage relationships. Appellees attempt to isolate § 29 from other state laws limiting marriage to heterosexual couples. But as we have explained, there is no fundamental right to be free of the political barrier a validly enacted constitutional amendment erects. If the many state laws limiting the persons who may marry are rationally related to a legitimate government interest, so is the reinforcing effect of § 29. The barrier created by § 29 was enough to confer standing, but Appellees' equal protection argument fails on the merits.

V. Conclusion

We hold that § 29 and other laws limiting the state-recognized institution of marriage to heterosexual couples are rationally related to legitimate state interests and therefore do not violate the Constitution of the United States.

NOTES

1. In *Bruning*, the State argued that the government interest that supported the challenged provision was "steering procreation into marriage." Because the constitutional amendment was enacted by referendum, there was no formal legislative history that could indicate the purpose of the law. The court cited no evidence as to the purpose of the enactment but simply accepted the post hoc rationalization put forward by the State in defending the case. In explaining the connection between the classification and this purpose, the court approved of the traditional notion that two committed heterosexuals are the optimal partnership for raising children. For the court, the statute was also sustained by a "responsible procreation" theory that justified conferring the inducements of marital recognition and benefits on opposite-sex couples, who can otherwise produce children by accident, but not on same-sex couples, who cannot. This may seem like an odd justification for heterosexual marriage--that a heterosexual couple can produce children "by accident." But it was enough given the deference accorded to the government by the court in this case.

The challengers to the law, on the other hand, questioned whether the amendment as written actually advanced the State's purpose of steering procreation into marriage. As a matter of logic, they argued, keeping gay people out of marriage was not likely to steer heterosexual persons into procreative marriages. The court, however, restated the purpose of traditional marriage laws: "to encourage *heterosexual* couples to bear and raise children in committed marriage relationships." In response to the argument that this last justification seemed to be based on prejudice against same-sex couples, the court explained that the amendment only "limits the class of people who may validly enter into marriage" and thus is not "'inexplicable by anything but animus' towards same-sex couples."

The *Bruning* court's decision is a classic version of deferential rationality. The court was not concerned with evidence of the actual purpose of the statute, it was not concerned with whether the statutory classification actually advanced a statutory purpose, and it easily rejected the argument that the enactment of the statute was motivated by prejudice against same-sex couples.

2. *Perry v. Brown*, the case that follows, applied a more demanding version of rational basis review to a similar amendment to a state constitution, and reached a different result.

Perry v. Brown
681 F.3d 1065 (9th Cir. 2012), *cert. granted, Hollingsworth v. Perry*, __U.S.__ (2012)

Prior to November 4, 2008, the California Constitution guaranteed the right to marry to opposite-sex couples and same-sex couples alike. On that day, the People of California adopted Proposition 8, which amended the state constitution to eliminate the right of same-sex couples to marry. We consider whether that amendment violates the Fourteenth Amendment to the United States Constitution. We conclude that it does.

Although the Constitution permits communities to enact most laws they believe to be desirable, it requires that there be at least a legitimate reason for the passage of a law that treats different classes of people differently. There was no such reason that Proposition 8 could have been enacted. Because under California statutory law, same-sex couples had all the rights of opposite-sex couples, regardless of their marital status, all parties agree that Proposition 8 had one effect only. It stripped same-sex couples of the ability they previously possessed to obtain from the State, or any other authorized party, an important right—the right to obtain and use the designation of 'marriage' to describe their relationships. Nothing more, nothing less. Proposition 8 therefore could not have been enacted to advance California's interests in childrearing or responsible procreation, for it had no effect on the rights of same-sex couples to raise children or on the procreative practices of other couples. Nor did Proposition 8 have any effect on religious freedom or on parents' rights to control their children's education; it could not have been enacted to safeguard these liberties.

All that Proposition 8 accomplished was to take away from same-sex couples the right to be granted marriage licenses and thus legally to use the designation of 'marriage,' which symbolizes state legitimization and societal recognition of their committed relationships. Proposition 8 serves no purpose, and has no effect, other than to lessen the status and human dignity of gays and lesbians in California, and to officially reclassify their relationships and families as inferior to those of opposite-sex couples. The Constitution simply does not allow for "laws of this sort." *Romer v. Evans*, 517 U.S. 620, 633 (1996).

A

The district court held Proposition 8 unconstitutional for two reasons: first, it deprives same-sex couples of the fundamental right to marry, which is guaranteed by the Due Process Clause, *see Perry IV*, 704 F.Supp.2d at 991–95; and second, it excludes same-sex couples from state-sponsored marriage while allowing opposite-sex couples access to that honored status, in violation of the Equal Protection Clause. Plaintiffs elaborate upon those arguments on appeal.

Plaintiffs and Plaintiff–Intervenor San Francisco also offer a third argument: Proposition 8 singles out same-sex couples for unequal treatment by *taking away* from them alone the right to marry, and this action amounts to a distinct constitutional violation because the Equal Protection Clause protects minority groups from being targeted for the deprivation of an existing right without a legitimate reason. *Romer*, 517 U.S. at 634–35. Because this third argument applies to the specific history of same-sex marriage in California, it is the narrowest ground for adjudicating the constitutional questions before us, while the first two theories, if correct, would apply on a broader basis. Because courts generally decide constitutional questions on the narrowest ground available, we consider the third argument first.

B

Proposition 8 worked a singular and limited change to the California Constitution: it stripped same-sex couples of the right to have their committed relationships recognized by the State with the designation of 'marriage,' which the state constitution had previously guaranteed them, while leaving in place all of their other rights and responsibilities as partners—rights and responsibilities that are identical to those of married spouses and form an integral part of the marriage relationship.

Both before and after Proposition 8, same-sex partners could enter into an official, state-recognized relationship that affords them "the same rights, protections, and benefits" as an opposite-sex union and subjects them "to the same responsibilities, obligations, and duties under law, whether they derive from statutes, administrative regulations, court rules, government policies, common law, or any other provisions or sources of law, as are granted to and imposed upon spouses." In adopting the amendment, the People simply took the designation of 'marriage' away from lifelong same-sex partnerships, and with it the State's authorization of that official status and the societal approval that comes with it.

By emphasizing Proposition 8's limited effect, we do not mean to minimize the harm that this change in the law caused to same-sex couples and their families. To the contrary, we emphasize the extraordinary significance of the official designation of 'marriage.' That designation is important because 'marriage' is the name that society gives to the relationship that matters most between two adults. A rose by any other name may smell as sweet, but to the couple desiring to enter into a committed lifelong relationship, a marriage by the name of 'registered domestic partnership' does not. The word 'marriage' is singular in connoting "a harmony in living," "a bilateral loyalty," and "a coming together for better or for worse, hopefully enduring, and intimate to the degree of being sacred." *Griswold v. Connecticut,* 381 U.S. 479, 486 (1965). As Proponents have admitted, "the word 'marriage' has a unique meaning," and "there is a significant symbolic disparity between domestic partnership and marriage." It is the designation of 'marriage' itself that expresses validation, by the state and the community, and that serves as a symbol, like a wedding ceremony or a wedding ring, of something profoundly important.

We need consider only the many ways in which we encounter the word 'marriage' in our daily lives and understand it, consciously or not, to convey a sense of significance. We are regularly given forms to complete that ask us whether we are "single" or "married." Newspapers run announcements of births, deaths, and marriages. We are excited to see someone ask, "Will you marry me?", whether on bended knee in a restaurant or in text splashed across a stadium Jumbotron. Certainly it would not have the same effect to see "Will you enter into a registered domestic partnership with me?" Groucho Marx's one-liner, "Marriage is a wonderful institution ... but who wants to live in an institution?" would lack its punch if the word 'marriage' were replaced with the alternative phrase. So too with Shakespeare's "A young man married is a man that's marr'd," Lincoln's "Marriage is neither heaven nor hell, it is simply purgatory," and Sinatra's "A man doesn't know what happiness is until he's married. By then it's too late." We see tropes like "marrying for love" versus "marrying for money" played out again and again in our films and literature because of the recognized importance and permanence of the marriage relationship. Had

Marilyn Monroe's film been called *How to Register a Domestic Partnership with a Millionaire*, it would not have conveyed the same meaning as did her famous movie, even though the underlying drama for same-sex couples is no different. The *name* 'marriage' signifies the unique recognition that society gives to harmonious, loyal, enduring, and intimate relationships. *See Knight v. Super. Ct.*, 128 Cal.App.4th 14 (2005) ("[M]arriage is considered a more substantial relationship and is accorded a greater stature than a domestic partnership."); *cf. Griswold,* 381 U.S. at 486.

The official, cherished status of 'marriage' is distinct from the incidents of marriage, such as those listed in the California Family Code. The incidents are both elements of the institution and manifestations of the recognition that the State affords to those who are in stable and committed lifelong relationships. We allow spouses but not siblings or roommates to file taxes jointly, for example, because we acknowledge the financial interdependence of those who have entered into an "enduring" relationship. The incidents of marriage, standing alone, do not, however, convey the same governmental and societal recognition, as does the designation of 'marriage' itself. We do not celebrate when two people merge their bank accounts; we celebrate when a couple marries. The designation of 'marriage' is the status that we recognize. It is the principal manner in which the State attaches respect and dignity to the highest form of a committed relationship and to the individuals who have entered into it.

We set this forth because we must evaluate Proposition 8's constitutionality in light of its actual and specific effects on committed same-sex couples desiring to enter into an officially recognized lifelong relationship. Before Proposition 8, California guaranteed gays and lesbians both the incidents and the status and dignity of marriage. Proposition 8 left the incidents but took away the status and the dignity. It did so by superseding the *Marriage Cases* and thus endorsing the "official statement that the family relationship of same-sex couples is not of comparable stature or equal dignity to the family relationship of opposite-sex couples." *Marriage Cases,* 76 Cal.Rptr.3d 683. The question we therefore consider is this: did the People of California have legitimate reasons for enacting a constitutional amendment that serves only to take away from same-sex couples the right to have their lifelong relationships dignified by the official status of 'marriage,' and to compel the State and its officials and all others authorized to perform marriage ceremonies to substitute the label of 'domestic partnership' for their relationships?

C

[The court referred to Colorado's Amendment 2 that had been found unconstitutional in *Romer v. Evans.*]

Proposition 8 is remarkably similar to Amendment 2. Like Amendment 2, Proposition 8 "single[s] out a certain class of citizens for disfavored legal status...." Like Amendment 2, Proposition 8 has the "peculiar property," of "withdraw[ing] from homosexuals, but no others," an existing legal right—here, access to the official designation of 'marriage'—that had been broadly available, notwithstanding the fact that the Constitution did not compel the state to confer it in the first place. Like Amendment 2, Proposition 8 denies "equal protection of the laws in the most literal sense," because it "carves out" an "exception" to California's equal protection clause, by removing equal access to marriage, which gays and lesbians had previously enjoyed, from the scope of that constitutional guarantee. *Strauss,* 93 Cal.Rptr.3d 591. Like Amendment 2, Proposition 8 "by state decree ... put[s] [homosexuals] in a solitary class with respect to" an important aspect of human relations, and accordingly "imposes a special disability upon [homosexuals] alone." *Romer,* 517 U.S. at 627, 631. And like Amendment 2, Proposition 8 constitutionalizes that disability, meaning that gays and lesbians may overcome it "only by enlisting the citizenry of [the state] to amend the State Constitution" for a second time. As we explain below, *Romer* compels that we affirm the judgment of the district court.

There is one further important similarity between this case and *Romer.* Neither case requires that the voters have stripped the state's gay and lesbian citizens of any federal constitutional right. In *Romer,* Amendment 2 deprived gays and lesbians of statutory protections against discrimination; here, Proposition 8 deprived same-sex partners of the right to use the designation of 'marriage.' There is no necessity in either case that the privilege, benefit, or protection at issue be a constitutional right. We therefore need not and do not consider whether same-sex couples have a fundamental right to marry, or whether states that fail to afford the right to marry to gays and lesbians must do so. Further, we express no view on those questions.

Ordinarily, "if a law neither burdens a fundamental right nor targets a suspect class, we will uphold the legislative classification so long as it bears a rational relation to some legitimate end." *Romer,* 517 U.S. at 631. Such was the case in *Romer,* and it is the case here as well. The end must be one that is legitimate for the *government* to pursue, not just one that would be legitimate for a private actor. The question here, then, is whether California had any more legitimate justification for withdrawing from gays and lesbians its constitutional protection with respect to the official designation of 'marriage' than Colorado did for withdrawing from that group all protection against discrimination generally.

Proposition 8, like Amendment 2, enacts a "'[d]iscrimination[ ] of an unusual character,'" which requires "'careful consideration to determine whether [it] [is] obnoxious to the'" Constitution. *Id.* at 633 (quoting *Louisville Gas & Elec. Co. v. Coleman,* 277 U.S. 32, 37–38). As in *Romer,* therefore, we must consider whether any *legitimate* state interest constitutes a rational basis for Proposition 8; otherwise, we must infer that it was enacted with only the constitutionally illegitimate basis of "animus toward the class it affects." *Romer,* 517 U.S. at 632.

[The court here rejected the claim that invalidating Proposition 8 would turn the Constitution into a "one-way ratchet." Rather, it would mean only that the Equal Protection Clause requires the state to have a legitimate reason for withdrawing a right or benefit *from one group but not others,* whether or not it was required to confer that right or benefit in the first place.]

D

We first consider four possible reasons offered by Proponents or amici to explain why Proposition 8 might have been enacted: (1) furthering California's interest in childrearing and responsible procreation, (2) proceeding with caution before making significant changes to marriage, (3) protecting religious freedom, and (4) preventing children from being taught about same-sex marriage in schools. To be credited, these rationales "must find some footing in the realities of the subject addressed by the legislation." *Heller v. Doe,* 509 U.S. 312, 321 (1993). They are, conversely, not to be credited if they "could not reasonably be conceived to be true by the governmental decisionmaker." *Vance v. Bradley,* 440 U.S. 93 (1979). Because Proposition 8 did not further any of these interests, we conclude that they cannot have been rational bases for this measure, whether or not they are legitimate state interests.

1

The primary rationale Proponents offer for Proposition 8 is that it advances California's interest in responsible procreation and childrearing. This rationale appears to comprise two distinct elements. The first is that children are better off when raised by two biological parents and that society can increase the likelihood of that family structure by allowing only potential biological parents—one man and one woman—to marry. The second is that marriage reduces the threat of "irresponsible procreation"—that is, unintended pregnancies out of wedlock—by providing an incentive for couples engaged in potentially procreative sexual activity to form stable family units. Because same-sex couples are not at risk of "irresponsible procreation" as a matter of biology, Proponents argue, there is simply no need to offer such couples the same incentives. Proposition 8 is not rationally related, however, to either of these purported interests, whether or not the interests would be legitimate under other circumstances.

We need not decide whether there is any merit to the sociological premise of Proponents' first argument—that families headed by two biological parents are the best environments in which to raise children—because even if Proponents are correct, Proposition 8 had absolutely no effect on the ability of same-sex couples to become parents or the manner in which children are raised in California. As we have explained, Proposition 8 in no way modified the state's laws governing parentage, which are distinct from its laws governing marriage. *See Strauss,* 93 Cal.Rptr.3d 591. Both before and after Proposition 8, committed opposite-sex couples ("spouses") and same-sex couples ("domestic partners") had identical rights with regard to forming families and raising children. *See* Cal. Fam.Code § 297.5(d)

Proponents' second argument is that there is no need to hold out the designation of 'marriage' as an encouragement for same-sex couples to engage in responsible procreation, because unlike opposite-sex couples, same-sex couples pose no risk of procreating accidentally. Proponents contend that California need not extend marriage to same-sex couples when the State's interest in responsible procreation would not be advanced by doing so, even if the interest would not be harmed, either. *See Johnson v. Robison,* 415 U.S. 361, 383 (1974) ("When ... the inclusion of one group promotes a legitimate governmental purpose, and the addition of other groups would not, we cannot say that the statute's classification of beneficiaries and nonbeneficiaries is invidiously discriminatory."). But Plaintiffs do not ask that marriage be *extended* to anyone. As we have by now made clear, the question is whether there is a legitimate governmental interest in *withdrawing* access to marriage from same-sex couples. We therefore need not decide whether, under *Johnson,* California would be justified in not extending the designation of 'marriage' to same-sex couples; that is not what Proposition 8 did. *Johnson* concerns decisions not to *add* to a legislative scheme a group that is unnecessary to the purposes of that scheme, but Proposition 8 *subtracted* a disfavored group from a scheme of which it already was a part.

Under *Romer,* it is no justification for taking something away to say that there was no need to provide it in the first place; instead, there must be some legitimate reason for the act of taking it away, a reason that overcomes the "inevitable inference that the disadvantage imposed is born of animosity toward the class of persons affected." *Romer,* 517 U.S. at 634. In order to explain how *rescinding* access to the designation of 'marriage' is rationally related to the State's interest in responsible procreation, Proponents would have had to argue that opposite-sex couples were *more* likely to procreate accidentally or irresponsibly when same-sex couples were allowed access to the designation of 'marriage.' We are aware of no basis on which this argument would be even conceivably plausible. There is no rational reason to think that taking away the designation of 'marriage' from same-sex couples would advance the goal of encouraging California's opposite-sex couples to procreate more responsibly. The *Johnson* argument, to put it mildly, does not help Proponents' cause.

Given the realities of California law, and of human nature, both parts of Proponents' primary rationale simply "find [no] footing in the realities of the subject addressed by the legislation," and thus cannot be credited as rational. *Heller,* 509 U.S. at 321. To the extent that it has been argued that withdrawing from same-sex couples access to the designation of 'marriage'—without in any way altering the substantive laws concerning their rights regarding childrearing or family formation—will encourage heterosexual couples to enter into matrimony, or will strengthen their matrimonial bonds, we believe that the People of California "could not reasonably" have "conceived" such an argument "to be true." *Vance,* 440 U.S. at 111. It is implausible to think that denying two men or two women the right to call themselves married could somehow bolster the stability of families headed by one man and one woman. While deferential, the rational-basis standard "is not a toothless one." *Mathews v. Lucas,* 427 U.S. 495, 510 (1976). "[E]ven the standard of rationality ... must find some footing in the realities of the subject addressed by the legislation." *Heller,* 509 U.S. at 321. Here, the argument that withdrawing the designation of 'marriage' from same-sex couples could on its own promote the strength or stability of opposite-sex marital relationships lacks any such footing in reality.

2

Proponents offer an alternative justification for Proposition 8: that it advances California's interest in "proceed[ing] with caution" when considering changes to the definition of marriage. But this rationale, too, bears no connection to the reality of Proposition 8. The amendment was enacted *after* the State had provided same-sex couples the right to marry and *after* more than 18,000 couples had married (and remain married even after Proposition 8, *Strauss,* 93 Cal.Rptr.3d 591).

3

We briefly consider two other potential rationales for Proposition 8, not raised by Proponents but offered by amici curiae. First is the argument that Proposition 8 advanced the State's interest in protecting religious liberty. There is no dispute that even before Proposition 8, "no religion [was] required to change its religious policies or practices with regard to same-sex couples, and no religious officiant [was] required to solemnize a marriage in contravention of his or her religious beliefs." *Marriage Cases,* 76 Cal.Rptr.3d 683, 183 P.3d at 451–52. Rather, the religious-liberty interest that Proposition 8 supposedly promoted was to decrease the likelihood that religious organizations would be penalized, under California's antidiscrimination laws and other government policies concerning sexual orientation, for refusing to provide services to families headed by same-sex spouses. But Proposition 8 did nothing to affect those laws. To the extent that California's antidiscrimination laws apply to various activities of religious organizations, their protections apply in the same way as before. Amicus's argument is thus more properly read as an appeal to the Legislature, seeking reform of the State's antidiscrimination laws to include greater accommodations for religious organizations. This argument is in no way addressed by Proposition 8 and could not have been the reason for Proposition 8.

Second is the argument, prominent during the campaign to pass Proposition 8, that it would "protect[ ] our children from being taught in public schools that 'same-sex marriage' is the same as traditional marriage." Yet again, California law belies the premise of this justification. Both before and after Proposition 8, schools have not been required to teach anything about same-sex marriage. And both before and after Proposition 8, schools and individual teachers have been prohibited from giving any instruction that discriminates on the basis of sexual orientation; now as before, students could not be taught the superiority or inferiority of either same- or opposite-sex marriage or other "committed relationships."

There is a limited sense in which the extension of the designation 'marriage' to same-sex partnerships might alter the content of the lessons that schools choose to teach. Schools teach about the world as it is; when the world changes, lessons change. A shift in the State's marriage law may therefore affect the content of classroom instruction just as would the election of a new governor, the discovery of a new chemical element, or the adoption of a new law permitting no-fault divorce: students learn about these as empirical facts of the world around them. But to protest the teaching of these facts is little different from protesting their very existence; it is like opposing the election of a particular governor on the ground that students would learn about his holding office, or opposing the legitimation of no-fault divorce because a teacher might allude to that fact if a course in societal structure were taught to graduating seniors. The prospect of children learning about the laws of the State and society's assessment of the legal rights of its members does not provide an *independent* reason for stripping members of a disfavored group of those rights they presently enjoy.

Proposition 8's only effect, we have explained, was to withdraw from gays and lesbians the right to employ the designation of 'marriage' to describe their committed relationships and thus to deprive them of a societal status that affords dignity to those relationships. Proposition 8 could not have reasonably been enacted to promote childrearing by biological parents, to encourage responsible procreation, to proceed with caution in social change, to protect religious liberty, or to control the education of schoolchildren. Simply taking away the designation of 'marriage' while leaving in place all the substantive rights and responsibilities of same-sex partners did not do any of the things its Proponents now suggest were its purposes. Proposition 8 "is so far removed from these particular justifications that we find it impossible to credit them." *Romer,* 517 U.S. at 635. We therefore need not, and do not, decide whether any of these purported rationales for the law would be "legitimate," *id.* at 632, or would suffice to justify Proposition 8 if the amendment actually served to further them.

E

1

We are left to consider why else the People of California might have enacted a constitutional amendment that takes away from gays and lesbians the right to use the designation of 'marriage.' One explanation is the desire to revert to the way things were prior to the *Marriage Cases,* when 'marriage' was available only to opposite-sex couples, as had been the case since the founding of the State and in other jurisdictions long before that. This purpose is one that Proposition 8 actually did accomplish: it "restore[d] the traditional definition of marriage as referring to a union between a man and a woman." *Strauss,* 93 Cal.Rptr.3d 591. But tradition alone is not a justification for *taking away* a right that had already been granted, even though that grant was in derogation of tradition. In *Romer,* it did not matter that at common law, gays and lesbians were afforded no protection from discrimination in the private sphere; Amendment 2 could not be justified on the basis that it simply repealed positive law and restored the "traditional" state of affairs. 517 U.S. at 627–29. Precisely the same is true here.

Laws may be repealed and new rights taken away if they have had unintended consequences or if there is some conceivable affirmative good that revocation would produce, but new rights may not be stripped away solely *because* they are new. Tradition is a legitimate consideration in policymaking, of course, but it cannot be an end unto itself. *Cf. Williams v. Illinois,* 399 U.S. 235, 239–40 (1970). "[T]he fact that the governing majority in a State has traditionally viewed a particular practice as immoral is not a sufficient reason for upholding a law prohibiting the practice; neither history nor tradition could save a law prohibiting miscegenation from constitutional attack." *Lawrence v. Texas,* 539 U.S. 558, 577–78 (2003); *see Loving v. Virginia,* 388 U.S. 1 (1967) (noting the historical pedigree of bans on interracial marriage but not even considering tradition as a possible justification for Virginia's law). If tradition alone is insufficient to justify *maintaining* a prohibition with a discriminatory effect, then it is necessarily insufficient to justify *changing* the law to revert to a previous state. A preference for the way things were before same-sex couples were allowed to marry, without any identifiable good that a return to the past would produce, amounts to an impermissible preference against same-sex couples themselves, as well as their families.

Absent any legitimate purpose for Proposition 8, we are left with "the inevitable inference that the disadvantage imposed is born of animosity toward," or, as is more likely with respect to Californians who voted for the Proposition, mere disapproval of, "the class of persons affected." *Romer,* 517 U.S. at 634. We do not mean to suggest that Proposition 8 is the result of ill will on the part of the voters of California. "Prejudice, we are beginning to understand, rises not from malice or hostile animus alone." *Bd. of Trustees of Univ. of Ala. v. Garrett,* 531 U.S. 356, 374 (2001) (Kennedy, J., concurring). Disapproval may also be the product of longstanding, sincerely held private beliefs. Still, while "[p]rivate biases may be outside the reach of the law, ... the law cannot, directly or indirectly, give them effect." *Palmore v. Sidoti,* 466 U.S. 429, 433 (1984). Ultimately, the "inevitable inference" we must draw in this circumstance is not one of ill will, but rather one of disapproval of gays and lesbians as a class. "[L]aws singling out a certain class of citizens for disfavored legal status or general hardships are rare." *Romer,* 517 U.S. at 633. Under *Romer,* we must infer from Proposition 8's effect on California law that the People took away from gays and lesbians the right to use the official designation of 'marriage'—and the societal status that accompanies it—because they disapproved of these individuals *as a class* and did not wish them to receive the same official recognition and societal approval of their committed relationships that the State makes available to opposite-sex couples.

Just as a "desire to harm ... cannot constitute a *legitimate* governmental interest," *Moreno,* 413 U.S. at 534, neither can a more basic disapproval of a class of people. *Romer,* 517 U.S. at 633–35. "The issue is whether the majority may use the power of the State to enforce these views on the whole society" through a law that abridges minority individuals' rights. *Lawrence,* 539 U.S. at 571. It may not. Without more, "[m]oral disapproval of [a] group, like a bare desire to harm the group, is an interest that is insufficient to satisfy rational basis review under the Equal Protection Clause." *Id.* at 582 (O'Connor, J., concurring). Society does sometimes draw classifications that likely are rooted partially in disapproval, such as a law that grants educational benefits to veterans but denies them to conscientious objectors who engaged in alternative civilian service. *See Johnson,* 415 U.S. at 362–64. Those classifications will not be invalidated so long as they can be justified by reference to some *independent* purpose they serve; in *Johnson,* they could provide an incentive for military service and direct assistance to those who needed the most help in readjusting to post-war life. Enacting a rule into law based solely on the disapproval of a group, however, "is a classification of persons undertaken for its own sake, something the Equal Protection Clause does not permit." *Romer,* 517 U.S. at 635. Like Amendment 2, Proposition 8 is a classification of gays and lesbians undertaken for its own sake.

VII

By using their initiative power to target a minority group and withdraw a right that it possessed, without a legitimate reason for doing so, the People of California violated the Equal Protection Clause. We hold Proposition 8 to be unconstitutional on this ground. We do not doubt the importance of the more general questions presented to us concerning the rights of same-sex couples to marry, nor do we doubt that these questions will likely be resolved in other states, and for the nation as a whole, by other courts. For now, it suffices to conclude that the People of California may not, consistent with the Federal Constitution, add to their state constitution a provision that has no more practical effect than to strip gays and lesbians of their right to use the official designation that the State and society give to committed relationships, thereby adversely affecting the status and dignity of the members of a disfavored class. The judgment of the district court is

AFFIRMED.

NOTES

1.   *Perry* is an extremely good example of heightened rational basis review. The *Perry* court did not discuss whether gay men and women are a suspect class or whether Proposition 8 implicated a fundamental right to marriage. The court treated the question as simply one of whether the classification excluding same-sex couples from marriage was rationally related to a permissible state interest. The court emphasized that Proposition 8, which took from same-sex couples a right to marry that they already had under state law, had one effect only: it stripped same-sex couples of the ability they previously possessed to obtain from the State an important right—the right to obtain and use the designation of 'marriage' to describe their relationships. "Nothing more, nothing less." The court explained that it would decide the case on the narrowest possible ground and that narrow ground turned out to be that Proposition 8 *took away* from same-sex couples alone the right to marry. Thus, it would not be sufficient to identify purposes that might justify a failure to *extend* marriage to same-sex couples; it would be necessary to identity purposes that justify *taking away* the existing right to marriage.

Even after the enactment of Proposition 8, same-sex couples, through the institution of "domestic partnerships," could have all the same rights and responsibilities that married couples had. So, did it really matter that what same-sex couples had was not called "marriage"? Yes, it mattered very much, since "'marriage' is the name that society gives to the relationship that matters most between two adults." The term has a unique meaning and it expresses validation, by the state and the community, and it serves as a symbol of something profoundly important; it is the unique recognition that society gives to harmonious, loyal, enduring, and intimate relationships. Thus, "marriage" is far more than the sum of the incidents of marriage as listed in the California Family Code.

The *Perry* court then identified the standard of review that it would apply: "we will uphold the legislative classification so long as it bears a rational relation to some legitimate end," citing *Romer*. The court then considered four possible purposes: (1) furthering California's interest in childrearing and responsible procreation, (2) proceeding with caution before making significant changes to marriage, (3) protecting religious freedom, and (4) preventing children from being taught about same-sex marriage in schools. The court determined that Proposition 8 did not further any of these interests, and therefore the court did not have to decide they are legitimate state interests.

Responsible procreation and childbearing failed as justifications since "Proposition 8 had absolutely no effect on the ability of same-sex couples to become parents or the manner in which children are raised in California." Proposition 8 had not modified the state's laws governing parentage, which are distinct from its laws governing marriage. As for the distinction that unlike opposite-sex couples, same-sex couples pose no risk of procreating accidentally, that was in no way related to *taking away* the existing right of same-sex couples to marry. For this to make sense, the argument would have to be made that opposite-sex couples were *more* likely to procreate accidentally or irresponsibly when same-sex couples were allowed access to the designation of 'marriage, an argument that the court found to be not even conceivably plausible. It was also implausible to think that denying two men or two women the right to call themselves married could somehow bolster the stability of families headed by one man and one woman.

The court also held that Proposition did not serve the other purposes advanced to justify it. How was "proceeding with caution" advanced when the amendment was enacted *after* 18,000 same-sex couples had already been married under the existing law of California? Proposition 8 did not advance the state's interest in protecting religious liberty because it would have no effect on religion: no religion was required to change its religious policies. It did not advance the interest of protecting children from being taught in public schools that same-sex marriage was equivalent to opposite-sex marriage. Both before and after Proposition 8, schools were not required to teach anything about same-sex marriage.

The court concluded "Proposition 8 could not have reasonably been enacted to promote childrearing by biological parents, to encourage responsible procreation, to proceed with caution in social change, to protect religious liberty, or to control the education of schoolchildren . . . Proposition 8 'is so far removed from these particular justifications that we find it impossible to credit them.'" With these four interests withdrawn from the argument, the court concluded that "we are left with 'the inevitable inference that the disadvantage imposed is born of animosity toward,' or . . . mere disapproval of, "the class of persons affected.'" Moral disapproval of a group is not a legitimate interest.

2. The *Bruning* and *Perry* cases are good examples of the extent to which the choice of a level of review will determine the outcome of the case. Both courts reviewed a state constitutional amendment that prohibited same-sex marriage. The *Bruning* court, applying the deferential version of rational basis review, had no problem upholding the amendment. The *Perry* court, on the other hand, applying the more demanding version of rational basis review, invalidated the amendment. Until the United States Supreme Court gives clear guidance on the proper standard of review for classifications that disadvantage gay men and women, we are likely to see more inconsistent decisions.

3. *THE FEDERAL DEFENSE OF MARRIAGE ACT*

The Defense of Marriage Act (DOMA) (Pub. L. No. 104-199, 110 Stat. 2419 (1996)) is a federal statute that provides that, for federal purposes, "the word 'marriage' means only a legal union between one man and one woman as husband and wife." It also provides that states need not give effect to proceedings of other states that recognize same sex marriage. The federal government's nonrecognition of same-sex marriage creates significant financial disadvantages for same-sex couples who have entered into valid marriages under the laws of their state. Since these couples will not be considered spouses, they will not qualify for spousal benefits under many federal programs, including Social Security, Medicare, veterans' programs, and federal government employment benefits, nor will they qualify as spouses under the federal income, gift, and estate tax laws, immigration laws, or bankruptcy law. The General Accounting Office of the United States has identified a total of 1,138 federal statutory provisions in the United States Code in which marital status is a factor in determining or receiving benefits, rights, and privileges. *See* http://www.gao.gov/new.items/d04353r.pdf.

Two federal courts in 2004 and 2005 upheld DOMA, using a very deferential rational basis review. *In re Kandu*, 315 B.R. 123, Bkrtc.W.D.Wash. (2004); *Wilson v. Ake*, 354 F.Supp.2d 1298 (M.D.Fla. 2005). More recently, federal appellate courts have been finding that DOMA violates the Equal Protection Clause. This section examines two cases that applied different standards of review and, correspondingly, reached different results.

In re Kandu
315 B.R. 123, Bkrtcy.W.D.Wash. (2004)

[Lee and Ann Kandu, two women, were United States citizens who married in Canada. They filed a joint petition for bankruptcy protection in the federal bankruptcy court. This matter came before the Court pursuant to an Order to Show Cause for Improper Joint Filing under 11 U.S.C. § 302. In support of the joint filing, the couple challenged the constitutionality of the Defense of Marriage Act (DOMA) as a violation of the equal protection component of the Fifth Amendment's Due Process Clause. The court initially rejected the argument that DOMA should be subject to heightened scrutiny because gay men and women are a suspect class.]

If a law neither burdens a fundamental right, nor targets a suspect class, the Supreme Court "will uphold the legislative classification so long as it bears a rational relation to some legitimate" governmental end. *Romer*, 517 U.S. at 631. This Court has determined that DOMA does not burden a fundamental right nor target a suspect class. The Supreme Court has provided thorough guidance to the courts for purposes of applying rational basis review. *See Heller v. Doe*, 509 U.S. 312 (1993); *FCC v. Beach Communications, Inc.*, 508 U.S. 307 (1993); *Aleman*, 217 F.3d 1191.

"In areas of social and economic policy, a statutory classification that neither proceeds along suspect lines nor infringes fundamental constitutional rights must be upheld against equal protection challenge *if there is any reasonably conceivable state of facts that could provide a rational basis for the classification.*" *Beach Communications,* 508 U.S. at 313 (emphasis added). Rational basis review is "a paradigm of judicial restraint" and "is not a license for courts to judge the wisdom, fairness, or logic of legislative choices." *Beach Communications,* 508 U.S. at 313–14. "Nor does it authorize 'the judiciary [to] sit as a superlegislature to judge the wisdom or desirability of legislative policy determinations made in areas that neither affect fundamental rights nor proceed along suspect lines.'" *Heller,* 509 U.S. at 319 (quoting *City of New Orleans v. Dukes,* 427 U.S. 297, 303 (1976) (per curiam)).

A statute is presumed constitutional. *Heller,* 509 U.S. at 320. "'[T]he burden of establishing the unconstitutionality of a statute rests on him who assails it.'" *Baker v. Carr,* 369 U.S. 186 (1962) (quoting *Metropolitan Cas. Ins. Co. v. Brownell,* 294 U.S. 580, 584 (1935)). The burden is to "'negative every conceivable basis which might support it,' whether or not the basis has a foundation in the record." *Heller,* 509 U.S. at 320–21 (quoting *Lehnhausen v. Lake Shore Auto Parts Co.,* 410 U.S. 356, 364 (1973)). The government "has no obligation to produce evidence to sustain the rationality of a statutory classification." *Heller,* 509 U.S. at 320. "[C]ourts are compelled under rational-basis review to accept a legislature's generalizations even when there is an imperfect fit between means and ends. A classification does not fail rational-basis review because it 'is not made with mathematical nicety or because in practice it results in some inequality.'" *Heller,* 509 U.S. at 321 (quoting *Dandridge v. Williams,* 397 U.S. 471, 485 (1970)). "A statutory classification fails rational-basis review only when it 'rests on grounds wholly irrelevant to the achievement of the State's objective.'" *Heller,* 509 U.S. at 324 (quoting *Holt Civic Club v. City of Tuscaloosa,* 439 U.S. 60, 71 (1978)).

As previously stated, since the Debtor does not have a fundamental right to enter into a same-sex marriage and is not within a quasi-suspect or suspect class, the constitutionality of DOMA is tested under a rational basis analysis. The UST argues that DOMA meets this test primarily because it furthers the legitimate government interest in encouraging the development of relationships optimal for procreating and raising children. Additionally, the legislative history of DOMA identifies four governmental interests advanced by this legislation: "(1) defending and nurturing the institution of traditional, heterosexual marriage; (2) defending traditional notions of morality; (3) protecting state sovereignty and democratic self-governance; and (4) preserving scarce government resources." H.R.Rep. No. 104–664, at 12, *reprinted in* 1996 U.S.C.C.A.N. at 2916.

The burden of proof is on the Debtor to establish that the rational basis test is not met. The Debtor contends that the interests advanced by the UST [United States Trustee] do not provide any rational justifications for excluding same-sex married couples from the rights extended to other married couples under federal law. The Debtor argues, (1) as to procreation, federal recognition of marriage has never been limited to couples willing or able to conceive and raise children; (2) the exclusion of all same-sex married couples from federal recognition undermines the state's goal to encourage responsible procreation, because same-sex couples can reproduce with outside assistance; (3) as to the raising of children by both biological parents, the Debtor alleges that because same-sex couples can now both be biological parents of a child, DOMA in reality undermines the state's goal; and (4) the Supreme Court has held that procreation is not a necessary or definitive aspect of marriage and has specifically rejected the notion that the purpose of marriage is to encourage the rearing of children by both of their biological parents.

To uphold the constitutionality of DOMA, the test is not whether Congress' rationale for enacting DOMA is persuasive, but whether it satisfies a minimal threshold of rationality. The review afforded under this rational basis standard is very deferential to the legislature, and does not permit this Court to interject or substitute its own personal views of DOMA or same-sex marriage. While courts have the authority to recognize rights supported by the Constitution, the creation of new and unique rights is more properly reserved for the people through the legislative process. As articulated by Justice Spina's in his dissent in *Goodridge,* 798 N.E.2d at 978, when courts extend a constitutional protection to a new right or liberty interest, they are to a great extent placing the matter outside the arena of public debate and legislative action.

The UST asserts that encouraging the development of relationships optimal for procreation is a primary government interest advanced by DOMA. Because a heterosexual union is the only one that can naturally produce a child, the UST states that government has an interest in encouraging the stability and legitimacy of this union for the benefit of the offspring. "Simply defined, marriage is a relationship within which the community socially approves and encourages sexual intercourse and the birth of children. It is society's way of signaling to would-be parents that their long-term relationship is socially important--a public concern, not simply a private affair." H.R.Rep. No. 104–664, at 14, *reprinted in* 1996 U.S.C.C.A.N. at 2918. "Marriage and procreation are fundamental to the very existence and survival of the race." *Skinner v. Oklahoma ex rel Williamson*, 316 U.S. 535, 541 (1942). Washington State, too, has recognized this interest: "[m]arriage exists as a protected legal institution primarily because of societal values associated with the propagation of the human race." *Singer,* 522 P.2d at 1195.

Authority exists that the promotion of marriage to encourage the maintenance of stable relationships that facilitate to the maximum extent possible the rearing of children by both of their biological parents is a legitimate congressional concern. *See, e.g., Bowen v. Gilliard,* 483 U.S. 587, 614 (1987) (Brennan J., dissenting) (noting that "'[t]he optimal situation for the child is to have both an involved mother and an involved father'") (quoting H. Biller, *Paternal Deprivation* 10 (1974)); *Lofton v. Secretary of the Dep't of Children and Family Servs.,* 358 F.3d 804, 819 (11th Cir.2004) (considering the state's argument that the presence of both male and female authority figures in the home is critical to optimal childhood development, the court held that "[i]t is hard to conceive an interest more legitimate and more paramount for the state than promoting an optimal social structure for educating, socializing, and preparing its future citizens to become productive participants in civil society"); *Adams,* 486 F.Supp. at 1124 (holding that it is beyond dispute that the state has a compelling interest in providing "status and stability to the environment in which children are raise"); *Standhardt,* 77 P.3d at 462–63 (holding that the state has an interest in promoting child-rearing by opposite-sex couples); *Singer,* 522 P.2d at 1197 (holding that "marriage is so clearly related to the public interest in affording a favorable environment for the growth of children that we are unable to say that there is not a rational basis upon which the state may limit the protection of its marriage laws to the legal union of one man and one woman"). This Court's personal view that children raised by same-sex couples enjoy benefits possibly different, but equal, to those raised by opposite-sex couples, is not relevant to the Court's ultimate decision. It is within the province of Congress, not the courts, to weigh the evidence and legislate on such issues, unless it can be established that the legislation is not rationally related to a legitimate governmental end. Thus, although this Court may not personally agree with the positions asserted by the UST in support of DOMA, applying the rational basis test as set forth by the Supreme Court, this Court cannot say that DOMA's limitation of marriage to one man and one woman is not wholly irrelevant to the achievement of the government's interest.

The Debtor and other critics however, argue that DOMA's definition of marriage permits heterosexual couples to marry regardless of whether they intend or are even able to have children. While this may be, the Supreme Court has made clear that, "[e]ven if the classification involved here is to some extent both underinclusive and overinclusive, and hence the line drawn by Congress imperfect, it is nevertheless the rule that in a case like this 'perfection is by no means required.'" *Vance v. Bradley,* 440 U.S. 93, 108 (1979) (quoting *Phillips Chem. Co. v. Dumas Indep. Sch. Dist.,* 361 U.S. 376, 385 (1960)). Congress is not required to provide identical forms of encouragement or endorsement to same-sex couples as to those in more traditional relationships. It need only to have a rational basis for its legislation. Moreover, if the government attempted to limit marriage solely to those able or desiring to produce children, the government would be required to make such inquires of couples prior to marriage. This would implicate constitutionally-rooted privacy concerns. *See Eisenstadt v. Baird,* 405 U.S. 438, 453–54 (1972); *Adams,* 486 F.Supp. at 1124–25 (recognizing government inquiry about couples' procreation plans or requiring sterility test before issuing marriage licenses would "raise serious constitutional questions."); *Standhardt,* 77 P.3d at 462 (citing *Griswold v. Connecticut,* 381 U.S. 479, 485–86 (1965)). Additionally, it would interfere with the fundamental right of opposite-sex couples to marry. *See Loving,* 388 U.S. at 12.

Furthermore, that same-sex couples also raise children does not negate the reasonableness of the link between opposite-sex marriage and child-rearing. That children in same-sex families could also benefit from the stability offered by marriage, as previously stated, rational classifications cannot be struck down merely because they are to some degree over- or underinclusive. *See Vance,* 440 U.S. at 108. Moreover, classifying governmental beneficiaries "inevitably requires that some persons who have an almost equally strong claim to favored treatment be placed on different sides of the line, and the fact [that] the line might have been drawn differently at some points is a matter for legislative, rather than judicial, consideration." *Beach Communications,* 508 U.S. at 315–16 (quoting *United States R.R. Ret. Bd. v. Fritz,* 449 U.S. 166, 179 (1980)). "[A]s long as plausible reasons exist for placement of the current line," the reasonableness of a classification cannot be set aside. *Standhardt,* 77 P.3d at 463.

The Debtor also argues that DOMA is like Colorado's Amendment 2 that was struck down in *Romer v. Evans* for failure to meet the rational basis test. *Romer v. Evans,* 517 U.S. 620 (1996). The Supreme Court held that the amendment had the "peculiar property of imposing a broad and undifferentiated disability on a single named group," and "its shear breadth is so discontinuous with the reasons offered for it that the amendment seems inexplicable by anything but animus toward the class it affects." *Romer,* 517 U.S. at 632.

In contrast, DOMA is not so exceptional and unduly broad as to render the UST's reasons for its enactment "inexplicable by anything but animus" towards same-sex couples. *See Standhardt,* 77 P.3d at 465 (rejecting *Romer* analogy on grounds that statute limiting marriage to opposite-sex couples furthers a proper legislative end and was not enacted simply to make same-sex couples unequal). Rather, DOMA simply codified that definition of marriage historically understood by society. *See Adams,* 486 F.Supp. at 1123 (observing that marriage historically has been defined as the union between persons of different sex).

The House Report indicates that Congress considered as interests in enacting DOMA, protecting state sovereignty and democratic self-governance, morality, and preserving scarce government resources. The UST, however, neither raises nor relies on these asserted interests as grounds to uphold the constitutionality of DOMA. Basing legislation on moral disapproval of same-sex couples may be questionable in light of *Lawrence.* The Debtor makes no mention or attack of these interests, but as the Court concludes that the government has a "conceivable" legitimate interest in enacting DOMA that is rationally related to promote an optimal social structure, the Court need not consider these additional interests advanced by Congress in its legislative history.

This Court concludes that DOMA does not violate [the] Equal Protection Clause of the Fifth Amendment.

NOTES

1. *In re Kandu* is a clear example of the deferential version of rational basis review. The court, citing both *Heller* and *Beach Communications,* held that the challenger's burden is to "'negative every conceivable basis which might support [the statute],' whether or not the basis has a foundation in the record." The bankruptcy trustee, defending DOMA, argued that DOMA satisfied

the rational-basis test because it "further[ed] the legitimate government interest in encouraging the development of relationships optimal for procreating and raising children." The court cited no evidence that these were the purposes of the statute other than the assertion of the trustee and it is not at all clear that the legislative classification was in fact related to these purposes. Under the deferential version of rational basis review, this did not matter. The *Kandu* case is discussed further, *supra* at Section C.1.

2. In the following case, the United States Court of Appeals for the First Circuit used the more demanding form of rational basis review in considering an equal protection challenge to DOMA.

Massachusetts v. U.S. Dept. of Health and Human Services
682 F.3d 1(1st Cir. 2012)

Boudin, Circuit Judge.

These appeals present constitutional challenges to section 3 of the Defense of Marriage Act ("DOMA"), 1 U.S.C. § 7, which denies federal economic and other benefits to same-sex couples lawfully married in Massachusetts and to surviving spouses from couples thus married. Rather than challenging the right of states to define marriage as they see fit, the appeals contest the right of Congress to undercut the choices made by same-sex couples and by individual states in deciding who can be married to whom.

Within three years after [a decision of the Hawaii Supreme Court which created the possibility of same-sex marriage in Hawaii], DOMA was enacted with strong majorities in both Houses and signed into law by President Clinton. Section 3 of DOMA, 1 U.S.C. § 7, defines "marriage" for purposes of federal law:

> In determining the meaning of any Act of Congress, or of any ruling, regulation, or interpretation of the various administrative bureaus and agencies of the United States, the word "marriage" means only a legal union between one man and one woman as husband and wife, and the word "spouse" refers only to a person of the opposite sex who is a husband or a wife.

Section 2, which is not at issue here, absolves states from recognizing same-sex marriages solemnized in other states. DOMA does not formally invalidate same-sex marriages in states that permit them, but its adverse consequences for such a choice are considerable. Notably, it prevents same-sex married couples from filing joint federal tax returns, which can lessen tax burdens, *see* 26 U.S.C. § 1(a)-(c), and prevents the surviving spouse of a same-sex marriage from collecting Social Security survivor benefits. DOMA also leaves federal employees unable to share their health insurance and certain other medical benefits with same-sex spouses.

DOMA affects a thousand or more generic cross-references to marriage in myriad federal laws. In most cases, the changes operate to the disadvantage of same-sex married couples in the half dozen or so states that permit same-sex marriage. The number of couples thus affected is estimated at more than 100,000. Further, DOMA has potentially serious adverse consequences, hereafter described, for states that choose to legalize same-sex marriage.

In *Gill v. OPM*, No. 10–2207, seven same-sex couples married in Massachusetts and three surviving spouses of such marriages brought suit in federal district court to enjoin pertinent federal agencies and officials from enforcing DOMA to deprive the couples of federal benefits available to opposite-sex married couples in Massachusetts. The Commonwealth brought a companion case, *Massachusetts v. DHHS,* No. 10–2204, concerned that DOMA will revoke federal funding for programs tied to DOMA's opposite-sex marriage definition — such as Massachusetts' state Medicaid program and veterans' cemeteries.

Certain suspect classifications—race, alienage and national origin—require what the Court calls strict scrutiny, which entails both a compelling governmental interest and narrow tailoring. *Adarand Constructors, Inc. v. Pena,* 515 U.S. 200 (1995). Gender-based classifications invoke intermediate scrutiny and must be substantially related to achieving an important governmental objective. Both are far more demanding than rational basis review as conventionally applied in routine matters of commercial, tax and like regulation.

Equal protection claims tested by this rational basis standard, famously called by Justice Holmes the "last resort of constitutional argument," *Buck v. Bell,* 274 U.S. 200, 208 (1927), rarely succeed. Courts accept as adequate any plausible factual basis, *Williamson v. Lee Optical of Oklahoma, Inc.,* 348 U.S. 483, 487–88 (1955), without regard to Congress' actual motives. *Beach Commc'ns,* 508 U.S. at 314. Means need not be narrowly drawn to meet—or even be entirely consistent with—the stated legislative ends. *Lee Optical,* 348 U.S. at 487–88.

Under such a rational basis standard, the *Gill* plaintiffs cannot prevail. Consider only one of the several justifications for DOMA offered by Congress itself, namely, that broadening the definition of marriage will reduce tax revenues and increase social security payments. This is the converse of the very advantages that the *Gill* plaintiffs are seeking, and Congress could rationally have believed that DOMA would reduce costs, even if newer studies of the actual economic effects of DOMA suggest that it may in fact raise costs for the federal government.

The federal defendants conceded that rational basis review leaves DOMA intact but now urge this court to employ the so-called intermediate scrutiny test used by Supreme Court for gender discrimination. Some similarity exists between the two situations along with some differences, *compare Frontiero v. Richardson,* 411 U.S. 677, 682–88 (1973) (plurality opinion) (describing criteria for categorization). But extending intermediate scrutiny to sexual preference classifications is not a step open to us.

First, this court in *Cook v. Gates,* 528 F.3d 42 (1st Cir.2008), *cert. denied,* —— U.S. ——, has already declined to create a major new category of "suspect classification" for statutes distinguishing based on sexual preference. *Cook* rejected an equal protection challenge to the now-superseded "Don't Ask, Don't Tell" policy adopted by Congress for the military, pointing out that *Romer* itself avoided the suspect classification label. *Cook,* 528 F.3d at 61–62. This binds the panel.

Second, to create such a new suspect classification for same-sex relationships would have far-reaching implications—in particular, by implying an overruling of *Baker,* which we are neither empowered to do nor willing to predict. Nothing indicates that the Supreme Court is about to adopt this new suspect classification when it conspicuously failed to do so in *Romer* — a case that could readily have been disposed by such a demarche. That such a classification could overturn marriage laws in a huge majority of individual states underscores the implications.

However, that is not the end of the matter. Without relying on suspect classifications, Supreme Court equal protection decisions have both intensified scrutiny of purported justifications where minorities are subject to discrepant treatment and have limited the permissible justifications. And (as we later explain), in areas where state regulation has traditionally governed, the Court may require that the federal government interest in intervention be shown with special clarity.

In a set of equal protection decisions, the Supreme Court has now several times struck down state or local enactments without invoking any suspect classification. In each, the protesting group was historically disadvantaged or unpopular, and the statutory justification seemed thin, unsupported or impermissible. It is these decisions—not classic rational basis review—that the *Gill* plaintiffs and the Justice Department most usefully invoke in their briefs (while seeking to absorb them into different and more rigid categorical rubrics).

[The Court here discussed *Moreno, Cleburne*, and *Romer v. Evans*.]

These three decisions did not adopt some new category of suspect classification or employ rational basis review in its minimalist form; instead, the Court rested on the case-specific nature of the discrepant treatment, the burden imposed, and the infirmities of the justifications offered. Several Justices have remarked on this — both favorably, *City of Cleburne,* 473 U.S. at 451–55 (1985) (Stevens, J., concurring), and unfavorably, *United States v. Virginia* (*VMI*), 518 U.S. 515, 567 (1996) (Scalia, J., dissenting).

Circuit courts, citing these same cases, have similarly concluded that equal protection assessments are sensitive to the circumstances of the case and not dependent entirely on abstract categorizations. As one distinguished judge observed:

> Judges and commentators have noted that the usually deferential "rational basis" test has been applied with greater rigor in some contexts, particularly those in which courts have had reason to be concerned about possible discrimination.

United States v. Then, 56 F.3d 464, 468 (2d Cir.1995) (Calabresi, J., concurring) (citing *City of Cleburne* as an example). There is nothing remarkable about this: categories are often approximations and are themselves constructed by weighing of underlying elements.

All three of the cited cases — *Moreno, City of Cleburne* and *Romer* — stressed the historic patterns of disadvantage suffered by the group adversely affected by the statute. As with the women, the poor and the mentally impaired, gays and lesbians have long been the subject of discrimination. *Lawrence,* 539 U.S. at 571. The Court has in these cases undertaken a more careful assessment of the justifications than the light scrutiny offered by conventional rational basis review.

As for burden, the combined effect of DOMA's restrictions on federal benefits will not prevent same-sex marriage where permitted under state law; but it will penalize those couples by limiting tax and social security benefits to opposite-sex couples in their own and all other states. For those married same-sex couples of which one partner is in federal service, the other cannot take advantage of medical care and other benefits available to opposite-sex partners in Massachusetts and everywhere else in the country.

These burdens are comparable to those the Court found substantial in *Moreno, City of Cleburne*, and *Romer*. *Moreno*, like this case, involved meaningful economic benefits; *City of Cleburne* involved the opportunity to secure housing; *Romer*, the chance to secure equal protection of the laws on the same terms as other groups. Loss of survivor's social security, spouse-based medical care and tax benefits are major detriments on any reckoning; provision for retirement and medical care are, in practice, the main components of the social safety net for vast numbers of Americans.

Accordingly, we conclude that the extreme deference accorded to ordinary economic legislation in cases like *Lee Optical* would not be extended to DOMA by the Supreme Court; and without insisting on "compelling" or "important" justifications or "narrow tailoring," the Court would scrutinize with care the purported bases for the legislation. Before providing such scrutiny, a separate element absent in *Moreno, City of Cleburne*, and *Romer* — federalism — must be considered.

Federalism.

[The court here determined that, given the longstanding understanding that the law of marriage and domestic relations was for the states and not the federal government, the federal intrusion into state law under DOMA—a departure from the traditional understanding of federalism--should not be given any deference by the court.]

DOMA's Rationales.

Despite its ramifying application throughout the U.S. Code, only one day of hearings was held on DOMA and none of the testimony concerned DOMA's effects on the numerous federal programs at issue. Some of the odder consequences of DOMA testify to the speed with which it was adopted. The statute, only a few paragraphs in length, is devoid of the express prefatory findings commonly made in major federal laws. Accordingly, in discerning and assessing Congress' basis for DOMA our main resort is the House Committee report and, in lesser measure, to variations of its themes advanced in the briefs before us. The committee report stated:

> [T]he Committee briefly discusses four of the governmental interests advanced by this legislation: (1) defending and nurturing the institution of traditional, heterosexual marriage; (2) defending traditional notions of morality; (3) protecting state sovereignty and democratic self-governance; and (4) preserving scarce government resources. H.R.Rep. No. 104–664, at 12 (1996), 1996 U.S.C.C.A.N. 2905, 2916.

The penultimate reason listed above was not directed to section 3 — indeed, is antithetical to it — but was concerned solely with section 2, which reserved a state's power not to recognize same-sex marriages performed in other states. Thus, we begin with the others, reserving for separate consideration the claim strongly pressed by the *Gill* plaintiffs that DOMA should be condemned because its unacknowledged but alleged central motive was hostility to homosexuality.

First, starting with the most concrete of the cited reasons — "preserving scarce government resources" — it is said that DOMA will save money for the federal government by limiting tax savings and avoiding social security and other payments to spouses. This may well be true, or at least might have been thought true; more detailed recent analysis indicates that DOMA is more likely on a net basis to cost the government money.

But, where the distinction is drawn against a historically disadvantaged group and has no other basis, Supreme Court precedent marks this as a reason undermining rather than bolstering the distinction. *Plyler v. Doe,* 457 U.S. 202, 227 (1982); *Romer,* 517 U.S. at 635. The reason, derived from equal protection analysis, is that such a group has historically been less able to protect itself through the political process. *Plyler,* 457 U.S. at 218 n. 14; *United States v. Carolene Prods. Co.,* 304 U.S. 144, 152 n. 4 (1938).

A second rationale of a pragmatic character, advanced by the Legal Group's brief and several others, is to support child-rearing in the context of stable marriage. The evidence as to child rearing by same-sex couples is the subject of controversy, but we need not enter the debate. Whether or not children raised by opposite-sex marriages are on average better served, DOMA cannot preclude same-sex couples in Massachusetts from adopting children or prevent a woman partner from giving birth to a child to be raised by both partners.

Although the House Report is filled with encomia to heterosexual marriage, DOMA does not increase benefits to opposite-sex couples — whose marriages may in any event be childless, unstable or both — or explain how denying benefits to same-sex couples will reinforce heterosexual marriage. Certainly, the denial will not affect the gender choices of those seeking marriage. This is not merely a matter of poor fit of remedy to perceived problem, *Lee Optical,* 348 U.S. at 487–88; *City of Cleburne,* 473 U.S. at 446–50, but a lack of any demonstrated connection between DOMA's treatment of same-sex couples and its asserted goal of strengthening the bonds and benefits to society of heterosexual marriage.

A third reason, moral disapproval of homosexuality, is one of DOMA's stated justifications:

> Civil laws that permit only heterosexual marriage reflect and honor a collective moral judgment about human sexuality. This judgment entails both *moral disapproval of homosexuality,* and a moral conviction that heterosexuality better comports with traditional (especially Judeo–Christian) morality.

H.R.Rep. No. 104–664, at 15–16 (emphasis added); *see also, e.g.,* 142 Cong. Rec. 16,972 (1996) (statement of Rep. Coburn) (homosexuality "morally wrong").

For generations, moral disapproval has been taken as an adequate basis for legislation, although usually in choices made by state legislators to whom general police power is entrusted. But, speaking directly of same-sex preferences, *Lawrence* ruled that moral disapproval alone cannot justify legislation discriminating on this basis. 539 U.S. at 577–78. Moral judgments can hardly be avoided in legislation, but *Lawrence* and *Romer* have undercut *this* basis. *Cf. Palmore v. Sidoti,* 466 U.S. 429, 433 (1984).

Finally, it has been suggested by the Legal Group's brief that, faced with a prospective change in state marriage laws, Congress was entitled to "freeze" the situation and reflect. But the statute was not framed as a temporary time-out; and it has no expiration date, such as one that Congress included in the Voting Rights Act. *See Nw. Austin,* 129 S.Ct. at 2510 (describing original expiration date and later extensions); *City of Boerne,* 521 U.S. at 533. The House Report's own arguments — moral, prudential and fiscal — make clear that DOMA was not framed as a temporary measure.

We conclude, without resort to suspect classifications' or any impairment of *Baker,* that the rationales offered do not provide adequate support for section 3 of DOMA. Several of the reasons given do not match the statute and several others are diminished by specific holdings in Supreme Court decisions more or less directly on point. If we are right in thinking that disparate impact on minority interests and federalism concerns both require somewhat more in this case than almost automatic deference to Congress' will, this statute fails that test.

In reaching our judgment, we do not rely upon the charge that DOMA's hidden but dominant purpose was hostility to homosexuality. The many legislators who supported DOMA acted from a variety of motives, one central and expressed aim being to preserve the heritage of marriage as traditionally defined over centuries of Western civilization. Preserving this institution is not the same as "mere moral disapproval of an excluded group," *Lawrence,* 539 U.S. at 585 (O'Connor, J., concurring), and that is singularly so in this case given the range of bipartisan support for the statute.

The opponents of section 3 point to selected comments from a few individual legislators; but the motives of a small group cannot taint a statute supported by large majorities in both Houses and signed by President Clinton. Traditions are the glue that holds society together, and many of our own traditions rest largely on belief and familiarity — not on benefits firmly provable in court. The desire to retain them is strong and can be honestly held.

For 150 years, this desire to maintain tradition would alone have been justification enough for almost any statute. This judicial deference has a distinguished lineage, including such figures as Justice Holmes, the second Justice Harlan, and Judges Learned Hand and Henry Friendly. But Supreme Court decisions in the last fifty years call for closer scrutiny of government action touching upon minority group interests and of federal action in areas of traditional state concern.

To conclude, many Americans believe that marriage is the union of a man and a woman, and most Americans live in states where that is the law today. One virtue of federalism is that it permits this diversity of governance based on local choice, but this applies as well to the states that have chosen to legalize same-sex marriage. Under current Supreme Court authority, Congress' denial of federal benefits to same-sex couples lawfully married in Massachusetts has not been adequately supported by any permissible federal interest.

The judgment of the district court is *affirmed* for the reasons and to the extent stated above. Anticipating that certiorari will be sought and that Supreme Court review of DOMA is highly likely, the mandate is *stayed,* maintaining the district court's stay of its injunctive judgment, pending further order of this court.

It is so ordered.

NOTES

1. In *Massachusetts v. HHS*, the court initially noted that, under the traditional, deferential rational basis standard, the plaintiffs could not prevail. Considering only one of the several justifications for DOMA—that broadening the definition of marriage would reduce tax revenues and increase social security payments—the court noted that Congress could rationally have believed that DOMA would reduce costs, even if newer studies of the actual economic effects of

DOMA suggest that it may in fact raise costs for the federal government. But the *Mass v. HHS* court decided that it would not apply that version of rational basis review. Instead, the court cited the most famous trio of heightened rationality—*Moreno, City of Cleburne,* and *Romer*—and noted the similarity in the groups disadvantaged. "As with the women, the poor and the mentally impaired, gays and lesbians have long been the subject of discrimination." Also similar was the burden imposed on those groups. The loss of substantial federal financial benefits was comparable to the loss of meaningful financial benefits in *Moreno,* the loss of opportunity to secure housing in *Cleburne,* and the loss of the chance to secure equal protection in *Romer.* Thus, the *Mass. v. HHS* court decided to apply heightened rationality.

The court noted that there was neither an express statutory finding nor much legislative history that would explain the purposes of DOMA. The court was therefore required to resort to the House Committee report which identified four governmental interests advanced by the legislation: (1) defending and nurturing the institution of traditional, heterosexual marriage; (2) defending traditional notions of morality; (3) protecting state sovereignty and democratic self-governance; and (4) preserving scarce government resources. The court dismantled each of this as an adequate justification.

The easiest purpose to get rid of was #3 — protecting state sovereignty. By taking away from states the power to determine who is married to whom, the statute was antithetical to that purpose. The last purpose--preserving government resources—is clearly a permissible purpose, but it does not explain at all why *this particular group* was singled out to bear the brunt of saving money. After all, excluding all Catholic spouses would also save money. The classification must be relevant to this particular purpose. The most significant purpose — to support child-rearing in the context of stable marriage — was not advanced by the law. "Although the House Report was filled with encomia to heterosexual marriage, DOMA does not increase benefits to opposite-sex couples — whose marriages may in any event be childless, unstable or both — or explain how denying benefits to same-sex couples will reinforce heterosexual marriage." The last reason — defending traditional notions of morality — can no longer, after *Lawrence,* justify legislation that discriminates on the basis of moral disapproval. None of the asserted purposes was advanced by the statute, and therefore, the statute failed the rational basis test.

2. *Is Respect for Tradition a Sufficient Government Purpose?* The *Massachusetts v. HHS* court noted its respect for traditions:

> Traditions are the glue that holds society together, and many of our own traditions rest largely on belief and familiarity — not on benefits firmly provable in court. The desire to retain them is strong and can be honestly held. For 150 years, this desire to maintain tradition would alone have been justification enough for almost any statute. This judicial deference has a distinguished lineage, including such figures as Justice Holmes, the second Justice Harlan, and Judges Learned Hand and Henry Friendly.

But tradition was an inadequate justification in this case, since "Supreme Court decisions in the last fifty years call for closer scrutiny of government action touching upon minority group interests and of federal action in areas of traditional state concern."

In *Tradition as Justification: The Case of Opposite-Sex Marriage,* 78 U. Chi. L. Rev. 281(2011), Professor Kim Forde-Mazrui argues that the tradition of opposite-sex marriage is sufficient to survive the most deferential standard of rational basis review. She explains:

CHAPTER 6: CLASSIFICATIONS BASED ON SEXUAL ORIENTATION

> [T]radition can serve as a legally sufficient basis on which to uphold discriminatory laws, including bans on same-sex marriage. More specifically, the benefits associated with tradition, such as time-tested wisdom, social-identity reinforcement, and avoiding unintended consequences, are legally permissible justifications for a law challenged under the Equal Protection Clause, provided that tradition is not relied on simply for its own sake and that the expected benefits that might result from preserving tradition are not premised on illegitimate purposes or beliefs.

However, Professor Forde-Mazrui thinks that courts should be skeptical of the tradition justification when it is used to disadvantage a historically stigmatized group:

> [C]ertain circumstances warrant skepticism toward the use of tradition when offered to justify a discriminatory law. A significant factor warranting suspicion is that a tradition serves beliefs that have become repudiated, such as antagonism toward a historically stigmatized group that has gained substantial social acceptance. In such circumstances, tradition may serve as a convenient justification for those who hold the attitudes that are no longer an acceptable justification for the discrimination in question. . . . That the concept of tradition is manipulable and has rhetorical appeal further contributes to its opportunistic usefulness to support a law that is in fact based on illegitimate or arbitrary motivations. As a result, tradition is as likely as not to reflect outmoded attitudes that are not expressed due to their current unacceptability. Courts should therefore be skeptical of a law justified by tradition, and should not uphold it absent a convincing showing of alternative, legitimate purposes.

2. *Kandu* and *Mass v. HHS* show how the two different versions of rational basis review lead to directly contradictory results on the same facts. The next case shows a court reviewing DOMA using heightened scrutiny.

Windsor v. United States
699 F.3d 169 (2d Cir. 2012), *cert. granted*, __ U.S. __ (2012)

[The portion of the court's opinion identifying gay men and women as a quasi-suspect class is reprinted in Section C.3 of this chapter. What follows is that part of the court's opinion that applies intermediate scrutiny to DOMA.]

To withstand intermediate scrutiny, a classification must be "substantially related to an important government interest." *Clark v. Jeter*, 486 U.S. 456, 461 (1988). "Substantially related" means that the explanation must be " 'exceedingly persuasive.' " *United States v. Virginia*, 518 U.S. 515, 533 (1996) (quoting *Mississippi Univ. for Women v. Hogan*, 458 U.S. 718, 724 (1982)). "The justification must be genuine, not hypothesized or invented post hoc in response to litigation."

BLAG [the Bipartisan Legal Advisory Group] advances two primary arguments for why Congress enacted DOMA. First, it cites "unique federal interests," which include maintaining a consistent federal definition of marriage, protecting the fisc, and avoiding "the unknown consequences of a novel redefinition of a foundational social institution." Second, BLAG argues that Congress enacted the statute to encourage "responsible procreation." At argument, BLAG's counsel all but conceded that these reasons for enacting DOMA may not withstand intermediate scrutiny.

A) Maintaining a "Uniform Definition" of Marriage

Statements in the Congressional Record express an intent to enforce uniform eligibility for federal marital benefits by insuring that same-sex couples receive—or lose—the same federal benefits across all states. However, the emphasis on uniformity is suspicious because Congress and the Supreme Court have historically deferred to state domestic relations laws, irrespective of their variations.

To the extent that there has ever been "uniform" or "consistent" rule in federal law concerning marriage, it is that marriage is "a virtually exclusive province of the States." *Sosna,* 419 U.S. at 404. As the Supreme Court has emphasized, "the states, at the time of the adoption of the Constitution, possessed full power over the subject of marriage and divorce. . . . [T]he Constitution delegated no authority to the Government of the United States on the subject of marriage and divorce." *Haddock v. Haddock,* 201 U.S. 562, 575 (1906) (emphasis added), overruled on other grounds by *Williams v. State of North Carolina,* 317 U.S. 287 (1942). DOMA was therefore an unprecedented intrusion "into an area of traditional state regulation." *Massachusetts,* 682 F.3d at 13. This is a reason to look upon Section 3 of DOMA with a cold eye. "The absence of precedent . . . is itself instructive; '[d]iscriminations of an unusual character especially suggest careful consideration to determine whether they are obnoxious to the constitutional provision .'" *Romer v. Evans,* 517 U.S. 620, 633 (1996) (*quoting Louisville Gas & Elec. Co. v. Coleman,* 277 U.S. 32, 37–38 (1928)).

Moreover, DOMA's sweep arguably creates more discord and anomaly than uniformity, as many amici observe. Because DOMA defined only a single aspect of domestic relations law, it left standing all other inconsistencies in the laws of the states, such as minimum age, consanguinity, divorce, and paternity. . . . The uniformity rationale is further undermined by inefficiencies that it creates. As a district court in this Circuit found, it was simpler—and more consistent—for the federal government to ask whether a couple was married under the law of the state of domicile, rather than adding "an additional criterion, requiring the federal government to identify and exclude all same-sex marital unions from federal recognition." *Pedersen,* —— F.Supp.2d at ——, 2012 WL 3113883, at 48; see *Golinski,* 824 F.Supp.2d at 1001–02 ("The passage of DOMA actually undermined administrative consistency by requiring that the federal government, for the first time, discern which state definitions of marriage are entitled to federal recognition and which are not.").

Because DOMA is an unprecedented breach of longstanding deference to federalism that singles out same-sex marriage as the only inconsistency (among many) in state law that requires a federal rule to achieve uniformity, the rationale premised on uniformity is not an exceedingly persuasive justification for DOMA.

B) Protecting the Fisc

Another professed goal of Congress is to save government resources by limiting the beneficiaries of government marital benefits. H.R.Rep. No. 104–664, at 18 (1996), reprinted in 1996 U.S.C.C.A.N. 2905, 2922. Fiscal prudence is undoubtedly an important government interest. Windsor and certain amici contest whether the measure will achieve a net benefit to the Treasury;

but in matters of the federal budget, Congress has the prerogative to err (if error it is), and cannot be expected to prophesy the future accurately. But the Supreme Court has held that "[t]he saving of welfare costs cannot justify an otherwise invidious classification." *Graham v. Richardson*, 403 U.S. 365, 375 (1971) As the district court observed, "excluding any arbitrarily chosen group of individuals from a government program conserves government resources." *Windsor*, 833 F.Supp.2d at 406.

Citing *Bowen v. Owens*, 476 U.S. 340, 348 (1986), BLAG draws the distinction that DOMA did not withdraw benefits from same-sex spouses; since DOMA was enacted before same-sex marriage was permitted in any state, DOMA operated to prevent the extension of benefits to people who never enjoyed them. However, *Bowen* was decided on rational basis grounds and did not involve an invidious classification. Moreover, DOMA is properly considered a benefit withdrawal in the sense that it functionally eliminated longstanding federal recognition of all marriages that are properly ratified under state law—and the federal benefits (and detriments) that come with that recognition.

Furthermore, DOMA is so broad, touching more than a thousand federal laws, that it is not substantially related to fiscal matters. As amicus Citizens for Responsibility and Ethics in Washington demonstrates, DOMA impairs a number of federal laws (involving bankruptcy and conflict-of-interest) that have nothing to do with the public fisc. DOMA transcends a legislative intent to conserve public resources. For these reasons, DOMA is not substantially related to the important government interest of protecting the fisc.

C) Preserving a Traditional Understanding of Marriage

Congress undertook to justify DOMA as a measure for preserving traditional marriage as an institution. 150 Cong. Rec. 14951. But "[a]ncient lineage of a legal concept does not give [a law] immunity from attack for lacking a rational basis." Heller, 509 U.S. at 326. A fortiori, tradition is hard to justify as meeting the more demanding test of having a substantial relation to an important government interest. Similar appeals to tradition were made and rejected in litigation concerning anti-sodomy laws. See *Lawrence*, 539 U.S. at 577–78 ("'[T]he fact that the governing majority in a State has traditionally viewed a particular practice as immoral is not a sufficient reason for upholding a law prohibiting the practice; neither history nor tradition could save a law prohibiting miscegenation from constitutional attack.'") (quoting *Bowers*, 478 U.S. at 216 (Stevens, J., dissenting)) (emphasis added).

Even if preserving tradition were in itself an important goal, DOMA is not a means to achieve it. As the district court found: "because the decision of whether same-sex couples can marry is left to the states, DOMA does not, strictly speaking, 'preserve' the institution of marriage as one between a man and a woman." *Windsor*, 833 F.Supp.2d at 403. Preservation of a traditional understanding of marriage therefore is not an exceedingly persuasive justification for DOMA.

D) Encouraging Responsible Procreation

Finally, BLAG presents three related reasons why DOMA advances the goals of "responsible childrearing": DOMA subsidizes procreation because only opposite-sex couples can procreate "naturally"; DOMA subsidizes biological parenting (for more or less the same reason); and DOMA facilitates the optimal parenting arrangement of a mother and a father. We agree that promotion of procreation can be an important government objective. But we do not see how DOMA is substantially related to it.

All three proffered rationales have the same defect: they are cast as incentives for heterosexual couples, incentives that DOMA does not affect in any way. DOMA does not provide any incremental reason for opposite-sex couples to engage in "responsible procreation." Incentives for opposite-sex couples to marry and procreate (or not) were the same after DOMA was enacted as they were before. Other courts have likewise been unable to find even a rational connection between DOMA and encouragement of responsible procreation and child-rearing. See *Massachusetts*, 682 F.3d at 14–15 (underscoring the "lack of any demonstrated connection between DOMA's treatment of same-sex couples and its asserted goal of strengthening the bonds and benefits to society of heterosexual marriage") (citations omitted); *Windsor*, 833 F.Supp.2d at 404–05; *Pedersen*, —— F.Supp.2d at —— – ——, 2012 WL 3113883, at 40–43. DOMA is therefore not substantially related to the important government interest of encouraging procreation.

DOMA's classification of same-sex spouses was not substantially related to an important government interest. Accordingly, we hold that Section 3 of DOMA violates equal protection and is therefore unconstitutional.

Our straightforward legal analysis sidesteps the fair point that same-sex marriage is unknown to history and tradition. But law (federal or state) is not concerned with holy matrimony. Government deals with marriage as a civil status—however fundamental—and New York has elected to extend that status to same-sex couples. A state may enforce and dissolve a couple's marriage, but it cannot sanctify or bless it. For that, the pair must go next door.

For the foregoing reasons, we AFFIRM the grant of Windsor's motion for summary judgment.

NOTES

1. The *Windsor* court examined all of the traditional justifications for nonrecognition of same-sex marriage and found that they are all wanting under intermediate scrutiny. The refusal to recognize same-sex marriage did not advance the *first* justification — maintaining a uniform definition of marriage. DOMA was in fact inimical to that goal, since, before DOMA, the federal government had uniformly recognized all marriages valid under state law but now had to determine which laws otherwise valid under state law would not meet this new federal standard. The court conceded that the *second* justification — protecting the fisc (conserving government resources)— was an important interest but, as the Supreme Court had made clear many times, "[t]he saving of welfare costs cannot justify an otherwise invidious classification," The government can always save money by excluding any group from a government benefit, but there needs to be a reason why that particular group was singled out to bear the burden.

The *third* justification — preserving a traditional understanding of marriage — was probably not important enough, and if it was important enough, DOMA did not advance it. Since *Lawrence*, it has been clear that appeals to tradition are not sufficient to justify invasions of personal rights. And, since DOMA leaves to the states the decision to recognize same-sex marriage, it does not actually preserve the institution of marriage as one between a man and a woman. The *fourth* justification — encouraging responsible procreation — was not advanced by DOMA. The justification was cast as creating incentives for heterosexual couples to procreate, but heterosexual couples are not affected in any way by DOMA and therefore it cannot create any incentives for them to procreate.

Ultimately, DOMA's refusal to recognize same-sex marriage was not substantially related to any important governmental interest.

2.   In *Pedersen v. Office of Personnel Management*, --- F.Supp.2d --- (D.Conn. 2012), the district court reviewed the constitutionality of DOMA. The court determined that gay persons are a quasi-suspect class. The court then determined that DOMA did not even satisfy rational basis review.

3.   *Is the constitutionality of same-sex marriage inevitable?* Since it decided the *Lawrence* case in 2003, the Supreme Court has been silent on the subject of classifications that disadvantage gay men and women. State supreme courts and the lower federal courts, however, have been quite busy in this area. Recent decisions, as reported in this chapter, are more and more likely to be favorable to gay persons. The Supreme Court has granted certiorari in the Perry and *Windsor* cases. What will be the result?

Professor Lawrence Tribe and Joshua Matz discuss the future of same-sex marriage in *The Constitutional Inevitability of Same-Sex Marriage*, 71 Maryland L. Rev. 471 (2012). They predict that same-sex marriage is coming:

> Whenever that momentous question finally arrives at the Supreme Court, the Justices should declare this right for the entire Nation. The reason is simple: if our Constitution's promises of liberty, equality, and dignity are to be realized for the millions of Americans whose most intimate lives are degraded by laws that set their love, their enduring commitments to one another, and their very sense of personhood apart as little more than second-class, then in the end the Justices must do their duty and recognize same-sex marriage rights. Such is their responsibility as faithful expositors of the Constitution. There is no other way.

CHAPTER 7

NONSUSPECT CLASSIFICATIONS

The Supreme Court has characterized classifications based on race and alienage as suspect, and therefore subject to strict scrutiny. In addition, the Court has characterized classifications based on gender and illegitimacy as quasi-suspect, and therefore subject to intermediate scrutiny. Further, although the issue has not been addressed in the Supreme Court, several state and lower federal courts have held that classifications based on sexual orientation are quasi-suspect, and thus also subject to intermediate scrutiny. The Supreme Court did almost all of its work in creating suspect classes and heightened scrutiny in the period beginning in 1968, when it decided *Levy v. Louisiana*, 391 U.S. 68 (1968), and ending in 1976, when it decided *Craig v. Boren*, 429 U.S. 190 (1976). Since that time, the Court has identified no additional suspect or quasi-suspect classifications. Thus, with the possible exception of classifications based on sexual orientation, the set of suspect or quasi-suspect classifications appears to be closed. This chapter will examine cases where the Court has explicitly decided that a particular classification is not suspect.

A. POVERTY IS NOT A SUSPECT CLASSIFICATION

1. THE COURT INITIALLY SUGGESTS THAT POVERTY IS AS SUSPECT AS RACE

In *Griffin v. Illinois*, 351 U.S. 12 (1956), the Court found unconstitutional a state practice under which those convicted at the trial level were not provided a trial transcript at state expense for purposes of appeal. The effect of this practice was that those who could not afford a transcript were effectively denied the chance to appeal their cases. If one looks back at the case with the benefit of subsequent Supreme Court precedents, it is very likely that the basis of the decision was the Court's concern for access to the judicial process, and the case is widely cited as a precedent for the claim of heightened scrutiny of state laws that limit access to the judicial process. *See* Chapter 8.D., *infra*.

At the time it was decided, however, *Griffin* might just as plausibly been viewed as a case that turned on the poverty of the litigants, rather than their lack of access to the court system. The Court introduced its discussion of the case by asserting that "Providing equal justice for poor and rich, weak and powerful alike is an age-old problem. People have never ceased to hope and strive to move closer to that goal." The Court then went on to describe the problem in more detail:

Surely no one would contend that either a State or the Federal Government could constitutionally provide that defendants unable to pay court costs in advance should be denied the right to plead not guilty or to defend themselves in court. Such a law would make the constitutional promise of a fair trial a worthless thing. Notice, the right to be heard, and the right to counsel would under such circumstances be meaningless promises to the poor. In criminal trials a State can no more discriminate on account of poverty than on account of religion, race, or color.

If one takes the Court at its word, then classifications that discriminate against the poor are as offensive as classifications that discriminate against racial minorities, and would thus be subject to strict scrutiny.

This understanding of *Griffin* would find subsequent support in *Douglas v. California*, 372 U.S. 353 (1963), where the Court found unconstitutional the state's unwillingness to pay for an attorney for a convicted person's first appeal, as of right. Again, the case today is seen more as part of the line of cases creating some sort of fundamental right to some level of access to the courts. Like *Griffin*, however, it could just as easily be read as a case that provides heightened scrutiny of classifications that disadvantage the poor. The *Douglas* Court said:

In either case the evil is the same: discrimination against the indigent. For there can be no equal justice where the kind of an appeal a man enjoys 'depends on the amount of money he has.' . . . Absolute equality is not required; lines can be and are drawn and we often sustain them. But where the merits of the one and only appeal an indigent has as of right are decided without benefit of counsel, we think an unconstitutional line has been drawn between rich and poor.

Thus, as of 1963, it was plausible to argue, on the basis of *Griffin* and *Douglas*, that the poor were a suspect class and that classifications that disadvantaged the poor would be subject to heightened scrutiny. The Supreme Court, however, soundly rejected that view in the 1970's.

2. THE COURT CONCLUDES THAT WEALTH IS NOT A SUSPECT CLASSIFICATION

In 1970, in *Dandridge v. Williams*, 397 U.S. 471 (1970), the Court reviewed a Maryland welfare statute under which the "standard of need" for each family was capped at a certain amount, with the effect that smaller families received state benefits equal to their standard of need but larger families received a benefit amount that was smaller than their standard of need. In response to the claim that this different treatment of differently-sized families violated the Equal Protection Clause, the Court responded:

In the area of economics and social welfare, a State does not violate the Equal Protection Clause merely because the classifications made by its laws are imperfect. If the classification has some 'reasonable basis,' it does not offend the Constitution simply because the classification 'is not made with mathematical nicety or because in practice it results in some inequality.' *Lindsley v. Natural Carbonic Gas Co.*, 220 U.S. 61, 78. 'The problems of government are practical ones and may justify, if they do not require, rough accommodations—illogical, it may be, and unscientific.' *Metropolis Theatre Co. v. City of Chicago*, 228 U.S. 61, 69—70. 'A statutory discrimination will not be set aside if any state of facts reasonably may be conceived to justify it.' *McGowan v. Maryland,* 366 U.S. 420, 426.

... To be sure, the cases cited, and many others enunciating this fundamental standard under the Equal Protection Clause, have in the main involved state regulation of business or industry. The administration of public welfare assistance, by contrast, involves the most basic economic needs of impoverished human beings. We recognize the dramatically real factual difference between the cited cases and this one, but we can find no basis for applying a different constitutional standard. It is a standard that has consistently been applied to state legislation restricting the availability of employment opportunities. *Goesaert v. Cleary,* 335 U.S. 464; *Kotch v. Board of River Port Pilot Com'rs,* 330 U.S. 552. See also *Flemming v. Nestor,* 363 U.S. 603. And it is a standard that is true to the principle that the Fourteenth Amendment gives the federal courts no power to impose upon the States their views of what constitutes wise economic or social policy.

The Court thus concluded that, even though the *Dandridge* case involved "the most basic economic needs of impoverished human beings," a legislative classification that affected those needs would not be subject to heightened scrutiny. The *Dandridge* Court never cited *Griffin*, and thus apparently did not see the need to distinguish that case's claim that discrimination on account of poverty is as objectionable as discrimination on the basis of race. Three years later, in *San Antonio Independent School Dist. v. Rodriguez,* 411 U.S. 1 (1973), the Court very explicitly held that the poor are not a suspect class.

San Antonio Independent School Dist. v. Rodriguez
411 U.S. 1 (1973)

[Low-income parents were residents of a school district that had a low property tax base, a high property tax rate, and low per pupil spending. They compared their situation with that of a neighboring district that had a high property tax base, a low property tax rate, and high per pupil spending. They brought a class action suit against various state defendants, alleging, *inter alia*, discrimination on the basis of wealth.]

Mr. Justice POWELL delivered the opinion of the Court.

[In a separate portion of the Court's opinion, reproduced in Chapter 8, the Court considered, and rejected, the claim that education was a fundamental right.]

We must decide, first, whether the Texas system of financing public education operates to the disadvantage of some suspect class, thereby requiring strict judicial scrutiny. If not, the Texas scheme must still be examined to determine whether it rationally furthers some legitimate, articulated state purpose and therefore does not constitute an invidious discrimination in violation of the Equal Protection Clause of the Fourteenth Amendment.

The wealth discrimination discovered by the District Court in this case, and by several other courts that have recently struck down school-financing laws in other States, is quite unlike any of the forms of wealth discrimination heretofore reviewed by this Court. Rather than focusing on the unique features of the alleged discrimination, the courts in these cases have virtually assumed their findings of a suspect classification through a simplistic process of analysis: since, under the traditional systems of financing public schools, some poorer people receive less expensive educations than other more affluent people, these systems discriminate on the basis of wealth. This approach largely ignores the hard threshold questions, including whether it makes a difference for purposes of consideration under the Constitution that the class of disadvantaged 'poor' cannot be identified or defined in customary equal protection terms, and whether the relative-rather than absolute-nature of the asserted deprivation is of significant consequence.

The Texas system of school financing might be regarded as discriminating (1) against 'poor' persons whose incomes fall below some identifiable level of poverty or who might be characterized as functionally 'indigent,' or (2) against those who are relatively poorer than others, or (3) against all those who, irrespective of their personal incomes, happen to reside in relatively poorer school districts. Our task must be to ascertain whether, in fact, the Texas system has been shown to discriminate on any of these possible bases and, if so, whether the resulting classification may be regarded as suspect.

The precedents of this Court provide the proper starting point. The individuals, or groups of individuals, who constituted the class discriminated against in our prior cases shared two distinguishing characteristics: because of their impecunity they were completely unable to pay for some desired benefit, and as a consequence, they sustained an absolute deprivation of a meaningful opportunity to enjoy that benefit. In *Griffin v. Illinois*, 351 U.S. 12 (1956), and its progeny, the Court invalidated state laws that prevented an indigent criminal defendant from acquiring a transcript, or an adequate substitute for a transcript, for use at several stages of the trial and appeal process. The payment requirements in each case were found to occasion de facto discrimination against those who, because of their indigency, were totally unable to pay for transcripts. And the Court in each case emphasized that no constitutional violation would have been shown if the State had provided some 'adequate substitute' for a full stenographic transcript.

Likewise, in *Douglas v. California*, 372 U.S. 353 (1963), a decision establishing an indigent defendant's right to court-appointed counsel on direct appeal, the Court dealt only with defendants who could not pay for counsel from their own resources and who had no other way of gaining representation. *Douglas* provides no relief for those on whom the burdens of paying for a criminal defense are relatively speaking, great but not insurmountable. Nor does it deal with relative differences in the quality of counsel acquired by the less wealthy.

Williams v. Illinois, 399 U.S. 235 (1970), and *Tate v. Short*, 401 U.S. 395 (1971), struck down criminal penalties that subjected indigents to incarceration simply because of their inability to pay a fine. Again, the disadvantaged class was composed only of persons who were totally unable to pay the demanded sum. Those cases do not touch on the question whether equal protection is denied to persons with relatively less money on whom designated fines impose heavier burdens. The Court has not held that fines must be structured to reflect each person's ability to pay in order to avoid disproportionate burdens. Sentencing judges may, and often do, consider the defendant's ability to pay, but in such circumstances they are guided by sound judicial discretion rather than by constitutional mandate.

Finally, in *Bullock v. Carter*, 405 U.S. 134 (1972), the Court invalidated the Texas filing-fee requirement for primary elections. Both of the relevant classifying facts found in the previous cases were present there. The size of the fee, often running into the thousands of dollars and, in at least one case, as high as $8,900, effectively barred all potential candidates who were unable to

CHAPTER 7: NONSUSPECT CLASSIFICATIONS

pay the required fee. As the system provided 'no reasonable alternative means of access to the ballot', inability to pay occasioned an absolute denial of a position on the primary ballot.

Only appellees' first possible basis for describing the class disadvantaged by the Texas school-financing system--discrimination against a class of definably 'poor' persons--might arguably meet the criteria established in these prior cases. Even a cursory examination, however, demonstrates that neither of the two distinguishing characteristics of wealth classifications can be found here. First, in support of their charge that the system discriminates against the 'poor,' appellees have made no effort to demonstrate that it operates to the peculiar disadvantage of any class fairly definable as indigent, or as composed of persons whose incomes are beneath any designated poverty level. Indeed, there is reason to believe that the poorest families are not necessarily clustered in the poorest property districts. A recent and exhaustive study of school districts in Connecticut concluded that '(i)t is clearly incorrect . . . to contend that the 'poor' live in 'poor' districts . . . . Thus, the major factual assumption of *Serrano*--that the educational financing system discriminates against the 'poor'--is simply false in Connecticut.' Defining 'poor' families as those below the Bureau of the Census 'poverty level,' the Connecticut study found, not surprisingly, that the poor were clustered around commercial and industrial areas-those same areas that provide the most attractive sources of property tax income for school districts. Whether a similar pattern would be discovered in Texas is not known, but there is no basis on the record in this case for assuming that the poorest people-defined by reference to any level of absolute impecunity--are concentrated in the poorest districts.

Second, neither appellees nor the District Court addressed the fact that, unlike each of the foregoing cases, lack of personal resources has not occasioned an absolute deprivation of the desired benefit. The argument here is not that the children in districts having relatively low assessable property values are receiving no public education; rather, it is that they are receiving a poorer quality education than that available to children in districts having more assessable wealth. Apart from the unsettled and disputed question whether the quality of education may be determined by the amount of money expended for it, a sufficient answer to appellees' argument is that, at least where wealth is involved, the Equal Protection Clause does not require absolute equality or precisely equal advantages. Nor indeed, in view of the infinite variables affecting the educational process, can any system assure equal quality of education except in the most relative sense. Texas asserts that the Minimum Foundation Program provides an 'adequate' education for all children in the State. By providing 12 years of free public-school education, and by assuring teachers, books, transportation, and operating funds, the Texas Legislature has endeavored to 'guarantee, for the welfare of the state as a whole, that all people shall have at least an adequate program of education. This is what is meant by 'A Minimum Foundation Program of Education." The State repeatedly asserted in its briefs in this Court that it has fulfilled this desire and that it now assures 'every child in every school district an adequate education.' No proof was offered at trial persuasively discrediting or refuting the State's assertion.

For these two reasons--the absence of any evidence that the financing system discriminates against any definable category of 'poor' people or that it results in the absolute deprivation of education--the disadvantaged class is not susceptible of identification in traditional terms.

As suggested above, appellees and the District Court may have embraced a second or third approach, the second of which might be characterized as a theory of relative or comparative discrimination based on family income. Appellees sought to prove that a direct correlation exists between the wealth of families within each district and the expenditures therein for education. That is, along a continuum, the poorer the family the lower the dollar amount of education received by the family's children.

The District Court, relying in major part upon [an] affidavit [found] a positive correlation between the wealth of school districts, measured in terms of assessable property per pupil, and their levels of per pupil expenditures and a similar correlation between district wealth and the personal wealth of its residents, measured in terms of median family income.

If, in fact, these correlations could be sustained then it might be argued that expenditures on education--equated by appellees to the quality of education--are dependent on personal wealth. Appellees' comparative-discrimination theory would still face serious unanswered questions, including whether a bare positive correlation or some higher degree of correlation is necessary to provide a basis for concluding that the financing system is designed to operate to the peculiar disadvantage of the comparatively poor, and whether a class of this size and diversity could ever claim the special protection accorded 'suspect' classes. These questions need not be addressed in this case, however, since appellees' proof fails to support their allegations or the District Court's conclusions.

This brings us, then, to the third way in which the classification scheme might be defined- district wealth discrimination. Since the only correlation indicated by the evidence is between district property wealth and expenditures, it may be argued that discrimination might be found without regard to the individual income characteristics of district residents. Assuming a perfect correlation between district property wealth and expenditures from top to bottom, the disadvantaged class might be viewed as encompassing every child in every district except the district that has the most assessable wealth and spends the most on education. Alternatively ... the class might be defined more restrictively to include children in districts with assessable property which falls below the statewide average, or median, or below some other artificially defined level.

However described, it is clear that appellees' suit asks this Court to extend its most exacting scrutiny to review a system that allegedly discriminates against a large, diverse, and amorphous class, unified only by the common factor of residence in districts that happen to have less taxable wealth than other districts. The system of alleged discrimination and the class it defines have none of the traditional indicia of suspectness: the class is not saddled with such disabilities, or subjected to such a history of purposeful unequal treatment, or relegated to such a position of political powerlessness as to command extraordinary protection from the majoritarian political process.

We thus conclude that the Texas system does not operate to the peculiar disadvantage of any suspect class.

NOTES

1. The trial court in the *Rodriguez* case had held that the Texas system of funding public schools by means of property taxes discriminated against a suspect class—the poor. In reversing that decision, the Supreme Court stated, "The District Court's opinion does not reflect the novelty and complexity of the constitutional questions posed by appellees' challenge to Texas' system of school financing." The Court distinguished *Griffin* and its progeny on the grounds that, in those cases, "The individuals, or groups of individuals, who constituted the class discriminated against in our prior cases shared two distinguishing characteristics: because of their impecunity they were completely unable to pay for some desired benefit, and as a consequence, they sustained an

absolute deprivation of a meaningful opportunity to enjoy that benefit." Thus, the test was whether the disadvantaged class was *completely* unable to pay for the desired benefit and whether there was an *absolute* deprivation of that benefit. By this measure, the students in poor districts were not suspect because taxpayers in their districts were able to make some payment and the students received some education.

In a sense, the *Rodriguez* case left the door slightly open for a future holding that the poor are a suspect class, if, for example, a case resulted from a situation where the disadvantaged persons were completely unable to pay for a benefit and thus were absolutely deprived of that benefit. But such a situation has never found its way into the Supreme Court and the Court has never found the poor to be a suspect class. In *Plyler v. Doe*, 457 U.S. 202 (1982), the Court was faced with a situation where there was an absolute deprivation of public education to undocumented aliens, but the Court avoided the question of heightened scrutiny of wealth discrimination by invalidating the statute on other grounds. *See* Chapter 8.F, *infra*.

3. GOVERNMENT'S FAILURE TO FUND THE POOR DOES NOT IMPLICATE A SUSPECT CLASS

Claims of wealth discrimination are usually interwoven with a claim of access to a right that the Court has found to be fundamental. These claims are most likely to be successful when the claim involves access to some benefit provided directly by the government only, like voting and access to the courts, and the claimants cannot obtain that benefit because they cannot afford to pay for the benefit. This was the context of successful claims in *Griffin v. Illinois*, 351 U.S. 12 (1956), *Douglas v. California*, 372 U.S. 353 (1963) and *Harper v. Virginia Sate Bd. of Elections*, 382 U.S. 663 (1965).

Shapiro v. Thompson, 394 U.S. 619 (1969) is something of an outlier in this context. In that case, the Court applied strict scrutiny to statutes that imposed durational residency requirements on welfare eligibility for those who had recently moved into a new state. *See* Chapter 8, *infra*. The *Shapiro* Court did not find, or even address the claim, that the poor were a suspect class. The case turned on the finding that the durational residency requirements infringed on the fundamental right to travel, in part by penalizing those who had recently exercised their right to travel, and were thus subject to strict scrutiny. But how was the requirement a penalty when the state had no obligation to have a welfare program at all, for any of its residents? Clearly, welfare benefits for poor people are not a fundamental right under the Constitution. In addition, the right to travel, although constitutionally fundamental, is not something that the state provides; it is rather something that the state is not supposed to interfere with. Somehow, however, the combination of a decision not to extend an existing welfare program to newcomers becomes a penalty on the exercise of a right that the state has no independent obligation to provide or fund.

By the logic of *Shapiro*, then, it might seem that the state cannot limit its existing welfare programs in a manner that, by not supporting an independent fundamental right, has the effect of penalizing it, and thus subjecting the government action to strict scrutiny. This was the basic argument made in the next two cases in which the claimants alleged that the failure of the state or federal government to fund abortion procedures in existing Medicaid and Medicare programs constituted a penalty on the exercise of a fundamental right and therefore triggered strict scrutiny.

In *Maher v. Roe*, 432 U.S. 464 (1977), the Court reviewed a regulation of the Connecticut Welfare Department that limited state Medicaid benefits for first trimester abortions to those that were medically necessary. The trial court had held that the regulation unconstitutionally interfered with a woman's fundamental right to terminate a pregnancy. The Supreme Court reversed. The Court began by dismissing the claim that a suspect class was involved:

> This case involves no discrimination against a suspect class. An indigent woman desiring an abortion does not come within the limited category of disadvantaged classes so recognized by our cases. Nor does the fact that the impact of the regulation falls upon those who cannot pay lead to a different conclusion. In a sense, every denial of welfare to an indigent creates a wealth classification as compared to nonindigents who are able to pay for the desired goods or services. But this Court has never held that financial need alone identifies a suspect class for purposes of equal protection analysis. See *Rodriguez, supra*, 411 U.S. at 29; *Dandridge v. Williams*, 397 U.S. 471(1970).[FN 6]

The Court here effectively limited the precedential effect of *Griffin* and *Douglas* to those situations that involved "a governmental monopoly in which participation is compelled." The Court also purported to distinguish its *Shapiro* holding on the failure to fund constituting a penalty. The Court stated:

> The Connecticut regulation before us is different in kind from the laws invalidated in our previous abortion decisions. The Connecticut regulation places no obstacles absolute or otherwise in the pregnant woman's path to an abortion. An indigent woman who desires an abortion suffers no disadvantage as a consequence of Connecticut's decision to fund childbirth; she continues as before to be dependent on private sources for the service she desires. The State may have made childbirth a more attractive alternative, thereby influencing the woman's decision, but it has imposed no restriction on access to abortions that was not already there. The indigency that may make it difficult and in some cases, perhaps, impossible for some women to have abortions is neither created nor in any way affected by the Connecticut regulation. We conclude that the Connecticut regulation does not impinge upon the fundamental right recognized in *Roe*.

> But the claim here is that the State "penalizes" the woman's decision to have an abortion by refusing to pay for it. *Shapiro* and *Maricopa County* did not hold that States would penalize the right to travel interstate by refusing to pay the bus fares of the indigent travelers. We find no support in the right-to-travel cases for the view that Connecticut must show a compelling interest for its decision not to fund elective abortions.

The Court confirmed this view three years later in *Harris v. McRae*, 448 U.S. 297 (1980), a case challenging a federal law that limited the use of federal funds to reimburse the cost of abortions under state Medicaid statutes. The Court refused to apply heightened scrutiny in upholding the restriction. The Court stated: "It is our view that the present case is indistinguishable from *Maher* in this respect. Here, as in *Maher*, the principal impact of the Hyde Amendment falls on the indigent. But that fact does not itself render the funding restriction

---

[FN 6] In cases such as *Griffin v. Illinois*, 351 U.S. 12 (1956) and *Douglas v. California*, 372 U.S. 353 (1963), the Court held that the Equal Protection Clause requires States that allow appellate review of criminal convictions to provide indigent defendants with trial transcripts and appellate counsel. These cases are grounded in the criminal justice system, a governmental monopoly in which participation is compelled. Our subsequent decisions have made it clear that the principles underlying *Griffin* and *Douglas* do not extend to legislative classifications generally.

constitutionally invalid, for this Court has held repeatedly that poverty, standing alone is not a suspect classification."

In looking at the factors that the Court has used to determine whether a classification is suspect, the poor do not fare well. First, as the *Rodriguez* Court noted, "the poor" are not a discrete and insular minority, that is, the groups of people who are poor in America are separate, diffuse, are rarely come together to act as a group. Being poor is not an immutable trait—although it is not unrelated to one's situation at birth, it is not something that cannot be changed. Individual persons can pass in and out of the class of "the poor" at different times in their lives. To the extent that there is a history of discrimination, it is discrimination that results from the *effect* of government action, not typically that the government intended. Thus, the decision to charge for a trial transcript for an appeal falls harder on the poor than the rich, but the decision to charge was likely enacted to finance the court system, not to harm the poor. Finally, although the Court in *Griffin* stated that one's wealth is not relevant to one's guilt or innocence, it surely is relevant to one's ability to pay for a government benefit such as access to the courts or access to medical care through the Medicaid program, and this kind of relevance may be what matters in terms of the poor being a suspect class. Ultimately, the *Rodriguez* court is probably correct: the poor do not fit within the Court's understanding of a suspect class.

B. MENTAL DISABILITY IS NOT A SUSPECT CLASSIFICATION

For those with mental disabilities, there is a long history of harsh treatment and the use of disparaging terminology. "At English common law there was a "marked distinction" in the treatment accorded 'idiots' (the mentally retarded) and 'lunatics' (the mentally ill)." *Heller v. Doe*, 509 U.S. 312 (1993). The *Heller* Court followed the usual practice of its time by referring to those with limited mental capacity as "mentally retarded." The Court in 1993 may have viewed the term "mentally retarded" as an upgrade from the common law term, "idiots." In the years since then, however, the term "mentally retarded" has come to be viewed as demeaning, and state and federal governments have worked to eliminate it from their statutory and regulatory language. Thus, in 2010, Congress passed "Rosa's Law," which ordered that all references in federal laws to "mental retardation" be changed to "intellectual disability." Rosa's Law, Pub. L. No. 111-256, 124 Stat. 2643 (2010). In 2010, New Jersey passed legislation that removed from all New Jersey statutes and regulations the terms "mental retardation," "mentally retarded," and "feeble-minded," and replaced them with the terms with "intellectual disability" or "developmental disability." 2010 New Jersey Senate Bill 1982. The American Association of Mental Retardation, founded in 1876, changed its name in 2007 to the American Association on Intellectual and Developmental Disabilities. The Associated Press Stylebook states that the term "mentally disabled" is to be preferred over "mentally retarded." The term "mentally retarded," however, is still widely used in court cases. In this section, the term "mentally retarded" will be used only to the extent that cases are being discussed in which the court uses that term.

In 1985, the Supreme Court reviewed a city's refusal to allow a group home for the mentally retarded in a certain section of the city. The case is reported in Chapter 1, *supra*, where the Court applied heightened rational basis review and found that the city had violated the Equal Protection Clause. The Court also considered whether or not the mentally retarded are a suspect class. That portion of the case follows.

City of Cleburne, Tex. v. Cleburne Living Center
473 U.S. 432 (1985)

Justice WHITE delivered the opinion of the Court.

The general [rational basis] rule gives way ... when a statute classifies by race, alienage, or national origin. These factors are so seldom relevant to the achievement of any legitimate state interest that laws grounded in such considerations are deemed to reflect prejudice and antipathy--a view that those in the burdened class are not as worthy or deserving as others. For these reasons and because such discrimination is unlikely to be soon rectified by legislative means, these laws are subjected to strict scrutiny and will be sustained only if they are suitably tailored to serve a compelling state interest. *McLaughlin v. Florida*, 379 U.S. 184, 192 (1964); *Graham v. Richardson*, 403 U.S. 365 (1971). Similar oversight by the courts is due when state laws impinge on personal rights protected by the Constitution. *Kramer v. Union Free School District No. 15*, 395 U.S. 621 (1969); *Shapiro v. Thompson*, 394 U.S. 618 (1969); *Skinner v. Oklahoma ex rel. Williamson*, 316 U.S. 535 (1942).

Legislative classifications based on gender also call for a heightened standard of review. That factor generally provides no sensible ground for differential treatment. "[W]hat differentiates sex from such nonsuspect statuses as intelligence or physical disability ... is that the sex characteristic frequently bears no relation to ability to perform or contribute to society." *Frontiero v. Richardson*, 411 U.S. 677, 686 (1973) (plurality opinion). Rather than resting on meaningful considerations, statutes distributing benefits and burdens between the sexes in different ways very likely reflect outmoded notions of the relative capabilities of men and women. A gender classification fails unless it is substantially related to a sufficiently important governmental interest. *Mississippi University for Women v. Hogan*, 458 U.S. 718 (1982); *Craig v. Boren*, 429 U.S. 190 (1976). Because illegitimacy is beyond the individual's control and bears "no relation to the individual's ability to participate in and contribute to society," *Mathews v. Lucas*, 427 U.S. 495, 505 (1976), official discriminations resting on that characteristic are also subject to somewhat heightened review. Those restrictions "will survive equal protection scrutiny to the extent they are substantially related to a legitimate state interest." *Mills v. Habluetzel*, 456 U.S. 91, 99 (1982).

We have declined, however, to extend heightened review to differential treatment based on age: "While the treatment of the aged in this Nation has not been wholly free of discrimination, such persons, unlike, say, those who have been discriminated against on the basis of race or national origin, have not experienced a 'history of purposeful unequal treatment' or been subjected to unique disabilities on the basis of stereotyped characteristics not truly indicative of their abilities." *Massachusetts Board of Retirement v. Murgia*, 427 U.S. 307, 313 (1976).

The lesson of *Murgia* is that where individuals in the group affected by a law have distinguishing characteristics relevant to interests the State has the authority to implement, the courts have been very reluctant, as they should be in our federal system and with our respect for the separation of powers, to closely scrutinize legislative choices as to whether, how, and to what extent those interests should be pursued. In such cases, the Equal Protection Clause requires only a rational means to serve a legitimate end.

III

Against this background, we conclude for several reasons that the Court of Appeals erred in holding mental retardation a quasi-suspect classification calling for a more exacting standard of judicial review than is normally accorded economic and social legislation. First, it is undeniable, and it is not argued otherwise here, that those who are mentally retarded have a reduced ability to cope with and function in the everyday world. Nor are they all cut from the same pattern: as the testimony in this record indicates, they range from those whose disability is not immediately evident to those who must be constantly cared for. They are thus different, immutably so, in relevant respects, and the States' interest in dealing with and providing for them is plainly a legitimate one. How this large and diversified group is to be treated under the law is a difficult and often a technical matter, very much a task for legislators guided by qualified professionals and not by the perhaps ill-informed opinions of the judiciary. Heightened scrutiny inevitably involves substantive judgments about legislative decisions, and we doubt that the predicate for such judicial oversight is present where the classification deals with mental retardation.

Second, the distinctive legislative response, both national and state, to the plight of those who are mentally retarded demonstrates not only that they have unique problems, but also that the lawmakers have been addressing their difficulties in a manner that belies a continuing antipathy or prejudice and a corresponding need for more intrusive oversight by the judiciary. Thus, the Federal Government has not only outlawed discrimination against the mentally retarded in federally funded programs, see § 504 of the Rehabilitation Act of 1973, 29 U.S.C. § 794, but it has also provided the retarded with the right to receive "appropriate treatment, services, and habilitation" in a setting that is "least restrictive of [their] personal liberty." Developmental Disabilities Assistance and Bill of Rights Act, 42 U.S.C. §§ 6010(1), (2). In addition, the Government has conditioned federal education funds on a State's assurance that retarded children will enjoy an education that, "to the maximum extent appropriate," is integrated with that of nonmentally retarded children. Education of the Handicapped Act, 20 U.S.C. § 1412(5)(B). The Government has also facilitated the hiring of the mentally retarded into the federal civil service by exempting them from the requirement of competitive examination. See 5 CFR § 213.3102(t) (1984). The State of Texas has similarly enacted legislation that acknowledges the special status of the mentally retarded by conferring certain rights upon them, such as "the right to live in the least restrictive setting appropriate to [their] individual needs and abilities," including "the right to live ... in a group home." Mentally Retarded Persons Act of 1977, Tex.Rev.Civ.Stat.Ann., Art. 5547-300, § 7 (Vernon Supp.1985).

Such legislation thus singling out the retarded for special treatment reflects the real and undeniable differences between the retarded and others. That a civilized and decent society expects and approves such legislation indicates that governmental consideration of those differences in the vast majority of situations is not only legitimate but also desirable. It may be, as CLC contends, that legislation designed to benefit, rather than disadvantage, the retarded would generally withstand examination under a test of heightened scrutiny. The relevant inquiry, however, is whether heightened scrutiny is constitutionally mandated in the first instance. Even assuming that many of these laws could be shown to be substantially related to an important governmental purpose, merely requiring the legislature to justify its efforts in these terms may lead it to refrain from acting at all. Much recent legislation intended to benefit the retarded also assumes the need for measures that might be perceived to disadvantage them. The Education of the Handicapped Act, for example, requires an "appropriate" education, not one that is equal in all respects to the education of nonretarded children; clearly, admission to a class that exceeded the abilities of a retarded child would not be appropriate. Similarly, the Developmental Disabilities Assistance Act and the Texas Act give the retarded the right to live only in the "least restrictive setting" appropriate to their abilities, implicitly assuming the need for at least some restrictions that would not be imposed on others. Especially given the wide variation in the abilities and needs of the retarded themselves, governmental bodies must have a certain amount of flexibility and freedom from judicial oversight in shaping and limiting their remedial efforts.

Third, the legislative response, which could hardly have occurred and survived without public support, negates any claim that the mentally retarded are politically powerless in the sense that they have no ability to attract the attention of the lawmakers. Any minority can be said to be powerless to assert direct control over the legislature, but if that were a criterion for higher level scrutiny by the courts, much economic and social legislation would now be suspect.

Fourth, if the large and amorphous class of the mentally retarded were deemed quasi-suspect for the reasons given by the Court of Appeals, it would be difficult to find a principled way to distinguish a variety of other groups who have perhaps immutable disabilities setting them off from others, who cannot themselves mandate the desired legislative responses, and who can claim some degree of prejudice from at least part of the public at large. One need mention in this respect only the aging, the disabled, the mentally ill, and the infirm. We are reluctant to set out on that course, and we decline to do so.

Doubtless, there have been and there will continue to be instances of discrimination against the retarded that are in fact invidious, and that are properly subject to judicial correction under constitutional norms. But the appropriate method of reaching such instances is not to create a new quasi-suspect classification and subject all governmental action based on that classification to more searching evaluation. Rather, we should look to the likelihood that governmental action premised on a particular classification is valid as a general matter, not merely to the specifics of the case before us. Because mental retardation is a characteristic that the government may legitimately take into account in a wide range of decisions, and because both State and Federal Governments have recently committed themselves to assisting the retarded, we will not presume that any given legislative action, even one that disadvantages retarded individuals, is rooted in considerations that the Constitution will not tolerate.

NOTES

1. The *Cleburne* Court focused on several factors that led it to conclude that the mentally retarded are not a suspect class:

(a) Relevance. While the Court had noted earlier that gender "bears no relation" to ability to perform or contribute to society, just the opposite is true with regard to the mentally retarded: "those who are mentally retarded have a reduced ability to cope with and function in the everyday world."

(b) Political Power. "[T]he legislative response [in enacting laws that address the problems of the mentally retarded], which could hardly have occurred and survived without public support, negates any claim that the mentally retarded are politically powerless in the sense that they have no ability to attract the attention of the lawmakers."

(c) Prejudice against a discrete and insular minority. "[T]he distinctive legislative response, both national and state, to the plight of those who are mentally retarded demonstrates not only that they have unique problems, but also that the lawmakers have been addressing their difficulties in a manner that belies a continuing antipathy or prejudice and a corresponding need for more intrusive oversight by the judiciary."

2. Somewhat ironically, the *Cleburne* Court determined that the mentally retarded were not a suspect class, but then overturned the government action using a heightened form of rational basis review. It may have seemed at the time the *Cleburne* Court was treating the mentally retarded as a quasi-suspect class, but in a disguised form, and thus would carefully scrutinize any subsequent classifications that disadvantaged the mentally retarded. That, however, turned out not to be the case.

Eight years later, in the 1993 case, *Heller v. Doe*, 509 U.S. 312 (1993), the Court upheld a classification that disadvantaged the mentally retarded; in doing so, the Court used an extremely deferential standard of review and virtually ignored *Cleburne*. *Heller* involved the statutory procedures for involuntary civil commitment in Kentucky. Under the statute, it was easier to commit a mentally retarded person than it was to commit a person who was mentally ill. The proceedings for both kinds of commitment were substantially similar with two exceptions. The burden of proof for involuntary commitment based on mental retardation was "clear and convincing evidence" while the standard for commitment based on mental illness was "beyond a reasonable doubt." Second, in commitment proceedings for mental retardation, but not for mental illness, guardians and immediate family members were allowed to participate as parties. The Court's opinion in *Heller* began with a survey of Supreme Court cases on rationality review that set forth the most deferential version of the standard. Rational basis review was "'not a license for courts to judge the wisdom, fairness, or logic of legislative choices.'" Classifications not involving fundamental rights or suspect lines are "accorded a strong presumption of validity," and will be upheld "if there is a rational relationship between the disparity of treatment and some legitimate governmental purpose." The legislature "need not 'actually articulate at any time the purpose or rationale supporting its classification'" which "'must be upheld ... if there is any reasonably conceivable set of facts that could provide a rational basis for the classification.'" Furthermore, a state was under "no obligation to produce evidence to sustain the rationality of a statutory classification," which "'may be based on rational speculation unsupported by evidence or empirical data.'" Rather, "'the burden is on the one attacking the legislative arrangement to negative every conceivable basis which might support it.'"

Once the Court in *Heller* had identified the extremely deferential standard that it was going to use, the analysis came easily. The lower standard of proof for commitment of the mentally retarded was justified, according to the Court, first, because mental retardation is easier to diagnose than mental illness, and second, because a finding of danger to the community is easier to establish for the mentally retarded. For the Court, this was sufficient because there was a "'reasonably conceivable set of facts'" from which the state could make these conclusions. In addition, the Court also found a third justification for the distinction, that the treatment of the mentally retarded who are committed is much less invasive than is the treatment for those who are committed as mentally ill. As for the involvement of guardian and family members as parties to the proceedings, the state "may have concluded" that family members have known the retarded person for many years and may have valuable insights that will help the commitment process. It was quite clear after *Heller* that the Supreme Court did not consider the mentally retarded a suspect class nor would it have to apply heightened scrutiny to classifications that disadvantaged the mentally retarded.

C. AGE IS NOT A SUSPECT CLASSIFICATION

Massachusetts Bd. of Retirement v. Murgia
427 U.S. 307 (1976)

[The part of this case that determined that a mandatory retirement for state troopers satisfied rational basis review is contained in Chapter 1. Here the Court considers whether age is a suspect classification.]

We need state only briefly our reasons for agreeing that strict scrutiny is not the proper test for determining whether the mandatory retirement provision denies appellee equal protection. *San Antonio School District v. Rodriguez*, 411 U.S. 1, (1973), reaffirmed that equal protection analysis requires strict scrutiny of a legislative classification only when the classification impermissibly interferes with the exercise of a fundamental right or operates to the peculiar disadvantage of a suspect class. Mandatory retirement at age 50 under the Massachusetts statute involves neither situation.

Nor does the class of uniformed state police officers over 50 constitute a suspect class for purposes of equal protection analysis. *Rodriguez, supra*, 411 U.S. at 28, observed that a suspect class is one "saddled with such disabilities, or subjected to such a history of purposeful unequal treatment, or relegated to such a position of political powerlessness as to command extraordinary protection from the majoritarian political process." While the treatment of the aged in this Nation has not been wholly free of discrimination, such persons, unlike, say, those who have been discriminated against on the basis of race or national origin, have not experienced a "history of purposeful unequal treatment" or been subjected to unique disabilities on the basis of stereotyped characteristics not truly indicative of their abilities. The class subject to the compulsory retirement feature of the Massachusetts statute consists of uniformed state police officers over the age of 50. It cannot be said to discriminate only against the elderly. Rather, it draws the line at a certain age in middle life. But even old age does not define a "discrete and insular" group, *United States v. Carolene Products Co.*, 304 U.S. 144, 152-153, n. 4 (1938), in need of "extraordinary protection from the majoritarian political process." Instead, it marks a stage that each of us will reach if we live out our normal span. Even if the statute could be said to impose a penalty upon a class defined as the aged, it would not impose a distinction sufficiently akin to those classifications that we have found suspect to call for strict judicial scrutiny.

Under the circumstances, it is unnecessary to subject the State's resolution of competing interests in this case to the degree of critical examination that our cases under the Equal Protection Clause recently have characterized as "strict judicial scrutiny."

NOTES

1. The elderly are not a suspect class. The *Murgia* Court focuses on the following:

(a) Discrete and insular minority. "But even old age does not define a 'discrete and insular' group, in need of 'extraordinary protection from the majoritarian political process.' Instead, it marks a stage that each of us will reach if we live out our normal span." If the elderly are a numerical minority, they are a very influential minority with a substantial influence on the political process. And while we are not all going eventually to become black or female, most of us will become elderly. It is not likely that the majority will substantially disadvantage a group that most members of the majority will eventually be members of.

(b) Relevance. "Physical ability generally declines with age."

(c) History of discrimination and stereotyping. "While the treatment of the aged in this Nation has not been wholly free of discrimination, such persons, unlike, say, those who have been discriminated against on the basis of race or national origin, have not experienced a 'history of purposeful unequal treatment' or been subjected to unique disabilities on the basis of stereotyped characteristics not truly indicative of their abilities."

2. In *Kimel v. Florida Bd. of Regents*, 528 U.S. 62 (2000), the Court confirmed that age is not a suspect classification. In that case, the Court considered whether Congress' power under Section 5 of the Fourteenth Amendment was sufficient to support the enactment of the Age Discrimination in Employment Act. The test of Congressional power was whether the conduct condemned by the Act was congruent and proportional to the conduct made unconstitutional under the Equal Protection Clause. *See* Chapter 9. The Court first had to determine the extent to which age discrimination violated the Equal Protection Clause. The Court stated:

> We have considered claims of unconstitutional age discrimination under the Equal Protection Clause three times. See *Gregory v. Ashcroft*, 501 U.S. 452 (1991); *Vance v. Bradley*, 440 U.S. 93 (1979); *Massachusetts Bd. of Retirement v. Murgia*, 427 U.S. 307 (1976) *(per curiam)*. In all three cases, we held that the age classifications at issue did not violate the Equal Protection Clause. See *Gregory, supra*, at 473; *Bradley, supra*, at 102–103, n. 20; *Murgia, supra*, at 317. Age classifications, unlike governmental conduct based on race or gender, cannot be characterized as "so seldom relevant to the achievement of any legitimate state interest that laws grounded in such considerations are deemed to reflect prejudice and antipathy." *Cleburne v. Cleburne Living Center, Inc.*, 473 U.S. 432, 440 (1985). Older persons, again, unlike those who suffer discrimination on the basis of race or gender, have not been subjected to a "history of purposeful unequal treatment." *Murgia, supra*, at 313 (quoting *San Antonio Independent School Dist. V. Rodriguez*, 411 U.S. 1, 28 (1973)). Old age also does not define a discrete and insular minority because all persons, if they live out their normal life spans, will experience it. 427 U.S., at 313–314. Accordingly, as we recognized in *Murgia, Bradley*, and *Gregory*, age is not a suspect classification under the Equal Protection Clause. See, *e.g., Gregory, supra*, at 470; *Bradley, supra*, at 97; *Murgia, supra*, at 313–314.

Since age was not a suspect class, there were few, if any, age classifications that would violate the Equal Protection Clause, and thus the Act failed the congruence and proportionality test.

3. In *Rethinking the Constitutionality of Age Discrimination: A Challenge to a Decades-Old Consensus*, 44 U.C. Davis L. Rev. 213 (2010), Professor Nina A. Kohn argues that "current Supreme Court precedent creates an opportunity for certain forms of age discrimination to be found to violate the Fourteenth Amendment's equal protection guarantees." She makes a case for intermediate scrutiny of age classifications. First, with regard to the *Murgia* Court's claim that the aged had not experienced a history of unequal treatment, she responds that "[t]his was flatly untrue," since there was evidence of "rampant age discrimination in employment based on unfounded stereotypes about older age." With regard to the Court's assertion that the elderly are

not a discrete and insular minority in need of protection from the majoritarian political process, she argues that the elderly should not be treated as a single, homogenous group but rather should be broken down into subcategories (the "young-old," the middle-old," and the "old-old.") With regard to the claim that age is not an immutable trait, she argues that, even though a person's age changes over time, it is immutable in the sense that the person has no control over it. Kohn identifies a common modern statute—the elder abuse reporting statute—that targets older adults and triggers a loss of their right to privacy in relation to medical records, and a lost expectation of confidentiality when dealing with doctors, lawyers, and clergy. A heightened level of review for age classifications would make it easier to challenge these statutes. Given, however, the current Supreme Court precedents in this area, heightened review of age classifications as they affect the elderly is very unlikely.

4. What about age classifications that treat *children* differently? There are a host of these. At age sixteen, one can get a driver's license. At age eighteen, one can vote. At age twenty-one, one can drink alcoholic beverages. Underlying these age distinctions for youth is the presumption that one's increasing age brings with it an increasing level of maturity so that the young person is likely to be ready to drive, vote, and drink.

The Supreme Court has not addressed the classifications that disadvantage children under the Equal Protection Clause but it has addressed the state's ability to treat children differently from adults. In *Planned Parenthood of Central Missouri v. Danforth*, 428 U.S. 52, 74 (1976), the Court stated that "Constitutional rights do not mature and come into being magically only when one attains the state-defined age of majority. Minors, as well as adults, are protected by the Constitution and possess constitutional rights." On the other hand, however, in *Prince v. Massachusetts*, 321 U.S. 158 (1944), the Court insisted "the power of the state to control the conduct of children reaches beyond the scope of its authority over adults."

Several lower courts have considered whether or not children are a suspect class and have determined that they are not. In *Cunningham v. Beavers*, 858 F.2d 269 (5rh Cir. 1988), the court, in determining that a school policy of allowing corporal punishment did not violate the Equal Protection Clause, declared that suspect classifications are "only those classifications which are likely to reflect deep seated prejudice rather than legislative rationality in pursuit of a legitimate objective. No cases have ever held, and we decline to hold, that children are a suspect class." *Id.* at 273. In *Bykofsky v. Borough of Middletown*, 401 F. Supp. 1242 (M.D. Pa. 1975), the court determined, with regard to a curfew ordinance aimed at teenagers, that age is not a suspect classification. The court explained why it is appropriate to treat children differently from adults:

> The age classification embodied in the ordinance is not arbitrary but rather rests on real and substantial differences between adults and minors which bear a just and reasonable relation to the statutory purposes of the enactment. Minors are a class founded on natural and intrinsic distinctions from adults—notably degree of maturity— and the court believes the state is free to give differential treatment to adults and youths based on inherent and practical differences . . .

> It is argued, why draw the line at eighteen instead of seventeen or twenty-one or some other age. The state can draw lines in a rational manner, and it is not unreasonable for a legislative body to conclude that those eighteen years of age or older as a class have achieved a sufficient degree of maturity so that there is no need to restrict their freedom of movement upon and activities on the street during the nighttime hours. Obviously, the

older the persons being regulated, the greater the burden on the state to justify the regulation in terms of reasonableness, and there would come an age beyond which a nocturnal curfew could not be constitutionally applied, absent extraordinary or emergency circumstances.

CHAPTER 8

IMPLIED FUNDAMENTAL RIGHTS & THE EQUAL PROTECTION CLAUSE

A. THE RELATIONSHIP BETWEEN IMPLIED FUNDAMENTAL RIGHTS UNDER THE DUE PROCESS CLAUSE AND IMPLIED FUNDAMENTAL RIGHTS UNDER THE EQUAL PROTECTION CLAUSE

The Constitution recognizes several explicit fundamental rights, such as the First Amendment's freedom of speech and freedom of religion, and the Fifth Amendment's protection against self-incrimination. In addition, there is a longstanding practice in the Court of recognizing implied fundamental rights, that is, rights considered of fundamental significance but not specifically identified in the text of the Constitution. For the most part, when the Court identifies an implied fundamental right, it looks to the term "liberty" in the Due Process Clause, a kind of reasoning that is called "substantive due process." Substantive due process claims are distinguished from "procedural due process" claims, which involve a requirement that the government provide a person some kind of notice and hearing when taking away life, liberty, or property.

The Court's earliest incursion into substantive due process reasoning was a series of cases at the end of the nineteenth century and the beginning of the twentieth in which the Court equated the term "liberty" in the Due Process Clause with "freedom of contract." In a line of cases epitomized by *Lochner v. New York*, 198 U.S. 45 (1905) (a case memorialized by its own verb — "Lochnerizing"), the Court found that state attempts to regulate contractual relations were an unconstitutional infringement on liberty. This meant that state statutes setting minimum wages or maximum hours in the workplace or protecting the right of workers to unionize were presumptively unconstitutional. The *Lochner* era ended in 1937 when the Court decided *West Coast Hotel v. Parrish,* 300 U.S. 379 (1937), a case that upheld a minimum wage statute and specifically overruled *Adkins v. Children's Hospital*, 261 U.S. 525 (1923), a *Lochner*-type case to the contrary. As the *Parrish* Court explained, "The Constitution does not speak of freedom of contract," and thus the "liberty" protected by the Constitution was not an "absolute and uncontrollable" liberty, but rather one subject to "regulation which is reasonable in relation to its subject."

Parrish effectively ended any kind of rigid scrutiny of government regulation of business and commercial matters in the name of protecting constitutional liberty. But substantive due process was not dead. During the 1920's, in the heart of the *Lochner* era, the Court had decided two cases—*Meyer v Nebraska*, 262 U.S. 290 (1923) and *Pierce v. Society of Sisters*, 268 U.S. 510 (1925)—in which the Court found that "liberty" in the Due Process Clause included the right of parents to some level of control over the upbringing and education of their children. The Court in these cases invalidated state statutes that prohibited the teaching of foreign languages and required parents to send their children to public schools. For the most part, however, the demise of the *Lochner* precedents meant that the Court's would not use the term "liberty" in the Due Process Clause to identify implied fundamental rights.

That changed in the 1960's and the 1970's, beginning with *Griswold v. Connecticut*, 381 U.S. 479 (1965) and then *Roe v. Wade*, 410 U.S. 113 (1973). In these cases, the Court developed a right to privacy that was, for the most part, derived from the term "liberty" in the Due Process Clause. This right to privacy included the right to use contraceptives and the right to terminate a pregnancy. As the Court explained in *Roe*, where these fundamental rights were involved, "regulation limiting these rights may be justified only by a compelling state interest." Although *Roe* remains a controversial decision, its finding of a fundamental right is anchored to the term "liberty" in the Due Process Clause.

Not so with the implied fundamental rights portion of equal protection doctrine. As a starting point, it is not at all apparent why there is any need for an equal protection version of the implied fundamental rights doctrine. At the conceptual level, the Due Process and Equal Protection Clauses are quite distinct and impose different types of limits on governmental conduct. The substantive version of the Due Process Clause imposes substantive limits on government when government action interferes with activity that is within a protected interest defined as "life," "liberty," or "property." On the other hand, the Equal Protection Clause imposes no substantive limitations on government. It works rather as a comparative limitation on government classifications, requiring that those similarly situated be treated similarly. While the rights found to be fundamental under the Due Process Clause must be traced to the word "liberty" in that clause, there is no comparable anchor that the Court can use to explain why it is treating certain rights as fundamental under the Equal Protection Clause. Notwithstanding these conceptual difficulties, however, the Court has in fact, in a long line of cases beginning in 1942, created an implied fundamental rights version of the Equal Protection Clause. And it has done so in a way that treats the two lines of precedents as interchangeable. Thus, although this chapter will focus on the Equal Protection's strain of fundamental rights reasoning, it will necessarily include references to the Court's Due Process precedents, for without those related Due Process cases, equal protection's implied fundamental rights cases would be incomplete and baffling.

The process begins in 1942 with *Skinner v. Oklahoma.*

B. PROCREATION AND MARRIAGE

Skinner v. Oklahoma
316 U.S. 535 (1942)

[Oklahoma had enacted a Habitual Criminal Sterilization Act that defined a "habitual criminal" as a person who had been convicted of three felonies involving moral turpitude. Under the act such persons were subject to compulsory sterilization, although those convicted of violating revenue

CHAPTER 8: IMPLIED FUNDAMENTAL RIGHTS & THE EQUAL PROTECTION CLAUSE

acts or of embezzlement were exempt. As a minor, Petitioner was convicted of the theft of chickens and, later, armed robbery. As a young adult, petitioner was also convicted of armed robbery. The Attorney General instituted proceedings that resulted in a court order requiring the state to perform a vasectomy on him. The petitioner challenged the Act as in violation of the Fourteenth Amendment.]

Mr. Justice DOUGLAS delivered the opinion of the Court.

This case touches a sensitive and important area of human rights. Oklahoma deprives certain individuals of a right which is basic to the perpetuation of a race-the right to have offspring. Oklahoma has decreed the enforcement of its law against petitioner, overruling his claim that it violated the Fourteenth Amendment. Because that decision raised grave and substantial constitutional questions, we granted the petition for certiorari. Several objections to the constitutionality of the Act have been pressed upon us. It is urged that the Act cannot be sustained as an exercise of the police power in view of the state of scientific authorities respecting inheritability of criminal traits. It is argued that due process is lacking because under this Act, unlike the act upheld in *Buck v. Bell*, 274 U.S. 200, the defendant is given no opportunity to be heard on the issue as to whether he is the probable potential parent of socially undesirable offspring. It is also suggested that the Act is penal in character and that the sterilization provided for is cruel and unusual punishment and violative of the Fourteenth Amendment. We pass those points without intimating an opinion on them, for there is a feature of the Act which clearly condemns it. That is its failure to meet the requirements of the equal protection clause of the Fourteenth Amendment.

We do not stop to point out all of the inequalities in this Act. A few examples will suffice. In Oklahoma grand larceny is a felony. Larceny is grand larceny when the property taken exceeds $20 in value. Embezzlement is punishable 'in the manner prescribed for feloniously stealing property of the value of that embezzled.' Hence he who embezzles property worth more than $20 is guilty of a felony. A clerk who appropriates over $20 from his employer's till and a stranger who steals the same amount are thus both guilty of felonies. If the latter repeats his act and is convicted three times, he may be sterilized. But the clerk is not subject to the pains and penalties of the Act no matter how large his embezzlements nor how frequent his convictions. A person who enters a chicken coop and steals chickens commits a felony; and he may be sterilized if he is thrice convicted. If, however, he is a bailee of the property and fraudulently appropriates it, he is an embezzler. Hence no matter how habitual his proclivities for embezzlement are and no matter how often his conviction, he may not be sterilized. Thus the nature of the two crimes is intrinsically the same and they are punishable in the same manner. Furthermore, the line between them follows close distinctions--distinctions comparable to those highly technical ones which shaped the common law as to 'trespass' or 'taking'. Bishop, Criminal Law, 9th Ed., Vol. 2, §§ 760, 799, *et seq*. There may be larceny by fraud rather than embezzlement even where the owner of the personal property delivers it to the defendant, if the latter has at that time 'a fraudulent intention to make use of the possession as a means of converting such property to his own use, and does so convert it.' If the fraudulent intent occurs later and the defendant converts the property, he is guilty of embezzlement. Whether a particular act is larceny by fraud or embezzlement thus turns not on the intrinsic quality of the act but on when the felonious intent arose - a question for the jury under appropriate instructions.

It was stated in *Buck v. Bell, supra,* that the claim that state legislation violates the equal protection clause of the Fourteenth Amendment is 'the usual last resort of constitutional arguments.' 274 U.S. page 208. Under our constitutional system the States in determining the reach and scope of particular legislation need not provide 'abstract symmetry'. *Patsone v.*

Pennsylvania, 232 U.S. 138, 144. They may mark and set apart the classes and types of problems according to the needs and as dictated or suggested by experience. See *People of State of New York ex rel. Bryant v. Zimmerman*, 278 U.S. 63, and cases cited. It was in that connection that Mr. Justice Holmes, speaking for the Court in *Bain Peanut Co. v. Pinson*, 282 U.S. 499, 501, stated, 'We must remember that the machinery of government would not work if it were not allowed a little play in its joints.' Only recently we reaffirmed the view that the equal protection clause does not prevent the legislature from recognizing 'degrees of evil' (*Truax v. Raich*, 239 U.S. 33, 43) by our ruling in *Tigner v. Texas*, 310 U.S. 141, 147, that 'the Constitution does not require things which are different in fact or opinion to be treated in law as though they were the same.' And see *Nashville, Chattanooga & St. Louis Ry. v. Browning*, 310 U.S. 362. Thus, if we had here only a question as to a State's classification of crimes, such as embezzlement or larceny, no substantial federal question would be raised. For a State is not constrained in the exercise of its police power to ignore experience which marks a class of offenders or a family of offenses for special treatment. Nor is it prevented by the equal protection clause from confining 'its restrictions to those classes of cases where the need is deemed to be clearest'. As stated in *Buck v. Bell, supra*, 274 U.S. page 208, 'the law does all that is needed when it does all that it can, indicates a policy, applies it to all within the lines, and seeks to bring within the lines all similarly situated so far and so fast as its means allow.'

But the instant legislation runs afoul of the equal protection clause, though we give Oklahoma that large deference which the rule of the foregoing cases requires. We are dealing here with legislation which involves one of the basic civil rights of man. Marriage and procreation are fundamental to the very existence and survival of the race. The power to sterilize, if exercised, may have subtle, farreaching and devastating effects. In evil or reckless hands it can cause races or types which are inimical to the dominant group to wither and disappear. There is no redemption for the individual whom the law touches. Any experiment which the State conducts is to his irreparable injury. He is forever deprived of a basic liberty. We mention these matters not to reexamine the scope of the police power of the States. We advert to them merely in emphasis of our view that strict scrutiny of the classification which a State makes in a sterilization law is essential, lest unwittingly or otherwise invidious discriminations are made against groups or types of individuals in violation of the constitutional guaranty of just and equal laws. The guaranty of 'equal protection of the laws is a pledge of the protection of equal laws.' *Yick Wo v. Hopkins*, 118 U.S. 356, 369. When the law lays an unequal hand on those who have committed intrinsically the same quality of offense and sterilizes one and not the other, it has made as an invidious a discrimination as if it had selected a particular race or nationality for oppressive treatment. *Yick Wo v. Hopkins, supra*; *Gaines v. Canada*, 305 U.S. 337. Sterilization of those who have thrice committed grand larceny with immunity for those who are embezzlers is a clear, pointed, unmistakable discrimination. Oklahoma makes no attempt to say that he who commits larceny by trespass or trick or fraud has biologically inheritable traits which he who commits embezzlement lacks. Oklahoma's line between larceny by fraud and embezzlement is determined, as we have noted, 'with reference to the time when the fraudulent intent to convert the property to the taker's own use' arises. We have not the slightest basis for inferring that that line has any significance in eugenics nor that the inheritability of criminal traits follows the neat legal distinctions which the law has marked between those two offenses. In terms of fines and imprisonment the crimes of larceny and embezzlement rate the same under the Oklahoma code. Only when it comes to sterilization are the pains and penalties of the law different. The equal protection clause would indeed be a formula of empty words if such conspicuously artificial lines could be drawn. In *Buck v. Bell, supra*, the Virginia statute was upheld though it applied only to feebleminded persons in institutions of the State. But it was pointed out that 'so far as the operations enable those who otherwise must be kept confined to be returned to the world, and thus open the asylum to others, the equality aimed at will be more nearly reached.' 274 U.S. page 208. Here there is no such saving feature. Embezzlers are forever free. Those who steal or take in other ways are not. If such a classification were permitted, the technical common law concept of a 'trespass' (Bishop, Criminal Law, 9th Ed., vol. 1, §§ 566, 567) based on distinctions which are 'very largely dependent upon history for explanation' (Holmes, The Common Law, p. 73) could readily become a rule of human genetics.

It is true that the Act has a broad severability clause. But we will not endeavor to determine whether its application would solve the equal protection difficulty. The Supreme Court of Oklahoma sustained the Act without reference to the severability clause. We have therefore a situation where the Act as construed and applied to petitioner is allowed to perpetuate the discrimination which we have found to be fatal. Whether the severability clause would be so applied as to remove this particular constitutional objection is a question which may be more appropriately left for adjudication by the Oklahoma court. That is reemphasized here by our uncertainty as to what excision, if any, would be made as a matter of Oklahoma law. It is by no means clear whether if an excision were made, this particular constitutional difficulty might be solved by enlarging on the one hand or contracting on the other (cf. Mr. Justice Brandeis dissenting, *National Life Insurance Co. v. United States*, 277 U.S. 508, 534, 535) the class of criminals who might be sterilized.

Reversed.

Mr. Chief Justice STONE concurring.

I concur in the result, but I am not persuaded that we are aided in reaching it by recourse to the equal protection clause. If Oklahoma may resort generally to the sterilization of criminals on the assumption that their propensities are transmissible to future generations by inheritance, I seriously doubt that the equal protection clause requires it to apply the measure to all criminals in the first instance, or to none. And so I think the real question we have to consider is not one of equal protection, but whether the wholesale condemnation of a class to such an invasion of personal liberty, without opportunity to any individual to show that his is not the type of case which would justify resort to it, satisfies the demands of due process.

NOTES

1. *Skinner* is the beginning of the fundamental rights branch of the Equal Protection Clause but the doctrine at this point is not yet fully formed. The Court noted that marriage and procreation are "fundamental to the very existence and survival of the race," and that, therefore, "strict scrutiny of the classification . . . is essential." The Court, however, did not explain in a satisfactory way why procreation is "fundamental" for constitutional purposes nor did it explain what "strict scrutiny" means. The Court also characterized procreation as a basic civil right and as a basic liberty, which would suggest that the case is about the Due Process Clause, but clearly the Court's holding is about equal protection, not due process.

The Court's final, cryptic words emphasized the equal protection foundation of the case. The Court noted, "[i]t is by no means clear whether if an excision were made, this particular constitutional difficulty might be solved by enlarging on the one hand or contracting on the other . . . the class of criminals who might be sterilized." This suggests that if Oklahoma had been willing to sterilize all thrice-convicted criminals, without exceptions for certain white-collar criminals, the Equal Protection Clause might not stand in the way. But the Equal Protection Clause imposes a comparative obligation on the state—it must treat all thrice-convicted criminals similarly, either by sterilizing all or by sterilizing none. And of course the very likely outcome is that, since the state would be unwilling to sterilize all in that class, it could not sterilize any.

2. As Chief Justice Stone's concurring opinion suggested, *Skinner* could more obviously be viewed as a due process rather than an equal protection case. In fact, if the case arose in the first instance after the 1973 case, *Roe v. Wade*, it very likely would have been a due process case in as much as *Roe* found that the right to procreate was part of the right to privacy protected by the term "liberty" in the Due Process Clause. *Skinner*, however was decided just five years after *West Coast Hotel v. Parrish*, the case that had effectively ended the *Lochner* kind of reasoning that had exalted the term "liberty" in a way that prevented most government regulation of commerce. The equal protection reasoning in *Skinner* was thus able to provide protection of a fundamental right without reviving the discredited *Lochner* doctrine. The decision to avoid *Lochner* effectively created a new equal protection doctrine but the Court neither then nor since has ever made it clear where the one doctrine ends and the other begins.

Zablocki v. Redhail
434 U.S. 374 (1978)

[A Wisconsin statute provided that any person having minor issue not in his custody and whom he was under obligation to support was not permitted to marry without first obtaining a court order granting permission to marry. Permission would not be granted unless the marriage applicant first proved compliance with the support obligation. While a high school student, Redhail fathered a child for whom he was not making support payments. He was denied a license to marry due to these child support arrearages. He filed suit challenging the statute as violative of the Equal Protection and Due Process Clauses of the Fourteenth Amendment.]

Mr. Justice MARSHALL delivered the opinion of the Court.

II

In evaluating [the Wisconsin statute] under the Equal Protection Clause, "we must first determine what burden of justification the classification created thereby must meet, by looking to the nature of the classification and the individual interests affected." *Memorial Hospital v. Maricopa County*, 415 U.S. 250, 253 (1974). Since our past decisions make clear that the right to marry is of fundamental importance, and since the classification at issue here significantly interferes with the exercise of that right, we believe that "critical examination" of the state interests advanced in support of the classification is required. *Massachusetts Board of Retirement v. Murgia*, 427 U.S. 307, 312, 314 (1976); see, *e. g., San Antonio Independent School Dist. v. Rodriguez*, 411 U.S. 1, 17 (1973).

The leading decision of this Court on the right to marry is *Loving v. Virginia*, 388 U.S. 1 (1967). In that case, an interracial couple who had been convicted of violating Virginia's miscegenation laws challenged the statutory scheme on both equal protection and due process grounds. The Court's opinion could have rested solely on the ground that the statutes discriminated on the basis of race in violation of the Equal Protection Clause. But the Court went on to hold that the laws arbitrarily deprived the couple of a fundamental liberty protected by the Due Process Clause, the freedom to marry. The Court's language on the latter point bears repeating:

"The freedom to marry has long been recognized as one of the vital personal rights essential to the orderly pursuit of happiness by free men.

"Marriage is one of the 'basic civil rights of man,' fundamental to our very existence and survival." *Id.*, at 12, quoting *Skinner v. Oklahoma ex rel. Williamson*, 316 U.S. 535, 541 (1942).

Although *Loving* arose in the context of racial discrimination, prior and subsequent decisions of this Court confirm that the right to marry is of fundamental importance for all individuals. Long ago, in *Maynard v. Hill*, 125 U.S. 190 (1888), the Court characterized marriage as "the most important relation in life," *id.*, at 205, and as "the foundation of the family and of society, without which there would be neither civilization nor progress," *id.*, at 211. In *Meyer v. Nebraska*, 262 U.S. 390 (1923), the Court recognized that the right "to marry, establish a home and bring up children" is a central part of the liberty protected by the Due Process Clause, *id.*, at 399, and in *Skinner v. Oklahoma ex rel. Williamson, supra*, 316 U.S. 535 (1942), marriage was described as "fundamental to the very existence and survival of the race," 316 U.S., at 541.

More recent decisions have established that the right to marry is part of the fundamental "right of privacy" implicit in the Fourteenth Amendment's Due Process Clause. In *Griswold v. Connecticut*, 381 U.S. 479 (1965), the Court observed:

> We deal with a right of privacy older than the Bill of Rights-older than our political parties, older than our school system. Marriage is a coming together for better or for worse, hopefully enduring, and intimate to the degree of being sacred. It is an association that promotes a way of life, not causes; a harmony in living, not political faiths; a bilateral loyalty, not commercial or social projects. Yet it is an association for as noble a purpose as any involved in our prior decisions.

Cases subsequent to *Griswold* and *Loving* have routinely categorized the decision to marry as among the personal decisions protected by the right of privacy. See generally *Whalen v. Roe*, 429 U.S. 589, 598-600 (1977). For example, last Term in *Carey v. Population Services International*, 431 U.S. 678 (1977), we declared:

> While the outer limits of [the right of personal privacy] have not been marked by the Court, it is clear that among the decisions that an individual may make without unjustified government interference are personal decisions 'relating to marriage, *Loving v. Virginia*, 388 U.S. 1, 12 (1967); procreation, *Skinner v. Oklahoma ex rel. Williamson*, 316 U.S. 535, 541-542 (1942); contraception, *Eisenstadt v. Baird*, 405 U.S. [438], at 453-454; family relationships, *Prince v. Massachusetts*, 321 U.S. 158, 166 (1944); and child rearing and education, *Pierce v. Society of Sisters*, 268 U.S. 510, 535 (1925); *Meyer v. Nebraska*, [262 U.S. 390, 399 (1923)].

See also *Cleveland Board of Education v. LaFleur*, 414 U.S. 632, 639-640 (1974) ("This Court has long recognized that freedom of personal choice in matters of marriage and family life is one of the liberties protected by the Due Process Clause of the Fourteenth Amendment").

It is not surprising that the decision to marry has been placed on the same level of importance as decisions relating to procreation, childbirth, child rearing, and family relationships. As the facts of this case illustrate, it would make little sense to recognize a right of privacy with respect to other matters of family life and not with respect to the decision to enter the relationship that is the foundation of the family in our society. The woman whom appellee desired to marry had a fundamental right to seek an abortion of their expected child, see *Roe v. Wade, supra,* or to bring the child into life to suffer the myriad social, if not economic, disabilities that the status of illegitimacy brings, see *Trimble v. Gordon,* 430 U.S. 762, 768-770, and n. 13 (1977); *Weber v. Aetna Casualty & Surety Co.,* 406 U.S. 164, 175-176 (1972). Surely, a decision to marry and raise the child in a traditional family setting must receive equivalent protection. And, if appellee's right to procreate means anything at all, it must imply some right to enter the only relationship in which the State of Wisconsin allows sexual relations legally to take place.

By reaffirming the fundamental character of the right to marry, we do not mean to suggest that every state regulation which relates in any way to the incidents of or prerequisites for marriage must be subjected to rigorous scrutiny. To the contrary, reasonable regulations that do not significantly interfere with decisions to enter into the marital relationship may legitimately be imposed. See *Califano v. Jobst,* 434 U.S. 47. The statutory classification at issue here, however, clearly does interfere directly and substantially with the right to marry.

Under the challenged statute, no Wisconsin resident in the affected class may marry in Wisconsin or elsewhere without a court order, and marriages contracted in violation of the statute are both void and punishable as criminal offenses. Some of those in the affected class, like appellee, will never be able to obtain the necessary court order, because they either lack the financial means to meet their support obligations or cannot prove that their children will not become public charges. These persons are absolutely prevented from getting married. Many others, able in theory to satisfy the statute's requirements, will be sufficiently burdened by having to do so that they will in effect be coerced into forgoing their right to marry. And even those who can be persuaded to meet the statute's requirements suffer a serious intrusion into their freedom of choice in an area in which we have held such freedom to be fundamental.

III

When a statutory classification significantly interferes with the exercise of a fundamental right, it cannot be upheld unless it is supported by sufficiently important state interests and is closely tailored to effectuate only those interests. See, *e. g., Carey v. Population Services International,* 431 U.S., at 686; *Memorial Hospital v. Maricopa County,* 415 U.S., at 262-263; *San Antonio Independent School Dist. v. Rodriguez,* 411 U.S., at 16-17; *Bullock v. Carter,* 405 U.S. 134, 144 (1972). Appellant asserts that two interests are served by the challenged statute: the permission-to-marry proceeding furnishes an opportunity to counsel the applicant as to the necessity of fulfilling his prior support obligations; and the welfare of the out-of-custody children is protected. We may accept for present purposes that these are legitimate and substantial interests, but, since the means selected by the State for achieving these interests unnecessarily impinge on the right to marry, the statute cannot be sustained.

[The Court determined that no counseling of applicants was in fact required or provided by the statue and that there were better means to safeguard the welfare of children. Thus, the interests advanced in support of it did not justify the statutory classification.]

The judgment of the District Court is, accordingly, *Affirmed.*

Mr. Justice STEWART, concurring in the judgment.

I cannot join the opinion of the Court. To hold, as the Court does, that the Wisconsin statute violates the Equal Protection Clause seems to me to misconceive the meaning of that constitutional guarantee. The Equal Protection Clause deals not with substantive rights or freedoms but with invidiously discriminatory classifications. *San Antonio Independent School Dist. v. Rodriguez,* 411 U.S. 1, 59 (concurring opinion). The paradigm of its violation is, of course, classification by race. *McLaughlin v. Florida,* 379 U.S. 184; *Loving v. Virginia,* 388 U.S. 1, 13 (concurring opinion).

Like almost any law, the Wisconsin statute now before us affects some people and does not affect others. But to say that it thereby creates "classifications" in the equal protection sense strikes me as little short of fantasy. The problem in this case is not one of discriminatory classifications, but of unwarranted encroachment upon a constitutionally protected freedom. I think that the Wisconsin statute is unconstitutional because it exceeds the bounds of permissible state regulation of marriage, and invades the sphere of liberty protected by the Due Process Clause of the Fourteenth Amendment.

II

In an opinion of the Court half a century ago, Mr. Justice Holmes described an equal protection claim as "the usual last resort of constitutional arguments." *Buck v. Bell,* 274 U.S. 200, 208. Today equal protection doctrine has become the Court's chief instrument for invalidating state laws. Yet, in a case like this one, the doctrine is no more than substantive due process by another name.

Although the Court purports to examine the bases for legislative classifications and to compare the treatment of legislatively defined groups, it actually erects substantive limitations on what States may do. Thus, the effect of the Court's decision in this case is not to require Wisconsin to draw its legislative classifications with greater precision or to afford similar treatment to similarly situated persons. Rather, the message of the Court's opinion is that Wisconsin may not use its control over marriage to achieve the objectives of the state statute. Such restrictions on basic governmental power are at the heart of substantive due process.

The Court is understandably reluctant to rely on substantive due process. See *Roe v. Wade,* 410 U.S., at 167-168 (concurring opinion). But to embrace the essence of that doctrine under the guise of equal protection serves no purpose but obfuscation. "[C]ouched in slogans and ringing phrases," the Court's equal protection doctrine shifts the focus of the judicial inquiry away from its proper concerns, which include "the nature of the individual interest affected, the extent to which it is affected, the rationality of the connection between legislative means and purpose, the existence of alternative means for effectuating the purpose, and the degree of confidence we may have that the statute reflects the legislative concern for the purpose that would legitimately support the means chosen." *Williams v. Illinois, supra,* 399 U.S., at 260 (Harlan, J., concurring in result).

To conceal this appropriate inquiry invites mechanical or thoughtless application of misfocused doctrine. To bring it into the open forces a healthy and responsible recognition of the nature and purpose of the extreme power we wield when, in invalidating a state law in the name of the Constitution, we invalidate *pro tanto* the process of representative democracy in one of the sovereign States of the Union.

NOTES

1. *Zablocki* is a good example of how interlocked the Court's due process and equal protection decisions have become with regard to marriage and procreation. *Zablocki* purports to be an equal protection decision and the Court therefore strains to find two different classes that are unequally treated. The Court identified the two classes as those who needed court permission to marry and those who did not. In terms of the precedents it cites, the *Zablocki* Court is quite inclusive, citing due process precedents in *Meyer v. Nebraska, Loving v. Virginia,* and *Griswold v. Connecticut,* as well as an equal protection precedent in *Skinner*. Justice Stewart's concurring opinion makes this illogic clear, identifying the problem as "not one of discriminatory classifications, but of unwarranted encroachment upon a constitutionally protected freedom," that is, not an equal protection problem, but a due process one.

2. Justice Marshall, who wrote the majority opinion, was never in favor of a rigid three-tier level of review in equal protection cases. He preferred a more flexible balancing approach, under which the Court would weigh the importance of the government issue advanced against the importance of the individual interest that was adversely affected. In *Zablocki*, Marshall stated the test as "[w]hen a statutory classification significantly interferes with the exercise of a fundamental right, it cannot be upheld unless it is supported by sufficiently important state interests and is closely tailored to effectuate only those interests." Marshall assumed that the two interests advanced by the state (counseling for the parent and providing support for the child) were sufficiently important but that the means selected to advance those interests were not closely enough tailored to advance those interests.

C. VOTING

Having effectively created in 1942 in *Skinner* an implied fundamental rights equal protection doctrine that covered procreation, the Court in the 1960's and 1970's identified additional implied fundamental rights under the Equal Protection Clause. The first of these cases was *Reynolds v. Sims*.

1. ACCESS TO THE VOTING BOOTH AND THE RIGHT TO HAVE ONE'S BALLOT COUNTED EQUALLY

Reynolds v. Sims
377 U.S. 533 (1964)

[Plaintiffs were residents, taxpayers, and voters of Jefferson County, Alabama. They filed a class action lawsuit alleging that, because seats in the state legislature were based on a 1900 census and did not consider sixty years of uneven population growth, Alabama's method of legislative apportionment was in violation of the Equal Protection Clause of the Fourteenth Amendment.]

Mr. Chief Justice WARREN delivered the opinion of the Court.

Involved in these cases are an appeal and two cross-appeals from a decision of the Federal District Court for the Middle District of Alabama holding invalid, under the Equal Protection Clause of the Federal Constitution, the existing and two legislative proposed plans for the apportionment of seats in the two houses of the Alabama Legislature, and ordering into effect a temporary reapportionment plan comprised of parts of the proposed but judicially disapproved measures.

II.

Undeniably the Constitution of the United States protects the right of all qualified citizens to vote, in state as well as in federal elections. A consistent line of decisions by this Court in cases involving attempts to deny or restrict the right of suffrage has made this indelibly clear. It has been repeatedly recognized that all qualified voters have a constitutionally protected right to vote, *Ex parte Yarbrough*, 110 U.S. 651, and to have their votes counted, *United States v. Mosley*, 238 U.S. 383. In *Mosley* the Court stated that it is 'as equally unquestionable that the right to have one's vote counted is as open to protection as the right to put a ballot in a box.' 238 U.S., at 386. The right to vote can neither be denied outright, *Guinn v. United States*, 238 U.S. 347, *Lane v. Wilson*, 307 U.S. 268, nor destroyed by alteration of ballots, see *United States v. Classic*, 313 U.S. 299, 315, nor diluted by ballot-box stuffing *Ex parte Siebold*, 100 U.S. 371, *United States v. Saylor*, 322 U.S. 385. As the Court stated in *Classic*, 'Obviously included within the right to choose, secured by the Constitution, is the right of qualified voters within a state to cast their ballots and have them counted.' 313 U.S., at 315. Racially based gerrymandering, *Gomillion v. Lightfoot*, 364 U.S. 339, and the conducting of white primaries, *Nixon v. Herndon*, 273 U.S. 536, *Nixon v. Condon*, 286 U.S. 73, *Smith v. Allwright*, 321 U.S. 649, *Terry v. Adams*, 345 U.S. 461, both of which result in denying to some citizens their right to vote, have been held to be constitutionally impermissible. And history has seen a continuing expansion of the scope of the right of suffrage in this country. The right to vote freely for the candidate of one's choice is of the essence of a democratic society, and any restrictions on that right strike at the heart of representative government. And the right of suffrage can be denied by a debasement or dilution of the weight of a citizen's vote just as effectively as by wholly prohibiting the free exercise of the franchise.

In *Baker v. Carr*, 369 U.S. 186, we held that a claim asserted under the Equal Protection Clause challenging the constitutionality of a State's apportionment of seats in its legislature, on the ground that the right to vote of certain citizens was effectively impaired since debased and diluted, in effect presented a justiciable controversy subject to adjudication by federal courts. The spate of similar cases filed and decided by lower courts since our decision in *Baker* amply shows that the problem of state legislative malapportionment is one that is perceived to exist in a large number of the States. In *Baker*, a suit involving an attack on the apportionment of seats in the Tennessee Legislature, we remanded to the District Court, which had dismissed the action, for consideration on the merits. We intimated no view as to the proper constitutional standards for evaluating the validity of a state legislative apportionment scheme. Nor did we give any consideration to the question of appropriate remedies. Rather, we simply stated:

> Beyond noting that we have no cause at this stage to doubt the District Court will be able to fashion relief if violations of constitutional rights are found, it is improper now to consider what remedy would be most appropriate if appellants prevail at the trial.

We indicated in *Baker*, however, that the Equal Protection Clause provides discoverable and manageable standards for use by lower courts in determining the constitutionality of a state legislative apportionment scheme, and we stated:

> Nor need the appellants, in order to succeed in this action, ask the Court to enter upon policy determinations for which judicially manageable standards are lacking. Judicial standards under the Equal Protection Clause are well developed and familiar, and it has

been open to courts since the enactment of the Fourteenth Amendment to determine, if on the particular facts they must, that a discrimination reflects no policy, but simply arbitrary and capricious action.

A predominant consideration in determining whether a State's legislative apportionment scheme constitutes an invidious discrimination violative of rights asserted under the Equal Protection Clause is that the rights allegedly impaired are individual and personal in nature. As stated by the Court in *United States v. Bathgate*, 246 U.S. 220, 227, '(t)he right to vote is personal.' While the result of a court decision in a state legislative apportionment controversy may be to require the restructuring of the geographical distribution of seats in a state legislature, the judicial focus must be concentrated upon ascertaining whether there has been any discrimination against certain of the State's citizens which constitutes an impermissible impairment of their constitutionally protected right to vote. Like *Skinner v. Oklahoma*, 316 U.S. 535, such a case 'touches a sensitive and important area of human rights,' and 'involves one of the basic civil rights of man,' presenting questions of alleged 'invidious discriminations against groups or types of individuals in violation of the constitutional guaranty of just and equal laws.' 316 U.S., at 536. Undoubtedly, the right of suffrage is a fundamental matter in a free and democratic society. Especially since the right to exercise the franchise in a free and unimpaired manner is preservative of other basic civil and political rights, any alleged infringement of the right of citizens to vote must be carefully and meticulously scrutinized. Almost a century ago, in *Yick Wo v. Hopkins*, 118 U.S. 356, the Court referred to 'the political franchise of voting' as 'a fundamental political right, because preservative of all rights.' 118 U.S., at 370.

Legislators represent people, not trees or acres. Voters, not farms or cities or economic interests, elect legislators. As long as ours is a representative form of government, and our legislatures are those instruments of government elected directly by and directly representative of the people, the right to elect legislators in a free and unimpaired fashion is a bedrock of our political system. It could hardly be gainsaid that a constitutional claim had been asserted by an allegation that certain otherwise qualified voters had been entirely prohibited from voting for members of their state legislature. And, if a State should provide that the votes of citizens in one part of the State should be given two times, or five times, or 10 times the weight of votes of citizens in another part of the State, it could hardly be contended that the right to vote of those residing in the disfavored areas had not been effectively diluted. It would appear extraordinary to suggest that a State could be constitutionally permitted to enact a law providing that certain of the State's voters could vote two, five, or 10 times for their legislative representatives, while voters living elsewhere could vote only once. And it is inconceivable that a state law to the effect that, in counting votes for legislators, the votes of citizens in one part of the State would be multiplied by two, five, or 10, while the votes of persons in another area would be counted only at face value, could be constitutionally sustainable. Of course, the effect of state legislative districting schemes that give the same number of representatives to unequal numbers of constituents is identical. Overweighting and overvaluation of the votes of those living here has the certain effect of dilution and undervaluation of the votes of those living there.

The resulting discrimination against those individual voters living in disfavored areas is easily demonstrable mathematically. Their right to vote is simply not the same right to vote as that of those living in a favored part of the State. Two, five, or 10 of them must vote before the effect of their voting is equivalent to that of their favored neighbor. Weighting the votes of citizens differently, by any method or means, merely because of where they happen to reside, hardly seems justifiable. One must be ever aware that the Constitution forbids 'sophisticated as well as simpleminded modes of discrimination.' *Lane v. Wilson*, 307 U.S. 268, 275; *Gomillion v. Lightfoot*, 364 U.S. 339, 342. As we stated in *Wesberry v. Sanders*, supra:

We do not believe that the Framers of the Constitution intended to permit the same vote-diluting discrimination to be accomplished through the device of districts containing widely varied numbers of inhabitants. To say that a vote is worth more in one district than in another would run counter to our fundamental ideas of democratic government.

Logically, in a society ostensibly grounded on representative government, it would seem reasonable that a majority of the people of a State could elect a majority of that State's legislators. To conclude differently, and to sanction minority control of state legislative bodies, would appear to deny majority rights in a way that far surpasses any possible denial of minority rights that might otherwise be thought to result. Since legislatures are responsible for enacting laws by which all citizens are to be governed, they should be bodies that are collectively responsive to the popular will. And the concept of equal protection has been traditionally viewed as requiring the uniform treatment of persons standing in the same relation to the governmental action questioned or challenged. With respect to the allocation of legislative representation, all voters, as citizens of a State, stand in the same relation regardless of where they live. Any suggested criteria for the differentiation of citizens are insufficient to justify any discrimination, as to the weight of their votes, unless relevant to the permissible purposes of legislative apportionment. Since the achieving of fair and effective representation for all citizens is concededly the basic aim of legislative apportionment, we conclude that the Equal Protection Clause guarantees the opportunity for equal participation by all voters in the election of state legislators. Diluting the weight of votes because of place of residence impairs basic constitutional rights under the Fourteenth Amendment just as much as invidious discriminations based upon factors such as race, *Brown v. Board of Education*, 347 U.S. 483, or economic status, *Griffin v. People of State of Illinois*, 351 U.S. 12, *Douglas v. People of State of California*, 372 U.S. 353. Our constitutional system amply provides for the protection of minorities by means other than giving them majority control of state legislatures. And the democratic ideals of equality and majority rule, which have served this Nation so well in the past, are hardly of any less significance for the present and the future.

We are told that the matter of apportioning representation in a state legislature is a complex and many-faceted one. We are advised that States can rationally consider factors other than population in apportioning legislative representation. We are admonished not to restrict the power of the States to impose differing views as to political philosophy on their citizens. We are cautioned about the dangers of entering into political thickets and mathematical quagmires. Our answer is this: a denial of constitutionally protected rights demands judicial protection; our oath and our office require no less of us. As stated in *Gomillion v. Lightfoot, supra*:

> When a State exercises power wholly within the domain of state interest, it is insulated from federal judicial review. But such insulation is not carried over when state power is used as an instrument for circumventing a federally protected right.

To the extent that a citizen's right to vote is debased, he is that much less a citizen. The fact that an individual lives here or there is not a legitimate reason for overweighting or diluting the efficacy of his vote. The complexions of societies and civilizations change, often with amazing rapidity. A nation once primarily rural in character becomes predominantly urban. Representation schemes once fair and equitable become archaic and outdated. But the basic principle of representative government remains, and must remain, unchanged—the weight of a citizen's vote cannot be made to depend on where he lives. Population is, of necessity, the starting point for consideration and the controlling criterion for judgment in legislative apportionment controversies. A citizen, a qualified voter, is no more nor no less so because he lives in the city or on the farm. This is the clear and strong command of our Constitution's Equal Protection Clause. This is an essential part of the concept of a government of laws and not men. This is at the heart of Lincoln's vision of 'government of the people, by the people, (and) for the people.' The Equal Protection Clause demands no less than substantially equal state legislative representation for all citizens, of all places as well as of all races.

We hold that, as a basic constitutional standard, the Equal Protection Clause requires that the seats in both houses of a bicameral state legislature must be apportioned on a population basis. Simply stated, an individual's right to vote for state legislators is unconstitutionally impaired when its weight is in a substantial fashion diluted when compared with votes of citizens living on other parts of the State.

By holding that as a federal constitutional requisite both houses of a state legislature must be apportioned on a population basis, we mean that the Equal Protection Clause requires that a State make an honest and good faith effort to construct districts, in both houses of its legislature, as nearly of equal population as is practicable. We realize that it is a practical impossibility to arrange legislative districts so that each one has an identical number of residents, or citizens, or voters. Mathematical exactness or precision is hardly a workable constitutional requirement.

NOTES

1. The Court in *Reynolds* described the right to vote as "fundamental matter in a free and democratic society," since that right is "preservative of other basic civil and political rights." Therefore, "any alleged infringement of the right of citizens to vote must be carefully and meticulously scrutinized." This line of reasoning echoed the Court's famous Footnote 4 in *United States v. Carolene Products*, 304 U.S. 144 (1938), in the which the Court noted that "legislation which restricts those political processes which can ordinarily be expected to bring about the repeal of undesirable legislation is to be subjected to more exacting judicial scrutiny." The Court was here suggesting that the right to vote is fundamental *because* it is preservative of all other rights. In a democracy subject to majority rule, the ordinary way that persons protect their rights is by supporting, and electing, candidates who will support their interests. In the ordinary case, courts should keep out of this process and accord deference to the actions of legislatures, But in a case like *Reynolds*, where the majority process has been gerrymandered so that a minority of voters control a majority of the legislature, it will be very difficult for a majority of the electorate ever to undo minority control. In this situation, judicial deference to the legislature is no longer warranted and the legislative scheme will be "carefully and meticulously scrutinized."

2. The language in *Reynolds* is suggestive of what we have come to call the "strict scrutiny" standard in that it speaks of a fundamental right and careful and meticulous scrutiny. But the exact language of our current strict scrutiny test—"necessary to serve a compelling interest" or "narrowly tailored to achieve a compelling interest"—has not yet appeared in the Court's opinion.

Harper v. Virginia State Bd. of Elections
383 U.S. 663 (1966)

[The Virginia Constitution directed the General Assembly to levy an annual poll tax not exceeding $1.50 on every resident of the State 21 years of age and over. The poll tax had to be paid at least six months prior to the election in which the voter sought to vote. The poll tax was usually assessed along with the personal property tax. Those who did not pay a personal property tax would not be assessed for a poll tax, it being their responsibility to take the initiative and request to be assessed.]

Mr. Justice DOUGLAS delivered the opinion of the Court.

These are suits by Virginia residents to have declared unconstitutional Virginia's poll tax.

While the right to vote in federal elections is conferred by Art. I, § 2, of the Constitution (*United States v. Classic*, 313 U.S. 299, 314-315), the right to vote in state elections is nowhere expressly mentioned. It is argued that the right to vote in state elections is implicit, particularly by reason of the First Amendment and that it may not constitutionally be conditioned upon the payment of a tax or fee. We do not stop to canvass the relation between voting and political expression. For it is enough to say that once the franchise is granted to the electorate, lines may not be drawn which are inconsistent with the Equal Protection Clause of the Fourteenth Amendment. That is to say, the right of suffrage 'is subject to the imposition of state standards which are not discriminatory and which do not contravene any restriction that Congress, acting pursuant to its constitutional powers, has imposed.' *Lassiter v. Northampton County Board of Elections*, 360 U.S. 45, 51. We were speaking there of a state literacy test which we sustained, warning that the result would be different if a literacy test, fair on its face, were used to discriminate against a class. But the *Lassiter* case does not govern the result here, because, unlike a poll tax, the 'ability to read and write has some relation to standards designed to promote intelligent use of the ballot.'

We conclude that a State violates the Equal Protection Clause of the Fourteenth Amendment whenever it makes the affluence of the voter or payment of any fee an electoral standard. Voter qualifications have no relation to wealth nor to paying or not paying this or any other tax. Our cases demonstrate that the Equal Protection Clause of the Fourteenth Amendment restrains the States from fixing voter qualifications which invidiously discriminate. Thus without questioning the power of a State to impose reasonable residence restrictions on the availability of the ballot (see *Pope v. Williams*, 193 U.S. 621), we held in *Carrington v. Rash*, 380 U.S. 89, that a State may not deny the opportunity to vote to a bona fide resident merely because he is a member of the armed services. 'By forbidding a soldier ever to controvert the presumption of non-residence, the Texas Constitution imposes an invidious discrimination in violation of the Fourteenth Amendment.' *Id.*, at 96. Previously we had said that neither homesite nor occupation 'affords a permissible basis for distinguishing between qualified voters within the State.' *Gray v. Sanders*, 372 U.S. 368, 380. We think the same must be true of requirements of wealth or affluence or payment of a fee.

Long ago in *Yick Wo v. Hopkins*, 118 U.S. 356, 370, the Court referred to 'the political franchise of voting' as a 'fundamental political right, because preservative of all rights.' Recently in *Reynolds v. Sims*, 377 U.S. 533, 561-562, we said, 'Undoubtedly, the right of suffrage is a fundamental matter in a free and democratic society. Especially since the right to exercise the franchise in a free and unimpaired manner is preservative of other basic civil and political rights, any alleged infringement of the right of citizens to vote must be carefully and meticulously scrutinized.' There we were considering charges that voters in one part of the State had greater representation per person in the State Legislature than voters in another part of the State. We concluded:

> A citizen, a qualified voter, is no more nor no less so because he lives in the city or on the farm. This is the clear and strong command of our Constitution's Equal Protection Clause. This is an essential part of the concept of a government of laws and not men. This is at the heart of Lincoln's vision of 'government of the people, by the people, (and) for the

people.' The Equal Protection Clause demands no less than substantially equal state legislative representation for all citizens, of all places as well as of all races.

We say the same whether the citizen, otherwise qualified to vote, has $1.50 in his pocket or nothing at all, pays the fee or fails to pay it. The principle that denies the State the right to dilute a citizen's vote on account of his economic status or other such factors by analogy bars a system which excludes those unable to pay a fee to vote or who fail to pay.

It is argued that a State may exact fees from citizens for many different kinds of licenses; that if it can demand from all an equal fee for a driver's license, it can demand from all an equal poll tax for voting. But we must remember that the interest of the State, when it comes to voting, is limited to the power to fix qualifications. Wealth, like race, creed, or color, is not germane to one's ability to participate intelligently in the electoral process. Lines drawn on the basis of wealth or property, like those of race (*Korematsu v. United States*, 323 U.S. 214, 216), are traditionally disfavored. See *Edwards v. People of State of California*, 314 U.S. 160, 184-185 (Jackson, J., concurring); *Griffin v. People of State of Illinois*, 351 U.S. 12; *Douglas v. People of State of California*, 372 U.S. 353. To introduce wealth or payment of a fee as a measure of a voter's qualifications is to introduce a capricious or irrelevant factor. The degree of the discrimination is irrelevant. In this context--that is, as a condition of obtaining a ballot--the requirement of fee paying causes an 'invidious' discrimination (*Skinner v. State of Oklahoma*, 316 U.S. 535, 514) that runs afoul of the Equal Protection Clause.

We agree, of course, with Mr. Justice Holmes that the Due Process Clause of the Fourteenth Amendment 'does not enact Mr. Herbert Spencer's Social Statics' (*Lochner v. People of State of New York*, 198 U.S. 45, 75). Likewise, the Equal Protection Clause is not shackled to the political theory of a particular era. In determining what lines are unconstitutionally discriminatory, we have never been confined to historic notions of equality, any more than we have restricted due process to a fixed catalogue of what was at a given time deemed to be the limits of fundamental rights. See *Malloy v. Hogan*, 378 U.S. 1, 5-6. Notions of what constitutes equal treatment for purposes of the Equal Protection Clause do change. This Court in 1896 held that laws providing for separate public facilities for white and Negro citizens did not deprive the latter of the equal protection and treatment that the Fourteenth Amendment commands. *Plessy v. Ferguson*, 163 U.S. 537. Seven of the eight Justices then sitting subscribed to the Court's opinion, thus joining in expressions of what constituted unequal and discriminatory treatment that sound strange to a contemporary ear. When, in 1954--more than a half-century later--we repudiated the 'separate-but-equal' doctrine of *Plessy* as respects public education we stated: 'In approaching this problem, we cannot turn the clock back to 1868 when the Amendment was adopted, or even to 1896 when *Plessy v. Ferguson* was written.' *Brown v. Board of Education*, 347 U.S. 483, 492.

In a recent searching re-examination of the Equal Protection Clause, we held, as already noted, that 'the opportunity for equal participation by all voters in the election of state legislators' is required. *Reynolds v. Sims, supra*, 377 U.S. at 566. We decline to qualify that principle by sustaining this poll tax. Our conclusion, like that in *Reynolds v. Sims*, is founded not on what we think governmental policy should be, but on what the Equal Protection Clause requires.

We have long been mindful that where fundamental rights and liberties are asserted under the Equal Protection Clause, classifications which might invade or restrain them must be closely scrutinized and carefully confined. See, e.g., *Skinner v. State of Oklahoma*, 316 U.S. 535, 541. Those principles apply here. For to repeat, wealth or fee paying has, in our view, no relation to voting qualifications; the right to vote is too precious, too fundamental to be so burdened or conditioned.

Reversed.

NOTES

1. The *Harper* Court initially noted that, unlike the explicitly protected Constitutional right to vote for member of the federal House of Representatives, "the right to vote in state elections is nowhere expressly mentioned." The Court alluded to the argument that the right to vote is implicitly protected since it is connected to the First Amendment's protection of political speech, but the Court did not need to address that claim. Whether or not there would be a constitutional problem if the state provided no elections at all, that was not the case before the Court. Virginia had in fact provided an elective process but had also adopted a poll tax that had the effect of excluding a number of voters. In this situation, according to the Court, "once the franchise is granted to the electorate, lines may not be drawn which are inconsistent with the Equal Protection Clause of the Fourteenth Amendment."

This line of reasoning suggests that in this, a fundamental rights case, the Court is in fact applying an equality argument. Assuming, without deciding, that the state could get by with no elections to state offices at all, once the state does choose to elect state representatives, the comparative claim of equality requires that all voters be treated equally. A law that excludes otherwise qualified voters because of their poverty does not meet this equality standard.

2. Citing *Reynolds v. Sims* and *Skinner v. Oklahoma*, the Court noted, "Where fundamental rights and liberties are asserted under the Equal Protection Clause, classifications which might invade or restrain them must be closely scrutinized and carefully confined."

3. *Harper* today still is cited for the proposition that voting is an implied fundamental right under the Equal Protection Clause. A different part of the Court's opinion has not withstood the test of time, that is, where the Court stated that "[l]ines drawn on the basis of wealth or property, like those of race . . . are traditionally disfavored." This sentence suggested that wealth is as suspect a classification as race is. In subsequent cases, the Court has clearly rejected this suggestion. *See* Chapter 7.A, *infra*.

Kramer v. Union Free School Dist. No. 15
395 U.S. 621 (1969)

[A New York statute provided that residents of certain school districts, otherwise eligible to vote, could vote in school district elections only if they owned or leased taxable real property in the school district, or were the parents of, or had custody of, children enrolled in the public schools. Appellant, a single, 31-year old male living in his parents' home and thus ineligible to vote, alleged that he was denied equal protection of the laws in violation of the Fourteenth Amendment.]

Mr. Chief Justice WARREN delivered the opinion of the Court.

The sole issue in this case is whether the additional requirements of § 2012-requirements which prohibit some district residents who are otherwise qualified by age and citizenship from participating in district meetings and school board elections-violate the Fourteenth Amendment's command that no State shall deny persons equal protection of the laws.

'In determining whether or not a state law violates the Equal Protection Clause, we must consider the facts and circumstances behind the law, the interests which the State claims to be protecting, and the interests of those who are disadvantaged by the classification.' *Williams v. Rhodes*, 393 U.S. 23, 30 (1968). And, in this case, we must give the statute a close and exacting examination. '(S)ince the right to exercise the franchise in a free and unimpaired manner is preservative of other basic civil and political rights, any alleged infringement of the right of citizens to vote must be carefully and meticulously scrutinized.' *Reynolds v. Sims*, 377 U.S. 533, 562. This careful examination is necessary because statutes distributing the franchise constitute the foundation of our representative society. Any unjustified discrimination in determining who may participate in political affairs or in the selection of public officials undermines the legitimacy of representative government.

Thus, state apportionment statutes, which may dilute the effectiveness of some citizens' votes, receive close scrutiny from this Court. *Reynolds v. Sims, supra*. No less rigid an examination is applicable to statutes denying the franchise to citizens who are otherwise qualified by residence and age. Statutes granting the franchise to residents on a selective basis always pose the danger of denying some citizens any effective voice in the governmental affairs which substantially affect their lives. Therefore, if a challenged state statute grants the right to vote to some bona fide residents of requisite age and citizenship and denies the franchise to others, the Court must determine whether the exclusions are necessary to promote a compelling state interest. See *Carrington v. Rash, supra*.

And, for these reasons, the deference usually given to the judgment of legislators does not extend to decisions concerning which resident citizens may participate in the election of legislators and other public officials. Those decisions must be carefully scrutinized by the Court to determine whether each resident citizen has, as far as is possible, an equal voice in the selections. Accordingly, when we are reviewing statutes which deny some residents the right to vote, the general presumption of constitutionality afforded state statutes and the traditional approval given state classifications if the Court can conceive of a 'rational basis' for the distinctions made are not applicable. See *Harper v. Virginia State Bd. of Elections*, 383 U.S. 663, 670 (1966). The presumption of constitutionality and the approval given 'rational' classifications in other types of enactments are based on an assumption that the institutions of state government are structured so as to represent fairly all the people. However, when the challenge to the statute is in effect a challenge of this basic assumption, the assumption can no longer serve as the basis for presuming constitutionality. And, the assumption is no less under attack because the legislature which decides who may participate at the various levels of political choice is fairly elected. Legislation which delegates decision making to bodies elected by only a portion of those eligible to vote for the legislature can cause unfair representation. Such legislation can exclude a minority of voters from any voice in the decisions just as effectively as if the decisions were made by legislators the minority had no voice in selecting.

The need for exacting judicial scrutiny of statutes distributing the franchise is undiminished simply because, under a different statutory scheme, the offices subject to election might have been filled through appointment. States do have latitude in determining whether certain public officials shall be selected by election or chosen by appointment and whether various questions shall be submitted to the voters. In fact, we have held that where a county school board is an administrative, not legislative, body, its members need not be elected. *Sailors v. Kent County Bd. of Education*, 387 U.S. 105, 108 (1967). However, 'once the franchise is granted to the electorate, lines may not be drawn which are inconsistent with the Equal Protection Clause of the Fourteenth Amendment.' *Harper v. Virginia Bd. of Elections, supra*.

Nor is the need for close judicial examination affected because the district meetings and the school board do not have 'general' legislative powers. Our exacting examination is not necessitated by the subject of the election; rather, it is required because some resident citizens are permitted to participate and some are not. For example, a city charter might well provide that the elected city council appoint a mayor who would have broad administrative powers. Assuming the council were elected consistent with the commands of the Equal Protection Clause, the delegation of power to the mayor would not call for this Court's exacting review. On the other hand, if the city charter made the office of mayor subject to an election in which only some resident citizens were entitled to vote, there would be presented a situation calling for our close review.

III.

Besides appellant and others who similarly live in their parents' homes, the statute also disenfranchises the following persons (unless they are parents or guardians of children enrolled in the district public school): senior citizens and others living with children or relatives; clergy, military personnel, and others who live on tax-exempt property; boarders and lodgers; parents who neither own nor lease qualifying property and whose children are too young to attend school; parents who neither own nor lease qualifying property and whose children attend private schools.

Appellant asserts that excluding him from participation in the district elections denies him equal protection of the laws. He contends that he and others of his class are substantially interested in and significantly affected by the school meeting decisions. All members of the community have an interest in the quality and structure of public education, appellant says, and he urges that 'the decisions taken by local boards may have grave consequences to the entire population.' Appellant also argues that the level of property taxation affects him, even though he does not own property, as property tax levels affect the price of goods and services in the community.

We turn therefore to question whether the exclusion is necessary to promote a compelling state interest. First appellees argue that the State has a legitimate interest in limiting the franchise in school district elections to 'members of the community of interest'-those 'primarily interested in such elections.' Second, appellees urge that the State may reasonably and permissibly conclude that 'property taxpayers' (including lessees of taxable property who share the tax burden through rent payments) and parents of the children enrolled in the district's schools are those 'primarily interested' in school affairs.

We do not understand appellees to argue that the State is attempting to limit the franchise to those 'subjectively concerned' about school matters. Rather, they appear to argue that the State's legitimate interest is in restricting a voice in school matters to those 'directly affected' by such decisions. The State apparently reasons that since the schools are financed in part by local property taxes, persons whose out-of-pocket expenses are 'directly' affected by property tax changes should be allowed to vote. Similarly, parents of children in school are thought to have a 'direct' stake in school affairs and are given a vote.

Appellees argue that it is necessary to limit the franchise to those 'primarily interested' in school affairs because 'the ever increasing complexity of the many interacting phases of the school system and structure make it extremely difficult for the electorate fully to understand the whys and wherefores of the detailed operations of the school system.' Appellees say that many communications of school boards and school administrations are sent home to the parents through the district pupils and are 'not broadcast to the general public'; thus, nonparents will be less informed than parents. Further, appellees argue, those who are assessed for local property taxes (either directly or indirectly through rent) will have enough of an interest 'through the burden on their pocketbooks, to acquire such information as they may need.'

We need express no opinion as to whether the State in some circumstances might limit the exercise of the franchise to those 'primarily interested' or 'primarily affected.' Of course, we therefore do not reach the issue of whether these particular elections are of the type in which the franchise may be so limited. For, assuming, arguendo, that New York legitimately might limit the franchise in these school district elections to those 'primarily interested in school affairs,' close scrutiny of the § 2012 classifications demonstrates that they do not accomplish this purpose with sufficient precision to justify denying appellant the franchise.

Whether classifications allegedly limiting the franchise to those resident citizens 'primarily interested' deny those excluded equal protection of the laws depends, inter alia, on whether all those excluded are in fact substantially less interested or affected than those the statute includes. In other words, the classifications must be tailored so that the exclusion of appellant and members of his class is necessary to achieve the articulated state goal. Section 2012 does not meet the exacting standard of precision we require of statutes which selectively distribute the franchise. The classifications in § 2012 permit inclusion of many persons who have, at best, a remote and indirect interest, in school affairs and, on the other hand, exclude others who have a distinct and direct interest in the school meeting decisions.

Nor do appellees offer any justification for the exclusion of seemingly interested and informed residents-other than to argue that the § 2012 classifications include those 'whom the State could understandably deem to be the most intimately interested in actions taken by the school board,' and urge that 'the task of balancing the interest of the community in the maintenance of orderly school district elections against the interest of any individual in voting in such elections should clearly remain with the Legislature.' But the issue is not whether the legislative judgments are rational. A more exacting standard obtains. The issue is whether the s 2012 requirements do in fact sufficiently further a compelling state interest to justify denying the franchise to appellant and members of his class. The requirements of s 2012 are not sufficiently tailored to limiting the franchise to those 'primarily interested' in school affairs to justify the denial of the franchise to appellant and members of his class.

The judgment of the United States District Court for the Eastern District of New York is therefore reversed. The case is remanded for further proceedings consistent with this opinion.

It is so ordered.

NOTES

1. The Court in *Kramer* makes clear exactly what the strict scrutiny of the fundamental right to vote means: whether the exclusion of certain persons from the voting process is "necessary to promote a compelling state interest." The system adopted by the school district in *Harper* did not meet this exacting standard. The school system insisted that its purpose was to limit the franchise to those who would be primarily interested in school district elections. As the Court often does when applying strict scrutiny, the Court was willing to assume, arguendo, that this was a compelling purpose. But the classification failed the other part of the strict scrutiny test—it was not *necessary* to promote that purpose, that is, it did not accomplish its purpose "with sufficient precision." As the Court explained, the classifications involved in the statute "permit inclusion of many persons who have, at best, a remote and indirect interest, in school affairs and, on the other

hand, exclude others who have a distinct and direct interest in the school meeting decisions." Overinclusion and underinclusion are not a problem when the Court is applying the rational basis standard. They are, however, fatal under strict scrutiny.

2. The *Kramer* Court confirmed the basic justification for strict scrutiny of the right to vote. "The presumption of constitutionality and the approval given 'rational' classifications in other types of enactments are based on an assumption that the institutions of state government are structured so as to represent fairly all the people. However, when the challenge to the statute is in effect a challenge of this basic assumption, the assumption can no longer serve as the basis for presuming constitutionality." In a situation like that in *Kramer*, the Court needs to intervene in the majoritarian democratic process in order to preserve the majoritarian democratic process.

2. RESTRICTIONS ON CANDIDATES

The foundational cases identifying the right to vote as fundamental involved the right of individual persons to cast their ballots and to have those ballots counted equally with all other ballots cast. The fundamental right to vote, however, also provides some protection in terms of who one can vote for. This aspect of the right to vote ends up creating certain protections for candidates in terms of having their names on the ballot.

Williams v. Rhodes
393 U.S. 23 (1968)

Mr. Justice BLACK delivered the opinion of the Court.

The State of Ohio in a series of election laws has made it virtually impossible for a new political party, even though it has hundreds of thousands of members, or an old party, which has a very small number of members, to be placed on the state ballot to choose electors pledged to particular candidates for the Presidency and Vice Presidency of the United States.

Ohio Revised Code, § 3517.01, requires a new party to obtain petitions signed by qualified electors totaling 15% of the number of ballots cast in the last preceding gubernatorial election. The detailed provisions of other Ohio election laws result in the imposition of substantial additional burdens. Together these various restrictive provisions make it virtually impossible for any party to qualify on the ballot except the Republican and Democratic Parties. These two Parties face substantially smaller burdens because they are allowed to retain their positions on the ballot simply by obtaining 10% of the votes in the last gubernatorial election and need not obtain any signature petitions. Moreover, Ohio laws make no provision for ballot position for independent candidates as distinguished from political parties. The State of Ohio claims the power to keep minority parties and independent candidates off the ballot under Art. II, § 1, of the Constitution, which provides that:

> Each State shall appoint, in such Manner as the Legislature thereof may direct, a Number of Electors, equal to the whole Number of Senators and Representatives to which the State may be entitled in the Congress.

The Ohio American Independent Party and the Socialist Labor Party both brought suit to challenge the validity of these Ohio laws as applied to them, on the ground that they deny these

Parties and the voters who might wish to vote for them the equal protection of the laws, guaranteed against state abridgment by the Equal Protection Clause of the Fourteenth Amendment.

III.

We turn ... to the question whether the court below properly held that the Ohio laws before us result in a denial of equal protection of the laws. It is true that this Court has firmly established the principle that the Equal Protection Clause does not make every minor difference in the application of laws to different groups a violation of our Constitution. But we have also held many times that 'invidious' distinctions cannot be enacted without a violation of the Equal Protection Clause. In determining whether or not a state law violates the Equal Protection Clause, we must consider the facts and circumstances behind the law, the interests which the State claims to be protecting, and the interests of those who are disadvantaged by the classification. In the present situation the state laws place burdens on two different, although overlapping, kinds of rights—the right of individuals to associate for the advancement of political beliefs, and the right of qualified voters, regardless of their political persuasion, to cast their votes effectively. Both of these rights, of course, rank among our most precious freedoms. We have repeatedly held that freedom of association is protected by the First Amendment. And of course this freedom protected against federal encroachment by the First Amendment is entitled under the Fourteenth Amendment to the same protection from infringement by the States. Similarly we have said with reference to the right to vote: 'No right is more precious in a free country than that of having a voice in the election of those who make the laws under which, as good citizens, we must live. Other rights, even the most basic, are illusory if the right to vote is undermined.'

No extended discussion is required to establish that the Ohio laws before us give the two old, established parties a decided advantage over any new parties struggling for existence and thus place substantially unequal burdens on both the right to vote and the right to associate. The right to form a party for the advancement of political goals means little if a party can be kept off the election ballot and thus denied an equal opportunity to win votes. So also, the right to vote is heavily burdened if that vote may be cast only for one of two parties at a time when other parties are clamoring for a place on the ballot. In determining whether the State has power to place such unequal burdens on minority groups where rights of this kind are at stake, the decisions of this Court have consistently held that 'only a compelling state interest in the regulation of a subject within the State's constitutional power to regulate can justify limiting First Amendment freedoms.' *NAACP v. Button*, 371 U.S. 415, at 438 (1963).

The State has here failed to show any 'compelling interest' which justifies imposing such heavy burdens on the right to vote and to associate.

The State asserts that the following interests are served by the restrictions it imposes. It claims that the State may validly promote a two-party system in order to encourage compromise and political stability. The fact is, however, that the Ohio system does not merely favor a 'two-party system'; it favors two particular parties—the Republicans and the Democrats—and in effect tends to give them a complete monopoly. There is, of course, no reason why two parties should retain a permanent monopoly on the right to have people vote for or against them. Competition in ideas and governmental policies is at the core of our electoral process and of the First Amendment freedoms. New parties struggling for their place must have the time and opportunity to organize in order to meet reasonable requirements for ballot position, just as the old parties have had in the past.

Ohio makes a variety of other arguments to support its very restrictive election laws. It points out, for example, that if three or more parties are on the ballot, it is possible that no one party would obtain 50% of the vote, and the runner-up might have been preferred to the plurality winner by a majority of the voters. Concededly, the State does have an interest in attempting to see that the election winner be the choice of a majority of its voters. But to grant the State power to keep all political parties off the ballot until they have enough members to win would stifle the growth of all new parties working to increase their strength from year to year. Considering these Ohio laws in their totality, this interest cannot justify the very severe restrictions on voting and associational rights which Ohio has imposed.

The State also argues that its requirement of a party structure and an organized primary insures that those who disagree with the major parties and their policies 'will be given a choice of leadership as well as issues' since any leader who attempts to capitalize on the disaffection of such a group is forced to submit to a primary in which other, possibly more attractive, leaders can raise the same issues and compete for the allegiance of the disaffected group. But while this goal may be desirable, Ohio's system cannot achieve it. Since the principal policies of the major parties change to some extent from year to year, and since the identity of the likely major party nominees may not be known until shortly before the election, this disaffected 'group' will rarely if ever be a cohesive or identifiable group until a few months before the election. Thus, Ohio's burdensome procedures, requiring extensive organization and other election activities by a very early date, operate to prevent such a group from ever getting on the ballot and the Ohio system thus denies the 'disaffected' not only a choice of leadership but a choice on the issues as well.

Finally Ohio claims that its highly restrictive provisions are justified because without them a large number of parties might qualify for the ballot, and the voters would then be confronted with a choice so confusing that the popular will could be frustrated. But the experience of many States, including that of Ohio prior to 1948, demonstrates that no more than a handful of parties attempts to qualify for ballot positions even when a very low number of signatures, such as 1% of the electorate, is required. It is true that the existence of multitudinous fragmentary groups might justify some regulatory control but in Ohio at the present time this danger seems to us no more than 'theoretically imaginable.' No such remote danger can justify the immediate and crippling impact on the basic constitutional rights involved in this case.

Of course, the number of voters in favor of a party, along with other circumstances, is relevant in considering whether state laws violate the Equal Protection Clause. And, as we have said, the State is left with broad powers to regulate voting, which may include laws relating to the qualification and functions of electors. But here the totality of the Ohio restrictive laws taken as a whole imposes a burden on voting and associational rights which we hold is an invidious discrimination, in violation of the Equal Protection Clause.

NOTES

1. Ohio's ballot restrictions raised both equal protection and First Amendment issues. The First Amendment issue was the right of individuals to associate for the advancement of political beliefs. The equal protection issue was the right of qualified voters, regardless of their political persuasion, to cast their votes effectively.

2. In specifying the proper standard of review of this restriction on ballot access, the *Rhodes* Court did not state the ordinary strict scrutiny standard—necessary to promote a compelling interest. Rather the Court suggested something of a balancing test—"we must consider the facts and circumstances behind the law, the interests which the State claims to be protecting, and the

interests of those who are disadvantaged by the classification." As the Court applied this balancing test, however, the test looked something close to strict scrutiny as the Court noted that "only a compelling state interest in the regulation of a subject within the State's constitutional power to regulate can justify limiting First Amendment freedoms," and that "[t]he State has here failed to show any 'compelling interest' which justifies imposing such heavy burdens on the right to vote and to associate."

3. The state asserted three interests that were served by the ballot restriction: (1) encouraging compromise and stability; (2) making it more likely that the election winner will be the choice of a majority of its voters; and (3) preventing confusion that would frustrate the popular will. None of these interests were sufficiently compelling to justify "imposing such heavy burdens on the right to vote and to associate."

Anderson v. Celebrezze
460 U.S. 780 (1983)

[John Anderson ran as an independent candidate for the office of President of the United States in the 1980 election. At the time when Anderson declared his candidacy, he had already missed the statutory filing deadlines in Ohio and in other states. Anderson and two registered voters filed an action to challenge the early registration deadlines.]

Justice STEVENS delivered the opinion of the Court.

The question presented by this case is whether Ohio's early filing deadline placed an unconstitutional burden on the voting and associational rights of Anderson's supporters.

I

After a date toward the end of March, even if intervening events create unanticipated political opportunities, no independent candidate may enter the Presidential race and seek to place his name on the Ohio general election ballot. Thus the direct impact of Ohio's early filing deadline falls upon aspirants for office. Nevertheless, as we have recognized, "the rights of voters and the rights of candidates do not lend themselves to neat separation; laws that affect candidates always have at least some theoretical, correlative effect on voters." *Bullock v. Carter*, 405 U.S. 134 (1972). Our primary concern is with the tendency of ballot access restrictions "to limit the field of candidates from which voters might choose." Therefore, "[i]n approaching candidate restrictions, it is essential to examine in a realistic light the extent and nature of their impact on voters."

The impact of candidate eligibility requirements on voters implicates basic constitutional rights.[FN 7] Writing for a unanimous Court in *NAACP v. Alabama*, 357 U.S. 449, 460 (1958),

---

[FN 7] In this case, we base our conclusions directly on the First and Fourteenth Amendments and do not engage in a separate Equal Protection Clause analysis. We rely, however, on the analysis in a number of our prior election cases resting on the Equal Protection Clause of the Fourteenth Amendment. These cases, applying the "fundamental rights" strand of equal protection analysis, have identified the First and Fourteenth Amendment rights implicated by restrictions on the eligibility of voters and candidates, and have considered the degree to which the State's restrictions further legitimate state interests. See, *e.g., Williams v. Rhodes*, 393 U.S. 23 (1968); *Bullock v. Carter*, 405 U.S. 134 (1972); *Lubin v. Panish*, 415 U.S. 709 (1974); *Illinois Elections Bd. v. Socialist Workers Party, supra.*

Justice Harlan stated that it "is beyond debate that freedom to engage in association for the advancement of beliefs and ideas is an inseparable aspect of the 'liberty' assured by the Due Process Clause of the Fourteenth Amendment, which embraces freedom of speech." In our first review of Ohio's electoral scheme, *Williams v. Rhodes,* 393 U.S. 23, 30-31 (1968), this Court explained the interwoven strands of "liberty" affected by ballot access restrictions:

> In the present situation the state laws place burdens on two different, although overlapping, kinds of rights-the right of individuals to associate for the advancement of political beliefs, and the right of qualified voters, regardless of their political persuasion, to cast their votes effectively. Both of these rights, of course, rank among our most precious freedoms.

As we have repeatedly recognized, voters can assert their preferences only through candidates or parties or both.

> It is to be expected that a voter hopes to find on the ballot a candidate who comes near to reflecting his policy preferences on contemporary issues.

Lubin v. Panish, 415 U.S. 709, 716 (1974). The right to vote is "heavily burdened" if that vote may be cast only for major-party candidates at a time when other parties or other candidates are "clamoring for a place on the ballot." *Ibid.; Williams v. Rhodes, supra,* 393 U.S., at 31. The exclusion of candidates also burdens voters' freedom of association, because an election campaign is an effective platform for the expression of views on the issues of the day, and a candidate serves as a rallying-point for like-minded citizens.

Although these rights of voters are fundamental, not all restrictions imposed by the States on candidates' eligibility for the ballot impose constitutionally-suspect burdens on voters' rights to associate or to choose among candidates. We have recognized that, "as a practical matter, there must be a substantial regulation of elections if they are to be fair and honest and if some sort of order, rather than chaos, is to accompany the democratic processes." *Storer v. Brown,* 415 U.S. 724, 730 (1974). To achieve these necessary objectives, States have enacted comprehensive and sometimes complex election codes. Each provision of these schemes, whether it governs the registration and qualifications of voters, the selection and eligibility of candidates, or the voting process itself, inevitably affects--at least to some degree--the individual's right to vote and his right to associate with others for political ends. Nevertheless, the state's important regulatory interests are generally sufficient to justify reasonable, nondiscriminatory restrictions.

Constitutional challenges to specific provisions of a State's election laws therefore cannot be resolved by any "litmus-paper test" that will separate valid from invalid restrictions. *Storer, supra,* 415 U.S., at 730. Instead, a court must resolve such a challenge by an analytical process that parallels its work in ordinary litigation. It must first consider the character and magnitude of the asserted injury to the rights protected by the First and Fourteenth Amendments that the plaintiff seeks to vindicate. It then must identify and evaluate the precise interests put forward by the State as justifications for the burden imposed by its rule. In passing judgment, the Court must not only determine the legitimacy and strength of each of those interests; it also must consider the extent to which those interests make it necessary to burden the plaintiff's rights. Only after weighing all these factors is the reviewing court in a position to decide whether the challenged provision is unconstitutional. See *Williams v. Rhodes, supra,* 393 U.S., at 30-31; *Bullock v. Carter, supra,* 405 U.S., at 142-143; *American Party of Texas v. White,* 415 U.S. 767, 780-781 (1974); *Illinois Elections Bd. v. Socialist Workers Party,* 440 U.S. 173, 183 (1979). The results of this evaluation will not be automatic; as we have recognized, there is "no substitute for the hard judgments that must be made." *Storer v. Brown, supra,* 415 U.S., at 730.

II

[The Court identified the difficulties that an independent candidate would face in Ohio if his campaign began to gain momentum only after mid-to late March.] If the State's filing deadline were later in the year, a newly-emergent independent candidate could serve as the focal point for a grouping of Ohio voters who decide, after mid-March, that they are dissatisfied with the choices within the two major parties.

Not only does the challenged Ohio statute totally exclude any candidate who makes the decision to run for President as an independent after the March deadline. It also burdens the signature-gathering efforts of independents who decide to run in time to meet the deadline. When the primary campaigns are far in the future and the election itself is even more remote, the obstacles facing an independent candidate's organizing efforts are compounded. Volunteers are more difficult to recruit and retain, media publicity and campaign contributions are more difficult to secure, and voters are less interested in the campaign.

It is clear, then, that the March filing deadline places a particular burden on an identifiable segment of Ohio's independent-minded voters. As our cases have held, it is especially difficult for the State to justify a restriction that limits political participation by an identifiable political group whose members share a particular viewpoint, associational preference, or economic status. "Our ballot access cases ... focus on the degree to which the challenged restrictions operate as a mechanism to exclude certain classes of candidates from the electoral process. The inquiry is whether the challenged restriction unfairly or unnecessarily burdens 'the availability of political opportunity.'" *Clements v. Fashing,* 457 U.S. 957, 964 (1982) (plurality opinion), quoting *Lubin v. Panish, supra,* 415 U.S., at 716.

A burden that falls unequally on new or small political parties or on independent candidates impinges, by its very nature, on associational choices protected by the First Amendment. It discriminates against those candidates and--of particular importance-against those voters whose political preferences lie outside the existing political parties. *Clements v. Fashing, supra,* 457 U.S., at ---- (plurality opinion). By limiting the opportunities of independent-minded voters to associate in the electoral arena to enhance their political effectiveness as a group, such restrictions threaten to reduce diversity and competition in the marketplace of ideas. Historically political figures outside the two major parties have been fertile sources of new ideas and new programs; many of their challenges to the status quo have in time made their way into the political mainstream. *Illinois Elections Bd. v. Socialist Workers Party, supra,* 440 U.S., at 186; *Sweezy v. New Hampshire,* 345 U.S. 234, 250-251 (1957) (opinion of Warren, C.J.). In short, the primary values protected by the First Amendment-"a profound national commitment to the principle that debate on public issues should be uninhibited, robust, and wide-open," *New York Times Co. v. Sullivan,* 376 U.S. 254, 270 (1964)--are served when election campaigns are not monopolized by the existing political parties.

III

The State identifies three separate interests that it seeks to further by its early filing deadline for independent Presidential candidates: voter education, equal treatment for partisan and independent candidates, and political stability. We now examine the legitimacy of these interests and the extent to which the March filing deadline serves them.

[The Court found that Ohio had an "important and legitimate interest in voter education" but that interest did not justify the early filing deadline, given modern communications and given that campaign spending and voter education occur largely in the month before the election. The Court found no merit in the Ohio's claim that the early filing deadline served the interest of treating all candidates alike, since candidates from the major parties followed a very different route than that of independents. In terms of political stability, the Court recognized the legitimacy of the State's interest in preventing "splintered parties and unrestrained factionalism." But that interest did not justify a political party invoking the powers of the State to assure monolithic control over its own members and supporters.]

IV

We began our inquiry by noting that our primary concern is not the interest of candidate Anderson, but rather, the interests of the voters who chose to associate together to express their support for Anderson's candidacy and the views he espoused. Under any realistic appraisal, the "extent and nature" of the burdens Ohio has placed on the voters' freedom of choice and freedom of association, in an election of nationwide importance, unquestionably outweigh the State's minimal interest in imposing a March deadline.

The judgment of the Court of Appeals is *reversed*.

NOTES

1. The *Celebrezze* Court initially noted "the rights of voters and the rights of candidates do not lend themselves to neat separation; laws that affect candidates always have at least some theoretical, correlative effect on voters," citing *Bullock v. Carter,* 405 U.S. 134 (1972). Thus, although this casebook attempts to separate those two issues in Subsections 1 and 2 of this Voting Section, the cases inevitably overlap.

2. *Celebrezze* is *not* an equal protection case. The Court made clear that it was deciding the case based on First Amendment associational rights. The Court, however, in Footnote 7, noted that although it was not engaging in a separate Equal Protection Clause analysis, it was relying on its analysis in a number of our prior election cases resting on the Equal Protection Clause, cases that had applied the "fundamental rights" strand of equal protection analysis. The Court's First Amendment analysis in *Celebrezze* ended up mirroring the reasoning in the equal protection cases it noted it was relying on.

3. The Court made clear that not every state regulation of the right to vote would trigger strict scrutiny. Even though the rights of voters are fundamental, "as a practical matter, there must be a substantial regulation of elections if they are to be fair and honest and if some sort of order, rather than chaos, is to accompany the democratic processes," and that, therefore, "the state's important regulatory interests are generally sufficient to justify reasonable, nondiscriminatory restrictions."

In terms of the exact standard of review to be applied, the *Celebrezze* Court, like the *Rhodes* Court before it, applied something of a balancing test:

> [The Court] must first consider the character and magnitude of the asserted injury to the rights protected by the First and Fourteenth Amendments that the plaintiff seeks to vindicate. It then must identify and evaluate the precise interests put forward by the State as justifications for the burden imposed by its rule. In passing judgment, the Court must

not only determine the legitimacy and strength of each of those interests; it also must consider the extent to which those interests make it necessary to burden the plaintiff's rights. Only after weighing all these factors is the reviewing court in a position to decide whether the challenged provision is unconstitutional.

This balancing test closely parallels the strict scrutiny test in that the more fundamental a right that is affected by government action, the more compelling must be the government interest that justifies the intrusion on the fundamental right, and the closer (the more narrowly tailored) must be the fit between the challenged classification and the identified compelling interest.

3. *WHEN THE STRICT SCRUTINY STANDARD APPLIES*

Clements v. Fashing
457 U.S. 957 (1982)

Justice REHNQUIST delivered the opinion of the Court with respect to Parts I, II, and V, and delivered an opinion with respect to Parts III and IV, in which THE CHIEF JUSTICE, Justice POWELL, and Justice O'CONNOR joined.

Appellees in this case challenge two provisions of the Texas Constitution that limit a public official's ability to become a candidate for another public office. The primary question in this appeal is whether these provisions violate the Equal Protection Clause of the Fourteenth Amendment. [The first challenged provision (Article III, § 19) prohibited certain elected officials from running for the legislature during the their current term, while the second (Article XVI, § 65) provided that if certain state officials announced their candidacy for elective office, that announcement constituted an automatic resignation from the current office.]

III

The Equal Protection Clause allows the States considerable leeway to enact legislation that may appear to affect similarly situated people differently. Legislatures are ordinarily assumed to have acted constitutionally. Under traditional equal protection principles, distinctions need only be drawn in such a manner as to bear some rational relationship to a legitimate state end. Classifications are set aside only if they are based solely on reasons totally unrelated to the pursuit of the State's goals and only if no grounds can be conceived to justify them. See, *e.g., McDonald v. Board of Election Comm'rs*, 394 U.S. 802, 808-809 (1969); *McGowan v. Maryland*, 366 U.S. 420, 425-426 (1961). We have departed from traditional equal protection principles only when the challenged statute places burdens upon "suspect classes" of persons or on a constitutional right that is deemed to be "fundamental." *San Antonio Independent School Dist. v. Rodriguez*, 411 U.S. 1, 17 (1973).

Thus, we must first determine whether the provisions challenged in this case deserve "scrutiny" more vigorous than that which the traditional principles would require.

Far from recognizing candidacy as a "fundamental right," we have held that the existence of barriers to a candidate's access to the ballot "does not of itself compel close scrutiny." *Bullock v. Carter*, 405 U.S. 134, 143 (1972). "In approaching candidate restrictions, it is essential to examine in a realistic light the extent and nature of their impact on voters." *Ibid.* In assessing challenges to state election laws that restrict access to the ballot, this Court has not formulated a "litmus-paper test for separating those restrictions that are valid from those that are invidious under the Equal

CHAPTER 8: IMPLIED FUNDAMENTAL RIGHTS & THE EQUAL PROTECTION CLAUSE 423

Protection Clause." *Storer v. Brown*, 415 U.S. 724, 730 (1974). Decision in this area of constitutional adjudication is a matter of degree, and involves a consideration of the facts and circumstances behind the law, the interests the State seeks to protect by placing restrictions on candidacy, and the nature of the interests of those who may be burdened by the restrictions. *Ibid.; Williams v. Rhodes*, 393 U.S. 23, 30 (1968).

Our ballot access cases, however, do focus on the degree to which the challenged restrictions operate as a mechanism to exclude certain classes of candidates from the electoral process. The inquiry is whether the challenged restriction unfairly or unnecessarily burdens the "availability of political opportunity." *Lubin v. Panish*, 415 U.S. 709, 716 (1974). This Court has departed from traditional equal protection analysis in recent years in two essentially separate, although similar, lines of ballot access cases.

One line of ballot access cases involves classifications based on wealth. In invalidating candidate filing-fee provisions, for example, we have departed from traditional equal protection analysis because such a "system falls with unequal weight on voters, as well as candidates, according to their economic status." *Bullock v. Carter, supra*, 405 U.S. at 144. "Whatever may be the political mood at any given time, our tradition has been one of hospitality toward all candidates without regard to their economic status." *Lubin v. Panish, supra*, 415 U.S. at 717-718. Economic status is not a measure of a prospective candidate's qualifications to hold elective office, and a filing fee alone is an inadequate test of whether a candidacy is serious or spurious. Clearly, the challenged provisions in the instant case involve neither filing fees nor restrictions that invidiously burden those of lower economic status. This line of cases therefore does not support a departure from the traditional equal protection principles.

The second line of ballot access cases involves classification schemes that impose burdens on new or small political parties or independent candidates. See, *e.g., Illinois State Bd. of Elections Bd. v. Socialist Workers Party*, 440 U.S. 173 (1979); *Storer v. Brown, supra; American Party of Texas v. White*, 415 U.S. 767 (1974); *Jenness v. Fortson*, 403 U.S. 431 (1971); *Williams v. Rhodes, supra.* These cases involve requirements that an independent candidate or minor party demonstrate a certain level of support among the electorate before the minor party or candidate may obtain a place on the ballot. In these cases, the Court has emphasized that the States have important interests in protecting the integrity of their political processes from frivolous or fraudulent candidacies, in ensuring that their election processes are efficient, in avoiding voter confusion caused by an overcrowded ballot, and in avoiding the expense and burden of run-off elections. To this end, the Court has upheld reasonable level-of-support requirements and classifications that turn on the political party's success in prior elections. See *Storer v. Brown, supra; American Party of Texas v. White, supra; Jenness v. Fortson, supra.* The Court has recognized, however, that such requirements may burden First Amendment interests in ensuring freedom of association, as these requirements classify on the basis of a candidate's association with particular political parties. Consequently, the State may not act to maintain the "status quo" by making it virtually impossible for any but the two major parties to achieve ballot positions for their candidates. See *Williams v. Rhodes, supra*, 393 U.S. at 25.

The provisions of the Texas Constitution challenged in this case do not contain any classification that imposes special burdens on minority political parties or independent candidates. The burdens placed on those candidates subject to § 19 and § 65 in no way depend upon political affiliation or political viewpoint.

It does not automatically follow, of course, that we must apply traditional equal protection principles in examining § 19 and § 65 merely because these restrictions on candidacy do not fall into the two patterns just described. But this fact does counsel against discarding traditional principles without first examining the nature of the interests that are affected and the extent of the burden these provisions place on candidacy. See *Bullock v. Carter, supra*, 405 U.S. at 143; *Storer v. Brown, supra*, 415 U.S. at 730. Not all ballot access restrictions require "heightened" equal protection scrutiny. The Court, for example, applied traditional equal protection principles to uphold a classification scheme that denied absentee ballots to inmates in jail awaiting trial. *McDonald v. Board of Election Comm'rs*, 394 U.S., at 807-811. Thus, it is necessary to examine the provisions in question in terms of the extent of the burdens that they place on the candidacy of current holders of public office.

IV

A

Section 19 applies only to candidacy for the Texas Legislature. Of the appellees, only Baca, a Justice of the Peace, alleged that he would run for the Texas Legislature. Of the plaintiffs in this case, only appellee Baca's candidacy for another public office has in any fashion been restricted by § 19. The issue in this case, therefore, is whether § 19 may be applied to a Justice of the Peace in a manner consistent with the Equal Protection Clause.

Section 19 merely prohibits officeholders from cutting short their current term of office in order to serve in the legislature. In Texas, the term of office for a Justice of the Peace is four years, while legislative elections are held every two years. Therefore, § 19 simply requires Baca to complete his 4-year term as Justice of the Peace before he may be eligible for the legislature. At most, therefore, Baca must wait two years--one election cycle--before he may run as a candidate for the legislature.

In making an equal protection challenge, it is the claimant's burden to "demonstrate in the first instance a discrimination against [him] of some substance." *American Party of Texas v. White*, 415 U.S., at 781. Classification is the essence of all legislation, and only those classifications which are invidious, arbitrary, or irrational offend the Equal Protection Clause of the Constitution. *Williamson v. Lee Optical Co.*, 348 U.S. 483, 489 (1955).

In establishing a maximum "waiting period" of two years for candidacy by a Justice of the Peace for the legislature, § 19 places a *de minimis* burden on the political aspirations of a *current* officeholder. Section 19 discriminates neither on the basis of political affiliation nor on any factor not related to a candidate's qualifications to hold political office. Unlike filing fees or the level-of-support requirements, § 19 in no way burdens access to the political process by those who are outside the "mainstream" of political life. In this case, § 19 burdens only a candidate who has successfully been elected to one office, but whose political ambitions lead him to pursue a seat in the Texas Legislature.

A "waiting period" is hardly a significant barrier to candidacy. In *Storer v. Brown*, 415 U.S., at 733-737, we upheld a statute that imposed a flat disqualification upon any candidate seeking to run in a party primary if he had been registered or affiliated with another political party within the 12 months preceding his declaration of candidacy. Similarly, we upheld a 7-year durational residency requirement for candidacy in *Chimento v. Stark*, 414 U.S. 802 (1973), summarily aff'g 353 F. Supp. 1211 (NH). We conclude that this sort of insignificant interference with access to the ballot need only rest on a rational predicate in order to survive a challenge under the Equal Protection Clause.

CHAPTER 8: IMPLIED FUNDAMENTAL RIGHTS & THE EQUAL PROTECTION CLAUSE

Section 19 clearly rests on a rational predicate. That provision furthers Texas' interests in maintaining the integrity of the State's Justices of the Peace. By prohibiting candidacy for the legislature until completion of one's term of office, § 19 seeks to ensure that a Justice of the Peace will neither abuse his position nor neglect his duties because of his aspirations for higher office. Texas has a legitimate interest in discouraging its Justices of the Peace from vacating their current terms of office.

B

Article XVI, § 65, of the Texas Constitution provides that the holders of certain offices automatically resign their positions if they become candidates for any other elected office, unless the unexpired portion of the current term is one year or less. The burdens that § 65 imposes on candidacy are even less substantial than those imposed by § 19. The two provisions, of course, serve essentially the same state interests. The District Court found § 65 deficient, however, not because of the nature or extent of the provision's restriction on candidacy, but because of the manner in which the offices are classified. According to the District Court, the classification system cannot survive equal protection scrutiny because Texas has failed to explain sufficiently why some elected public officials are subject to § 65 and why others are not. As with the case of § 19, we conclude that § 65 survives a challenge under the Equal Protection Clause unless appellees can show that there is no rational predicate to the classification scheme.

The history behind § 65 shows that it may be upheld consistent with the "one step at a time" approach that this Court has undertaken with regard to state regulation not subject to more vigorous scrutiny than that sanctioned by the traditional principles. Section 65 was enacted in 1954 as a transitional provision applying only to the 1954 election. Section 65 extended the terms of those offices enumerated in the provision from two to four years. The provision also staggered the terms of other offices so that at least some county and local offices would be contested at each election. The automatic resignation proviso to § 65 was not added until 1958. In that year, a similar automatic resignation provision was added in Art. XI, § 11, which applies to officeholders in home rule cities who serve terms longer than two years. Section 11 allows home rule cities the option of extending the terms of municipal offices from two to up to four years.

Thus, the automatic resignation provision in Texas is a creature of the State's electoral reforms of 1958. That the State did not go further ... is not the sort of malfunctioning of the State's lawmaking process forbidden by the Equal Protection Clause. See *McDonald v. Board of Election Comm'rs, supra,* at 809. A regulation is not devoid of a rational predicate simply because it happens to be incomplete. See *Williamson v. Lee Optical Co., supra,* at 489. The Equal Protection Clause does not forbid Texas to restrict one elected officeholder's candidacy for another elected office unless and until it places similar restrictions on other officeholders. *Broadrick v. Oklahoma,* 413 U.S., at 607, n. 5. Cf. *Minnesota v. Clover Leaf Creamery Co.*, 449 U.S. 456, 466 (1981). The provision's language and its history belie any notion that § 65 serves the invidious purpose of denying access to the political process to identifiable classes of potential candidates.

V

Neither the Equal Protection Clause nor the First Amendment authorizes this Court to review in cases such as this the manner in which a State has decided to govern itself. Constitutional limitations arise only if the classification scheme is invidious or if the challenged provision significantly impairs interests protected by the First Amendment. Our view of the wisdom of a state constitutional provision may not color our task of constitutional adjudication. The judgment of the Court of Appeals is

Reversed.

NOTES

1. The first set of cases in this section on voting demonstrated that the Court considers the right to vote to be a fundamental right. Those initial cases, however, did not make clear what follows from that determination. This section examines what kind of scrutiny follows from the finding of voting as a fundamental right. In *Clements*, the Court made clear that not every regulation of the right to vote, including the right of access to the ballot, will be subject to strict scrutiny. It should be noted that Sections III and IV of the *Clements* opinion, the portions that appear above, were only a plurality, rather than a majority, opinion of the Court.

2. The plurality opinion suggests that it will apply a balancing test, under which it will examine "the nature of the interests that are affected and the extent of the burden these provisions place on candidacy." Not all ballot access restrictions will require heightened scrutiny. The plurality thus considered it essential to examine the extent of the burdens that the challenged provisions placed on the candidacy of current holders of public office. The Court determined that the waiting periods established by the challenged provisions were *de minimis*, and that this "insignificant interference with access to the ballot need only rest on a rational predicate." The Court then determined that the provisions did in fact have a rational predicate, since Texas has a legitimate interest in discouraging its office holders from vacating their current terms of office.

3. The *Clements* plurality makes clear that not every regulation of voting or ballot access will be subject to strict scrutiny and it suggests the beginning of a framework for determining the proper level of review—insignificant interference will be subject only to rational basis review. Ten years later, in *Burdick v. Takushi*, the Court set forth in greater detail the test to determine when heightened scrutiny would apply.

Burdick v. Takushi
504 U.S. 428 (1992)

Justice WHITE delivered the opinion of the Court.

The issue in this case is whether Hawaii's prohibition on write-in voting unreasonably infringes upon its citizens' rights under the First and Fourteenth Amendments. Petitioner contends that the Constitution requires Hawaii to provide for the casting, tabulation, and publication of write-in votes. The Court of Appeals for the Ninth Circuit disagreed, holding that the prohibition, taken as part of the State's comprehensive election scheme, does not impermissibly burden the right to vote. 937 F.2d 415, 422 (1991). We affirm.

I

Petitioner is a registered voter in the city and county of Honolulu. In 1986, only one candidate filed nominating papers to run for the seat representing petitioner's district in the Hawaii House of Representatives. Petitioner wrote to state officials inquiring about Hawaii's write-in voting policy and received a copy of an opinion letter issued by the Hawaii Attorney General's Office stating that the State's election law made no provision for write-in voting.

Petitioner then filed this lawsuit, claiming that he wished to vote in the primary and general elections for a person who had not filed nominating papers and that he wished to vote in future elections for other persons whose names might not appear on the ballot.

II

Petitioner proceeds from the erroneous assumption that a law that imposes any burden upon the right to vote must be subject to strict scrutiny. Our cases do not so hold.

It is beyond cavil that "voting is of the most fundamental significance under our constitutional structure." *Illinois Bd. of Elections v. Socialist Workers Party,* 440 U.S. 173, 184 (1979). It does not follow, however, that the right to vote in any manner and the right to associate for political purposes through the ballot are absolute. *Munro v. Socialist Workers Party,* 479 U.S. 189, 193 (1986). The Constitution provides that States may prescribe "[t]he Times, Places and Manner of holding Elections for Senators and Representatives," Art. I, § 4, cl. 1, and the Court therefore has recognized that States retain the power to regulate their own elections. *Sugarman v. Dougall,* 413 U.S. 634, 647 (1973); *Tashjian v. Republican Party of Connecticut,* 479 U.S. 208, 217 (1986). Common sense, as well as constitutional law, compels the conclusion that government must play an active role in structuring elections; "as a practical matter, there must be a substantial regulation of elections if they are to be fair and honest and if some sort of order, rather than chaos, is to accompany the democratic processes." *Storer v. Brown,* 415 U.S. 724, 730 (1974).

Election laws will invariably impose some burden upon individual voters. Each provision of a code, "whether it governs the registration and qualifications of voters, the selection and eligibility of candidates, or the voting process itself, inevitably affects--at least to some degree--the individual's right to vote and his right to associate with others for political ends." *Anderson v. Celebrezze,* 460 U.S. 780, 788 (1983). Consequently, to subject every voting regulation to strict scrutiny and to require that the regulation be narrowly tailored to advance a compelling state interest, as petitioner suggests, would tie the hands of States seeking to assure that elections are operated equitably and efficiently. Accordingly, the mere fact that a State's system "creates barriers ... tending to limit the field of candidates from which voters might choose ... does not of itself compel close scrutiny." *Bullock v. Carter,* 405 U.S. 134, 143 (1972); *Anderson, supra,* 460 U.S., at 788; *McDonald v. Board of Election Comm'rs of Chicago,* 394 U.S. 802 (1969).

Instead, as the full Court agreed in *Anderson,* 460 U.S., at 788-789; *id.* at 808, 817, (REHNQUIST, J., dissenting), a more flexible standard applies. A court considering a challenge to a state election law must weigh "the character and magnitude of the asserted injury to the rights protected by the First and Fourteenth Amendments that the plaintiff seeks to vindicate" against "the precise interests put forward by the State as justifications for the burden imposed by its rule," taking into consideration "the extent to which those interests make it necessary to burden the plaintiff's rights." *Id.* at 789; *Tashjian, supra,* 479 U.S., at 213-214.

Under this standard, the rigorousness of our inquiry into the propriety of a state election law depends upon the extent to which a challenged regulation burdens First and Fourteenth Amendment rights. Thus, as we have recognized when those rights are subjected to "severe" restrictions, the regulation must be "narrowly drawn to advance a state interest of compelling importance." *Norman v. Reed,* 502 U.S. 279, 289 (1992). But when a state election law provision imposes only "reasonable, nondiscriminatory restrictions" upon the First and Fourteenth Amendment rights of voters, "the State's important regulatory interests are generally sufficient to justify" the restrictions. *Anderson,* 460 U.S., at 788; see also *id.* at 788-789, n. 9. We apply this standard in considering petitioner's challenge to Hawaii's ban on write-in ballots.

A

There is no doubt that the Hawaii election laws, like all election regulations, have an impact on the right to vote, but it can hardly be said that the laws at issue here unconstitutionally limit access to the ballot by party or independent candidates or unreasonably interfere with the right of voters to associate and have candidates of their choice placed on the ballot. Indeed, petitioner understandably does not challenge the manner in which the State regulates candidate access to the ballot.

[The Court here explains the three mechanisms by means of which a candidate can have his name placed on the primary ballot. The Court concludes that, given the three rather generous methods of having one's name placed on the ballot, any burden on voters' freedom of choice and association is borne only by those who fail to identify their candidate of choice until days before the primary.]

But in *Storer v. Brown,* we gave little weight to "the interest the candidate and his supporters may have in making a late rather than an early decision to seek independent ballot status." We think the same reasoning applies here and therefore conclude that any burden imposed by Hawaii's write-in vote prohibition is a very limited one. "To conclude otherwise might sacrifice the political stability of the system of the State, with profound consequences for the entire citizenry, merely in the interest of particular candidates and their supporters having instantaneous access to the ballot."

Because he has characterized this as a voting rights rather than ballot access case, petitioner submits that the write-in prohibition deprives him of the opportunity to cast a meaningful ballot, conditions his electoral participation upon the waiver of his First Amendment right to remain free from espousing positions that he does not support, and discriminates against him based on the content of the message he seeks to convey through his vote. At bottom, he claims that he is entitled to cast and Hawaii required to count a "protest vote" for Donald Duck, and that any impediment to this asserted "right" is unconstitutional.

Petitioner's argument is based on two flawed premises. First, in *Bullock v. Carter,* we minimized the extent to which voting rights cases are distinguishable from ballot access cases, stating that "the rights of voters and the rights of candidates do not lend themselves to neat separation." 405 U.S., at 143. Second, the function of the election process is "to winnow out and finally reject all but the chosen candidates," *Storer,* 415 U.S., at 735, not to provide a means of giving vent to "short-range political goals, pique, or personal quarrel[s]." Attributing to elections a more generalized expressive function would undermine the ability of States to operate elections fairly and efficiently.

Accordingly, we have repeatedly upheld reasonable, politically neutral regulations that have the effect of channeling expressive activity at the polls. See *Munro,* 479 U.S., at 199. Petitioner offers no persuasive reason to depart from these precedents. Reasonable regulation of elections *does not* require voters to espouse positions that they do not support; it *does* require them to act in a timely fashion if they wish to express their views in the voting booth. And there is nothing content based about a flat ban on all forms of write-in ballots.

The appropriate standard for evaluating a claim that a state law burdens the right to vote is set forth in *Anderson.* Applying that standard, we conclude that, in light of the adequate ballot access afforded under Hawaii's election code, the State's ban on write-in voting imposes only a limited burden on voters' rights to make free choices and to associate politically through the vote.

B

[The Court here identified the interests that the state asserted would justify the limits it placed on write-in voting: avoiding unrestrained factionalism, averting divisive sore-loser candidacies, and guarding against party-raiding. Since the burden on voters was slight, the state did not need to establish a compelling interest to justify restraint. The Court determined that the state had legitimate interests in preventing these sorts of maneuvers, and that the write-in voting ban was a reasonable way of accomplishing these goals.]

Indeed, the foregoing leads us to conclude that when a State's ballot access laws pass constitutional muster as imposing only reasonable burdens on First and Fourteenth Amendment rights--as do Hawaii's election laws--a prohibition on write-in voting will be presumptively valid, since any burden on the right to vote for the candidate of one's choice will be light and normally will be counterbalanced by the very state interests supporting the ballot access scheme.

Accordingly, the judgment of the Court of Appeals is *affirmed*.

NOTES

1.   The Court in Burdick clarified when a restriction on the right to vote would trigger strict scrutiny and when it would be reviewed under a more deferential standard. Citing the balancing test announced by the Court in *Anderson v. Celebrezze*, the Court adopted the following distinction: when the state subjects voting rights to "severe" restrictions, the regulation must be "narrowly drawn to advance a state interest of compelling importance." But when a state election law provision imposes only "reasonable, nondiscriminatory restrictions" upon the First and Fourteenth Amendment rights of voters, "the State's important regulatory interests are generally sufficient to justify" the restrictions. Of course, the line between "severe restrictions" and "reasonable, nondiscriminatory restrictions" will not always be clear, but that is the line that the Supreme Court has drawn here and, thus, the line that lower courts must identify in voting rights cases.

2.   When the Court applied its test to the facts of *Burdick*, it determined that the State's ban on write-in voting imposed only a limited burden on voters' rights and was justified by Hawaii's important regulatory interests. Those interests included avoiding the possibility of unrestrained factionalism, averting divisive sore-loser candidacies, and guarding against "party raiding."

3.   Going forward from *Burdick*, the Court now had a clearly enunciated standard for determining when to apply strict scrutiny in voting cases. As the next two cases demonstrate, however, that standard has been very difficult to apply in an evenhanded manner.

Crawford v. Marion County Election Bd.
553 U.S. 181 (2008)

Justice STEVENS announced the judgment of the Court and delivered an opinion in which THE CHIEF JUSTICE and Justice KENNEDY join.

At issue in these cases is the constitutionality of an Indiana statute requiring citizens voting in person on election day, or casting a ballot in person at the office of the circuit court clerk prior to election day, to present photo identification issued by the government.

Referred to as either the "Voter ID Law" or "SEA 483," the statute applies to in-person voting at both primary and general elections. The requirement does not apply to absentee ballots submitted by mail, and the statute contains an exception for persons living and voting in a state-licensed facility such as a nursing home. A voter who is indigent or has a religious objection to being photographed may cast a provisional ballot that will be counted only if she executes an appropriate affidavit before the circuit court clerk within 10 days following the election. A voter who has photo identification but is unable to present that identification on election day may file a provisional ballot that will be counted if she brings her photo identification to the circuit county clerk's office within 10 days. No photo identification is required in order to register to vote, and the State offers free photo identification to qualified voters able to establish their residence and identity.

[The Indiana Democratic Party filed suit in federal court seeking a judgment that the Voter ID law violated the Equal Protection Clause.]

I

In *Harper v. Virginia Bd. of Elections*, 383 U.S. 663 (1966), the Court held that Virginia could not condition the right to vote in a state election on the payment of a poll tax of $1.50. We rejected the dissenters' argument that the interest in promoting civic responsibility by weeding out those voters who did not care enough about public affairs to pay a small sum for the privilege of voting provided a rational basis for the tax. Applying a stricter standard, we concluded that a State "violates the Equal Protection Clause of the Fourteenth Amendment whenever it makes the affluence of the voter or payment of any fee an electoral standard." We used the term "invidiously discriminate" to describe conduct prohibited under that standard, noting that we had previously held that while a State may obviously impose "reasonable residence restrictions on the availability of the ballot," it "may not deny the opportunity to vote to a bona fide resident merely because he is a member of the armed services." *Id.* at 666–667 (citing *Carrington v. Rash*, 380 U.S. 89, 96 (1965)). Although the State's justification for the tax was rational, it was invidious because it was irrelevant to the voter's qualifications.

Thus, under the standard applied in *Harper*, even rational restrictions on the right to vote are invidious if they are unrelated to voter qualifications. In *Anderson v. Celebrezze*, 460 U.S. 780 (1983), however, we confirmed the general rule that "evenhanded restrictions that protect the integrity and reliability of the electoral process itself" are not invidious and satisfy the standard set forth in *Harper*. 460 U.S., at 788, n. 9. Rather than applying any "litmus test" that would neatly separate valid from invalid restrictions, we concluded that a court must identify and evaluate the interests put forward by the State as justifications for the burden imposed by its rule, and then make the "hard judgment" that our adversary system demands.

In later election cases we have followed *Anderson*'s balancing approach. Thus, in *Norman v. Reed*, 502 U.S. 279, 288–289 (1992), after identifying the burden Illinois imposed on a political party's access to the ballot, we "called for the demonstration of a corresponding interest sufficiently weighty to justify the limitation," and concluded that the "severe restriction" was not justified by a narrowly drawn state interest of compelling importance. Later, in *Burdick v. Takushi*, 504 U.S. 428 (1992), we applied *Anderson*'s standard for "'reasonable, nondiscriminatory restrictions,'" 504 U.S., at 434, and upheld Hawaii's prohibition on write-in voting despite the fact that it prevented a significant number of "voters from participating in Hawaii elections in a meaningful manner," *id.* at 443 (KENNEDY, J., dissenting). We reaffirmed

Anderson's requirement that a court evaluating a constitutional challenge to an election regulation weigh the asserted injury to the right to vote against the "'precise interests put forward by the State as justifications for the burden imposed by its rule.'" 504 U.S., at 434 (quoting *Anderson,* 460 U.S., at 789).

In neither *Norman* nor *Burdick* did we identify any litmus test for measuring the severity of a burden that a state law imposes on a political party, an individual voter, or a discrete class of voters. However slight that burden may appear, as *Harper* demonstrates, it must be justified by relevant and legitimate state interests "sufficiently weighty to justify the limitation." *Norman,* 502 U.S., at 288–289. We therefore begin our analysis of the constitutionality of Indiana's statute by focusing on those interests.

II

The State has identified several state interests that arguably justify the burdens that SEA 483 imposes on voters and potential voters. While petitioners argue that the statute was actually motivated by partisan concerns and dispute both the significance of the State's interests and the magnitude of any real threat to those interests, they do not question the legitimacy of the interests the State has identified. Each is unquestionably relevant to the State's interest in protecting the integrity and reliability of the electoral process.

The first is the interest in deterring and detecting voter fraud. The State has a valid interest in participating in a nationwide effort to improve and modernize election procedures that have been criticized as antiquated and inefficient. The State also argues that it has a particular interest in preventing voter fraud in response to a problem that is in part the product of its own maladministration—namely, that Indiana's voter registration rolls include a large number of names of persons who are either deceased or no longer live in Indiana. Finally, the State relies on its interest in safeguarding voter confidence. Each of these interests merits separate comment.

[With regard to election modernization, the Court determined that photo identification is one effective method of establishing a voter's qualification to vote and that the integrity of elections is enhanced through improved technology. With regard to voter fraud, the Court determined that the state had a legitimate and important interest in counting only the votes of eligible voters. With regard to safeguarding voter confidence, the Court determined that public confidence in the integrity of the electoral process has significance independent of the state's interest in promoting voter fraud.]

III

States employ different methods of identifying eligible voters at the polls. Some merely check off the names of registered voters who identify themselves; others require voters to present registration cards or other documentation before they can vote; some require voters to sign their names so their signatures can be compared with those on file; and in recent years an increasing number of States have relied primarily on photo identification. A photo identification requirement imposes some burdens on voters that other methods of identification do not share. For example, a voter may lose his photo identification, may have his wallet stolen on the way to the polls, or may not resemble the photo in the identification because he recently grew a beard. Burdens of that sort arising from life's vagaries, however, are neither so serious nor so frequent as to raise any question about the constitutionality of SEA 483; the availability of the right to cast a provisional ballot provides an adequate remedy for problems of that character.

The burdens that are relevant to the issue before us are those imposed on persons who are eligible to vote but do not possess a current photo identification that complies with the requirements of SEA 483. The fact that most voters already possess a valid driver's license, or some other form of acceptable identification, would not save the statute under our reasoning in *Harper,* if the State required voters to pay a tax or a fee to obtain a new photo identification. But just as other States provide free voter registration cards, the photo identification cards issued by Indiana's BMV are also free. For most voters who need them, the inconvenience of making a trip to the BMV, gathering the required documents, and posing for a photograph surely does not qualify as a substantial burden on the right to vote, or even represent a significant increase over the usual burdens of voting.

Both evidence in the record and facts of which we may take judicial notice, however, indicate that a somewhat heavier burden may be placed on a limited number of persons. They include elderly persons born out of state, who may have difficulty obtaining a birth certificate; persons who because of economic or other personal limitations may find it difficult either to secure a copy of their birth certificate or to assemble the other required documentation to obtain a state-issued identification; homeless persons; and persons with a religious objection to being photographed. If we assume, as the evidence suggests, that some members of these classes were registered voters when SEA 483 was enacted, the new identification requirement may have imposed a special burden on their right to vote.

The severity of that burden is, of course, mitigated by the fact that, if eligible, voters without photo identification may cast provisional ballots that will ultimately be counted. To do so, however, they must travel to the circuit court clerk's office within 10 days to execute the required affidavit. It is unlikely that such a requirement would pose a constitutional problem unless it is wholly unjustified. And even assuming that the burden may not be justified as to a few voters, that conclusion is by no means sufficient to establish petitioners' right to the relief they seek in this litigation.

IV

Given the fact that petitioners have advanced a broad attack on the constitutionality of SEA 483, seeking relief that would invalidate the statute in all its applications, they bear a heavy burden of persuasion. Only a few weeks ago we held that the Court of Appeals for the Ninth Circuit had failed to give appropriate weight to the magnitude of that burden when it sustained a preelection, facial attack on a Washington statute regulating that State's primary election procedures. *Washington State Grange v. Washington State Republican Party,* 552 U.S. 442 (2008). Our reasoning in that case applies with added force to the arguments advanced by petitioners in these cases.

Petitioners ask this Court, in effect, to perform a unique balancing analysis that looks specifically at a small number of voters who may experience a special burden under the statute and weighs their burdens against the State's broad interests in protecting election integrity. Petitioners urge us to ask whether the State's interests justify the burden imposed on voters who cannot afford or obtain a birth certificate and who must make a second trip to the circuit court clerk's office after voting. But on the basis of the evidence in the record it is not possible to quantify either the magnitude of the burden on this narrow class of voters or the portion of the burden imposed on them that is fully justified.

First, the evidence in the record does not provide us with the number of registered voters without photo identification; Judge Barker found petitioners' expert's report to be "utterly incredible and unreliable." 458 F.Supp.2d, at 803. Much of the argument about the numbers of such voters comes from extrarecord, postjudgment studies, the accuracy of which has not been tested in the trial court.

Further, the deposition evidence presented in the District Court does not provide any concrete evidence of the burden imposed on voters who currently lack photo identification ... The record includes depositions of two case managers at a day shelter for homeless persons and the depositions of members of the plaintiff organizations, none of whom expressed a personal inability to vote under SEA 483. A deposition from a named plaintiff describes the difficulty the elderly woman had in obtaining an identification card, although her testimony indicated that she intended to return to the BMV since she had recently obtained her birth certificate and that she was able to pay the birth certificate fee. Judge Barker's opinion makes reference to six other elderly named plaintiffs who do not have photo identifications, but several of these individuals have birth certificates or were born in Indiana and have not indicated how difficult it would be for them to obtain a birth certificate. One elderly named plaintiff stated that she had attempted to obtain a birth certificate from Tennessee, but had not been successful, and another testified that he did not know how to obtain a birth certificate from North Carolina. The elderly in Indiana, however, may have an easier time obtaining a photo identification card than the nonelderly, and although it may not be a completely acceptable alternative, the elderly in Indiana are able to vote absentee without presenting photo identification.

The record says virtually nothing about the difficulties faced by either indigent voters or voters with religious objections to being photographed. While one elderly man stated that he did not have the money to pay for a birth certificate, when asked if he did not have the money or did not wish to spend it, he replied, "both." From this limited evidence we do not know the magnitude of the impact SEA 483 will have on indigent voters in Indiana. The record does contain the affidavit of one homeless woman who has a copy of her birth certificate, but was denied a photo identification card because she did not have an address. But that single affidavit gives no indication of how common the problem is.

In sum, on the basis of the record that has been made in this litigation, we cannot conclude that the statute imposes "excessively burdensome requirements" on any class of voters. See *Storer v. Brown*, 415 U.S. 724, 738 (1974). A facial challenge must fail where the statute has a "'plainly legitimate sweep.'" *Washington State Grange*, 552 U.S., at —— (quoting *Washington v. Glucksberg*, 521 U.S. 702, 739–740, and n. 7 (1997) (STEVENS, J., concurring in judgments)). When we consider only the statute's broad application to all Indiana voters we conclude that it "imposes only a limited burden on voters' rights." *Burdick*, 504 U.S., at 439. The "'precise interests'" advanced by the State are therefore sufficient to defeat petitioners' facial challenge to SEA 483. *Id.* at 434.

In their briefs, petitioners stress the fact that all of the Republicans in the General Assembly voted in favor of SEA 483 and the Democrats were unanimous in opposing it. In her opinion rejecting petitioners' facial challenge, Judge Barker noted that the litigation was the result of a partisan dispute that had "spilled out of the state house into the courts." 458 F.Supp.2d, at 783. It is fair to infer that partisan considerations may have played a significant role in the decision to enact SEA 483. If such considerations had provided the only justification for a photo identification requirement, we may also assume that SEA 483 would suffer the same fate as the poll tax at issue in *Harper*. But if a nondiscriminatory law is supported by valid neutral justifications, those justifications should not be disregarded simply because partisan interests may have provided one motivation for the votes of individual legislators. The state interests identified as justifications for SEA 483 are both neutral and sufficiently strong to require us to reject petitioners' facial attack on the statute. The application of the statute to the vast majority of Indiana voters is amply justified by the valid interest in protecting "the integrity and reliability of the electoral process." *Anderson,* 460 U.S., at 788, n. 9. The judgment of the Court of Appeals is affirmed.

It is so ordered.

Justice SCALIA, with whom Justice THOMAS and Justice ALITO join, concurring in the judgment.

The lead opinion assumes petitioners' premise that the voter-identification law "may have imposed a special burden on" some voters, but holds that petitioners have not assembled evidence to show that the special burden is severe enough to warrant strict scrutiny. That is true enough, but for the sake of clarity and finality (as well as adherence to precedent), I prefer to decide these cases on the grounds that petitioners' premise is irrelevant and that the burden at issue is minimal and justified.

To evaluate a law respecting the right to vote—whether it governs voter qualifications, candidate selection, or the voting process—we use the approach set out in *Burdick v. Takushi,* 504 U.S. 428 (1992). This calls for application of a deferential "important regulatory interests" standard for nonsevere, nondiscriminatory restrictions, reserving strict scrutiny for laws that severely restrict the right to vote. The lead opinion resists the import of *Burdick* by characterizing it as simply adopting "the balancing approach" of *Anderson v. Celebrezze,* 460 U.S. 780 (1983) (majority opinion of STEVENS, J.). Although *Burdick* liberally quoted *Anderson, Burdick* forged *Anderson*'s amorphous "flexible standard" into something resembling an administrable rule. Since *Burdick,* we have repeatedly reaffirmed the primacy of its two-track approach. See *Timmons v. Twin Cities Area New Party,* 520 U.S. 351, 358 (1997); *Clingman v. Beaver,* 544 U.S. 581, 586–587 (2005). "[S]trict scrutiny is appropriate only if the burden is severe. " Thus, the first step is to decide whether a challenged law severely burdens the right to vote. Ordinary and widespread burdens, such as those requiring "nominal effort" of everyone, are not severe. Burdens are severe if they go beyond the merely inconvenient. See *Storer v. Brown,* 415 U.S. 724, 728–729 (1974) (characterizing the law in *Williams v. Rhodes,* 393 U.S. 23 (1968), as "severe" because it was "so burdensome" as to be "'virtually impossible'" to satisfy).

Of course, we have to identify a burden before we can weigh it. The Indiana law affects different voters differently, but what petitioners view as the law's several light and heavy burdens are no more than the different *impacts* of the single burden that the law uniformly imposes on all voters. To vote in person in Indiana, *everyone* must have and present a photo identification that can be obtained for free. The State draws no classifications, let alone discriminatory ones, except to establish *optional* absentee and provisional balloting for certain poor, elderly, and institutionalized voters and for religious objectors. Nor are voters who already have photo identifications exempted from the burden, since those voters must maintain the accuracy of the information displayed on the identifications, renew them before they expire, and replace them if they are lost.

The Indiana photo-identification law is a generally applicable, nondiscriminatory voting regulation, and our precedents refute the view that individual impacts are relevant to determining the severity of the burden it imposes. In the course of concluding that the Hawaii laws at issue in *Burdick* "impose[d] only a limited burden on voters' rights to make free choices and to associate politically through the vote," we considered the laws and their reasonably foreseeable effect on *voters generally.* We did not discuss whether the laws had a severe effect on Mr. Burdick's own right to vote, given his particular circumstances. That was essentially the approach of the *Burdick* dissenters, who would have applied strict scrutiny to the laws because of their effect on "some voters." Subsequent cases have followed *Burdick* 's generalized review of nondiscriminatory election laws. See, *e.g., Timmons, supra,* at 361–362; *Clingman, supra,* at 590–591, 592–593. Indeed, *Clingman* 's holding that burdens are not severe if they are ordinary and widespread would be rendered meaningless if a single plaintiff could claim a severe burden.

The universally applicable requirements of Indiana's voter-identification law are eminently reasonable. The burden of acquiring, possessing, and showing a free photo identification is simply not severe, because it does not "even represent a significant increase over the usual burdens of voting." And the State's interests are sufficient to sustain that minimal burden. That should end the matter. That the State accommodates some voters by permitting (not requiring) the casting of absentee or provisional ballots is an indulgence — not a constitutional imperative that falls short of what is required.

NOTES

1. There is no majority opinion for the Court in *Crawford*. The dispute between the plurality opinion of Justice Stevens and the concurring opinion of Justice Scalia is over the proper standard of review. Justice Stevens' opinion applied the balancing test of *Anderson v. Celebrezze* while Justice Scalia's opinion applied the strict two-tiered test set forth in *Burdick*. These two tests substantially overlap, in that, under both tests, the more important the individual interest burdened, the more important must be the interest that the state is advancing. The difference between the two tests is that the balancing approach is a flexible, sliding-scale approached that could accommodate different levels of importance in individual interests and different levels of importance of government interests, while the two-tiered test identifies only two levels, either strict scrutiny or a deferential "important regulatory interests" standard. The Stevens' opinion in its citation of *Anderson v. Celebrezze* indicated that *Celebrezze* has survived *Burdick*, while the Scalia opinion assumed that *Burdick* has replaced *Celebrezze*.

2. Under either test, the Court must determine how much of a burden is imposed on the right to vote and how significant is the state interest that is advanced by imposing that burden. In measuring these two factors, the Court is inconsistent. With regard to the state interest in preventing voter fraud, the Court does not consider factual evidence of that interest to be particularly important. Thus the Court notes that the only kind of voter fraud that the challenged statute addresses is in-person voter impersonation at polling places but that "[t]he record contains no evidence of any such fraud actually occurring in Indiana at any time in its history." The only evidence of fraud before the Court was fraud in the use of absentee ballots, not in-person fraud. Yet, even though there was no evidence before the Court that in-person voting fraud existed at all, the Court was willing to conclude that "[t]here is no question about the legitimacy or importance of the State's interest in counting only the votes of eligible voters, and thus preventing in-person vote is a sufficiently substantial interest of the state."

On the other hand, when the Court went about measuring the extent of the burden that is imposed on voters by the photo ID requirement, it combed the record carefully and determined that there was not an adequate factual basis to find any substantial burden. Thus, the Court noted:

> [T]he evidence in the record does not provide us with the number of registered voters without photo identification; . . . [m]uch of the argument about the numbers of such voters comes from extrarecord, postjudgment studies, the accuracy of which has not been tested in the trial court; [and that] . . . the deposition evidence presented in the District

Court does not provide any concrete evidence of the burden imposed on voters who currently lack photo identification ...[and that] on the basis of the record that has been made in this litigation, we cannot conclude that the statute imposes "excessively burdensome requirements" on any class of voters.

What this means is that the Court has assumed to be true, without evidence, the facts supporting the statute, but rejected as inadequate the evidence that call into question the statute's reasonableness. The Court rejects as irrelevant that fact that "all of the Republicans in the General Assembly voted in favor of SEA 483 and the Democrats were unanimous in opposing it." But this fact by itself calls into question the claim that the law is in fact designed to eliminate voter fraud.

3. In *Is the Right to Vote Really Fundamental*, 18 Cornell J.L Pub. Pol'y 143, Joshua A. Douglas critiques the Court's voting cases: "For over forty years, the Supreme Court has fostered confusion surrounding the right to vote by creating two lines of election law cases. In one breath the Court calls the right to vote fundamental and applies strict scrutiny review. In another, the Court fails to recognize the right as fundamental and uses a lower level of scrutiny. These two lines of cases have coexisted, leaving lower courts and litigants with little guidance on how to approach future election law disputes. The problem inherent in this approach is that it derogates the value of having an individual right to vote and poses significant questions about the efficacy of our notion of democratic self-governance."

4. THE CASE THAT MUST NOT BE NAMED

Bush v. Gore
531 U.S. 98 (2000)

[In the year 2000, Vice President Albert Gore, Jr., a Democrat, and Texas Governor George W. Bush, a Republican, were candidates for the office of President of the United States. The outcome of the national election turned on the outcome of the vote count in Florida. George Bush was initially victorious in the Florida count, but it was by a margin of less than one half of one per cent. Although this triggered an automatic machine recount, Vice-President Gore challenged the accuracy of mechanical vote tallies in four Florida counties, alleging that votes for the Democratic candidates were not counted because the automated process was unable to detect the clear intent of many voters who cast their ballot for Gore. The litigation proceeded in several stages back and forth between the Florida circuit court, the Florida Supreme Court, and the United States Supreme Court.]

PER CURIAM.

On December 8, 2000, the Supreme Court of Florida ordered that the Circuit Court of Leon County tabulate by hand 9,000 ballots in Miami-Dade County. It also ordered the inclusion in the certified vote totals of 215 votes identified in Palm Beach County and 168 votes identified in Miami-Dade County for Vice President Albert Gore, Jr., and Senator Joseph Lieberman, Democratic candidates for President and Vice President. The State Supreme Court noted that petitioner George W. Bush asserted that the net gain for Vice President Gore in Palm Beach County was 176 votes, and directed the Circuit Court to resolve that dispute on remand. *Gore v. Harris,* 772 So.2d 1243, 1248, n. 6. The court further held that relief would require manual recounts in all Florida counties where so-called "undervotes" had not been subject to manual tabulation. The court ordered all manual recounts to begin at once. Governor Bush and Richard Cheney, Republican candidates for President and Vice President, filed an emergency application for a stay of this mandate. On December 9, we granted the application, treated the application as a petition for a writ of certiorari, and granted certiorari.

The petition presents the following questions: whether the Florida Supreme Court established new standards for resolving Presidential election contests, thereby violating Art. II, § 1, cl. 2, of the United States Constitution and failing to comply with 3 U.S.C. § 5, and whether the use of standardless manual recounts violates the Equal Protection and Due Process Clauses. With respect to the equal protection question, we find a violation of the Equal Protection Clause.

II

A

The closeness of this election, and the multitude of legal challenges which have followed in its wake, have brought into sharp focus a common, if heretofore unnoticed, phenomenon. Nationwide statistics reveal that an estimated 2% of ballots cast do not register a vote for President for whatever reason, including deliberately choosing no candidate at all or some voter error, such as voting for two candidates or insufficiently marking a ballot. In certifying election results, the votes eligible for inclusion in the certification are the votes meeting the properly established legal requirements.

This case has shown that punchcard balloting machines can produce an unfortunate number of ballots which are not punched in a clean, complete way by the voter. After the current counting, it is likely legislative bodies nationwide will examine ways to improve the mechanisms and machinery for voting.

B

The individual citizen has no federal constitutional right to vote for electors for the President of the United States unless and until the state legislature chooses a statewide election as the means to implement its power to appoint members of the electoral college. U.S. Const., Art. II, § 1. This is the source for the statement in *McPherson v. Blacker,* 146 U.S. 1, 35 (1892), that the state legislature's power to select the manner for appointing electors is plenary; it may, if it so chooses, select the electors itself, which indeed was the manner used by state legislatures in several States for many years after the framing of our Constitution. History has now favored the voter, and in each of the several States the citizens themselves vote for Presidential electors. When the state legislature vests the right to vote for President in its people, the right to vote as the legislature has prescribed is fundamental; and one source of its fundamental nature lies in the equal weight accorded to each vote and the equal dignity owed to each voter. The State, of course, after granting the franchise in the special context of Article II, can take back the power to appoint electors.

The right to vote is protected in more than the initial allocation of the franchise. Equal protection applies as well to the manner of its exercise. Having once granted the right to vote on equal terms, the State may not, by later arbitrary and disparate treatment, value one person's vote over that of another. See, *e.g., Harper v. Virginia Bd. of Elections,* 383 U.S. 663, 665 (1966) ("[O]nce the franchise is granted to the electorate, lines may not be drawn which are inconsistent with the Equal Protection Clause of the Fourteenth Amendment"). It must be remembered that "the right of suffrage can be denied by a debasement or dilution of the weight of a citizen's vote just as effectively as by wholly prohibiting the free exercise of the franchise." *Reynolds v. Sims,* 377 U.S. 533, 555 (1964).

There is no difference between the two sides of the present controversy on these basic propositions. Respondents say that the very purpose of vindicating the right to vote justifies the recount procedures now at issue. The question before us, however, is whether the recount procedures the Florida Supreme Court has adopted are consistent with its obligation to avoid arbitrary and disparate treatment of the members of its electorate.

Much of the controversy seems to revolve around ballot cards designed to be perforated by a stylus but which, either through error or deliberate omission, have not been perforated with sufficient precision for a machine to register the perforations. In some cases a piece of the card-a chad-is hanging, say, by two corners. In other cases there is no separation at all, just an indentation.

The Florida Supreme Court has ordered that the intent of the voter be discerned from such ballots. For purposes of resolving the equal protection challenge, it is not necessary to decide whether the Florida Supreme Court had the authority under the legislative scheme for resolving election disputes to define what a legal vote is and to mandate a manual recount implementing that definition. The recount mechanisms implemented in response to the decisions of the Florida Supreme Court do not satisfy the minimum requirement for nonarbitrary treatment of voters necessary to secure the fundamental right. Florida's basic command for the count of legally cast votes is to consider the "intent of the voter." 772 So.2d, at 1262. This is unobjectionable as an abstract proposition and a starting principle. The problem inheres in the absence of specific standards to ensure its equal application. The formulation of uniform rules to determine intent based on these recurring circumstances is practicable and, we conclude, necessary.

The law does not refrain from searching for the intent of the actor in a multitude of circumstances; and in some cases the general command to ascertain intent is not susceptible to much further refinement. In this instance, however, the question is not whether to believe a witness but how to interpret the marks or holes or scratches on an inanimate object, a piece of cardboard or paper which, it is said, might not have registered as a vote during the machine count. The factfinder confronts a thing, not a person. The search for intent can be confined by specific rules designed to ensure uniform treatment.

The want of those rules here has led to unequal evaluation of ballots in various respects. See *id.* at 1267 (Wells, C.J., dissenting) ("Should a county canvassing board count or not count a 'dimpled chad' where the voter is able to successfully dislodge the chad in every other contest on that ballot? Here, the county canvassing boards disagree"). As seems to have been acknowledged at oral argument, the standards for accepting or rejecting contested ballots might vary not only from county to county but indeed within a single county from one recount team to another.

The record provides some examples. A monitor in Miami-Dade County testified at trial that he observed that three members of the county canvassing board applied different standards in defining a legal vote. And testimony at trial also revealed that at least one county changed its evaluative standards during the counting process. Palm Beach County, for example, began the process with a 1990 guideline which precluded counting completely attached chads, switched to a rule that considered a vote to be legal if any light could be seen through a chad, changed back to the 1990 rule, and then abandoned any pretense of a *per se* rule, only to have a court order that the county consider dimpled chads legal. This is not a process with sufficient guarantees of equal treatment.

An early case in our one-person, one-vote jurisprudence arose when a State accorded arbitrary and disparate treatment to voters in its different counties. *Gray v. Sanders,* 372 U.S. 368

(1963). The Court found a constitutional violation. We relied on these principles in the context of the Presidential selection process in *Moore v. Ogilvie,* 394 U.S. 814 (1969), where we invalidated a county-based procedure that diluted the influence of citizens in larger counties in the nominating process. There we observed that "[t]he idea that one group can be granted greater voting strength than another is hostile to the one man, one vote basis of our representative government."

The State Supreme Court ratified this uneven treatment. It mandated that the recount totals from two counties, Miami-Dade and Palm Beach, be included in the certified total. The court also appeared to hold *sub silentio* that the recount totals from Broward County, which were not completed until after the original November 14 certification by the Secretary, were to be considered part of the new certified vote totals even though the county certification was not contested by Vice President Gore. Yet each of the counties used varying standards to determine what was a legal vote. Broward County used a more forgiving standard than Palm Beach County, and uncovered almost three times as many new votes, a result markedly disproportionate to the difference in population between the counties.

In addition, the recounts in these three counties were not limited to so-called undervotes but extended to all of the ballots. The distinction has real consequences. A manual recount of all ballots identifies not only those ballots which show no vote but also those which contain more than one, the so-called overvotes. Neither category will be counted by the machine. This is not a trivial concern. At oral argument, respondents estimated there are as many as 110,000 overvotes statewide. As a result, the citizen whose ballot was not read by a machine because he failed to vote for a candidate in a way readable by a machine may still have his vote counted in a manual recount; on the other hand, the citizen who marks two candidates in a way discernible by the machine will not have the same opportunity to have his vote count, even if a manual examination of the ballot would reveal the requisite indicia of intent. Furthermore, the citizen who marks two candidates, only one of which is discernible by the machine, will have his vote counted even though it should have been read as an invalid ballot. The State Supreme Court's inclusion of vote counts based on these variant standards exemplifies concerns with the remedial processes that were under way.

That brings the analysis to yet a further equal protection problem. The votes certified by the court included a partial total from one county, Miami-Dade. The Florida Supreme Court's decision thus gives no assurance that the recounts included in a final certification must be complete. Indeed, it is respondents' submission that it would be consistent with the rules of the recount procedures to include whatever partial counts are done by the time of final certification, and we interpret the Florida Supreme Court's decision to permit this. See 772 So.2d, at 1261-1262, n. 21 (noting "practical difficulties" may control outcome of election, but certifying partial Miami-Dade total nonetheless). This accommodation no doubt results from the truncated contest period established by the Florida Supreme Court in *Palm Beach County Canvassing Bd. v. Harris,* at respondents' own urging. The press of time does not diminish the constitutional concern. A desire for speed is not a general excuse for ignoring equal protection guarantees.

In addition to these difficulties the actual process by which the votes were to be counted under the Florida Supreme Court's decision raises further concerns. That order did not specify who would recount the ballots. The county canvassing boards were forced to pull together ad hoc teams of judges from various Circuits who had no previous training in handling and interpreting ballots. Furthermore, while others were permitted to observe, they were prohibited from objecting during the recount.

The recount process, in its features here described, is inconsistent with the minimum procedures necessary to protect the fundamental right of each voter in the special instance of a statewide recount under the authority of a single state judicial officer. Our consideration is limited to the present circumstances, for the problem of equal protection in election processes generally presents many complexities.

The question before the Court is not whether local entities, in the exercise of their expertise, may develop different systems for implementing elections. Instead, we are presented with a situation where a state court with the power to assure uniformity has ordered a statewide recount with minimal procedural safeguards. When a court orders a statewide remedy, there must be at least some assurance that the rudimentary requirements of equal treatment and fundamental fairness are satisfied.

Given the Court's assessment that the recount process underway was probably being conducted in an unconstitutional manner, the Court stayed the order directing the recount so it could hear this case and render an expedited decision. The contest provision, as it was mandated by the State Supreme Court, is not well calculated to sustain the confidence that all citizens must have in the outcome of elections. The State has not shown that its procedures include the necessary safeguards. The problem, for instance, of the estimated 110,000 overvotes has not been addressed, although Chief Justice Wells called attention to the concern in his dissenting opinion.

Upon due consideration of the difficulties identified to this point, it is obvious that the recount cannot be conducted in compliance with the requirements of equal protection and due process without substantial additional work. It would require not only the adoption (after opportunity for argument) of adequate statewide standards for determining what is a legal vote, and practicable procedures to implement them, but also orderly judicial review of any disputed matters that might arise. In addition, the Secretary has advised that the recount of only a portion of the ballots requires that the vote tabulation equipment be used to screen out undervotes, a function for which the machines were not designed. If a recount of overvotes were also required, perhaps even a second screening would be necessary. Use of the equipment for this purpose, and any new software developed for it, would have to be evaluated for accuracy by the Secretary, as required by Fla. Stat. Ann. § 101.015 (Supp.2001).

The Supreme Court of Florida has said that the legislature intended the State's electors to "participat[e] fully in the federal electoral process," as provided in 3 U.S.C. § 5. That statute, in turn, requires that any controversy or contest that is designed to lead to a conclusive selection of electors be completed by December 12. That date is upon us, and there is no recount procedure in place under the State Supreme Court's order that comports with minimal constitutional standards. Because it is evident that any recount seeking to meet the December 12 date will be unconstitutional for the reasons we have discussed, we reverse the judgment of the Supreme Court of Florida ordering a recount to proceed.

Seven Justices of the Court agree that there are constitutional problems with the recount ordered by the Florida Supreme Court that demand a remedy. See *post,* at 545 (SOUTER, J., dissenting); *post,* at 551-552 (BREYER, J., dissenting). The only disagreement is as to the remedy. Because the Florida Supreme Court has said that the Florida Legislature intended to obtain the safe-harbor benefits of 3 U.S.C. § 5, Justice BREYER's proposed remedy-remanding to the Florida Supreme Court for its ordering of a constitutionally proper contest until December 18-contemplates action in violation of the Florida Election Code, and hence could not be part of an "appropriate" order authorized by Fla. Stat. Ann. § 102.168(8) (Supp.2001).

* * *

None are more conscious of the vital limits on judicial authority than are the Members of this Court, and none stand more in admiration of the Constitution's design to leave the selection of the President to the people, through their legislatures, and to the political sphere. When contending parties invoke the process of the courts, however, it becomes our unsought responsibility to resolve the federal and constitutional issues the judicial system has been forced to confront.

The judgment of the Supreme Court of Florida is reversed, and the case is remanded for further proceedings not inconsistent with this opinion. *It is so ordered.*

Justice STEVENS, with whom Justice GINSBURG and Justice BREYER join, dissenting.

The Constitution assigns to the States the primary responsibility for determining the manner of selecting the Presidential electors. See Art. II, § 1, cl. 2. When questions arise about the meaning of state laws, including election laws, it is our settled practice to accept the opinions of the highest courts of the States as providing the final answers. On rare occasions, however, either federal statutes or the Federal Constitution may require federal judicial intervention in state elections. This is not such an occasion.

The federal questions that ultimately emerged in this case are not substantial. Article II provides that "[e]ach *State* shall appoint, in such Manner as the Legislature *thereof* may direct, a Number of Electors." It does not create state legislatures out of whole cloth, but rather takes them as they come--as creatures born of, and constrained by, their state constitutions. Lest there be any doubt, we stated over 100 years ago in *McPherson v. Blacker,* 146 U.S. 1, 25 (1892), that "[w]hat is forbidden or required to be done by a State" in the Article II context "is forbidden or required of the legislative power under state constitutions as they exist." In the same vein, we also observed that "[t]he [State's] legislative power is the supreme authority except as limited by the constitution of the State." *Ibid.;* cf. *Smiley v. Holm,* 285 U.S. 355, 367 (1932). The legislative power in Florida is subject to judicial review pursuant to Article V of the Florida Constitution, and nothing in Article II of the Federal Constitution frees the state legislature from the constraints in the State Constitution that created it. Moreover, the Florida Legislature's own decision to employ a unitary code for all elections indicates that it intended the Florida Supreme Court to play the same role in Presidential elections that it has historically played in resolving electoral disputes. The Florida Supreme Court's exercise of appellate jurisdiction therefore was wholly consistent with, and indeed contemplated by, the grant of authority in Article II.

Nor are petitioners correct in asserting that the failure of the Florida Supreme Court to specify in detail the precise manner in which the "intent of the voter," Fla. Stat. Ann. § 101.5614(5) (Supp.2001), is to be determined rises to the level of a constitutional violation. We found such a violation when individual votes within the same State were weighted unequally, see, *e.g., Reynolds v. Sims,* 377 U.S. 533, 568 (1964), but we have never before called into question the substantive standard by which a State determines that a vote has been legally cast. And there is no reason to think that the guidance provided to the factfinders, specifically the various canvassing boards, by the "intent of the voter" standard is any less sufficient-or will lead to results any less uniform-than, for example, the "beyond a reasonable doubt" standard employed every day by ordinary citizens in courtrooms across this country.

Even assuming that aspects of the remedial scheme might ultimately be found to violate the Equal Protection Clause, I could not subscribe to the majority's disposition of the case. As the majority explicitly holds, once a state legislature determines to select electors through a popular vote, the right to have one's vote counted is of constitutional stature. As the majority further acknowledges, Florida law holds that all ballots that reveal the intent of the voter constitute valid votes. Recognizing these principles, the majority nonetheless orders the termination of the contest proceeding before all such votes have been tabulated. Under their own reasoning, the appropriate course of action would be to remand to allow more specific procedures for implementing the legislature's uniform general standard to be established.

In the interest of finality, however, the majority effectively orders the disenfranchisement of an unknown number of voters whose ballots reveal their intent--and are therefore legal votes under state law--but were for some reason rejected by ballot-counting machines. It does so on the basis of the deadlines set forth in Title 3 of the United States Code. *Ante,* at 532. But, as I have already noted, those provisions merely provide rules of decision for Congress to follow when selecting among conflicting slates of electors. They do not prohibit a State from counting what the majority concedes to be legal votes until a bona fide winner is determined. Indeed, in 1960, Hawaii appointed two slates of electors and Congress chose to count the one appointed on January 4, 1961, well after the Title 3 deadlines. See Josephson & Ross, Repairing the Electoral College, 22 J. Legis. 145, 166, n. 154 (1996). Thus, nothing prevents the majority, even if it properly found an equal protection violation, from ordering relief appropriate to remedy that violation without depriving Florida voters of their right to have their votes counted. As the majority notes, "[a] desire for speed is not a general excuse for ignoring equal protection guarantees."

What must underlie petitioners' entire federal assault on the Florida election procedures is an unstated lack of confidence in the impartiality and capacity of the state judges who would make the critical decisions if the vote count were to proceed. Otherwise, their position is wholly without merit. The endorsement of that position by the majority of this Court can only lend credence to the most cynical appraisal of the work of judges throughout the land. It is confidence in the men and women who administer the judicial system that is the true backbone of the rule of law. Time will one day heal the wound to that confidence that will be inflicted by today's decision. One thing, however, is certain. Although we may never know with complete certainty the identity of the winner of this year's Presidential election, the identity of the loser is perfectly clear. It is the Nation's confidence in the judge as an impartial guardian of the rule of law.

I respectfully dissent.

Justice SOUTER, with whom Justice BREYER joins, and with whom Justice STEVENS and Justice GINSBURG join as to all but Part III, dissenting.

As will be clear, I am in substantial agreement with the dissenting opinions of Justice STEVENS, Justice GINSBURG, and Justice BREYER. I write separately only to say how straightforward the issues before us really are.

Petitioners have raised an equal protection claim (or, alternatively, a due process claim, see generally *Logan v. Zimmerman Brush Co.,* 455 U.S. 422 (1982)), in the charge that unjustifiably disparate standards are applied in different electoral jurisdictions to otherwise identical facts. It is true that the Equal Protection Clause does not forbid the use of a variety of voting mechanisms within a jurisdiction, even though different mechanisms will have different levels of effectiveness in recording voters' intentions; local variety can be justified by concerns about cost, the potential value of innovation, and so on. But evidence in the record here suggests that a different order of disparity obtains under rules for determining a voter's intent that have been applied (and could continue to be applied) to identical types of ballots used in identical brands of machines and exhibiting identical physical characteristics (such as "hanging" or "dimpled" chads). I can conceive of no legitimate state interest served by these differing treatments of the expressions of voters' fundamental rights. The differences appear wholly arbitrary.

CHAPTER 8: IMPLIED FUNDAMENTAL RIGHTS & THE EQUAL PROTECTION CLAUSE 443

In deciding what to do about this, we should take account of the fact that electoral votes are due to be cast in six days. I would therefore remand the case to the courts of Florida with instructions to establish uniform standards for evaluating the several types of ballots that have prompted differing treatments, to be applied within and among counties when passing on such identical ballots in any further recounting (or successive recounting) that the courts might order.

Unlike the majority, I see no warrant for this Court to assume that Florida could not possibly comply with this requirement before the date set for the meeting of electors, December 18.

Justice GINSBURG, with whom Justice STEVENS joins, and with whom Justice SOUTER and Justice BREYER join as to Part I, dissenting.

I agree with Justice STEVENS that petitioners have not presented a substantial equal protection claim. Ideally, perfection would be the appropriate standard for judging the recount. But we live in an imperfect world, one in which thousands of votes have not been counted. I cannot agree that the recount adopted by the Florida court, flawed as it may be, would yield a result any less fair or precise than the certification that preceded that recount.

Justice BREYER, with whom Justice STEVENS and Justice GINSBURG join except as to Part I-A-1, and with whom Justice SOUTER joins as to Part I, dissenting.

The Court was wrong to take this case. It was wrong to grant a stay. It should now vacate that stay and permit the Florida Supreme Court to decide whether the recount should resume.

The political implications of this case for the country are momentous. But the federal legal questions presented, with one exception, are insubstantial.

The majority raises three equal protection problems with the Florida Supreme Court's recount order: first, the failure to include overvotes in the manual recount; second, the fact that *all* ballots, rather than simply the undervotes, were recounted in some, but not all, counties; and third, the absence of a uniform, specific standard to guide the recounts. As far as the first issue is concerned, petitioners presented no evidence, to this Court or to any Florida court, that a manual recount of overvotes would identify additional legal votes. The same is true of the second, and, in addition, the majority's reasoning would seem to invalidate any state provision for a manual recount of individual counties in a statewide election.

The majority's third concern does implicate principles of fundamental fairness. The majority concludes that the Equal Protection Clause requires that a manual recount be governed not only by the uniform general standard of the "clear intent of the voter," but also by uniform subsidiary standards (for example, a uniform determination whether indented, but not perforated, "undervotes" should count). The opinion points out that the Florida Supreme Court ordered the inclusion of Broward County's undercounted "legal votes" even though those votes included ballots that were not perforated but simply "dimpled," while newly recounted ballots from other counties will likely include only votes determined to be "legal" on the basis of a stricter standard . . . . I agree that, in these very special circumstances, basic principles of fairness may well have counseled the adoption of a uniform standard to address the problem.

Nonetheless, there is no justification for the majority's remedy, which is simply to reverse the lower court and halt the recount entirely. An appropriate remedy would be, instead, to remand this case with instructions that, even at this late date, would permit the Florida Supreme Court to require recounting *all* undercounted votes in Florida, including those from Broward, Volusia, Palm Beach, and Miami-Dade Counties, whether or not previously recounted prior to the end of the protest period, and to do so in accordance with a single uniform standard.

By halting the manual recount, and thus ensuring that the uncounted legal votes will not be counted under any standard, this Court crafts a remedy out of proportion to the asserted harm. And that remedy harms the very fairness interests the Court is attempting to protect.

NOTES

1. *Bush v. Gore* is a very controversial decision. It had the effect of deciding the 2000 Presidential election in favor of George W. Bush. The decision has been derided as partisan—designed to reach a specific political result rather than to apply neutral principles of law. Even without resolving the question of partisanship, the case clearly leaves much to be desired in terms of legal argument, internal consistency, and precedential effect.

2. With regard to the legal argument, although the majority opinion on four occasions refers to the right to vote as "fundamental," it is not at all clear what standard of review the Court is applying. The majority makes no reference to the two-tiered standard of *Burdick v. Takushi*, nor to the balancing test set forth in *Calabrezze*. Rather, the Court seems to identify the problem with the Florida recount as one of "arbitrary and disparate treatment" of the right to vote and also speaks of "the minimum requirement for nonarbitrary treatment of voters necessary to secure the fundamental right." But a requirement of "nonarbitrariness" is usually associated with rational basis review and ordinarily results in a very deferential standard of review.

The Court forecasts the result of the case when it initially describes the issue as "whether the use of standardless manual recounts violates the Equal Protection and Due Process Clauses." But of course the Supreme Court of Florida would not have described the review that they had prescribed as "standardless, for that court had required vote counters to determine "the intent of the voter." As Justice Stevens pointed out, that requirement is neither any less standardless, nor any more likely to lead to nonuniform results, than the "beyond a reasonable doubt standard" that is employed every day in criminal courtrooms across the country. And if the Court were in fact applying something like rational basis review, it would not ordinarily demand evidence that the "intent of the voter" standard in fact produced uniform results, but only that the Florida court could reasonably have assumed that to be true.

3. The majority opinion could also be criticized for lacking internal consistency. The majority opinion concluded that the recount process that was underway violated the Equal Protection Clause, in that "[h]aving once granted the right to vote on equal terms, the State may not, by later arbitrary and disparate treatment, value one person's vote over that of another." If this is the rule of the case, then the result reached by the majority had the effect of producing a result that contradicted that rule. The effect of *Bush v. Gore* was to value one person's vote over that of another on a statewide basis. That is, when the Supreme Court stopped the vote recount, it left in place a statewide system in which the value of one's vote varied widely depending on type of vote-counting system that was used in the county where the voter lived. Thus, for example, Justice Stevens pointed out in dissent that the percentage of nonvotes in this election in counties using a punchcard system was 3.92% while the rate of error under the more modern optical-scan systems was only 1.43%. This meant that a voter living in a county that used a punchcard system was almost three times as likely to have his vote not count as was a voter in a county that used the

optical scanning method. But the majority's opinion gave effect to these results and thus validated a result that appeared to be inconsistent with the rule it was announcing in the case.

4. With regard to precedential effect, the majority stated, "Our consideration is limited to the present circumstances, for the problem of equal protection in election processes generally presents many complexities." The Supreme Court itself has never cited its own opinion in *Bush v. Gore*. This has led Adam Cohen to call it "The Case That Must Not Be Named." N.Y. Times, Aug 15, 2006. Cohen noted that "[t]here are several problems with trying to airbrush *Bush v. Gore* from the law. It undermines the courts' legitimacy when they depart sharply from rules of precedent, and it gives support to those who have said that *Bush v. Gore* was not a legal decision but a raw assertion of power."

This attempt by the Court to limit the effect of the decision to the facts before it is highly unusual in our legal system. Ordinarily, our system of precedent provides that earlier court decisions are viewed as stating rules that will become precedents for future cases. When the Supreme Court stated that its *Bush v. Gore* decision was to be limited to the present circumstances, that language is almost surely dictum, that is, language not necessary to the result in the case, and therefore not binding on lower courts. The "present circumstances" language also calls into question the soundness of the majority opinion by giving the impression that the majority wanted to reach a particular result in the case before it, but was concerned that any justification it adopted for stopping the Florida recount could be used as a new standard that would invalidate the voting mechanisms used in the majority of states.

Professor Richard L. Hasen, in *The Untimely Death of Bush v. Gore*, 60 Stan L. Rev. 1 (2007), notes that some lower courts have taken the rule of *Bush v. Gore* seriously. He cites two cases in which the Courts of Appeal for the Sixth and Ninth Circuits cited *Bush v. Gore* to invalidate election systems that selectively used punchcard ballots. *Id.* at 10-15. In each case, however, the decision of the three-judge panel was overruled by a majority of the circuit judges sitting *en banc*.

D. ACCESS TO THE JUDICIAL PROCESS

The Due Process Clauses of the Fifth and Fourteenth Amendments require that the government provide a certain process, usually made up of notice and a hearing, in connection with the government's taking a person's life, liberty, or property. This right of due process clearly includes some measure of access to the courts. It would therefore have been possible for the Supreme Court to create a body of law in this area based entirely on the Due Process Clause. As it turns out, however, that has not been the case. Rather, the Court has developed a set of precedents on access to the courts that is a mixture of due process and equal protection reasoning, beginning with *Griffin v. Illinois*.

Griffin v. Illinois
351 U.S. 12 (1956)

[Following a joint trial and conviction for armed robbery, Petitioners Crenshaw and Griffin requested that the court provide a certified copy of the entire court record, including a stenographic transcript of the proceedings. Asserting indigence, they asked the court to waive the customary fees for these records. The state conceded that it was sometimes impossible to prepare an appeal without a stenographic transcript of the trial proceedings, but the request for a fee waiver was denied. The petitioners alleged that this denial violated the Due Process and Equal Protection Clauses of the Fourteenth Amendment.]

Mr. Justice BLACK announced the judgment of the Court and an opinion in which THE CHIEF JUSTICE, Mr. Justice DOUGLAS, and Mr. Justice CLARK, join.

Illinois law provides that 'Writs of error in all criminal cases are writs of right and shall be issued of course.' The question presented here is whether Illinois may, consistent with the Due Process and Equal Protection Clauses of the Fourteenth Amendment, administer this statute so as to deny adequate appellate review to the poor while granting such review to all others.

Counsel for Illinois concedes that these petitioners needed a transcript in order to get adequate appellate review of their alleged trial errors. There is no contention that petitioners were dilatory in their efforts to get appellate review, or that the Illinois Supreme Court denied review on the ground that the allegations of trial error were insufficient. We must therefore assume for purposes of this decision that errors were committed in the trial which would merit reversal, but that the petitioners could not get appellate review of those errors solely because they were too poor to buy a stenographic transcript. The sole question for us to decide, therefore, is whether due process or equal protection has been violated.

Providing equal justice for poor and rich, weak and powerful alike is an age-old problem. People have never ceased to hope and strive to move closer to that goal. This hope, at least in part, brought about in 1215 the royal concessions of Magna Charta: 'To no one will we sell, to no one will we refuse, or delay, right or justice. * * * No free man shall be taken or imprisoned, or disseised, or outlawed, or exiled, or anywise destroyed; nor shall we go upon him nor send upon him, but by the lawful judgment of his peers or by the law of the land.' These pledges were unquestionably steps toward a fairer and more nearly equal application of criminal justice. In this tradition, our own constitutional guaranties of due process and equal protection both call for procedures in criminal trials that allow no invidious discriminations between persons and different groups of persons. Both equal protection and due process emphasize the central aim of our entire judicial system-all people charged with crime must, so far as the law is concerned, 'stand on an equality before the bar of justice in every American court.' *Chambers v. Florida*, 309 U.S. 227, 241. See also *Yick Wo v. Hopkins*, 118 U.S. 356, 369.

Surely no one would contend that either a State or the Federal Government could constitutionally provide that defendants unable to pay court costs in advance should be denied the right to plead not guilty or to defend themselves in court. Such a law would make the constitutional promise of a fair trial a worthless thing. Notice, the right to be heard, and the right to counsel would under such circumstances be meaningless promises to the poor. In criminal trials a State can no more discriminate on account of poverty than on account of religion, race, or color. Plainly the ability to pay costs in advance bears no rational relationship to a defendant's guilt or innocence and could not be used as an excuse to deprive a defendant of a fair trial. Indeed, a provision in the Constitution of Illinois of 1818 provided that every person in Illinois 'ought to obtain right and justice freely, and without being obliged to purchase it, completely and without denial, promptly and without delay, conformably to the laws.

There is no meaningful distinction between a rule which would deny the poor the right to defend themselves in a trial court and one which effectively denies the poor an adequate appellate review accorded to all who have money enough to pay the costs in advance. It is true that a State is not required by the Federal Constitution to provide appellate courts or a right to appellate review at all. See, e.g., *McKane v. Durston*, 153 U.S. 684, 687-688. But that is not to say that a State that does grant appellate review can do so in a way that discriminates against some convicted defendants on account of their poverty. Appellate review has now become an integral part of the Illinois trial system for finally adjudicating the guilt or innocence of a defendant. Consequently at all stages of the proceedings the Due Process and Equal Protection Clauses protect persons like petitioners from invidious discriminations.

All of the States now provide some method of appeal from criminal convictions, recognizing the importance of appellate review to a correct adjudication of guilt or innocence. Statistics show that a substantial proportion of criminal convictions are reversed by state appellate courts. Thus to deny adequate review to the poor means that many of them may lose their life, liberty or property because of unjust convictions which appellate courts would set aside. Many States have recognized this and provided aid for convicted defendants who have a right to appeal and need a transcript but are unable to pay for it. A few have not. Such a denial is a misfit in a country dedicated to affording equal justice to all and special privileges to none in the administration of its criminal law. There can be no equal justice where the kind of trial a man gets depends on the amount of money he has. Destitute defendants must be afforded as adequate appellate review as defendants who have money enough to buy transcripts.

The Illinois Supreme Court denied these petitioners relief under the Post-Conviction Act because of its holding that no constitutional rights were violated. In view of our holding to the contrary the State Supreme Court may decide that petitioners are now entitled to a transcript, as the State's brief suggests. We do not hold, however, that Illinois must purchase a stenographer's transcript in every case where a defendant cannot buy it. The Supreme Court may find other means of affording adequate and effective appellate review to indigent defendants. For example, it may be that bystanders' bills of exceptions or other methods of reporting trial proceedings could be used in some cases. The Illinois Supreme Court appears to have broad power to promulgate rules of procedure and appellate practice. We are confident that the State will provide corrective rules to meet the problem which this case lays bare.

The judgment of the Supreme Court of Illinois is vacated and the cause is remanded to that court for further action not inconsistent with the foregoing paragraph. Vacated and remanded.

NOTES

1. Since the claim in *Griffin* is about a trial transcript that is to be used to make an appeal, the case has the initial look of a due process case, in that the state cannot deprive the defendants of their liberty without providing them an adequate hearing. The problem with the due process claim, however, is that the precedents make clear that while due process would require a fair trial before a criminal conviction, the defendants have already been given that fair trial, and due process does not require that there be any appellate process at all. Therefore, the Court needs to treat the claim as a kind of hybrid—"our own constitutional guaranties of due process and equal protection both call for procedures in criminal trials which allow no invidious discriminations between persons and different groups of persons. Both equal protection and due process emphasize the central aim of our entire judicial system--all people charged with crime must, so far as the law is concerned, 'stand on an equality before the bar of justice in every American court.'" Illinois had in fact provided for an appellate process, and although due process would not have required appellate review at all, once that appellate process has been created, the state cannot grant it "in a way that discriminates against some convicted defendants on account of their poverty."

2. The *Griffin* decision suggests that the poor are a suspect class: "In criminal trials a State can no more discriminate on account of poverty than on account of religion, race, or color." This language will turn out to be complete dictum, completely rejected by the Court in its later decision in *San Antonio School District v. Rodriguez*. *See* Chapter VII.A. *supra*.

3. Although the *Griffin* Court seems to be applying some kind of heightened standard of review because of the importance of the appellate process, it clearly does not use the language of "fundamental right" or "strict scrutiny." In fact, the Court says that "the ability to pay costs in advance bears no rational relationship to a defendant's guilt or innocence." This is of course the language of rationality review. But the *Griffin* decision is the first of the Court's precedents that give close scrutiny to limitations on access to the judicial process.

4. *Douglas* decided that a State's obligation to provide appellate counsel to poor defendants faced with incarceration applies to appeals of right. In *Ross v. Moffitt*, 417 U.S. 600 (1974), however, the Court held that neither the Due Process Clause nor the Equal Protection Clause required a State to provide counsel at state expense to an indigent prisoner pursuing a discretionary appeal in the state system or petitioning for review in the United States Supreme Court.

Douglas v. California
372 U.S. 353 (1963)

[Petitioners Bennie Will Meyes and William Douglas were jointly tried in a California state court, convicted, and sentenced to prison terms on thirteen felony counts that included robbery, assault with a deadly weapon, and assault with intent to commit murder. Petitioners requested, and were denied, the assistance of counsel on appeal, even though it plainly appeared they were indigents. The request was denied in accordance with a California rule of criminal procedure which provided that state appellate courts, upon the request of an indigent for counsel, may make an independent investigation of the record and determine whether it would be of advantage to the defendant or helpful to the appellate court to have counsel appointed. After such investigation, appellate courts should appoint counsel if in their opinion it would be helpful to the defendant or the court, and should deny the appointment of counsel only if in their judgment such appointment would be of no value.]

Mr. Justice DOUGLAS delivered the opinion of the Court.

We agree ... with Justice Traynor of the California Supreme Court, who said that the '(d)enial of counsel on appeal (to an indigent) would seem to be a discrimination at least as invidious as that condemned in *Griffin v. People of State of Illinois*.' *People v. Brown*, 55 Cal.2d 64, 71 (concurring opinion). In *Griffin v. Illinois*, 351 U.S. 12, we held that a State may not grant appellate review in such a way as to discriminate against some convicted defendants on account of their poverty. There, as in *Draper v. Washington*, 372 U.S. 487, the right to a free transcript on appeal was in issue. Here the issue is whether or not an indigent shall be denied the assistance of counsel on appeal. In either case the evil is the same: discrimination against the indigent. For there can be no equal justice where the kind of an appeal a man enjoys 'depends on the amount of money he has.' *Griffin v. Illinois*, *supra*, at p. 19.

In spite of California's forward treatment of indigents, under its present practice the type of an appeal a person is afforded in the District Court of Appeal hinges upon whether or not he can pay for the assistance of counsel. If he can the appellate court passes on the merits of his case only after having the full benefit of written briefs and oral argument by counsel. If he cannot the appellate court is forced to prejudge the merits before it can even determine whether counsel should be provided. At this stage in the proceedings only the barren record speaks for the indigent, and, unless the printed pages show that an injustice has been committed, he is forced to go without a champion on appeal. Any real chance he may have had of showing that his appeal has hidden merit is deprived him when the court decides on an ex parte examination of the record that the assistance of counsel is not required.

We are not here concerned with problems that might arise from the denial of counsel for the preparation of a petition for discretionary or mandatory review beyond the stage in the appellate process at which the claims have once been presented by a lawyer and passed upon by an appellate court. We are dealing only with the first appeal, granted as a matter of right to rich and poor alike from a criminal conviction. We need not now decide whether California would have to provide counsel for an indigent seeking a discretionary hearing from the California Supreme Court after the District Court of Appeal had sustained his conviction or whether counsel must be appointed for an indigent seeking review of an appellate affirmance of his conviction in this Court by appeal as of right or by petition for a writ of certiorari which lies within the Court's discretion. But it is appropriate to observe that a State can, consistently with the Fourteenth Amendment, provide for differences so long as the result does not amount to a denial of due process or an 'invidious discrimination.' *Williamson v. Lee Optical of Oklahoma*, 348 U.S. 483, 489; *Griffin v. Illinois, supra*, p. 18. Absolute equality is not required; lines can be and are drawn and we often sustain them. See *Tigner v. Texas*, 310 U.S. 141; *Goesaert v. Cleary*, 335 U.S. 464. But where the merits of the one and only appeal an indigent has as of right are decided without benefit of counsel, we think an unconstitutional line has been drawn between rich and poor.

When an indigent is forced to run this gantlet of a preliminary showing of merit, the right to appeal does not comport with fair procedure. In the federal courts, on the other hand, an indigent must be afforded counsel on appeal whenever he challenges a certification that the appeal is not taken in good faith. *Johnson v. United States*, 352 U.S. 565. The federal courts must honor his request for counsel regardless of what they think the merits of the case may be; and 'representation in the role of an advocate is required.' *Ellis v. United States*, 356 U.S. 674, 675. In California, however, once the court has 'gone through' the record and denied counsel, the indigent has no recourse but to prosecute his appeal on his own, as best he can, no matter how meritorious his case may turn out to be. The present case, where counsel was denied petitioners on appeal, shows that the discrimination is not between 'possibly good and obviously bad cases,' but between cases where the rich man can require the court to listen to argument of counsel before deciding on the merits, but a poor man cannot. There is lacking that equality demanded by the Fourteenth Amendment where the rich man, who appeals as of right, enjoys the benefit of counsel's examination into the record, research of the law, and marshalling of arguments on his behalf, while the indigent, already burdened by a preliminary determination that his case is without merit, is forced to shift for himself. The indigent, where the record is unclear or the errors are hidden, has only the right to a meaningless ritual, while the rich man has a meaningful appeal.

We vacate the judgment of the District Court of Appeal and remand the case to that court for further proceedings not inconsistent with this opinion. *It is so ordered.*

Mr. Justice HARLAN, whom Mr. Justice STEWART joins, dissenting.

In holding that an indigent has an absolute right to appointed counsel on appeal of a state criminal conviction, the Court appears to rely both on the Equal Protection Clause and on the guarantees of fair procedure inherent in the Due Process Clause of the Fourteenth Amendment, with obvious emphasis on 'equal protection.' In my view the Equal Protection Clause is not apposite, and its application to cases like the present one can lead only to mischievous results. This case should be judged solely under the Due Process Clause, and I do not believe that the California procedure violates that provision.

EQUAL PROTECTION.

To approach the present problem in terms of the Equal Protection Clause is, I submit, but to substitute resounding phrases for analysis. I dissented from this approach in Griffin v. Illinois, 351 U.S. 12, 29, 34-36, and I am constrained to dissent from the implicit extension of the equal protection approach here--to a case in which the State denies no one an appeal, but seeks only to keep within reasonable bounds the instances in which appellate counsel will be assigned to indigents.

Every financial exaction which the State imposes on a uniform basis is more easily satisfied by the well-to-do than by the indigent. Yet I take it that no one would dispute the constitutional power of the State to levy a uniform sales tax, to charge tuition at a state university, to fix rates for the purchase of water from a municipal corporation, to impose a standard fine for criminal violations, or to establish minimum bail for various categories of offenses. Nor could it be contended that the State may not classify as crimes acts which the poor are more likely to commit than are the rich. And surely, there would be no basis for attacking a state law which provided benefits for the needy simply because those benefits fell short of the goods or services that others could purchase for themselves.

Laws such as these do not deny equal protection to the less fortunate for one essential reason: the Equal Protection Clause does not impose on the States 'an affirmative duty to lift the handicaps flowing from differences in economic circumstances.' To so construe it would be to read into the Constitution a philosophy of leveling that would be foreign to many of our basic concepts of the proper relations between government and society. The State may have a moral obligation to eliminate the evils of poverty, but it is not required by the Equal Protection Clause to give to some whatever others can afford.

NOTES

1. The focus of the majority opinion in *Douglas* is clearly the problem of discrimination against the poor—an equal protection problem—rather than access to the judicial system—a due process problem. Thus, the Court identified the problem as "discrimination against the indigent. For there can be no equal justice where the kind of an appeal a man enjoys 'depends on the amount of money he has.'" (Citing *Griffin*). The Court concluded that "an unconstitutional line has been drawn between rich and poor." Thus, as in *Griffin*, the holding of the case has as much to do with discrimination against the poor as it does with access to the judicial process. With the benefit of subsequent cases, however, where the Court has reversed course on the notion that the poor are a suspect class but has provided additional precedents supporting a claim of some access to the judicial process, the *Douglas* case does appear to provide some support for the right of some level of access to the judicial process.

2. Justice Harlan, dissenting, rejects the notion that the Equal Protection Clause imposes on the states "an affirmative duty to lift the handicaps flowing from differences in economic circumstances." In his view, such an interpretation of equal protection would be "to read into the Constitution a philosophy of leveling that would be foreign to many of our basic concepts of the

proper relations between government and society." Harlan's understanding that the state has no "affirmative duty to lift the handicaps flowing from differences in economic circumstances" turns out to be the view of the majority of the Court when we are speaking of rights that the government is not required to provide (*see, supra*, Chapter VII.A.3) but it is not true where the government is the only provider of an important service, such as voting or a court system.

Boddie v. Connecticut
401 U.S. 371 (1971)

[Appellants were welfare recipients, married and unable to obtain a divorce because of an inability to pay required court fees and costs of about $60.]

Mr. Justice HARLAN delivered the opinion of the Court.

Our conclusion is that, given the basic position of the marriage relationship in this society's hierarchy of values and the concomitant state monopolization of the means for legally dissolving this relationship, due process does prohibit a State from denying, solely because of inability to pay, access to its courts to individuals who seek judicial dissolution of their marriages.

I

At its core, the right to due process reflects a fundamental value in our American constitutional system. Our understanding of the value is the basis upon which we have resolved this case.

Perhaps no characteristic of an organized and cohesive society is more fundamental than its erection and enforcement of a system of rules defining the various rights and duties of its members, enabling them to govern their affairs and definitively settle their differences in an orderly, predictable manner. Without such a 'legal system,' social organization and cohesion are virtually impossible; with the ability to seek regularized resolution of conflicts individuals are capable of interdependent action that enables them to strive for achievements without the anxieties that would beset them in a disorganized society. Put more succinctly, it is this injection of the rule of law that allows society to reap the benefits of rejecting what political theorists call the 'state of nature.'

American society, of course, bottoms its systematic definition of individual rights and duties, as well as its machinery for dispute settlement, not on custom or the will of strategically placed individuals, but on the common-law model. It is to courts, or other quasi-judicial official bodies, that we ultimately look for the implementation of a regularized, orderly process of dispute settlement. Within this framework, those who wrote our original Constitution, in the Fifth Amendment, and later those who drafted the Fourteenth Amendment recognized the centrality of the concept of due process in the operation of this system. Without this guarantee that one may not be deprived of his rights, neither liberty nor property, without due process of law, the State's monopoly over techniques for binding conflict resolution could hardly be said to be acceptable under our scheme of things. Only by providing that the social enforcement mechanism must function strictly within these bounds can we hope to maintain an ordered society that is also just. It is upon this premise that this Court has through years of adjudication put flesh upon the due process principle.

Such litigation has, however, typically involved rights of defendants--not, as here, persons seeking access to the judicial process in the first instance. This is because our society has been so structured that resort to the courts is not usually the only available, legitimate means of resolving private disputes. Indeed, private structuring of individual relationships and repair of their breach is largely encouraged in American life, subject only to the caveat that the formal judicial process, if resorted to, is paramount. Thus, this Court has seldom been asked to view access to the courts as an element of due process. The legitimacy of the State's monopoly over techniques of final dispute settlement, even where some are denied access to its use, stands unimpaired where recognized, effective alternatives for the adjustment of differences remain. But the successful invocation of this governmental power by plaintiffs has often created serious problems for defendants' rights. For at that point, the judicial proceeding becomes the only effective means of resolving the dispute at hand and denial of a defendant's full access to that process raises grave problems for its legitimacy.

Recognition of this theoretical framework illuminates the precise issue presented in this case. As this Court on more than one occasion has recognized, marriage involves interests of basic importance in our society. See, e.g., *Loving v. Virginia*, 388 U.S. 1 (1967); *Skinner v. Oklahoma, ex rel. Williamson*, 316 U.S. 535 (1942); *Meyer v. Nebraska*, 262 U.S. 390 (1923). It is not surprising, then, that the States have seen fit to oversee many aspects of that institution. Without a prior judicial imprimatur, individuals may freely enter into and rescind commercial contracts, for example, but we are unaware of any jurisdiction where private citizens may covenant for or dissolve marriages without state approval. Even where all substantive requirements are concededly met, we know of no instance where two consenting adults may divorce and mutually liberate themselves from the constraints of legal obligations that go with marriage, and more fundamentally the prohibition against remarriage, without invoking the State's judicial machinery.

Thus, although they assert here due process rights as would-be plaintiffs, we think appellants' plight, because resort to the state courts is the only avenue to dissolution of their marriages, is akin to that of defendants faced with exclusion from the only forum effectively empowered to settle their disputes. Resort to the judicial process by these plaintiffs is no more voluntary in a realistic sense than that of the defendant called upon to defend his interests in court. For both groups this process is not only the paramount dispute-settlement technique, but, in fact, the only available one. In this posture we think that this appeal is properly to be resolved in light of the principles enunciated in our due process decisions that delimit rights of defendants compelled to litigate their differences in the judicial forum.

II

These due process decisions, representing over a hundred years of effort by this Court to give concrete embodiment to this concept, provide, we think, complete vindication for appellants' contentions. In particular, precedent has firmly embedded in our due process jurisprudence two important principles upon whose application we rest our decision in the case before us.

A

Prior cases establish, first, that due process requires, at a minimum, that absent a countervailing state interest of overriding significance, persons forced to settle their claims of right and duty through the judicial process must be given a meaningful opportunity to be heard.

Due process does not, of course, require that the defendant in every civil case actually have a hearing on the merits. A State, can, for example, enter a default judgment against a defendant who, after adequate notice, fails to make a timely appearance, see *Windsor, supra*, 93 U.S. at 278, or who, without justifiable excuse, violates a procedural rule requiring the production of evidence necessary for orderly adjudication, *Hammond Packing Co. v. Arkansas*, 212 U.S. 322, 351 (1909). What the Constitution does require is 'an opportunity granted at a meaningful time and in a meaningful manner,' *Armstrong v. Manzo*, 380 U.S. 545, 552 (1965), 'for (a) hearing appropriate to the nature of the case,' *Mullane v. Central Hanover Bank & Trust Co., supra*, 339 U.S. at 313. The formality and procedural requisites for the hearing can vary, depending upon the importance of the interests involved and the nature of the subsequent proceedings. That the hearing required by due process is subject to waiver, and is not fixed in form does not affect its root requirement that an individual be given an opportunity for a hearing before he is deprived of any significant property interest, except for extraordinary situations where some valid governmental interest is at stake that justifies postponing the hearing until after the event. In short, 'within the limits of practicability,' a State must afford to all individuals a meaningful opportunity to be heard if it is to fulfill the promise of the Due Process Clause.

B

Our cases further establish that a statute or a rule may be held constitutionally invalid as applied when it operates to deprive an individual of a protected right although its general validity as a measure enacted in the legitimate exercise of state power is beyond question. Thus, in cases involving religious freedom, free speech or assembly, this Court has often held that a valid statute was unconstitutionally applied in particular circumstances because it interfered with an individual's exercise of those rights.

No less than these rights, the right to a meaningful opportunity to be heard within the limits of practicality, must be protected against denial by particular laws that operate to jeopardize it for particular individuals. See *Mullane v. Central Hanover Bank & Trust Co., supra; Covey v. Town of Somers*, 351 U.S. 141 (1956).

Just as a generally valid notice procedure may fail to satisfy due process because of the circumstances of the defendant, so too a cost requirement, valid on its face, may offend due process because it operates to foreclose a particular party's opportunity to be heard. The State's obligations under the Fourteenth Amendment are not simply generalized ones; rather, the State owes to each individual that process which, in light of the values of a free society, can be characterized as due.

III

Drawing upon the principles established by the cases just canvassed, we conclude that the State's refusal to admit these appellants to its courts, the sole means in Connecticut for obtaining a divorce, must be regarded as the equivalent of denying them an opportunity to be heard upon their claimed right to a dissolution of their marriages, and, in the absence of a sufficient countervailing justification for the State's action, a denial of due process.

The arguments for this kind of fee and cost requirement are that the State's interest in the prevention of frivolous litigation is substantial, its use of court fees and process costs to allocate scarce resources is rational, and its balance between the defendant's right to notice and the plaintiff's right to access is reasonable.

In our opinion, none of these considerations is sufficient to override the interest of these plaintiff-appellants in having access to the only avenue open for dissolving their allegedly untenable marriages. Not only is there no necessary connection between a litigant's assets and the seriousness of his motives in bringing suit, but it is here beyond present dispute that appellants bring these actions in good faith. Moreover, other alternatives exist to fees and cost requirements as a means for conserving the time of courts and protecting parties from frivolous litigation, such as penalties for false pleadings or affidavits, and actions for malicious prosecution or abuse of process, to mention only a few. In the same vein we think that reliable alternatives exist to service of process by a state-paid sheriff if the State is unwilling to assume the cost of official service. This is perforce true of service by publication which is the method of notice least calculated to bring to a potential defendant's attention the pendency of judicial proceedings. See *Mullane v. Central Hanover Bank & Trust Co., supra.* We think in this case service at defendant's last known address by mail and posted notice is equally effective as publication in a newspaper.

We are thus left to evaluate the State's asserted interest in its fee and cost requirements as a mechanism of resource allocation or cost recoupment. Such a justification was offered and rejected in *Griffin v. Illinois*, 351 U.S. 12 (1956). In *Griffin* it was the requirement of a transcript beyond the means of the indigent that blocked access to the judicial process. While in *Griffin* the transcript could be waived as a convenient but not necessary predicate to court access, here the State invariably imposes the costs as a measure of allocating its judicial resources. Surely, then, the rationale of *Griffin* covers this case.

IV

In concluding that the Due Process Clause of the Fourteenth Amendment requires that these appellants be afforded an opportunity to go into court to obtain a divorce, we wish to re-emphasize that we go no further than necessary to dispose of the case before us, a case where the bona fides of both appellants' indigency and desire for divorce are here beyond dispute. We do not decide that access for all individuals to the courts is a right that is, in all circumstances, guaranteed by the Due Process Clause of the Fourteenth Amendment so that its exercise may not be placed beyond the reach of any individual, for, as we have already noted, in the case before us this right is the exclusive precondition to the adjustment of a fundamental human relationship. The requirement that these appellants resort to the judicial process is entirely a state-created matter. Thus we hold only that a State may not, consistent with the obligations imposed on it by the Due Process Clause of the Fourteenth Amendment, pre-empt the right to dissolve this legal relationship without affording all citizens access to the means it has prescribed for doing so.

Reversed.

NOTES

1. As the Court made clear, *Boddie* is a due process case, with no explicit equal protection references. But the Court did cite both *Skinner v. Oklahoma* and *Griffin v. Illinois*, both equal protection cases. A further complicating factor in explaining the Court's reasoning is that, to the extent the case involves an implied fundamental right, the Court made reference both to the right of some level of access to the judicial process as well as to the right to marriage.

2. *Boddie* is a civil, not a criminal case, so its reasoning would not automatically follow from the rights of criminal defendants in *Griffin* and *Douglas*. The Court, however, explains the nature

of the connection between two lines of cases. Just as in the criminal cases, defendants had no choice but to defend their liberty in the state's court system, so also with regard to divorce, the state has a monopoly on the dissolution of marriage and, unlike other contractual arrangements, which can be privately rescinded, only the state through its court system can terminate a marriage.

3. Since the Court in *Boddie* essentially uses a procedural due process reasoning, it makes no reference to strict scrutiny. It does, however, cite *Skinner, inter alia*, to the effect that "marriage involves interests of basic importance in our society."

Mayer v. City of Chicago
404 U.S. 189 (1971)

[Appellant was convicted of nonfelony charges of disorderly conduct and interference with a police officer. He was sentenced to a $250 fine on each offense; violation of each ordinance carried a maximum penalty of $500. Desiring to appeal, he petitioned the Circuit Court for a free transcript of the proceedings of his trial. The Circuit Court found that he was indigent, but denied his application because, under the existing court rules, a free transcript was only provided in case of felony convictions.]

Mr. Justice BRENNAN delivered the opinion of the Court.

I

Griffin v. Illinois, 351 U.S. 12 (1956), is the watershed of our transcript decisions. We held there that '(d)estitute defendants must be afforded as adequate appellate review as defendants who have money enough to buy transcripts.' This holding rested on the 'constitutional guaranties of due process and equal protection both (of which) call for procedures in criminal trials which allow no invidious discriminations between persons and different groups of persons.' We said that '(p)lainly the ability to pay costs in advance bears no rational relationship to a defendant's guilt or innocence,' and concluded that '(t)here can be no equal justice where the kind of trial a man gets depends on the amount of money he has.' Appellee city of Chicago urges that we re-examine *Griffin*. We decline to do so. For 'it is now fundamental that, once established avenues (of appellate review) must be kept free of unreasoned distinctions that can only impede open and equal access to the courts.' *Rinaldi v. Yeager*, 384 U.S. 305, 310 (1966). Therefore, '(i)n all cases the duty of the State is to provide the indigent as adequate and effective an appellate review as that given appellants with funds.' *Draper v. Washington*, 372 U.S. 487, 496 (1963). In terms of a trial record, this means that the State must afford the indigent a "record of sufficient completeness' to permit proper consideration of (his) claims.' *Id.*, at 499 (quoting *Coppedge v. United States*, 369 U.S. 438 (1962)).

A 'record of sufficient completeness' does not translate automatically into a complete verbatim transcript. We said in *Griffin* that a State 'may find other means (than providing stenographic transcripts for) affording adequate and effective appellate review to indigent defendants.' 351 U.S., at 20. We considered this more fully in *Draper v. Washington, supra*, 372 U.S., at 495-496:

> Alternative methods of reporting trial proceedings are permissible if they place before the appellate court an equivalent report of the events at trial from which the appellant's contentions arise. A statement of facts agreed to by both sides, a full narrative statement

based perhaps on the trial judge's minutes taken during trial or on the court reporter's untranscribed notes, or a bystander's bill of exceptions might all be adequate substitutes, equally as good as a transcript.

We emphasize, however, that the State must provide a full verbatim record where that is necessary to assure the indigent as effective an appeal as would be available to the defendant with resources to pay his own way. Moreover, where the grounds of appeal, as in this case, make out a colorable need for a complete transcript, the burden is on the State to show that only a portion of the transcript or an 'alternative' will suffice for an effective appeal on those grounds. This rationale underlies our statement in *Draper, supra,* at 498, that:

> (T)he State could have endeavored to show that a narrative statement or only a portion of the transcript would be adequate and available for appellate consideration of petitioners' contentions. The trial judge would have complied with *** the constitutional mandate *** in limiting the grant accordingly on the basis of such a showing by the State.

II

The distinction between felony and nonfelony offenses drawn by [the challenged court rule] can no more satisfy the requirements of the Fourteenth Amendment than could the like distinction in the Wisconsin law, held invalid in *Groppi v. Wisconsin,* 400 U.S. 505 (1971), which permitted a change of venue in felony but not in misdemeanor trials. The size of the defendant's pocketbook bears no more relationship to his guilt or innocence in a nonfelony than in a felony case. The distinction drawn by [the rule] is, therefore, an 'unreasoned distinction' proscribed by the Fourteenth Amendment. *Rinaldi v. Yeager, supra,* 384 U.S., at 310. That conclusion follows directly from our decision in *Williams v. Oklahoma City,* 395 U.S. 458, 459 (1969), rejecting the argument "that an indigent person, convicted for a violation of a city ordinance, quasi criminal in nature and often referred to as a petty offense, is (not) entitled to a case-made or transcript at city expense in order to perfect an appeal."

III

The city of Chicago urges another distinction to set this case apart from Griffin and its progeny. The city notes that the defendants in all the transcript cases previously decided by this Court were sentenced to some term of confinement. Where the accused, as here, is not subject to imprisonment, but only a fine, the city suggests that his interest in a transcript is outweighed by the State's fiscal and other interests in not burdening the appellate process. This argument misconceives the principle of *Griffin* no less than does the line that [the rule] expressly draws. Griffin does not represent a balance between the needs of the accused and the interests of society; its principle is a flat prohibition against pricing indigent defendants out of as effective an appeal as would be available to others able to pay their own way. The invidiousness of the discrimination that exists when criminal procedures are made available only to those who can pay is not erased by any differences in the sentences that may be imposed. The State's fiscal interest is, therefore, irrelevant. *Cf. Shapiro v. Thompson,* 394 U.S. 618, 633 (1969).

We add that even approaching the problem in the terms the city suggests hardly yields the answer the city tenders. The practical effects of conviction of even petty offenses of the kind involved here are not to be minimized. A fine may bear as heavily on an indigent accused as forced confinement. The collateral consequences of conviction may be even more serious, as when (as was apparently a possibility in this case) the impecunious medical student finds himself barred from the practice of medicine because of a conviction he is unable to appeal for lack of funds. Moreover, the State's long-term interest would not appear to lie in making access to appellate processes from even its most inferior courts depend upon the defendant's ability to pay. It has been aptly said:

> (F)ew citizens ever have contact with the higher courts. In the main, it is the police and the lower court Bench and Bar that convey the essence of our democracy to the people.
>
> Justice, if it can be measured, must be measured by the experience the average citizen has with the police and the lower courts.

Arbitrary denial of appellate review of proceedings of the State's lowest trial courts may save the State some dollars and cents, but only at the substantial risk of generating frustration and hostility toward its courts among the most numerous consumers of justice.

IV

We conclude that appellant cannot be denied a 'record of sufficient completeness' to permit proper consideration of his claims. We repeat that this does not mean that he is automatically entitled to a full verbatim transcript. We hold today that a denial of appellant's motion, either on the basis of the rule, or, in the context of his grounds of appeal, on the basis that he did not meet the burden of showing the inadequacy of the alternatives, would constitute constitutional error.

It is so ordered.

NOTES

1. The specific constitutional underpinning of *Mayer* is at least mixed if not unclear. The Court begins by citing *Griffin*, calling it "the watershed of our transcript decisions" and noting that it rested on both due process and equal protection grounds. The *Mayer* Court also emphasized that unequal treatment of the poor in the context of appellate review was a major element of the constitutional violation. The city attempted to distinguish the earlier cases on two grounds—first, that the case at hand involved a nonfelony while the earlier cases had all involved felonies, and second that the punishment in the case at hand only amounted to a fine while the previous cases had imposed imprisonment. The Court rejected both distinctions, noting first that "[t]he size of the defendant's pocketbook bears no more relationship to his guilt or innocence in a nonfelony than in a felony case," and second, that the "collateral consequences of conviction may be even more serious, as when (as was apparently a possibility in this case) the impecunious medical student finds himself barred from the practice of medicine because of a conviction he is unable to appeal for lack of funds."

M.L.B. v. S.L.J.
519 U.S. 102 (1996)

[M.L.B. was the mother, and S.L.J. the father, of two minor children. When they divorced in 1992, the parents agreed that the children would reside with the father. He re-married the next year and petitioned the court to terminate M.L.B.'s parental rights so their stepmother could adopt the children. In his petition, the father argued that the mother did not maintain regular visitation and was in arrears on her child support obligation. The mother unsuccessfully countersued for primary custody, alleging that the father obstructed her visitation rights. By order of a Mississippi Chancery Court, petitioner M. L. B.'s parental rights to her two minor children were forever terminated. M. L. B. sought to appeal from the termination decree, but Mississippi required that she pay in advance record preparation fees estimated at $2,352.36. Because M. L. B. lacked funds to pay the fees, her appeal was dismissed.]

Justice GINSBURG delivered the opinion of the Court.

Urging that the size of her pocketbook should not be dispositive when "an interest far more precious than any property right" is at stake, *Santosky v. Kramer,* 455 U.S. 745, 758–759 (1982), M. L. B. tenders this question, which we agreed to hear and decide: May a State, consistent with the Due Process and Equal Protection Clauses of the Fourteenth Amendment, condition appeals from trial court decrees terminating parental rights on the affected parent's ability to pay record preparation fees? We hold that, just as a State may not block an indigent petty offender's access to an appeal afforded others, see *Mayer v. Chicago,* 404 U.S. 189, 195–196 (1971), so Mississippi may not deny M. L. B., because of her poverty, appellate review of the sufficiency of the evidence on which the trial court found her unfit to remain a parent.

II

Courts have confronted, in diverse settings, the "age-old problem" of "[p]roviding equal justice for poor and rich, weak and powerful alike." *Griffin v. Illinois,* 351 U.S. 12, 16 (1956). Concerning access to appeal in general, and transcripts needed to pursue appeals in particular, *Griffin* is the foundation case.

Griffin involved an Illinois rule that effectively conditioned thoroughgoing appeals from criminal convictions on the defendant's procurement of a transcript of trial proceedings. Indigent defendants, other than those sentenced to death, were not excepted from the rule, so in most cases, defendants without means to pay for a transcript had no access to appellate review at all. Although the Federal Constitution guarantees no right to appellate review, once a State affords that right, *Griffin* held, the State may not "bolt the door to equal justice."

The plurality in *Griffin* recognized "the importance of appellate review to a correct adjudication of guilt or innocence." "[T]o deny adequate review to the poor," the plurality observed, "means that many of them may lose their life, liberty or property because of unjust convictions which appellate courts would set aside." Judging the Illinois rule inconsonant with the Fourteenth Amendment, the *Griffin* plurality drew support from the Due Process and Equal Protection Clauses.

Justice Frankfurter, concurring in the judgment in *Griffin,* emphasized and explained the decision's equal protection underpinning:

> Of course a State need not equalize economic conditions.... But when a State deems it wise and just that convictions be susceptible to review by an appellate court, it cannot by force of its exactions draw a line which precludes convicted indigent persons, forsooth erroneously convicted, from securing such a review.

See also *Ross v. Moffitt,* 417 U.S. 600, 607 (1974) (*Griffin* and succeeding decisions "stand for the proposition that a State cannot arbitrarily cut off appeal rights for indigents while leaving open avenues of appeal for more affluent persons."). Summarizing the *Griffin* line of decisions regarding an indigent defendant's access to appellate review of a conviction, we said in *Rinaldi v. Yeager,* 384 U.S. 305, 310 (1966): "This Court has never held that the States are required to establish avenues of appellate review, but it is now fundamental that, once established, these avenues must be kept free of unreasoned distinctions that can only impede open and equal access to the courts."

Of prime relevance to the question presented by M. L. B.'s petition, *Griffin*'s principle has not been confined to cases in which imprisonment is at stake. The key case is *Mayer v. Chicago,* 404 U.S. 189 (1971). *Mayer* involved an indigent defendant convicted on nonfelony charges of violating two city ordinances. Fined $250 for each offense, the defendant petitioned for a transcript to support his appeal. He alleged prosecutorial misconduct and insufficient evidence to convict. The State provided free transcripts for indigent appellants in felony cases only. We declined to limit *Griffin* to cases in which the defendant faced incarceration. "The invidiousness of the discrimination that exists when criminal procedures are made available only to those who can pay," the Court said in *Mayer,* "is not erased by any differences in the sentences that may be imposed." 404 U.S., at 197. Petty offenses could entail serious collateral consequences, the *Mayer* Court noted. The *Griffin* principle, *Mayer* underscored, "is a flat prohibition," 404 U.S., at 196, against "making access to appellate processes from even [the State's] most inferior courts depend upon the [convicted] defendant's ability to pay." An impecunious party, the Court ruled, whether found guilty of a felony or conduct only "quasi criminal in nature," "cannot be denied a record of sufficient completeness to permit proper [appellate] consideration of his claims."

In contrast to the "flat prohibition" of "bolted doors" that the *Griffin* line of cases securely established, the right to counsel at state expense, as delineated in our decisions, is less encompassing. A State must provide trial counsel for an indigent defendant charged with a felony, *Gideon v. Wainwright,* 372 U.S. 335, 339 (1963), but that right does not extend to nonfelony trials if no term of imprisonment is actually imposed, *Scott v. Illinois,* 440 U.S. 367, 373–374 (1979). A State's obligation to provide appellate counsel to poor defendants faced with incarceration applies to appeals of right. *Douglas v. California,* 372 U.S. 353, 357 (1963). In *Ross v. Moffitt,* however, we held that neither the Due Process Clause nor the Equal Protection Clause requires a State to provide counsel at state expense to an indigent prisoner pursuing a discretionary appeal in the state system or petitioning for review in this Court. 417 U.S., at 610, 612, 616–618.

III

We have also recognized a narrow category of civil cases in which the State must provide access to its judicial processes without regard to a party's ability to pay court fees. In *Boddie v. Connecticut,* 401 U.S. 371 (1971), we held that the State could not deny a divorce to a married couple based on their inability to pay approximately $60 in court costs. Crucial to our decision in *Boddie* was the fundamental interest at stake. "[G]iven the basic position of the marriage relationship in this society's hierarchy of values and the concomitant state monopolization of the means for legally dissolving this relationship," we said, due process "prohibit[s] a State from denying, solely because of inability to pay, access to its courts to individuals who seek judicial dissolution of their marriages;" see also *Little v. Streater,* 452 U.S. 1, 13–17 (1981) (State must pay for blood grouping tests sought by an indigent defendant to enable him to contest a paternity suit).

Soon after *Boddie,* in *Lindsey v. Normet,* 405 U.S. 56 (1972), the Court confronted a double-bond requirement imposed by Oregon law only on tenants seeking to appeal adverse decisions in eviction actions. We referred first to precedent recognizing that, "if a full and fair trial on the merits is provided, the Due Process Clause of the Fourteenth Amendment does not require a State to provide appellate review." We next stated, however, that "[w]hen an appeal is afforded, ... it cannot be granted to some litigants and capriciously or arbitrarily denied to others without violating the Equal Protection Clause." Oregon's double-bond requirement failed equal protection measurement, we concluded, because it raised a substantial barrier to appeal for a particular class of litigants—tenants facing eviction—a barrier "faced by no other civil litigant in Oregon." The Court pointed out in *Lindsey* that the classification there at issue disadvantaged nonindigent as well as indigent appellants; the *Lindsey* decision, therefore, does not guide our inquiry here.

The following year, in *United States v. Kras,* 409 U.S. 434 (1973), the Court clarified that a constitutional requirement to waive court fees in civil cases is the exception, not the general rule. *Kras* concerned fees, totaling $50, required to secure a discharge in bankruptcy. The Court recalled in *Kras* that "[o]n many occasions we have recognized the fundamental importance ... under our Constitution" of "the associational interests that surround the establishment and dissolution of th[e] [marital] relationship." But bankruptcy discharge entails no "fundamental interest," we said. Although "obtaining [a] desired new start in life [is] important," that interest, the Court explained, "does not rise to the same constitutional level" as the interest in establishing or dissolving a marriage. Nor is resort to court the sole path to securing debt forgiveness, we stressed; in contrast, termination of a marriage, we reiterated, requires access to the State's judicial machinery.

In *Ortwein v. Schwab,* 410 U.S. 656 (1973) *(per curiam),* the Court adhered to the line drawn in *Kras.* The appellants in *Ortwein* sought court review of agency determinations reducing their welfare benefits. Alleging poverty, they challenged, as applied to them, an Oregon statute requiring appellants in civil cases to pay a $25 fee. We summarily affirmed the Oregon Supreme Court's judgment rejecting appellants' challenge. As in *Kras,* the Court saw no "'fundamental interest ... gained or lost depending on the availability' of the relief sought by [the complainants]." 410 U.S., at 659 (quoting *Kras,* 409 U.S., at 445). Absent a fundamental interest or classification attracting heightened scrutiny, we said, the applicable equal protection standard "is that of rational justification," a requirement we found satisfied by Oregon's need for revenue to offset the expenses of its court system. 410 U.S., at 660. We expressly rejected the *Ortwein* appellants' argument that a fee waiver was required for all civil appeals simply because the State chose to permit *in forma pauperis* filings in special classes of civil appeals, including appeals from terminations of parental rights.

In sum, as *Ortwein* underscored, this Court has not extended *Griffin* to the broad array of civil cases. But tellingly, the Court has consistently set apart from the mine run of cases those involving state controls or intrusions on family relationships. In that domain, to guard against undue official intrusion, the Court has examined closely and contextually the importance of the governmental interest advanced in defense of the intrusion. Cf. *Moore v. East Cleveland,* 431 U.S. 494 (1977).

IV

Choices about marriage, family life, and the upbringing of children are among associational rights this Court has ranked as "of basic importance in our society," *Boddie,* 401 U.S., at 376, rights sheltered by the Fourteenth Amendment against the State's unwarranted usurpation, disregard, or disrespect. See, for example, *Turner v. Safley,* 482 U.S. 78 (1987), *Zablocki v. Redhail,* 434 U.S. 374 (1978), and *Loving v. Virginia,* 388 U.S. 1 (1967) (marriage); *Skinner v. Oklahoma ex rel. Williamson,* 316 U.S. 535 (1942) (procreation); *Pierce v. Society of Sisters,* 268 U.S. 510 (1925), and *Meyer v. Nebraska,* 262 U.S. 390 (1923) (raising children). M. L. B.'s case, involving the State's authority to sever permanently a parent-child bond, demands the close consideration the Court has long required when a family association so undeniably important is at stake. We approach M. L. B.'s petition mindful of the gravity of the sanction imposed on her and in light of two prior decisions most immediately in point: *Lassiter v. Department of Social Servs. of Durham Cty.,* 452 U.S. 18 (1981), and *Santosky v. Kramer,* 455 U.S. 745 (1982).

Lassiter concerned the appointment of counsel for indigent persons seeking to defend against the State's termination of their parental status. The Court held that appointed counsel was not routinely required to assure a fair adjudication; instead, a case-by-case determination of the need for counsel would suffice, an assessment to be made "in the first instance by the trial court, subject ... to appellate review." 452 U.S., at 32.

For probation-revocation hearings where loss of conditional liberty is at issue, the *Lassiter* Court observed, our precedent is not doctrinaire; due process is provided, we have held, when the decision whether counsel should be appointed is made on a case-by-case basis. See *Gagnon v. Scarpelli,* 411 U.S. 778, 790 (1973). In criminal prosecutions that do not lead to the defendant's incarceration, however, our precedent recognizes no right to appointed counsel. See *Scott v. Illinois,* 440 U.S., at 373–374. Parental termination cases, the *Lassiter* Court concluded, are most appropriately ranked with probation-revocation hearings: While the Court declined to recognize an automatic right to appointed counsel, it said that an appointment would be due when warranted by the character and difficulty of the case. See *Lassiter,* 452 U.S., at 31–32.

Significant to the disposition of M. L. B.'s case, the *Lassiter* Court considered it "plain ... that a parent's desire for and right to 'the companionship, care, custody, and management of his or her children' is an important interest," one that "'undeniably warrants deference and, absent a powerful countervailing interest, protection.'" The object of the proceeding is "not simply to infringe upon [the parent's] interest," the Court recognized, "but to end it"; thus, a decision against the parent "work[s] a unique kind of deprivation." *Lassiter,* 452 U.S., at 27. For that reason, "[a] parent's interest in the accuracy and justice of the decision ... is ... a commanding one."

Santosky held that a "clear and convincing" proof standard is constitutionally required in parental termination proceedings. 455 U.S., at 769–770. In so ruling, the Court again emphasized that a termination decree is "*final* and irrevocable." "Few forms of state action," the Court said, "are both so severe and so irreversible." *Ibid.* As in *Lassiter,* the Court characterized the parent's interest as "commanding," indeed, "far more precious than any property right." 455 U.S., at 758–759.

Although both *Lassiter* and *Santosky* yielded divided opinions, the Court was unanimously of the view that "the interest of parents in their relationship with their children is sufficiently fundamental to come within the finite class of liberty interests protected by the Fourteenth Amendment." 455 U.S., at 774 (REHNQUIST, J., dissenting). It was also the Court's unanimous view that "[f]ew consequences of judicial action are so grave as the severance of natural family ties." *Id.* at 787.

V

Guided by this Court's precedent on an indigent's access to judicial processes in criminal and civil cases, and on proceedings to terminate parental status, we turn to the classification question this case presents: Does the Fourteenth Amendment require Mississippi to accord M. L. B. access to an appeal—available but for her inability to advance required costs—before she is forever branded unfit for affiliation with her children? Respondents urge us to classify M. L. B.'s case with the generality of civil cases, in which indigent persons have no constitutional right to proceed *in forma pauperis.* See *supra,* at 562–564. M. L. B., on the other hand, maintains that the accusatory state action she is trying to fend off is barely distinguishable from criminal condemnation in view of the magnitude and permanence of the loss she faces. For the purpose at hand, M. L. B. asks us to treat her parental termination appeal as we have treated petty offense appeals; she urges us to adhere to the reasoning in *Mayer v. Chicago,* 404 U.S. 189 (1971), and rule that Mississippi may not withhold the transcript M. L. B. needs to gain review of the order ending her parental status. Guided by *Lassiter* and *Santosky,* and other decisions acknowledging the primacy of the parent-child relationship, *e.g., Stanley v. Illinois,* 405 U.S., at 651; *Meyer v. Nebraska,* 262 U.S., at 399, we agree that the *Mayer* decision points to the disposition proper in this case.

We observe first that the Court's decisions concerning access to judicial processes, commencing with *Griffin* and running through *Mayer,* reflect both equal protection and due process concerns. See *Ross v. Moffitt,* 417 U.S., at 608–609. As we said in *Bearden v. Georgia,* 461 U.S. 660, 665 (1983), in the Court's *Griffin*-line cases, "[d]ue process and equal protection principles converge." The equal protection concern relates to the legitimacy of fencing out would-be appellants based solely on their inability to pay core costs. See *Griffin,* 351 U.S., at 23 (Frankfurter, J., concurring in judgment). The due process concern homes in on the essential fairness of the state-ordered proceedings anterior to adverse state action. See *Ross,* 417 U.S., at 609. A "precise rationale" has not been composed because cases of this order "cannot be resolved by resort to easy slogans or pigeonhole analysis," *Bearden,* 461 U.S., at 666. Nevertheless, "[m]ost decisions in this area," we have recognized, "res[t] on an equal protection framework," as M. L. B.'s plea heavily does, for, as we earlier observed, due process does not independently require that the State provide a right to appeal. We place this case within the framework established by our past decisions in this area. In line with those decisions, we inspect the character and intensity of the individual interest at stake, on the one hand, and the State's justification for its exaction, on the other. See *Bearden,* 461 U.S., at 666–667.

We now focus on *Mayer* and the considerations linking that decision to M. L. B.'s case. *Mayer* applied *Griffin* to a petty offender, fined a total of $500, who sought to appeal from the trial court's judgment. An "impecunious medical student," the defendant in *Mayer* could not pay for a transcript. We held that the State must afford him a record complete enough to allow fair appellate consideration of his claims. The defendant in *Mayer* faced no term of confinement, but the conviction, we observed, could affect his professional prospects and, possibly, even bar him from the practice of medicine. The State's pocketbook interest in advance payment for a transcript, we concluded, was unimpressive when measured against the stakes for the defendant.

Similarly here, the stakes for petitioner M. L. B. — forced dissolution of her parental rights—are large, "'more substantial than mere loss of money.'" *Santosky,* 455 U.S., at 756 (quoting *Addington v. Texas,* 441 U.S. 418, 424 (1979)). In contrast to loss of custody, which does not sever the parent-child bond, parental status termination is "irretrievabl[y] destructi[ve]" of the most fundamental family relationship. *Santosky,* 455 U.S., at 753. And the risk of error, Mississippi's experience shows, is considerable.

Consistent with *Santosky,* Mississippi has, by statute, adopted a "clear and convincing proof" standard for parental status termination cases. Nevertheless, the Chancellor's termination order in this case simply recites statutory language; it describes no evidence, and otherwise details no reasons for finding M. L. B. "clear[ly] and convincing[ly]" unfit to be a parent. Only a transcript can reveal to judicial minds other than the Chancellor's the sufficiency, or insufficiency, of the evidence to support his stern judgment.

CHAPTER 8: IMPLIED FUNDAMENTAL RIGHTS & THE EQUAL PROTECTION CLAUSE   463

The countervailing government interest, as in *Mayer,* is financial. Mississippi urges, as the justification for its appeal cost prepayment requirement, the State's legitimate interest in offsetting the costs of its court system. But in the tightly circumscribed category of parental status termination cases, appeals are few, and not likely to impose an undue burden on the State.

Several States deal discretely with *in forma pauperis* appeals, including transcripts, in parental status termination cases. In States providing criminal appeals, as we earlier recounted, an indigent's access to appeal, through a transcript of relevant trial proceedings, is secure under our precedent. That equal access right holds for petty offenses as well as for felonies. But counsel at state expense, we have held, is a constitutional requirement, even in the first instance, only when the defendant faces time in confinement. When deprivation of parental status is at stake, however, counsel is sometimes part of the process that is due. See *Lassiter,* 452 U.S., at 31–32. It would be anomalous to recognize a right to a transcript needed to appeal a misdemeanor conviction—though trial counsel may be flatly denied — but hold, at the same time, that a transcript need not be prepared for M. L. B. — though were her defense sufficiently complex, state-paid counsel, as *Lassiter* instructs, would be designated for her.

In aligning M. L. B.'s case and *Mayer* — parental status termination decrees and criminal convictions that carry no jail time — for appeal access purposes, we do not question the general rule, stated in *Ortwein,* that fee requirements ordinarily are examined only for rationality. The State's need for revenue to offset costs, in the mine run of cases, satisfies the rationality requirement, see *Ortwein,* 410 U.S., at 660; States are not forced by the Constitution to adjust all tolls to account for "disparity in material circumstances." *Griffin,* 351 U.S., at 23 (Frankfurter, J., concurring in judgment).

But our cases solidly establish two exceptions to that general rule. The basic right to participate in political processes as voters and candidates cannot be limited to those who can pay for a license. Nor may access to judicial processes in cases criminal or "quasi criminal in nature," *Mayer,* 404 U.S., at 196, turn on ability to pay. In accord with the substance and sense of our decisions in *Lassiter* and *Santosky,* see *supra,* at 564–566, we place decrees forever terminating parental rights in the category of cases in which the State may not "bolt the door to equal justice," *Griffin,* 351 U.S., at 24 (Frankfurter, J., concurring in judgment); see *supra,* at 560–561.

Notably, the Court in *Harper* recognized that "a State may exact fees from citizens for many different kinds of licenses." For example, the State "can demand from all an equal fee for a driver's license." But voting cannot hinge on ability to pay, the Court explained, for it is a "'fundamental political right ... preservative of all rights.'" *Bullock* rejected as justifications for excluding impecunious persons, the State's concern about unwieldy ballots and its interest in financing elections. *Lubin* reaffirmed that a State may not require from an indigent candidate "fees he cannot pay."

VI

In numerous cases, respondents point out, the Court has held that government "need not provide funds so that people can exercise even fundamental rights." Brief for Respondents 12; see, *e.g., Lyng v. Automobile Workers,* 485 U.S. 360, 363, n. 2 (1988) (rejecting equal protection attack on amendment to Food Stamp Act providing that no household could become eligible for benefits while a household member was on strike); *Regan v. Taxation with Representation of Wash.,* 461 U.S. 540, 543–544, 550–551 (1983) (rejecting nonprofit organization's claims of free speech and equal protection rights to receive tax deductible contributions to support its lobbying activity); *Harris v. McRae,* 448 U.S. 297, 321–326 (1980) (Medicaid funding need not be provided for women seeking medically necessary abortions). A decision for M. L. B., respondents contend, would dishonor our cases recognizing that the Constitution "generally confer[s] no affirmative right to governmental aid, even where such aid may be necessary to secure life, liberty, or property interests of which the government itself may not deprive the individual." *DeShaney v. Winnebago County Dept. of Social Servs.,* 489 U.S. 189, 196 (1989).

Complainants in the cases on which respondents rely sought state aid to subsidize their privately initiated action or to alleviate the consequences of differences in economic circumstances that existed apart from state action. M. L. B.'s complaint is of a different order. She is endeavoring to defend against the State's destruction of her family bonds, and to resist the brand associated with a parental unfitness adjudication. Like a defendant resisting criminal conviction, she seeks to be spared from the State's devastatingly adverse action. That is the very reason we have paired her case with *Mayer,* not with *Ortwein* or *Kras,* discussed *supra,* at 562–564.

Respondents and the dissenters urge that we will open floodgates if we do not rigidly restrict *Griffin* to cases typed "criminal." But we have repeatedly noticed what sets parental status termination decrees apart from mine run civil actions, even from other domestic relations matters such as divorce, paternity, and child custody. To recapitulate, termination decrees "wor[k] a unique kind of deprivation." *Lassiter,* 452 U.S., at 27. In contrast to matters modifiable at the parties' will or based on changed circumstances, termination adjudications involve the awesome authority of the State "to destroy permanently all legal recognition of the parental relationship." *Rivera,* 483 U.S., at 580. Our *Lassiter* and *Santosky* decisions, recognizing that parental termination decrees are among the most severe forms of state action, *Santosky,* 455 U.S., at 759, have not served as precedent in other areas. See *supra,* at 565, n. 11. We are therefore satisfied that the label "civil" should not entice us to leave undisturbed the Mississippi courts' disposition of this case. Cf. *In re Gault,* 387 U.S., at 50.

For the reasons stated, we hold that Mississippi may not withhold from M. L. B. "a 'record of sufficient completeness' to permit proper [appellate] consideration of [her] claims." *Mayer,* 404 U.S., at 198. Accordingly, we reverse the judgment of the Supreme Court of Mississippi and remand the case for further proceedings not inconsistent with this opinion.

It is so ordered.

NOTES

1. The Court's opinion in *M.L.B.* is both an extremely good summary and review of the Court's cases on access to the judicial process and a good explanation of the interplay between due process and equal protection doctrines. The question before the Court was how to fit the issue of appeals from trial court decrees terminating parental rights in with previous precedents. The Court described *Griffin* as the "foundation case," and *Mayer* as the "key case" in making clear that "*Griffin*'s principle has not been confined to cases in which imprisonment is at stake." The Court summarized other important cases that had extended *Griffin/Mayer*:

- *Ross v. Moffitt,* 417 U.S. 600 (1974), holding that neither the Due Process Clause nor the Equal Protection Clause requires a state to provide counsel at state expense to an indigent prisoner pursuing a discretionary appeal in the state system or petitioning for review in the Supreme Court.

- *United States v. Kras,* 409 U.S. 434 (1973), clarifying that a constitutional requirement to waive court fees in civil cases is the exception, not the general rule. *Kras* concerned fees, totaling $50, required to secure a discharge in bankruptcy. The Court noted in *Kras* that "[o]n many occasions we have recognized the fundamental importance ... under our Constitution" of "the associational interests that surround the establishment and dissolution of th[e] [marital] relationship." But bankruptcy discharge entails no "fundamental interest." Although "obtaining [a] desired new start in life [is] important," that interest, the Court explained, "does not rise to the same constitutional level" as the interest in establishing or dissolving a marriage.

- *Ortwein v. Schwab,* 410 U.S. 656 (1973), rejecting a challenge to an Oregon statute requiring appellants in civil cases to pay a $25 fee. "Absent a fundamental interest or classification attracting heightened scrutiny, we said, the applicable equal protection standard 'is that of rational justification,' a requirement we found satisfied by Oregon's need for revenue to offset the expenses of its court system."

In terms of extending *Griffin* to civil cases, the *M.L.B.* Court summarized its history: "this Court has not extended *Griffin* to the broad array of civil cases. But tellingly, the Court has consistently set apart from the mine run of cases those involving state controls or intrusions on family relationships. In that domain, to guard against undue official intrusion, the Court has examined closely and contextually the importance of the governmental interest advanced in defense of the intrusion."

2. In terms of the overlap between due process and equal protection reasoning, the Court noted:

> We observe first that the Court's decisions concerning access to judicial processes, commencing with *Griffin* and running through *Mayer,* reflect both equal protection and due process concerns. As we said in *Bearden v. Georgia,* 461 U.S. 660, 665 (1983), in the Court's *Griffin*-line cases, "[d]ue process and equal protection principles converge." The equal protection concern relates to the legitimacy of fencing out would-be appellants based solely on their inability to pay core costs. The due process concern homes in on the essential fairness of the state-ordered proceedings anterior to adverse state action. A "precise rationale" has not been composed because cases of this order "cannot be resolved by resort to easy slogans or pigeonhole analysis," *Bearden,* 461 U.S., at 666. Nevertheless, "[m]ost decisions in this area," we have recognized, "res[t] on an equal protection framework," *id.* at 665, as M. L. B.'s plea heavily does, for, as we earlier observed, see *supra,* at 560, due process does not independently require that the State provide a right to appeal. We place this case within the framework established by our past decisions in this area. In line with those decisions, we inspect the character and intensity of the individual interest at stake, on the one hand, and the State's justification for its exaction, on the other. See *Bearden,* 461 U.S., at 666–667.

This explanation also makes clearer that some kind of heightened judicial scrutiny is at work in the *Griffin* line of cases. The Court does not use the exact language of strict scrutiny—narrowly tailored and compelling interest—but it does, as in some of the voting cases, suggest a balancing test, where the Court will weigh "the character and intensity of the individual interest at stake, on the one hand, and the State's justification for its exaction, on the other." This balancing test will usually result in something close to strict scrutiny where, as here, the individual interest (termination of parental rights) is extremely significant.

E. THE RIGHT TO TRAVEL

1. *THE COURT APPLIES STRICT SCRUTINY TO INFRINGEMENTS ON THE RIGHT TO TRAVEL*

Shapiro v. Thompson
394 U.S. 618 (1969)

[This case consolidated three appeals in which federal trial courts had held unconstitutional statutes that denied welfare benefits to residents who failed to meet a one-year durational residency requirement.]

Mr. Justice BRENNAN delivered the opinion of the Court.

II.

There is no dispute that the effect of the waiting-period requirement in each case is to create two classes of needy resident families indistinguishable from each other except that one is composed of residents who have resided a year or more, and the second of residents who have resided less than a year, in the jurisdiction. On the basis of this sole difference the first class is granted and the second class is denied welfare aid upon which may depend the ability of the families to obtain the very means to subsist--food, shelter, and other necessities of life ... [A]ppellees' central contention is that the statutory prohibition of benefits to residents of less than a year creates a classification which constitutes an invidious discrimination denying them equal protection of the laws. We agree. The interests which appellants assert are promoted by the classification either may not constitutionally be promoted by government or are not compelling governmental interests.

III.

Primarily, appellants justify the waiting-period requirement as a protective device to preserve the fiscal integrity of state public assistance programs. It is asserted that people who require welfare assistance during their first year of residence in a State are likely to become continuing burdens on state welfare programs. Therefore, the argument runs, if such people can be deterred from entering the jurisdiction by denying them welfare benefits during the first year, state programs to assist long-time residents will not be impaired by a substantial influx of indigent newcomers.[FN 7]

[FN 7] The waiting-period requirement has its antecedents in laws prevalent in England and the American Colonies centuries ago which permitted the ejection of individuals and families if local authorities thought they might become public charges. For example, the preamble of the English Law of Settlement and Removal of 1662 expressly recited the concern, also said to justify the three statutes before us, that large numbers of the poor were moving to parishes where more liberal relief policies were in effect. See generally Coll, Perspectives in Public Welfare: The English Heritage, 4 Welfare in Review No. 3, p. 1 (1966). The 1662 law and the earlier Elizabethan Poor Law of 1601 were the models adopted by the American Colonies. Newcomers to a city, town, or county who might become public charges were 'warned out' or 'passed on' to the next locality. Initially, the funds for welfare payments were raised by local taxes, and the controversy as to responsibility for particular indigents was between localities in the same State. As States-first alone and then with federal grants-assumed the major responsibility, the contest of nonresponsibility became interstate.

There is weighty evidence that exclusion from the jurisdiction of the poor who need or may need relief was the specific objective of these provisions. In the Congress, sponsors of federal legislation to eliminate all residence requirements have been consistently opposed by representatives of state and local welfare agencies who have stressed the fears of the States that elimination of the requirements would result in a heavy influx of individuals into States providing the most generous benefits. The sponsor of the Connecticut requirement said in its support: 'I doubt that Connecticut can and should continue to allow unlimited migration into the state on the basis of offering instant money and permanent income to all who can make their way to the state regardless of their ability to contribute to the economy.' In Pennsylvania, shortly after the enactment of the one-year requirement, the Attorney General issued an opinion construing the one-year requirement strictly because '(a)ny other conclusion would tend to attract the dependents of other states to our Commonwealth.' In the District of Columbia case, the constitutionality of § 3-203 was frankly defended in the District Court and in this Court on the ground that it is designed to protect the jurisdiction from an influx of persons seeking more generous public assistance than might be available elsewhere.

We do not doubt that the one-year waiting period device is well suited to discourage the influx of poor families in need of assistance. An indigent who desires to migrate, resettle, find a new job, and start a new life will doubtless hesitate if he knows that he must risk making the move without the possibility of falling back on state welfare assistance during his first year of residence, when his need may be most acute. But the purpose of inhibiting migration by needy persons into the State is constitutionally impermissible.

This Court long ago recognized that the nature of our Federal Union and our constitutional concepts of personal liberty unite to require that all citizens be free to travel throughout the length and breadth of our land uninhibited by statutes, rules, or regulations which unreasonably burden or restrict this movement. That proposition was early stated by Chief Justice Taney in the Passenger Cases, 7 How. 283, 492, 12 L .Ed. 702 (1849):

> For all the great purposes for which the Federal government was formed, we are one people, with one common country. We are all citizens of the United States; and, as members of the same community, must have the right to pass and repass through every part of it without interruption, as freely as in our own States.

We have no occasion to ascribe the source of this right to travel interstate to a particular constitutional provision. It suffices that, as Mr. Justice Stewart said for the Court in United *States v. Guest*, 383 U.S. 745, 757-758 (1966):

> The constitutional right to travel from one State to another occupies a position fundamental to the concept of our Federal Union. It is a right that has been firmly established and repeatedly recognized.

> (The) right finds no explicit mention in the Constitution. The reason, it has been suggested, is that a right so elementary was conceived from the beginning to be a necessary concomitant of the stronger Union the Constitution created. In any event, freedom to travel throughout the United States has long been recognized as a basic right under the Constitution.

Thus, the purpose of deterring the in-migration of indigents cannot serve as justification for the classification created by the one-year waiting period, since that purpose is constitutionally impermissible. If a law has 'no other purpose than to chill the assertion of constitutional rights by penalizing those who choose to exercise them, then it (is) patently unconstitutional.' *United States v. Jackson*, 390 U.S. 570, 581 (1968).

Alternatively, appellants argue that even if it is impermissible for a State to attempt to deter the entry of all indigents, the challenged classification may be justified as a permissible state attempt to discourage those indigents who would enter the State solely to obtain larger benefits. We observe first that none of the statutes before us is tailored to serve that objective. Rather, the class of barred newcomers is all-inclusive, lumping the great majority who come to the State for other purposes with those who come for the sole purpose of collecting higher benefits. In actual operation, therefore, the three statutes enact what in effect are non-rebuttable presumptions that every applicant for assistance in his first year of residence came to the jurisdiction solely to obtain higher benefits. Nothing whatever in any of these records supplies any basis in fact for such a presumption.

More fundamentally, a State may no more try to fence out those indigents who seek higher welfare benefits than it may try to fence out indigents generally. Implicit in any such distinction is the notion that indigents who enter a State with the hope of securing higher welfare benefits are somehow less deserving than indigents who do not take this consideration into account. But we do not perceive why a mother who is seeking to make a new life for herself and her children should be regarded as less deserving because she considers, among others factors, the level of a State's public assistance. Surely such a mother is no less deserving than a mother who moves into a particular State in order to take advantage of its better educational facilities.

Appellants argue further that the challenged classification may be sustained as an attempt to distinguish between new and old residents on the basis of the contribution they have made to the community through the payment of taxes. We have difficulty seeing how long-term residents who qualify for welfare are making a greater present contribution to the State in taxes than indigent residents who have recently arrived. If the argument is based on contributions made in the past by the long-term residents, there is some question, as a factual matter, whether this argument is applicable in Pennsylvania where the record suggests that some 40% of those denied public assistance because of the waiting period had lengthy prior residence in the State. But we need not rest on the particular facts of these cases. Appellants' reasoning would logically permit the State to bar new residents from schools, parks, and libraries or deprive them of police and fire protection. Indeed it would permit the State to apportion all benefits and services according to the past tax contributions of its citizens. The Equal Protection Clause prohibits such an apportionment of state services.

We recognize that a State has a valid interest in preserving the fiscal integrity of its programs. It may legitimately attempt to limit its expenditures, whether for public assistance, public education, or any other program. But a State may not accomplish such a purpose by invidious distinctions between classes of its citizens. It could not, for example, reduce expenditures for education by barring indigent children from its schools. Similarly, in the cases before us, appellants must do more than show that denying welfare benefits to new residents saves money. The saving of welfare costs cannot justify an otherwise invidious classification.

In sum, neither deterrence of indigents from migrating to the State nor limitation of welfare benefits to those regarded as contributing to the State is a constitutionally permissible state objective.

IV.

Appellants next advance as justification certain administrative and related governmental objectives allegedly served by the waiting-period requirement. They argue that the requirement (1) facilitates the planning of the welfare budget; (2) provides an objective test of residency; (3) minimizes the opportunity for recipients fraudulently to receive payments from more than one jurisdiction; and (4) encourages early entry of new residents into the labor force.

At the outset, we reject appellants' argument that a mere showing of a rational relationship between the waiting period and these four admittedly permissible state objectives will suffice to justify the classification. See *Lindsley v. Natural Carbonic Gas Co.*, 220 U.S. 61, 78 (1911); *Flemming v. Nestor*, 363 U.S. 603, 611 (1960); *McGowan v. Maryland*, 366 U.S. 420, 426 (1961). The waiting-period provision denies welfare benefits to otherwise eligible applicants solely because they have recently moved into the jurisdiction. But in moving from State to State or to the District of Columbia appellees were exercising a constitutional right, and any classification which serves to penalize the exercise of that right, unless shown to be necessary to promote a compelling governmental interest, is unconstitutional. Cf. *Skinner v. Oklahoma*, 316 U.S. 535, 541 (1942); *Korematsu v. United States*, 323 U.S. 214, 216 (1944); *Bates v. Little Rock*, 361 U.S. 516, 524 (1960); *Sherbert v. Verner*, 374 U.S. 398, 406 (1963).

The argument that the waiting-period requirement facilitates budget predictability is wholly unfounded. The records in all three cases are utterly devoid of evidence that either State or the District of Columbia in fact uses the one-year requirement as a means to predict the number of people who will require assistance in the budget year. None of the appellants takes a census of new residents or collects any other data that would reveal the number of newcomers in the State less than a year. Nor are new residents required to give advance notice of their need for welfare assistance. Thus, the welfare authorities cannot know how many new residents come into the jurisdiction in any year, much less how many of them will require public assistance. In these circumstances, there is simply no basis for the claim that the one-year waiting requirement serves the purpose of making the welfare budget more predictable.

The argument that the waiting period serves as an administratively efficient rule of thumb for determining residency similarly will not withstand scrutiny. The residence requirement and the one-year waiting-period requirement are distinct and independent prerequisites for assistance under these three statutes, and the facts relevant to the determination of each are directly examined by the welfare authorities. Before granting an application, the welfare authorities investigate the applicant's employment, housing, and family situation and in the course of the inquiry necessarily learn the facts upon which to determine whether the applicant is a resident.

Similarly, there is no need for a State to use the one-year waiting period as a safeguard against fraudulent receipt of benefits; for less drastic means are available, and are employed, to minimize that hazard. Of course, a State has a valid interest in preventing fraud by any applicant, whether a newcomer or a long-time resident. It is not denied, however, that the investigations now conducted entail inquiries into facts relevant to that subject.

Pennsylvania suggests that the one-year waiting period is justified as a means of encouraging new residents to join the labor force promptly. But this logic would also require a similar waiting period for long-term residents of the State. A state purpose to encourage employment provides no rational basis for imposing a one-year waiting-period restriction on new residents only.

We conclude therefore that appellants in these cases do not use and have no need to use the one-year requirement for the governmental purposes suggested. Thus, even under traditional equal protection tests a classification of welfare applicants according to whether they have lived in the State for one year would seem irrational and unconstitutional. But, of course, the traditional criteria do not apply in these cases. Since the classification here touches on the fundamental right of interstate movement, its constitutionality must be judged by the stricter standard of whether it promotes a compelling state interest. Under this standard, the waiting-period requirement clearly violates the Equal Protection Clause.

NOTES

1. There is a lot of law in *Shapiro v. Thompson*. First, the Court identifies the right to interstate travel as fundamental. Why is the right to travel fundamental? The Court concedes that it will make no effort "to ascribe the source of this right to travel interstate to a particular constitutional provision." Rather, it is fundamental because the right "to travel from one State to another occupies a position fundamental to the concept of our Federal Union," and because "the nature of our Federal Union and our constitutional concepts of personal liberty unite to require that all citizens be free to travel throughout the length and breadth of our land uninhibited by statutes, rules, or regulations which unreasonably burden or restrict this movement." The right to travel, then, is a classic "implied" fundamental right, that is, one not mentioned explicitly in the Constitution, but necessary to give effect to the grand design of the Constitution. But if the right to travel is fundamental in and of itself, why is *Shapiro* an equal protection case? Why do we have to compare the class of those who have recently exercised their right to travel with the class of long-term state residents? Isn't it enough that one person's right to travel has been infringed without regard to how others have been treated? The Court does not address the issue but, for a long time, the Court's right to travel cases were all equal protection cases. That changed in *Saenz v. Roe*, *infra*.

2. The Court's *Shapiro* opinion provides one of the clearest statements of the strict scrutiny standard: "But in moving from State to State or to the District of Columbia appellees were exercising a constitutional right, and any classification which serves to penalize the exercise of that right, unless shown to be necessary to promote a compelling governmental interest, is unconstitutional." Once the Court announced that it would apply this very demanding standard, the result in the case followed easily. Certain of the state's purposes are not even permissible, much less compelling: thus, "the purpose of deterring the in-migration of indigents cannot serve as justification for the classification created by the one-year waiting period, since that purpose is constitutionally impermissible. If a law has 'no other purpose than to chill the assertion of constitutional rights by penalizing those who choose to exercise them, then it (is) patently unconstitutional." And as to a more limited version of that deterring migration purpose, that is, deterring only those who move to a state to acquire welfare benefits, "a State may no more try to fence out those indigents who seek higher welfare benefits than it may try to fence out indigents generally." As to the purpose of distinguishing between new and old residents on the basis of the contribution they have made to the community through the payment of taxes, "[t]he Equal Protection Clause prohibits such an apportionment of state services."

Finally, the state sought to justify the statute in that it promoted fiscal integrity and served several other administrative and government objectives. But here the Court noted that the states did not need to use the durational residence requirement to achieve these ends and thus the challenged statutes did not meet the demands of strict scrutiny.

Dunn v. Blumstein
405 U.S. 330 (1972)

[James Blumstein accepted a position as Assistant Professor of Law at Vanderbilt University and, upon moving to Tennessee, applied to vote in an election scheduled for the following month. The county registrar denied his registration on the ground that Tennessee law authorizes the registration of only those persons who, at the time of the next election, will have been residents of the State for a year and residents of the county for three months. Blumstein filed a complaint alleging that this durational residency requirement for voting violated the Equal Protection Clause of the Constitution.]

Mr. Justice MARSHALL delivered the opinion of the Court.

The subject of this lawsuit is the durational residence requirement. Appellee does not challenge Tennessee's power to restrict the vote to bona fide Tennessee residents. Nor has Tennessee ever disputed that appellee was a bona fide resident of the State and county when he attempted to register. But Tennessee insists that, in addition to being a resident, a would-be voter must have been a resident for a year in the State and three months in the county. It is this additional durational residence requirement that appellee challenges.

Durational residence laws penalize those persons who have traveled from one place to another to establish a new residence during the qualifying period. Such laws divide residents into two classes, old residents and new residents, and discriminate against the latter to the extent of totally denying them the opportunity to vote. The constitutional question presented is whether the Equal Protection Clause of the Fourteenth Amendment permits a State to discriminate in this way among its citizens.

To decide whether a law violates the Equal Protection Clause, we look, in essence, to three things: the character of the classification in question; the individual interests affected by the classification; and the governmental interests asserted in support of the classification. Cf. *Williams v. Rhodes*, 393 U.S. 23, 30 (1968). In considering laws challenged under the Equal Protection Clause, this Court has evolved more than one test, depending upon the interest affected or the classification involved. First, then, we must determine what standard of review is appropriate. In the present case, whether we look to the benefit withheld by the classification (the opportunity to vote) or the basis for the classification (recent interstate travel) we conclude that the State must show a substantial and compelling reason for imposing durational residence requirements.

[The Court initially noted that Tennessee's durational residence requirement restricted the implied fundamental right to vote.]

This exacting test is appropriate for another reason: Tennessee's durational residence laws classify bona fide residents on the basis of recent travel, penalizing those persons, and only those persons, who have gone from one jurisdiction to another during the qualifying period. Thus, the durational residence requirement directly impinges on the exercise of a second fundamental personal right, the right to travel.

'(F)reedom to travel throughout the United States has long been recognized as a basic right under the Constitution.' *United States v. Guest*, 383 U.S. 745, 758 (1966). And it is clear that the freedom to travel includes the 'freedom to enter and abide in any State in the Union,' *id.*, at 285.

Obviously, durational residence laws single out the class of bona fide state and county residents who have recently exercised this constitutionally protected right, and penalize such travelers directly. We considered such a durational residence requirement in *Shapiro v. Thompson, supra,* where the pertinent statutes imposed a one-year waiting period for interstate migrants as a condition to receiving welfare benefits. Although in *Shapiro* we specifically did not decide whether durational residence requirements could be used to determine voting eligibility, we concluded that since the right to travel was a constitutionally protected right, 'any classification which serves to penalize the exercise of that right, unless shown to be necessary to promote a compelling governmental interest, is unconstitutional.' This compelling-state-interest test was also adopted in the separate concurrence of Mr. Justice Stewart. Preceded by a long line of cases recognizing the constitutional right to travel, and repeatedly reaffirmed in the face of attempts to disregard it, see *Wyman v. Bowens,* 397 U.S. 49 (1970), and *Wyman v. Lopez,* 404 U.S. 1055 (1972), *Shapiro* and the compelling-state-interest test it articulates control this case.

Tennessee attempts to distinguish *Shapiro* by urging that 'the vice of the welfare statute in *Shapiro* . . . was its objective to deter interstate travel.' In Tennessee's view, the compelling-state-interest test is appropriate only where there is 'some evidence to indicate a deterrence of or infringement on the right to travel . . . .' Thus, Tennessee seeks to avoid the clear command of *Shapiro* by arguing that durational residence requirements for voting neither seek to nor actually do deter such travel. In essence, Tennessee argues that the right to travel is not abridged here in any constitutionally relevant sense.

This view represents a fundamental misunderstanding of the law. It is irrelevant whether disenfranchisement or denial of welfare is the more potent deterrent to travel. *Shapiro* did not rest upon a finding that denial of welfare actually deterred travel. Nor have other 'right to travel' cases in this Court always relied on the presence of actual deterrence. In *Shapiro* we explicitly stated that the compelling state interest test would be triggered by 'any classification which serves to penalize the exercise of that right (to travel) . . . .' While noting the frank legislative purpose to deter migration by the poor, and speculating that '(a)n indigent who desires to migrate . . . will doubtless hesitate if he knows that he must risk' the loss of benefits, the majority found no need to dispute the 'evidence that few welfare recipients have in fact been deterred (from moving) by residence requirements.' Indeed, none of the litigants had themselves been deterred. Only last Term, it was specifically noted that because a durational residence requirement for voting 'operates to penalize those persons, and only those persons, who have exercised their constitutional right of interstate migration . . ., (it) may withstand constitutional scrutiny only upon a clear showing that the burden imposed is necessary to protect a compelling and substantial governmental interest.' *Oregon v. Mitchell,* 400 U.S., at 238 (separate opinion of Brennan, White, and Marshall, JJ.).

Of course, it is true that the two individual interests affected by Tennessee's durational residence requirements are affected in different ways. Travel is permitted, but only at a price; voting is prohibited. The right to travel is merely penalized, while the right to vote is absolutely denied. But these differences are irrelevant for present purposes. *Shapiro* implicitly realized what this Court has made explicit elsewhere:

> 'It has long been established that a State may not impose a penalty upon those who exercise a right guaranteed by the Constitution. . . . 'Constitutional rights would be of little value if they could be . . . indirectly denied,' . . . .' *Harman v. Forssenius,* 380 U.S. 528, 540 (1965).

See also *Garrity v. New Jersey,* 385 U.S. 493 (1967), and cases cited therein; *Spevack v. Klein,*

385 U.S. 511, 515 (1967). The right to travel is an 'unconditional personal right,' a right whose exercise may not be conditioned. *Shapiro v. Thompson*, 394 U.S., at 643 (Stewart, J., concurring); *Oregon v. Mitchell, supra*, 400 U.S., at 292 (Stewart, J., concurring and dissenting, Burger, C.J., and Blackmun, J., joined). Durational residence laws impermissibly condition and penalize the right to travel by imposing their prohibitions on only those persons who have recently exercised that right. In the present case, such laws force a person who wishes to travel and change residences to choose between travel and the basic right to vote. Cf. *United States v. Jackson*, 390 U.S. 570, 582-583 (1968). Absent a compelling state interest, a State may not burden the right to travel in this way.

In sum, durational residence laws must be measured by a strict equal protection test: they are unconstitutional unless the State can demonstrate that such laws are 'necessary to promote a compelling governmental interest.' *Shapiro v. Thompson*, 394 U.S., at 634; *Kramer v. Union Free School District No. 15*, 395 U.S., at 627. Thus phrased, the constitutional question may sound like a mathematical formula. But legal 'tests' do not have the precision of mathematical formulas. The key words emphasize a matter of degree: that a heavy burden of justification is on the State, and that the statute will be closely scrutinized in light of its asserted purposes.

It is not sufficient for the State to show that durational residence requirements further a very substantial state interest. In pursuing that important interest, the State cannot choose means that unnecessarily burden or restrict constitutionally protected activity. Statutes affecting constitutional rights must be drawn with 'precision,' *NAACP v. Button*, 371 U.S. 415, 438 (1963); *United States v. Robel*, 389 U.S. 258, 265 (1967), and must be 'tailored' to serve their legitimate objectives. *Shapiro v. Thompson, supra*, 394 U.S., at 631. And if there are other, reasonable ways to achieve those goals with a lesser burden on constitutionally protected activity, a State may not choose the way of greater interference. If it acts at all, it must choose 'less drastic means.' *Shelton v. Tucker*, 364 U.S. 479, 488 (1960).

II

We turn, then, to the question of whether the State has shown that durational residence requirements are needed to further a sufficiently substantial state interest.

[Tennessee argued that the two purposes of the durational residence requirement were to insure the purity of the ballot box and to assure that voters would be knowledgeable about community interests. The Court determined that "purity of the ballot box," concerned with voting by nonresidents, was a compelling government goal, but the durational residence requirements were not necessary to achieve that goal. The prevention of vote fraud by nonresidents could be achieved by a system of voter registration, wherein the new voter must, at least thirty days before the election, establish by oath that he or she is a bona fide resident. With regard to the further the goal of having 'knowledgeable voters,' the Court identified three separate claims: (1) that the durational residence requirement assures that the voter has, in fact, become member of the community, (2) that the requirement assures that the voter has a common interest in all matters pertaining to the community's government, and (3) that the requirement assures that the voter is more likely to exercise his right to vote intelligently. The Court determined that the first of these confused an impermissible durational residence requirement with a permissible bona fide residence requirement, that the second impermissibly attempted to fence out newer opinions so that all voters would have a local point of view, and that the third was too crudely served by a durational residence requirement.]

Concluding that Tennessee has not offered an adequate justification for its durational residence laws, we affirm the judgment of the court below.

Affirmed.

NOTES

1. In the majority opinion, Justice Marshall, as was his custom, insisted that equal protection analysis amounted to a balancing test: "To decide whether a law violates the Equal Protection Clause, we look, in essence, to three things: the character of the classification in question; the individual interests affected by the classification; and the governmental interests asserted in support of the classification." As noted earlier, this balancing test is not inconsistent with the strict scrutiny standard, but is simply a more flexible version of that standard. When, however, Marshall had reviewed the relevant precedents and was ready actually to decide the case, he stated the standard in a very traditional way: "In sum, durational residence laws must be measured by a strict equal protection test: they are unconstitutional unless the State can demonstrate that such laws are 'necessary to promote a compelling governmental interest.'"

2. The *Dunn* case actually involved infringement of *two* constitutional rights—the right to vote and the right to travel. Infringement on either one of these would have been sufficient to trigger strict scrutiny.

3. Two years after *Dunn*, in *Memorial Hospital v. Maricopa County*, 415 U.S. 250 (1974), the Court invalidated a one-year durational residence requirement for eligibility for medical care at the county's expense. The Court applied strict scrutiny and determined both that the state's interests were not compelling and that in pursuing legitimate objectives, the state had chosen means that impinged on constitutionally protected interests.

4. In 1974, then, after the Court's decisions in *Shapiro*, *Dunn*, and *Memorial Hospital*, it appeared that durational residence requirements were very likely unconstitutional. These three cases seemed to make clear that a classification would be subjected to strict scrutiny because of its negative impact on the right to travel in three situations: (1) if the *purpose* of the law was to inhibit interstate travel; (2) if the *effect* of the law was to *deter* interstate travel; or (3) if the law served as a *penalty* on the exercise of the right to interstate travel.

The first of these grounds for heightened review was a legislative *purpose* to inhibit interstate travel. The attorneys defending the durational residence requirement in *Shapiro* sought to defend the statute on the grounds that it would prevent indigents from moving into the state in order to qualify for generous welfare benefits. The Court's response was that a law enacted with such a purpose was "patently unconstitutional." The second ground for heightened scrutiny identified by the Court's early decisions was the possibility of *deterrence* of the right to travel. An indigent currently receiving welfare assistance in State A would likely be deterred from moving to State B if the price of that move was the loss of basic subsistence for the period of one year. Such deterrence of the fundamental right to travel would trigger strict scrutiny. However, it would be a rare case in which actual deterrence of a specific individual could be demonstrated. To the extent a residence requirement is successful in deterring the resident of State A from moving to State B, it is also likely to deter lawsuits challenging the waiting period. The deterred resident of State A, still residing in State A, is not likely to bring a lawsuit challenging the residence requirement of State B. Given the improbability of finding an actual plaintiff who would claim that she had been deterred from moving, the Court did not insist on actual deterrence in order to trigger strict scrutiny, just the likelihood of deterrence. These difficulties make the deterrence argument a seldom-used tactic.

The third, the most important, and the most frequent ground for heightened scrutiny in this area is that a law *penalizes* those who have recently exercised their right to travel from one state to another. The *Shapiro-Dunn-Memorial Hospital* line of cases made no attempt to define the parameters of this penalty analysis, but did identify two specific kinds of impermissible penalties on recent arrivals. The first was the denial, even though temporary, of basic necessities of life, such as welfare or medical care. The second was the denial of a fundamental right such as voting. These decisions left open substantial questions concerning the penalty analysis. Most importantly, the opinions did not make clear how much negative impact a state may attach to the recent exercise of the right to travel before that state action becomes a penalty. The Court conceded that some waiting periods might not be penalties, but did not explain how to distinguish a waiting period that is a penalty from one that is not. These three opinions did, however, leave the impression that durational residence requirements would be very difficult to defend under the Constitution. *Sosna v. Iowa*, the next opinion, showed that this impression was incorrect.

2. THE COURT APPLIES LESS DEMANDING SCRUTINY TO INFRINGEMENTS ON THE RIGHT TO TRAVEL

Sosna v. Iowa
419 U.S. 393 (1975)

[Carol and Michael Sosna were married in 1964 and lived together in New York from 1967 through 1971, after which time they separated but continued to live in New York. In August of 1972 Carol moved from New York to Iowa with their three children and, one month later, petitioned the Iowa district court for a divorce. Although the court obtained personal jurisdiction over Michael Sosna during a visit with his children, the suit was nonetheless dismissed because Carol failed to meet the statutory requirement that the petitioner in a divorce action have been a resident of the state for at least one year. Sosna then brought suit in federal court, alleging that the one-year durational residence requirement violated the Equal Protection Clause.]

Mr. Justice REHNQUIST delivered the opinion of the Court.

II

The durational residency requirement under attack in this case is a part of Iowa's comprehensive statutory regulation of domestic relations, an area that has long been regarded as a virtually exclusive province of the States. Cases decided by this Court over a period of more than a century bear witness to this historical fact. In *Barber v. Barber*, 21 How. 582, 584 (1859), the Court said: 'We disclaim altogether any jurisdiction in the courts of the United States upon the subject of divorce . . . .' In *Penoyer v. Neff*, 95 U.S. 714, 734-735 (1878), the Court said: 'The State . . . has absolute right to prescribe the conditions upon which the marriage relation between its own citizens shall be created, and the causes for which it may be dissolved,' and the same view was reaffirmed in *Simms v. Simms*, 175 U.S. 162, 167 (1899).

The statutory scheme in Iowa, like those in other States, sets forth in considerable detail the grounds upon which a marriage may be dissolved and the circumstances in which a divorce may be obtained. Jurisdiction over a petition for dissolution is established by statute in 'the county where either party resides,' and the Iowa courts have construed the term 'resident' to have much the same meaning as is ordinarily associated with the concept of domicile. *Korsrud v. Korsrud*, 242 Iowa 178 (1951). Iowa has recently revised its divorce statutes, incorporating the no-fault concept, but it retained the one-year durational residency requirement.

The imposition of a durational residency requirement for divorce is scarcely unique to Iowa, since 48 States impose such a requirement as a condition for maintaining an action for divorce. As might be expected, the periods vary among the States and range from six weeks to two years. The one-year period selected by Iowa is the most common length of time prescribed.

Appellant contends that the Iowa requirement of one year's residence is unconstitutional for two separate reasons: first, because it establishes two classes of persons and discriminates against those who have recently exercised their right to travel to Iowa, thereby contravening the Court's holdings in *Shapiro v. Thompson*, 394 U.S. 618 (1969); *Dunn v. Blumstein*, 405 U.S. 330 (1972); and *Memorial Hospital v. Maricopa County*, 415 U.S. 250 (1974); and, second, because it denies a litigant the opportunity to make an individualized showing of bona fide residence and therefore denies such residents access to the only method of legally dissolving their marriage. *Vlandis v. Kline*, 412 U.S. 441 (1973); *Boddie v. Connecticut*, 401 U.S. 371 (1971).

State statutes imposing durational residency requirements were, of course, invalidated when imposed by States as a qualification for welfare payments, *Shapiro, supra*; for voting, *Dunn, supra*; and for medical care, *Maricopa County, supra*. But none of those cases intimated that the States might never impose durational residency requirements, and such a proposition was in fact expressly disclaimed. What those cases had in common was that the durational residency requirements they struck down were justified on the basis of budgetary or recordkeeping considerations which were held insufficient to outweigh the constitutional claims of the individuals. But Iowa's divorce residency requirement is of a different stripe. Appellant was not irretrievably foreclosed from obtaining some part of what she sought, as was the case with the welfare recipients in *Shapiro*, the voters in *Dunn*, or the indigent patient in *Maricopa County*. She would eventually qualify for the same sort of adjudication which she demanded virtually upon her arrival in the State. Iowa's requirement delayed her access to the courts, but, by fulfilling it, she could ultimately have obtained the same opportunity for adjudication which she asserts ought to have been hers at an earlier point in time.

Iowa's residency requirement may reasonably be justified on grounds other than purely budgetary considerations or administrative convenience. Cf. *Kahn v. Shevin*, 416 U.S. 351 (1974). A decree of divorce is not a matter in which the only interested parties are the State as a sort of 'grantor,' and a divorce petitioner such as appellant in the role of 'grantee.' Both spouses are obviously interested in the proceedings, since it will affect their marital status and very likely their property rights. Where a married couple has minor children, a decree of divorce would usually include provisions for their custody and support. With consequences of such moment riding on a divorce decree issued by its courts, Iowa may insist that one seeking to initiate such a proceeding have the modicum of attachment to the State required here.

Such a requirement additionally furthers the State's parallel interests both in avoiding officious intermeddling in matters in which another State has a paramount interest, and in minimizing the susceptibility of its own divorce decrees to collateral attack. A State such as Iowa may quite reasonably decide that it does not wish to become a divorce mill for unhappy spouses who have lived there as short a time as appellant had when she commenced her action in the state court after having long resided elsewhere. Until such time as Iowa is convinced that appellant intends to remain in the State, it lacks the 'nexus between person and place of such permanence as to control the creation of legal relations and responsibilities of the utmost significance.' *Williams v. North Carolina*, 325 U.S. 226, 229 (1945). Perhaps even more important, Iowa's interests extend beyond its borders and include the recognition of its divorce decrees by other States under the Full Faith and Credit Clause of the Constitution, Art. IV, § 1. For that purpose, this Court has often stated that 'judicial power to grant a divorce-jurisdiction, strictly speaking-is founded on domicil.' *Williams, supra*; *Andrews v. Andrews*, 188 U.S. 14 (1903); *Bell v. Bell*, 181 U.S. 175 (1901). Where a divorce decree is entered after a finding of domicile in ex parte proceedings, this Court has held that the finding of domicile is not binding upon another State and may be disregarded in the face of 'cogent evidence' to the contrary. *Williams, supra*, 325 U.S. at 236. For that reason, the State asked to enter such a decree is entitled to insist that the putative divorce petitioner satisfy something more than the bare minimum of constitutional requirements before a divorce may be granted. The State's decision to exact a one-year residency requirement as a matter of policy is therefore buttressed by a quite permissible inference that this requirement not only effectuates state substantive policy but likewise provides a greater safeguard against successful collateral attack than would a requirement of bona fide residence alone. This is precisely the sort of determination that a State in the exercise of its domestic relations jurisdiction is entitled to make.

We therefore hold that the state interest in requiring that those who seek a divorce from its courts be genuinely attached to the State, as well as a desire to insulate divorce decrees from the likelihood of collateral attack, requires a different resolution of the constitutional issue presented than was the case in *Shapiro, supra, Dunn, supra*, and *Maricopa County, supra*.

Affirmed.

NOTES

1. The Court's opinion in *Sosna* is remarkable. The Court never mentions the Equal Protection Clause, the right to travel, the word "penalty," or what standard of review it was applying. The Court's holding was that the case "requires a different resolution of the constitutional issue" than was the case in *Shapiro, Dunn*, and *Memorial Hospital*. One was left to surmise why the case required a different resolution. The court at one point suggested that the plaintiff in *Sosna* was different from the plaintiffs in *Shapiro, Dunn*, and *Memorial Hospital*, in that she was not "irretrievably foreclosed" from obtaining some part of what she sought. That is, after one year, she could get her divorce. But the same could be said of the plaintiffs in the other cases. After one year, they would qualify for welfare benefits, be eligible to vote, or qualify for medical care. What was lost, permanently, was the receipt of those benefits for the first year. Likewise, Ms. Sosna permanently lost the ability to be legally divorced from her husband during her first year of residence. The Court's attempt to identify a factual distinction was thus extremely weak.

After the Court's decision in *Sosna*, the framework from which to measure the constitutional validity of durational residence requirements was anything but settled. The Court had sent contradictory signals concerning the amount of impact to the right to travel required to trigger strict scrutiny and on whether that test could be satisfied. Indeed, the Court implicitly suggested that the issue need not be considered at all. The most one could say after *Sosna* was that one-year durational residence requirements are invalid when imposed for welfare, voting, and medical care, but valid when imposed for in-state tuition, *see Vlandis v. Kline*, 442 U.S. 441 (1973); high elective office, *see Sununu v. Stark*, 383 F. Supp. 1287 (D.N.H. 1974), *aff'd*, 420 U.S. 958 (1975); and divorce actions, *see Sosna*. The Court had given no guidance to explain the different conclusions and then, perhaps prudently given its conceptual disarray, retired from this area of the law for a period of time. When the Court finally returned to the fray in 1999, in *Saenz v. Roe*, the underpinnings of the right to travel were to change substantially.

3.   THE COURT RECONCEPTUALIZES THE IMPLIED FUNDAMENTAL RIGHT TO TRAVEL

Saenz v. Roe
526 U.S. 489 (1999)

Justice STEVENS delivered the opinion of the Court.

In 1992, California enacted a statute limiting the maximum welfare benefits available to newly arrived residents. The scheme limits the amount payable to a family that has resided in the State for less than 12 months to the amount payable by the State of the family's prior residence. The questions presented by this case are whether the 1992 statute was constitutional

III

The word "travel" is not found in the text of the Constitution. Yet the "constitutional right to travel from one State to another" is firmly embedded in our jurisprudence. *United States v. Guest*, 383 U.S. 745, 757 (1966). Indeed, as Justice Stewart reminded us in *Shapiro v. Thompson*, 394 U.S. 618 (1969), the right is so important that it is "assertable against private interference as well as governmental action ... a virtually unconditional personal right, guaranteed by the Constitution to us all." *Id.*, at 643 (concurring opinion).

In *Shapiro,* we reviewed the constitutionality of three statutory provisions that denied welfare assistance to residents of Connecticut, the District of Columbia, and Pennsylvania, who had resided within those respective jurisdictions less than one year immediately preceding their applications for assistance. Without pausing to identify the specific source of the right, we began by noting that the Court had long "recognized that the nature of our Federal Union and our constitutional concepts of personal liberty unite to require that all citizens be free to travel throughout the length and breadth of our land uninhibited by statutes, rules, or regulations which unreasonably burden or restrict this movement." We squarely held that it was "constitutionally impermissible" for a State to enact durational residency requirements for the purpose of inhibiting the migration by needy persons into the State. We further held that a classification that had the effect of imposing a penalty on the exercise of the right to travel violated the Equal Protection Clause "unless shown to be necessary to promote a *compelling* governmental interest," and that no such showing had been made.

In this case California argues that § 11450.03 was not enacted for the impermissible purpose of inhibiting migration by needy persons and that, unlike the legislation reviewed in *Shapiro,* it does not penalize the right to travel because new arrivals are not ineligible for benefits during their first year of residence. California submits that, instead of being subjected to the strictest scrutiny, the statute should be upheld if it is supported by a rational basis and that the State's legitimate interest in saving over $10 million a year satisfies that test.

IV

The "right to travel" discussed in our cases embraces at least three different components. It protects the right of a citizen of one State to enter and to leave another State, the right to be treated

CHAPTER 8: IMPLIED FUNDAMENTAL RIGHTS & THE EQUAL PROTECTION CLAUSE

as a welcome visitor rather than an unfriendly alien when temporarily present in the second State, and, for those travelers who elect to become permanent residents, the right to be treated like other citizens of that State.

It was the right to go from one place to another, including the right to cross state borders while en route, that was vindicated in *Edwards v. California,* 314 U.S. 160 (1941), which invalidated a state law that impeded the free interstate passage of the indigent. We reaffirmed that right in *United States v. Guest,* 383 U.S. 745 (1966), which afforded protection to the "'right to travel freely to and from the State of Georgia and to use highway facilities and other instrumentalities of interstate commerce within the State of Georgia.'" Given that § 11450.03 imposed no obstacle to respondents' entry into California, we think the State is correct when it argues that the statute does not directly impair the exercise of the right to free interstate movement. For the purposes of this case, therefore, we need not identify the source of that particular right in the text of the Constitution. The right of "free ingress and regress to and from" neighboring States, which was expressly mentioned in the text of the Articles of Confederation, may simply have been "conceived from the beginning to be a necessary concomitant of the stronger Union the Constitution created."

The second component of the right to travel is, however, expressly protected by the text of the Constitution. The first sentence of Article IV, § 2, provides:

> "The Citizens of each State shall be entitled to all Privileges and Immunities of Citizens in the several States."

Thus, by virtue of a person's state citizenship, a citizen of one State who travels in other States, intending to return home at the end of his journey, is entitled to enjoy the "Privileges and Immunities of Citizens in the several States" that he visits. This provision removes "from the citizens of each State the disabilities of alienage in the other States." *Paul v. Virginia,* 8 Wall. 168, 180 (1868) ("[W]ithout some provision ... removing from the citizens of each State the disabilities of alienage in the other States, and giving them equality of privilege with citizens of those States, the Republic would have constituted little more than a league of States; it would not have constituted the Union which now exists"). It provides important protections for nonresidents who enter a State whether to obtain employment, *Hicklin v. Orbeck,* 437 U.S. 518 (1978), to procure medical services, *Doe v. Bolton,* 410 U.S. 179 (1973), or even to engage in commercial shrimp fishing, *Toomer v. Witsell,* 334 U.S. 385 (1948). Those protections are not "absolute," but the Clause "does bar discrimination against citizens of other States where there is no substantial reason for the discrimination beyond the mere fact that they are citizens of other States." There may be a substantial reason for requiring the nonresident to pay more than the resident for a hunting license, see *Baldwin v. Fish and Game Comm'n of Mont.,* 436 U.S. 371, 390-391 (1978), or to enroll in the state university, see *Vlandis v. Kline,* 412 U.S. 441, 445 (1973), but our cases have not identified any acceptable reason for qualifying the protection afforded by the Clause for "the 'citizen of State A who ventures into State B' to settle there and establish a home." *Zobel,* 457 U.S., at 74 (O'CONNOR, J., concurring in judgment). Permissible justifications for discrimination between residents and nonresidents are simply inapplicable to a nonresident's exercise of the right to move into another State and become a resident of that State.

What is at issue in this case, then, is this third aspect of the right to travel-the right of the newly arrived citizen to the same privileges and immunities enjoyed by other citizens of the same State. That right is protected not only by the new arrival's status as a state citizen, but also by her status as a citizen of the United States.[FN 15] That additional source of protection is plainly identified in the opening words of the Fourteenth Amendment:

> "All persons born or naturalized in the United States, and subject to the jurisdiction thereof, are citizens of the United States and of the State wherein they reside. No State shall make or enforce any law which shall abridge the privileges or immunities of citizens of the United States; ..."

Despite fundamentally differing views concerning the coverage of the Privileges or Immunities Clause of the Fourteenth Amendment, most notably expressed in the majority and dissenting opinions in the *Slaughter-House Cases,* 16 Wall. 36 (1872), it has always been common ground that this Clause protects the third component of the right to travel. Writing for the majority in the *Slaughter-House Cases,* Justice Miller explained that one of the privileges conferred by this Clause "is that a citizen of the United States can, of his own volition, become a citizen of any State of the Union by a *bona fide* residence therein, with the same rights as other citizens of that State." Justice Bradley, in dissent, used even stronger language to make the same point:

> The states have not now, if they ever had, any power to restrict their citizenship to any classes or persons. A citizen of the United States has a perfect constitutional right to go to and reside in any State he chooses, and to claim citizenship therein, and an equality of rights with every other citizen; and the whole power of the nation is pledged to sustain him in that right. He is not bound to cringe to any superior, or to pray for any act of grace, as a means of enjoying all the rights and privileges enjoyed by other citizens.

That newly arrived citizens "have two political capacities, one state and one federal," adds special force to their claim that they have the same rights as others who share their citizenship. Neither mere rationality nor some intermediate standard of review should be used to judge the constitutionality of a state rule that discriminates against some of its citizens because they have been domiciled in the State for less than a year. The appropriate standard may be more categorical than that articulated in *Shapiro,* see *supra,* at 1524-1525, but it is surely no less strict.

V

Because this case involves discrimination against citizens who have completed their interstate travel, the State's argument that its welfare scheme affects the right to travel only "incidentally" is beside the point. Were we concerned solely with actual deterrence to migration, we might be persuaded that a partial withholding of benefits constitutes a lesser incursion on the right to travel than an outright denial of all benefits. See *Dunn v. Blumstein,* 405 U.S. 330, 339 (1972). But since the right to travel embraces the citizen's right to be treated equally in her new State of residence, the discriminatory classification is itself a penalty.

[FN 15] The Framers of the Fourteenth Amendment modeled this Clause upon the "Privileges and Immunities" Clause found in Article IV. Cong. Globe, 39th Cong., 1st Sess., 1033-1034 (1866) (statement of Rep. Bingham). In *Dred Scott v. Sandford,* 19 How. 393 (1856), this Court had limited the protection of Article IV to rights under state law and concluded that free blacks could not claim citizenship. The Fourteenth Amendment overruled this decision. The Amendment's Privileges or Immunities Clause and Citizenship Clause guaranteed the rights of newly freed black citizens by ensuring that they could claim the state citizenship of any State in which they resided and by precluding that State from abridging their rights of national citizenship.

It is undisputed that respondents and the members of the class that they represent are citizens of California and that their need for welfare benefits is unrelated to the length of time that they have resided in California. We thus have no occasion to consider what weight might be given to a citizen's length of residence if the bona fides of her claim to state citizenship were questioned. Moreover, because whatever benefits they receive will be consumed while they remain in California, there is no danger that recognition of their claim will encourage citizens of other States to establish residency for just long enough to acquire some readily portable benefit, such as a divorce or a college education, that will be enjoyed after they return to their original domicile. See, *e.g., Sosna v. Iowa,* 419 U.S. 393 (1975); *Vlandis v. Kline,* 412 U.S. 441 (1973).

The classifications challenged in this case--and there are many-- are defined entirely by (a) the period of residency in California and (b) the location of the prior residences of the disfavored class members. The favored class of beneficiaries includes all eligible California citizens who have resided there for at least one year, plus those new arrivals who last resided in another country or in a State that provides benefits at least as generous as California's. Thus, within the broad category of citizens who resided in California for less than a year, there are many who are treated like lifetime residents. And within the broad subcategory of new arrivals who are treated less favorably, there are many smaller classes whose benefit levels are determined by the law of the States from whence they came. To justify § 11450.03, California must therefore explain not only why it is sound fiscal policy to discriminate against those who have been citizens for less than a year, but also why it is permissible to apply such a variety of rules within that class.

These classifications may not be justified by a purpose to deter welfare applicants from migrating to California for three reasons. First, although it is reasonable to assume that some persons may be motivated to move for the purpose of obtaining higher benefits, the empirical evidence reviewed by the District Judge, which takes into account the high cost of living in California, indicates that the number of such persons is quite small-surely not large enough to justify a burden on those who had no such motive. Second, California has represented to the Court that the legislation was not enacted for any such reason. Third, even if it were, as we squarely held in *Shapiro v. Thompson,* 394 U.S. 618 (1969), such a purpose would be unequivocally impermissible.

Disavowing any desire to fence out the indigent, California has instead advanced an entirely fiscal justification for its multitiered scheme. The enforcement of § 11450.03 will save the State approximately $10.9 million a year. The question is not whether such saving is a legitimate purpose but whether the State may accomplish that end by the discriminatory means it has chosen. An evenhanded, across-the-board reduction of about 72 cents per month for every beneficiary would produce the same result. But our negative answer to the question does not rest on the weakness of the State's purported fiscal justification. It rests on the fact that the Citizenship Clause of the Fourteenth Amendment expressly equates citizenship with residence: "That Clause does not provide for, and does not allow for, degrees of citizenship based on length of residence." *Zobel,* 457 U.S., at 69. It is equally clear that the Clause does not tolerate a hierarchy of 45 subclasses of similarly situated citizens based on the location of their prior residence. Thus § 11450.03 is doubly vulnerable: Neither the duration of respondents' California residence, nor the identity of their prior States of residence, has any relevance to their need for benefits. Nor do those factors bear any relationship to the State's interest in making an equitable allocation of the funds to be distributed among its needy citizens. As in *Shapiro,* we reject any contributory rationale for the denial of benefits to new residents:

> But we need not rest on the particular facts of these cases. Appellants' reasoning would logically permit the State to bar new residents from schools, parks, and libraries or

deprive them of police and fire protection. Indeed it would permit the State to apportion all benefits and services according to the past tax contributions of its citizens. 394 U.S., at 632-633.

See also *Zobel,* 457 U.S., at 64. In short, the State's legitimate interest in saving money provides no justification for its decision to discriminate among equally eligible citizens.

VI

Citizens of the United States, whether rich or poor, have the right to choose to be citizens "of the State wherein they reside." U.S. Const., Amdt. 14, § 1. The States, however, do not have any right to select their citizens. The Fourteenth Amendment, like the Constitution itself, was, as Justice Cardozo put it, "framed upon the theory that the peoples of the several states must sink or swim together, and that in the long run prosperity and salvation are in union and not division." *Baldwin v. G.A.F. Seelig, Inc.,* 294 U.S. 511, 523 (1935).

The judgment of the Court of Appeals is affirmed.

It is so ordered.

NOTES

1.   It is very likely that the drafters of the statute challenged in *Saenz* had the Court's opinion in *Shapiro* in mind when they crafted its provisions. In *Shapiro,* the Court had treated the complete denial of welfare benefits for one year as a *penalty* on the right to travel, thus triggering strict scrutiny. The California statute, on the other hand, did not completely deny benefits during the first year; it simply limited the amount of the benefit to the level the recipient was eligible for in his previous state for residence. How could this be described as a penalty when the recipient was receiving the same benefit that he had been receiving in the previous state of residence? As it turned out, that level of benefits *was* a penalty, since the proper comparison was not with the residents of the previous state but rather with the residents of the current state, California. In relation to residents of the current state, the new arrivals were clearly being penalized.

2.   The Court's reasoning in *Saenz* is a significant departure from its earlier analysis of the right to travel. In the earlier cases, the Court had not identified any particular provision of the Constitution that created a right to travel but rather had insisted that the right to travel was implicit in the concept of a federal union. In *Saenz,* the Court breaks down the right to travel into three components, each of which has a separate constitutional source.

The first component of the right to travel is right to go from one place to another, including the right to cross state borders while en route. For this aspect of the right to travel, as before, there is no specific constitutional underpinning; it is an essential component of a federal union. This aspect of the right to travel is not at issue in *Saenz.*

The second component of the right to travel is one's right as a citizen of one state to be treated as a welcome visitor rather than an unfriendly alien when temporarily present in a second state. The Privileges and Immunities Clause of Article IV, § 2 expressly protects this aspect of the right to travel and it was not at issue in *Saenz.*

The third component of the right to travel is one's right as a citizen of the United States to move permanently from one state to another and, immediately upon arrival in the new state, to be treated equally with the state's existing citizens. This component of the right to travel, protected by the Privileges or Immunities Clause of the Fourteenth Amendment, is what is at issue in *Saenz*. Since the right to travel embraces the citizen's right to be treated equally in a new state of residence, the discriminatory classification is itself a penalty. The Fourteenth Amendment expressly equates citizenship with residence: it does not provide for, and does not allow for, degrees of citizenship based on length of residence.

3. Is the right to travel still an equal protection doctrine? After *Saenz*, the answer to this question is not at all clear. Since express provisions of the Constitution protect the second and third components of the right to travel, there seems to be no need to imply any rights or necessarily any need to make comparative equality arguments. But the Court is not clear on this point. Having identified the specific sources of the right to travel, the Court does engage in a comparative analysis of residents recently arrived in California from lower benefit states with all other residents. The Court speaks of the "classifications challenged in this case" and of "discrimination" against this new class in order to explain why there is a penalty against those who had recently exercised their right to travel. And the third aspect of the right to travel includes the right "to be treated equally in her new state of residence." It seems that the right to travel protected by the Privileges or Immunities Clause of the Fourteenth Amendment is inherently an equality standard.

F. INTERESTS THAT ARE NOT FUNDAMENTAL

The previous sections of this Chapter have examined interests that the Court has found to be impliedly fundamental. This section explores interests that the Court has determined are not fundamental and for which, therefore, heightened scrutiny is not necessary.

1. *FOOD AND SHELTER*

Dandridge v. Williams
397 U.S (1970)

Mr. Justice STEWART delivered the opinion of the Court.

This case involves the validity of a method used by Maryland, in the administration of an aspect of its public welfare program, to reconcile the demands of its needy citizens with the finite resources available to meet those demands. Like every other State in the Union, Maryland participates in the Federal Aid to Families With Dependent Children (AFDC program). Under this jointly financed program, a State computes the so-called 'standard of need' of each eligible family unit within its borders. [Maryland provided grants to most families in full accord with the ascertained standard of need, but imposed an upper limit on the total amount of money any one family unit could receive. This meant that large families would not receive an amount equal to their standard of need as calculated by the state.] This suit was brought by several AFDC recipients to enjoin the application of the Maryland maximum grant regulation on the ground that it is in conflict with the Social Security Act of 1935 and with the Equal Protection Clause of the Fourteenth Amendment.

Although a State may adopt a maximum grant system in allocating its funds available for AFDC payments without violating the Act, it may not, of course, impose a regime of invidious discrimination in violation of the Equal Protection Clause of the Fourteenth Amendment. Maryland says that its maximum grant regulation is wholly free of any invidiously discriminatory purpose or effect, and that the regulation is rationally supportable on at least four entirely valid grounds. The regulation can be clearly justified, Maryland argues, in terms of legitimate state interests in encouraging gainful employment, in maintaining an equitable balance in economic status as between welfare families and those supported by a wage-earner, in providing incentives for family planning, and in allocating available public funds in such a way as fully to meet the needs of the largest possible number of families. The District Court, while apparently recognizing the validity of at least some of these state concerns, nonetheless held that the regulation 'is invalid on its face for overreaching,'--that it violates the Equal Protection Clause '(b)ecause it cuts too broad a swath on an indiscriminate basis as applied to the entire group of AFDC eligibles to which it purports to apply.'

If this were a case involving government action claimed to violate the First Amendment guarantee of free speech, a finding of 'overreaching' would be significant and might be crucial. For when otherwise valid governmental regulation sweeps so broadly as to impinge upon activity protected by the First Amendment, its very overbreadth may make it unconstitutional. See, e.g., *Shelton v. Tucker*, 364 U.S. 479. But the concept of 'overreaching' has no place in this case. For here we deal with state regulation in the social and economic field, not affecting freedoms guaranteed by the Bill of Rights, and claimed to violate the Fourteenth Amendment only because the regulation results in some disparity in grants of welfare payments to the largest AFDC families. For this Court to approve the invalidation of state economic or social regulation as 'overreaching' would be far too reminiscent of an era when the Court thought the Fourteenth Amendment gave it power to strike down state laws 'because they may be unwise, improvident, or out of harmony with a particular school of thought.' *Williamson v. Lee Optical of Oklahoma, Inc.*, 348 U.S. 483, 488. 563. That era long ago passed into history. *Ferguson v. Skrupa*, 372 U.S. 726.

In the area of economics and social welfare, a State does not violate the Equal Protection Clause merely because the classifications made by its laws are imperfect. If the classification has some 'reasonable basis,' it does not offend the Constitution simply because the classification 'is not made with mathematical nicety or because in practice it results in some inequality.' *Lindsley v. Natural Carbonic Gas Co.*, 220 U.S. 61, 78. 'The problems of government are practical ones and may justify, if they do not require, rough accommodations-illogical, it may be, and unscientific.' *Metropolis Theatre Co. v. City of Chicago*, 228 U.S. 61, 69-70. 'A statutory discrimination will not be set aside if any state of facts reasonably may be conceived to justify it.' *McGowan v. Maryland*, 366 U.S. 420, 426.

To be sure, the cases cited, and many others enunciating this fundamental standard under the Equal Protection Clause, have in the main involved state regulation of business or industry. The administration of public welfare assistance, by contrast, involves the most basic economic needs of impoverished human beings. We recognize the dramatically real factual difference between the cited cases and this one, but we can find no basis for applying a different constitutional standard. See *Snell v. Wyman*, D.C., 281 F. Supp. 853, aff'd, 393 U.S. 323. It is a standard that has consistently been applied to state legislation restricting the availability of employment opportunities. *Goesaert v. Cleary*, 335 U.S. 464; *Kotch v. Board of River Port Pilot Com'rs*, 330 U.S. 552. See also *Flemming v. Nestor*, 363 U.S. 603. And it is a standard that is true to the principle that the Fourteenth Amendment gives the federal courts no power to impose upon the States their views of what constitutes wise economic or social policy.

Under this long-established meaning of the Equal Protection Clause, it is clear that the Maryland Maximum grant regulation is constitutionally valid. We need not explore all the reasons that the State advances in justification of the regulation. It is enough that a solid foundation for the regulation can be found in the State's legitimate interest in encouraging employment and in avoiding discrimination between welfare families and the families of the working poor. By combining a limit on the recipient's grant with permission to retain money earned, without reduction in the amount of the grant, Maryland provides an incentive to seek gainful employment. And by keying the maximum family AFDC grants to the minimum wage a steadily employed head of a household receives, the State maintains some semblance of an equitable balance between families on welfare and those supported by an employed breadwinner.

It is true that in some AFDC families there may be no person who is employable. It is also true that with respect to AFDC families whose determined standard of need is below the regulatory maximum, and who therefore receive grants equal to the determined standard, the employment incentive is absent. But the Equal Protection Clause does not require that a State must choose between attacking every aspect of a problem or not attacking the problem at all. *Lindsley v. Natural Carbonic Gas Co.*, 220 U.S. 61. It is enough that the State's action be rationally based and free from invidious discrimination. The regulation before us meets that test.

We do not decide today that the Maryland regulation is wise, that it best fulfills the relevant social and economic objectives that Maryland might ideally espouse, or that a more just and humane system could not be devised. Conflicting claims of morality and intelligence are raised by opponents and proponents of almost every measure, certainly including the one before us. But the intractable economic, social, and even philosophical problems presented by public welfare assistance programs are not the business of this Court. The Constitution may impose certain procedural safeguards upon systems of welfare administration, *Goldberg v. Kelly*, 397 U.S. 254. But the Constitution does not empower this Court to second-guess state officials charged with the difficult responsibility of allocating limited public welfare funds among the myriad of potential recipients. Cf. *Charles C. Steward Mach. Co. v. Davis*, 301 U.S. 548, 584-585; *Helvering v. Davis*, 301 U.S. 619, 644.

The judgment is *reversed*.

NOTES

1. In *Skinner*, the Court announced that procreation was a fundamental right because it was essential for the survival of the race. Isn't food essential for the survival of the race? Of course it is—for it "involves the most basic economic needs of impoverished human beings." But that doesn't make a right to food fundamental. The Court ignores the language in *Skinner* that suggests that a thing is constitutionally fundamental because it is essential for the survival of the race. *Skinner* perhaps could be distinguished in that the fundamental right there simply required the government to keep out of the way and take no affirmative act while the claim in *Dandridge* would have required the government take the affirmative steps to support poor people. But the Court makes no attempt to distinguish *Skinner*. It simply ignores it.

Lindsey v. Normet
405 U.S. 56 (1972)

[The Lindseys were month-to-month tenants living in a home that was declared unfit for habitation by the Portland, Oregon Bureau of Buildings. They withheld rent, demanding that various repairs be made to the dwelling. The landlord, Normet, refused to comply with the request and threatened eviction. The Lindseys, however, filed a preemptive suit in federal court alleging that the Oregon Forcible Entry and Wrongful Detainer (FED) Statute, on which an eviction action would be based, violated the Due Process and Equal Protection Clauses of the Fourteenth Amendment.]

Mr. Justice WHITE delivered the opinion of the Court.

This case presents the question of whether Oregon's judicial procedure for eviction of tenants after nonpayment of rent violates ... the Equal Protection Clause ... of the Fourteenth Amendment.

The Oregon Forcible Entry and Wrongful Detainer Statute establishes a procedure intended to insure that any entry upon real property 'shall be made in a peaceable manner and without force.'

[The Court here identified the three defining characteristics of the FED statute: (1) trial within six days of service of the complaint; (2) limitation of triable issues to tenant default; and (3) the requirement of posting a double bond on appeal.]

We cannot agree that the FED Statute is invalid on its face under the Equal Protection Clause. It is true that Oregon FED suits differ substantially from other litigation, where the time between complaint and trial is substantially longer, and where a broader range of issues may be considered. But it does not follow that the Oregon statute invidiously discriminates against defendants in FED actions.

The statute potentially applies to all tenants, rich and poor, commercial and noncommercial; it cannot be faulted for over-exclusiveness or under-exclusiveness. And classifying tenants of real property differently from other tenants for purposes of possessory actions will offend the equal protection safeguard 'only if the classification rests on grounds wholly irrelevant to the achievement of the State's objective,' *McGowan v. Maryland*, 366 U.S. 420, 425 (1961), or if the objective itself is beyond the State's power to achieve, *Gomillion v. Lightfoot*, 364 U.S. 339 (1960); *N.A.A.C.P. v. Alabama ex rel. Flowers*, 377 U.S. 288 (1964); *Douglas v. California*, 372 U.S. 353 (1963). It is readily apparent that prompt as well as peaceful resolution of disputes over the right to possession of real property is the end sought by the Oregon statute. It is also clear that the provisions for early trial and simplification of issues are closely related to that purpose. The equal protection claim with respect to these provisions thus depends on whether the State may validly single out possessory disputes between landlord and tenant for especially prompt judicial settlement. In making such an inquiry a State is 'presumed to have acted within (its) constitutional power despite the fact that, in practice, (its) laws result in some inequality.' *McGowan v. Maryland*, *supra*, 366 U.S., at 425-426.

[The Court explains the challenged statute was enacted to replace the landlord's common law right of self-help and thus to help resolve landlord/tenant disputes in a peaceable manner.]

Before a tenant is forcibly evicted from property the Oregon statute requires a judicial determination that he is not legally entitled to possession. 'The action of forcible entry and detainer is intended for the benefit of him whose possession is invaded.' *Taylor v. Scott*, 10 Or. 483, 485 (1883). The objective of achieving rapid and peaceful settlement of possessory disputes between landlord and tenant has ample historical explanation and support. It is not beyond the State's power to implement that purpose by enacting special provisions applicable only to possessory disputes between landlord and tenant.

Appellants argue, however, that a more stringent standard than mere rationality should be applied both to the challenged classification and its stated purpose. They contend that the 'need for decent shelter' and the 'right to retain peaceful possession of one's home' are fundamental interests which are particularly important to the poor and which may be trenched upon only after the State demonstrates some superior interest. They invoke those cases holding that certain classifications based on unalterable traits such as race and lineage are inherently suspect and must be justified by some 'overriding statutory purpose.' They also rely on cases where classifications burdening or infringing constitutionally protected rights were required to be justified as 'necessary to promote a compelling governmental interest.'

We do not denigrate the importance of decent, safe, and sanitary housing. But the Constitution does not provide judicial remedies for every social and economic ill. We are unable to perceive in that document any constitutional guarantee of access to dwellings of a particular quality, or any recognition of the right of a tenant to occupy the real property of his landlord beyond the term of his lease without the payment of rent or otherwise contrary to the terms of the relevant agreement. Absent constitutional mandate, the assurance of adequate housing and the definition of landlord-tenant relationships are legislative, not judicial, functions. Nor should we forget that the Constitution expressly protects against confiscation of private property or the income therefrom.

Since the purpose of the Oregon Forcible Entry and Wrongful Detainer Statute is constitutionally permissible and since the classification under attack is rationally related to that purpose, the statute is not repugnant to the Equal Protection Clause of the Fourteenth Amendment.

IV

[The Court here found that the double-bond prerequisite for appealing an FED action violated their right to the equal protection of the laws, since it heavily burdened the statutory right to appeal.]

The judgment of the District Court is affirmed in part and reversed in part.

NOTES

1. The *Lindsey* plaintiffs who challenged that process called for heightened scrutiny, arguing "the 'need for decent shelter' and the 'right to retain peaceful possession of one's home' were fundamental interests of particular important to the poor "which may be trenched upon only after the State demonstrates some superior interest." Although this reasoning was used successfully in *Skinner*, this time the Court rejected the claim, saying, "We do not denigrate the importance of decent, safe, and sanitary housing. But the Constitution does not provide judicial remedies for every social and economic ill. We are unable to perceive in that document any constitutional guarantee of access to dwellings of a particular quality." The Court went on to use a very

deferential form of review and upheld the summary process action.

The *Lindsey* Court made no mention of *Skinner*, so there was no need to distinguish *Skinner's* reasoning. Further, the Court made the telling reference to its inability to perceive "in that document" (the Constitution) any guarantee of housing. Of course, it ought not to be surprising that an alleged implied fundamental right will not be found "in that document." By definition, an implied fundamental right will not be found explicitly in the Constitution itself. Further, as a matter of loyalty to precedent, the Court in *Lindsey* was overlooking the fact that the Court in *Skinner* likewise could not have found "in that document" a right to procreate. But the *Lindsey* opinion was consistent with the Court's views in *Dandridge*, and it also served as a bridge to the next case, *San Antonio Independent School District v. Rodriguez*, in which the Court appeared to bury the Skinner methodology.

2. EDUCATION

a. Not a Fundamental Right

San Antonio Independent School Dist. v. Rodriguez
411 U.S. 1 (1973)

[The plaintiffs in the original case were low-income parents who were residents of a school district with a low property tax base, a high property tax rate, and low per pupil spending. They compared their situation with that of a neighboring district that had a high property tax base, a low property tax rate, and high per pupil spending. They brought a class action suit against various state defendants, alleging a violation of the Equal Protection Clause. In Chapter 7, *supra*, the portion of the case that discussed the issue of the poor as a suspect class was included. What follows is the portion of the case that discusses education as a fundamental right.]

Mr. Justice POWELL delivered the opinion of the Court.

This suit attacking the Texas system of financing public education was initiated by Mexican-American parents whose children attend the elementary and secondary schools in the Edgewood Independent School District, an urban school district in San Antonio, Texas. They brought a class action on behalf of schoolchildren throughout the State who are members of minority groups or who are poor and reside in school districts having a low property tax base. Texas virtually concedes that its historically rooted dual system of financing education could not withstand the strict judicial scrutiny that this Court has found appropriate in reviewing legislative judgments that interfere with fundamental constitutional rights or that involve suspect classifications. If, as previous decisions have indicated, strict scrutiny means that the State's system is not entitled to the usual presumption of validity, that the State rather than the complainants must carry a 'heavy burden of justification,' that the State must demonstrate that its educational system has been structured with 'precision,' and is 'tailored' narrowly to serve legitimate objectives and that it has selected the 'less drastic means' for effectuating its objectives, the Texas financing system and its counterpart in virtually every other State will not pass muster. The State candidly admits that '(n)o one familiar with the Texas system would contend that it has yet achieved perfection.' Apart from its concession that educational financing in Texas has 'defects' and 'imperfections,' the State defends the system's rationality with vigor and disputes the District Court's finding that it lacks a 'reasonable basis.'

[The Court determined that wealth discrimination alone did not provide an adequate basis for invoking strict scrutiny. But the plaintiffs] also assert that the State's system impermissibly interferes with the exercise of a 'fundamental' right and that accordingly the prior decisions of this Court require the application of the strict standard of judicial review. *Graham v. Richardson*, 403 U.S. 365, 375-376 (1971); *Kramer v. Union Free School District*, 395 U.S. 621 (1969); *Shapiro v. Thompson*, 394 U.S. 618 (1969). It is this question--whether education is a fundamental right, in the sense that it is among the rights and liberties protected by the Constitution--which has so consumed the attention of courts and commentators in recent years.

B

In *Brown v. Board of Education*, 347 U.S. 483 (1954), a unanimous Court recognized that 'education is perhaps the most important function of state and local governments.' *Id.*, at 493. What was said there in the context of racial discrimination has lost none of its vitality with the passage of time:

> Compulsory school attendance laws and the great expenditures for education both demonstrate our recognition of the importance of education to our democratic society. It is required in the performance of our most basic public responsibilities, even service in the armed forces. It is the very foundation of good citizenship. Today it is a principal instrument in awakening the child to cultural values, in preparing him for later professional training, and in helping him to adjust normally to his environment. In these days, it is doubtful that any child may reasonably be expected to succeed in life if he is denied the opportunity of an education. Such an opportunity, where the state has undertaken to provide it, is a right which must be made available to all on equal terms.

This theme, expressing an abiding respect for the vital role of education in a free society, may be found in numerous opinions of Justices of this Court writing both before and after Brown was decided. *Wisconsin v. Yoder*, 406 U.S. 205, 213 (Burger, C.J.), 237, 238-239 (White, J.), (1972); *Abington School Dist. v. Schempp*, 374 U.S. 203 (1963) (Brennan, J.); *People of State of Illinois ex rel. McCollum v. Board of Education*, 333 U.S. 203, 212 (1948) (Frankfurter, J.); *Pierce v. Society of Sisters*, 268 U.S. 510 (1925); *Meyer v. Nebraska*, 262 U.S. 390 (1923); *Interstate Consolidated Street R. Co. v. Massachusetts*, 207 U.S. 79 (1907).

Nothing this Court holds today in any way detracts from our historic dedication to public education. We are in complete agreement with the conclusion of the three-judge panel below that 'the grave significance of education both to the individual and to our society' cannot be doubted. But the importance of a service performed by the State does not determine whether it must be regarded as fundamental for purposes of examination under the Equal Protection Clause. Mr. Justice Harlan, dissenting from the Court's application of strict scrutiny to a law impinging upon the right of interstate travel, admonished that '(v)irtually every state statute affects important rights.' *Shapiro v. Thompson*, 394 U.S., at 655, 661. In his view, if the degree of judicial scrutiny of state legislation fluctuated, depending on a majority's view of the importance of the interest affected, we would have gone 'far toward making this Court a 'super-legislature.'' We would, indeed, then be assuming a legislative role and one for which the Court lacks both authority and competence. But Mr. Justice Stewart's response in Shapiro to Mr. Justice Harlan's concern correctly articulates the limits of the fundamental-rights rationale employed in the Court's equal protection decisions:

> The Court today does not 'pick out particular human activities, characterize them as 'fundamental,' and give them added protection . . ..' To the contrary, the Court simply

recognizes, as it must, an established constitutional right, and gives to that right no less protection than the Constitution itself demands.

Mr. Justice Stewart's statement serves to underline what the opinion of the Court in *Shapiro* makes clear. In subjecting to strict judicial scrutiny state welfare eligibility statutes that imposed a one-year durational residency requirement as a precondition to receiving AFDC benefits, the Court explained:

> [I]n moving from State to State . . . appellees were exercising a constitutional right, and any classification which serves to penalize the exercise of that right, unless shown to be necessary to promote a compelling governmental interest, is unconstitutional.

The right to interstate travel had long been recognized as a right of constitutional significance, and the Court's decision, therefore, did not require an ad hoc determination as to the social or economic importance of that right. *Lindsey v. Normet*, 405 U.S. 56 (1972), decided only last Term, firmly reiterates that social importance is not the critical determinant for subjecting state legislation to strict scrutiny. [The Court here summarized the *Lindsey* case.]

Similarly, in *Dandridge v. Williams*, 397 U.S. 471 (1970), the Court's explicit recognition of the fact that the 'administration of public welfare assistance . . . involves the most basic economic needs of impoverished human beings,' provided no basis for departing from the settled mode of constitutional analysis of legislative classifications involving questions of economic and social policy. As in the case of housing, the central importance of welfare benefits to the poor was not an adequate foundation for requiring the State to justify its law by showing some compelling state interest. See also *Jefferson v. Hackney*, 406 U.S. 535 (1972); *Richardson v. Belcher*, 404 U.S. 78 (1971).

The lesson of these cases in addressing the question now before the Court is plain. It is not the province of this Court to create substantive constitutional rights in the name of guaranteeing equal protection of the laws. Thus, the key to discovering whether education is 'fundamental' is not to be found in comparisons of the relative societal significance of education as opposed to subsistence or housing. Nor is it to be found by weighing whether education is as important as the right to travel. Rather, the answer lies in assessing whether there is a right to education explicitly or implicitly guaranteed by the Constitution. *Eisenstadt v. Baird*, 405 U.S. 438 (1972); *Dunn v. Blumstein*, 405 U.S. 330 (1972); *Police Dept. of City of Chicago v. Mosley*, 408 U.S. 92 (1972); *Skinner v. Oklahoma ex rel. Williamson*, 316 U.S. 535 (1942).

Dunn fully canvasses this Court's voting rights cases and explains that 'this Court has made clear that a citizen has a constitutionally protected right to participate in elections on an equal basis with other citizens in the jurisdiction.' 405 U.S., at 336. The constitutional underpinnings of the right to equal treatment in the voting process can no longer be doubted even though, as the Court noted in *Harper v. Virginia Bd. of Elections*, 383 U.S., at 665, 'the right to vote in state elections is nowhere expressly mentioned.'

Education, of course, is not among the rights afforded explicit protection under our Federal Constitution. Nor do we find any basis for saying it is implicitly so protected. As we have said, the undisputed importance of education will not alone cause this Court to depart from the usual standard for reviewing a State's social and economic legislation. It is appellees' contention, however, that education is distinguishable from other services and benefits provided by the State because it bears a peculiarly close relationship to other rights and liberties accorded protection under the Constitution. Specifically, they insist that education is itself a fundamental personal right because it is essential to the effective exercise of First Amendment freedoms and to intelligent utilization of the right to vote. In asserting a nexus between speech and education, appellees urge that the right to speak is meaningless unless the speaker is capable of articulating his thoughts intelligently and persuasively. The 'marketplace of ideas' is an empty forum for those lacking basic communicative tools. Likewise, they argue that the corollary right to receive information becomes little more than a hollow privilege when the recipient has not been taught to read, assimilate, and utilize available knowledge.

A similar line of reasoning is pursued with respect to the right to vote. Exercise of the franchise, it is contended, cannot be divorced from the educational foundation of the voter. The electoral process, if reality is to conform to the democratic ideal, depends on an informed electorate: a voter cannot cast his ballot intelligently unless his reading skills and thought processes have been adequately developed.

We need not dispute any of these propositions. The Court has long afforded zealous protection against unjustifiable governmental interference with the individual's rights to speak and to vote. Yet we have never presumed to possess either the ability or the authority to guarantee to the citizenry the most effective speech or the most informed electoral choice. That these may be desirable goals of a system of freedom of expression and of a representative form of government is not to be doubted. These are indeed goals to be pursued by a people whose thoughts and beliefs are freed from governmental interference. But they are not values to be implemented by judicial instruction into otherwise legitimate state activities.

Even if it were conceded that some identifiable quantum of education is a constitutionally protected prerequisite to the meaningful exercise of either right, we have no indication that the present levels of educational expenditures in Texas provide an education that falls short. Whatever merit appellees' argument might have if a State's financing system occasioned an absolute denial of educational opportunities to any of its children, that argument provides no basis for finding an interference with fundamental rights where only relative differences in spending levels are involved and where--as is true in the present case--no charge fairly could be made that the system fails to provide each child with an opportunity to acquire the basic minimal skills necessary for the enjoyment of the rights of speech and of full participation in the political process.

Furthermore, the logical limitations on appellees' nexus theory are difficult to perceive. How, for instance, is education to be distinguished from the significant personal interests in the basics of decent food and shelter? Empirical examination might well buttress an assumption that the ill-fed, ill-clothed, and ill-housed are among the most ineffective participants in the political process, and that they derive the least enjoyment from the benefits of the First Amendment. If so, appellees' thesis would cast serious doubt on the authority of *Dandridge v. Williams, supra* and *Lindsey v. Normet, supra*.

We have carefully considered each of the arguments supportive of the District Court's finding that education is a fundamental right or liberty and have found those arguments unpersuasive. In one further respect we find this a particularly inappropriate case in which to subject state action to strict judicial scrutiny. The present case, in another basic sense, is significantly different from any of the cases in which the Court has applied strict scrutiny to state or federal legislation touching upon constitutionally protected rights. Each of our prior cases involved legislation which 'deprived,' 'infringed,' or 'interfered' with the free exercise of some such fundamental personal right or liberty. See *Skinner v. Oklahoma, ex rel. Williamson, supra*, 316 U.S. at 536; *Shapiro v. Thompson, supra*, 394 U.S. at 634; *Dunn v. Blumstein, supra*, 405 U.S.

at 338-343. A critical distinction between those cases and the one now before us lies in what Texas is endeavoring to do with respect to education.

The Texas system of school financing is not unlike the federal legislation involved in *Katzenbach* in this regard. Every step leading to the establishment of the system Texas utilizes today-including the decisions permitting localities to tax and expend locally, and creating and continuously expanding the state aid--was implemented in an effort to extend public education and to improve its quality. Of course, every reform that benefits some more than others may be criticized for what it fails to accomplish. But we think it plain that, in substance, the thrust of the Texas system is affirmative and reformatory and, therefore, should be scrutinized under judicial principles sensitive to the nature of the State's efforts and to the rights reserved to the States under the Constitution.

C

It should be clear, for the reasons stated above and in accord with the prior decisions of this Court, that this is not a case in which the challenged state action must be subjected to the searching judicial scrutiny reserved for laws that create suspect classifications or impinge upon constitutionally protected rights.

We need not rest our decision, however, solely on the inappropriateness of the strict-scrutiny test. A century of Supreme Court adjudication under the Equal Protection Clause affirmatively supports the application of the traditional standard of review, which requires only that the State's system be shown to bear some rational relationship to legitimate state purposes. This case represents far more than a challenge to the manner in which Texas provides for the education of its children. We have here nothing less than a direct attack on the way in which Texas has chosen to raise and disburse state and local tax revenues. We are asked to condemn the State's judgment in conferring on political subdivisions the power to tax local property to supply revenues for local interests. In so doing, appellees would have the Court intrude in an area in which it has traditionally deferred to state legislatures. This Court has often admonished against such interferences with the State's fiscal policies under the Equal Protection Clause.

In addition to matters of fiscal policy, this case also involves the most persistent and difficult questions of educational policy, another area in which this Court's lack of specialized knowledge and experience counsels against premature interference with the informed judgments made at the state and local levels. Education, perhaps even more than welfare assistance, presents a myriad of 'intractable economic, social, and even philosophical problems.' *Dandridge v. Williams*, 397 U.S., at 487. The very complexity of the problems of financing and managing a statewide public school system suggests that 'there will be more than one constitutionally permissible method of solving them,' and that, within the limits of rationality, 'the legislature's efforts to tackle the problems' should be entitled to respect. *Jefferson v. Hackney*, 406 U.S., at 546-547.

It must be remembered, also, that every claim arising under the Equal Protection Clause has implications for the relationship between national and state power under our federal system. Questions of federalism are always inherent in the process of determining whether a State's laws are to be accorded the traditional presumption of constitutionality, or are to be subjected instead to rigorous judicial scrutiny. While '(t)he maintenance of the principles of federalism is a foremost consideration in interpreting any of the pertinent constitutional provisions under which this Court examines state action,' it would be difficult to imagine a case having a greater potential impact on our federal system than the one now before us, in which we are urged to abrogate systems of financing public education presently in existence in virtually every State.

The foregoing considerations buttress our conclusion that Texas' system of public school finance is an inappropriate candidate for strict judicial scrutiny. These same considerations are relevant to the determination whether that system, with its conceded imperfections, nevertheless bears some rational relationship to a legitimate state purpose. It is to this question that we next turn our attention.

III

[The Court, applying rational basis review, determined that the Texas system of financing schools with substantial reliance on local property taxes was rationally related to the state's permissible interest in local control of schools.]

NOTES

1.   The plaintiffs in *Rodriguez* argued that the Court should strictly scrutinize the disparities in education funding since the right to education with which they interfered was a fundamental one. The Court's initial response appeared to be very favorable to the plaintiffs and consistent with *Skinner's* notion that the importance of an interest made it fundamental. The Court conceded that "education is perhaps the most important function of state and local governments," that it "is required in the performance of our most basic public responsibilities," and that it is "the foundation of good citizenship." Ultimately, however, in terms of the standard of review that the Court would apply, none of that mattered, for "the importance of a service performed by the State does not determine whether it must be regarded as fundamental for purposes of examination under the Equal Protection Clause."

What then was the test? According to the Court, "the key to discovering whether education is 'fundamental' is not to be found in comparisons of the relative societal significance of education as opposed to subsistence or housing. Nor is it to be found by weighing whether education is as important as the right to travel. Rather, the answer lies in assessing whether there is a right to education explicitly or implicitly guaranteed by the Constitution."

Since this new *Rodriguez* test directly conflicted with the method the Court had followed in *Skinner*, one might have expected the Court to overrule or distinguish Skinner. Surprisingly, the Court cited *Skinner* as supporting authority for its claim that the true test of a fundamental right was not its societal significance but whether it was "explicitly or implicitly guaranteed by the Constitution." This turns the *Skinner* holding on its head. The Court attempted to explain this away with the claim that "[i]mplicit in the Court's opinion [in *Skinner*] is the recognition that the right of procreation is among the rights of personal privacy protected under the Constitution. See *Roe v. Wade*." This purported explanation is entirely unconvincing. The *Skinner* opinion, of course, had nothing to do with privacy, nothing to do with liberty, nothing to do with the Due Process Clause, and could not possibly have envisioned the Court's due process opinion forty-one years later in *Roe*. The Court in *Skinner*, of course, made no attempt to ground the fundamental right to procreate in any language in the Constitution, but the *Rodriguez* Court saw a very different *Skinner*.

2.   The absolute nature of the language in *Rodriguez* and its outright rejection of "societal significance" as relevant to the search for implied fundamental rights would seem to have put an end to the matter. It didn't. Twelve years later, in *Plyler v. Doe*, the Court once again considered the proper standard of review of government action that deprived young persons of access to

public education.

b. But Not Just Another Benefit

Plyler v. Doe
457 U.S. 202 (1982)

Justice BRENNAN delivered the opinion of the Court.

The question presented by these cases is whether, consistent with the Equal Protection Clause of the Fourteenth Amendment, Texas may deny to undocumented school-age children the free public education that it provides to children who are citizens of the United States or legally admitted aliens.

I

Since the late 19th century, the United States has restricted immigration into this country. Unsanctioned entry into the United States is a crime, 8 U.S.C. § 1325, and those who have entered unlawfully are subject to deportation. But despite the existence of these legal restrictions, a substantial number of persons have succeeded in unlawfully entering the United States, and now live within various States, including the State of Texas.

In May 1975, the Texas Legislature revised its education laws to withhold from local school districts any state funds for the education of children who were not "legally admitted" into the United States. The 1975 revision also authorized local school districts to deny enrollment in their public schools to children not "legally admitted" to the country. These cases involve constitutional challenges to those provisions.

II

The Fourteenth Amendment provides that "[n]o State shall ... deprive any person of life, liberty, or property, without due process of law; nor deny to *any person within its jurisdiction* the equal protection of the laws." (Emphasis added.) Appellants argue at the outset that undocumented aliens, because of their immigration status, are not "persons within the jurisdiction" of the State of Texas, and that they therefore have no right to the equal protection of Texas law. We reject this argument. Whatever his status under the immigration laws, an alien is surely a "person" in any ordinary sense of that term. Aliens, even aliens whose presence in this country is unlawful, have long been recognized as "persons" guaranteed due process of law by the Fifth and Fourteenth Amendments. *Shaughnessy v. Mezei*, 345 U.S. 206, 212 (1953); *Wong Wing v. United States*, 163 U.S. 228, 238 (1896); *Yick Wo v. Hopkins*, 118 U.S. 356, 369 (1886). Indeed, we have clearly held that the Fifth Amendment protects aliens whose presence in this country is unlawful from invidious discrimination by the Federal Government. *Mathews v. Diaz*, 426 U.S. 67, 77 (1976).

Our conclusion that the illegal aliens who are plaintiffs in these cases may claim the benefit of the Fourteenth Amendment's guarantee of equal protection only begins the inquiry. The more difficult question is whether the Equal Protection Clause has been violated by the refusal of the State of Texas to reimburse local school boards for the education of children who cannot demonstrate that their presence within the United States is lawful, or by the imposition by those school boards of the burden of tuition on those children. It is to this question that we now turn.

III

The Equal Protection Clause directs that "all persons similarly circumstanced shall be treated alike." *F. S. Royster Guano Co. v. Virginia*, 253 U.S. 412, 415 (1920). But so too, "[t]he Constitution does not require things which are different in fact or opinion to be treated in law as though they were the same." *Tigner v. Texas*, 310 U.S. 141, 147 (1940). The initial discretion to determine what is "different" and what is "the same" resides in the legislatures of the States. A legislature must have substantial latitude to establish classifications that roughly approximate the nature of the problem perceived, that accommodate competing concerns both public and private, and that account for limitations on the practical ability of the State to remedy every ill. In applying the Equal Protection Clause to most forms of state action, we thus seek only the assurance that the classification at issue bears some fair relationship to a legitimate public purpose.

But we would not be faithful to our obligations under the Fourteenth Amendment if we applied so deferential a standard to every classification. The Equal Protection Clause was intended as a restriction on state legislative action inconsistent with elemental constitutional premises. Thus we have treated as presumptively invidious those classifications that disadvantage a "suspect class," or that impinge upon the exercise of a "fundamental right."[FN 15] With respect to such classifications, it is appropriate to enforce the mandate of equal protection by requiring the State to demonstrate that its classification has been precisely tailored to serve a compelling governmental interest. In addition, we have recognized that certain forms of legislative classification, while not facially invidious, nonetheless give rise to recurring constitutional difficulties; in these limited circumstances we have sought the assurance that the classification reflects a reasoned judgment consistent with the ideal of equal protection by inquiring whether it may fairly be viewed as furthering a substantial interest of the State. We turn to a consideration of the standard appropriate for the evaluation of § 21.031.

A

Sheer incapability or lax enforcement of the laws barring entry into this country, coupled with the failure to establish an effective bar to the employment of undocumented aliens, has resulted in the creation of a substantial "shadow population" of illegal migrants--numbering in the millions--within our borders. This situation raises the specter of a permanent caste of undocumented resident aliens, encouraged by some to remain here as a source of cheap labor, but nevertheless denied the benefits that our society makes available to citizens and lawful residents. The existence of such an underclass presents most difficult problems for a Nation that prides itself on adherence to principles of equality under law.

The children who are plaintiffs in these cases are special members of this underclass. Persuasive arguments support the view that a State may withhold its beneficence from those

---

[FN 15] In determining whether a class-based denial of a particular right is deserving of strict scrutiny under the Equal Protection Clause, we look to the Constitution to see if the right infringed has its source, explicitly or implicitly, therein. But we have also recognized the fundamentality of participation in state "elections on an equal basis with other citizens in the jurisdiction," *Dunn v. Blumstein*, 405 U.S. 330, 336 (1972), even though "the right to vote, *per se*, is not a constitutionally protected right." *San Antonio Independent School Dist., supra*, at 35, n. 78. With respect to suffrage, we have explained the need for strict scrutiny as arising from the significance of the franchise as the guardian of all other rights. See *Harper v. Virginia Bd. of Elections*, 383 U.S. 663, 667 (1966); *Reynolds v. Sims*, 377 U.S. 533, 562 (1964); *Yick Wo v. Hopkins*, 118 U.S. 356, 370 (1886).

whose very presence within the United States is the product of their own unlawful conduct. These arguments do not apply with the same force to classifications imposing disabilities on the minor *children* of such illegal entrants. At the least, those who elect to enter our territory by stealth and in violation of our law should be prepared to bear the consequences, including, but not limited to, deportation. But the children of those illegal entrants are not comparably situated. Their "parents have the ability to conform their conduct to societal norms," and presumably the ability to remove themselves from the State's jurisdiction; but the children who are plaintiffs in these cases "can affect neither their parents' conduct nor their own status." *Trimble v. Gordon*, 430 U.S. 762, 770 (1977). Even if the State found it expedient to control the conduct of adults by acting against their children, legislation directing the onus of a parent's misconduct against his children does not comport with fundamental conceptions of justice.

> [V]isiting ... condemnation on the head of an infant is illogical and unjust. Moreover, imposing disabilities on the ... child is contrary to the basic concept of our system that legal burdens should bear some relationship to individual responsibility or wrongdoing. Obviously, no child is responsible for his birth and penalizing the ... child is an ineffectual-as well as unjust-way of deterring the parent." *Weber v. Aetna Casualty & Surety Co.*, 406 U.S. 164, 175 (1972).

Of course, undocumented status is not irrelevant to any proper legislative goal. Nor is undocumented status an absolutely immutable characteristic since it is the product of conscious, indeed unlawful, action. But § 21.031 is directed against children, and imposes its discriminatory burden on the basis of a legal characteristic over which children can have little control. It is thus difficult to conceive of a rational justification for penalizing these children for their presence within the United States. Yet that appears to be precisely the effect of § 21.031.

Public education is not a "right" granted to individuals by the Constitution. *San Antonio Independent School Dist. v. Rodriguez*, 411 U.S. 1, 35 (1973). But neither is it merely some governmental "benefit" indistinguishable from other forms of social welfare legislation. Both the importance of education in maintaining our basic institutions, and the lasting impact of its deprivation on the life of the child, mark the distinction. The "American people have always regarded education and [the] acquisition of knowledge as matters of supreme importance." *Meyer v. Nebraska*, 262 U.S. 390, 400 (1923). We have recognized "the public schools as a most vital civic institution for the preservation of a democratic system of government," *Abington School District v. Schempp*, 374 U.S. 203, 230 (1963) (BRENNAN, J., concurring), and as the primary vehicle for transmitting "the values on which our society rests." *Ambach v. Norwick*, 441 U.S. 68, 76 (1979). "[A]s ... pointed out early in our history, ... some degree of education is necessary to prepare citizens to participate effectively and intelligently in our open political system if we are to preserve freedom and independence." *Wisconsin v. Yoder*, 406 U.S. 205, 221 (1972). And these historic "perceptions of the public schools as inculcating fundamental values necessary to the maintenance of a democratic political system have been confirmed by the observations of social scientists." *Ambach v. Norwick, supra*, 411 U.S., at 77. In addition, education provides the basic tools by which individuals might lead economically productive lives to the benefit of us all. In sum, education has a fundamental role in maintaining the fabric of our society. We cannot ignore the significant social costs borne by our Nation when select groups are denied the means to absorb the values and skills upon which our social order rests.

In addition to the pivotal role of education in sustaining our political and cultural heritage, denial of education to some isolated group of children poses an affront to one of the goals of the Equal Protection Clause: the abolition of governmental barriers presenting unreasonable obstacles to advancement on the basis of individual merit. Paradoxically, by depriving the children of any disfavored group of an education, we foreclose the means by which that group might raise the level of esteem in which it is held by the majority. But more directly, "education prepares individuals to be self-reliant and self-sufficient participants in society." *Wisconsin v. Yoder, supra*, 406 U.S., at 221. Illiteracy is an enduring disability. The inability to read and write will handicap the individual deprived of a basic education each and every day of his life. The inestimable toll of that deprivation on the social economic, intellectual, and psychological well-being of the individual, and the obstacle it poses to individual achievement, make it most difficult to reconcile the cost or the principle of a status-based denial of basic education with the framework of equality embodied in the Equal Protection Clause. [The Court here quoted *Brown v. Board of Education* to the effect that "education is perhaps the most important function of state and local governments."]

B

These well-settled principles allow us to determine the proper level of deference to be afforded § 21.031. Undocumented aliens cannot be treated as a suspect class because their presence in this country in violation of federal law is not a "constitutional irrelevancy." Nor is education a fundamental right; a State need not justify by compelling necessity every variation in the manner in which education is provided to its population. See *San Antonio Independent School Dist. v. Rodriguez, supra*, at 28-39. But more is involved in these cases than the abstract question whether § 21.031 discriminates against a suspect class, or whether education is a fundamental right. Section 21.031 imposes a lifetime hardship on a discrete class of children not accountable for their disabling status. The stigma of illiteracy will mark them for the rest of their lives. By denying these children a basic education, we deny them the ability to live within the structure of our civic institutions, and foreclose any realistic possibility that they will contribute in even the smallest way to the progress of our Nation. In determining the rationality of § 21.031, we may appropriately take into account its costs to the Nation and to the innocent children who are its victims. In light of these countervailing costs, the discrimination contained in § 21.031 can hardly be considered rational unless it furthers some substantial goal of the State.

IV

It is the State's principal argument, and apparently the view of the dissenting Justices, that the undocumented status of these children *vel non* establishes a sufficient rational basis for denying them benefits that a State might choose to afford other residents. The State notes that while other aliens are admitted "on an equality of legal privileges with all citizens under non-discriminatory laws," *Takahashi v. Fish & Game Comm'n*, 334 U.S. 410, 420 (1948), the asserted right of these children to an education can claim no implicit congressional imprimatur. Indeed, in the State's view, Congress' apparent disapproval of the presence of these children within the United States, and the evasion of the federal regulatory program that is the mark of undocumented status, provides authority for its decision to impose upon them special disabilities. Faced with an equal protection challenge respecting the treatment of aliens, we agree that the courts must be attentive to congressional policy; the exercise of congressional power might well affect the State's prerogatives to afford differential treatment to a particular class of aliens. But we are unable to find in the congressional immigration scheme any statement of policy that might weigh significantly in arriving at an equal protection balance concerning the State's authority to deprive these children of an education.

[The Court here explained that it is primarily the federal government, not the states, that has the power to regulate immigration.]

We are reluctant to impute to Congress the intention to withhold from these children, for so long as they are present in this country through no fault of their own, access to a basic education. In other contexts, undocumented status, coupled with some articulable federal policy, might enhance state authority with respect to the treatment of undocumented aliens. But in the area of special constitutional sensitivity presented by these cases, and in the absence of any contrary indication fairly discernible in the present legislative record, we perceive no national policy that supports the State in denying these children an elementary education. The State may borrow the federal classification. But to justify its use as a criterion for its own discriminatory policy, the State must demonstrate that the classification is reasonably adapted to "*the purposes for which the state desires to use it.*" *Oyama v. California*, 332 U.S. 633, 664-665 (1948) (Murphy, J., concurring) (emphasis added). We therefore turn to the state objectives that are said to support § 21.031.

V

Appellants argue that the classification at issue furthers an interest in the "preservation of the state's limited resources for the education of its lawful residents." Of course, a concern for the preservation of resources standing alone can hardly justify the classification used in allocating those resources. *Graham v. Richardson*, 403 U.S. 365, 374-375 (1971). The State must do more than justify its classification with a concise expression of an intention to discriminate. *Examining Board v. Flores de Otero*, 426 U.S. 572, 605 (1976). Apart from the asserted state prerogative to act against undocumented children solely on the basis of their undocumented status--an asserted prerogative that carries only minimal force in the circumstances of these cases--we discern three colorable state interests that might support § 21.031.

First, appellants appear to suggest that the State may seek to protect itself from an influx of illegal immigrants. While a State might have an interest in mitigating the potentially harsh economic effects of sudden shifts in population, § 21.031 hardly offers an effective method of dealing with an urgent demographic or economic problem. There is no evidence in the record suggesting that illegal entrants impose any significant burden on the State's economy. To the contrary, the available evidence suggests that illegal aliens underutilize public services, while contributing their labor to the local economy and tax money to the state fisc. The dominant incentive for illegal entry into the State of Texas is the availability of employment; few if any illegal immigrants come to this country, or presumably to the State of Texas, in order to avail themselves of a free education. Thus, even making the doubtful assumption that the net impact of illegal aliens on the economy of the State is negative, we think it clear that "[c]harging tuition to undocumented children constitutes a ludicrously ineffectual attempt to stem the tide of illegal immigration," at least when compared with the alternative of prohibiting the employment of illegal aliens.

Second, while it is apparent that a State may "not ... reduce expenditures for education by barring [some arbitrarily chosen class of] children from its schools," *Shapiro v. Thompson*, 394 U.S. 618, 633 (1969), appellants suggest that undocumented children are appropriately singled out for exclusion because of the special burdens they impose on the State's ability to provide high-quality public education. But the record in no way supports the claim that exclusion of undocumented children is likely to improve the overall quality of education in the State. As the District Court in No. 80-1934 noted, the State failed to offer any "credible supporting evidence that a proportionately small diminution of the funds spent on each child [which might result from devoting some state funds to the education of the excluded group] will have a grave impact on the quality of education." 501 F. Supp., at 583. And, after reviewing the State's school financing mechanism, the District Court in No. 80-1538 concluded that barring undocumented children from local schools would not necessarily improve the quality of education provided in those schools.

458 F. Supp., at 577. Of course, even if improvement in the quality of education were a likely result of barring some *number* of children from the schools of the State, the State must support its selection of *this* group as the appropriate target for exclusion. In terms of educational cost and need, however, undocumented children are "basically indistinguishable" from legally resident alien children.

Finally, appellants suggest that undocumented children are appropriately singled out because their unlawful presence within the United States renders them less likely than other children to remain within the boundaries of the State, and to put their education to productive social or political use within the State. Even assuming that such an interest is legitimate, it is an interest that is most difficult to quantify. The State has no assurance that any child, citizen or not, will employ the education provided by the State within the confines of the State's borders. In any event, the record is clear that many of the undocumented children disabled by this classification will remain in this country indefinitely, and that some will become lawful residents or citizens of the United States. It is difficult to understand precisely what the State hopes to achieve by promoting the creation and perpetuation of a subclass of illiterates within our boundaries, surely adding to the problems and costs of unemployment, welfare, and crime. It is thus clear that whatever savings might be achieved by denying these children an education, they are wholly insubstantial in light of the costs involved to these children, the State, and the Nation.

VI

If the State is to deny a discrete group of innocent children the free public education that it offers to other children residing within its borders, that denial must be justified by a showing that it furthers some substantial state interest. No such showing was made here. Accordingly, the judgment of the Court of Appeals in each of these cases is

Affirmed.

NOTES

1. When the Court reviewed the statute excluding undocumented aliens from the public schools, it might have been expected to follow *Rodriguez,* finding the statute implicated no fundamental right and then upholding it with minimal scrutiny. In fact, the *Plyler* Court initially paid lip service to *Rodriguez*, stating that "[p]ublic education is not a right granted to individuals by the Constitution." The Court, however, then added:

> But neither is it merely some governmental 'benefit' indistinguishable from other forms of social welfare legislation. Both the importance of education in maintaining our basic institutions, and the lasting impact of its deprivation on the life of the child, mark the distinction . . . . In sum, education has a fundamental role in maintaining the fabric of our society.

Having thus announced the importance of education, the Court adopted a somewhat heightened level of scrutiny and invalidated the statute. The standard of review that the Court announced was a hybrid. On the one hand, the Court stated that it would determine the "rationality" of the statute, but it also declared that the statute could "hardly be considered rational unless it furthers some substantial goal of the State." The reference to "substantial" goals and the requirement that the statute actually "further" those goals very much tracks the language of intermediate scrutiny, not rational basis review. Additionally, in assessing whether the exclusion of undocumented aliens from the school system was related to the alleged statutory purposes, the Court made several references to the fact that there was no evidence "in the record" of such a connection. Under rational basis review, however, it is clear that there need not be any evidence in the record to support a legislative classification. Essentially, the *Plyler* Court created a kind of intermediate scrutiny for the quasi-fundamental right to education.

And how did the Court determine that education was quasi-fundamental? The *Plyler* Court seemed to weigh the value of education to the students educated and to society as a whole. This sounds quite a bit like a test of "societal significance," without any reference to the text of the Constitution, the very test rejected in *Rodriguez*. Thus, the original *Skinner* test--it's fundamental because it's important--is not really dead after all. But *Plyler* seems to be the only post-*Skinner* case to apply it.

CHAPTER 9

CONGRESSIONAL POWER TO ENFORCE THE EQUAL PROTECTION CLAUSE

A. CONGRESSIONAL POWER UNDER THE COMMERCE CLAUSE AND UNDER SECTION 5 OF THE FOURTEENTH AMENDMENT

The federal government is a government of enumerated powers; it has no inherent sovereign authority. This means that, whenever the federal government acts, it must trace its authority for that action to a particular provision of the Constitution.

The Commerce Clause, Art. I, Sec. 8, which grants to Congress the power "to regulate Commerce with foreign Nations, and among the several States, and with Indian Tribes," is one of the broadest grants of authority to Congress. The Commerce Clause has been the basis of a substantial amount of federal regulation of economic activity. In addition, it has also been used as a source of authority for certain civil rights statutes. Thus, for example, in *Heart of Atlanta Motel v. United States*, 379 U.S. 241 (1964), the Supreme Court held that Congress' power under the Commerce Clause extended to enacting the Civil Rights Act of 1964, which prohibited discrimination in places of public accommodation. Further, in EEOC v. Wyoming, 460 U.S. 226 (1983), the Court determined that the extension of the Age Discrimination in Employment Act to cover state and local governments was a valid exercise of Congress' powers under the Commerce Clause. As long as Congress could rely on the Commerce Clause as constitutional authority for the enactment of civil rights statutes, it need not look for authority elsewhere in the Constitution.

That changed with the Court's decision in *Seminole Tribe of Florida v. Florida*, 517 U.S. 44 (1996), in which the Court considered the extent to which the Eleventh Amendment limited Congress' power under the Commerce Clause. The Eleventh Amendment provides that "The Judicial power of the United States shall not be construed to extend to any suit in law or equity, commenced or prosecuted against one of the United States by Citizens of another State, or by Citizens or Subjects of any Foreign State." As the Court explained, "Although the text of the Amendment would appear to restrict only the Article III diversity jurisdiction of the federal courts, "we have understood the Eleventh Amendment to stand not so much for what it says, but for the presupposition ... which it confirms"—that a state cannot be sued without its consent." The Court then determined that the Eleventh Amendment limited Congress' power under the Commerce Clause and that, therefore, the act in question (The Indian Gaming Regulatory Act) which gave tribes a cause of action against unconsenting states, was unconstitutional.

The Court's decision in *Seminole Tribe* affected civil rights legislation in the following way. To the extent that a civil rights bill was directed at private parties, the Commerce Clause would continue to be an appropriate basis for the legislation. But to the extent the statute was also directed at the state, the Commerce Clause could no longer be appropriate constitutional authority. This created problems in that many federal anti-discrimination statutes-- including the Age Discrimination in Employment Act, the Americans with Disabilities Act, and the Family and Medical Leave Act—are directed, *inter alia*, at state actors.

Fortunately, there was an alternate source of constitutional authority for federal civil rights statutes—Section 5 of the Fourteenth Amendment, which provides that "The Congress shall have power to enforce, by appropriate legislation, the provisions of this article." In an earlier decision, *Fitzpatrick v. Bitzer*, 427 U.S. 445 (1976), the Court had held that Congress' Section 5 power was *not* limited by the Eleventh Amendment. The Court's later opinion in *Seminole* Tribe explains the effect of the *Fitzpatrick* decision:

> In *Fitzpatrick,* we recognized that the Fourteenth Amendment, by expanding federal power at the expense of state autonomy, had fundamentally altered the balance of state and federal power struck by the Constitution. We noted that § 1 of the Fourteenth Amendment contained prohibitions expressly directed at the States and that § 5 of the Amendment expressly provided that "The Congress shall have power to enforce, by appropriate legislation, the provisions of this article." We held that through the Fourteenth Amendment, federal power extended to intrude upon the province of the Eleventh Amendment and therefore that § 5 of the Fourteenth Amendment allowed Congress to abrogate the immunity from suit guaranteed by that Amendment. *Seminole Tribe*, 517 U.S. at 59.

After *Seminole Tribe*, then, it became all the more important for the Court to explicate exactly what Congress' power under Section 5 was. That issue is examined in this chapter.

B. THE PRINCIPLE OF CONGRUENCE AND PROPORTIONALITY

City of Boerne v. Flores
521 U.S. 507 (1997)

Justice KENNEDY delivered the opinion of the Court.

A decision by local zoning authorities to deny a church a building permit was challenged under the Religious Freedom Restoration Act of 1993 (RFRA or Act), 107 Stat. 1488, 42 U.S.C. § 2000bb *et seq*. The case calls into question the authority of Congress to enact RFRA. We conclude the statute exceeds Congress' power.

[A Catholic church applied for a city permit to construct an addition to its church building. Since the building was considered an historic landmark, approval of the city's Historic Landmark Commission was required. City authorities denied the application and the church brought this suit challenging the permit denial.]

Congress enacted RFRA in direct response to the Court's decision in *Employment Div., Dept. of Human Resources of Oregon v. Smith,* 494 U.S. 872 (1990). [In *Smith,* the Court had declined to apply the "compelling government interest" test to generally applicable prohibitions of socially harmful conduct even if they burdened a religious practice.]

These points of constitutional interpretation were debated by Members of Congress in hearings and floor debates. Many criticized the Court's reasoning, and this disagreement resulted in the passage of RFRA. RFRA prohibits "[g]overnment" from "substantially burden[ing]" a person's exercise of religion even if the burden results from a rule of general applicability unless the government can demonstrate the burden "(1) is in furtherance of a compelling governmental interest; and (2) is the least restrictive means of furthering that compelling governmental interest."

Under our Constitution, the Federal Government is one of enumerated powers. *M'Culloch v. Maryland,* 4 Wheat. 316, 405 (1819); see also The Federalist No. 45, p. 292 (C. Rossiter ed. 1961) (J. Madison). The judicial authority to determine the constitutionality of laws, in cases and controversies, is based on the premise that the "powers of the legislature are defined and limited; and that those limits may not be mistaken, or forgotten, the constitution is written." *Marbury v. Madison,* 1 Cranch 137, 176 (1803).

Congress relied on its Fourteenth Amendment enforcement power in enacting the most far-reaching and substantial of RFRA's provisions, those which impose its requirements on the States. The parties disagree over whether RFRA is a proper exercise of Congress' § 5 power "to enforce" by "appropriate legislation" the constitutional guarantee that no State shall deprive any person of "life, liberty, or property, without due process of law" nor deny any person "equal protection of the laws."

In defense of the Act, respondent the Archbishop contends, with support from the United States, that RFRA is permissible enforcement legislation. Congress, it is said, is only protecting by legislation one of the liberties guaranteed by the Fourteenth Amendment's Due Process Clause, the free exercise of religion, beyond what is necessary under *Smith.* It is said the congressional decision to dispense with proof of deliberate or overt discrimination and instead concentrate on a law's effects accords with the settled understanding that § 5 includes the power to enact legislation designed to prevent, as well as remedy, constitutional violations. It is further contended that Congress' § 5 power is not limited to remedial or preventive legislation.

All must acknowledge that § 5 is "a positive grant of legislative power" to Congress, *Katzenbach v. Morgan,* 384 U.S. 641, 651 (1966). In *Ex parte Virginia,* 100 U.S. 339, 345–346 (1879), we explained the scope of Congress' § 5 power in the following broad terms:

> Whatever legislation is appropriate, that is, adapted to carry out the objects the amendments have in view, whatever tends to enforce submission to the prohibitions they contain, and to secure to all persons the enjoyment of perfect equality of civil rights and the equal protection of the laws against State denial or invasion, if not prohibited, is brought within the domain of congressional power.

Legislation which deters or remedies constitutional violations can fall within the sweep of Congress' enforcement power even if in the process it prohibits conduct which is not itself unconstitutional and intrudes into "legislative spheres of autonomy previously reserved to the States." *Fitzpatrick v. Bitzer,* 427 U.S. 445, 455 (1976). For example, the Court upheld a suspension of literacy tests and similar voting requirements under Congress' parallel power to enforce the provisions of the Fifteenth Amendment see U.S. Const., Amdt. 15, § 2, as a measure to combat racial discrimination in voting, *South Carolina v. Katzenbach,* 383 U.S. 301, 308 (1966), despite the facial constitutionality of the tests under *Lassiter v. Northampton County Bd. of Elections,* 360 U.S. 45 (1959). We have also concluded that other measures protecting voting rights are within Congress' power to enforce the Fourteenth and Fifteenth Amendments, despite the burdens those measures placed on the States. *South Carolina v. Katzenbach, supra* (upholding several provisions of the Voting Rights Act of 1965); *Katzenbach v. Morgan, supra* (upholding ban on literacy tests that prohibited certain people schooled in Puerto Rico from voting); *Oregon v. Mitchell,* 400 U.S. 112 (1970) (upholding 5-year nationwide ban on literacy tests and similar voting requirements for registering to vote); *City of Rome v. United States,* 446 U.S. 156, 161 (1980) (upholding 7-year extension of the Voting Rights Act's requirement that certain jurisdictions preclear any change to a " 'standard, practice, or procedure with respect to voting'"); see also *James Everard's Breweries v. Day,* 265 U.S. 545 (1924) (upholding ban on medical prescription of intoxicating malt liquors as appropriate to enforce Eighteenth Amendment ban on manufacture, sale, or transportation of intoxicating liquors for beverage purposes).

It is also true, however, that "[a]s broad as the congressional enforcement power is, it is not unlimited." *Oregon v. Mitchell, supra,* at 128 (opinion of Black, J.). In assessing the breadth of § 5's enforcement power, we begin with its text. Congress has been given the power "to enforce" the "provisions of this article." We agree with respondent, of course, that Congress can enact legislation under § 5 enforcing the constitutional right to the free exercise of religion. The "provisions of this article," to which § 5 refers, include the Due Process Clause of the Fourteenth Amendment. Congress' power to enforce the Free Exercise Clause follows from our holding in *Cantwell v. Connecticut,* 310 U.S. 296, 303 (1940), that the "fundamental concept of liberty embodied in [the Fourteenth Amendment's Due Process Clause] embraces the liberties guaranteed by the First Amendment." See also *United States v. Price,* 383 U.S. 787, 789 (1966) (there is "no doubt of the power of Congress to enforce by appropriate criminal sanction every right guaranteed by the Due Process Clause of the Fourteenth Amendment" (internal quotation marks and citation omitted)).

Congress' power under § 5, however, extends only to "enforc[ing]" the provisions of the Fourteenth Amendment. The Court has described this power as "remedial," *South Carolina v. Katzenbach, supra,* at 326. The design of the Amendment and the text of § 5 are inconsistent with the suggestion that Congress has the power to decree the substance of the Fourteenth Amendment's restrictions on the States. Legislation which alters the meaning of the Free Exercise Clause cannot be said to be enforcing the Clause. Congress does not enforce a constitutional right by changing what the right is. It has been given the power "to enforce," not the power to determine what constitutes a constitutional violation. Were it not so, what Congress would be enforcing would no longer be, in any meaningful sense, the "provisions of [the Fourteenth Amendment]."

While the line between measures that remedy or prevent unconstitutional actions and measures that make a substantive change in the governing law is not easy to discern, and Congress must have wide latitude in determining where it lies, the distinction exists and must be observed. There must be a congruence and proportionality between the injury to be prevented or remedied and the means adopted to that end. Lacking such a connection, legislation may become substantive in operation and effect. History and our case law support drawing the distinction, one apparent from the text of the Amendment.

Any suggestion that Congress has a substantive, non-remedial power under the Fourteenth Amendment is not supported by our case law. In *Oregon v. Mitchell, supra*, a majority of the Court concluded Congress had exceeded its enforcement powers by enacting legislation lowering the minimum age of voters from 21 to 18 in state and local elections. The five Members of the Court who reached this conclusion explained that the legislation intruded into an area reserved by the Constitution to the States.

If Congress could define its own powers by altering the Fourteenth Amendment's meaning, no longer would the Constitution be "superior paramount law, unchangeable by ordinary means." It would be "on a level with ordinary legislative acts, and, like other acts, ... alterable when the legislature shall please to alter it." *Marbury v. Madison,* 1 Cranch, at 177. Under this approach, it is difficult to conceive of a principle that would limit congressional power. See Van Alstyne, The Failure of the Religious Freedom Restoration Act under Section 5 of the Fourteenth Amendment, 46 Duke L.J. 291, 292–303 (1996). Shifting legislative majorities could change the Constitution and effectively circumvent the difficult and detailed amendment process contained in Article V.

We now turn to consider whether RFRA can be considered enforcement legislation under § 5 of the Fourteenth Amendment.

B

[The Court determined that the challenged statute could not be considered remedial, preventive legislation. Rather, it was so out of proportion to a supposed remedial or preventive object that it could not be understood as responsive to, or designed to prevent, unconstitutional behavior. It appeared, instead, to attempt a substantive change in constitutional protections. The stringent test that the statute demanded of state laws reflected a lack of proportionality or congruence between the means adopted and the legitimate end to be achieved. The Court thus concluded that Congress lacked authority under Section 5 to enact RFRA.]

NOTES

1. Since *Marbury v. Madison,* 1 Cranch 137, 176 (1803), it has been clear that it is the role of the Judiciary to say what the law is and the Judiciary's word is final. In one sense, then, *City of Boerne* is simply an application of that historic principle, that is, the Court rather than Congress is determining what the First Amendment means. *City of Boerne*, however, can also be characterized quite differently—as a power grab by the Supreme Court at the expense of Congress.

This second reading of *City of Boerne* rises from the fact that the case is a substantial departure from the Court's earlier precedent on Congress' Section 5 power. In *Katzenbach v. Morgan,* 384 U.S. 641(1966), the Court had given broad effect to Congressional power to enforce the Fourteenth Amendment. The Court had specifically approved of Congress' power to enact the Voting Rights Act of 1965, even though the Act prohibited certain conduct that the Court had not found to be in violation of the Equal Protection Clause. The Court explained:

A construction of § 5 that would require a judicial determination that the enforcement of the state law precluded by Congress violated the Amendment, as a condition of sustaining the congressional enactment, would depreciate both congressional resourcefulness and congressional responsibility for implementing the Amendment. It would confine the legislative power in this context to the insignificant role of abrogating only those state laws that the judicial branch was prepared to adjudge unconstitutional, or of merely informing the judgment of the judiciary by particularizing the 'majestic generalities' of s 1 of the Amendment . . . It is not for us to review the congressional resolution of these factors. It is enough that we be able to perceive a basis upon which the Congress might resolve the conflict as it did.

Thirty years later, in *City of Boerne*, the Court reached a much narrower result that substantially limited Congressional power. Professors Robert C. Post and Reva B. Siegel, in *Legislative Constitutionalism and the Section Five Power: Policentric Interpretation of the Family and Medical Leave Act*, 112 Yale L.J. 1943 (2003), are critical of this interpretation:

The Rehnquist Court now views Section 5 power as a potential threat to the Court's role as "the ultimate expositor of the constitutional text." Beginning with its 1997 decision in *City of Boerne v. Flores*, the Court has repeatedly affirmed that Section 5 does not authorize Congress "to determine what constitutes a constitutional violation" or "to rewrite the Fourteenth Amendment law laid down by this Court." . . . We call this view of separation of powers the "enforcement model." The Rehnquist Court has used the enforcement model to strike down path-breaking civil rights legislation enacted under the quite different understanding of Section 5 that prevailed during the thirty years that preceded *Boerne*. *Id.* at 1945-46.

2. The *City of Boerne* opinion introduced the "congruence and proportionality" test as a standard for measuring Congressional power under Section 5 of the Fourteenth Amendment: "There must be a congruence and proportionality between the injury to be prevented or remedied and the means adopted to that end." What this means is that the Court looks to see what kind of conduct the Fourteenth Amendment itself makes unconstitutional—"the injury to be prevented or remedied"—and then compares that conduct with the conduct made unlawful by the statute—"the means adopted to that end." Although the prohibited acts under the two standards need not be identical, there must be a very substantial overlap in order to make the statute "congruent and proportional" to the Fourteenth Amendment. As the next cases will show, the Court has construed this standard very strictly and this narrow construction has had the effect of narrowing Congressional power under Section 5.

3. *City of Boerne* is, of course, not an equal protection case. It arises under the Due Process Clause of the Fourteenth Amendment because the First Amendment protection of religious liberty has been incorporated against the states through the Due Process Clause. Section 5 gives Congress power to enforce "the provisions of this article." Those provisions include the Equal Protection Clause, the Due Process Clause, and the Privileges or Immunities Clause. *Kimel v. Florida Bd. of Regents*, the next case, is the first case in which the Court applied the "congruence and proportionality" test in an equal protection context.

CHAPTER 9: CONGRESSIONAL POWER TO ENFORCE THE EQUAL PROTECTION CLAUSE

Kimel v. Florida Bd. of Regents
528 U.S. 62 (2000)

[Three sets of plaintiffs filed suit against state defendants, seeking damages for alleged violations of the federal Age Discrimination in Employment Act (ADEA). The Court considered whether Section 5 of the Fourteenth Amendment gave Congress authority to enact the ADEA.]

Justice O'CONNOR delivered the opinion of the Court.

The Age Discrimination in Employment Act of 1967 (ADEA or Act), makes it unlawful for an employer, including a State, "to fail or refuse to hire or to discharge any individual or otherwise discriminate against any individual ... because of such individual's age." In these cases, three sets of plaintiffs filed suit under the Act, seeking money damages for their state employers' alleged discrimination on the basis of age. In each case, the state employer moved to dismiss the suit on the basis of its Eleventh Amendment immunity. [W]e are asked to consider whether the ADEA contains a clear statement of Congress' intent to abrogate the States' Eleventh Amendment immunity and, if so, whether the ADEA is a proper exercise of Congress' constitutional authority. We conclude that the ADEA does contain a clear statement of Congress' intent to abrogate the States' immunity, but that the abrogation exceeded Congress' authority under § 5 of the Fourteenth Amendment.

When first passed in 1967, the ADEA applied only to private employers. See 29 U.S.C. § 630(b) (1964 ed., Supp. III) (defining term "employer" to exclude "the United States, a corporation wholly owned by the Government of the United States, or a State or political subdivision thereof"). In 1974 ...Congress extended application of the ADEA's substantive requirements to the States ... by a simple amendment to the definition of "employer" contained in 29 U.S.C. § 630(b): "The term [employer] also means ... a State or political subdivision of a State and any agency or instrumentality of a State or a political subdivision of a State. . . ."

II

The Eleventh Amendment states:

> "The Judicial power of the United States shall not be construed to extend to any suit in law or equity, commenced or prosecuted against one of the United States by Citizens of another State, or by Citizens or Subjects of any Foreign State."

Although today's cases concern suits brought by citizens against their own States, this Court has long "'understood the Eleventh Amendment to stand not so much for what it says, but for the presupposition ... which it confirms.'" *Seminole Tribe of Fla. v. Florida,* 517 U.S. 44, 54 (1996). Accordingly, for over a century now, we have made clear that the Constitution does not provide for federal jurisdiction over suits against nonconsenting States. *College Savings Bank v. Florida Prepaid Postsecondary Ed. Expense Bd.,* 527 U.S. 666, 669–670 (1999); *Seminole Tribe, supra,* at 54. Petitioners nevertheless contend that the States of Alabama and Florida must defend the present suits on the merits because Congress abrogated their Eleventh Amendment immunity in the ADEA. To determine whether petitioners are correct, we must resolve two predicate questions: first, whether Congress unequivocally expressed its intent to abrogate that immunity; and second, if it did, whether Congress acted pursuant to a valid grant of constitutional authority. *Seminole Tribe, supra,* at 55.

III

To determine whether a federal statute properly subjects States to suits by individuals, we apply a "simple but stringent test: 'Congress may abrogate the States' constitutionally secured immunity from suit in federal court only by making its intention unmistakably clear in the language of the statute.'" *Dellmuth v. Muth,* 491 U.S. 223, 228 (1989) (quoting *Atascadero State Hospital v. Scanlon,* 473 U.S. 234, 242 (1985)). We agree with petitioners that the ADEA satisfies that test.

IV

This is not the first time we have considered the constitutional validity of the 1974 extension of the ADEA to state and local governments. In *EEOC v. Wyoming,* 460 U.S. 226, 243 (1983), we held that the ADEA constitutes a valid exercise of Congress' power "[t]o regulate Commerce ... among the several States," Art. I, § 8, cl. 3, and that the Act did not transgress any external restraints imposed on the commerce power by the Tenth Amendment. Because we found the ADEA valid under Congress' Commerce Clause power, we concluded that it was unnecessary to determine whether the Act also could be supported by Congress' power under § 5 of the Fourteenth Amendment. Resolution of today's cases requires us to decide that question.

In *Seminole Tribe,* we held that Congress lacks power under Article I to abrogate the States' sovereign immunity. 517 U.S., at 72–73. "Even when the Constitution vests in Congress complete lawmaking authority over a particular area, the Eleventh Amendment prevents congressional authorization of suits by private parties against unconsenting States." *Id.,* at 72.

Section 5 of the Fourteenth Amendment, however, does grant Congress the authority to abrogate the States' sovereign immunity. In *Fitzpatrick v. Bitzer,* 427 U.S. 445 (1976), we recognized that "the Eleventh Amendment, and the principle of state sovereignty which it embodies, are necessarily limited by the enforcement provisions of § 5 of the Fourteenth Amendment." Since our decision in *Fitzpatrick,* we have reaffirmed the validity of that congressional power on numerous occasions. See, *e.g., College Savings Bank, supra,* at 670; *Florida Prepaid, supra,* at 636–637; *Alden, supra,* at 756; *Seminole Tribe, supra,* at 59. Accordingly, the private petitioners in these cases may maintain their ADEA suits against the States of Alabama and Florida if, and only if, the ADEA is appropriate legislation under § 5.

B

The Fourteenth Amendment provides, in relevant part:

"Section 1. ... No State shall make or enforce any law which shall abridge the privileges or immunities of citizens of the United States; nor shall any State deprive any person of life, liberty, or property, without due process of law; nor deny to any person within its jurisdiction the equal protection of the laws."

....

"Section 5. The Congress shall have power to enforce, by appropriate legislation, the provisions of this article."

As we recognized most recently in *City of Boerne v. Flores,* 521 U.S. 507, 517 (1997), § 5 is an affirmative grant of power to Congress. "It is for Congress in the first instance to 'determin[e] whether and what legislation is needed to secure the guarantees of the Fourteenth Amendment,' and its conclusions are entitled to much deference." *Id.,* at 536 (quoting *Katzenbach v. Morgan,* 384 U.S. 641, 651 (1966)). Congress' § 5 power is not confined to the enactment of legislation that merely parrots the precise wording of the Fourteenth Amendment. Rather, Congress' power "to enforce" the Amendment includes the authority both to remedy and to deter violation of rights guaranteed thereunder by prohibiting a somewhat broader swath of conduct, including that which is not itself forbidden by the Amendment's text.

Nevertheless, we have also recognized that the same language that serves as the basis for the affirmative grant of congressional power also serves to limit that power. For example, Congress cannot "decree the *substance* of the Fourteenth Amendment's restrictions on the States. . . . It has been given the power 'to enforce,' not the power to determine *what constitutes* a constitutional violation." *Id.,* at 519 (emphases added). The ultimate interpretation and determination of the Fourteenth Amendment's substantive meaning remains the province of the Judicial Branch. In *City of Boerne,* we noted that the determination whether purportedly prophylactic legislation constitutes appropriate remedial legislation, or instead effects a substantive redefinition of the Fourteenth Amendment right at issue, is often difficult. The line between the two is a fine one. Accordingly, recognizing that "Congress must have wide latitude in determining where [that line] lies," we held that "[t]here must be a congruence and proportionality between the injury to be prevented or remedied and the means adopted to that end."

In *City of Boerne,* we applied that "congruence and proportionality" test and held that the Religious Freedom Restoration Act of 1993 (RFRA) was not appropriate legislation under § 5. We first noted that the legislative record contained very little evidence of the unconstitutional conduct purportedly targeted by RFRA's substantive provisions. Rather, Congress had uncovered only "anecdotal evidence" that, standing alone, did not reveal a "widespread pattern of religious discrimination in this country." Second, we found that RFRA is "so out of proportion to a supposed remedial or preventive object that it cannot be understood as responsive to, or designed to prevent, unconstitutional behavior."

C

Applying the same "congruence and proportionality" test in these cases, we conclude that the ADEA is not "appropriate legislation" under § 5 of the Fourteenth Amendment. Initially, the substantive requirements the ADEA imposes on state and local governments are disproportionate to any unconstitutional conduct that conceivably could be targeted by the Act. We have considered claims of unconstitutional age discrimination under the Equal Protection Clause three times. See *Gregory v. Ashcroft,* 501 U.S. 452 (1991); *Vance v. Bradley,* 440 U.S. 93 (1979); *Massachusetts Bd. of Retirement v. Murgia,* 427 U.S. 307 (1976) *(per curiam).* In all three cases, we held that the age classifications at issue did not violate the Equal Protection Clause. See *Gregory, supra,* at 473; *Bradley, supra,* at 102–103, n. 20; *Murgia, supra,* at 317. Age classifications, unlike governmental conduct based on race or gender, cannot be characterized as "so seldom relevant to the achievement of any legitimate state interest that laws grounded in such considerations are deemed to reflect prejudice and antipathy." *Cleburne v. Cleburne Living Center, Inc.,* 473 U.S. 432, 440 (1985). Older persons, again, unlike those who suffer discrimination on the basis of race or gender, have not been subjected to a " 'history of purposeful unequal treatment.' " *Murgia, supra,* at 313 (quoting *San Antonio Independent School Dist. v. Rodriguez,* 411 U.S. 1, 28 (1973)). Old age also does not define a discrete and insular minority because all persons, if they live out their normal life spans, will experience it. 427 U.S., at 313–314. Accordingly, as we recognized in *Murgia, Bradley,* and *Gregory,* age is not a suspect classification under the Equal Protection

Clause. See, *e.g., Gregory, supra,* at 470; *Bradley, supra,* at 97; *Murgia, supra,* at 313–314.

States may discriminate on the basis of age without offending the Fourteenth Amendment if the age classification in question is rationally related to a legitimate state interest. The rationality commanded by the Equal Protection Clause does not require States to match age distinctions and the legitimate interests they serve with razorlike precision. As we have explained, when conducting rational basis review "we will not overturn such [government action] unless the varying treatment of different groups or persons is so unrelated to the achievement of any combination of legitimate purposes that we can only conclude that the [government's] actions were irrational." *Bradley, supra,* at 97. In contrast, when a State discriminates on the basis of race or gender, we require a tighter fit between the discriminatory means and the legitimate ends they serve. See, *e.g., Adarand Constructors, Inc. v. Peña,* 515 U.S. 200, 227 (1995) ("[Racial] classifications are constitutional only if they are narrowly tailored measures that further compelling governmental interests"); *Mississippi Univ. for Women v. Hogan,* 458 U.S. 718, 724 (1982) (holding that gender classifications are constitutional only if they serve " 'important governmental objectives and ... the discriminatory means employed' are 'substantially related to the achievement of those objectives' " (citation omitted)). Under the Fourteenth Amendment, a State may rely on age as a proxy for other qualities, abilities, or characteristics that are relevant to the State's legitimate interests. The Constitution does not preclude reliance on such generalizations. That age proves to be an inaccurate proxy in any individual case is irrelevant. "[W]here rationality is the test, a State 'does not violate the Equal Protection Clause merely because the classifications made by its laws are imperfect.' " *Murgia, supra,* at 316 (quoting *Dandridge v. Williams,* 397 U.S. 471, 485 (1970)). Finally, because an age classification is presumptively rational, the individual challenging its constitutionality bears the burden of proving that the "facts on which the classification is apparently based could not reasonably be conceived to be true by the governmental decisionmaker." *Bradley, supra,* at 111; see *Gregory, supra,* at 473.

Judged against the backdrop of our equal protection jurisprudence, it is clear that the ADEA is "so out of proportion to a supposed remedial or preventive object that it cannot be understood as responsive to, or designed to prevent, unconstitutional behavior." *City of Boerne,* 521 U.S., at 532. The Act, through its broad restriction on the use of age as a discriminating factor, prohibits substantially more state employment decisions and practices than would likely be held unconstitutional under the applicable equal protection, rational basis standard. The ADEA makes unlawful, in the employment context, all "discriminat[ion] against any individual ... because of such individual's age." 29 U.S.C. § 623(a)(1). Petitioners, relying on the Act's exceptions, dispute the extent to which the ADEA erects protections beyond the Constitution's requirements. They contend that the Act's prohibition, considered together with its exceptions, applies only to arbitrary age discrimination, which in the majority of cases corresponds to conduct that violates the Equal Protection Clause. We disagree.

Petitioners stake their claim on § 623(f)(1). That section permits employers to rely on age when it "is a bona fide occupational qualification reasonably necessary to the normal operation of the particular business." Petitioners' reliance on the "bona fide occupational qualification" (BFOQ) defense is misplaced. Our interpretation of § 623(f)(1) in *Western Air Lines, Inc. v. Criswell,* 472 U.S. 400 (1985), conclusively demonstrates that the defense is a far cry from the rational basis standard we apply to age discrimination under the Equal Protection Clause. The petitioner in that case maintained that, pursuant to the BFOQ defense, employers must be permitted to rely on age when such reliance has a "rational basis in fact." We rejected that argument, explaining that "[t]he BFOQ standard adopted in the statute is one of 'reasonable necessity,' not reasonableness," and that the ADEA standard and the rational basis test are "significantly different."

Under the ADEA, even with its BFOQ defense, the State's use of age is prima facie unlawful. See 29 U.S.C. § 623(a)(1); *Western Air Lines,* 472 U.S., at 422 ("Under the Act, employers are to evaluate employees ... on their merits and not their age"). Application of the Act therefore starts with a presumption in favor of requiring the employer to make an individualized determination. In *Western Air Lines,* we concluded that the BFOQ defense, which shifts the focus from the merits of the individual employee to the necessity for the age classification as a whole, is "'meant to be an extremely narrow exception to the general prohibition' of age discrimination contained in the ADEA." We based that conclusion on both the restrictive language of the statutory BFOQ provision itself and the EEOC's regulation interpreting that exception. See 29 CFR § 1625.6(a) (1998) ("It is anticipated that this concept of a [BFOQ] will have limited scope and application. Further, as this is an exception to the Act it must be narrowly construed"). To succeed under the BFOQ defense, we held that an employer must demonstrate either "a substantial basis for believing that *all or nearly all employees* above an age lack the qualifications required for the position," or that reliance on the age classification is necessary because "it is *highly impractical* for the employer to insure by individual testing that its employees will have the necessary qualifications for the job." 472 U.S., at 422–423 (emphases added). Measured against the rational basis standard of our equal protection jurisprudence, the ADEA plainly imposes substantially higher burdens on state employers. Thus, although it is true that the existence of the BFOQ defense makes the ADEA's prohibition of age discrimination less than absolute, the Act's substantive requirements nevertheless remain at a level akin to our heightened scrutiny cases under the Equal Protection Clause.

That the ADEA prohibits very little conduct likely to be held unconstitutional, while significant, does not alone provide the answer to our § 5 inquiry. Difficult and intractable problems often require powerful remedies, and we have never held that § 5 precludes Congress from enacting reasonably prophylactic legislation. Our task is to determine whether the ADEA is in fact just such an appropriate remedy or, instead, merely an attempt to substantively redefine the States' legal obligations with respect to age discrimination. One means by which we have made such a determination in the past is by examining the legislative record containing the reasons for Congress' action. See, *e.g., Florida Prepaid,* 527 U.S., at 640–647; *City of Boerne,* 521 U.S., at 530–531. "The appropriateness of remedial measures must be considered in light of the evil presented. Strong measures appropriate to address one harm may be an unwarranted response to another, lesser one." *Id.,* at 530 (citing *South Carolina v. Katzenbach,* 383 U.S. 301, 308 (1966)).

Our examination of the ADEA's legislative record confirms that Congress' 1974 extension of the Act to the States was an unwarranted response to a perhaps inconsequential problem. Congress never identified any pattern of age discrimination by the States, much less any discrimination whatsoever that rose to the level of constitutional violation. The evidence compiled by petitioners to demonstrate such attention by Congress to age discrimination by the States falls well short of the mark. That evidence consists almost entirely of isolated sentences clipped from floor debates and legislative reports.

A review of the ADEA's legislative record as a whole, then, reveals that Congress had virtually no reason to believe that state and local governments were unconstitutionally discriminating against their employees on the basis of age. Although that lack of support is not determinative of the § 5 inquiry, Congress' failure to uncover any significant pattern of unconstitutional discrimination here confirms that Congress had no reason to believe that broad prophylactic legislation was necessary in this field. In light of the indiscriminate scope of the Act's substantive requirements, and the lack of evidence of widespread and unconstitutional age discrimination by the States, we hold that the ADEA is not a valid exercise of Congress' power under § 5 of the Fourteenth Amendment. The ADEA's purported abrogation of the States' sovereign immunity is accordingly invalid.

D

Our decision today does not signal the end of the line for employees who find themselves subject to age discrimination at the hands of their state employers. We hold only that, in the ADEA, Congress did not validly abrogate the States' sovereign immunity to suits by private individuals. State employees are protected by state age discrimination statutes, and may recover money damages from their state employers, in almost every State of the Union. Those avenues of relief remain available today, just as they were before this decision.

Because the ADEA does not validly abrogate the States' sovereign immunity, however, the present suits must be dismissed. Accordingly, the judgment of the Court of Appeals is affirmed.

It is so ordered.

NOTES

1. The *Kimel* Court explains that Congress' Section 5 power is to *enforce* the Fourteenth Amendment, not to decree the *substance* of it. In applying the congruence and proportionality test, the Court compared the age classifications that would violate the Equal Protection Clause with the age classifications that were a violation of the ADEA. The Court found that the conduct prohibited by the statute was substantially greater than that prohibited by the Equal Protection Clause. Since age classifications are subjected to only a very deferential version of rational basis review, virtually any age classification will survive constitutional scrutiny. In fact, the Supreme Court has never invalidated an age classification under the Equal Protection Clause. All that is required for Equal Protection purposes is that the legislature might reasonably have believed that there is a correlation between age and some other trait, like fitness. Thus, "Under the Fourteenth Amendment, a State may rely on age as a proxy for other qualities, abilities, or characteristics that are relevant to the State's legitimate interests. The Constitution does not preclude reliance on such generalizations. That age proves to be an inaccurate proxy in any individual case is irrelevant."

By contrast, the ADEA "prohibits substantially more state employment decisions and practices than would likely be held unconstitutional under the applicable equal protection, rational basis standard." The ADEA makes unlawful, in the employment context, all discrimination against any individual "because of such individual's age." This statutory standard seems to prohibit the use even of reasonable classifications, if the classification is not accurate in an individual case.

The practical effect of *Kimel* is that, when Congress is using its Section 5 power to enact a statute that prohibits a certain kind of discrimination, if that discrimination is subject to only rational basis review under the Equal Protection Clause, it is likely that Congress does not have Section 5 power to enact that statute.

Board of Trustees of University of Alabama v. Garrett
531 U.S. 356 (2001)

[Two petitioners filed suit against state defendants seeking money damages under the Americans with Disabilities Act (ADA). The state defendants argued that the suits were barred by the Eleventh Amendment and that Congress lacked authority under Section 5 of the Fourteenth Amendment to enact the ADA.]

Chief Justice REHNQUIST delivered the opinion of the Court.

We decide here whether employees of the State of Alabama may recover money damages by reason of the State's failure to comply with the provisions of Title I of the Americans with Disabilities Act of 1990 (ADA or Act). We hold that such suits are barred by the Eleventh Amendment.

The ADA prohibits certain employers, including the States, from "discriminat[ing] against a qualified individual with a disability because of the disability of such individual in regard to job application procedures, the hiring, advancement, or discharge of employees, employee compensation, job training, and other terms, conditions, and privileges of employment.". To this end, the Act requires employers to "mak[e] reasonable accommodations to the known physical or mental limitations of an otherwise qualified individual with a disability who is an applicant or employee, unless [the employer] can demonstrate that the accommodation would impose an undue hardship on the operation of the [employer's] business."

I

[The Court summarized its precedents on Eleventh Amendment immunity and Congress' Section 5 power.]

Section 5 of the Fourteenth Amendment grants Congress the power to enforce the substantive guarantees contained in § 1 by enacting "appropriate legislation." See *City of Boerne v. Flores,* 521 U.S. 507, 536 (1997). Congress is not limited to mere legislative repetition of this Court's constitutional jurisprudence. "Rather, Congress' power 'to enforce' the Amendment includes the authority both to remedy and to deter violation of rights guaranteed thereunder by prohibiting a somewhat broader swath of conduct, including that which is not itself forbidden by the Amendment's text." *Kimel, supra,* at 81; *City of Boerne, supra,* at 536.

City of Boerne also confirmed, however, the long-settled principle that it is the responsibility of this Court, not Congress, to define the substance of constitutional guarantees. 521 U.S., at 519–524. Accordingly, § 5 legislation reaching beyond the scope of § 1's actual guarantees must exhibit "congruence and proportionality between the injury to be prevented or remedied and the means adopted to that end."

II

The first step in applying these now familiar principles is to identify with some precision the scope of the constitutional right at issue. Here, that inquiry requires us to examine the limitations § 1 of the Fourteenth Amendment places upon States' treatment of the disabled. As we did last Term in *Kimel,* see 528 U.S., at 83, we look to our prior decisions under the Equal Protection Clause dealing with this issue.

In *Cleburne v. Cleburne Living Center, Inc.,* 473 U.S. 432 (1985), we considered an equal protection challenge to a city ordinance requiring a special use permit for the operation of a group home for the mentally retarded. The specific question before us was whether the Court of Appeals had erred by holding that mental retardation qualified as a "quasi-suspect" classification under our equal protection jurisprudence. We answered that question in the affirmative, concluding instead that such legislation incurs only the minimum "rational-basis" review applicable to general social and economic legislation.

Under rational-basis review, where a group possesses "distinguishing characteristics relevant to interests the State has the authority to implement," a State's decision to act on the basis of those differences does not give rise to a constitutional violation. "Such a classification cannot run afoul of the Equal Protection Clause if there is a rational relationship between the disparity of treatment and some legitimate governmental purpose." *Heller v. Doe,* 509 U.S. 312, 320 (1993) (citing *Nordlinger v. Hahn,* 505 U.S. 1 (1992); *New Orleans v. Dukes,* 427 U.S. 297, 303 (1976) (*per curiam*)). Moreover, the State need not articulate its reasoning at the moment a particular decision is made. Rather, the burden is upon the challenging party to negative "'any reasonably conceivable state of facts that could provide a rational basis for the classification.'" *Heller, supra,* at 320 (quoting *FCC v. Beach Communications, Inc.,* 508 U.S. 307, 313 (1993)).

Thus, the result of *Cleburne* is that States are not required by the Fourteenth Amendment to make special accommodations for the disabled, so long as their actions toward such individuals are rational. They could quite hardheadedly--and perhaps hardheartedly--hold to job-qualification requirements which do not make allowance for the disabled. If special accommodations for the disabled are to be required, they have to come from positive law and not through the Equal Protection Clause.

III

Once we have determined the metes and bounds of the constitutional right in question, we examine whether Congress identified a history and pattern of unconstitutional employment discrimination by the States against the disabled. Just as § 1 of the Fourteenth Amendment applies only to actions committed "under color of state law," Congress' § 5 authority is appropriately exercised only in response to state transgressions. The legislative record of the ADA, however, simply fails to show that Congress did in fact identify a pattern of irrational state discrimination in employment against the disabled.

Congress made a general finding in the ADA that "historically, society has tended to isolate and segregate individuals with disabilities, and, despite some improvements, such forms of discrimination against individuals with disabilities continue to be a serious and pervasive social problem." 42 U.S.C. § 12101(a)(2). The record assembled by Congress includes many instances to support such a finding. But the great majority of these incidents do not deal with the activities of States.

Even were it possible to squeeze out of these examples a pattern of unconstitutional discrimination by the States, the rights and remedies created by the ADA against the States would raise the same sort of concerns as to congruence and proportionality as were found in *City of Boerne, supra.* For example, whereas it would be entirely rational (and therefore constitutional) for a state employer to conserve scarce financial resources by hiring employees who are able to use existing facilities, the ADA requires employers to "mak[e] existing facilities used by employees readily accessible to and usable by individuals with disabilities." 42 U.S.C. §§ 12112(5)(B), 12111(9). The ADA does except employers from the "reasonable accommodatio[n]" requirement where the employer "can demonstrate that the accommodation would impose an undue hardship on the operation of the business of such covered entity." § 12112(b)(5)(A). However, even with this exception, the accommodation duty far exceeds what is constitutionally required in that it makes unlawful a range of alternative responses that would be reasonable but would fall short of imposing an "undue burden" upon the employer. The Act also makes it the employer's duty to prove that it would suffer such a burden, instead of requiring (as the Constitution does) that the complaining party negate reasonable bases for the employer's decision.

Congressional enactment of the ADA represents its judgment that there should be a "comprehensive national mandate for the elimination of discrimination against individuals with disabilities." 42 U.S.C. § 12101(b)(1). Congress is the final authority as to desirable public policy, but in order to authorize private individuals to recover money damages against the States, there must be a pattern of discrimination by the States which violates the Fourteenth Amendment, and the remedy imposed by Congress must be congruent and proportional to the targeted violation. Those requirements are not met here, and to uphold the Act's application to the States would allow Congress to rewrite the Fourteenth Amendment law laid down by this Court in *Cleburne*. Section 5 does not so broadly enlarge congressional authority. The judgment of the Court of Appeals is therefore

Reversed.

NOTES

1. The *Garrett* Court reaches the same result as the *Kimel* Court—the conduct prohibited by the challenged statute is not congruent and proportional with the conduct prohibited by the Equal Protection Clause. Just as age classifications are subject only to rational basis review, so too are classifications concerning the disabled. Thus, "States are not required by the Fourteenth Amendment to make special accommodations for the disabled, so long as their actions toward such individuals are rational. They could quite hardheadedly-- and perhaps hardheartedly--hold to job-qualification requirements which do not make allowance for the disabled." This means that very little governmental conduct that affects the disabled will violate the Equal Protection Clause. On the other hand, the ADA "requires employers to "mak[e] existing facilities used by employees readily accessible to and usable by individuals with disabilities," and makes unlawful a substantial amount of conduct that is unaffected by the Equal Protection Clause. This fails the congruence and proportionality test.

2. There is one difficulty with the above analysis that the Court does not mention. While rational basis is the proper standard to review classifications that affect the disabled, there is one case, *City of Cleburne v. Cleburne Living Center*, where the Court, applying that standard, invalidated the classification. This result suggests that, at least in relation to the disabled, the amount of conduct that would violate the Equal Protection Clause is broader than one would expect under rational basis review, and would thus provide greater support for a statute that prohibited discrimination against the disabled. The Court, however, did not consider this argument.

3. Kenji Yoshino points out that the *Garrett* case further constricts Congress' power under Section 5:

> The *Garrett* Court added two evidentiary requirements to the basic inquiry set forth in *Boerne*. First, the *Garrett* Court required that the scope of the constitutional right in question be identified "with some precision." Second, it required that Congress produce evidence that this constitutional right had been systematically violated. In the case of Title I of the Americans with Disabilities Act, this standard meant Congress needed to have "identified a history and pattern of unconstitutional employment discrimination by the States against the disabled." These evidentiary requirements further conscribed the civil rights legislation Congress could pass under section 5. Kenji Yoshino, *The New Equal Protection*, 124 Harv. L. Rev. 747, 772 (2011).

Nevada Dept. of Human Resources v. Hibbs
538 U.S. 721 (2003)

[William Hibbs took a leave of absence from his position with the Welfare Division of the Nevada Department of Human Resources in order to care for his wife after she was injured in a car accident. When Hibbs failed to return to work after exhausting the twelve weeks of leave to which he was entitled under the Family and Medical Leave Act (FMLA), he was dismissed. Hibbs brought suit in federal court against the state to recover money damages, alleging violation of the Family and Medical Leave Act.]

Chief Justice REHNQUIST delivered the opinion of the Court.

The Family and Medical Leave Act of 1993 (FMLA or Act) entitles eligible employees to take up to 12 work weeks of unpaid leave annually for any of several reasons, including the onset of a "serious health condition" in an employee's spouse, child, or parent. 107 Stat. 9, 29 U.S.C. § 2612(a)(1)(C). The Act creates a private right of action to seek both equitable relief and money damages "against any employer (including a public agency) in any Federal or State court of competent jurisdiction," § 2617(a)(2), should that employer "interfere with, restrain, or deny the exercise of" FMLA rights, § 2615(a)(1). We hold that employees of the State of Nevada may recover money damages in the event of the State's failure to comply with the family-care provision of the Act.

[The Court summarized its precedents on Eleventh Amendment immunity and Congress' Section 5 power.]

Congress may, however, abrogate such immunity in federal court if it makes its intention to abrogate unmistakably clear in the language of the statute and acts pursuant to a valid exercise of its power under § 5 of the Fourteenth Amendment. The clarity of Congress' intent here is not fairly debatable. This case turns, then, on whether Congress acted within its constitutional authority when it sought to abrogate the States' immunity for purposes of the FMLA's family-leave provision.

In enacting the FMLA, Congress relied on two of the powers vested in it by the Constitution: its Article I commerce power and its power under § 5 of the Fourteenth Amendment to enforce that Amendment's guarantees. Congress may not abrogate the States' sovereign immunity pursuant to its Article I power over commerce. *Seminole Tribe, supra.* Congress may, however, abrogate States' sovereign immunity through a valid exercise of its § 5 power, for "the Eleventh Amendment, and the principle of state sovereignty which it embodies, are necessarily limited by the enforcement provisions of § 5 of the Fourteenth Amendment." *Fitzpatrick v. Bitzer,* 427 U.S. 445, 456 (1976) (citation omitted). See also *Garrett, supra,* at 364; *Kimel, supra,* at 80.

Two provisions of the Fourteenth Amendment are relevant here: Section 5 grants Congress the power "to enforce" the substantive guarantees of § 1—among them, equal protection of the laws—by enacting "appropriate legislation." Congress may, in the exercise of its § 5 power, do more than simply proscribe conduct that we have held unconstitutional. "'Congress' power "to enforce" the Amendment includes the authority both to remedy and to deter violation of rights guaranteed thereunder by prohibiting a somewhat broader swath of conduct, including that which is not itself forbidden by the Amendment's text.'" In other words, Congress may enact so-called prophylactic legislation that proscribes facially constitutional conduct, in order to prevent and deter unconstitutional conduct.

City of Boerne also confirmed, however, that it falls to this Court, not Congress, to define the substance of constitutional guarantees. "The ultimate interpretation and determination of the Fourteenth Amendment's substantive meaning remains the province of the Judicial Branch." *Kimel,* 528 U.S., at 81. Section 5 legislation reaching beyond the scope of § 1's actual guarantees must be an appropriate remedy for identified constitutional violations, not "an attempt to substantively redefine the States' legal obligations." We distinguish appropriate prophylactic legislation from "substantive redefinition of the Fourteenth Amendment right at issue," by applying the test set forth in *City of Boerne:* Valid § 5 legislation must exhibit "congruence and proportionality between the injury to be prevented or remedied and the means adopted to that end," 521 U.S., at 520.

The FMLA aims to protect the right to be free from gender-based discrimination in the workplace. We have held that statutory classifications that distinguish between males and females are subject to heightened scrutiny. See, *e.g., Craig v. Boren,* 429 U.S. 190, 197–199 (1976). For a gender-based classification to withstand such scrutiny, it must "serv[e] important governmental objectives," and "the discriminatory means employed [must be] substantially related to the achievement of those objectives." *United States v. Virginia,* 518 U.S. 515, 533 (1996). The State's justification for such a classification "must not rely on overbroad generalizations about the different talents, capacities, or preferences of males and females." We now inquire whether Congress had evidence of a pattern of constitutional violations on the part of the States in this area.

The history of the many state laws limiting women's employment opportunities is chronicled in—and, until relatively recently, was sanctioned by—this Court's own opinions. For example, in *Bradwell v. State,* 16 Wall. 130 (1873) (Illinois), and *Goesaert v. Cleary,* 335 U.S. 464 (1948) (Michigan), the Court upheld state laws prohibiting women from practicing law and tending bar, respectively. State laws frequently subjected women to distinctive restrictions, terms, conditions, and benefits for those jobs they could take. In *Muller v. Oregon,* 208 U.S. 412, 419, n. 1 (1908), for example, this Court approved a state law limiting the hours that women could work for wages, and observed that 19 States had such laws at the time. Such laws were based on the related beliefs that (1) a woman is, and should remain, "the center of home and family life," *Hoyt v. Florida,* 368 U.S. 57, 62 (1961), and (2) "a proper discharge of [a woman's] maternal functions—having in view not merely her own health, but the well-being of the race—justif[ies] legislation to protect her from the greed as well as the passion of man," *Muller, supra,* at 422. Until our decision in

Reed v. Reed, 404 U.S. 71 (1971), "it remained the prevailing doctrine that government, both federal and state, could withhold from women opportunities accorded men so long as any 'basis in reason' "—such as the above beliefs—"could be conceived for the discrimination." *Virginia, supra,* at 531.

Congress responded to this history of discrimination by abrogating States' sovereign immunity in Title VII of the Civil Rights Act of 1964, 78 Stat. 255, 42 U.S.C. § 2000e–2(a), and we sustained this abrogation in *Fitzpatrick.* But state gender discrimination did not cease. "[I]t can hardly be doubted that ... women still face pervasive, although at times more subtle, discrimination ... in the job market." *Frontiero v. Richardson,* 411 U.S. 677, 686 (1973). According to evidence that was before Congress when it enacted the FMLA, States continue to rely on invalid gender stereotypes in the employment context, specifically in the administration of leave benefits. Reliance on such stereotypes cannot justify the States' gender discrimination in this area. *Virginia, supra,* at 533. The long and extensive history of sex discrimination prompted us to hold that measures that differentiate on the basis of gender warrant heightened scrutiny; here, as in *Fitzpatrick,* the persistence of such unconstitutional discrimination by the States justifies Congress' passage of prophylactic § 5 legislation.

Congress also heard testimony that "[p]arental leave for fathers ... is rare. Even ... [w]here child-care leave policies do exist, men, *both in the public and private sectors,* receive notoriously discriminatory treatment in their requests for such leave." Joint Hearing 147 (Washington Council of Lawyers) (emphasis added). Many States offered women extended "maternity" leave that far exceeded the typical 4– to 8–week period of physical disability due to pregnancy and childbirth, but very few States granted men a parallel benefit: Fifteen States provided women up to one year of extended maternity leave, while only four provided men with the same. M. Lord & M. King, The State Reference Guide to Work–Family Programs for State Employees 30 (1991). This and other differential leave policies were not attributable to any differential physical needs of men and women, but rather to the pervasive sex-role stereotype that caring for family members is women's work.

Evidence pertaining to parenting leave is relevant here because state discrimination in the provision of both types of benefits is based on the same gender stereotype: that women's family duties trump those of the workplace. Justice KENNEDY's dissent ignores this common foundation that, as Congress found, has historically produced discrimination in the hiring and promotion of women. Consideration of such evidence does not, as the dissent contends, expand our § 5 inquiry to include "*general* gender-based stereotypes in employment." To the contrary, because parenting and family leave address very similar situations in which work and family responsibilities conflict, they implicate the same stereotypes.

Finally, Congress had evidence that, even where state laws and policies were not facially discriminatory, they were applied in discriminatory ways. It was aware of the "serious problems with the discretionary nature of family leave," because when "the authority to grant leave and to arrange the length of that leave rests with individual supervisors," it leaves "employees open to discretionary and possibly unequal treatment." H.R.Rep. No. 103–8, pt. 2, pp. 10–11 (1993). Testimony supported that conclusion, explaining that "[t]he lack of uniform parental and medical leave policies in the work place has created an environment where [sex] discrimination is rampant."

In sum, the States' record of unconstitutional participation in, and fostering of, gender-based discrimination in the administration of leave benefits is weighty enough to justify the enactment of prophylactic § 5 legislation.

We reached the opposite conclusion in *Garrett* and *Kimel.* In those cases, the § 5 legislation under review responded to a purported tendency of state officials to make age- or disability-based distinctions. Under our equal protection case law, discrimination on the basis of such characteristics is not judged under a heightened review standard, and passes muster if there is "a rational basis for doing so at a class-based level, even if it 'is probably not true' that those reasons are valid in the majority of cases." *Kimel,* 528 U.S., at 86 (quoting *Gregory v. Ashcroft,* 501 U.S. 452, 473 (1991)). See also *Garrett,* 531 U.S., at 367 ("States are not required by the Fourteenth Amendment to make special accommodations for the disabled, so long as their actions toward such individuals are rational"). Thus, in order to impugn the constitutionality of state discrimination against the disabled or the elderly, Congress must identify, not just the existence of age- or disability-based state decisions, but a "widespread pattern" of irrational reliance on such criteria. *Kimel, supra,* at 90. We found no such showing with respect to the ADEA and Title I of the Americans with Disabilities Act of 1990(ADA). *Kimel, supra,* at 89; *Garrett, supra,* at 368.

Here, however, Congress directed its attention to state gender discrimination, which triggers a heightened level of scrutiny. See, *e.g., Craig,* 429 U.S., at 197–199. Because the standard for demonstrating the constitutionality of a gender-based classification is more difficult to meet than our rational-basis test—it must "serv[e] important governmental objectives" and be "substantially related to the achievement of those objectives," *Virginia,* 518 U.S., at 533 — it was easier for Congress to show a pattern of state constitutional violations. Congress was similarly successful in *South Carolina v. Katzenbach,* 383 U.S. 301, 308–313 (1966), where we upheld the Voting Rights Act of 1965: Because racial classifications are presumptively invalid, most of the States' acts of race discrimination violated the Fourteenth Amendment.

The impact of the discrimination targeted by the FMLA is significant. Congress determined:

> Historically, denial or curtailment of women's employment opportunities has been traceable directly to the pervasive presumption that women are mothers first, and workers second. This prevailing ideology about women's roles has in turn justified discrimination against women when they are mothers or mothers-to-be.

Stereotypes about women's domestic roles are reinforced by parallel stereotypes presuming a lack of domestic responsibilities for men. Because employers continued to regard the family as the woman's domain, they often denied men similar accommodations or discouraged them from taking leave. These mutually reinforcing stereotypes created a self-fulfilling cycle of discrimination that forced women to continue to assume the role of primary family caregiver, and fostered employers' stereotypical views about women's commitment to work and their value as employees. Those perceptions, in turn, Congress reasoned, lead to subtle discrimination that may be difficult to detect on a case-by-case basis.

We believe that Congress' chosen remedy, the family-care leave provision of the FMLA, is "congruent and proportional to the targeted violation," *Garrett, supra,* at 374. Congress had already tried unsuccessfully to address this problem through Title VII and the amendment of Title VII by the Pregnancy Discrimination Act, 42 U.S.C. § 2000e(k). Here, as in *Katzenbach, supra,* Congress again confronted a "difficult and intractable proble[m]," *Kimel, supra,* at 88, where previous legislative attempts had failed. See *Katzenbach, supra,* at 313 (upholding the Voting

Rights Act). Such problems may justify added prophylactic measures in response. *Kimel, supra,* at 88.

By creating an across-the-board, routine employment benefit for all eligible employees, Congress sought to ensure that family-care leave would no longer be stigmatized as an inordinate drain on the workplace caused by female employees, and that employers could not evade leave obligations simply by hiring men. By setting a minimum standard of family leave for *all* eligible employees, irrespective of gender, the FMLA attacks the formerly state-sanctioned stereotype that only women are responsible for family caregiving, thereby reducing employers' incentives to engage in discrimination by basing hiring and promotion decisions on stereotypes.

For the above reasons, we conclude that § 2612(a)(1)(C) is congruent and proportional to its remedial object, and can "be understood as responsive to, or designed to prevent, unconstitutional behavior." *City of Boerne, supra,* at 532.

The judgment of the Court of Appeals is therefore *affirmed.*

NOTES

1. The key to understanding the result in *Hibbs* is that the Court characterizes the family care provisions of FMLA as designed to address the problem of a gender stereotype in the workplace—that family care was women's work. Once the Court identified the problem being addressed as a gender classification, then immediately the "congruence and proportionality" test was much easier to satisfy. While virtually no conduct violates the deferential version of rationality review, the intermediate scrutiny standard that is applied to gender classifications has the effect of invalidating a substantial number of gender classifications. Thus, when the Court in *Hibbs* is comparing the conduct that violates the Equal Protection Clause with the conduct that is prohibited by the statute, it is far easier to find a match between the two. In *Kimel* and *Garrett*, on the other hand, the challenged statute had attempted to prohibit discrimination on the basis of a classification that would only receive rational basis review under the Equal Protection Clause. Since in those cases so little conduct would be constitutionally prohibited, the statutes failed the congruence and proportionality test.

Tennessee v. Lane
541 U.S. 509 (2004)

Justice STEVENS delivered the opinion of the Court.

Title II of the Americans with Disabilities Act of 1990 (ADA or Act) provides that "no qualified individual with a disability shall, by reason of such disability, be excluded from participation in or be denied the benefits of the services, programs or activities of a public entity, or be subjected to discrimination by any such entity." The question presented in this case is whether Title II exceeds Congress' power under § 5 of the Fourteenth Amendment.

I

[Respondents, both of whom are paraplegics who use wheelchairs for mobility, claimed that they were denied access to, and the services of, the state court system by reason of their disabilities. Lane alleged that he was compelled to appear to answer a set of criminal charges on the second floor of a county courthouse that had no elevator. When he refused to crawl up the stairs or be carried by officers to the courtroom, he was arrested and jailed for failure to appear. Jones, a certified court reporter, alleged that she has not been able to gain access to a number of county courthouses, and, as a result, has lost both work and an opportunity to participate in the judicial process.]

The State moved to dismiss the suit on the ground that it was barred by the Eleventh Amendment.

II

The ADA was passed by large majorities in both Houses of Congress after decades of deliberation and investigation into the need for comprehensive legislation to address discrimination against persons with disabilities. In the years immediately preceding the ADA's enactment, Congress held 13 hearings and created a special task force that gathered evidence from every State in the Union. The conclusions Congress drew from this evidence are set forth in the task force and Committee Reports, described in lengthy legislative hearings, and summarized in the preamble to the statute. Central among these conclusions was Congress' finding that

> individuals with disabilities are a discrete and insular minority who have been faced with restrictions and limitations, subjected to a history of purposeful unequal treatment, and relegated to a position of political powerlessness in our society, based on characteristics that are beyond the control of such individuals and resulting from stereotypic assumptions not truly indicative of the individual ability of such individuals to participate in, and contribute to, society. 42 U.S.C. § 12101(a)(7).

Invoking "the sweep of congressional authority, including the power to enforce the fourteenth amendment and to regulate commerce," the ADA is designed "to provide a clear and comprehensive national mandate for the elimination of discrimination against individuals with disabilities." It forbids discrimination against persons with disabilities in three major areas of public life: employment, which is covered by Title I of the statute; public services, programs, and activities, which are the subject of Title II; and public accommodations, which are covered by Title III.

Title II, §§ 12131-12134, prohibits any public entity from discriminating against "qualified" persons with disabilities in the provision or operation of public services, programs, or activities. The Act defines the term "public entity" to include state and local governments, as well as their agencies and instrumentalities. § 12131(1). Persons with disabilities are "qualified" if they, "with or without reasonable modifications to rules, policies, or practices, the removal of architectural, communication, or transportation barriers, or the provision of auxiliary aids and services, mee[t] the essential eligibility requirements for the receipt of services or the participation in programs or activities provided by a public entity." § 12131(2).

III

[The Court summarized its precedents on Eleventh Amendment immunity and Congress' Section 5 power.]

Congress' § 5 power is not, however, unlimited. Section 5 legislation is valid if it exhibits "a congruence and proportionality between the injury to be prevented or remedied and the means adopted to that end." Applying the *Boerne* test in *Garrett,* we concluded that Title I of the ADA was not a valid exercise of Congress' § 5 power to enforce the Fourteenth Amendment's prohibition on unconstitutional disability discrimination in public employment. In view of the significant differences between Titles I and II, however, *Garrett* left open the question whether Title II is a valid exercise of Congress' § 5 enforcement power. It is to that question that we now turn.

IV

The first step of the *Boerne* inquiry requires us to identify the constitutional right or rights that Congress sought to enforce when it enacted Title II. *Garrett,* 531 U.S., at 365. In *Garrett* we identified Title I's purpose as enforcement of the Fourteenth Amendment's command that "all persons similarly situated should be treated alike." *Cleburne v. Cleburne Living Center, Inc.,* 473 U.S. 432, 439 (1985). As we observed, classifications based on disability violate that constitutional command if they lack a rational relationship to a legitimate governmental purpose. *Garrett,* 531 U.S., at 366 (citing *Cleburne,* 473 U.S., at 446).

Title II, like Title I, seeks to enforce this prohibition on irrational disability discrimination. But it also seeks to enforce a variety of other basic constitutional guarantees, infringements of which are subject to more searching judicial review. See, *e.g., Dunn v. Blumstein,* 405 U.S. 330, 336-337 (1972); *Shapiro v. Thompson,* 394 U.S. 618, 634 (1969); *Skinner v. Oklahoma ex rel. Williamson,* 316 U.S. 535, 541 (1942). These rights include some, like the right of access to the courts at issue in this case, that are protected by the Due Process Clause of the Fourteenth Amendment. The Due Process Clause and the Confrontation Clause of the Sixth Amendment, as applied to the States via the Fourteenth Amendment, both guarantee to a criminal defendant such as respondent Lane the "right to be present at all stages of the trial where his absence might frustrate the fairness of the proceedings." *Faretta v. California,* 422 U.S. 806, 819, n. 15 (1975). The Due Process Clause also requires the States to afford certain civil litigants a "meaningful opportunity to be heard" by removing obstacles to their full participation in judicial proceedings. *Boddie v. Connecticut,* 401 U.S. 371, 379 (1971); *M.L.B. v. S.L.J.,* 519 U.S. 102 (1996). We have held that the Sixth Amendment guarantees to criminal defendants the right to trial by a jury composed of a fair cross section of the community, noting that the exclusion of "identifiable segments playing major roles in the community cannot be squared with the constitutional concept of jury trial." *Taylor v. Louisiana,* 419 U.S. 522, 530 (1975). And, finally, we have recognized that members of the public have a right of access to criminal proceedings secured by the First Amendment. *Press-Enterprise Co. v. Superior Court of Cal., County of Riverside,* 478 U.S. 1, 8-15 (1986).

Whether Title II validly enforces these constitutional rights is a question that "must be judged with reference to the historical experience which it reflects." *South Carolina v. Katzenbach,* 383 U.S. 301, 308 (1966). While § 5 authorizes Congress to enact reasonably prophylactic remedial legislation, the appropriateness of the remedy depends on the gravity of the harm it seeks to prevent. "Difficult and intractable problems often require powerful remedies," *Kimel,* 528 U.S., at 88, but it is also true that "[s]trong measures appropriate to address one harm may be an unwarranted response to another, lesser one," *Boerne,* 521 U.S., at 530.

It is not difficult to perceive the harm that Title II is designed to address. Congress enacted

Title II against a backdrop of pervasive unequal treatment in the administration of state services and programs, including systematic deprivations of fundamental rights. For example, "[a]s of 1979, most States ... categorically disqualified 'idiots' from voting, without regard to individual capacity." The majority of these laws remain on the books, and have been the subject of legal challenge as recently as 2001. Similarly, a number of States have prohibited and continue to prohibit persons with disabilities from engaging in activities such as marrying and serving as jurors. The historical experience that Title II reflects is also documented in this Court's cases, which have identified unconstitutional treatment of disabled persons by state agencies in a variety of settings, including unjustified commitment, *e.g., Jackson v. Indiana,* 406 U.S. 715 (1972); the abuse and neglect of persons committed to state mental health hospitals, *Youngberg v. Romeo,* 457 U.S. 307 (1982); and irrational discrimination in zoning decisions, *Cleburne v. Cleburne Living Center, Inc.,* 473 U.S. 432 (1985). The decisions of other courts, too, document a pattern of unequal treatment in the administration of a wide range of public services, programs, and activities, including the penal system, public education, and voting.

With respect to the particular services at issue in this case, Congress learned that many individuals, in many States across the country, were being excluded from courthouses and court proceedings by reason of their disabilities. A report before Congress showed that some 76% of public services and programs housed in state-owned buildings were inaccessible to and unusable by persons with disabilities, even taking into account the possibility that the services and programs might be restructured or relocated to other parts of the buildings. Congress itself heard testimony from persons with disabilities who described the physical inaccessibility of local courthouses. And its appointed task force heard numerous examples of the exclusion of persons with disabilities from state judicial services and programs, including exclusion of persons with visual impairments and hearing impairments from jury service, failure of state and local governments to provide interpretive services for the hearing impaired, failure to permit the testimony of adults with developmental disabilities in abuse cases, and failure to make courtrooms accessible to witnesses with physical disabilities.

In any event, our cases have recognized that evidence of constitutional violations on the part of nonstate governmental actors is relevant to the § 5 inquiry. To be sure, evidence of constitutional violations by the States themselves is particularly important when, as in *Florida Prepaid Postsecondary Ed. Expense Bd. v. College Savings Bank,* 527 U.S. 627 (1999), *Kimel v. Florida Bd. of Regents,* 528 U.S. 62 (2000), and *Garrett,* the sole purpose of reliance on § 5 is to place the States on equal footing with private actors with respect to their amenability to suit. But much of the evidence in *South Carolina v. Katzenbach,* 383 U.S. 301, 312-315 (1966), to which THE CHIEF JUSTICE favorably refers, *post,* at 2003, involved the conduct of county and city officials, rather than the States.

Given the sheer volume of evidence demonstrating the nature and extent of unconstitutional discrimination against persons with disabilities in the provision of public services, the dissent's contention that the record is insufficient to justify Congress' exercise of its prophylactic power is puzzling, to say the least. Just last Term in *Hibbs,* we approved the family-care leave provision of the FMLA as valid § 5 legislation based primarily on evidence of disparate provision of parenting leave, little of which concerned unconstitutional state conduct. 538 U.S., at 728-733. We explained that because the FMLA was targeted at sex-based classifications, which are subject to a heightened standard of judicial scrutiny, "it was easier for Congress to show a pattern of state constitutional violations" than in *Garrett* or *Kimel,* both of which concerned legislation that targeted classifications subject to rational-basis review. 538 U.S., at 735-737. Title II is aimed at the enforcement of a variety of basic rights, including the right of access to the courts at issue in this case, that call for a standard of judicial review at least as searching, and in some cases more searching, than the standard that applies to sex-based classifications. And in any event, the record of constitutional violations in this case--including judicial findings of unconstitutional state action, and statistical, legislative, and anecdotal evidence of the widespread exclusion of persons with disabilities from the enjoyment of public services--far exceeds the record in *Hibbs.*

The conclusion that Congress drew from this body of evidence is set forth in the text of the ADA itself: "[D]iscrimination against individuals with disabilities persists in such critical areas as ... education, transportation, communication, recreation, institutionalization, health services, voting, and *access to public services.*" 42 U.S.C. § 12101(a)(3) (emphasis added). This finding, together with the extensive record of disability discrimination that underlies it, makes clear beyond peradventure that inadequate provision of public services and access to public facilities was an appropriate subject for prophylactic legislation.

V

The only question that remains is whether Title II is an appropriate response to this history and pattern of unequal treatment. At the outset, we must determine the scope of that inquiry. Title II-unlike RFRA, the Patent Remedy Act, and the other statutes we have reviewed for validity under § 5-reaches a wide array of official conduct in an effort to enforce an equally wide array of constitutional guarantees. Petitioner urges us both to examine the broad range of Title II's applications all at once, and to treat that breadth as a mark of the law's invalidity. According to petitioner, the fact that Title II applies not only to public education and voting-booth access but also to seating at state-owned hockey rinks indicates that Title II is not appropriately tailored to serve its objectives. But nothing in our case law requires us to consider Title II, with its wide variety of applications, as an undifferentiated whole. Whatever might be said about Title II's other applications, the question presented in this case is not whether Congress can validly subject the States to private suits for money damages for failing to provide reasonable access to hockey rinks, or even to voting booths, but whether Congress had the power under § 5 to enforce the constitutional right of access to the courts. Because we find that Title II unquestionably is valid § 5 legislation as it applies to the class of cases implicating the accessibility of judicial services, we need go no further. See *United States v. Raines,* 362 U.S. 17, 26 (1960).

Congress' chosen remedy for the pattern of exclusion and discrimination described above, Title II's requirement of program accessibility, is congruent and proportional to its object of enforcing the right of access to the courts. The unequal treatment of disabled persons in the administration of judicial services has a long history, and has persisted despite several legislative efforts to remedy the problem of disability discrimination. Faced with considerable evidence of the shortcomings of previous legislative responses, Congress was justified in concluding that this "difficult and intractable proble[m]" warranted "added prophylactic measures in response." *Hibbs.*

For these reasons, we conclude that Title II, as it applies to the class of cases implicating the fundamental right of access to the courts, constitutes a valid exercise of Congress' § 5 authority to enforce the guarantees of the Fourteenth Amendment. The judgment of the Court of Appeals is therefore affirmed.

It is so ordered.

NOTES

1. The Court in *Garrett* had already held that *Title I* of the ADA, which forbids discrimination against persons with disabilities in employment, is beyond Congress' Section 5 power, because the statutory prohibitions were not congruent and proportional to the constitutional violation. In *Lane*, the Court determined that *Title II* of the ADA, which forbids discrimination against persons with disabilities in public services, programs, and activities, was within Congress Section 5 power. If the ADA is viewed simply as a statute that prohibits discrimination against the disabled, then the *Garrett* Court had made clear that the statute was beyond Congress' power. Since the Court only applies a deferential rational basis standard to disability classifications, there is very little disability discrimination that would violate the Equal Protection Clause, and thus very little conduct to which the statute's prohibitions could be congruent and proportional.

The issue in *Lane*, however, was different. According to the *Lane* Court, "Title II, like Title I, seeks to enforce this prohibition on irrational disability discrimination. But it also seeks to enforce a variety of other basic constitutional guarantees, infringements of which are subject to more searching judicial review. These rights include some, like the right of access to the courts at issue in this case, that are protected by the Due Process Clause of the Fourteenth Amendment." Since Title II was concerned, at least in the *Lane* case, with access to the courts, that was a right that called for "for a standard of judicial review at least as searching, and in some cases more searching, than the standard that applies to sex-based classifications." This meant that the relevant precedent was not *Garrett*, which involved a classification that was subject to rational basis review, but *Hibbs*, which involved a gender classification that was subject to intermediate scrutiny.

2. The Court identified the constitutional harm that Title II was designed to address: "With respect to the particular services at issue in this case, Congress learned that many individuals, in many States across the country, were being excluded from courthouses and court proceedings by reason of their disabilities." One of the problems with this analysis was that Title II's provisions were not limited to access to courthouses, but rather extended to every public building that provided "public services, programs, and activities." As the petitioners pointed out, the coverage of Title II would extend not just to courts, public schools, and voting booths, but also state-owned hockey rinks. Surely there was no constitutional right of access to hockey rinks that would trigger heightened scrutiny. The Court did not need to address this issue because it did not have to decide the constitutionality of the statute as a whole; it need only address the constitutionality of limited access to courts. It is very likely that the extension of Title II to all publicly-owned buildings is beyond Congress' Section 5 power. But that was not the issue before the Court. As to the particular facts before it, the Court determined that "Title II's requirement of program accessibility is congruent and proportional to its object of enforcing the right of access to the courts."

Coleman v. Court of Appeals of Maryland
132 S.Ct.1327 (2012)

Justice KENNEDY announced the judgment of the Court and delivered an opinion, in which THE CHIEF JUSTICE, Justice THOMAS, and Justice ALITO joined.

The question in this case is whether a state employee is allowed to recover damages from the state entity that employs him by invoking one of the provisions of a federal statute that, in express terms, seeks to abrogate the States' immunity from suits for damages. The statute in question is the Family and Medical Leave Act of 1993, 107 Stat. 6, 29 U.S.C. § 2601 *et seq*. The provision at issue requires employers, including state employers, to grant unpaid leave for self care for a serious medical condition, provided other statutory requisites are met, particularly requirements that the total amount of annual leave taken under all the Act's provisions does not exceed a stated maximum. In agreement with every Court of Appeals to have addressed this question, this Court now holds that suits against States under this provision are barred by the States' immunity as sovereigns in our federal system.

[The Court summarized the provisions of the Family and Medical Leave Act (FMLA), including the family care provisions upheld in *Nevada Dept. of Human Resources v. Hibbs* (the right to take up to 12 weeks of unpaid leave per year to care for a newborn or adopted child or for a spouse, child, or parent with a serious health condition) and the self-care provision (the right to take that leave for the employee's own serious health condition).]

The question then becomes whether the self-care provision and its attempt to abrogate the States' immunity are a valid exercise of congressional power under § 5 of the Fourteenth Amendment.

Under this analysis *Hibbs* permitted employees to recover damages from States for violations of subparagraph (C). In enacting the FMLA, Congress relied upon evidence of a well-documented pattern of sex-based discrimination in family-leave policies.

The same cannot be said for requiring the States to give all employees the opportunity to take self-care leave. Petitioner advances three arguments for allowing employees to recover damages from States that violate the FMLA's self-care provision: The self-care provision standing alone addresses sex discrimination and sex stereotyping; the provision is a necessary adjunct to the family-care provision sustained in *Hibbs*; and the provision eases the burden on single parents. But what the family-care provisions have to support them, the self-care provision lacks, namely evidence of a pattern of state constitutional violations accompanied by a remedy drawn in narrow terms to address or prevent those violations.

Standing alone, the self-care provision is not a valid abrogation of the States' immunity from suit. When the FMLA was enacted, "ninety-five percent of full-time state- and local-government employees were covered by paid sick leave plans and ninety-six percent of such employees likewise enjoyed short-term disability protection." The evidence did not suggest States had facially discriminatory self-care leave policies or that they administered neutral self-care leave policies in a discriminatory way. And there is scant evidence in the legislative history of a purported stereotype harbored by employers that women take self-care leave more often than men. Congress considered evidence that "men and women are out on medical leave approximately equally." Nothing in the record shows employers formulated self-care leave policies based on a contrary view.

It is true the self-care provision offers some women a benefit by allowing them to take leave for pregnancy-related illnesses; but as a remedy, the provision is not congruent and proportional to any identified constitutional violations . . . To abrogate the States' immunity from suits for damages under § 5, Congress must identify a pattern of constitutional violations and tailor a remedy congruent and proportional to the documented violations. It failed to do so when it allowed employees to sue States for violations of the FMLA's self-care provision. The judgment of the Court of Appeals is affirmed.

It is so ordered.

NOTES

1.   Once again, the result in a case on Congress' Section 5 power turns on the level of scrutiny that the classification would receive under the Equal Protection Clause. Since the self-care provision is not a gender classification, it is not possible to identify a pattern of constitutional violations to which the statutory provisions could be congruent and proportional.